# THE UNDIVINE *COMEDY*

## DETHEOLOGIZING DANTE

*TEODOLINDA BAROLINI*

PRINCETON UNIVERSITY PRESS

PRINCETON, NEW JERSEY

*Library of Congress Cataloging-in-Publication Data*
Barolini, Teodolinda, 1951–
The undivine *Comedy* : detheologizing Dante / Teodolinda Barolini.
p.    cm.
Includes bibliographical references and index.
ISBN 0-691-06953-0 (cloth)
ISBN 0-691-01528-7 (pbk.)
1. Dante Alighieri, 1265–1321. Divina commedia.
2. Dante Alighieri, 1265–1321—Religion. 3. Dante Alighieri,
1265–1321—Criticism and interpretation—History. 4. Religion in literature.
I. Title.

PQ4416.B37   1992   851'.1—dc20   92-11859   CIP

For Douglas Gardner Caverly, beloved fellow traveler

# CONTENTS

# PREFACE

ONE THINKS of strange things reading the *Commedia*: that Dante's spires of poetic life—terza rima—bear a resemblance to modern science's spires of biological life, DNA; that his long obsession with the new is echoed in current research on the brain, which shows that the new things that we live actually become who we are. Dante is no naturalist, but he is the ultimate realist, preoccupied with rendering reality—even surreality—in language, "sì che dal fatto il dir non sia diverso." It is to Erich Auerbach that we owe the profound insight that Dante's content was finally ruptured by its form, his theology imperiled by his mimetic genius. I have endeavored in what follows to show some of the paths trodden by a master of mimesis, some of the ways in which Dante's poetic adventuring is indeed, according to his own lights, Ulyssean—a journey "di retro al sol, del mondo sanza gente."

# EDITIONS AND ACKNOWLEDGMENTS

Citations of Dante's texts are from the following editions:

"*La Commedia*" *secondo l'antica vulgata*, ed. Giorgio Petrocchi, 4 vols. (Milan: Mondadori, 1966–1967).

*Vita Nuova*, ed. Domenico De Robertis (Milan: Ricciardi, 1980).

*Convivio*, ed. Cesare Vasoli, in Dante Alighieri, *Opere minori*, vol. 5, tomo I, parte II, *La letteratura italiana: Storia e testi* (Milan: Ricciardi, 1988).

*De vulgari eloquentia*, ed. Pier Vincenzo Mengaldo, in Dante Alighieri, *Opere minori*, vol. 5, tomo II, *La letteratura italiana: Storia e testi* (Milan: Ricciardi, 1979).

*Monarchia*, ed. Bruno Nardi, in *Opere minori*, tomo II.

*Epistole*, ed. Arsenio Frugoni and Giorgio Brugnoli, in *Opere minori*, tomo II.

*Egloge*, ed. Enzo Cecchini, in *Opere minori*, tomo II.

*Questio de aqua et terra*, ed. Francesco Mazzoni, in *Opere minori*, tomo II.

The following abbreviations are used:

ED    *Enciclopedia Dantesca*, 6 vols. (Rome: Istituto dell'Enciclopedia Italiana, 1970–1978).

ST    Thomas Aquinas, *Summa Theologiae*, in the Blackfriars edition, 61 vols. (New York: McGraw-Hill; London: Eyre and Spottiswoode, 1964–1981).

Translations are mine unless otherwise stated. All italics present both in the Italian and the English translation are mine. A substantially less evolved version of chapter 1 appeared in *Quaderni d'italianistica* 10 (1988): 35–53. Chapter 4 appeared in *Annali d'italianistica* 8 (1990): 314–344, and, in Italian, in *Lettere italiane* 42 (1990): 173–207. Shorter forms of chapter 6 appeared in *Dante Studies* 105 (1987): 43–62, and, in Italian, in *Studi americani su Dante*, ed. Gian Carlo Alessio and Robert Hollander (Milan: Franco Angeli, 1989). Chapter 9 appeared in *Lettere italiane* 40 (1988): 3–36. Mary Refling compiled the index.

I would like also to take this opportunity to thank Joan M. Ferrante for her friendship, enthusiasm, and generosity over the by now twenty years of our Dante dialogue.

# THE UNDIVINE *COMEDY*

# DETHEOLOGIZING DANTE:
# REALISM, RECEPTION, AND THE
# RESOURCES OF NARRATIVE

> vellem quippe, si tunc ego essem Moyses—ex eadem namque
> massa omnes venimus; et quid est homo, nisi quia memor es
> eius?—vellem ergo, si tunc ego essem quod ille, et mihi abs te
> Geneseos liber scribendus adiungeretur, talem mihi eloquendi
> facultatem dari et eum texendi sermonis modum . . .
>
> (Augustine, *Confessions*)

> Sì ch'egli è nuovo Apollo e nuovo Apelle:
> Tacete unquanco, pallide viole,
> E liquidi cristalli e fiere snelle;
> *E' dice cose, e voi dite parole*
> (Francesco Berni on Michelangelo,
> "Capitolo a Fra Bastian dal Piombo")

IN HIS CAPITAL and underutilized "Dante profeta," published in
1941, Bruno Nardi threw down a critical gauntlet and challenged us to
look at the *Commedia* not through a glass darkly but face to face.[1] He
begins where all such discussions must begin, with the *Commedia*'s most
overtly prophetic moments, its political prophecies; situating them within
the context of Joachimism and Franciscan spiritualism, he moves to a discussion of medieval attitudes toward prophecy, dreams, and divination.
Calling to our attention Albert the Great's teaching that some people
"sognano il vero, e, a differenza di altri, hanno visioni veraci, talchè non di
rado pronunziano perfino chiarissime profezie" ("dream the truth and, differently from others, have true visions, so that not rarely they even pro-
nounce very clear prophecies" [368]), Nardi claims that Dante considered
his own experience one such *visione verace*,[2] with the result that those who
view the poem as a literary fiction misread it: "Chi considera la visione dantesca e il rapimento del poeta al cielo come finzioni letterarie, travisa il
senso" ("Those who consider Dante's vision and the poet's abduction to
heaven as literary fictions distort the sense" [392]). Moreover, Nardi persists
in asking the inelegant questions that are the logical consequence of his

position, not only, "Si deve dunque credere colle donnicciole di Verona, che Dante scendesse davvero all'Inferno, e davvero salisse all'Empireo?" ("Must we therefore believe with the women of Verona that Dante really descended to Hell and really ascended to the Empyrean?" [392]), but even, "Ma fu veramente un profeta, Dante?" ("Was Dante truly a prophet?" [405]). Given that his answer to the first query is a qualified yes ("Non precisamente questo; bensì che Dante credette gli fossero mostrati in visione l'Inferno, il Purgatorio, il Paradiso terrestre, come veramente sono nella realtà" ["Not precisely this; rather that Dante believed that Hell, Purgatory, and the Earthly Paradise were shown to him in vision, as they truly are in reality" (392)]), Nardi's next step is to take on Croce, for whom to admit such a hallucination on Dante's part is to suggest—impossibly—that the lucid poet was a madman.[3] If this is madness, says Nardi, Dante was in good company: "Dobbiamo confessare che di demenza è impastata la psicologia religiosa; e dementi furono del pari Mosè, Zarathrustra e Maometto, dementi Geremia, Ezechiele e san Paolo, non meno del protomartire Stefano e dell'autore dell'Apocalisse" ("We must admit that the religious psychology is compounded with madness; and that equally mad were Moses, Zarathrustra and Mohammed, Jeremiah, Ezekiel and St. Paul, no less than the protomartyr Stephen and the author of the Apocalypse" [396]). Faced with the obvious similarity between Dante's claims and those of previous prophets, Nardi courageously—especially in that he was not an American academic but an Italian ex-seminarian—vaults the barrier that, by segregating Dante from his precursors, preserves modern believers from the unpalatable necessity of accepting with regard to a medieval poet what they find less distasteful with regard to various earlier claimants: namely, authentic divine inspiration. In this Nardi was most unusual, for there are complex cultural factors indisposing Italian scholars from objectivity regarding the Commedia's truth claims: either, as believers, they are incapable of taking Dante's prophetic pretensions at face value; or, as lapsed believers (and frequently converts to a militant secularism), they do not want to. But, if Nardi is more rational than is decorous among believers, he is also more believing than is decorous among rationalists; indeed, the very posing of his final query (to which he offers another qualified assent)[4] may have limited the influence of his essay.

In this chapter I will trace, in broad outline, the history of our recent handling of what I take to be the fundamental question for all readers of Dante's poem: How are we to respond to the poet's insistence that he is telling us the truth? Logically prior to this query stands another that we cannot answer, but on which we may speculate: Did Dante himself believe in the literal truth of those things for which he claims literal truth?

In the wake of the American querelle regarding the allegory of poets versus the allegory of theologians (the Convivio's terminology for allegorical signifying presumed to be man-made and invented versus allegorical signifying presumed to be intrinsic and divine), we seem to have reached an impasse in which the question of Dante's truth claims has been effectively put to one side, begged by some of us, ignored by others, treated as settled by many. This is not to say that the issue is never raised; in our attempts to understand the Commedia's intertextuality, for instance, it is frequently touched upon.[5] But there is no consensus—merely, in North America, an undiscussed and acritical assumption of allegiance to Charles Singleton's teachings. As to how we have arrived at such an impasse, I submit that a major cause has been the issue, still unresolved, of the authorship of the Epistle to Cangrande. The impasse has been compounded, moreover, by cultural differences that prevent adherents to essentially the same point of view from benefiting from each other's work: it is my belief that Nardi's contributions regarding "Dante profeta" and Singleton's regarding the Commedia's use of the allegory of theologians are essentially complementary. Since Singleton, in the wake of Erich Auerbach, emphasizes the validity of the literal sense as historically true, and the issue of Dante as profeta ultimately goes beyond the specific prophecies within the text to encompass the much larger problem of the poet's view of himself as a teller of truth, these two traditions are in effect parallel ways of discussing the one central issue of the poet's truth claims.[6] They have not been viewed as such because neither side has been particularly receptive to the other's mode of framing the question. In the United States we have tended to vex the issue of allegory as a mode, genre, or method, evolving a critical discourse regarding the allegory of the Commedia that barely refers to the text. Hence the Italian accusation that we are engaged in sterile allegorizing at the expense of the poetry—an ironic response given that our insistence on the allegory of theologians was intended to reinvest the literal sense with a poetic worth denied it by the traditional reading based on the allegory of poets. Nor could it be said that we have given the Nardian position its due: in "Dante Theologus-Poeta," Robert Hollander chides those dantisti who "have no difficulty in understanding that Dante claims literal truth for his poem, but then go on to make this Dante a 'prophet,' thus avoiding, as did Bruno Nardi, the way in which the poem is rooted in fourfold exegesis in the name of a single aspect of the biblical possibilities."[7] But Nardi was not engaged in avoidance; he was formulating the issue in terms that were more congenial to one who was less a literary critic than a historian and philosopher, steeped in thirteenth-century controversies wherein Franciscans, for instance, regularly impugned the truth of other Franciscans, and the charge of "false prophet" was not uncommon. Indeed, if we interrogate the Commedia as we have in the past interrogated the Convivio and the Epistle to Cangrande, we will find that Nardi's way of framing the issue of the poet's truth claims is far from inappropriate.

In his later "Il punto sull'Epistola a Cangrande," Nardi moves from stating his case regarding Dante's claims to examining how the poet's claims have traditionally been evaded.[8] In other words, he formulates a theory of evasive reception. Due to its emphasis on reception, and thus on the Trecento commentators—the earliest "recipients" of record—Nardi's theory involves a shift of focus from the *Commedia* to the Epistle to Cangrande. Noting the accusations of heresy that were leveled at Dante, called a vessel of the devil by the Dominican Guido Vernani,[9] and culminating in the Dominican ban of 1335, he points out that all of Dante's early commentators (among whom Nardi places the author of the expository part of the Epistle, a point to which we shall return) feel obliged to protect their poet from the charge of heresy. Their defense is invariably based on distinguishing the *poeta* from the *theologus*, the literal sense contrived by the poet from the allegorical sense employed by the moralist: "E tutti lo mettono al riparo da questa accusa nello stesso modo, cioè distinguendo quello che Dante scrive come poeta (*poetizans*) da quello che Dante pensa come teologo 'nullius dogmatis expers,' ossia, in sostanza, fra il senso letterale, intenzionalmente svalutato, e il senso allegorico, il solo vero, cioè quello che si cela sotto il velo delle parole fittizie, 'sotto il velame de li versi strani,' come dice Dante stesso in uno dei luoghi del poema veramente allegorici" ("Everyone shelters him from this accusation in the same way, distinguishing what Dante writes as a poet from what Dante thinks as a theologian, or rather, in substance, between the literal sense, intentionally devalued, and the allegorical sense, the only true sense, the one that is hidden under the veil of fictitious words, 'under the veil of the strange verses,' as Dante himself says in one of the truly allegorical moments of his poem" [27]). The early commentators thus deflected attention from the literal sense and its preposterous claims by intentionally devaluing it, equating it with the allegedly fictitious imaginings of the poet. This stratified division of the text's authorial persona along allegorical lines, with the moralist responsible for the allegorical truth that is hidden under the *bella menzogna* of the poet's fanciful inventions, creates a deplorable dichotomy that persists to this day, yielding critics who "pur riconoscendo a Dante la tempra di vero poeta, ne svalutano l'altissima ispirazione religiosa da cui la poesia sgorga" ("while acknowledging in Dante the fiber of a true poet, yet devalue the high religious inspiration from which his poetry flows" [30]). In Nardi's opinion, the disastrous lesson on how to protect the poet by devaluing the literal sense of his poem is first provided by the well-intentioned theologian who, he believes, is responsible for the expository section of the Epistle to Cangrande.

At this point, the parallels between Nardi and Singleton become more evident, as do the ironies inherent in our story. Nardi is as determined a defender of the literal sense of the *Commedia* as is Singleton; like Singleton, he is deeply aware of the significance of the Epistle to Cangrande as a hermeneutic document. But their approach to the document could not be more different. While Singleton grounds his defense of the *Commedia*'s literal sense in an appeal to the Epistle to Cangrande—"The allegory of the *Divine Comedy* is so clearly the 'allegory of theologians' (as the Letter to Cangrande by its example says it is) that one may only wonder at the continuing efforts made to see it as the 'allegory of poets'"[10]—Nardi refuses to acknowledge the Dantesque paternity of much of the Epistle because he thinks that it treats the poem's literal sense as mere *fictio*. In this, Nardi took what seemed at the time a particularly idiosyncratic stand, since—as Singleton had in fact astutely observed[11]—it was only to be expected that attacks on the allegory of theologians as the *Commedia*'s dominant mode would take the form of attacks on the authenticity of the Epistle, as indeed proved to be the case. Before turning to the complications caused by Nardi's stand regarding the Epistle, another profound confluence between his ideas and Singleton's should be noted, a confluence that is the logical outcome of their defenses of the poem's literal sense.[12] Nardi's emphasis on the detrimental effects of separating the *theologus* from the *poeta* may be considered responsible for the lack of response to "Dante profeta" in Italy:[13] Italian *dantismo*'s protectionist attitude toward what it calls the "poetry" is a Crocean legacy, and Croce's reading—motivated by his legitimate disgust with deracinated allegorizing—represents in its essence nothing but a willed and consistent application of a method already canonical in Dante studies, to wit, the dichotomized *theologus-poeta*. Although he did not lay as great a stress on the evils of this dichotomy as Nardi, Singleton too was aware of it as a problem and indeed viewed the matter in a Nardian focus that was not passed on to his heirs, who have instead preserved the dichotomy and privileged the *theologus*—precisely as Italian critics, who have done the opposite, have accused them of doing. Thus, Singleton writes that "if we must choose between Dante as theologian and Dante as poet, then, I suppose, we take the poet" (86), adding, apropos "Boccaccio and many others [who] have preferred the theologian": "To see the poet as a 'theologian' is to see him essentially as one who constructs an 'allegory of poets' hiding under a veil the truths of theology—a view that has a long history in Dante interpretation" (95).

Both symptom and cause of the deadlock we have reached with respect to the issue of Dante's truth claims (a formulation that I prefer, in the interests both of clarity and a more ecumenical approach to Dante studies, to either its allegorical or prophetic precursor) are the acrimony and inflexibility displayed by those who, unwittingly, reflect the old dichotomy in extreme form: as Singleton's heirs dig ever more deeply into the cultural and theological humus from which the *Commedia* grows, they make the poet appear more and more a theologian, unleashing a backlash from those who would have us remember that he is a poet.[14] As a group, we are interested in the

*Commedia*'s poetry, meaning its rhetoric and philology, and in its theology, meaning its moral philosophy, aspects of the poem that we keep resolutely apart; we shy away from the underlying crucible where the two coincide—in a poet who models himself on David, the "humble psalmist" ("l'umile salmista" [*Purg.* 10.65]), who like David composes a *tëodia* and speaks as *scriba Dei* of "that matter of which I am made the scribe" ("quella materia ond'io son fatto scriba" [*Par.* 10.27]), with what he considers a theologically-vested authority at least equal to that of the author of the Apocalypse (John agrees with him on a visionary detail in *Purgatorio* 29—not the other way around!). To the extent that we do speak of these matters, we view them not as prerequisites for all investigation of the *Commedia* but as independent strands of Dante studies, devoted to allegory, *profetismo*, apocalyptic literature, mysticism, and the like.[15] Greatly to blame for our critical disarray has been what I consider the red herring issue of the Epistle to Cangrande's paternity. The linking of the Epistle to the issue of the *Commedia*'s mode of signifying has had the unfortunate effect of allowing the question of the Epistle's authorship to seem decisive for our reading of the poem. This skewing of the critical discourse is implicit in Singleton's contribution, which gives the impression of being most vulnerable in its reliance on the Epistle, and is explicit in Nardi.

The issue of the Epistle's authorship has distracted us from the text we are trying to understand and has bred unnecessary confusion. Thus, Nardi's principal antagonist in the debate over the paternity of the Epistle was Francesco Mazzoni, a scholar who is far from a supporter of the "prophetic" reading of the *Commedia*; it is ironic that Nardi and Mazzoni should respond to the Epistle in the same way, as in no way inimical to the fictitiousness of the poem it glosses. To complicate matters, in "La 'mirabile visione' di Dante e l'Epistola a Cangrande," Giorgio Padoan enters the fray on Mazzoni's side, in that he undertakes to defend the authenticity of the entire Epistle, but in Nardi's cause:[16] Nardi denies the authenticity of the expository part of the Epistle because he believes that it promotes the idea of the *Commedia* as mere *fictio*; Padoan sustains the Epistle's authenticity because he believes that exactly the opposite is true, i.e., that in tone and content the expository part of the Epistle supports the idea that Dante intentionally represented his text's literal sense as true. In contrast to other commentaries on the opening of the *Paradiso*, which respond to the first canto's audacious patterning of the poet's ascent on St. Paul's *raptus*, "whether in the body I do not know, or out of the body I do not know, God knows," with cautious appeals to poetic fiction,[17] Padoan points out that the Epistle to Cangrande contains no such disclaimers: "Il fatto essenziale per questo discorso è che nell'*Epistola*—proprio come abbiamo visto per la *Comedìa*—si afferma esplicitamente che non di viaggio metaforico si tratta, né di immaginazione di fantasia, bensì di vera e propria 'elevatio ad coelum'" ("The essential fact is that the Epistle—precisely as we have seen for the *Comedìa*—explicitly affirms that it treats not a metaphoric voyage, or the imagination of fantasy, but rather a true 'elevation to heaven'" [43]). Even more telling for Padoan are the authentic biblical visions invoked by the Epistle as models for the *Commedia*, "tre esempi biblici di visioni (ancora una volta) realmente avvenute: (1) il *raptus* al cielo di S. Paolo; (2) la visione che S. Pietro, S. Giacomo e S. Giovanni ebbero della trasfigurazione di Cristo; (3) la visione della gloria di Dio avuta da Ezechiele" ("three biblical examples of visions that, yet again, really occurred: (1) the abduction to heaven of St. Paul; (2) the vision that St. Peter, St. James, and St. John had of the transfiguration of Christ; (3) the vision of God's glory experienced by Ezekiel" [44]), examples that in turn are buttressed with references to three authorities on visionary experience, Richard of St. Victor, St. Bernard, and St. Augustine.

Prodding us to confront and openly discuss the issues raised by Nardi, Padoan poses the key question for Dante studies: "Ma questo insistere sulla realtà della visione e questo tono profetico sono essi ad imporsi a Dante per la forza insita nel suo stesso realismo e per la foga della sua appassionata polemica, oppure derivano da una scelta deliberata e consapevole dell'autore, da una sua ben meditata convinzione?" ("Are this insistence on the reality of the vision and this prophetic tone imposed on Dante by the force inherent in his realism and by the impetuosity of his impassioned polemic, or do they stem from a deliberate and self-conscious choice of the author, from a well thought-out conviction?" [39]). Why is it that this question, articulated almost thirty years ago, whose implications broach representational concerns on the one hand and authorial intentionality on the other, still haunts us today? As I have suggested, one of the reasons that Padoan's arguments have not been able to penetrate and focus critical thought as fully as their author would have wished is their connection to the Epistle; to the extent that his arguments engage the Epistle more than the *Commedia*, and to the extent that they are presented in the context of a defense of the Epistle's Dantesque authorship, they are the more easily discounted. Moreover, by linking a tangential issue (the Epistle's authorship) to the main issue (the *Commedia*'s mode of signifying) and then blurring the lines between the two, we have allowed the critical waters to become fearfully muddied. A case in point is a 1986 book by Peter Dronke, in which the author (like Padoan a student of Nardi's) inveighs against the exegetical approach to which we have been giving the label allegory of poets, which he thinks ill serves the *Commedia*'s imaginative power.[18] Following Nardi, he argues that Dante's claims are not derisable in their historical context: "the great prophet-visionaries of the twelfth and thirteenth centuries—Hildegard and Joachim, Mechthild and Marguerite—made unflinching claims to truth. I believe it is their kind of claim that Dante makes"

(127). However, he argues against Dante's penning of the Epistle, whose author he considers an inept allegorist, and hence against Padoan;[19] moreover, he lumps Singleton and Hollander among that "majority of scholars since Croce [who] have continued to think of the *Commedia* in terms of fiction" (127), an assessment that hardly does justice to their positions or strengthens the cause in which he is fighting. Greater individuation is required if we are to promote clarity vis-à-vis the complex critical tradition we inherit. Dronke's book, which also conflates Dante's prophetic claims with those of Alanus, without acknowledging that a major tenet of Nardi's supporters has been the distance they posit between Dante and those poets for whom the literal sense is explicitly less important than the allegorical, illustrates the confusion to which our lack of critical consensus has led.

I suggested earlier that, if we were to interrogate the *Commedia* as we have the *Convivio* and the Epistle, we would find support for both Nardi and Singleton. Any metatextual study of the *Commedia* has to come to terms with the poet's presentation of himself as truth-teller, and thus with "Dante profeta" in the larger sense. Indeed, one result of interrogating the *Commedia* regarding itself may be to collapse the distinctions between the "allegorical" and the "prophetic" approach by suggesting that, from Dante's perspective, they amount to the same thing. In other words, what one could call Dante's prophetic mode corresponds to Singleton's allegory of theologians or Auerbach's figural mode. This claim is the more readily made in that it is less the fourfold method per se, as a practical exegetical technique, that is important for Dante, than what that method radically signifies. What is significant in Singleton's thesis regards the use of an allegorical approach, called "allegory of theologians" in the *Convivio* but "figura" elsewhere, in which the literal sense is considered historically true. There is no need to infer that Dante intended his poem to be consistently decoded according to a method to which even exegetes of the Bible more often paid lip service than actually used. Moreover, there is no need to hold that the *Commedia*'s imitation of God's way of writing requires the Epistle to Cangrande or any other external document for its substantiation; the poem itself furnishes sufficient and incontrovertible evidence of how it wants to be read. By this I do not mean to say that I find the Epistle uninteresting; for the record, my own sense of it is that it is Dante's, nor have I yet seen anything that convinces me it is not. It should be noted, however, that the critical climate has altered to the point of making Nardi's once idiosyncratic position seem nothing short of prophetic; recently, Zygmunt G. Barański argued against the authenticity of the Epistle because he believes it presents the *Commedia* as "an ordinary fictional poem with an ethically useful message."[20] My point is that the Epistle's authorship, were the matter one day to be definitively decided against Dante, need not in any way impinge on our reading of the *Commedia*.

The distance between Nardi and Singleton regards not so much their ideas on how the poem intends to be received as their response to the second of my initial queries; with respect to Dante's view of himself, Singleton presents a less "naive" persona than Nardi, hewing more closely to the Crocean path: "But to attribute to a critical and reflective Dante the belief that he was another Aeneas or another St. Paul is simply to unload on him our own disinclination to face the myth directly and to understand it" (78). In this matter, I follow the Nardian school of thought, which I think in fact "faces the myth more directly"; thus, my approval for Singleton's famous formula that "the fiction of the *Divine Comedy* is that it is not a fiction" (62) does not extend to the suggestion that Dante himself thought his poem a fiction in any simple sense.[21] In my opinion, Dante self-consciously used the means of fiction—poetic and narrative strategies—in the service of a vision he believed to be true, thus creating the hybrid he defined a "truth that has the face of a lie"—"un ver c'ha faccia di menzogna." We should remember that the use of rhetorical techniques in the service of a divinely inspired message is explicitly defended by Augustine in the *De doctrina Christiana*, who furnishes examples of Paul's rhetorical prowess and asks: "Does the Apostle contradict himself when he says that men are made teachers by the operation of the Holy Spirit and at the same time tells them what and how they should teach?" (4.16.33).[22] In other words, Augustine discredits the common misapprehension that a "prophet" cannot also be a "poet," that one who is inspired need not also attend to the "how" of language and rhetoric.

The belief in the incompatibility of poetry and prophecy is durable, nonetheless, and has taken deep root in Dante exegesis. Recently, Peter Hawkins has commented on the extraordinary self-consciousness of *Purgatorio* 29 and has voiced his concern that the literary self-consciousness of the canto is at odds with Dante's prophetic claims: "But at the same time that the poet makes these claims, so too does he make them problematic. He habituates us to what Battaglia Ricci calls the 'forma letteraria della Bibbia,' but then he abjures his spell with instances of literary self-reference (be they invocations to the Muses or addresses to the reader) that are utterly foreign to the Bible, or to the 'great prophet visionaries of the twelfth and thirteenth centuries' whom Peter Dronke educes as Dante's peers."[23] Although I endorse Hawkins's conclusion regarding Dante's "utter confounding of the categories that Croce sought to separate" (91), I do not share his belief that in this respect Dante is so different from all other prophets, from whose texts Hawkins maintains that literary self-consciousness is entirely absent. The self-conscious use of rhetoric is not foreign to the Bible, or to later prophet-visionaries: the Apocalypse, the prophetic text that is the most immediate precursor of *Purgatorio* 29, is hardly innocent of literary self-referencing; rather, its author repeatedly refers to himself as a writer and to us as

his readers, without being concerned that by so doing he "abjures his spell."
And Augustine is convinced of the rhetorical eloquence of the prophets, to
whom he passes after treating the eloquence of St. Paul: "But perhaps someone thinks that I have selected the Apostle Paul as our one eloquent
speaker. . . . It is therefore incumbent upon me to say something of the
eloquence of the Prophets, where many things are obscured by tropes" (*De
doctrina Christiana* 4.7.15). Not even relatively unsophisticated visionary
texts are lacking in self-consciousness regarding their status as verbal fab-
rications. The author of *Tundale's Vision*, for instance, sets himself certain
narrative precepts: he believes in selectivity ("Since we ought to try to
be brief, not all that we hear is worth writing down"), does not want to be
repetitive ("Since we described this before, we should not repeat it again"),
is aware of his limitations ("Neither could your humble writer understand it
nor his tongue tell of it"), and also of the service he performs, noting that he
has recorded Tundale's vision "for the benefit of our readers."[24] The author
of the *Commedia* is not a solitary exception in being both *poeta* and *theologus*, both one who uses metaphoric language with its attendant dangers
and one who claims knowledge of a supernatural order; any prophet, visionary, or mystic who tries to render received truth in language is constrained
to wrestle with the medium's inherent limitations.[25]

Augustine puts his finger on the nub of the problem in his treatment of
the truth value of Genesis. After acknowledging the uncertainties that will
always attend the reception of a truth that is delivered through signs ("per
signa" [12.23]), and stipulating that a truth need not be reducible to a single
true interpretation (12.24), he frames in the most personal possible terms
the need for eloquence in delivering a true message. Had Augustine himself
been entrusted by God with the task of writing Genesis, he says, he would
have wished for the rhetorical skills to create a polysemous truth:

> if I had been Moses and you had made it my task to write the book of Genesis, I
> should have wished you to give me such skill in writing and such power in framing
> words, that not even those who as yet cannot understand how God creates should
> reject my words as beyond their comprehension, and those who can should find
> expressed in the few words of your servant whatever true conclusions they had
> reached by their own reasoning; and if, in the light of truth, another man saw a
> different meaning in those words, it should not be impossible to understand this
> meaning too in those same words. (*Conf.* 12.26)[26]

Here Augustine, a man who actively imagined being called to fashion divine
truth in language, one moreover who has succeeded in persuading many
readers that he was up to the task, tells us that in the service of a polysemous
truth eloquence and rhetoric are desirable. We come back thus to his point
about Paul: the Apostle should not be seen as contradicting himself when he
says that men are made teachers by the operation of the Holy Spirit and at

the same time tells them what and how they should teach. In other words, if Dante views himself as one who was made a teacher by the operation of the Holy Spirit, he is not thereby prevented from fully exploiting his poetic genius as to what—and especially *how*—to teach; if a poet is charged with what he believes is a prophetic mission, he may legitimately put all his poetic cunning to work. Aware, like Augustine, of the apparent tension between divine inspiration and poetic praxis, Dante describes his poem as a "ver c'ha faccia di menzogna," situating the *menzogna* of art within the framework of a prophetic stature that guarantees truth. A further paradox furnishes the poet's definition of his poem: the *Commedia* is a nonfalse error, a *non falso errore*, not a fiction that pretends to be true but a fiction that IS true. The phrase "non falsi errori" (*Purg.* 15.117), used to describe the ecstatic visions of the terrace of wrath (i.e., the local equivalents of the encompassing ecstatic vision that induces the sleep to which the poet refers at the beginning and end of his poem) provides a means to understand Dante's own understanding of his achievement: not polarized as either *theologus* or *poeta*, Dante holds the aporias and contradictions of a prophetically inspired poem—a work that as art may be error but that as prophecy is nonfalse—within the rigorous embrace of paradox.

In sum, I suggest we accept Dante's insistence that he is telling the truth and move on to the consequences, which we can only do by accepting that he intends to represent his fiction as credible, believable, true. How to cut the Gordian knot of a true fiction? We could, like Jeremy Tambling in his 1988 study of a Derridean Dante for whom meaning is always relativized and deferred, remove the problem of belief altogether on the basis that "the problem of belief is never relevant since belief entails a hierarchy of meanings."[27] This reading of the poem in terms of Derridean openendedness and free-floating signifiers creates a monolith of relativity to take the place of the traditional totem of certainty. While I agree that Dante is acutely aware of texts generating texts, signs leading to more signs, in my opinion he handles his awareness not by relativizing his own claims but by absolutizing them (to say that Dante tries to do this is not, of course, to say that he succeeds). As I have tried to show previously, Dante works to cut himself out of the chain of infinitely regressive semiosis by erecting a wall between his textuality and that of all but his biblical precursors; by impugning the credibility of their signs he desperately seeks to carve out a realm of stability and truth for his own. We cannot skirt the problem of belief because Dante does not skirt it; rather, he forcibly addresses it, directly in his truth claims and indirectly in his strategies vis-à-vis other texts, other attempts to command belief. Although we must be aware that the *Commedia* is made of signs, that "nothing in the vision escapes representation" (68), in order to further our understanding of that representation we must acknowledge that a major feature of it is that it claims to be a representation of truth.

The topic at hand is Dante's realism. Although Dante shares with other narrators the concern to authenticate his narrative, his religious pretensions make this concern particularly pressing; for, as Morton Bloomfield remarks, the "basic problem of all revealed religions is just this authentication."[28] Bloomfield further notes that this problem is in the minds of the authors of the Bible, where, we might add, it articulates itself precisely in the terms that Nardi formulated in "Dante profeta": "The end of Chapter 18 of Deuteronomy frankly discusses the problem of how to distinguish true prophecy from false" (344). This is the node at which the problems of discussing the *Commedia* intersect with the problems of discussing all realistic narrative: because of its biblical and prophetic pretensions the *Commedia* poses the basic narrative issue of its truth value in aggravated form. At the same time, however, Dante does not seek to hide the fact that he is crafting the word of God in language; he draws attention to his role as narrator in a multitude of ways, including the celebrated addresses to the reader. It is of great relevance to our discussion that Auerbach finds in Dante's addresses to the reader the urgency of a prophet;[29] in other words, typically, Dante has used what could have been moments of vulnerability, moments of exposed narrativity, to forge his most authoritative voice. Leo Spitzer rejects Auerbach's insistence on prophecy in favor of a reading that puts the emphasis on mimesis, on the addresses as aids in the reader's visualization and thus in the poem's realism. Tellingly, Spitzer does not understand that Auerbach is able to arrive at his formulation (Dante as a new prophet capable of inventing the essentially new topos of the address to the reader in the service of his prophetic vision) precisely because he had so long been thinking in terms of Dantesque realism: in Dante the prophetic stance is indissolubly wedded to the poet's concern with achieving supreme mimesis.[30] The formulation Dante-prophet disturbs Spitzer as one who is interested in understanding how the *Commedia* works as art; it does not occur to him that in order to see how it works as art, we have first to accept—not believe!—its prophetic claims on its own terms. Only then can we discern the pressures such claims exert upon a poet. One of the great problems of studying Dante is reflected in Spitzer's taking to task of Auerbach: critics, like Nardi and Auerbach, who take the poem's pretensions seriously, are criticized for not seeing an artifact, for believing Dante too much. In fact, they are seeing the artifact most clearly and are on the road to believing Dante least.

The *Commedia*'s remarkable fusion of absolute certainty about content with self-consciousness about the human artistry that is its vehicle has continually fostered new variants of the ancient either/or critical stand, variants expressed in the critical language of their day: in his 1985 study, Jesse Gellrich (sounding like a deconstructionist version of Spitzer critiquing Auerbach) argues against what he calls Singleton's sense of the *Commedia* as myth in favor of its self-consciousness, claiming that "an awareness of illusion making is inevitable" and that the poem "does not protect itself from such awareness but encourages it."[31] I would say, rather, that Dante creates a poem in which such encouragements may constitute one of its most effective forms of self-protection.[32] As with the addresses to the reader, Dante protects himself most when he seems most exposed; he neutralizes the betrayal of self-consciousness implicit in all narrative authenticating devices by making his authenticating devices outrageously inauthentic (we need only remember Geryon, who is literally a figure for fraud, i.e., inauthenticity).[33] Gellrich mistakes Singleton's position in an instructive fashion: he accuses Singleton of really thinking that Dante imitated God's way of writing, of falling for the "myth," while Singleton was in fact saying that Dante would have us believe that he imitated God's way of writing. In other words, Gellrich conflates what Singleton himself believes with what Singleton says that Dante wants us to believe. This occurs because of the enormous effort required to keep the two apart; one of the effects of Dante's realism—and one of its most insidious forms of self-protection—is that it causes people to think one agrees with him when one paraphrases him (as all teachers of the Commedia know, it is difficult to persuade one's students otherwise).[34] By the same token, the reverse is also true: Dante's realism causes critics to tend to "believe" Dante without knowing that they believe him, i.e., to pose their critical questions and situate their critical debates within the very presuppositions of the fiction they are seeking to understand.

An example of such behavior is the common defensive move that could be called the collocation fallacy: the set of assumptions that permit a critic to argue against a given point of view with regard to a particular soul on the basis of that soul's collocation within the fictive possible world of the Commedia. Thus, reading X is not tenable with regard to character X because, if it were operative, character X would be located elsewhere; for example, Ulysses cannot be guilty of false discourse, because then he would be with Sinon among the falsifiers of words.[35] But why should collocation be elevated to a heuristic device? Only because we approach the poem through the lens of its own fiction treated as dogma. When we approach the poem in this way, treating its fiction as objective reality, we neglect to remember that Dante is a creator and that his system of classification, for all its apparent objectivity, is a representation (and a rather arbitrary and idiosyncratic one at that) designed to promote the illusion of objectivity. The fact that Dante's hell is made to look like a penal colony does not mean that the poet who constructed it functioned literally like a warden. He functioned like a poet whose job includes the construction of the illusion of a penal colony, following infinitely more complex and fluid principles of construction than the deployment of the argument by collocation would suggest. Once more, the conniving specularity of the "ver c'ha faccia di menzogna" has cast its spell, leading us to pay its creator the ultimate compliment of forgetting that he is indeed creating the world he describes.

The *Commedia* makes narrative believers of us all. By this I mean that we accept the possible world (as logicians call it) that Dante has invented; we do not question its premises or assumptions except on its own terms. We read the *Commedia* as Fundamentalists read the Bible, as though it were true, and the fact that we do this is not connected to our religious beliefs, for on a narrative level, we believe the *Commedia* without knowing that we do so. The history of the *Commedia*'s reception offers a sustained demonstration of our narrative credulity, our readerly incapacity to suspend our suspension of disbelief in front of the poet-creator's masterful deployment of what are essentially techniques of verisimilitude. Thus, the poet manages our scandalized reaction to encountering his beloved teacher among the sodomites by staging his own scandalized reaction: "Siete voi qui, ser Brunetto?" creates a complicity between reader and pilgrim that masks the artifice always present in what is, after all, a text, an artifact. Thus, the poet constructs in Vergil a fictive construct so "real" and compelling that not only do generations of readers wish that he were saved (a legitimate response), but periodically—and less legitimately—the issue is raised by scholars who debate the matter in terms of its theological plausibility rather than the textual reality. Rarely do we think in terms of the narrative exigencies that require Vergil's damnation or the narrative uses to which he is put as a tool in Dante's struggle against a severely overdetermined plot.[36] In other words, we discuss Vergil's salvation as though the issue belonged to the real world, rather than to a text whose narrative powers have generated our concern. Whatever else Dante may have had in mind, his ability to make a text that we treat as a real world constitutes his essential "allegory of theologians"; indeed, it is possible that rather than continuing to attempt to ascertain Dante's mode of signifying in the abstract, we should begin with what the poem actually does, and how it accomplishes what it does, and extrapolate backward to its theoretical mode of signifying.

Standing resolutely outside of the fiction's mirror games, we can begin to examine the formal structures that manipulate the reader so successfully that even now we are blinded, prevented by the text's fulfillment of its self-imposed goals from fully appreciating its achievements as artifact. What is needed to get some purchase on this poem is not a "new historicism," which is an effective tool vis-à-vis texts that have always been read as texts, i.e., as false, but a "new formalism": a tool that will not run aground on the text's presentation of itself as true. As has been pointed out in the context of African American literary studies, the most effective approach at any given moment in any given discipline depends not on what is happening elsewhere but on the history of that discipline: "At a time when theorists of European and Anglo-American literature were offering critiques of Anglo-American formalism, scholars of black literature, responding to the history of their own discipline, found it 'radical' to teach formal methods of reading."[37] Mutatis mutandis, I would suggest that a formal method of reading—in the sense of Gian Biagio Conte's call for a "philology of the narrative structure"[38]—could be particuliarly useful in Dante studies, allowing us to go through the looking glass, to get behind the author's theological *speculum*. We must detheologize our reading if we are to understand what makes the theology stick. For the final irony of our tradition of Dante exegesis is that, as a direct result of our *theologus-poeta* dichotomy, and frequently in the name of preserving the poetry, we have obscured its greatness by accepting uncritically its directives and its premises, its "theology." To the extent that we read as the poet directs us to read we have not fully appreciated the magnificence of his direction. To the extent that we hearken always to what Dante says rather than take note of what he has done, we treat him as he would have us treat him—not as a poet, but as an authority, a "theologian."[39]

The chapters that follow propose a detheologized reading of the *Commedia*. This is not to say that they eschew theology. Detheologizing is not antitheological; it is not a call to abandon theology or to excise theological concerns from Dante criticism. Rather, detheologizing is a way of reading that attempts to break out of the hermeneutic guidelines that Dante has structured into his poem, hermeneutic guidelines that result in theologized readings whose outcomes have been overdetermined by the author. Detheologizing, in other words, signifies releasing our reading of the *Commedia* from the author's grip, finding a way out of Dante's hall of mirrors. In order to accomplish this, I privilege form over content, remembering that when Beatrice says, "Anzi è formale" (*Par.* 3.79) she is saying, "Anzi è essenziale": form *is* the essence. Form, in this sense, is not less deep than metaphysics; it is not abstractable as a surface value.[40] Like all poets, Dante is subject to the exigencies of form, but he is supremely gifted at camouflaging the fact that form can dictate poetic choices; he ideologizes form in such a way as to draw our attention from it to the ideology it serves. Therefore, the formal reading that follows differs from earlier formal readings, essentially stylistic, in that, in my reading, form is never disengaged from content; it never slips the traces of the ideology it serves.[41] It is precisely in the ideology of the form that we can perceive the means through which Dante controls his readers and shapes their readings, and that we can locate the wellsprings of his mimetic art.

It is not enough to declare an interest in narrative to detheologize one's reading of the *Commedia*, as Robin Kirkpatrick's 1987 book on the *Inferno* testifies. Kirkpatrick's interest in the poem's narrative properties is skewed by the moral lens through which he views formal concerns; his interest in "the ethical act of writing" leads him to confuse the text's content with its form—admittedly a confusion Dante encourages in his readers, but one from which the study of the narrative dimension should help to free us.[42] He thus claims that the *Inferno* was the most difficult of the three canticles for the poet to write—by the same token, the *Paradiso* was the least difficult— and that it is literally "dead poetry," of which Dante is ashamed. Within Dante's hall of mirrors, Kirkpatrick has taken an extra turn: rather than merely theologizing what has been represented, as Dante works to have us do, he theologizes the act of representation itself. In his earlier study of the *Paradiso* too, Kirkpatrick strenuously denies the ideological implications of Dante's formal decisions; thus, for example, he stresses the "modest voice" that dictates the third canticle's recurrent ineffability topoi and comments on the "modesty" implicit in canto 28's palinode regarding the order of the angelic ranks.[43] Let us remember: Dante here retracts Gregory the Great's angelic hierarchy, which he had followed in the *Convivio*, and adopts Dionysius's instead. But rather than say as much, Dante, being God's scribe, can instead have Beatrice relate how Gregory laughed at himself when, arriving in paradise, he saw his mistake. I am not calling into question the sincerity of Dante's visionary vocation when I note that this move, as a poetic strategy, is hardly modest—how can it be, when it substitutes for the reality of the poet's change of mind another "reality" whereby Gregory learned that he should have changed his? But to argue in these terms is to acknowledge that Dante wishes to persuade us of a reality he has to offer, a possible world he has seen and then made, while Kirkpatrick's concern to rehabilitate the "ornamental" leads him to deny, in the name of formalism, the ideology of Dante's form.[44]

In *Dante's Poets*, I had occasion to note that "if, in Singleton's formula, the fiction of the *Comedy* is that it is no fiction, then it follows that the strategy of the *Comedy* is that there is no strategy" (90). My concern now is to more fully identify the workings of this strategy that would deny its own existence. Previously, I used the example of Cacciaguida, whose explanation that the pilgrim has been shown only famous souls, "anime che son di fama note," is frequently cited by critics; less frequently have they noted—Auerbach is one exception that comes to mind—that Cacciaguida's statement is not true.[45] As I have pointed out, most of the souls we meet in the *Commedia* are famous because the *Commedia* has made them famous, and Cacciaguida's anticipation of this process effects a contamination between text and life that is precisely what Dante seeks to achieve.[46] Another example of this self-denying strategy is the inscription on the gate of hell, analyzed by John Freccero in terms of the poet's successful attempt to "establish the fiction of immediacy."[47] Reminding us that "*vision* is the province of the prophet, but the task of the poet is *representation*" (95), Freccero seeks to "dispel the unexamined assumption, encouraged by the fiction, of an innocent author describing an infernal reality rather than constructing it" (104). Like the representation of God's art on purgatory's terrace of pride, which confronts the reader with the conundrum of the poet's verisimilar art representing an art defined as the *ver* itself, Cacciaguida creates an "optical illusion" within the text, as do the verses that affect to present God's words on the gates of hell. It is important to note that these examples come from all three canticles: my point is that on the representational front the poem is neutral; in the mimetic realm collocation does not imply value, as it does in the thematic sphere. In Freccero's reading, by contrast, form remains subservient to theology, as is indicated by the distinctions he attempts to draw between the mimesis of the three canticles. Thus, he begins "Infernal Irony" by (1) invoking the *De genesi ad litteram*'s three kinds of vision—corporeal, spiritual, and intellectual—as analogies for the kinds of representation found in each canticle, and by (2) suggesting that "mimesis is peculiarly infernal and represents Dante's effort to render corporeal vision" (96). While irony may be peculiarly infernal, mimesis poses a problem for the poet throughout the poem—one that if anything escalates as the poem proceeds. To associate the three canticles with Augustine's three types of vision is to address the matter of their content, not the matter of their form.[48]

The three examples cited above—the gate of hell, the art of the terrace of pride, Cacciaguida's injunction—are taken from *Inferno*, *Purgatorio*, and *Paradiso* to make the point that we cannot approach these issues by invoking the theological grid that we have become so accustomed to imposing on the *Commedia*, whereby whatever happens in hell is "bad," problematic, and whatever happens in heaven is "good," problem-free. Whereas this formulation may be accurate with respect to the text's content, its plot, and therefore the pilgrim, it need not be accurate with respect to its form, and therefore the poet. The *Paradiso* is not more serene, narratologically, than the *Inferno*, nor do Dante's representational anxieties lessen as the poem proceeds. Two logical fallacies have led to these critical clichés, which have recently been given a Derridean spin. First, the *Commedia*'s content is projected onto its form, so that difficult or dangerous fictional encounters (which do indeed lessen as the poem proceeds) are translated into difficult or dangerous representational experiences.[49] Second, the *Inferno* is viewed as the only "narrative" canticle, because of its dramatic vigor, as though philosophy, history, theology, cosmology, etcetera did not constitute forms of narrative.[50]

Dante consistently manipulates narrative in ways that authenticate his text, making it appear inevitable, a "fatale andare," and conferring upon himself the authority that in fact we have rarely denied him. Our tendency has been to listen to what Dante says, accepting it as true—as though he were a "theologian"—rather than looking at, and learning from, the gap that exists between what he says and what he has actually wrought. To the extent, then, that we have not dealt with the implications of Dante's claims to be a second St. Paul, a second St. John, we have not put ourselves in a position to fully grasp the genius of his poetry—of its ability to construct a textual metaphysics so enveloping that it prevents us from analyzing the conditions that give rise to the illusion that such a metaphysics is possible. In "The Irreducible Dove," Singleton answers the charges of critics who fear that his approach to the question of Dante's allegory puts him "in danger of succumbing so completely to the illusion of reality in Dante's poem as to forget that it is illusion."[51] Although he did not realize it, preferring as he did to think in terms of restoring a medieval *forma mentis* that authorized such illusion, and thus being "allowed to recover from the Renaissance, if only for a brief reader's moment" (135), Singleton's attempt to locate the source of the illusion in the fiction that pretends it is not a fiction is a first step to dismantling the *Commedia*'s textual metaphysics. His critics, precisely in proportion to their levelheaded and rational refusal to succumb to a preposterous theory about a preposterous claim, revealed themselves to be the more fully duped by an author whose cunning they had not begun to penetrate. What follows is an attempt to analyze the textual metaphysics that makes the *Commedia*'s truth claims credible and to show how the illusion is constructed, forged, made—by a man who is precisely, after all, "only" a *fabbro*, a maker . . . a poet.

## Chapter 2

# INFERNAL INCIPITS: THE POETICS OF THE NEW

> But half a jiffy. I'm forgetting that you haven't the foggiest what
> all this is about. It so often pans out that way when you begin a
> story. You whizz off the mark all pep and ginger, like a mettle-
> some charger going into its routine, and the next thing you know,
> the customers are up on their hind legs, yelling for footnotes.
> (P. G. Wodehouse, *The Mating Season*)

> The first proceeding of the historian is to select at random a
> series of successive events and examine them apart from others,
> though there is and can be no *beginning* to any event, for one
> event flows without any break in continuity from another.
> (Leo Tolstoy, *War and Peace*)

THE COMMEDIA, perhaps more than any other text ever written,
consciously seeks to imitate life, the conditions of human existence.
Not surprisingly, then, the narrative journey begins with the problem of beginnings.[1] Dante's beginning, "Nel mezzo del cammin di nostra
vita" ("In the middle of the path of our life"), evokes biblical and classical
precedents for not beginning at the beginning. As Frank Kermode reminds
us, "Men, like poets, rush 'into the middest,' *in medias res*, when they are
born; they also die *in mediis rebus*."[2] This is to say that we exist in time,
which, according to Aristotle, "is a kind of middle-point, uniting in itself
both a beginning and an end, a beginning of future time and an end of
past time."[3] It is further to say that we exist in history, a middleness that,
according to Kermode, men try to mitigate by making "fictive concords
with origins and ends, such as give meaning to lives and to poems." Time
and history are the media Dante invokes to begin a text whose narrative
journey will strive to imitate—not escape—the journey it undertakes to
represent, "il cammin di nostra vita." The poet's will to make a text in which
we make choices within a simulacrum of reality, rather than within a fictive
concord, a text that mirrors the conditions of time and history, in which
men are born and die "nel mezzo," finds immediate expression in his handling of his text's beginning, which is distended and immaterialized to the
point of becoming nonlocatable, a nonevent. In other words, a good part of
the narrative journey in the first part of the poem is involved with constructing a textual fabric that implicitly counters the artifice of beginning. Dante

does this not by trying not to begin, which would be impossible, but by creating multiple beginnings, so that each beginning undermines the absolute status of the previous beginning. In this way the poet mimics our middleness, our existence in time, and creates a possible world that is not too sweet, that can tolerate the hard truths of the reality he represents. In this way, moreover, the text is accorded a pulse that is the pulse of life itself, in whose ceaseless temporal flow beginnings multiply, jostling one another for priority. Like the pilgrim on the path of life, the reader of the *Commedia* must assess reality within a context that seeks to recreate the destabilizing flux of time: as the unceasing forward motion of linear time is punctuated by the daily cycle of dawns and dusks, so the narrative line of the poem, which discloses "le vite spiritali *ad una ad una*" ("spiritual lives *one by one*" [*Par.* 33.24]), is punctuated by the cyclical rhythm of cantos that begin and end.

The poem's narrative journey, like the pilgrim's represented journey, is predicated on a principle of sequentiality, on encounters that occur one by one, "ad una ad una," in which each new event displaces the one that precedes it. Like all narrative (indeed like all language),[4] but more self-consciously than most, the *Commedia* is informed by a poetics of the new, a poetics of time, its narrative structured like a voyage in which the traveler is continually waylaid by the new things that cross his path. Life is just such a voyage: it is the "nuovo e mai non fatto cammino di questa vita" ("new and never before traveled path of this life" [*Conv.* 4.12.15]),[5] in which our forward progress is articulated by our successive encounters with the new. The text is also such a voyage: the equivalences life = voyage = text are implied in verses where the pilgrim's life is a "corso," and his "corso" is a "testo" ("Ciò che narrate di mio corso scrivo, / e serbolo a chiosar con altro testo" ["That which you narrate of my race I write, and save it to gloss with another text" (*Inf.* 15.88–89)]). Therefore, if the path of life is the "nuovo e mai non fatto cammino di questa vita," so too a text may achieve, in precisely the same language, "novum aliquid atque intentatum artis" ("something new and never before tried in art" [*DVE* 2.13.13]). In other words, human experience is conceptualized as a linear path affording encounters with the new, a line of becoming intercepted by newness. This view of human experience—and human textuality—may be extrapolated from a passage in the *Paradiso* that denies the faculty of memory to angels. Because angels never turn their faces from the face of God and see all things in his eternal present, their sight is uninterrupted by new things, and they have no need of memory (which we use to store the new things once they are no longer new):[6]

> Queste sustanze, poi che fur gioconde
> de la faccia di Dio, non volser viso
> da essa, da cui nulla si nasconde:

*però non hanno vedere interciso*
  *da novo obietto, e però non bisogna*
  *rememorar per concetto diviso. . . .*

These substances, since they were gladdened by the face of God, have never turned their faces from it, from which nothing is hidden; *therefore their sight is not intercepted by new objects,* and therefore they have no need *to remember by means of divided thought. . . .*

(*Par.* 29.76–81)

This passage is of particular relevance to an author who, as early as the *Vita Nuova*'s "libro de la mia memoria," acknowledges the narrativity inherent in remembering, which is to say the narrativity of the human condition. The condition of angels, "[che] non hanno vedere interciso / da novo obietto," is precisely not the human condition; our condition, the "cammin di nostra vita," imitated by the *cammino* of the poem, is precisely "vedere interciso da novo obietto."[7] The "novo obietto," moreover, requires a mental structure that can accommodate it, and so "concetto diviso" is born; since we do not see everything all at once, but must see and remember many new things sequentially, "ad una ad una," human beings think differentiatedly, by way of divided thoughts, "per concetto diviso." In answer to the questions "does an angel know by discursive thinking" ("utrum angelus cognoscat discurrendo" [*ST* 1a.58.3]) and "does an angel know by distinguishing and combining concepts" ("utrum angeli intelligant componendo et dividendo" [1a.58.4]; "dividendo" here is analogous to Dante's "diviso"), Aquinas points out that whereas humans acquire knowledge rationally, through a discursive process ("Discursive thinking implies a sort of movement, and all movement is from a first point to a second one distinct from it" [153]), angels acquire knowledge intellectually, by intuiting first principles.[8] Likewise, "just as an angel does not understand discursively, by syllogisms, so he does not understand by combining and distinguishing . . . For he sees manifold things in a simple way" (156–57). The new ("novo obietto") comports difference ("concetto diviso"), and both are essentially human.[9] Thus, the pilgrim's eyes are happy to gaze because of their innate desire for newness ("Li occhi miei, ch'a mirare eran contenti / per veder novitadi ond'e' son vaghi" ["My eyes, which were pleased to gaze in order to see new things that they desire" (*Purg.* 10.103–4)]), and his path is strewn with *novi obietti*, with difference. For him alone, in hell, there are "novi tormenti e novi tormentati" ("new sufferings and new sufferers" [*Inf.* 6.4]), "nove travaglie e pene" ("new travails and pains" [7.20]), "nova pieta, / novo tormento e novi frustatori" ("new anguish, new torment, and new scourgers" [18.22–23]). For the sinners, instead—as for the angels, but for opposite reasons, and with opposite results—there is no difference, nothing is ever new: "regola e qualità mai non l'è nova" ("measure and quality are never new" [*Inf.* 6.9]).

The pilgrim and the narrator are both committed to forward motion, to the new.[10] Analogous to the pilgrim's experience of "novi tormenti e novi tormentati" is the narrator's task to "ben manifestar le cose nove" ("manifest well the new things" [14.7]), recalled later in his statement that "Di nova pena mi conven far versi" ("Of new pain I must make verses" [20.1]). In contrast to the motion of the pilgrim who, by dint of continually "passing beyond" ("Noi passamm' oltre" [27.133]),[11] will keep meeting new things until one day hell will be a memory, confined to the past absolute ("quando ti gioverà dicere 'I' *fui'*" ["when it will please you to say 'I *was*'" (16.84)]), stand both the deathly stasis of hell and the vital *quies* of heaven. God is "Colui che mai non vide cosa nova" (*Purg.* 10.94), a periphrasis whose emphatic negation echoes the description of hell where "regola e qualità mai non l'è nova." "He who never saw a new thing" underscores the difference between divine and human artists in temporal terms, reminding us that representation is a temporal issue, a question of priority or, better, of not having priority, since, as Aquinas puts it, "semper enim quod naturalius est prius est" ("what is more natural is always first" [*ST* 1a2ae.49.2]).[12] For God, who knows all things, who sees everything before it happens, before it comes into existence and takes its historical place as new, there are no surprises in store, no new things ever on the (narrative) horizon; for us, instead, all things are new, and we require to know the newest of new things, the one most capable of leading toward relative priority in the absence of absolute priority. This is preeminently so if we are artists, dedicated to representation, the act of reinvesting an object with "originality," its original newness. In the key canzone of the *Vita Nuova* (a work whose title yields but one of many lexical attestations to Dante's long obsession with the new),[13] Beatrice is a "cosa nova," a new thing: "Poi la reguarda, e fra se stesso giura / che Dio ne 'ntenda di far cosa nova" ("Then he looks at her, and swears within himself that God intended to make of her a new thing" ["Donne ch'avete intelletto d'amore," 45–46]). What is this "cosa nova"? Too frequently we move on from the primary meaning of "new," glossed by Dante himself in "nuovo e *mai non fatto* cammino," to an extrapolated meaning, forgetting that, in Dante's usage, *nuovo*'s temporal resonance is always present.[14] As the creator, God is an artist who presents rather than re-presents; his is a vantage that precedes newness, that is always *prius*. Dante is an artist who, desiring to eliminate the artifice of the represented, of that which comes later, creates for himself a Beatrice, a "cosa nova" so new—so miraculous and unparalleled—as to preclude any newer new thing following in her wake.

The new is at the core of the *Commedia*'s narrative structure, and of its very rhyme scheme. Terza rima, which Dante invented for the *Commedia*, mimics the voyage of life by providing both unceasing forward motion and recurrent backward glances. If we consider *aba/bcb/cdc*, we see that in each tercet the new enters in the form of the second or middle rhyme, while the rhyme that was "new" in the previous tercet becomes "old," becomes the base onto which the newer new is added. This process, whereby an alterity, the new rhyme, becomes the identity of the subsequent tercet, imitates the genealogical flow of human history, in which the creation of each new identity requires the grafting of alterity onto a previous identity. Terza rima's imitation of our history extends to its essential middleness, its need to have beginnings and endings (in the form of the double rather than triple rhymes that appear at a canto's opening and closing; *a* only appears twice above, *b* three times) imposed onto its unbridled sequentiality.[15] Like time in Aristotle's definition, each tercet could be seen as "a kind of middle-point, uniting in itself both a beginning and an end, a beginning of future time [the new rhyme] and an end of past time [the old rhyme]." This combining of past and future, old and new, motion progressive and regressive, is also found in the spiral, the shape that defines the pilgrim's voyage through hell and purgatory and has been proposed as the geometric analogue to terza rima.[16] If the new is fundamental to terza rima, it must be fundamental to the spiral as well, and indeed, the connection between the spiral and the new is made explicit by Vergil, who explains that because guide and pilgrim travel in spirals, without ever traversing a circle's entire perimeter, Dante need not be amazed if a new thing—a "cosa nova"—should suddenly appear:

> Ed elli a me: "Tu sai che 'l loco è tondo;
>   e tutto che tu sie venuto molto,
>   pur a sinistra, giù calando al fondo,
> non se' ancor per tutto 'l cerchio vòlto;
>   per che, *se cosa n'apparisce nova,*
>   non de' addur maraviglia al tuo volto."

And he to me: "You know that the place is round, and, for all that you have come far, always to the left, dropping down to the bottom, you haven't yet turned round the whole circle; so that, *if a new thing appears*, it should not bring wonder to your face."

(Inf. 14.124–29)

The new functions in the economy of the spiral as the forward thrust that overrides the backward pull, that breaks with the status quo, converting what is into what was, into the old, the no longer new, and thereby pushing the soul ahead: turning it, in Benvenuto's words, "ad rem novam."[17] The new is the force of conversion, in the relative sense of all the little reconversions that shape life's spiral path; the prefix *ri-* in the poem's first verb, "ritrovai," echoes the form of the spiral, in which no conversion is final.[18] The new is desire, defined in the *Convivio* as that which we lack: "ché nullo desidera quello che ha, ma quello che non ha, che è manifesto difetto" ("for no one desires what he has, but what he does not have, which is manifest lack" [*Conv.* 3.15.3]). Desire is defective, while the cessation of desire is happiness, beatitude, in a word perfection. Beatitude as spiritual auton-omy—as emancipation from the new—is introduced as early as the *Vita Nuova*, where Dante learns to place his *beatitudine* not in Beatrice's greet-ing, which can be removed (thus causing him to desire, to exist defectively), but in that which cannot fail him: "quello che non mi puote venire meno" (18.4). Since nothing mortal can satisfy these conditions, we either learn from the failure of one object of desire to cease to desire mortal objects altogether, or we move forward along the path of life toward something else, something new;[19] this is the case of Dante in the *Vita Nuova*, for in-stance, who proceeds in Beatrice's absence to the *donna gentile*. Desire is thus the imperative of forward motion, the imperative of the new, both the void, and also the spiritual motion in which we engage to fill the void: "di-sire, / ch'è moto spiritale" ("desire, which is spiritual motion" [*Purg.* 18.31–32]). Ultimately, therefore, the new denotes time, the medium that robs all the previous new things of their ability to remain new, that confers the mortality—motion, change, absence of being[20]—that condemns us always to desire. These principles govern the temporal journey of life, the "cammin di nostra vita," and are imitated by the temporal journey of the poem, by its very narrative pulse: "Omne quod movetur, movetur propter aliquid quod non habet, quod est terminus sui motus ... Omne quod movetur est in aliquo defectu, et non habet totum suum esse simul" ("Everything that moves, moves because of what it does not have, which is the end of its motion ... Everything that moves exists in some defect, and does not pos-sess all its being at once" [*Ep.* 13.71–72]).

. . . . .

According to the poetics of the new, Dante handles the *Commedia*'s begin-ning by accommodating time not just passively, as all texts must, but by actively working to structure time, succession, and difference into his text, with the result that the *Inferno*'s first six cantos can be read as a graduated series of textual *cose nove, novi obietti*, new beginnings. The text's first be-ginning initiates the narrative technique whereby new beginnings are piled up so that the absolute beginning is blurred. *Inferno* 1 is structurally divisi-ble into two halves, pre-Vergil and post-Vergil; its first half consists of a series of starts and stops, "beginnings" and "ends," that could be viewed as up and down curves on a graph, with the up curve signifying hope and the down curve despair. There are three such curves, each ending on a down note. After the preliminary twelve line sequence, there are two twenty-four line sequences, both of which begin hopefully, depict a gradual loss of ground, and conclude despairingly:

| | | |
|---|---|---|
| 1–12 | first beginning and first fall | 12 lines |
| 13–36 | second beginning and second fall | 24 lines |
| 37–60 | third beginning and third fall | 24 lines |

The poem begins with a tercet whose magnificent simplicity works like a stone thrown into a pond; what follows are concentric ripples that retell its story in widening detail and scope. Thus, after enlarging the narrative field by introducing the issue of his own speech ("quanto a dir" [4], "ma per trattar" [8], "dirò" [9], "non so ben ridir" [10]), the poet circles back to end the first sequence with "che la verace via abbandonai" ("I abandoned the true way" [12]), which echoes "ché la diritta via era smarritta" ("the straight way was lost" [3]) from the opening tercet. The verse that marks the base of the first curve, "che la verace via abbandonai," yields to a new beginning in verse 13, "Ma poi ch'i' fui al piè d'un colle giunto" ("But when I had reached the foot of a hill"); here begins a sequence whose upward momentum encompasses the pilgrim's arrival at the sun-covered hill and the poem's first simile, that of the shipwrecked man who looks back at the dangerous waters he has just escaped. After resting, he sets out again in line 29, "ripresi via per la piaggia diserta" ("I took up the way again along the deserted shore"), only to be interrupted by the leopard, whose appearance in line 31 triggers the second sequence's downward spiral.

The leopard's arrival occurs when the pilgrim is "quasi al cominciar de l'erta" ("almost at the beginning of the slope" [31]). Such impediments to beginning—this is the poem's first use of *cominciare*—confer a stilted quality on the text (evidenced by stiff transitional markers like "Ma" [13], "Allor" [19], "Ed ecco" [31]), making the poem at this point the textual analogue to the limping pilgrim, whose awkward gait is suggested by the fact that his "piè fermo sempre era 'l più basso" ("firm foot was always the lower" [30]).[21] The second nadir, the second halt in the pilgrim's progress, occurs in verse 36, "ch'i' fui per ritornar più volte vòlto" ("so that more than once I was turned round to go back"), where the paronomasia underscores the feeling of impotence, of constrained return, of moving backward rather than forward. Again, the low point is followed by a new high; but, whereas the second sequence proceeds positively for eighteen of its twenty-four lines before encountering the leopard, the third sequence barely registers the pilgrim's new reasons for hope, "l'ora del tempo e la dolce stagione" ("the hour of the day and the sweet season" [43]), before giving him, in its eighth verse, new cause for fear in the sight of the lion. From there it is all downhill: the lion is followed by the wolf. The loss that the pilgrim sustains is immediately registered—"ch'io perdei la speranza de l'altezza" ("I lost hope of the height" [54])—and then emphasized by the canto's second simile ("E qual è quei che volontieri acquista, / e giugne 'l tempo che perder lo face" ["And like one who willingly gains, when the time comes that makes him lose" (55–56)]); while the earlier simile was devoted to the pilgrim's preservation, the second concentrates on his perdition (note the recurrence of *perdere*, verses 54 and 56). As the wolf comes toward him, it pushes him slowly back whence he came: "a poco a poco / mi ripigneva là dove 'l sol tace" ("little by little, it again pushed me back where the sun is silent" [59–60]). With this last verse we reach the sunless dark of total loss, total despair; the next tercet takes the matter out of the pilgrim's hands by recounting how, through no effort of his own, upon reaching the canto's lowest point ("Mentre ch'i' rovinava in basso loco" ["While I plunged down to a low place" (61)]), salvation is offered to him in the form of Vergil. So, before the gradual uplifting brought about by Vergil in the canto's second half, we must just as gradually—"a poco a poco"—spiral downward and hit rock bottom—"basso loco"—in the canto's first half, in the same way that before the climb up purgatory we must go down to the pit of hell.[22]

The beginning of the *Commedia*, then, is a carefully constructed sequence of ups and downs, starts and stops; it is a beginning subject to continual new beginnings. The subversion of absolute beginning that we find within *Inferno* 1 occurs on a larger scale in the opening cantos as a group: only in canto 2 do we find the poet's invocation to the Muses, and only in canto 3 does the pilgrim approach the gate of hell and does the actual voyage get under way. Moreover, although the first souls we see are those in hell's vestibule, in canto 3, we do not reach the first circle, and thus the first souls of hell proper, until canto 4, and the first prolonged infernal interview does not occur until canto 5, when the pilgrim meets Francesca. This programmatic serialization of the poem's beginning, whereby a new beginning is accorded to each of these early cantos, is most dramatically evidenced by canto 2, which effectively succeeds in postponing, and at least temporarily derailing, the beginning provided by the end of canto 1. The last verse of the first canto, "Allor si mosse, e io li tenni dietro" ("Then he moved off, and I followed behind him"), initiates a journey that is called to a halt as soon as it has begun; action gives way to talk in canto 2, where the pilgrim voices his doubts and is reassured by his guide. Vergil provides as a divine warrant for the enterprise words previously uttered by Beatrice, in an encounter with the Roman poet that is described as having taken place before the events recorded in the second half of canto 1, i.e., before Vergil's appearance in the poem, in a past that is outside the scope of the *Commedia*'s narrative action but that is invoked in the form of discursive history. Indeed, canto 2 is about the relation of the past, necessarily recalled as speech, to the events of the present, the relation of narrative to the events being narrated. Although the canto's invocation of the past through language is the bedrock for any further action, and in this sense may be viewed as a form of action itself, its immediate effect is to cause all forward motion to cease. Not only does it constitute a new beginning, an exploration of matters not dealt with in canto 1 (which is fully employed in establishing the basic semantic and narrative blueprints for the poem as a whole), but it mandates a restaging of the pilgrim's actual setting forth as represented at the end of canto 1. The result is the provision of a newer new beginning in the last verse of canto 2: "intrai per lo cammino alto e silvestro" ("I entered on the high and wooded path").[23]

While canto 1 enacts a series of beginnings, canto 2 constitutes a meditation on beginnings. The canto's status with respect to the architecture of the *Commedia* is unclear: if canto 1 is, as has traditionally been argued, the prologue to the poem as a whole, thus justifying the first canticle's inclusion of a thirty-fourth canto, then canto 2 is, equally traditionally, the prologue to the *Inferno*.[24] Canto 2 is certainly fitted for its role as prologue to the first canticle by its invocation, corresponding to the invocations found in the first cantos of *Purgatorio* and *Paradiso*, but in other respects it seems less suited than canto 3. In fact, canto 2 functions both as a beginning to the *Inferno* proper and, with canto 1, as part of a general beginning to the poem as a whole. It shares with canto 1 the task of setting up premises fundamental to the entire *Commedia*, which it develops in a more personal vein (emblematic in this regard are verses 62–64, where a host of key words from canto 1—"diserta piaggia," "cammin," "vòlto," "paura," "smarrito"—are transferred from the narrator to Beatrice). Although it also deals, like canto 3, with issues specific to the first canticle, the allegiance of canto 2 is more to its predecessor than to its successor; it tends to be read in concert with canto 1, with which it seems to form a proemial package, cordoned off from the rest of hell.[25] This structural ambiguity, caused by the disjunction between the role that would seem to be conferred upon canto 2 by the canticle's overall structure and the role that it actually performs, feeds into the canto's concerns with "beginningness": its interest in the historical causes of action, in the verbal wellsprings that give rise to events, is reflected in the repeated juxtaposing of speech and motion and in the use of *cominciare*, which appears here with singularly high frequency.[26] Most notably, *cominciare* appears in concert with the *Commedia*'s first use of *novo*, in the image of the man who disconverts, who exemplifies backward motion by unwanting what he wanted ("E qual è quei che disvuol ciò che volle" [37]); his "novi pensier" (38) cause him to keep changing his mind and prevent him from beginning by consigning him to endless stops and starts, "sì che dal cominciar tutto si tolle" ("so that from beginning he utterly desisted"

[39]). As in canto 1's "che nel pensier rinova la paura" (6), which anticipates the situation of canto 2 by coupling *novo* with *pensier* to create the image of impasse, so here the new does not move the pilgrim forward but keeps him circling upon himself, unable to break out of circular motion into the spiral that denotes voyage: the renewal of fear leads not to motion but to stasis. A further sign of the canto's anomalous functioning is its use of a narrative flashback; by inscribing the past where we had expected the future, and thereby greatly reinforcing the nonincipience he worked to create in canto 1, the poet both dramatizes the problematic nature of all beginnings and brilliantly handles his own problems as a reluctant beginner of this text.

Only at the canto's end do we find the desire, registered by the poem's first use of "disiderio," that will move the pilgrim forward along the path, allowing the journey to continue: "Tu m'hai con disiderio il cor disposto / sì al venir con le parole tue, / ch'i' son tornato nel primo proposto" ("You have so disposed my heart with desire, and your words have so inclined me to come, that I have returned to my first intention" [136–38]).[27] Here the man of verse 38, who "per novi pensier cangia proposta" ("because of new thoughts changes his intention"), returns "nel primo proposto"; by coming full circle, back to where he was at the canto's beginning, he puts himself in a position to move out of the (nonvirtuous) circularity that has governed his actions thus far. In a canto where motion is accomplished by not moving, where the new prevents action rather than initiating it, to return to the beginning, "nel *primo* proposto," is finally to begin. Thus, the relation between action and discourse that has obtained throughout the canto, summed up by Beatrice's "amor mi mosse, che mi fa parlare" ("love moved me, and makes me speak" [72]), is reversed at the canto's end.[28] The canto is predicated on unrepresented motion that sets the stage for represented speech: the relation between words and deeds established by Lucy, who "si mosse" (101) and then "Disse" (103), is anticipated by the Virgin, practiced by Beatrice, and enjoined upon Vergil, who is told "Or movi, e con la tua parola ornata" ("Now move, and with your ornate speech" [67]). But while Beatrice and Vergil move in order to talk, Vergil's talk disposes the pilgrim to move: "Tu m'hai con disiderio il cor disposto / sì al venir con le parole tue." The canto's last two verses, "Così li dissi; e poi che mosso fue, / intrai per lo cammino alto e silvestro" ("So I spoke to him, and after he had moved, I entered on the high and wooded path"), where speech is the prerequisite for action rather than the other way around, signify the end of stasis and the readiness of the narrative to recommence, to move now that it has spoken. The action that was begun and aborted at the end of canto 1 may now begin again; "intrai" in the last verse of canto 2 signals not only a recoup of the original beginning but an advance upon it, an engagement with and entrance into the new that will be the topic of canto 3.

*Entrare*, which will denote transition throughout the *Commedia* (each of the first five cantos contains at least one instance), sets the stage for a canto that is about transition.[29] If *Inferno* 2 is about the act of beginning, *Inferno* 3 is about the state that immediately follows that act, a moment we could think of as the beginning-*ire* of having begun. Transition—*trans-ire*—going beyond, will be figured most explicitly in the crossing of the river, the *trapassare* that takes place at the canto's end; it is immediately present in the "si va," "si va," "si va" of the canto's first three verses (echoing "Or va" from 2.139), a verbal propulsion that culminates in the irreversibility of "Lasciate ogne speranza, voi ch'*intrate*" ("Leave all hope, you who *enter*" [3.9]). The words on the gate of hell signal the newest new beginning in a form that is far from subtle: this is the entrance, this is the way forward, this is the beginning, they tell us. These verses employ one of the *Commedia*'s basic techniques, that of imparting crucial information which the pilgrim/reader is not yet in a position to appreciate, so that they accrete greater significance with hindsight.[30] Thus, although we are duly informed that "Giustizia mosse il mio alto fattore" ("Justice moved my high maker" [4]), this is information that we will internalize—if at all—only after completing much of the voyage through hell, not here at the outset; nor would the poet want it otherwise. In fact, the poet counts on our not internalizing the information that he so carefully places on the record; the *Inferno*'s power, as poetry, derives from the tension that exists between abstract verities such as these and the palpable sympathy for the damned that the poet manipulates the reader into feeling. The text's aliveness comes from this ability to work at cross purposes to itself, to create living situations rather than fictive concords: although we are told about justice by the words on the gate, we shall nonetheless be persuaded to see mistreated victims by the words in the sinners' mouths; although we are told about hell's impotence by Beatrice, who reveals that its misery cannot harm her, we shall nonetheless be persuaded to feel fear as the events of the first canticle unfold.[31] Thus, the pilgrim forgets about justice when he meets Francesca, and both guide and charge forget Beatrice's words when challenged by the devils at the gates of Dis.

Another signpost marking the new beginning of *Inferno* 3 is the repetition of locative adverbs we find early on, in the form of *qui* ("Qui si convien lasciare ogne sospetto; / ogne viltà convien che qui sia morta" ["Here it is necessary to leave all fear; here all cowardice must die" (14–15)]) or *quivi*, in one case linked to *cominciare*:[32] "Quivi sospiri, pianti, e alti guai / risonavan per l'aere sanza stelle, / per ch'io al cominciar ne lagrimai" ("There sighs, crying, and high wails resounded through the air without stars, so that I at the beginning wept at it" [22–24]). The reiterated locatives stress the place where we have arrived, where we are now, at the expense of previous locations; they serve to differentiate our experience of the journey thus far, to mark it off into discrete segments, distinct new experiences that must be ordered by divided thoughts, "per concetto diviso." Techniques of this kind are employed so unremittingly throughout the *Commedia* that we barely notice them; they function as tiny and remarkably effective subliminal contributors to a textual metaphysics that seeks to persuade us to accord it the status of reality. In *Inferno* 3, moreover, the idea of difference insinuated by way of the recurrent *qui* is a major theme of the canto as a whole, which represents a place that is the space between other places, a place for creatures who are, Vergil tells us, accepted neither in heaven nor in hell: "Cac-cianli i ciel per non esser men belli, / né lo profondo inferno li riceve" ("The heavens drive them out in order not to be less beautiful, nor does deep hell receive them" [40–41]). In these verses the words "profondo inferno" are hallmarks of the poetics of the new, which requires a continual redefining of implicit boundaries in order to keep us moving forward: in canto 2, where what matters is the distinction between Beatrice's point of origin and her point of arrival, indeterminate place markers like "qua giuso" (83), "qua entro" (87), "qua giù" (112) are sufficient; in canto 3, on the other hand, our position must be distinguished not just from heaven but from the place in canto 2 and, at least *grosso modo*, from the rest of hell. Thus, we find the phrase "profondo inferno," which serves the immediate purpose but will run counter to later distinctions between "lower" and "upper" hell, distinctions that in their turn will be subject to continual modification, as the pressure to mark the new escalates: Dante keeps redefining the idea of lower hell the lower in hell we get. By marking the spot to which we have come as a spot that is within the gate of hell but different from *profondo inferno*, the poet distinguishes and blurs simultaneously; he lets us know that this is a new and different place while leaving us retrospectively confused as to the status of this place within the whole. When, in canto 4, we learn that we are entering the first circle of hell, we are able to infer what the place in canto 3 is not. But what is it? The structural confusion that afflicts canto 2—is it the pro-logue to the whole poem or to the first canticle?—has resurfaced in canto 3 as a topographical and moral confusion: are these souls in hell and, if not, where are they?[33]

The place in canto 3 is transition incarnate. Its identity is conferred by what it is between: it is between the gate of hell and the river Acheron, which the pilgrim will cross at canto's end.[34] To reach that crossing, that point of commitment, that Rubicon at which transition is ratified, the pil-grim must transit the place of transitions in canto 3. It is also a place that tells us a great deal about the character and methods of our poet. Morally, this place serves as an index of engagement, dramatizing his commitment to commitment by creating a category for those who rejected both good and evil (but who are, we note, by no means positioned equally between the two). Narratologically, this place serves as a way of once more postponing the elusive beginning that seemed so definite as we faced the words on hell's gate; what was delayed in canto 2 by the pilgrim's moral cowardice, the "viltade" of which Vergil accuses him in 2.45, is delayed in canto 3 by the thematically related *viltà* of the first souls he sees. Moreover, Dante's invention of the theologically nonwarranted and unprecedented category of cowardly neutrals demonstrates the lengths to which he will go in his use of distinction to forge a beginning as hard to pinpoint as any in life itself.[35] The vestibule of hell, or "antehell" as it is sometimes called (a locution whose very coining betrays critical uneasiness with and rationalization of Dante's program of deliberate obfuscation), performs a function that will be performed later, on a larger scale, by a similarly motivated Dantesque invention, "antepurgatory" (a liminal area that we have baptized without sufficiently considering the significance of the label, which again insists on difference within similarity), and still later by the three earth-shadowed heavens: the function of instituting difference where otherwise there would be an undifferentiated expanse. The result of all these distinctions is to blur absolute distinction in the narrative sphere, and thus in the moral sphere as well; the reader's confusion in "placing" the souls of *Inferno* 3 is mirrored by later attempts to distinguish the souls of lower hell generally from the souls of upper hell, and later still by attempts to distinguish the souls of antepurgatory from those of purgatory proper, and finally by attempts to distinguish the souls in the lower heavens from those higher up.

The institutionalizing of difference throughout this text, mandated by the poetics of the new, is the source of a deep-seated confusion that has launched at least a thousand critical debates, which take the form of discussing individual souls but in fact reflect basic perplexities: Are the souls of upper hell in any way "better" than those lower down, any less damned? (Vergil suggests as much when he tells the pilgrim that "incontenenza / men Dio offende e men biasimo accatta" ["incontinence offends God less and incurs less blame" (*Inf.* 11.83–84)].) Are the souls in antepurgatory, and by extension those in the lower heavens, any less saved than those higher up? Ultimately, Francesca is as damned as Ugolino, Belacqua as redeemed as Forese, and Piccarda as saved as Beatrice, but Dante has created a system in which these truths compete with other truths (most problematically, as we shall see, in the *Paradiso*). He confronts us with absolute truths, while simultaneously rehearsing all the differentiating factors that apparently conflict with those truths. The excessive ingenuity that marks so many critical attempts to account for the collocation of this or that soul or group of souls is symptomatic of the double bind in which Dante places his reader, who must register difference while never losing sight of the larger units that subsume these differences. Dante's method tempts the reader into an absolutism not in fact displayed by the poet, into ascribing to him a dogmatism that he has in actual practice not endorsed. Vis-à-vis the uncodified second realm, in particular, Dante enjoys an ideological freedom that gives him carte blanche for the creation of difference and the consequent blurring of distinction.[36] He exploits this freedom to the hilt in the creation of antepurgatory: as an authorially invented space for which there is absolutely no constraining theological precedent, Dante's antepurgatory has generated sustained critical bewilderment, with regard, for instance, to its geographical extension (should it include the banks of the Tiber?) and its moral taxonomy (should its four types of sinners all be considered negligent?). The solitary and unplaceable figure of Sordello (scholars have debated whether he should be grouped with those who died violently or with the princes in the valley) is emblematic of the ambiguities raised by this liminal space.[37]

We are confused by Dante's love of difference, by his cultivation of the new: students must frequently be reminded that the souls of antepurgatory are indeed saved, while critics succumb to the temptation to make the distinction between antepurgatory and purgatory too hard and fast, too rigidly black and white (Peter Armour, for instance, makes too much of the "negative, waiting world of Antepurgatory," as distinct from the positive world of purgatory proper).[38] It is easy to conceive of these differences as more clear-cut than Dante makes them, picking up suggestions that Dante does not fail to offer, such as Vergil's request to be directed "là dove purgatorio ha dritto *inizio*" ("there where purgatory has its true *beginning*" [*Purg.* 7.39]). By the same token, much emphasis is placed on the transition from antepurgatory to purgatory: the hinges of the door resound, the angel warns the pilgrim not to look back. But all the souls in antepurgatory, without exception, will eventually pass this way, so that what we have is another instance of Dante's art of gradation: to create his newest new beginning, his newest "dritto inizio," the poet must institute difference, must draw a line between what was and what is to come—the new. And, in fact, the cantos that mark the end of antepurgatory—the end of the beginning of the purgatorial journey—demonstrate with peculiar clarity Dante's art of highlighting, institutionalizing, and exploiting transition: while *Purgatorio* 8 marks the end of antepurgatory, *Purgatorio* 9 embodies transition to purgatory, and *Purgatorio* 10 provides the new beginning of purgatory proper.[39] The gradations thus expressed should not be hardened into absolute moral categories; for in fact they exist less by virtue of the moral order than by virtue of the needs of the narrative, itself a kind of macro–terza rima that conjoins (almost) every new beginning with the ending/beginning that precedes it. The exception is the ending constituted by *Inferno* 34 and the beginning constituted by *Purgatorio* 1, an ending and beginning that correspond to the only absolute difference in this world: the difference between damnation and salvation. The wonder is that Dante's art of transition makes us believe in so many other differences along the way.

In each of the poem's early cantos the art of transition is particularly in evidence, as Dante works to make each new beginning the real new beginning at the expense of its predecessor, thus creating the illusion of a deferral of beginning while at the same time relaying information essential to the creation of the possible world that is, in fact, beginning to take shape. Canto 3 is no exception, and a key "first" to which the canto introduces us is the contrapasso,[40] the principle whereby the poet fashions the form that damnation (or purgation) takes by transforming the sinners' spiritual condition while alive into their literal condition after death, either making their later suffering like their earlier sin or setting up a contrast between past and present. Although contrapasso by analogy is more usual in hell, in canto 3 we find the other variety: the souls are stimulated by flies and wasps as they run after a banner symbolizing the beliefs and commitments they never embraced. Of greater significance, from the perspective of the narrative journey, is that Dante takes the opportunity to inaugurate not only the contrapasso in its simple sense but also what I think of as the "textual contrapasso," a technique whereby the text inflicts a distinct punishment of its own—with the result that it becomes an instrument of God's justice in its own right, and the poet has engineered a conflation of the "reality" the text represents with the vehicle that represents it. In the case of the neutrals, the textual contrapasso is the poet's deliberate suppression of information regarding souls whom he tells us he recognizes, especially the one of whom he says "vidi e conobbi l'ombra di colui / che fece per viltade il gran rifiuto" ("I saw and I knew the shade of him who made through cowardice the great refusal" [59–60]).[41] By withholding the soul's identity and guaranteeing the insoluble enigma that has resulted from his reticence, the poet acts on and indeed gives life—life outside the text—to Vergil's injunction, "non ragioniam di lor, ma guarda e passa" ("let us not speak of them, but look and pass on" [51]). Although Dante has not been able to prevent scholarly discussion, he has effectively ensured that all discourse regarding this figure remain hypothetical, shadowed by the text's contempt. Thus, the real and eternal anonymity of the soul "che fece per viltade il gran rifiuto" is his true contrapasso, and it is conferred not within the fiction of the poem but within the reality of the text's reception, by the poet.[42] Techniques of this sort, intended to blur our sense of the distinction between the fabricated text and the allegedly nonfabricated reality of which it tells, belong to a kind of representational mirror game first played in the opening verses of canto 3, where we encounter verses that are allegedly written by the gate of hell itself, rather than by the author of the poem. A measure of the poet's success in using such tactics is provided by the history of our response to these verses, for we have rarely stopped to consider how they invest the subjective author of the *Inferno* with the objective authority of the divine "author"— i.e., maker—of hell.[43]

In the second part of canto 3, after viewing the neutrals, Dante treats the paradoxical desire of those souls who are destined for "real" hell to cross the Acheron. Twice he indicates the souls' eagerness to make the transition by pairing the verb *trapassare* with the adjective *pronto*: "e qual costume / le fa di trapassar parer sì pronte" ("what instinct makes them seem so ready to cross over" [73–74]); "e pronti sono a trapassar lo rio" ("and they are ready to cross the river" [124]). Again, as with Beatrice's statement on the inability of hell or its denizens to harm her, we find passages that lay the groundwork for all of hell. The sinners' basic psychological posture as victims of anyone but themselves, subject to anything but free will, is schematically rendered in their curses: "Bestemmiavano Dio e lor parenti, / l'umana spezie e 'l loco e 'l tempo e 'l seme / di lor semenza e di lor nascimenti" ("They cursed God and their parents, and the human species and the place and the time and the seed of their sowing and of their birth" [103–5]). The violence with which the souls throw themselves one by one from the shore—"gittansi di quel lito ad una ad una" (116)—is matched by the violence of the divine justice that spurs them ("la divina giustizia li sprona" [125]), turning their fear into desire ("sì che la tema si volve in disio" [126]). The fierce and mysterious dialectic between what the souls want for themselves and what God wants for them denotes the dialectic between free will and justice that underpins the entire poem: the fear that is converted to desire reminds us that fear creates a standstill, as we saw in cantos 1 and 2, while desire creates forward motion. The text thus comes back to desire as the narrative's motive force, echoing the pilgrim's "disiderio" from the end of canto 2 and anticipating the later definition of desire as "moto spirituale." The spiritual motion that hurls the souls "ad una ad una" from the banks of the Acheron confirms this canto's key role within the economy of a narrative journey that will proceed by representing such souls "ad una ad una," and will eventually, at its end, define itself as the unveiling of "le vite spirituali ad una ad una," in an exact and unique evocation of the expression first used in *Inferno* 3.

In the same way that the presence of an "antehell" adds a distinction to the underworld that blurs the contours of the whole, obscuring hell's boundaries and leaving us confused as to precisely where it begins and precisely whom it embraces, so Dante's handling of limbo is governed by an insistence on distinction that again confuses rather than clarifies. Canto 3 ends with an earthquake that causes the pilgrim to faint, a swoon that is the first of many instances in which Dante uses sleep as a metaphor for the problematic of transition. (In a passage in *Purgatorio* 32 to which we shall return, the poet wishes that he could represent the act of falling asleep; essentially, what he wishes—hardly surprising for the maker of the unbroken chain that is terza rima—is that he could represent transition, the in-between spaces in a life or narrative.) Canto 4 begins with a thunderclap that violently awakens him, "breaking" his sleep. The emphatically non-smooth transition from canto 3 to canto 4 (signaled by canto 4's initial "Ruppemi"), and from one shore of the Acheron to the other, is not only a way of maintaining a focus on transition as the subject of canto 3 but also of marking our newest new beginning, once more made to correspond with the beginning of a new canto: it is a characteristic of these early cantos to highlight each canto as a new beginning by maintaining a rigid symmetry between the boundaries of the cantos—the legs of the narrative journey, as it were—and the boundaries or legs of the actual (represented) journey. Again we find the verbal markers of newness, the words that stress this place and this moment at the expense of the last place and the last moment. "Or discendiam qua giù nel cieco mondo" ("Now let us descend down here into the blind world" [13]), says Vergil, articulating the new both temporally ("Or") and spatially ("qua giù"). We note the repetition of "qua giù" a few verses later ("L'angoscia de le genti / che son qua giù" ["The anguish of the people who are down here" (19–20)]) and the use of "Quivi" to lead off a tercet differentiating the sounds of this new place from the place we just left: with "Quivi, secondo che per ascoltare, / non avea pianto mai che di sospiri" ("There, from what could be heard, there was no lament greater than sighs" [25–26]), the poet asserts a new reality to replace the "Quivi sospiri, pianti e alti guai" of a similarly aural tercet on the threshold of the previous canto. The methods employed for differentiating a new place from previous places now expand to include number, our most precise denoter of difference, here used for the first time (in collaboration with the by now standard *intrare*) to tag Limbo as the "primo cerchio": "Così si mise e così mi fé intrare / nel primo cerchio che l'abisso cigne" ("So he entered and so he made me enter the first circle that girds the abyss" [23–24]).

Locating it with numerical precision, Dante has distinguished limbo in a way that seems straightforward, clear, and not susceptible to confusion: it is the first circle of hell. And yet, master of the manipulation of narrative—i.e., textual time—to create dialectical perspectives, Dante will dedicate the rest of canto 4 to making us disbelieve this simple fact, and indeed, how many readers "forget" that limbo is hell's first circle! As I have already indicated, the technique involved is basic to the *Inferno*, a means of structuring tension into the discourse (which in the other canticles Dante obtains by other means), and it is based on the exploitation of the text's temporal dimension: first the poet presents a truth, a "warning" directed at the reader (e.g., hell cannot hurt us, in canto 2; hell's maker was moved by justice, in canto 3; the souls we are about to meet are carnal sinners, in canto 5); then he does everything in his power to make us disregard the warning we have received. *Inferno* 4 is in any case a curiously absent canto, from a narrative point of view, more than usually dependent on the textual future to reveal its subterranean tension and complexity; not a canto that most first-time readers find particularly exciting or dramatic, its drama unfolds as the story of Vergil and the virtuous pagans unfolds, and culminates in *Paradiso* 19's agonized questioning of the justice that condemns those deprived of the knowledge of God through no fault of their own. Since Dante has chosen to keep the larger issues of canto 4 muffled, so that they can be unfolded slowly, literally accompanying Vergil, the figure who embodies them, as he moves through the poem, topography is once more the focal point for the canto's more overt tensions: on the one hand it is established that limbo is hell, on the other hand a great deal is done to make us think of limbo as not hell, in other words to offset the clarity of "così mi fé intrare / nel primo cerchio che l'abisso cigne." We have already seen how, upon entering limbo, the poet notes the difference in sound: where before sighs were accompanied by more violent laments ("sospiri, pianti e alti guai" [3.22]), now there are sighs alone ("non avea pianto mai che di sospiri" [4.26]). We have entered a place where "duol sanza martìri" ("sorrow without torments" [28]) afflicts the "turbe, ch'eran molte e grandi, / d'infanti e di femmine e di viri" ("crowds, that were many and great, of infants, women, and men" [29–30]). The key difference, as presented by Vergil, is that these souls did not sin ("Or vo' che sappi, innanzi che più andi, / ch'ei non peccaro" ["Now I want you to know, before you go any further, that they did not sin" (33–34)]), an anomalous condition underscored by Vergil's own anomalous aggressiveness (note his repetition of "vo' che sappi" in line 62).[44]

The most significant physical indicator of limbo's metaphysical difference is the light cast by the "foco / ch'emisperio di tenebre vincia" ("fire that conquered a hemisphere of shadows" [68–69]), a light that contrasts sharply with the darkness of the abyss on whose edge the pilgrim finds himself at the canto's beginning. While the opening obscurity is so profound that it prevents him from discerning anything below (10–12), the light that they reach later reveals a "loco aperto, luminoso e alto, / sì che veder si potien tutti quanti" ("place that was open, luminous and high, so that we could see everybody" [116–17]). It is true that the light carved out of the shadows by the fire is reserved, like the noble castle that they enter to reach the open and luminous place in which all can be seen, for the special souls of limbo, the "honorable folk" ("orrevol gente" [72])—predominantly classical figures—whose fame has acquired them this special dispensation: "L'onrata nominanza / che di lor suona sù ne la tua vita, / grazïa acquista in ciel che sì li avanza" ("Their honored name, which resounds up above in your life, acquires grace in heaven that accrues for them thus" [76–78]). But the net result of the special dispensation, for all that it mandates an entrance within an entrance ("per sette porte intrai con questi savi" ["through seven gates I entered with these sages" (110)]), is less to differentiate between the souls within limbo than to differentiate all of limbo from the rest of hell, reinforcing those aspects of the first circle that are unlike what we have seen previously and what we expect to see later on. The pilgrim's query, "questi chi son c'hanno cotanta onranza, / che dal modo de li altri li diparte" ("who are these who have so much honor that it sets them apart from the way of the others" [74–75]), aptly expresses the special status of limbo as a whole. The difference that distinguishes limbo's honored few from its unnamed crowds provides an emblem for the difference that sets the whole first circle apart from hell's other circles, *che dal modo de li altri lo diparte*, a difference that is stressed at the end of canto 4: "per altra via mi mena il savio duca, / fuor de la queta, ne l'aura che trema. / E vegno in parte ove non è che luca" ("by another path my wise leader leads me, out of the quiet, into the air that trembles. And I come to a part where there is nothing that shines" [149–51]). In order to express the new, i.e., the place they find upon leaving limbo, the poet rehearses those aspects of limbo that are no more, that make it forever different: now we embark on an "altra via" that takes us beyond limbo's quiet, and—most emphatically, in the canto's last verse—beyond its light, "ove non è che luca."[45]

It is the light, then, the light that no longer shines in canto 5, that gives us the feeling that we are not really in hell when we are in limbo, and that reinforces limbo's literally marginal status: *limbo*, like its modern derivative *lembo*, means border or edge.[46] Thus, when the pilgrim awakes at the beginning of canto 4 he finds himself "'n su la proda" (7)—on the edge or brink—of the abyss. As with the place in canto 3, which is within the gate of hell but not yet beyond the Acheron, here Dante creates a first circle whose position as the first circle he undercuts by emphasizing everything that is on the edge, marginal, liminal, different about it.[47] This is an ideologically motivated topography, informed not only by the desire to destabilize the boundaries of hell but also by the poet's underlying polemic about the value of classical culture: while it is true, as scholars of the Renaissance never tire of pointing out, that Dante places Aristotle and the others in hell, it is also true, and much more relevant to Dante's contemporaries, that he places them—counter to all theological precedent—in limbo.[48] The tranquil and undramatic pace of *Inferno* 4 should not cause us to overlook the exceedingly dramatic nature of the canto's implied poetic choices, its suppression of unbaptized infants, mentioned only once in passing (infants for whom, if for anyone, theologians declared their sympathies) in favor of pagan poets and philosophers. Dante invents—in the same way that he invents the category and topography of an antehell for his neutrals—a special condition for the honorable folk of the noble castle. This special condition is as theologically willful as his decision to place virtuous pagans in limbo in the first place, along with the theologically orthodox unbaptized infants to whom he pays virtually no attention (a lack of attention that is underscored by the interestingly discrepant behavior of Vergil, who in his description of limbo for Sordello in *Purgatorio* 7 devotes a tercet each to the infants and to the virtuous pagans). The topography of the first circle perfectly adumbrates Dante's relation to classical antiquity throughout the *Commedia*; limbo's "limbic" position, within hell but not of hell, figures his simultaneous damnation and exaltation of classical culture, most fully articulated in his treatment of Vergil.[49]

For our present purposes, however, the chief point is that Dante's handling of limbo constitutes another deferral of the beginning, once more conjuring in us the sensation that we have not yet reached "true" hell, a sensation that the opening of canto 5 will reinforce. The last verses of canto 4, in which Vergil leads the pilgrim "per altra via . . . fuor de la queta . . . ove non è che luca," implicitly set up the second circle as everything that the first circle is not;[50] the implication is that in canto 5 we will finally reach hell. Canto 5's first thirty-nine verses strenuously reaffirm the difference that is implied by canto 4's conclusion; affirmation of the difference between hell's first and second circles is the task of the opening tercet: "Così discesi del cerchio primaio / giù nel secondo, che men loco cinghia / e tanto più dolor, che punge a guaio" ("So I descended from the first circle down into the second, which holds less space and so much more suffering that goads to lamentation"). Immediately the new beginning is marked by the downward plunge of "Così discesi" (underscored by "giù"), and difference is driven home by the numbers "primaio" and "secondo," whose differentiating function is strengthened by their correlation with the quantifying adverbs "più" and "meno"; the second circle is different from the first in that it holds less space but more suffering. All this is then buttressed by the presence of Minos, the infernal judge who warns the travelers to beware the entrance ("guarda com'*entri* e di cui tu ti fide; / non t'inganni l'ampiezza de l'*intrare*!" ["watch how you *enter* and in whom you trust; do not be deceived by the width of the *entrance*!" (19–20)]) of which he is the guardian: "Stavvi Minòs orribilmente, e ringhia: / essamina le colpe ne l'*intrata*" ("Minos stands there horribly, and snarls; he examines the sins in the *entrance*" [4–5]). Minos stands at the entrance of a new beginning as a sentient marker of difference, constituting a barrier between the souls who do not have to submit to his judgment and those who do, a barrier that cuts between canto 5 and all that precedes it, putting canto 5 on the wrong side of the divide, in the same way that the Acheron cuts between canto 4 and its predecessors, to the detriment of those in canto 4. Minos's differentiating function will be recalled much later by Vergil, who is all too happy to upgrade himself by reminding us that he is among the souls whom Minos does not bind, in verses that provide a retrospective gloss on the way that the beginning of *Inferno* 5 reinforces limbo's outsider status: "Minòs me non lega; / ma son del cerchio ove son li occhi casti / di Marzia tua" ("Minos does not bind me; for I am of the circle where are the chaste eyes of your Marcia" [*Purg.* 1.77–79]). Since Minos's job institutionalizes difference by assigning each soul to its precise location, it is not surprising that the language that describes his duties anticipates the canto that will be devoted to institutionalizing difference in the *Inferno* as a whole, namely canto 11; in canto 5 we are first introduced to degree and gradation—the notions summed up by *più* and *meno*—through Minos's determinations and assignments: "vede *qual loco* d'inferno è da essa; / cignesi con la coda *tante volte* / *quantunque gradi* vuol che giù sia messa" ("he sees *which part* of hell is for it, and girds himself with his tail *as many times as the grades* that he wants it to be sent down" [10–12]).

Once beyond Minos, we reach the initial descriptions of the second circle, again concentrated on sound. As the "orribili favelle" ("horrible sounds" [3.25]) of the vestibule mediate between Beatrice's angelic "favella" (2.57) and the sighs of limbo, so in canto 5 change is again marked aurally, in a tercet that registers difference in the emphatically repeated particle "or" (linked to *cominciare*, as was *quivi* in a similar tercet in canto 3): "Or incomincian le dolenti note / a farmisi sentire; or son venuto / là dove molto pianto mi percuote" ("Now the sorrowful notes begin to make themselves heard; now I have come to where much weeping hits me" [25–27]). The next tercet continues to characterize the second circle as in every way different from the first, even explicitly recalling canto 4's last verse; where there was light, now there is darkness, where there was quiet, now there is roaring noise: "Io venni in loco d'ogne luce muto, / che mugghia come fa mar per tempesta" ("I came to a place mute of all light, which roars like the sea in a storm" [28–29]). However, after describing the souls being whipped about by the infernal storm and cursing God in a way reminiscent of the souls in canto 3, and after noting that the damned of the second circle are carnal sinners, who submit reason to desire ("enno dannati i peccator carnali, / che la ragion sommettono al talento" [38–39]), thus reminding us that this is the first circle to treat a positive sin, the tonality—and apparent morality— of canto 5 begin to shift. With the first bird simile, the poet begins the portrayal of these souls as buffetted victims of love, tossed by their passions like starlings by the wind. Slowly his voice takes on the lyric and romance modalities that will erupt in Francesca's speeches, to leave their imprint on the pilgrim and the reader. Indeed, the infernal ambience that we find in the opening section of canto 5 is effectively dissipated by the poet's change of register, which is virtually complete by the time we reach the transitional tercet that literally romanticizes the sinners, making them "donne antiche e ' cavalieri" ("ladies of old and knights" [71]).

Once again Dante has found a way of blurring his sharply drawn distinctions. Although in the case of canto 5 he creates his chiaroscuro not topographically but poetically, the effect is the same: he manipulates the level of textual tension by endowing Francesca with beautiful, irresistible language, language that has caused generations of readers to swoon like the pilgrim at the canto's end. After Francesca has spoken, we forget the coarse brutality of Minos's tail and the harsh indictment of "peccator carnali"; the clear distinctions wrought by the canto's opening have been obscured, as once more Dante subverts the absolute in order to charge moral issues with the difficulty they possess for the living. The *Inferno*, which challenges us by alternating between sinners for whom we feel little or no sympathy and sinners to whom we must respond, provides in its first great individual encounter a striking instance of the poet's manipulation of the reader's affective response, which was not similarly stimulated by the abject neutrals or the stern sages. Our acceptance of the damned as damned is not overdetermined by the text, which cuts across its own grain to achieve its goal; the narrative journey engages us dialectically, with the result that readers resist Francesca's sinfulness, perhaps not correctly, but certainly abetted by the text. The history of the episode's reception testifies to Dante's willingness to sacrifice clarity of dogma to a "living" textuality: not surprisingly, the critical impasse discussed in the preceding chapter is exemplified by our handling of Francesca. She divides critics into champions of theology and defenders of poetry, a dichotomy further reflected in the poet vs. pilgrim formulation, according to which the stern moralizing poet (ironically, this "poet" is not susceptible to the charms of poetry) damns the woman for whom the pilgrim feels sympathy. Interpretation is thus fractured by the text's kinetic dimension, which programmatically undermines our ability to focus on the poem's single creator, who in the case of *Inferno* 5 has done (at least) two things, for both of which we must give him credit: he wrote the poetry with which Francesca seduces the pilgrim/reader, and he put her into hell.

*Inferno* 6 is a modest and unprepossessing canto whose new beginning is particularly forceful, benefiting from the lyrical atmosphere of the Francesca episode, its deliberate lack of attention to the sordid realities of hell, to conjure by contrast a properly hellish environment. The first canto that does not strive to further defer the beginning of hell, canto 6 begins by underscoring hell's reality. On the one hand, there is the ostentatious emphasis on the newness that barrages the pilgrim, and on the present tense in which he alone is not stuck: "novi tormenti e novi tormentati, / mi veggio intorno, come ch'io mi mova / e ch'io mi volga, e come che io guati" ("new sufferings and new sufferers I see around me, whichever way I move, and whichever way I turn, and whichever way I look" [4–6]). On the other, there is the static, totally adjectival verse that describes the eternally not new conditions of this circle: the "piova / etterna, maladetta, fredda e greve" ("rain eternal, cursed, cold and heavy" [7–8]) whose "regola e qualità mai non l'è nova" (9). Like canto 5, canto 6 uses its first thirty-nine verses to set the stage; but unlike canto 5, canto 6 does not then proceed to graft a whole new sensibility onto that of its opening section. Rather, its poetic identity is determined by contrast to that of the preceding canto, whose mysteries it immediately recasts in its own language: "Al tornar de la mente, che si chiuse / dinanzi a la pietà d'i due cognati" ("At the return of my mind, which had closed itself before the piteousness of the two in-laws" [1–2]). Here canto 5's oft-reiterated *pietà* is experienced not at the plight of two *amanti* but at that of "due cognati," in a transfer that is symptomatic of Dante's handling of the third circle; in place of the refined Francesca, whose very name is redolent of the courtly French romances on which she models her story, we find Ciacco, whose porcine nickname encapusulates the shift in register from lyric lust to prosaic gluttony. "Io sono al terzo cerchio" ("I am in the third circle" [7]), the narrator announces, and suddenly everything has changed: while Francesca, although not a Florentine, is known to the pilgrim, who importunes her twice, the second time by name, Ciacco, a fellow Florentine, must accost the pilgrim, hoping to be recognized. But to no avail; Ciacco is forced to instruct the pilgrim that "Voi cittadini mi chiamaste Ciacco" ("You citizens called me Ciacco" [52]), thus introducing the theme of Florence, the true protagonist of canto 6 (perhaps it is not coincidental that in the canto where we "reach hell," we reach Florence as well),[51] and using the concise and stringent syntax that will characterize his speech, in contrast to Francesca's more literary diction.[52] Where his speech echoes hers, the result is to strengthen the contrast: if the words *bocca* and *persona* recall Francesca, who uses both in an erotic context, we now find, in place of the lovers' kiss on the mouth, the mouths of Cerberus, and in place of a beloved body, the insubstantial bodies of the gluttonous souls, limply prostrate beneath the pelting rain. By the same token, while in canto 5 the pilgrim falls at the end of the encounter, thus preserving Francesca's tragic dignity, in canto 6 Ciacco squints and collapses among his companions. His ignominious departure is typical of a circle that causes the pilgrim to comment of the pain he sees that "s'altra è maggio, nulla è sì spiacente" ("if another is greater, none is so unpleasant" [48]). This ranking of the circle's suffering, for all that it borders on the comic, is a way of definitively enrolling it in the hierarchy of hell: we may be at the beginning, but we have arrived.

A full appreciation of canto 6's role within the economy of the narrative journey, its position as the last "infernal incipit," the last canto to function according to the rules that have governed the narrative thus far, requires a brief discussion of canto endings. There are three basic types of canto ending in the *Inferno*: (1) endings that denote, with respect to the journey being represented, forward motion and transition; (2) endings where transition is delayed but initiated; (3) endings that provide no transition at all.[53] Thus far, all canto endings, i.e., moments of formal transition, have been correlated with moments of thematic transition; in other words, there have been no examples of the third type of ending. The first type of ending may be further subdivided: either it denotes pure forward motion, as in canto 1 ("Allor si mosse, e io li tenni dietro"), or it denotes forward motion that has already become an entry into the new, as in canto 4 ("E vegno in parte ove non è che luca"); in the case of canto 2 we find forward motion that has been stiffened by the use of *intrare* ("intrai per lo cammino alto e silvestro"), but is not yet the full-fledged description of the new that we find in canto 4. The second type of ending relies on a pause that delays the transition but lays the foundation on which it takes place; although later in the canticle there will be more subtle means of achieving this effect, up to now it has been achieved by stopping the action in almost melodramatic fashion. The result is to create a situation that must be resolved in the next canto before moving forward; transition, which is implied in the canto ending, is in this way delayed beyond the first verse of the succeeding canto. Thus, the pilgrim's faint at the end of canto 3 ("e caddi come l'uom cui sonno piglia") delays transition until verse 4 of canto 4 but is also the vehicle that allows transition to occur. The same may be said for the similar faint that overcomes the pilgrim at the end of canto 5 ("E caddi come corpo morto cade"), which again delays transition until verse 4 of the subsequent canto: only after rehearsing the pity that had caused him to swoon does the action proceed with the "novi tormenti e novi tormentati" that he sees all about him.

The ending of canto 6 does not disrupt the pattern established by previous canto endings. It is of the first type; specifically, it belongs to the subset that records not just transition but transition accomplished, arrival into the new. Like canto 4's "E vegno in parte ove non è che luca," which marks departure from the first circle and entry into the second, the last verse of canto 6 registers departure from the third circle and entrance into the fourth, where the misers and spendthrifts are guarded by the god of wealth: "quivi trovammo Pluto, il gran nemico" ("there we found Plutus, the great enemy"). The ending of canto 6 also maintains the narrative status quo by conforming to the strict symmetry that has obtained thus far between canto and circle: to each formal unit, the canto, is assigned one geographical or episodic unit. Canto 7 marks a turning point, where for the first time the rigid correlation between the narrative journey and the pilgrim's journey is relaxed; it is the first canto not to confine itself to the circle that we enter at its beginning.[54] Thus, after viewing the fruits of avarice and prodigality and listening to Vergil's discourse on Fortune, transition is signaled in the language to which we are accustomed: Vergil's "Or discendiam omai a maggior pietà"[55] ("Now let us descend to greater anguish" [7.97]) leads to "intrammo giù per una via diversa"[56] ("we entered down by a different path" [105]), which in turn leads to the description of the muddy souls who are immersed in the Styx. What is new is not the language but the "deregulated" way in which this language is deployed, occurring three-quarters of the way through canto 7 rather than at its end. In other words, a transition in the pilgrim's journey—his passage from the fourth to the fifth circle—has for the first time occurred out of synchrony with the formal transitions of canto beginnings and endings.[57] Thematic transitions are no longer tied to the transitions enacted by the form. This narrative deregulation will be allowed further scope at the end of canto 7: the apparently straightforward motion of the last verse, "Venimmo al piè d'una torre al da sezzo" ("We came finally to the foot of a tower"), will be complicated by the insertion of a flashback in the opening verses of canto 8, with the result that we are for the first time rendered retrospectively uncertain as to precisely how far forward we have moved.

With *Inferno* 7, then, the narrative spiral delineated by the beginnings and endings of the first six cantos, whereby each new canto comes into being by looking back and defining itself as different from what came before, becomes less visible. The process does not cease to exist; as we shall see in the next chapter, the episodes of *Inferno* 8–9 and 16–17 serve as prologues to new beginnings on a large scale, marking respectively transition from the upper hell that houses the sins of incontinence to the lower hell ("basso inferno" [8.75; 12.35]) beyond the walls of Dis, and the boundary that separates the realm of fraud from all that precedes it. On a smaller scale as well, narrative progression will continue to be articulated in terms of new beginnings, following the principles established in the first six cantos of the *Inferno*. These principles receive their most explicit theoretical airing in *Inferno* 11,[58] the canto that expounds difference, clustering quantifiers in an effort to give verbal shape to the hierarchy of hell: "tre cerchietti" ("three little circles" [17]), "primo cerchio" ("first circle" [28]), "tre gironi" ("three rings" [30]), "lo giron primo" ("the first ring" [39]), "secondo /giron" ("second ring" [41–42]), "cerchio secondo" ("second circle" [57]). We find as well an impressive spate of the adverbs first used in canto 5 to render difference, *più* and *meno*: since fraud "più spiace a Dio" ("displeases God more" [26]), the fraudulent are assailed by "più dolor" ("more suffering" [27]); since incontinence, on the other hand, "men Dio offende e men biasimo accatta" ("offends God less and incurs less blame" [84]), God's vengeance is "men crucciata" ("less wrathful" [89]) in smiting such sinners. We find expressions that convey difference geographically, dividing those who are below and within from those who are above and without: while the fraudulent "stan di sotto" ("are below" [26]), the incontinent are not within the city of Dis ("dentro da la città roggia" ["inside the flaming city" (73)]) but "sù di fuor" ("up outside" [87]). We find phrases like "di grado in grado" ("from grade to grade" [18]) and "per diverse schiere" ("in different groups" [39]), and verbs that denote differentiation, such as *distinguere* and *dipartire*: the circle of violence "in tre gironi è distinto" ("is divided into three rings" [30]), and the incontinent are "dipartiti" ("divided" [89]) from the souls of lower hell. Vergil is a differentiator, his discourse an act of differentiation, which "ben distingue / questo baràtro e 'l popol ch'e' possiede" ("clearly distinguishes this abyss and the people it possesses" [68–69]). And if it is with some impatience that Vergil expects the pilgrim to grasp his point about the incontinent ("tu vedrai ben perché da questi felli / sien dipartiti" ["you see clearly why they are divided from these felons" (88–89)]), we should remember that he has recently spoken to his charge with even greater asperity, replying to the pilgrim's question (why the souls in the first five circles are not within the city of Dis) with an unusually harsh "Perché tanto delira . . . lo 'ngegno tuo da quel che sòle?" ("Why does your intelligence so deviate from its accustomed path?" [76–77]). Vergil is essentially asking Dante how he can have failed to grasp the principle that underlies all created existence, the principle of difference, the principle that the poet of the *Commedia* renders through his masterful use of the poetics of the new.

*Inferno* 11 is usually considered a boring canto. Let us conclude this chapter on Dante's art of *gradatio* by observing that, as codifier of difference and institutionalizer of the poetics of the new, canto 11 is in fact a safeguard against boredom: a prime bulwark against the narrative parataxis—and resulting boredom—that afflicts earlier texts of this ilk. Visions of hell before the *Inferno* suffer from lack of difference: all the sinners seem the same, all the punishments merge into one sadistic blur. Although critics refer to the plastic realism that Dante brings to the genre,[59] they have paid little attention to his importation of narrative structure and order, to the advent of narrative cunning. Where parataxis reigned, both stylistically and structurally, Dante—with passages like *Inferno* 11—imposes hypotaxis. In so doing, he eliminates the random—and he precludes our boredom. Where, in earlier visions of hell, sins and sinners are piled one upon the other with minimal differentiation, so that the reader has no way of distinguishing the first from the second, third, or fourth, and consequently little incentive to see who comes next, in the *Inferno* we know the order in which sins will be encountered and the moral value that has been assigned to each. (Nor does Dante commit the opposite mistake of relaying such information too soon; he waits until he has taken us through all the circles based on the seven deadly sins, whose logic is easy enough to follow, and has begun to complicate matters in such a way that we require assistance.)[60] As a result the reader can anticipate the narrative and is thereby induced to proceed, propelled by the subliminal desire to see how cogently the author's rendering will conform to his earlier declarations, as well as by the urge to participate in a possible world that seems to make sense, or that can be challenged if it does not, because its structuring principles have been made known to us. By the same token, the contrapasso is less a theological device, as it is usually considered, than, in Dante's hands, a narrative stroke of genius: if we look at previous visions from which the contrapasso is lacking, we can see by contrast to what extent its presence anchors the narrative, working with the narrative *gradatio* to deflect the random, to create a sense of order and confer a persuasiveness on the text. The comparative effectiveness of *Tundale's Vision*, for example, derives in no small measure from its rudimentary deployment of the notion that certain punishments befit certain sinners: "Which souls in particular might this punishment be for?" asks Tundale of his angel guide, thus acknowledging a curiosity that the ideology of moral decorum—the ideology of the contrapasso—succeeds in projecting onto the reader as well. This vision also displays an understanding of the need for narrative subordination in order to create differentiation (Tundale is frequently told that the newest punishment will be greater than any he has seen before); moreover, the concern to differentiate has reached the point that the author imagines categories of souls called the "not-very-bad" and the "not-very-good."[61] Such procedures, for all their crudity, lend this text a force that its predecessors lack, and remind us that not least among the secrets of Dante's greatness is his unsurpassed subtlety in deploying the not-so-simple staples of the narrator's art: hypotaxis, gradation, difference, the new, desire, time.

*Chapter 3*

# ULYSSES, GERYON, AND THE AERONAUTICS
# OF NARRATIVE TRANSITION

> What Song the Syrens sang, or what name Achilles assumed
> when he hid himself among women, though puzling
> Questions are not beyond all conjecture.
> (Sir Thomas Browne, *Hydriotaphia, or Urne-Burial*)

> The sin of man is that he seeks to make himself God.
> (Reinhold Niebuhr, *The Nature and Destiny of Man*)

> Io mi credea del tutto esser partito
> da queste nostre rime, messer Cino,
> ché si conviene omai altro cammino
> a la mia nave più lungi dal lito
> *(Dante to Cino da Pistoia)*

> Su per la costa, Amor, de l'alto monte,
> drieto a lo stil del nostro ragionare
> or chi potrà montare,
> poi che son rotte l'ale d'ogni ingegno?
> *(Cino da Pistoia on Dante's death)*

ULYSSES IS AS fundamental to the *Commedia* as the voyage theme that he incarnates and dramatizes, as irrepressible as the trope whose most living embodiment within the poem he is. He is linked to the poem's metaphorization of desire as flight, a metaphor whose origin is the celebrated verse from Ulysses' oration, in which the adventurer indicates the extent of the enthusiasm he had solicited from his aged crew by saying "de' remi facemmo ali al folle volo" ("of our oars we made wings for the mad flight" [*Inf.* 26.125]).[1] Ulysses and his surrogates, other failed flyers like Phaeton and Icarus, are thus connected to one of the *Commedia*'s most basic metaphorical assumptions: if we desire sufficiently, we fly. In other words, if we desire sufficiently, our quest takes on wings; if we desire sufficiently, we vault all obstacles, we cross all boundaries (perhaps we even trans-gress, vaulting in a *varco folle*). Thus the passage in the *Purgatorio* in which the narrator overtly establishes the metaphorical identity between desire and flight, saying that in order to climb the steep grade of lower purgatory one needs to fly with the wings of desire: "ma qui convien ch'om voli; / dico con l'ale snelle e con le piume / del gran disio" ("but here a man must fly—I mean with the slender wings and with the feathers of great desire" [Purg. 4.27–29]). The pilgrim flies on the "piume del gran disio," and the saturation of the Commedia with flight imagery—Ulyssean flight imagery—is due to the importance of desire as the impulse that governs all questing, all voyaging, all coming to know. Desire and the search for understanding are intimately linked, indeed ultimately one: desire is spiritual motion, "disire è moto spiritale." This equivalence, desire = spiritual motion, crucially recasts in the metaphorical language of voyage and pilgrimage the Aristotelian precept that stands on the Convivio's threshold, where we already find articulated the link between desiderio and sapere: "tutti li uomini naturalmente desiderano di sapere" ("all men naturally desire to know" [Conv. 1.1.1]). The treatise's abstract conceptual pairing returns in the Commedia's metaphorical copulae: the wingéd oars, the plumage of great desire. Desire—Ulyssean ardore—is the motor propelling all voyage: both right voyages, conversions, and those that, like Ulysses' own, tend toward the left, the "lato mancino" (Inf. 26.126). Readings of Dante's Ulysses thus focus on his desires as appropriate or transgressive, as well as on the way his desires reflect those of the poem's other voyager, Dante himself.

Dante criticism has been divided on the subject of Ulysses essentially since its inception. Among the early commentators, Buti takes a moralizing position critical of the Homeric hero, while Benvenuto sees him as exciting Dante's admiration.[2] We could sketch the positions of various modern critics around the same polarity: there is a pro-Ulysses group, spearheaded by Fubini, who maintains that Dante feels only admiration for the folle volo, the desire for knowledge it represents, and the oration that justifies it;[3] and there is a less unified group that emphasizes the Greek hero's sinfulness and seeks to determine the primary cause for his infernal abode (rendered less clear by the poet's avoidance of the eighth bolgia's label until the end of his colloquy with Guido da Montefeltro in the next canto).[4] This second group could be divided into those who see the folle volo itself as the chief of Ulysses' sins, and those who concentrate instead on the sin of fraudulent counsel as described by Guido and the hero's rhetorical deceitfulness as manifested in the orazion picciola.[5] Most influential in the first category has been the position of Nardi, who argues that Dante's Ulysses is a new Adam, a new Lucifer, and that his sin is precisely Adam's, namely "il trapassar del segno."[6] Ulysses is thus a transgressor, whose pride incites him to seek a knowledge that is beyond the limits set for man by God, in the same way that Adam's pride drove him to a similar transgression, also in pursuit of a knowledge that would make him Godlike. Ulysses rebels against the limits marked by the pillars of Hercules, and his rebellion is akin to that of Lucifer and the rebel angels. To account for Ulysses' heroic stature within the poem, Nardi posits a split within Dante himself, whereby the poet is moved by what the theologian condemns.[7] Nardi's reading has much in common with that of an earlier critic, Luigi Valli, who also considered Ulysses deeply embedded within the symbolism of the *Commedia* and representative of the perilous pride that besets mankind.[8] Valli too sees the sin of Dante's Ulysses as akin to Adam's eating of the tree of knowledge, as a *trapassar del segno* analogous to the original sin. The key difference between the two is that Valli relates the figure of Ulysses to Dante's sense of a peril within himself, rather than arguing for an unconsciously divided Dante; indeed, Valli goes so far as to invoke the *Convivio* as an example of Dante's own propensities toward intellectual pride, thus anticipating the positions of such critics as Freccero, Thompson, and Corti.[9]

As is frequently the case in Dante criticism, the Ulysses *querelle* abounds in ironies, which in this instance are centered on the much bandied charge of romantic reading. Fubini and Sapegno attempt to discredit Nardi by charging him with imposing an anachronistically Promethean shape onto Dante's character, with unwittingly falling into a romantic trap, the nonmedieval pitfall of glorifying the quest for knowledge and the rebellious hero who pursues it.[10] By invoking antiromanticism in the name of a purer medievalism, critics who are at pains to demonstrate that Ulysses is not a typical sinner, that he is instead someone for whom Dante feels a special admiration, draw very near to those who originally were at the furthest remove from them on the ideological spectrum, namely the sternest moralists: those, like Anthony Cassell, who deny any special importance to Ulysses at all.[11] For, if at one extreme we place those who argue that Dante feels only admiration for Ulysses' voyage and that it has nothing whatever to do with his damnation (and here the hero's crimes as listed by Vergil and the issue of the nature of this *bolgia* and Ulysses' relation to Guido are brought into play), since his shipwreck cannot be considered a punishment nor the pillars of Hercules to be limits,[12] at the other extreme we find those who urge us not to be taken in by the hero's rhetoric, who tell us that the poet feels nothing but scorn for his creature and that to see anything else at work in the canto is to read it through romantic, DeSanctisian eyes. Ironically, both these extreme positions use an alleged romanticism as their foil: the pro-Ulysseans by insisting that to make the *folle volo* into a sin is to romanticize it, and the moralists by claiming that to see anything special or positive about the hero is to invest him with an anachronistic romantic glamour. These extreme readings have yet more in common: both rob the episode of its tension and deflate it of its energy, on the one hand by making the fact that Ulysses is in hell irrelevant, and on the other by denying that this particular sinner means more to the poem than do his companions. Fubini's simple admiration fails to deal with the fact that Dante places Ulysses in hell;

Cassell's simple condemnation fails to take into account the structural and thematic significance that the Greek hero bears for the whole poem.

In a further irony, it should be noted that Nardi and Fubini, despite their critical wrangling, share a major conviction, to wit that Ulysses cannot be entirely defined by the *bolgia* in which we find him, that he is a thematic pillar of the poem who cannot be reduced but must be understood in his complex integrity. A key sign of Ulysses' irreducibility, of the fact that he is not just any sinner in Malebolge, is his sustained presence in the poem: he is the only single-episode sinner—with the exception of Nimrod, whom I consider an echoing talisman of overweening pride in human endeavor[13]—to be named in each canticle. The fact that Ulysses has been invested with a significance that goes beyond one *bolgia*, or even one *cantica*, is thus a matter of record, not of impressionistic interpretation: if, to the unique number of episodes in which he is referred to by name (*Inferno* 26, *Purgatorio* 19, *Paradiso* 27), we add the many instances in which he is invoked—through surrogate figures like Phaeton and Icarus; through semantic tags, like *folle*, that Dante has taken care to associate with him; and, most encompassingly, through Ulyssean flight imagery—our sense of his textual weight is confirmed.[14] The many readers who have glorified Ulysses (like those who have glorified Francesca, Farinata, Brunetto, and Ugolino) were privileging a figure who is indeed privileged by the poet, not morally or eschatologically but textually and poetically. Rather than argue against the testimony of centuries of readers who tell us that they react more passionately to this particular narrative, it seems more profitable to ask why the poet confers on some of his characters a greater textual resonance, a more inviolate ability to seduce. Dante deliberately manipulates the level of his poem's textual tension by making it more difficult not to react affectively to some sinners than to others. Moreover, such sinners invariably signify in a "larger," more metaphoric mode than their fellows (and are frequently coordinated in a textual *variatio* with souls who signify more simply and literally, as Francesca with Ciacco and Ulysses with Guido): not simply lust, in Francesca's case, but an *in malo* exploration of the poem's basic premises—the possibility of transcendence through love and the salvific mission of the word; not simply fraudulent counsel, in Ulysses' case, but the seductive dangers of disobedience and transgression, and a meditation on pride as the sin most capable of bringing the life-voyage to disaster. The textual privileging of these sinners is, accordingly, a way of underlining them, of pointing to the significance they bear—and that love and pride bear—for life and for the *Commedia* as a whole. This notion of textual privileging could be seen, moreover, as a reformulation of Croce's fundamental insight. There are indeed narrative highs and lows in the *Commedia*, but since these are a function of narrative itself—one could not have the one without the other—it makes little sense to accord value as "poesia" and "non poesia" to what is all part of the same narrative continuum.[15]

In my opinion, then, the *folle volo* cannot be overlooked in an assessment of Ulysses' role within the poem, and to this extent I follow Nardi, whose reading echoes those of Dante's contemporaries. Dante's Adam explains that his banishment was caused by his overreaching, a trespass the poem has long coded as Ulyssean: "non il gustar del legno / fu per sé la cagion di tanto essilio, / ma solamente il trapassar del segno" ("the tasting of the tree was not in itself the cause of so long an exile, but solely the going beyond the bound" [*Par.* 26.115–17]). Boccaccio echoes the Adamic "trapassar del segno" in his characterization of the Greek hero, who "per voler veder trapassò il segno / dal qual nessun poté mai in qua reddire" ("in his desire to see went beyond the bound from which no one has ever been able to return" [*Amorosa visione*, redaction A, 27.86–87]). For Petrarch, too, Ulysses "desiò del mondo veder troppo" ("desired to see too much of the world" [*Triumphus fame* 2.18]). Far from being anachronistic, as claimed by Fubini, Nardi is reviving a contemporary insight when he associates Ulysses with Adam.[16] I disagree, however, with Nardi's formulation of an unconsciously divided poet, believing instead that Ulysses reflects Dante's conscious concern for himself. The perception of a profound autobiographical alignment between the poet and his creation seems also to have early roots; Umberto Bosco shows that Dante's intransigence in not accepting Florentine terms for repatriation despite the suffering of his family elicited contrasting reactions from Boccaccio, who defended him, and Petrarch, whose criticism implicitly brands him a Ulysses.[17] In sum, then, the Dante who is implicated in the figure of Ulysses is not solely the Dante of the *Convivio*, a Dante of the past, but also the Dante of the *Commedia*. By the Dante of the *Commedia*, I refer not to the pilgrim, who, as many studies have shown, is related to Ulysses as an inverse type, his negative double.[18] I refer rather to the poet, who has embarked on a voyage whose Ulyssean component he recognizes, fears, and never fully overcomes.[19]

Ulysses is the lightning rod Dante places in his poem to attract and defuse his own consciousness of the presumption involved in anointing oneself God's scribe. In other words, Ulysses documents Dante's self-awareness: Dante *knows* that, in constructing a system whose fiction is that it is not fictional, he has given himself a license to write the world, to play God unchecked. In the "Amor mi spira" passage of *Purgatorio* 24, Dante establishes a conduit between himself and Love, transcendent authority and poetic dictator, which is precisely analogous to the conduit established in *Paradiso* 10 between himself and God, also a poetic dictator, the *dittatore* of "quella materia ond'io son fatto scriba" ("that matter of which I am made the scribe" [27]).[20] As Amor's inspiration gives the poet the vantage to assess the history of the love lyric, so his scribal relation to God—also Amor, indeed "l'amor che move il sole e l'altre stelle" ("the love that moves the sun and the other stars" [*Par.* 33.145])—permits an assessment of universal history. The vantage of *scriba Dei* confers a breathtaking advantage.[21] From it the poet is able to claim knowledge of the truth not only with respect to the historical moment but also *sub specie aeternitatis*, for to know what happens after death, in the context of the Christian afterlife, is to know what every action really accomplished, what every thought really contributed, what every thing, in short, really signifies. "Vo significando" is no exaggeration in this context. I cannot, as none of us can, speak authoritatively regarding what Dante believed he saw; in my opinion, he believed that he was inspired by God with a true vision. However, although I believe that he believed, I do not think Dante was an unconscious visionary; on the contrary, I think he was fully aware—and afraid—of the implications that follow from believing that what one writes is true. The Ulyssean component of the poem is thus related to the basic representational *impresa* of the *Commedia*, which involves transgressing the boundary between life and death: "ché non è impresa da pigliare a gabbo / discriver fondo a tutto l'universo" ("for it is not an enterprise to take in jest, to describe the bottom of all the universe" [*Inf.* 32.7–8]).[22] The Ulysses theme, as Dante uses it, is in fact intimately related to the practical exigencies of writing the *Commedia*, if by practical we refer to the actual praxis of the poet in the construction and composition of a text that claims to tell truth.

The Ulysses theme, if looked at from the angle of the poet rather than the pilgrim, forces us to challenge the theological grid with which we read the *Commedia* (following interpretative guidelines suggested by the text itself), whereby whatever happens in hell is "bad," problematic, and whatever happens in heaven is "good," problem-free. As noted in the first chapter, this formulation may be accurate with respect to the text's content, its plot, but it need not be accurate with respect to its form. Critics who have posited the Ulyssean tendencies of the poet have generally been led by the theological grid to a reading that confuses what the poet says he is doing with what he has actually done, forgetting that how Dante chooses to portray the experience of writing the *Commedia*—how the poet chooses to describe being a poet—is one thing, while the actual experience of being the *Commedia*'s author, to the extent that it can be reconstructed from the evidence of the poem, is another. Thus, it has been argued that Dante-poet's Ulyssean tendencies are confronted in the *Inferno* and resolved before we reach the other canticles: Peter Hawkins claims that the Ulyssean virtuosity displayed in the *bolgia* of the thieves is corrected later in the poem; Karla Taylor, too, while going further than Hawkins in recognizing the hubris that underlies the humility of the terrace of pride, simply postpones the venue of correction, moving it from *Purgatorio* to *Paradiso*.[23] Giuliana Carugati, who insists on the poet as a Ulyssean maker of *menzogna*, nonetheless believes that the mendacious texture of Dante's poetic language is progressively frayed as he approaches the redemptive silence of *Paradiso*.[24] The critical assumptions that back up these readings are stated straightforwardly by James T. Chiampi: "Because it is the key to the poem's immanent typology, the *Paradiso* is to the *Inferno* as criticism is to poetry. The *Paradiso* is the very center of the poem's structure of values because it is the locus of the proper object of representation, the good."[25] Once again, form and content have been conflated, and we have forgotten that a "good" object of representation does not guarantee a "good" representation. As Marguerite Mills Chiarenza puts it in her salutary reminder: "In the *Inferno* and the *Purgatorio* the poet's struggle is secondary to the pilgrim's and the danger is essentially in the voyage. In the *Paradiso* it is the poet who struggles while the pilgrim is safe."[26]

The poetic humility of which the later canticles tell cannot simply be taken at face value. Such a procedure constitutes an extrapolation from the content—the declared humility that overwhelms both pilgrim and poet in paradise—to a conclusion for which there is no textual basis, namely that Dante-poet actually is more humble in writing *Paradiso*. I see no signs of this oft-imputed humility; indeed, the only real way to have practiced humility in writing *Paradiso* would have been not to write it. By the same token, the silence that the *Paradiso* will eventually attain cannot be factored in before it occurs, which is not until the entire *Paradiso*—not incidentally, the longest of the three canticles—has been written. The real story of the *Paradiso* is in the words that are written, not in the incapacity to find such words of which its author repeatedly writes. Neither Carugati's notion of a mystical passage through linguistic fraudulence to silence, nor Jeremy Tambling's Derridean paraphrasing of Dante's own ineffability topoi, whereby *Paradiso* has "given up the possibility of literal referentiality,"[27] deal with the reality of Dante's struggle with referentiality in the third canticle, where rather than surrendering at the outset he seeks repeatedly to wed the "essemplo" to the "essemplare." Dante himself tells us that he cannot represent his vision; rather than paraphrase him, it seems more worthwhile to try to understand how Dante did what he said could not be done, how he vaults the limits that he was the first to declare.

Nor does the intractable problem of self-legitimization, self-investiture, disappear in the *Paradiso*: again, Dante is aware of a fact that we tend to forget, namely that he is writing what Bonagiunta says, what Beatrice says, what Cacciaguida says, what St. Peter says. Far from diminishing as the pilgrim draws nearer to his goal, the poet's problems become ever more acute: if the pilgrim learns to be not like Ulysses, the poet is conscious of having to be ever more like him. The *Paradiso*, if it is to exist at all, cannot fail to be transgressive; its poet cannot fail to be a Ulysses, since only a *trapassar del segno* will be able to render the experience of *trasumanar*. In a context where "significar *per verba* / non si poria" ("signifying through words cannot be done" [*Par.* 1.70–71]), and where "l'essemplo / e l'essemplare non vanno d'un modo" ("the model and the copy do not match" [*Par.* 28.55–56]), a representational process that is avowedly based on the principles of mimesis, on the seamless match of "essemplo" and "essemplare," becomes ever more arduous. In such a context signs must be trespassed, since only a trespass of the sign can render an experience for which no signs are sufficient. If the poet cannot express a thousandth part of the truth of Beatrice's smile ("al millesmo del vero / non si verria, cantando il santo riso" [*Par.* 23.58–59]), his only solution is a going beyond the sign, the poetic equivalent of the *varcare* (passing beyond, crossing over) associated with Ulysses and his mad flight: "il varco / folle d'Ulisse" (*Par.* 27.82–83). And so the poem is forced to jump ("convien saltar lo sacrato poema")—*saltare* being a kind of homely "comedic" version of *varcare*—as the narrator announces the need to trespass the normative linearity of narrative signifying in the Ulyssean outburst of *Paradiso* 23:

> e così, figurando il paradiso,
> > convien saltar lo sacrato poema,
> > come chi trova suo cammin riciso.
> Ma chi pensasse il ponderoso tema
> > e l'omero mortal che se ne carca,
> > nol biasmerebbe se sott'esso trema:
> non è pareggio da picciola barca
> > quel che fendendo va l'ardita prora,
> > né da nocchier ch'a sé medesmo parca.

And so, figuring paradise, the sacred poem is forced to jump, like one who finds his path cut off. But he who thinks of the ponderous theme and the mortal shoulder that is burdened with it will not blame it for trembling beneath the load; it is not a crossing for a little boat, this which my bold prow now cleaves, nor for a helmsman who would spare himself.

> (*Par.* 23.61–69)

The *Paradiso*'s Ulyssean *materia* first manifests itself in the great address to the reader that stands at the canticle's threshold, where Dante (putting a new spin on the rhetoric of persuasion) challenges us to follow him by telling us that we are not up to the task:[28]

> O voi che siete in piccioletta barca,
> > desiderosi d'ascoltar, seguiti
> > dietro al mio legno che cantando varca,
> tornate a riveder li vostri liti:
> > non vi mettete in pelago, ché forse,
> > perdendo me, rimarreste smarriti.

L'acqua ch'io prendo già mai non si corse;
  Minerva spira, e conducemi Appollo,
  e nove Muse mi dimostran l'Orse.
Voialtri pochi che drizzaste il collo
  per tempo al pan de li angeli, del quale
  vivesi qui ma non sen vien satollo,
metter potete ben per l'alto sale
  vostro navigio, servando mio solco
  dinanzi a l'acqua che ritorna equale.
Que' glorïosi che passaro al Colco
  non s'ammiraron come voi farete,
  quando Iasón vider fatto bifolco.

O you that are in little boats, desiring to hear, having followed behind my ship that singing leaps, turn back to see again your shores; don't set out for the deep lest, perhaps, losing me, you find yourselves astray. The water that I draw has never yet been coursed; Minerva breathes and Apollo guides me, and nine [new][29] Muses show me the Bears. You other few who straightened your necks in time for the bread of the angels (on which you live here without ever growing sated), you may indeed set your course for the high sea, keeping to my wake ahead of the water that always comes back equal. Those glorious ones who crossed to Colchis were not as amazed as you will be, when they saw Jason turned ploughman.

(*Par.* 2.1–18)

Here Ulyssean imagery is fused around a specific mythological figure, Jason, whose metamorphosis into a ploughman will cause his crew no greater amazement than that for which the reader of the *Paradiso* is destined; there is an implicit analogy between Jason, a sailor, and the poet, also a sailor on his "legno che cantando varca," whose account will awaken wonder in us. Jason returns in the poem's last canto, where the compound of oblivion and remembered wonder experienced by the pilgrim at his momentary insight into the universal form of creation is rendered by analogy with Neptune, who was similarly struck with wonder at the sight of the first ship passing overhead: "Un punto solo m'è maggior letargo / che venticinque secoli a la 'mpresa / che fé Nettuno ammirar l'ombra d'Argo" ("A single moment is to me greater oblivion than are twenty-five centuries to the enterprise that made Neptune wonder at the shadow of the Argo" [*Par.* 33.94–96]). Both pilgrim and god experience an astounding vision—an ultimately new thing, as indeed the Argo is a literal *cosa nova*—which is irretrievable but whose impress remains indelibly: the pilgrim's amazement at what he perceives about the "great sea of being" ("gran mar de l'essere" [*Par.* 1.113]), the metaphorical waters of the cosmos, finds its counterpart in Neptune's amazement at seeing the uncharted waters over his head shadowed for the first time by a ship. Here too then, as in the earlier address to the reader, although the reference is to the pilgrim's experience, which is compared to Neptune's, it is the poet's ability to recount that experience, to create the "legno che cantando varca" that will rescue it from oblivion, that is at stake. If the pilgrim is like Neptune (by virtue of the *trasumanar* that has made him a sea god, made him, like Glaucus, a lesser Neptune), then the poet is like Jason, a Ulysses bent on his most daring *impresa*.[30]

The Ulysses theme enters the *Commedia* in its first verse, in the word *cammino*, and more pointedly in its first simile, in which the pilgrim compares himself to one who (unlike Dante's Ulysses) emerges from dangerous waters, "del pelago a la riva" ("from the deep to the shore" [*Inf.* 1.23]) and turns to look at what he has escaped: "si volse a retro a rimirar lo passo / che non lasciò già mai persona viva" ("he turned back to look at the pass that never yet let any go alive" [26–27]).[31] The beginnings of a contrastive Ulyssean lexicon are here established: from "pelago" to "passo," which will be given its Ulyssean twist in canto 2 when Dante asks his guide to ascertain his courage before entrusting him to the "alto passo" (12), thus anticipating the "alto passo" (*Inf.* 26.132) that leads to Ulysses' death. It is the task of *Inferno* 2 to show us, in retrospect, that the pilgrim is not Ulysses, that his *impresa* and Ulysses'—their respective *alti passi*—are related as inverse types. Recapitulating what is by now critical dogma, the pilgrim is an anti-Ulysses, whose voyage is charted in great part by a counter-Ulyssean emulation: "se del venire io m'abbandono, / temo che la venuta non sia folle" ("if I yield and come, I fear that my coming may be mad" [*Inf.* 2.34–35]). He is afraid of abandoning himself to this voyage, as he had in the past abandoned the true path ("che la verace via abbandonai" [*Inf.* 1.12]), and as Phaeton abandoned the chariot reins that served to keep his horses on the straight way ("abbandonò li freni" [*Inf.* 17.107]). All this fear, which it is the agenda of *Inferno* 2 to defuse, keeps us focused on the difference between the self-willed adventurer and the pilgrim touched by grace, but it should also alert us to the poet's awareness of his potentially Ulyssean trespasses: if there were no such potential, there would be no need of a Ulyssean agenda to defuse it, no need for the poet to stage the pilgrim's momentary disconversion, his fear that he is not Aeneas or St. Paul. Indeed, the pilgrim's concern that "Io non Enëa, io non Paulo sono" (*Inf.* 2.32) is a supreme example of the double bind in which Dante is placed as the guarantor of his own prophetic status: the very act by which the pilgrim demonstrates humility serves the poet as a vehicle for recording his visionary models and for telling us, essentially, that "Io sì Enëa, io sì Paulo sono."[32] Thus, the poet's voyage runs not counter to Ulysses' but parallel to it: Ulysses persuades his tired old men to pass the markers set by Hercules, "dov' Ercule segnò li suoi riguardi" (*Inf.* 26.108); Dante persuades us to pass the markers set by death. Both are linguistic transgressions, grounded in the "trespass of the sign": "il trapassar del segno" hearkens back to the Ulysses episode, where we find not only *segnare* but also an injunction containing *oltre* (Hercules places his markers "acciò che l'uom più oltre non si metta" ["so that man should not pass beyond" (109)]), a term that works throughout the *Commedia* as the adverbial correlative of *trapassare*.

In sum, then, the Ulyssean component of the poem is ultimately related to the *impresa* of the *Commedia* itself, to the poet's transgressing of the boundary between life and death, between God and man.[33] The Ulysses episode is not unique in reflecting Dante's awareness of the dangers of his position: such awareness informs the canto of the false prophets, for instance, which is governed by a need to disavow any connection with what Dante knows he could be considered.[34] The diviners also seek to cross the boundary between divine and human prerogatives; their attempt to read the future in God's "magno volume" (*Par.* 15.50) is an attempt to reach a vantage from which they, like God, "Colui che mai non vide cosa nova," will never see a new thing.[35] And so, these sinners, who would have obliterated by foretelling all the new things before they occurred, whose attitude of conquest toward life's manifold *cose nove* is like Ulysses' toward the "nova terra" (*Inf.* 26.137) he burns to reach,[36] are reduced to being one more instance of the new on the poet's narrative path: "Di nova pena mi conven far versi" (*Inf.* 20.1). But most important from this perspective is Ulysses, most important because the poet makes him so, investing him not only with the unforgettable language of *Inferno* 26 but making his name a hermeneutic lodestone of the *Commedia*, associating it with the voyage metaphor that keeps the Ulyssean thematic alive even in the hero's absence. Ulysses is designed as a recurring presence because the issue of the *trapassar del segno*, of Adam's sin conceived not literally as the eating of the tree but metaphorically as a transgression, is one that Dante cannot discount. It is an issue that does not belong safely to the past, like the *Convivio* and his excessive adoration of Lady Philosophy. No matter how orthodox his theology (and it is not so orthodox), no matter how fervently Dante believes in and claims the status of true prophet, of directly inspired poet, of *scriba Dei*, the very fiber of the *Commedia* consists of a going beyond. Thus Ulysses dies, over and over again, for Dante's sins.

· · · · ·

The locus classicus for textual self-awareness in the *Commedia* is the passage in *Inferno* 16 where the poet announces the arrival of Geryon, a monster derived from classical mythology whose patently fictional characteristics Dante first heightens and then uses as the stake on which to gamble the veracity of his poem:

Sempre a quel ver c'ha faccia di menzogna
   de' l'uom chiuder le labbra fin ch'el puote,
   però che sanza colpa fa vergogna;
ma qui tacer nol posso; e per le note
   di questa comedìa, lettor, ti giuro,
   s'elle non sien di lunga grazia vòte,
ch'i' vidi per quell'aere grosso e scuro
   venir notando una figura in suso,
   maravigliosa ad ogne cor sicuro

To that truth which has the face of a lie a man should always close his lips as long
as he can, since without fault it brings him shame, but here I cannot be silent; and
by the notes of this comedy, reader, I swear to you—so may they not be empty of
long grace—that I saw through that dense and dark air a figure come swimming
upward, a cause for marvel to even the most secure of hearts

(*Inf.* 16.124–32)

Keeping in mind that "narrative verisimilitude tends to flaunt rather than
mask its fictitious nature," and that there is a "constant coincidence between textual features declaring the fictionality of a story and a reassertion
of the truth of that story,"[37] I propose that Geryon serves as an outrageously
paradoxical authenticating device: one that, by being so overtly inauthentic—so literally a figure for inauthenticity, a figure for "fraud"—confronts
and attempts to defuse the belatedness or inauthenticity to which the need
for an authenticating device necessarily testifies. Geryon also serves as the
poem's very baptismal font: this is the passage in which Dante first anoints
his poem a *comedìa*, using a term that he will contrast to *tragedìa* later in the
*Inferno*. In the *Paradiso* this same term will be implicitly redefined a *sacrato
poema*, indeed a *tëodia*. Without attempting to reproduce the detail of my
earlier argumentation on this subject,[38] I will simply note that the poet
achieves his redefinition of the term *comedìa* by contextualizing it vis-à-vis
*tragedìa* in ways that align *comedìa* (Dante) with truth, and *tragedìa* (Vergil)
with falsehood, *menzogna*. Key to this process of redefinition and to the
significance with which the poet intends to endow his "new" genre—the
*comedìa/tëodia* for which he has invented both a new life-based form and a
new truth-based content—is the phrase used to designate the act of representing Geryon: the discourse that undertakes to represent that in-credible
beast is a "ver c'ha faccia di menzogna," a "truth that has the face of a lie."
In other words, although a *comedìa* may at times, as when representing
Geryon, have the "face of a lie"—give the appearance of lying—it is intractably always truth: "VER c'ha faccia di menzogna." By explicitly confronting
the inauthenticity inherent in all narrative, Dante attempts to neutralize it
with respect to his own narrative truth claims.

The Geryon episode is fundamental to the *Commedia*'s poetics, which is

a poetics of realism, with its concomitant surrealism, not a poetics of natu-
ralism. It establishes a precedent that has important repercussions for the
rest of the poem: the least credible (i.e., least naturalistic) of Dante's representations will be supported by the most unyielding and overt of authorial
interventions. This is the poetics of the "mira vera," true marvels, to use the
expression Dante coins in his second eclogue for another encounter with a
magically heightened reality, in this case a miraculous flute that produces
not sounds but sung words. Here Dante, personified as the aged Tityrus,
receives the young Melibeus, who plays him Mopsus's (Giovanni del Virgilio's) new eclogue on his flute. The wonder is that, when Melibeus lifts the
instrument to his lips, it sings Mopsus's opening verse; describing this miracle of the singing flute, the narrator inserts the phrase, "I tell of marvels, but
they are nonetheless true" ("mira loquar, sed vera tamen" [4.40]).[39] The
poetics of the incredible and nonetheless true—"Io dirò cosa incredibile e
vera" says Cacciaguida in Par. 16.124—is the poetics of the "ver c'ha faccia
di menzogna." The oxymoronic formulations—"mira vera," "incredibile e
vera"—demonstrate the poet's awareness of his own intransigence and correspond precisely to the equally oxymoronic juxtaposition of "maravigliosa"
("mira") with "io vidi" ("vera") in the Geryon episode. Far from giving quar-
ter, backing off when the materia being represented is too "maravigliosa" to
be credible, Dante raises the ante by using such moments to underscore his
poem's veracity, its status as historical scribal record of what he saw. Thus,
just as in the Geryon episode Dante weds "maravigliosa" with "vidi,"
thereby closing off all escape routes to himself and his reader by insisting
that he actually sees something that he acknowledges is "maravigliosa"—
fantastic, incredible—so, faced with the equally fantastic sight of the
thieves' metamorphoses, the poet opts for another bold frontal attack on
the reader's credulity, again arming himself with the verb vedere:[40] "Se tu se'
or, lettore, a creder lento / ciò ch'io dirò, non sarà maraviglia, / ché io che 'l
vidi, a pena il mi consento" ("If you are now, reader, slow to believe what I
will say, it is no wonder, since I who saw it hardly consent to it myself" [Inf.
25.46–48]). Similarly, in another of the Inferno's moments of greatest maraviglia, as the narrator sets out to represent the headless Bertran de Born, he
reapplies the Geryon principle, once again challenging the reader to disbelieve him:

> Ma io rimasi a riguardar lo stuolo,
>     e vidi cosa ch'io avrei paura,
>     sanza più prova, di contarla solo;
> se non che coscïenza m'assicura,
>     la buona compagnia che l'uom francheggia
>     sotto l'asbergo del sentirsi pura.
> Io vidi certo, e ancor par ch'io 'l veggia,
>     un busto sanza capo . . .

But I remained to look over the troop, and I saw a thing that I would be afraid even to recount without more proof, except that my conscience—the good companion that gives a man courage under the hauberk of feeling itself pure—reassures me. I certainly saw, and still seem to see, a trunk without a head . . .

(*Inf.* 28.112–19)

Dante's strategy is bold, but it is also logical. By underlining what is apparently least verisimilar in his representation, and by letting us know that he fully shares our assessment regarding this material's lack of verisimilitude, which he does by posing as reluctant to represent it lest we lose confidence in him, the narrator secures our confidence for the rest of his story. Why is the plight of the lustful or the gluttonous any more verisimilar, or any more credible, than the plight of the thieves or the schismatics? Is being blown for all eternity by an infernal wind or pelted by filthy rain really more verisimilar than exchanging shapes with a serpent or carrying one's head in one's hand? By urging us to identify heightened drama with decreased verisimilitude and credibility, Dante is subtly encouraging us to accept his text's basic fictions and assumptions: sodomites dancing in a circle under a pouring rain of fire or usurers sitting on the edge of an abyss with purses around their necks (to mention just the groups of sinners who bracket Geryon's arrival) are acceptable, but flying monsters are not and therefore require the author's direct intervention. In this way the poet becomes the arbiter of our skepticism, allowing it to blossom forth only in authorially-sanctioned moments of high drama. Far from demonstrating humor or Ariostesque irony (as per Hollander's suggestion that the Geryon episode involves an "authorial wink"),[41] these passages are the most exposed weapons in a massive and unrelenting campaign to coerce our suspension of disbelief, a campaign that the history of the *Commedia*'s reception shows to have been remarkably successful. The Geryon episode, however, constitutes an even more profound poetic gamble for the poet of the *Commedia* than we have hitherto noted, for its emblematic verse is a double-edged sword and may be approached from the perspective of its last word, "menzogna," as well as from the perspective of its first word, "ver." Rather than emphasize the poet's claim that his poem is a *ver* and remains such no matter what marvels it is forced to recount, we could ask: Why does this truth, this *comedìa*, have a *faccia di menzogna*? The answer is that even a *comedìa*, in order to come into existence as text, must to some extent accommodate that human and thus ultimately fraudulent construct, language.

Within the metapoetic discourse that this supremely self-conscious author has inscribed into his poem, Geryon, "quella sozza imagine di froda" ("that filthy image of fraud" [*Inf.* 17.7]), is, as Franco Ferrucci has noted, an image of representational fraud:[42] he is the vehicle required for the naming—the coming into being—of even this text. Let us look at the verses that precede the monster's arrival. The sequence begins with the crux in which

Dante removes from his waist a cord of whose existence we were previously unaware; specifying that with this cord he once thought to take the painted leopard, in an overt reference to the second of the opening canto's three beasts, he hands the knotted skein to Vergil at his guide's behest:

> Io avea una corda intorno cinta,
>   e con essa pensai alcuna volta
>   prender la lonza a la pelle dipinta.
> Poscia ch'io l'ebbi tutta da me sciolta,
>   sì come 'l duca m'avea comandato,
>   porsila a lui aggroppata e ravvolta.

I had a cord tied around me, and with it I on occasion thought to take the leopard with the painted skin. After I had completely loosened it from me, as my leader had commanded, I handed it to him knotted and coiled.

(*Inf.* 16.106–11)

Vergil throws the cord into the abyss, while the pilgrim thinks about the novelty that so remarkable a signal must command:

> Ond'ei si volse inver' lo destro lato,
>   e alquanto di lunge da la sponda
>   la gittò giuso in quell'alto burrato.
> "E' pur convien che novità risponda,"
>   dicea fra me medesmo, "al novo cenno
>   che 'l maestro con l'occhio sì seconda."

Then he turned to the right and threw it some distance from the edge down into that deep ravine. "Surely," I said to myself, "something strange [new] must answer to the strange [new] sign that my master follows with his eye."

(*Inf.* 16.112–17)

At this point the poet interrupts the action with a tercet on the caution that should govern our behavior in the company of those who can read our thoughts, followed by Vergil's confirmation that he has in fact divined the pilgrim's excitement regarding the "novità" that will respond to the "novo cenno." He announces the arrival of such a thing as dreams are made of, such a thing as the writer fishes for in the deep waters of the imagination with the thin cord of reason: "Tosto verrà di sovra / ciò ch'io attendo e che il tuo pensier sogna; / tosto convien ch'al tuo viso si scovra" ("Soon will come up what I await and what your mind dreams; soon it must be discovered to your sight" [*Inf.* 16.121–23]). This long crescendo concludes with the verses cited earlier, in which the narrator first compares himself to one who should keep silent but cannot, then appeals directly to the reader, and finally presents Geryon. The canto closes with a brief simile in which the monster is compared to a diver who returns from the depths of the sea.

Because of the intrusion of elements that seem entirely disconnected from the literal story line, this passage has always been read allegorically; besides Buti, who takes the cord as the Franciscan cordon and thus proof of Dante's belonging to minor orders, interpretations range from the cord as a symbol of chastity contrasted to lust (the leopard), the cord as truth contrasted to fraud (Geryon), and the cord as the pity that the pilgrim must shed before venturing into lower hell.[43] In a study that analyzes the language of the Geryon episode for its biblical and patristic valences, Roberto Mercuri proposes that taking off the cord represents a renunciation of sin as the pilgrim completes the conversion begun in the poem's first canto.[44] I would advance instead the following metapoetic interpretation, based on the traditional interpretation of the cord as a symbol of fraud.[45] The cord is knotted and tortuous ("aggroppata e ravvolta"), signifying the deceit of language; it was used for catching the leopard, lust, because Dante comes out of a tradition where language serves to deal with—capture—eros: his major previous experience with poetic language is the experience of love poetry. He hands the cord to Vergil, thus signifying the development of his discourse, its enlargement from the lyric to the epic—"Vergilian"—mode. Only this mode can provide the new language, the new signs ("novo cenno") required to bring forth a *novità*, because only this mode imitates life, defined as a path punctuated by the continual arrival of new things. The use of a *novo cenno* to elicit a *novità* is thus a paradigm for the writing of a new kind of poetry, a poetry founded on the poetics of the new. The knotty skein of an exclusively erotic textuality (of Petrarchan *dolci nodi*) calls forth the even knottier, supremely embellished emblem of a new and larger textuality:

> lo dosso e 'l petto e ambedue le coste
> dipinti avea di nodi e di rotelle.
> Con più color, sommesse e sovraposte
> non fer mai drappi Tartari né Turchi,
> né fuor tai tele per Aragne imposte.

His back and chest and both his sides were painted with knots and circlets. Never did Tartars or Turks make fabrics with more colors, more threads of warp and woof; nor were such webs loomed by Arachne.

(*Inf.* 17.14–18)

Everything about this description speaks to the identification of "la sozza imagine di froda" with textuality ("imagine" virtually authorizes us to read Geryon in a representational key, as does this canto's unusually high proportion of *imagines*, i.e., similes):[46] the monster's knotty surface, reminiscent of the knots of discourse that imprison Pier della Vigna;[47] the emphasis on painting and color, reminiscent of the *colores retorici*;[48] the reference to weaving, to the warp and woof of a woven fabric, which reminds us that the poet on occasion speaks of his *testo* in terms of weaving or *tessere*, the activity that lies at the etymological roots of textuality;[49] and finally, the name that brings all the above into focus, that of Arachne. By comparing the designs woven on Geryon's flanks to the *tele* woven by Arachne, Dante summons the mythological figure who more than any other is an emblem for textuality, for weaving the webs of discourse. Her *tele* are the webs of textuality, of art: they signify the inherent deceptiveness of an art that can deceive through its mimetic perfection, its achievement of verisimilitude (art, therefore, as "craft" in both its senses, as handiwork and Ulyssean guile); also, because Arachne challenged Minerva, her webs signify our hubris (again Ulyssean), our will to challenge, to go beyond. In other words, Arachne is the textual/artistic correlative of Ulysses, and also therefore of those surrogates for Ulysses who figure so prominently at the end of the Geryon episode. In his own moment of flight, Dante likens the fear he experiences on Geryon's back first to that of Phaeton when he let go the reins and doomed his ride in his father's chariot to perdition—"Maggior paura non credo che fosse / quando Fetonte abbandonò li freni" ("Greater fear I do not think there was when Phaeton abandoned the reins" [*Inf.* 17.106–7])—and then to that of Icarus, as his wings melt: "né quando Icaro misero le reni / sentì spennar per la scaldata cera, / gridando il padre a lui 'Mala via tieni!'" ("nor while poor Icarus felt his sides unfeathering on account of the heated wax, while his father cried to him 'You're on the wrong path!'" [*Inf.* 17.109–11]). Thus, Ulysses is proleptically evoked in the Geryon episode: first by Arachne, at the beginning of canto 17, and then by Phaeton and Icarus, at the canto's end.[50]

It is worth noting, moreover, that the image cluster we associate with Ulysses, the conflation of sailing with flying epitomized by "de' remi facemmo ali al folle volo," is also used for the presentation of Geryon. As we recall, Geryon both flies and swims, or rather—although we know that he is flying, since the element in which he navigates is air, not water—he is presented as swimming. The narrator recounts seeing "per quell'*aere* grosso e scuro / venir *notando* una figura in suso" and then reinforces the swimming image with the simile of the diver that closes canto 16:

> sì come torna colui che va giuso
>   talora a solver l'àncora ch'aggrappa
>   o scoglio o altro che nel mare è chiuso,
> che 'n sù si stende e da piè si rattrappa.

as one returns who sometimes goes down to release the anchor caught on a reef or on something else hidden in the sea, who stretches himself upward and pushes off with his feet.

(*Inf.* 16.133–36)

In the opening sequence of canto 17, describing the monster's position on the edge of the abyss, the poet compares him first to boats that are banked on the shore, part in the water and part on land, and then to the beaver:

> Come talvolta stanno a riva i burchi,
>   che parte sono in acqua e parte in terra,
>   e come là tra li Tedeschi lurchi
> lo bivero s'assetta a far sua guerra

as boats sometimes lie along the shore, part in the water and part on land, and as there among the gluttonous Germans the beaver makes ready to wage its war

(*Inf.* 17.19–22)

And, in order to describe the way in which Geryon backs up from the edge and turns around, Dante again pairs the image of a boat, a "navicella," with a marine animal, the eel:

> Come la navicella esce di loco
>   in dietro in dietro, sì quindi si tolse;
>   e poi ch'al tutto si sentì a gioco,
> là 'v'era 'l petto, la coda rivolse,
>   e quella tesa, come anguilla, mosse,
>   e con le branche l'aere a sé raccolse.

As the little ship backs out of its place a little at a time, so did Geryon take himself from there; and as soon as he felt himself completely in the clear he turned his tail to where his chest had been and, having stretched it, moved it like an eel and with his paws gathered the air to himself.

(*Inf.* 17.100–105)

In the passage that follows Dante reconflates navigation by air and by sea, telling us that the *fera* "sen va notando lenta lenta; / rota e discende, ma non me n'accorgo / se non che al viso e di sotto mi venta" ("goes swimming slowly on; he wheels and descends, but I can make out nothing but the wind blowing on my face and from below" [17.115–17]). The canto closes with an image of unadulterated flight; as though to balance the ascent of the swimming diver at the end of canto 16, here we find the descent of a flying falcon.

From this welter of navigational images, I would like to isolate one as particularly important for my present purposes, that of the *navicella*. The word occurs only thrice in the poem; undoubtedly the most conspicuous of its three appearances is that of *Purgatorio* 1, where it serves in the canticle's second verse as an image for the text itself, about to sail onto better waters: "Per correr miglior acque alza le vele / omai la navicella del mio ingegno, / che lascia dietro a sé mar sì crudele" ("To course over better waters the little ship of my intellect now lifts its sails, leaving behind her a sea so cruel" [*Purg.* 1.1–3]).[51] I would suggest that there is an analogy between the poem, "la navicella del mio ingegno," sailed by Dante poet, and Geryon, also a "navicella," sailed by Dante pilgrim. Much of what is said about Geryon in *Inferno* 16 and 17 could be taken as a description of the poem. Geryon—who like God, Lucifer, and the *Commedia* possesses both a single and a triple nature (the Latin poets call him *tergeminus*, threefold, three-bodied)—concedes his strong shoulders (the "omeri forti" of *Inf.* 17.42 bring to mind the poet's "omero mortal" in the metapoetic Ulyssean passage of *Paradiso* 23) for a spiraling voyage that synthesizes the journey through hell: the verses "lo scendere e 'l girar per li gran mali / che s'appressavan da diversi canti" ("the descending and the turning through the great evils that drew near on different sides" [*Inf.* 17.125–26]) provide a punning description not only of the pilgrim's flight but of the reader's narrative descent through the text's *diversi canti*.[52] We have already noted the emblematic value for the poem as a whole of "quel ver c'ha faccia di menzogna," a phrase that prepares the reader for Geryon; also significant are Vergil's words describing the unknown new object as "ciò ch'io attendo e che il tuo pensier sogna," which cast Dante as a visionary and Geryon as what he has created, envisioned, imagined, dreamed up. As we shall see, there are ample grounds for believing that Dante viewed his vision as the product of a waking dream, and himself as akin both to St. Paul, confused regarding the status of his otherworldly experience, and to Christ's disciples upon witnessing their master's transfiguration; it is worth noting that Guido da Pisa glosses "ver c'ha faccia di menzogna" with the examples of Paul's *raptus*, which he dared not reveal lest it be thought a lie, and the disciples' similar concern to hide what they had seen until after the resurrection, lest their truth be considered false.[53] Finally, if we look at the similes of the diver and the falcon in this light, we are struck by the extent to which they are paradigms for the action of the poem as a whole. Thus, Geryon arrives "sì come torna colui che va giuso / talora a solver l'àncora ch'aggrappa / o scoglio o altro che nel mare è chiuso," in verses that seem to gloss the return of the pilgrim from hell, that "mar sì crudele" into which he dove in order to free his own ship's anchor from the reef of sin. Likewise, the image of the falcon that falls to earth without having seen its master's lure—"Come 'l falcon ch'è stato assai su l'ali, / che sanza veder logoro o uccello / fa dire al falconiere 'Omè, tu cali!'" ("As the falcon that has been long upon the wing, that without seeing lure or bird makes the falconer cry 'Alas, you fall!'" [*Inf.* 17.127–29])—glosses the fall of the soul that refuses the upward lure set out by God and insists on heading downward, a condition Dante refers to, using the same falcon imagery, in the *Purgatorio*.[54]

With respect to the analogy between Geryon and the Ulyssean "navicella del mio ingegno," I would argue that Geryon both is the poem and is its antithesis, in the same way that Ulysses both is Dante and is his antithesis. On the one hand, the poem is defined as truth, Geryon is defined as mendacity, fraud; therefore, Geryon and the poem are opposites, Geryon is the

*Commedia*'s antithesis. A passage with great bearing on this reading may be found, significantly, immediately preceding Geryon's arrival, in the context of the pilgrim's meeting with the three noble Florentine sodomites. To their request for a statement regarding the condition of Florence, the pilgrim replies with the famous verses about the "gente nuova e i sùbiti guadagni" ("new people and sudden gains" [*Inf.* 16.73]) that have corrupted his city. Less noted are the verses that follow, in which Dante characterizes himself as one who speaks in the posture of an angry prophet—"Così gridai con la faccia levata" ("So I cried with uplifted face" [76])—and with a prophet's claim to truth: "e i tre, che ciò inteser per risposta, / guardar l'un l'altro *com'al ver si guata*" ("and the three, who took this as my answer, looked at each other *as one looks at the truth*" [77–78]). This "ver," like the "ver c'ha faccia di menzogna" to be introduced shortly, is the part of the poem that will triumph over the fraudulence of the medium to which it is tied, because its truth has been secured by one who transcends the mendacity of language. Because, in fact, he is using the lying medium of language to write a truth, Dante dares to confront the "faccia di menzogna" that is his necessary vehicle, which he does precisely by tackling head-on the representation of the vehicle itself: Geryon. Thus it is not surprising that Vergil should much later single out the ride on Geryon, the ride that made Dante akin to Phaeton and Icarus, the ride that made him a Ulyssean aeronaut, as emblematic of all the dangers they have encountered together in the course of their journey: "Ricorditi, ricorditi! E se io / sovresso Gerïon ti guidai salvo, / che farò ora presso più a Dio?" ("Remember, remember! And if on Geryon I guided you safely, what shall I do now nearer to God?" [*Purg.* 27.22–24]). The encounter with Geryon dramatizes the text's confrontation with its own necessary representational fraud, and as such is the moment of maximum peril, when the text gambles all on being accepted as a "ver c'ha faccia di menzoga," a *comedìa*. Dante establishes the parallel between Geryon and Ulysses because he knows that with respect to the textual voyage the Ulyssean component is finally inevitable: the text is a ship, a "navicella" identified with Geryon, and it is sailed by a Dante afraid of being Ulysses, a Dante who hears in simile the words "Mala via tieni!" shouted by Daedalus at his erring son and fears lest they be directed at him.

·  ·  ·  ·  ·

Now that we can integrate the Ulysses theme with the issue of new beginnings treated in the preceding chapter, we are in a position to discuss *Inferno* 8–9 and 16–17 as moments of narrative transition. In the wake of the relentless creation of infernal incipits in the opening cantos, by canto 7 the rhythmic pulse of the *Commedia*'s forward motion has been somewhat quieted, if only because it has been established as continual and is therefore less noticeable. In cantos 8–9 and 16–17 the text's forward moving energy, its will to begin again, reemerges, chaneled by interruptions that require noticeable new beginnings to offset them. These cantos evoke *Inferno* 1 and 2, where too forward motion was coordinated with fearful stasis: cantos 8 and 9 recount the pilgrim's crossing of the Styx and fearful arrival at the city of Dis, his transition from the circles of incontinence to "questo basso inferno" (*Inf.* 8.75), while cantos 16 and 17 narrate his encounter with Geryon and fearful transition from the circle of violence to the realm of fraud.[55] What interests me here is the poet's handling of these transitional cantos, his playing with narrative in ways that expose the lineaments of the narrative journey more than is usual. It is as though Dante wants us to recognize that there is a narrative voyage alongside the pilgrim's voyage, that the text's thematics will always be mirrored by its poetics. In the *Commedia*, the text's attention to itself, to its own voyage, is figured, as we have seen, by nautical, indeed aeronautical, imagery, in the same way that the narrator's presence is figured through Ulyssean language. Although the *Inferno*'s boats, beginning with Charon's in canto 3, appear, as is to be expected, in episodes where they are required to assist in physical transition, they also signal increased attention to the poet and his problems. Thus, Charon's Ulyssean characterization of the pilgrim as a sailor, about to board the first of many boats ("Per altra via, per altri porti / verrai a piaggia, non qui, per passare: / più lieve legno convien che ti porti" ["By another path, by other ports, you will come to shore, not here shall you pass; a lighter ship must carry you" (3.91–93)]) is coordinated with one of the poem's least smooth transitions, accomplished by way of a quake and a swoon; the very roughness of this transition draws attention to the narrating poet, who a few verses later will indulge for the first time in one of his favorite narrative devices, opening a sentence with "Vero è" (4.7). In canto 8 too, the reader finds a boat and a boatman—a "nave" and a "nocchier"[56]—and language that, with hindsight, reveals itself as provocatively metapoetical: no arrow ever coursed through the air as fast as this little ship ("nave piccioletta" [15]) piloted by a furious helmsman ("galeoto" [17], "nocchier" [80]), this boat ("barca" [25]) that cuts through the murky water with its ancient stern ("antica prora" [29]).[57] The arrow simile offers the rudiments of the aeronautics that will be more developed in the cases of Geryon and Ulysses, and fully achieved in the case of the angel's boat in *Purgatorio* 2;[58] that winged sailor, a "celestial nocchiero" (43), will share with Phlegyas, and with no one else, the designation "galeotto" (27). Phlegyas's "nave piccioletta" anticipates the *navicelle* of *Inferno* 17 and *Purgatorio* 1,[59] as well as the "piccioletta barca" of *Paradiso* 2 and the "picciola barca" of *Paradiso* 23, whose more metaphorical "ardita prora" (as compared to Phlegyas's "antica prora") is also guided by a *nocchier*: the poet.

Nautical language, even at this stage of the poem, where it has not yet achieved the metaphorical resonance it will accrete later on, is linked to the self-conscious presence of the poet, a presence testified to at once by canto 8's uniquely self-conscious opening words, "Io dico." The story the poet tells here is new, a tense drama spread over two cantos that interrupts the pilgrim's progress by invoking the possibility, whose narrative antecedents derive from canto 2, of his unsuitability for the journey. The encounter with the devils who block the pilgrim's path, who try to send him back unescorted and unfulfilled, is different from the encounters engineered thus far, and so the poet does new and different things with his narrative. Indeed, cantos 8 and 9 are a display of the author's narrative prowess, a resolute breaking with the narrative conventions established heretofore. The first break is the self-conscious authorial flashback that begins canto 8, in which the narrator presents events that occurred before the events narrated at the end of the previous canto; before the travelers reached the foot of the tower described in canto 7's last verse ("Venimmo al piè d'una torre al da sezzo"), they had seen and discussed ominous signals passed between that tower and one further distant:[60]

> Io dico, seguitando, ch'assai prima
>   che noi fossimo al piè de l'alta torre,
>   li occhi nostri n'andar suso a la cima
> per due fiammette che i vedemmo porre,
>   e un'altra da lungi render cenno,
>   tanto ch'a pena il potea l'occhio tòrre.

I say, following, that long before we had reached the foot of the high tower, our eyes went up to its top because of two little flames we saw set there, and another tower returned the signal from such a distance that the eye could barely catch it.

(*Inf.* 8.1–6)

This flashback requires an overt manipulation of narrative time (as indicated by "Io dico, seguitando, ch'assai prima," where "seguitando," a word that moves forward, is paired with "assai prima," words that look back); it highlights the narrator, the one arranging the sequence according to his own rules, the one who says "Io dico" and who will announce, regarding Filippo Argenti, "Quivi il lasciammo, che più non ne narro" ("There we left him, and I tell no more of him" [64]). This narrator, a term we use more advisedly than usual, since "narro" in line 64 represents the poem's first instance of the verb *narrare*, is in control: he can withhold or dispense narrative attention, textual time, as he chooses. Canto 8 concludes—it is, significantly, the first canto to end transitionally, *in medias res*—with Vergil's reference to the heavenly messenger whose assistance they anxiously await; his final verses are projected forward, using the adverb *già* and the future tense to forecast the angel's arrival:[61] "e già di qua da lei discende l'erta, / passando per li cerchi sanza scorta, / tal che per lui ne fia la terra aperta" ("and already on this side of the gate is descending the steep path, passing without guide through the circles, one by whom the city will be opened to us" [128–30]). We note the careful coordination of the canto's beginning and end: at the beginning, the narrator looks into the past, via flashback, while at the end he looks (through Vergil) into the future, via suspense. The beginning goes back, and the end goes forward, creating a kind of narrative spiral and emphasizing, once more, the narrator's control over his text.

The narrator's presence is felt throughout this sequence, which also contains the poem's first two addresses to the reader and, in canto 8, the interpolated episode of Filippo Argenti, which complicates the narrative line in an unprecedented fashion by occurring after Phlegyas has picked up the travelers and before he deposits them at the gates of Dis.[62] Once arrived, the devils suggest that the temerarious pilgrim, "che sì ardito intrò per questo regno" ("who so daring entered in this kingdom" [*Inf.* 8.90]), return alone on the reckless path by which he came: "Sol si ritorni per la folle strada" (91). By denoting the pilgrim's path as "folle," the devils capitalize on his fears, attempting to diminish his resolve, to reduce him, psychologically, to the condition of canto 2, when he feared that the trip would be Ulyssean: *folle*.[63] The fears that in canto 2 were allayed by Vergil's assurance of grace will soon be swept away by the celestial messenger. But, if the devils are wrong regarding the pilgrim's "folle strada," one wonders if they might not have a point regarding the poet, whose "dead poetry" ("morta poesì" [*Purg.* 1.7]) seems calculated to fill in the blanks of what Vergil now calls, referring to the writing on hell's gate, God's "dead script" ("scritta morta" [*Inf.* 8.127]).[64] Conscious of the Ulyssean dimension of his project, Dante takes particular pains in this episode to distinguish diabolic from angelic sign systems. Besides the relay of threatening diabolic signs with which canto 8 opens,[65] the devils are characterized as creators of "parole maladette" whose effect would be to prevent the pilgrim's progress, to dead-end him: "Pensa, lettor, se io mi sconfortai / nel suon de le *parole maladette*, / ché non credetti ritornarci mai" ("Think, reader, if I was discomforted by the sound of the *cursed words*, for I did not think I should ever return here" [*Inf.* 8.94–96]). Conversely, the angel, who appears after the devils have played their semiotic trump card in canto 9 by bringing forth Medusa, is the bearer of "parole sante," words invested with the power to convert a dead end into a new beginning:[66] "e noi movemmo i piedi inver' la terra, / sicuri appresso le *parole sante*" ("and we moved our feet toward the city, secure in the wake of the *holy words*" [*Inf.* 9.104–5]). While Vergil, whose own mutilated word ("parola tronca" [*Inf.* 9.14]) mediates between the *parole maladette* and the *parole sante*, subscribes to the power of the diabolic signifiers and tells the pilgrim to turn back,[67] the angel—God's sign, his messenger—knows that the divine will is never *tronca*, that it is "quella voglia / a cui non puote il fin mai esser mozzo" ("that will whose end can never be cut off" [9.94–95]). Thus, while the devils are destined to remain forever impotently insolent

("Questa lor tracotanza *non è nova*" ["This their arrogance *is not new*" (*Inf.* 8.124)]), forever exchanging signs that accomplish nothing, forever "not new," the poet will successfully navigate his transition, moving forward along the narrative path, along the signpost of the new.

Vergil's heralding of Phlegyas's arrival—"Su per le sucide onde / già scorger puoi quello che s'aspetta" ("Over the filthy waves you can already discern what is expected" [*Inf.* 8.10–11])—anticipates his later preannouncement of Geryon: "Tosto verrà di sovra / ciò ch'io attendo e che il tuo pensier sogna." The metapoetic content of the later verses is less latent, as indeed everything about the poet's meditation on narrative is less latent in cantos 16–17 than it was in cantos 8–9. Once more the poet's concerns have surfaced in a moment of narrative stress; once more he adopts narrative devices that dramatize the very nature of transition as a passing of the baton from the old to the new, a forging of the new out of the old.[68] If we look at the sequence as a whole, we see how the narrative is spliced: canto 16 begins with a new beginning, the waterfall that signals the passage to the eighth circle; this new beginning is staved off by the arrival of the three Florentine sodomites, recommences when Geryon ascends at the canto's end, and is again postponed by the encounter with the usurers in canto 17. These interruptions serve to make the sequence's formal structure a commentary on the nature of ending and beginning: the intercalatory narrative underlines the new beginning by simultaneously announcing and delaying it. All this is worked out textually with great care. Canto 16 introduces change with its first word, the proleptic adverb "Già" that marks the point of transition to the new, an "altro giro": "Già era in loco onde s'udia 'l rimbombo / de l'acqua che cadea ne l'altro giro" ("Already I was in a place where one could hear the crashing of the water that fell into the next circle" [*Inf.* 16.1–2]). The Florentine sodomites, representatives not of the new circle of fraud that seemed so imminent but of the old circle of violence, appear within the same sentence, ushered by "quando": "quando tre ombre insieme si partiro, / correndo, d'una torma che passava / sotto la pioggia de l'aspro martiro" ("when three shades together broke off, running, from a troop that was passing under the rain of the fierce torment" [4–6]). This description is calculated to bring us back, mentally, to the condition of the sodomites— inhabitants of the third *girone* of the seventh circle, a place we thought we were leaving—as presented at the end of the preceding canto, when we watched Brunetto rejoin his companions; the political conversation that ensues with the Florentine nobles also echoes the meeting with Brunetto. This encounter with the old, or with a variation thereof, continues until line 90, when the travelers again set off; they are soon overwhelmed by the sound of crashing water that this time receives its due in a lengthy simile (lines 94– 105) whose key element for us is the verb "rimbomba" (100), which echoes "rimbombo" in line 1 and repositions us at the waterfall, precisely where we

were at the outset of canto 16: we are once more prepared for a new beginning, which now arrives in the form of Geryon. After Geryon's arrival, however, and after the opening of a new canto that seems to make the new
beginning embodied by Geryon definitive, the narrative cuts back to the
seventh circle with the pilgrim's visit to the usurers, who represent a more
complex intertwining of the old with the new: the usurers are a new group—
no longer sodomites—inhabiting the old place, namely the same third ring
of the seventh circle. Finally, the actual entry into the new takes place in the
last section of canto 17.

The straight narrative line is interrupted in these cantos, much as it was
in canto 8 by the various narrative manipulations noted earlier. Like canto
8, canto 16 ends *in medias res*; here we wait not for an arrival, as in the earlier
instance, but for an identification of the creature that has just arrived. In
canto 17, which begins with Vergil's exclamatory verses identifying Geryon,
verses that only make sense if one has read the end of canto 16, the disjunctions of the narrative are rendered even more vividly than in the preceding
canto.[69] This is a land of transition, and proximity to the boundary between
old and new is stressed: Geryon is on the edge ("su l'orlo" [*Inf.* 17.24]) of the
abyss, with his tail in the void ("Nel vano" [25]); in order to reach him the
travelers must move ten paces along the extremity ("in su lo stremo" [32]).
Transition is further dramatized in the overlapping events whereby Vergil
stays behind to negotiate with Geryon while Dante goes, "tutto solo" ("all
alone" [44]) for the first time since setting forth on his journey,[70] to gain full
knowledge—Ulyssean *esperienza piena*—of this ring at his guide's behest:
"Acciò che tutta piena / esperïenza d'esto giron porti" ("so that you may
have full experience of this ring" [37–38]). By the same token, he will return
to find Vergil "già su la groppa del fiero animale" ("already on the back of
the fierce animal" [80]). Most telling is Dante's presentation of the usurers,
who are used as vehicles of narrative transition; as representatives of a third
group of sinners within the seventh circle's third *girone*, they are precise
embodiments of the grafting of the new onto the old. Thus, they sit next to
the edge of the seventh circle ("propinqua al loco scemo" [36]), so that the
pilgrim is obliged to go even further along, "su per la strema testa / di quel
settimo cerchio" ("up along the extreme margin of that seventh circle" [43–
44]), in order to speak to them. Not only are they geographically positioned
on the outer limits of the seventh circle, on the boundary dividing the seventh circle from the eighth as befits practitioners of a sin that seems to
partake more of fraud than of violence, but they are linguistically and dramatically characterized in eighth circle terms: the usurers' low language,
rough rhymes, vulgar gestures, and desire to incriminate each other are all
narrative features of Malebolge.[71] They are the sequence's most explicit in-
carnations of the problematic Dante is dealing with: how do we distinguish
the end from the beginning when all ends are beginnings and all beginnings

are endings? How to render the mysterious process whereby time is accreted and a human being comes to say "I' *fui*"—"I *was*"—the process whereby the new imperceptibly becomes the old and the present imperceptibly becomes the past?[72] This process, represented microcosmically by terza rima, is here dramatized and writ large by the narrative structure of these cantos. Not surprisingly, it is a structure that takes the form of a spiral, i.e., of a dialectic between old and new:

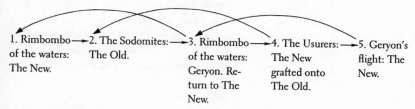

1. Rimbombo→2. The Sodomites:→3. Rimbombo→4. The Usurers:→5. Geryon's
of the waters:    The Old.         of the waters:    The New       flight: The
The New.                           Geryon. Re-    grafted onto  New.
                                  turn to The     The Old.
                                  New.

The structure of these transitional cantos is spiral-like because transition, history, life itself are spiral-like, ever going backward in order to go forward (as the pilgrim goes anomalously backward from the usurers to Geryon, and as Geryon backs into his spiral),[73] ever finding the new within the old. The poet who designed these cantos was attempting to discover the shape of life, to register the form of things and the rhythm of existence in his verse. He was a Ulysses.

## Chapter 4

# NARRATIVE AND STYLE IN LOWER HELL

> But of such a diffused nature, and so large is the Empire of Truth,
> that it hath place within the walls of Hell, and the Devils
> themselves are daily forced to practise it . . . although they
> deceive us, they lie not unto each other; as well understanding
> that all community is continued by Truth, and that of Hell
> cannot consist without it.
>
> (Sir Thomas Browne, *Pseudodoxia epidemica*)

I NTRODUCED BY the complex transition of cantos 16 and 17, *Inferno* 18 constitutes an emphatic new beginning situated at the canticle's midpoint, at its narrative "mezzo del cammin." "Luogo è in inferno detto Malebolge" ("There is a place in hell called Malebolge") begins the canto, with a verse that is crisply informative, explicitly introductory, and patently devoted to differentiation:[1] this is a new place, a new locus. Following the *descriptio loci* heralded by the opening "Luogo è,"[2] the narrator's focus shifts to the travelers. In two apparently very simple tercets, he activates the poetics of the new, founded on the discreteness of "questo luogo," this place as distinct from any other:

> In questo luogo, de la schiena scossi
>     di Gerïon, trovammoci; e 'l poeta
>     tenne a sinistra, e io dietro mi mossi.
> A la man destra vidi nova pieta,
>     novo tormento e novi frustatori,
>     di che la prima bolgia era repleta.

In this place, shaken off Geryon's back, we found ourselves; the poet kept to the left, and I moved after him. To the right I saw new anguish, new torment and new scourgers, of which the first pouch was replete.

(*Inf.* 18.19–24)

Besides the triple use of *novo*, echoing the double use at the beginning of canto 6, we note the numerical precision of "prima bolgia," which builds on the earlier "distinto in dieci valli" ("divided into ten valleys" [*Inf.* 18.9]); numbers will be used throughout lower hell to convey the sense of a suffocatingly precise system of order. In this canto alone we find not only "prima bolgia" but also "prima valle" ("first valley" [98]), and "argine secondo" ("second embankment" [101]); in canto 19 we find "terza bolgia" ("third pouch" [6]), "l'argine quarto" ("fourth embankment" [40]), and "dal quarto al quinto argine" ("from the fourth to the fifth embankment" [129]). These numbers prepare us for the smaller and more numerous containers, the more frequent encounters with the new that will characterize lower hell; again, canto 18 sets the pace for this more intense narrative rhythm by presenting us, uniquely, with two pouches, the first of which is further subdivided into two distinct groups of sinners, the panderers and seducers. Finally, we note that canto 18's proemial function, its enactment of a new beginning with almost *Inferno* 1 pretensions, is underscored by verse 21, which echoes in recombinatory fashion the first canto's last verse: "Allor si mosse, e io li tenni dietro" has become "'l poeta / tenne a sinistra, e io dietro mi mossi." Once more, then, as at the end of canto 1, the journey has begun.

However, it has begun again in a post-Geryon world, as the careful insertion of "de la schiena scossi / di Gerïon" into the new beginning's preamble testifies. The cantos of Malebolge, in fact the cantos of all lower hell, since fraud governs both the eighth and the ninth circles, are written under the sign of Geryon: a representation of fraud that calls into question the very representational values used to figure it forth. Thus, on the one hand these cantos rely on the same kind of representational illusionism that was inaugurated by the writing on hell's gate; the line, "Luogo è in inferno detto Malebolge," for instance, confers truth status on the locus it names by implying that it is so named by others—by whom, after all, is this place "called" Malebolge? When the poet speaks in his own voice in verse 6—"di cui *suo loco* dicerò l'ordigno" ("of whose structure I will speak in its place")—his "dicerò" is made authoritative by the anonymous "detto" that precedes; he is telling us what is known, and therefore what is true. At the same time, however, that the truth status of his own representation continues to be maintained, Dante will use these cantos to question the basis of all human representation, to probe relentlessly the fraud inherent in language and indeed in all sign systems. In these cantos fraud is consistently treated as a semiotic sin, a sin in which sign systems must be breached in order for the fraudulent act to be committed.[3] Canto 18, with its linguistically oriented seducers and flatterers, sets the stage for a meditation on representational falsehood that extends throughout Malebolge (a circle that culminates, let us not forget, with the falsifiers of words); this meditation generates both content—the types of sins Dante includes under the rubric of fraud, the concern to characterize these sins linguistically—and poetic form. From the stylistic perspective, these cantos run the gamut from the lowest of low styles to the highest of high; here too, canto 18 is paradigmatic, moving in its brief compass from vulgar black humor ("Ahi come facean lor levar le berze / a le prime percosse! già nessuno / le seconde aspettava né le terze" ["Oh, how they made them lift their heels at the first blows! Truly none awaited the second or the third" (37–39)]) to the solemnity with which Vergil displays Jason ("Guarda quel grande che vene" ["Look at that great one who comes" (83)]) to the nastiness of the *merda* in which the flatterers are plunged. For Barchiesi, such transitions constitute the essence of canto 18; he suggests that the canto's most singular aspect is its violent juxtapositioning of elevated language with realistic language, of the Latinate "Luogo è" with the plebeian neologism "Malebolge."[4] This insight can be extended to the cantos of Malebolge as a group, whose violent stylistic transitions provide an implicit commentary on the questions of genre and style that were opened up for the poem by the use of the term *comedìa* in the Geryon episode.

Transitions in style and register occur with singular frequency in Malebolge.[5] These marked and sudden changes in style signal an exploration of the bounds of representational decorum that is connected to the poet's first formulation, in canto 16, of genre. His use of *comedìa* in canto 16 will be answered, in canto 20, by a unique use of *tragedìa*: "alta tragedìa" is *Inferno* 20's designation for the *Aeneid*. In my previous reading of the poem's Vergilian narrative, I attempted to show that the running critique of Vergil that is found in the *Inferno* is also, necessarily, a critique of *tragedìa*; the poem works to demonstrate that *alta tragedìa* is inferior to—because less true than—*bassa comedìa*. *Comedìa*, the textuality that undertakes to represent such as Geryon, may appear to be a lie, but is always truth: it is a "ver c'ha faccia di menzogna," a "mirum verum," a "cosa incredibile e vera." What I intend to focus on here is the stylistic correlative to the *comedìa's* truth claims, which I take to be its manifoldness; the ultimate point of lower hell's dizzying array of register and style is that the *comedìa* is a voracious genre, one that—because it tells the truth—is committed to embracing and representing all of reality. My concern is no longer to demonstrate the implicit contrast Dante establishes between *comedìa* and *tragedìa*, *verità* and *menzogna*; however, I am obliged to remind the reader that all formulations of what *comedìa* is occur, in this poem, in tandem with what it is not. Thus, it is no accident that Malebolge contains a series of classical/contemporary couples; these couples serve to highlight the disjunction that is at the root of Dante's meditation on genre and style, the disjunction between *comedìa* and *tragedìa*.

Returning to canto 18, which again is paradigmatic for Malebolge as a whole, Sanguineti notes that the canto contains a modern and a classical figure in each of its two pouches; Barchiesi comments on the symmetry whereby the pilgrim addresses both contemporaries, while Vergil takes it upon himself to describe both classical sinners.[6] We could further note that the two classical/contemporary couples of Malebolge's first canto (Venedico Caccianemico and Jason, Alessio Interminelli and Thaïs) are matched by the two classical/contemporary couples of Malebolge's last canto, canto 30 (Gianni Schicchi and Myrrha, Master Adam and Sinon). Bracketed by these sets of classical/contemporary figures, is the *pièce de résistance*, Ulysses and Guido da Montefeltro, where the alignment between Vergil and Ulysses on the one hand and Dante and Guido on the other is pronounced; Vergil feels that he should address the Greek hero, while the pilgrim may speak to his Italian counterpart. In this crucial central diptych the classical/contemporary coupling signals a stylistic disjunction on a grand scale, as we move from the heroic discourse of canto 26 to the quotidian language of canto 27.[7] The disjunction between cantos 26 and 27 is programmatic, a signpost to Malebolgian poetics, and it is already implicit on a smaller scale in the similar disjunctions that make up the stylistic texture of *Inferno* 18.

The classical/contemporary couples that punctuate Malebolge are emblems of the mixed style that is the essence of the "comedic" mode.[8] While Jason deceived Hypsipyle "with signs and ornate words" ("con segni e con parole ornate" [*Inf.* 18.91])—a phrasing that draws attention to the semiotic nature of his sin—the pilgrim adopts a "plain speech" that forces Venedico to reveal himself ("ma sforzami la tua chiara favella" [53]), and the poet's language could not be further from the ornate as he describes Alessio's head "di merda lordo" ("filthy with shit" [116]) and Thaïs's "unghie merdose" ("shitty nails" [131]). The connection between Vergil and Jason is established by the Latin poet's own predilection for *parola ornata*, an aspect of his persona to which we were introduced by Beatrice in *Inferno* 2;[9] in canto 18, then, changes in stylistic register work to associate classical culture (Jason, Vergil) with linguistic ornament and deceit, with the "flattery" of which Cato will accuse Vergil in *Purgatorio* 1.[10] It seems no accident that, within the economy of canto 18, the poet's language becomes most vulgar in the final sequence, as he treats those who are punished for their *lusinghe* (the very word Cato will so harshly throw at Vergil), after the encounter with classical *parola ornata*. Using low language and the type of harsh rhyme that in *Inferno* 32 he will explicitly invoke as a means of representing the pit of hell,[11] Dante begins in canto 18 to clarify poetically the enigmatic word used for the first time at the end of canto 16, the word *comedìa*: it is a genre capable of exploiting the lowest of styles. But the lesson in comedic style is an ongoing one; were we to think that its province is exclusively low, we would be mistaken, as canto 19—a great outburst of comedic high style—demonstrates.[12] Again, the point is the stylistic discrepancy between the two cantos: from the relatively simple, unadorned, plain style of canto 18 to the rhetorical profusion of canto 19. The transition from a literal and rhetorically unelaborated style to a language of great metaphorical density finds its emblem in the transition from the literal "puttana" of 18.133, Thaïs, to the metaphorical "puttaneggiar coi regi" ("whoring with kings" [19.108]) of the Church on behalf of the pimping popes. The back-to-back use of *puttana* and *puttaneggiar* (the former used only twice more, both times in *Purgatorio* 32 for the Church, the latter a hapax), underscores the transition from literal to metaphorical whoring and thus the rhetorical differences between cantos: the straightforward narrative of 18 contrasts sharply with the grandiloquence of 19, a canto that contains three apostrophes, that indeed opens with the apostrophic trumpet blast directed at Simon Magus and his fellow prostituters of "the things of God."[13]

I refer to a trumpet blast advisedly, since this is the metaphor the poet adopts for his attack on the simonists, for whom his trumpet must now sound: "or convien che per voi suoni la tromba, / però che ne la terza bolgia state" ("now the trumpet must sound for you, since you are in the third pouch" [5–6]). Calling his poetic discourse a trumpeting, Dante aligns his text with the "angelic trumpet" ("angelica tromba" [*Inf.* 6.95]) that will sound on the Judgment Day, as later in the canto he will buttress his denunciation of the simonist popes by invoking St. John the Evangelist, for him the writer of the Apocalypse. The Apocalypse is Dante's preferred source in canto 19, as it will be also in the cantos that narrate the procession and *tableaux vivants* of the earthly paradise; the pilgrim specifically cites St. John as his authority when he accuses the popes in language taken directly from the Apocalypse: "Di voi pastor s'accorse il Vangelista, / quando colei che siede sopra l'acque / puttaneggiar coi regi a lui fu vista" ("The Evangelist thought of pastors such as you when she who sits upon the waters was seen by him to whore with kings" [*Inf.* 19.106–8]). St. John too was a trumpeter; in *Paradiso* 26 Dante calls his Gospel "l'alto preconio che grida l'arcano / di qui là giù sovra ogne altro bando" ("the high announcement that more than any other heralding cries out the mystery of here down there" [44–45]), and in the *Monarchia* as well Dante refers to the "trumpet of the gospels" ("tuba evangelica").[14] There is thus ample cause to associate the poet's trumpeting with inspired art, the kind of art that a few verses further on will cause Dante to break into canto 19's second apostrophe, celebrating the art displayed throughout the universe by God's wisdom: "O somma sapïenza, quanta è l'arte / che mostri in cielo, in terra e nel mal mondo" ("Oh supreme wisdom, how great is the art that you show in heaven, on earth, and in the evil world" [10–11]). *Comedìa* in this canto is shown to be crafted in the high style of biblical invective, replete with apostrophes, rhetorical questions, exclamations, biting sarcasm, and metaphoric density; it is, moreover, shown to be an art that is analogous to the evangelical proclamation, the art displayed (or the *tuba* played) by God. Canto 19 therefore also contains the requisite signs of the poet's "Ulyssean" anxiety, to wit a double defensive move that encompasses both narrative past and present: the narrator sets the record straight regarding the potentially sacreligious breaking of a baptismal font in the Florentine Baptistery, using his poetic authority to give the lie to all other recountings of the event ("e questo sia suggel ch'ogn'omo sganni" ["and let this be the seal to undeceive all men" (21)]);[15] he also prefaces the pilgrim's outburst against Nicholas III with an authorial disclaimer marked by the Ulyssean word "folle": "Io non so s'i' mi fui qui troppo folle" ("I do not know if I was here too rash" [88]). As usual in the *Commedia*, such moves serve to defuse the poet's anxieties about his enormous claims and thus allow him to be even more explicit; after the pilgrim has finished denouncing the pope, we learn that Vergil listened with pleasure to his true words: "lo suon de le parole vere espresse" ("the sound of the true words expressed" [123]).[16]

The poet's words are "parole vere" because what he recounts was revealed to him, as the contents of the Book of Revelation were revealed to St. John, by whom the Church's whorish behavior was seen, "fu vista"; the passive voice stresses the prophet's function as a recipient of divine revelation. The pilgrim's similar posture is emphasized by his passive acceptance of revelation in canto 19's last verse: "Indi un altro vallon mi fu scoperto" ("Thence another valley was revealed to me"). What is revealed to this man whose words have just been expressly defined as true is the pouch that contains those sinners who claimed falsely to be the recipients of divine revelation, lying prophets whose words were not true but false. Canto 20, the canto of the false prophets, thus follows a canto in which our poet's identity as a true prophet has been validated, not least by canto 19's own comedic—and in this instance also mordantly comic—version of true prophecy, to wit Nicholas III's expectations regarding the eventual arrival to this pouch of the still living Boniface VIII. The issue of false prophecy will in canto 20 be viewed in a textual focus: the prophets we encounter are mainly classical figures from classical texts; the presentation of Manto occasions the poem's most explicit revision of the *Aeneid* in the very canto where Vergil's text is baptized "alta tragedìa."[17] Canto 20's textual focus is anticipated in canto 19, where Nicholas reacts to what he presumes to be the arrival of his successor by saying, "Di parecchi anni mi mentì lo scritto" ("By several years the text has lied to me" [19.54]), thus broaching the theme of lying texts versus truthful texts, which is the main topic of canto 20. Canto 20's insistence on the technical aspects of textual construction—its unique use of textual jargon such as "ventesimo canto / de la prima canzon" ("twentieth canto of the first canticle" [2–3]) and the term "tragedìa" (113)—is also anticipated in canto 19, where we find "metro" and "note" framing the pilgrim's great outburst (89, 118). Explicit textual self-consciousness of this sort was ushered into the poem by the Geryon episode, where first the poet writes of the "notes of this comedy," and where first (after implicitly raising the issue in the Pier della Vigna episode) he overtly poses the question of his text's credibility. The question of the *Commedia*'s truthfulness is dramatically reprised in canto 19, where Dante's text is associated with that of the evangelist, and it is again the center of attention in canto 20, where Dante's text is forcefully *dis*associated from the classical texts that provide the pouch's lying prophets. In canto 19 Dante insists on his own credibility; with regard to the incident at the Baptistery, he instructs us to let his version be the "seal that undeceives all men." In canto 20 Vergil uses similar language to imply the fraudulence of his own version of the founding of Mantova in *Aeneid* 10; he tells us to "let no lie defraud the truth" (99)—in other words, to credit no version other than the one recounted in *Inferno* 20. Both these lapidary imperatives—"questo sia suggel ch'ogn'omo sganni" and "la verità nulla menzogna frodi"—stress the relation of language to fraud: language is a medium that can both deceive—*frodare*—and undeceive—*sgannare*.

The relation of language to fraud is a central concern of the pouch of the barraters. Although the sin of graft is less overtly linguistic than flattery or prophecy, Dante takes care to characterize these sinners by provenance and speech patterns: as the pimps were labeled Bolognese and Bologna was indicated by a linguistic periphrasis ("che tante lingue non son ora apprese / a dicer 'sipa' tra Sàvena e Reno" ["so many tongues are not now taught to say 'sipa' between Savena and Reno" (18.60–61)]), so the grafters are characterized by linguistic traits, first as men of Lucca, where "no" becomes "yes" for money ("del no, per li denar, vi si fa *ita*" [21.42]), and further as Sardinians, whose speech is laden with regionalisms and whose tongues never weary of talking of Sardinia ("e a dir di Sardigna / le lingue lor non si sentono stanche" [22.89–90]). The unnamed Navarrese barrater (the unusual absence of a signifier for this character is in itself a way of drawing attention to the value of signs) adds to the climate of linguistic regionalism by boasting that he can bring Tuscans and Lombards out of the pitch for Dante to interrogate.[18] The semiotic sin par excellence of this pouch, of course, is Malacoda's "truthful" lie.[19] This fraudulent use of linguistic signs spearheads a sequence that deals in particular depth with the issue of signs, as manifested by the diabolic signs registered at the end of canto 21: "ma prima avea ciascun la lingua stretta / coi denti, verso lor duca, *per cenno*; / ed elli avea del cul fatto *trombetta*" ("But first each pressed his tongue between his teeth at their leader *as a signal*, and he had made a *trumpet* of his ass" [137–39]). These *cenni* are picked up in the mock-epic opening of canto 22, where the military imagery that runs through the pouch of barratry (civic graft being a kind of war against the state) becomes a focused rehearsal of various signs;[20] the significance of this passage for the *Commedia* at large, for the poem's sustained discourse on signs, is manifested by its concluding evocation of a ship whose voyage is governed by signs from earth and sky, including the sign—"stella"—that will greet us as we emerge from hell:

Io vidi già cavalier muover campo

. . . . . . . . . . .

quando con *trombe*, e quando con *campane*,
 con *tamburi* e con *cenni di castella*,
 e con cose nostrali e con istrane;

né già con sì diversa *cennamella*
  cavalier vidi muover né pedoni,
  né nave a *segno di terra o di stella.*

I have seen before horsemen move camp ... now with *trumpets*, and now with *bells*, with *drums* and with *signals from castles*, with things native and foreign; but never have I seen horsemen move to so strange a *bugle*, or footmen, or ship by *sign of land or star.*

(*Inf.* 22.1, 7–12)

The "signals from castles"—"cenni di castella"—recall the ominous signals passed between the demonic towers at the outset of *Inferno* 8;[21] we also find the *Commedia*'s last use of *tromba*, following the poet's evangelically attuned trumpet of canto 19 and Barbariccia's antiangelic bugle of canto 21. Again, the point seems to be that the voracious genre *comedìa* encompasses all manner of semiotic activity; the discourse of realism requires both the angelic *tromba* and the demonic *trombetta*.

At the beginning of the *bolgia* of the barraters we learn of the "divine art" that makes the purposeful pitch in which the sinners stew ("tal, non per foco ma per divin'arte, / bollia là giuso una pegola spessa" ["so, not by fire but by divine art, a thick pitch was boiling there below" (*Inf.* 21.16–17)]); in the same opening sequence, we learn that Dante's art is similarly purposeful, that it records nothing but what is necessary: "Così di ponte in ponte, altro parlando / che la mia comedìa cantar non cura" ("So from bridge to bridge, speaking of other things that my comedy does not care to sing" [1–2]). We note that *comedìa*, which appears here for the last time, is inserted into a clause that functions as a subliminal garnerer of verisimilitude: the verses give life to the text by casually insisting on a life outside the text, an independent reality that the text does not choose to reveal to us. We note further the association of *comedìa* with the divine art whose work it records,[22] an association that introduces a sequence notable for its stylistic plenitude, for its fearless veering from high to low, emblematized by the mock-epic—neither high nor low—exordium of canto 22. Pietro di Dante considered the exordium a way of making amends for the offensively low conclusion of the preceding canto;[23] instead, the passage draws attention to the purposefulness of that conclusion and to these cantos as an intentional recital of the disparate elements that make up the mixed style.[24] These cantos are in fact a manifesto for the mixed style; their precept of stylistic decorum is canto 22's proverbial "ma ne la chiesa / coi santi, e in taverna coi ghiottoni" ("But with saints in church and with gluttons in a tavern" [*Inf.* 22.14–15]). A striking example of the stylistic counterpoint mandated by the proverb is provided by the contrast between the high Latinate word *ludo* ("O tu che leggi, udirai nuovo ludo" ["O you who read, you will hear a new game" (*Inf.* 22.118)]) and its vernacular equivalent, the low *buffa* ("Irato Calcabrina de la buffa" ["Calcabrina, angered by the trick" (*Inf.* 22.133)]) or *beffa* ("Questi per noi / sono scherniti con danno e con beffa" ["Because of us they have been fooled with hurt and trickery" (*Inf.* 23.13–14)]). All three terms are used to refer to the series of events in which Ciampolo tricks the devils into allowing him to jump back into the pitch, a scenario whose telling takes up the final third of canto 22. The tale told here is a low one, replete with animal imagery—a Boccaccian *beffa* but for the eschatological dimension that draws in the high "tragic" language: this is a *nuovo ludo*, a game in which there are no winners.[25] The *beffa* played by Ciampolo on his tormentors leads to the brawl between devils at the end of 22, wherein the cooks are cooked; this segment constitutes a rather straightforward novella-like recounting of what are hardly "high" events. However, the opening of canto 23 will retrospectively complicate and intellectualize the apparently simple ending of canto 22 by comparing the devils' brawl to a text.

The "presente rissa," the current brawl, is interpreted by the pilgrim in such a way as to sustain the remarkable semiotic density of these cantos; his uneasiness regarding the humiliated devils causes him to think of the story of the frog and the mouse from Aesop's *Fables*:

> Vòlt'era in su la favola d'Isopo
>   lo mio pensier per la presente rissa,
>   dov'el parlò de la rana e del topo;
> ché più non si pareggia 'mo' e 'issa'
>   che l'un con l'altro fa, se ben s'accoppia
>   principio e fine con la mente fissa.

> My thoughts were turned by the present brawl onto the fable of Aesop where he spoke of the frog and the mouse; for "mo" and "issa" are not more alike than the one is to the other, if one matches the beginning and the ending well with an attentive mind.

> (*Inf.* 23.4–9)

The implicit parallel between the tale told by the *Commedia* and the fable that glosses it sustains the identification between Dante's text and the low style, a style that does not eschew cooks, animals, or brawls, that is no more afraid to humble itself than are the Franciscans to whom the two travelers are compared at the outset of canto 23: "Taciti, soli, sanza compagnia / n'andavam l'un dinanzi e l'altro dopo, / come frati minor vanno per via" ("Silent, alone, without company, we went along the one ahead and the other behind, as Friars Minor go along the road" [*Inf.* 23.1–3]).[26] Indeed, the vulgar *rissa* to which the poet refers in 23.5 has been recounted unashamedly and at length. It is interesting to note that the only other usage of *rissa* is the verbal form adopted by Vergil in response to what he considers the pilgrim's excessive interest in the *piato* or quarrel between Sinon and maestro Adamo: "Or pur mira, / che per poco che teco non mi risso!" ("Just keep on looking, and it will take very little before I quarrel with you myself!" [*Inf.* 30.131–32]). So Vergil elicits the pilgrim's shame for his interest in watching a *rissa*, but the poet shows no shame at having narrated a similar *rissa* in canto 22; rather he situates his representation within the humble morality of the Aesopic tradition. This passage therefore supports my previous reading of canto 30, in which I sustained that Vergil was wrong to reprimand the pilgrim for confronting all the reality that hell has to offer; if he does not look and listen, how will he later recount?[27] Also significant as emblems of the low style are the humble words signifying "now"—the moment of conversion, of understanding—that represent the two terms of the comparison: *mo* is used throughout the *Commedia*, while *issa* is aligned first with Aesop's fable, second with Guido da Montefeltro's deflation of Vergil's exalted heroic language, and finally with Bonagiunta's tribute to a transcendentally plain style, the sweet new style that will ultimately lead to the new style par excellence, the *comedìa*.[28]

For all its implications regarding the value of the low style, the parallel between the "presente rissa" narrated at the end of canto 22 and the fable of the frog and the mouse does not generate textual clarity. Let us reconstruct the sequence of events. Ciampolo proposes to whistle up some fellow grafters, requesting that the devils withdraw from the edge of the bank where they can be seen; when the devils comply, urged on by Alichino, Ciampolo dives back into the pitch, prompting Alichino to dive in after him, to no avail. Calcabrina, angered at Ciampolo's escape, follows Alichino, not to help him but to attack him; they fight and at canto's end are embroiled in the pitch. These events are declared as similar as *mo* is to *issa* to those recounted in a fable about a mouse who asks a frog for help in crossing a river; tying the mouse to his leg with a string, the frog sets out and, at midstream, begins to dive, intending to kill the mouse. The mouse resists; a kite flying by seizes the mouse and, because of the string, is rewarded with the malicious frog as well. The most common interpretation of this passage views Alichino as the mouse, Calcabrina as the frog who should have come to his aid, and the pitch as the kite who triumphs over both. More recently, scholars have begun to focus on a second level of meaning, suggesting a proleptic analogy between the fable and the pursuit that is about to occur, whereby Dante is the mouse, Vergil is an unwitting frog leading the mouse into danger, and the Malebranche are the kite. What interests me here, however, is not the correct interpretation of the passage, but the fact that its interpretation has traditionally proved so arduous. Establishing the equivalences between the two sets of signs—or, indeed, three sets, if we add the story of Dante, Vergil, and the devils—has resulted in as many interpretations as there are ways of combining the variables—signs—

Dante has given us. Thus, in addition to the most popular reading mentioned above, the exegetical record as summarized by Hollander includes the following combinations:[29] Ciampolo as mouse, Alichino as frog, Calcabrina as kite; Alichino as frog, Calcabrina as kite; Ciampolo as frog, devils as mouse; Alichino as mouse, Calcabrina as frog, Barbariccia as kite; Dante and Vergil as mouse, devils as frog, with the sometime addition of Ciampolo as kite; Ciampolo as frog at beginning, Calcabrina as frog at end; Alichino and Dante as mouse, Calcabrina and Vergil as frog, devils twice as kite; Ciampolo and Dante as mouse, Alichino and Vergil as frog, Calcabrina and devils as kite. Undoubtedly, some of these equivalences are more plausible than others; nonetheless, it is significant that Dante has planted a semiotic terrain fertile enough for all of them—even the most farfetched—to spring up. In other words, the historical lack of critical consensus regarding the application of the fable to the events of the poem is part of Dante's point, which is the ambiguity—the Geryonesque fraudulence—of all signs, all representation. Applying one set of signs (the text of the fable) to another (the text of the poem) results not in clarity but in confusion. And, in fact, the two signs—*mo* and *issa*—whose likeness is declared the basis of the comparison between the larger sets of signs, are themselves irreducibly different.[30]

The opening sequence of canto 23 is notable also for the narrative suspense created vis-à-vis the devils' pursuit; although from a theological perspective the travelers would seem to be invulnerable, protected by divine warrant, from a diegetic perspective it is important that the poet be able to deflect the narrative from the potential tedium of an entirely preordained story line. A first instance of such authorial intervention occurs in the sequence at the gates of Dis, where Dante succeeds in insinuating concern about the outcome of events into his story, most dramatically by way of Vergil's partially expressed doubt as he awaits the arrival of the heavenly messenger: "'Pur a noi converrà vincer la punga,' / cominciò el, 'se non . . .'" ("'Yet we must win this fight,' he began, 'or else . . .'" [*Inf.* 9.7–8]). The anomalous ellipsis with which Vergil interrupts himself creates an atmosphere of negative suspense, which balances the positive suspense created by the confidence with which he had asserted the *messo's* imminent arrival at the end of the preceding canto: "e già di qua da lei discende l'erta . . . tal che per lui ne fia la terra aperta" ("and *already* on this side of it descends the steep path one by whom this land will be opened for us" [*Inf.* 8.128, 130]). The manipulation of narrative time to create suspense—literally the suspension of events in order to generate uncertainty as to their outcome—is signaled, in canto 8, by the poet's use of *già*. In *Inferno* 23 we witness an accelerated use of the same technique: "*Già* mi sentia tutti arricciar li peli / de la paura" ("*Already* I felt my hair curling with fear" [23.19]) is the verse that begins the buildup of narrative suspense; the pilgrim then alerts Vergil as to his fear of the Malebranche, saying, "Noi li avem *già* dietro; / io li 'magino sì, che *già* li sento" ("*Already* we have them behind us; I so imagine them that I *already* hear them" [23–24]). As soon as Vergil has suggested a way for them to flee "the imagined chase" ("l'imaginata caccia" [33]), the narrator cuts in with another *già*: "*Già* non compié di tal consiglio rendere, / ch'io li vidi venir con l'ali tese" ("*Not yet* had he finished giving me such counsel than I saw them coming with wings outstretched" [34–35]). Here *già* must do what the narrator, constrained by temporal order, cannot; the adverb insinuates simultaneity, gives us the impression that the devils are upon the travelers before Vergil has finished speaking (while in actual fact, of course, the narrator has been obliged to register all of Vergil's words, and only then can pass on to the pursuers). Throughout the episode there is a tension between, on the one hand, temporal adverbs that denote urgency and immediacy (not only *già*, but *tostamente* [22], *tosto* [27], *pur mo* [28], *sùbito* [37], *sì tosto* [46], *a pena* [52]) and, on the other, the word *imaginare*, which relegates the devils to the pilgrim's overheated imagination ("io li 'magino sì," "imaginata caccia").

This tension mirrors the fundamental ambivalence of the sequence, brought about by the conflict between theological and narrative principles: Can the pilgrim be harmed? Do the devils constitute a real danger? Dante manipulates his narrative in such a way as to suggest that they do, while at the same time covering himself theologically: the episode's conclusion proclaims the total impotence of the demons outside of their own pouch, but the poet never clarifies whether they could have harmed him while he was within it. The poet tells us that the pilgrim's arrival in the sixth pouch removes all cause for fear: "ma non lì era sospetto" ("there was nothing to fear there" [23.54]), for providence has denied the devils the power of entrance. But by telling us so emphatically that there is no cause for *sospetto* in the sixth *bolgia*, the poet if anything implies that there was reason for fear while in the fifth; he at any rate does nothing to defuse the illusion of the presence of danger within the fifth pouch. The illusion of the presence of danger in hell is akin to the illusion of the presence of sin in purgatory, as dramatized by the arrival of the serpent in the valley of princes. Like the devils' pursuit, the serpent's threat constitutes a narrative sleight of hand, serving as a way of creating tension and generating suspense in what would otherwise risk being a flat textual experience. All the souls in purgatory, including all the souls in antepurgatory and all the souls in the valley, are saved. They are no longer subject to temptation by sin, but only to the pain of remembering past temptations and past succumbings. The pain of remembrance is ritualized by means of the recurrent arrival of the serpent into their valley, their ultimate resistance by the defending angels who drive it out again. Had Dante been willing—or able!—to narrate the daily repetitive arrivals and departures of the serpent, its ritualized aspect would gain in focus and its dramatic impact would lessen. As it is, however, the pressure is on us to find a way to accommodate the apparently contradictory realities of temptation and salvation, to hold these different and competing truths simultaneously in our minds, savoring Dante's art of *gradatio*, rather than to yield to the simplistic assumption that the souls in the valley are in fact being tempted. Like the devils, the serpent demonstrates Dante's willingness to take steps to counter his overdetermined plot, although by so doing he blurs the sharp moral contours of his narrative.

Between the Aesop's fable analogy and the "imaginata caccia" of the devils, *Inferno* 23's opening sequence deals with both semantic and structural ambiguities. The extended simile of the *villanello* that opens *Inferno* 24 hearkens back to the ambiguity of meaning generated by the comparison of the fable to the *rissa, mo* to *issa*. To describe the pilgrim's dismay at Vergil's anger and subsequent reassurance when his guide resumes his normal demeanor, Dante introduces the simile in which the peasant is first dismayed by what he thinks is snow and then reassured by the discovery that the snow is frost:

> In quella parte del giovanetto anno
>   che 'l sole i crin sotto l'Aquario tempra
>   e già le notti al mezzo dì sen vanno,
> quando la brina in su la terra assempra
>   l'imagine di sua sorella bianca,
>   ma poco dura a la sua penna tempra,
> lo villanello a cui la roba manca,
>   si leva, e guarda, e vede la campagna
>   biancheggiar tutta; ond'ei si batte l'anca,
> ritorna in casa, e qua e là si lagna,
>   come 'l tapin che non sa che si faccia;
>   poi riede, e la speranza ringavagna,
> veggendo 'l mondo aver cangiata faccia
>   in poco d'ora, e prende suo vincastro
>   e fuor le pecorelle a pascer caccia.

In that part of the young year when the sun refreshes his locks under Aquarius and already the nights move toward half the day, when the frost on the ground imitates the image of its white sister, but little lasts the point of its pen, the peasant, lacking food, gets up and looks and sees the countryside all white; at which he hits his thigh, returns into the house, and here and there goes about complaining, like the wretch who knows not what to do; then goes out again and recovers hope, seeing that the world has changed face in a brief time, and takes his staff and drives his sheep out to pasture.

(*Inf.* 24.1–15)

To the most obvious interpretation, whereby Dante is the stricken peasant and Vergil is the countryside, first a cause for consternation and then benign, at least one other set of equivalences can be added, whereby Vergil is the peasant (lied to by the frost as Vergil is by Malacoda) and Dante is the sheep, frightened by his protector's demeanor and then "led out to pasture" by his sweet look.[31] The possibility of more than one interpretation serves again to dramatize the shifting and hence ultimately deceptive nature of language, further reinforced by the use of *rime equivoche* (tempra/tempra, faccia/faccia), whereby identical sounds possess different meanings. Moreover, although this simile presents us with less sheer multivalence than the Aesop's fable analogy, it begins to explore the implications of semiotic failure in a way that the earlier passage does not, by raising the larger issue of representation through its use of artistic/mimetic language. The peasant mistakenly believes the frost to be snow because the frost has imitated the snow; borrowing from the lexicon of mimesis, the poet tells us that the frost "copies the image of its white sister." Attempting to represent snow, the frost appropriates the mode of art, and it fails, for like all art—all human representation—it is nondurable, subject to time: "little lasts the point of its pen." As compared to *Purgatorio* 10, where art is assimilated to nature and becomes real, infallible, here nature is assimilated to art, becoming fallible, corruptible, subject to time.[32] From a concern with the shifting values of signs, Dante's meditation broadens to engage the constraints of human representation.

The *villanello* simile, which has been criticized for its erudition and preciosity, also serves to mark the transition from the generally lower novellistic style that characterizes cantos 21–23 to the higher, classically inspired style that characterizes cantos 24–25. In the pouch of the thieves the poet dramatizes metamorphosis that is rebirth, change, and forward motion—the wellsprings of this poem—by depicting its infernal variant: metamorphosis that is not change, not rebirth, not forward motion. Here we find souls eternally subject to a grotesque copulation in which men become serpents or fuse with serpents to form an ungodly union of the two, only to revert and repeat the same process over and over again. To represent these exchanges Dante forges some of the most graphically and obscenely realistic language in the poem:[33]

Co' piè di mezzo li avvinse la pancia
   e con li anterïor le braccia prese;
   poi li addentò e l'una e l'altra guancia;
li diretani a le cosce distese,
   e miseli la coda tra 'mbedue
   e dietro per le ren sù la ritese.

With the middle feet it gripped his belly and with those in front took his arms, then set its teeth in one and the other cheek; the rear feet it stretched on the thighs and placed its tail between them and pulled it up over the loins behind.

(*Inf.* 25.52–57)

At the same time he endows the contrapasso with full classical regalia, explicitly relating his metamorphoses to the classical epics that are his models, boasting of his superiority to Lucan and Ovid. A particularly aggravated stylistic hybridity comes into focus in these cantos: not a sustained high style, nor a sustained low style, but a hybrid that could be considered the stylistic correlative of the metamorphoses of canto 25.[34] The language that describes those metamorphoses aptly renders the hybrid style: we could think in terms of a loss of stylistic identity and call it a fusion of two forms that results in an unclassifiable perversion, so that, as with the monster created in the first metamorphosis, "due e nessun l'imagine perversa /parea" ("both two and nothing the perverse image seemed" [*Inf.* 25.77–78]); or we could think of the way the two styles contaminate each other, so that they end up strangely mirrored, exchanging their natures as in the second metamorphosis, where "amendue le forme / a cambiar lor matera fosser pronte" ("both forms were ready to change their substance" [25.101–2]). From Vergil's eloquently classicized exhortation on fame and the Pharsalian catalogue of exotic reptiles to the linguistic and semiotic vulgarity of Vanni Fucci, the *mulo* who hurls his obscene gesture at God (but who is also capable of grand prophetic oratory), these cantos achieve a peculiar synthesis, a new breed of style that can imitate God's horrid making, the obscene sculpting that redistributes matter according to perverse notions of genre and form. If, as the poet claims, his pen at times puts things together confusedly ("e qui mi scusi / la novità se fior la penna abborra" ["let the novelty excuse me here if my pen somewhat bungles" (25.143–44)]), it is because he is called upon to represent confusion; the hybrids he must shape call forth a hybrid art that is indeed a "novità."

Canto 24 is the seventh—central—canto of Malebolge's thirteen; it initiates a series of four cantos that are central to the series as a whole. The fact that canto 24 marks a narrative new beginning is signaled by the pilgrim's response to his guide's exhortation; his "Va, ch'i' son forte e ardito" ("Go on, for I am strong and daring" [*Inf.* 24.60]) echoes Vergil's earlier injunction, uttered on the threshold of Malebolge as the travelers prepare to mount Geryon, "Or sie forte e ardito. / Omai si scende per sì fatte scale" ("Now be strong and daring; from now on we must descend on stairs made like these" [17.81–82]). The second of these verses is also picked up in canto 24, where Vergil reminds his charge that "Più lunga scala convien che si saglia" ("A longer ladder must be climbed" [24.55]); the following verse, "non basta da costoro esser partito" (56), cogently states the incessant imperative of the new: it is not enough to have left the hypocrites behind, for the essence of the travelers' forward motion is to be "nuovi / di compagnia ad ogne mover d'anca" ("new in company at every step" [23.71–72]). This new beginning initiates a central cluster that contains not only the hybrid style of the metamorphoses but also the central classical/contemporary couple of Male-

bolge, Ulysses and Guido: since Malebolge's pairings of classical with contemporary figures articulate the hybrid style at the level of content, cantos
26 and 27 may be said to recapitulate cantos 24 and 25 in radically different
form. What cantos 24–25 accomplish as a unit, by way of their remarkably
homogeneous stylistic heterogeneity, cantos 26 and 27 achieve dialectically,
playing off each other stylistically as the two protagonists play off each other
historically. The protagonists are the vehicles by which all stylistic concerns
are conveyed in these cantos, which are as psychologically dense as the preceding cantos are psychologically shallow. In fact, cantos 26 and 27 are
linked not only because both represent the same pouch but because they
represent in a similar way that is anomolous in Malebolge: these are the only
cantos of the thirteen where human dramas are fleshed out and where there
are overriding personalities with which we become emotionally involved.
The fact that these two episodes form a package, occurring in tandem, confers upon them an extraordinary weight within the narrative economy of
Malebolge. Of the two, canto 26 is pivotal (nor is it surprising that it is the
ninth—central—canto of the seventeen that make up the second half of the
*Inferno*): for if on the one hand its high style will be unmasked by the vernacular mode of its successor, on the other its high style constitutes a genuine achievement, is—like the hero to whom it belongs—truly and consistently "great," limited only and precisely by knowing no limitations, by its
greatness. Here there is no mixture: nothing is *picciolo*, everything is *alto*; in
comparison to canto 25's flashy fireworks, the rhetoric of canto 26 is austere,
sublimely simple. The opening apostrophe to Florence carries over from the
oratorical flourishes and virtuoso displays of the preceding *bolgia*; as the
canto progresses the narrative voice takes on more and more the note of
dispassionate passion that will characterize its hero, that indeed makes him
a hero, until finally the voice flattens out, assumes the divine flatness of
God's voice, like the flat surface of the sea that will submerge the speaker,
pressing down his high ambitions. The anti-oratorical high style that culminates at the end of canto 26 is perhaps the most telling index of the poet's
commitment to the canto's protagonist, upon whom he endows at least the
cadences of authentic grandeur.

For all their disparity, cantos 26 and 27 present a united front because
they are so different from the cantos that bracket them; canto 28 is in fact
very similar to 25, psychologically shallow and visually dazzling. Rhetorically
too, it signals its flashiness from the outset, starting off with a rhetorical
question (unusual enough as an opening gambit) that highlights the narrator and his art: "Chi poria mai pur con parole sciolte / dicer del sangue e de
le piaghe a pieno / ch'i' ora vidi, per narrar più volte?" ("Who could ever
fully tell of the blood and wounds that I now saw, even if in prose [loosened
words] and after numerous narrative attempts?" [*Inf.* 28.1–3]). There follows the quintessentially Dantesque strategic move of the disclaimer; the

limits of human speech and memory are such that any tongue that attempted this narration ("narrar" in verse 3 is the third and last use of this verb in *Inferno*) would surely fail: "Ogne lingua per certo verria meno / per lo nostro sermone e per la mente" (4–5). And yet the poet narrates, and his narration is notably literary. We now encounter the lengthy accumulation of Romans, Anjevins, and other mutilated combatants who have fallen on the battlefields of southern Italy; if they were all assembled and each demonstrated his wounds, "d'aequar sarebbe nulla / il modo de la nona bolgia sozzo" ("it would be nothing to equal the foul mode of the ninth pouch" [20–21]). Again we note the text's self-consciousness regarding its representational mission; its task is to equal in its textual mode the foul mode adopted by infernal reality, which is labeled as though it too were a genre or style, a "foul style." The suggestive label *modo sozzo* could be seen as another way of describing the special hybridity that characterizes Malebolgian poetics; as in the pouch of the thieves, here we find a foully realistic matter wedded to elevated rhetoric, conjoined in a style whose hallmark is its ability to encompass within a 20-verse span references both to Livy and to the "tristo sacco / che merda fa di quel che si trangugia" ("sad sack that makes shit of what is swallowed" [26–27]).

Cantos 25 and 28 are also similar—and typical of a post-Geryon infernal poetics—in their insistence on the truth of their fantastic representations. As in canto 25 we find the poet intervening to address the reader ("Se tu se' or, lettore, a creder lento / ciò ch'io dirò, non sarà maraviglia, / ché io che 'l vidi, a pena il mi consento" ["If you are now, reader, slow to believe what I will say, it is no wonder, since I who saw it hardly consent to it myself" (*Inf.* 25.46–48)]), so too in canto 28 the following emphatic intervention precedes the arrival of Bertran de Born: "Io vidi certo, ed ancor par ch'io 'l veggia, / un busto sanza capo" ("I certainly saw, and still seem to see, a trunk without a head" [28.118–19]). Here the application of the Geryon principle is further strengthened by the use of the present tense with the adverb *ancora* carrying the full weight of the poet's visionary authority. Moreover, a variation in the Geryon strategy is introduced; whereas in canto 16 Geryon was a fantastic truth (a "ver c'ha faccia di menzogna," a "mirum verum," a "cosa incredibile e vera") to be assimilated by the pilgrim, now the roles are reversed. Now the pilgrim becomes the source of wonder to the souls; he causes the "maraviglia" in them that Geryon caused for him: "s'arrestaron nel fosso a riguardarmi / per maraviglia, oblïando il martiro" ["they stopped in the ditch to look at me, out of wonder, forgetting their torment" (53–54)]). Here Vergil takes on the role of the poet, insisting on the truth of what he has just recounted, namely the pilgrim's remarkable itinerary: "e quest'è ver così com'io ti parlo" ("and this is true just as I say" [51]). Vergil is akin to the poet, the pilgrim to the unbelievable truth, the "ver c'ha faccia di menzogna" that the poet narrates, and the sinners are akin to us, the readers who must believe. Dante thus tropes the already enormous self-consciousness of the Geryon episode with an—if possible—even greater self-consciousness that covers its traces by remaining entirely within the fiction, at the same time that it subliminally affects us by dramatizing our response, assigning us hidden roles within his text.

The hybrid style reaches its apogee in the cantos devoted to the falsifiers, whose grotesque pathologies are the backdrop for a narrative art that encompasses Cavalcantian laments that pierce like arrows, homely similes of pots and pigs, a disgusting *captatio benevolentiae* based on descaling oneself like a fish, erudite Ovidian reminiscences, biblical echoes, and the vulgar brawl between Sinon and maestro Adamo. The juxtaposition of the crude verb "leccar" to a precious periphrasis for water, "the mirror of Narcissus," creates the verse "e per leccar lo specchio di Narcisso" (*Inf.* 30.128), singled out by Battaglia Ricci as emblematic of the poetics that govern these cantos.[35] Most important, however, is the way the last pouch brings to a head the eighth circle's theme of semiotic and representational fraudulence; grouping together alchemists, impersonators, counterfeiters, and liars under the general rubric of "falsador" (*Inf.* 29.57), Dante comments on misrepresentation, imitation for false purposes, the perils of mimesis. These concerns come particularly close to the surface in the encounter with the alchemists:

> Vero è ch'i' dissi lui, parlando a gioco:
>    "I' mi saprei levar per l'aere a volo";
>       e quei, ch'avea vaghezza e senno poco,
> volle ch'i' li mostrassi l'arte; e solo
>    perch'io nol feci Dedalo, mi fece
>    ardere a tal che l'avea per figliuolo.

> It is true that I said to him, speaking in jest: "I know how to raise myself through the air in flight," and he, who had desire and little wisdom, wanted me to show him the art; and only because I did not make him Daedalus, he had me burned by one who held him as a son.

(Inf. 29.112–17)

Griffolino here raises the specter of a Ulyssean art: the "arte" that he was supposed to teach Albero of Siena, the art of rising through the air in flight, the art of being Daedalus. Dante is referring to a consummate mimesis that can transgress the boundaries between art and nature, permitting men to do what they were not endowed by nature to do: to fly, as Vergil puts it of Daedalus, on "the rowing of his wings" ("remigium alarum"), as Dante's Ulysses is able to fly "on the wings of his oars."[36] To be Daedalus is, according to the Ovidian account, to be able to set your mind upon unknown arts and change the laws of nature ("ignotas animum dimittit in artes / naturamque novat"), to create by imitation wings that look and work like real birds' wings ("ut veras imitetur aves"), to possess fatal arts ("damnosas . . . artes") that enable one to be taken for a god ("credidit esse deos"), and that one ends by cursing ("devovitque suas artes").[37] The fact that these transgressive arts are mimetic is emphasized by the second alchemist, Capocchio, who reminds the pilgrim how good an ape he was of nature—"com'io fui di natura buona scimia" (*Inf.* 29.139)—thus essentially furnishing us with a definition of mimesis.[38] But if Dante here condemns the falsifiers' mimesis as a misrepresentation, he simultaneously insists on the exemption of his own mimesis, whose unique status is reaffirmed in this canto by alignment with infallible justice, which alone is responsible for punishing the sinners registered here, in this text: "infallibil giustizia / punisce i falsador che qui registra" (*Inf.* 29.56–57).[39] Once more Dante has confronted the problem of his realism, of his Daedalan pretensions, demonstrating his awareness of the Ulyssean dimension of his project, only to reconfirm his warrant to practice such arts legitimately.

Canto 31 is less dramatic than expository, a canto of transition (from the eighth to the ninth circle) and anticipation (of Lucifer, named for the first time in 31.143), which foregrounds the *Commedia*'s ideology of pride; pride is essentially a rebellion, and hence a transgression, a *trapassar del segno* as in the case of Ephialtes: "Questo superbo volle esser esperto / di sua potenza contra 'l sommo Giove" ("This prideful one wanted experience of his power against high Jove" [*Inf.* 31.91–92]).[40] Not insignificantly, in light of the semiotic meditation that we have been tracing, pride and the losses that it procures here find a linguistic focus, vis-à-vis Nimrod's prideful construction of the tower of Babel, because of which "pur un linguaggio nel mondo non s'usa" ("only one language is not used in the world" [78]). Nimrod's transgression, his desire to be as "high" as God (note the opposition of his "alto corno" [12] and the giants' "alta guerra" [119] to the "santa gesta" [17] of Charlemagne), results in the linguistic fall that afflicts mankind in the form of difference, lack of sameness, loss of "una medesma lingua" ("one same language" [1]).[41] Moreover, failure in this realm is necessarily communicable; Nimrod's incomprehensible babbling threatens the travelers with incomprehensibility, as Vergil suggests: "Lasciànlo stare e non parliamo a vòto; / ché così è a lui ciascun linguaggio / come 'l suo ad altrui, ch'a nullo è noto" ("Let us leave him alone and not speak emptily, for to him every language is as his is to others, which is known to none" [79–81]). The phrase *parlare a vuoto* indicates the insurpassable gulf, the empty space between *res* and *signum* that is part of man's fallen condition. As is usual for Dante, acknowledgment of radical representational inadequacy reinforces his dedication to overcome such lacks, to be "di natura buona scimia," to find the language that will eliminate difference, traversing the space between what the *De vulgari eloquentia* calls the rational and the sensual aspects of language, i.e., the meaning and the sound, the signified and signifier, "sì che dal fatto il dir non sia diverso" ("so that speech is not different from fact" [*Inf.* 32.12]).[42] Achieving a language that is indivisible from reality, that accomplishes the goal of "discriver fondo a tutto l'universo," is the task, "impresa," which the poet explicitly sets himself in the great exordium that marks the last of hell's divisions, almost its last new beginning, indeed the beginning of its end:

> S'ïo avessi le rime aspre e chiocce,
>   come si converrebbe al tristo buco
>   sovra 'l qual pontan tutte l'altre rocce,
> io premerei di mio concetto il suco
>   più pienamente; ma perch'io non l'abbo,
>   non sanza tema a dicer mi conduco;
> ché non è impresa da pigliare a gabbo
>   discriver fondo a tutto l'universo,
>   né da lingua che chiami mamma o babbo.
> Ma quelle donne aiutino il mio verso
>   ch'aiutaro Anfïone a chiuder Tebe,
>   sì che dal fatto il dir non sia diverso.

If I had rhymes as harsh and raucous as would be suited to the sad pit over which all other rocks converge, then I would press out the juice of my thought more fully; but because I do not have them, not without fear do I begin to speak, since it is not a task to be taken in jest to describe the bottom of all the universe, nor for a tongue that calls mommy or daddy. But may those ladies aid my verse who aided Amphion to close Thebes, so that my speech will not be different from the fact.

(*Inf.* 32.1–12)

This great cascade of metapoetic language celebrates the fundamental principle of Dantesque stylistic decorum: language must not differ from reality. What is stylistically *conveniens* ("come si *converrebbe* al tristo buco")[43] is what best fits the reality being represented, "sì che dal fatto il dir non sia diverso." Accordingly, we have reached a place where speech is hard ("loco onde parlare è duro" [*Inf.* 32.14]), where language must be as unflinching as that which it describes.[44]

The narrator is nearing the end of the first leg of his journey. His desire to make his "dir" coincide with the "fatto" hearkens back to the journey's beginning, when he voiced his concern that "molte volte al *fatto* il *dir* vien meno" ("many times my *speech* falls short of the *fact*" [*Inf.* 4.147]). As this part of the narrative journey reaches its conclusion, it recapitulates and mirrors itself, as though the glassy ice of Cocytus provided a mirror for the self-scrutiny of poet as well as pilgrim. Thus, a figure within the representation, Bocca degli Abati, figures forth the representation itself, mirroring the poet's representational techniques; to the pilgrim who has cast himself as truth-teller, saying "io porterò di te vere novelle" ("I will carry true news of you" [*Inf.* 32.111]), Bocca replies by appropriating the *Commedia*'s most fundamental strategy, that of saying "I saw": "'Io vidi,' potrai dir, 'quel da Duera / là dove i peccatori stanno freschi'" ("'I saw,' you can say, 'the one from Duera there where the sinners stay cold'" [*Inf.* 32.116–17]). He—a character within a fiction that maintains that its protagonist indeed saw what he says he saw—tells the protagonist what to say he saw, with the result that once again Dante tropes one of his authenticating devices: either he does this by drawing attention to them as outrageously inauthentic (in the case of Geryon), or he buries them within the fiction, so that we are manipulated by them without knowing they are there. A technique of this sort demonstrates Dante's formidable ability to play the textual mirror game to the advantage of his fiction. A supreme instance of such textual self-awareness and specularity is found at the end of *Inferno* 33, where Dante highlights the scandal at the base of his fiction—its flouting of the mysteries of damnation and salvation—by proposing, even more scandal-ously, that a soul can be already damned and in hell while apparently still alive. Dante ventures onto very thin ice when he prepares a place in hell for Boniface VIII, alive in 1300, thus denying him the exercise of free will until the moment of death. But in the hierarchy of Dantesque deviations from orthodoxy, the case of Branca Doria, the soul whom Dante actually places in hell before his death, is the most outrageous and is sufficiently scandalous to have provoked a reaction: there is a tradition according to which Branca (who seems to have been still alive as late as 1325) took revenge on the poet by having him beaten.[45]

Frate Alberigo explains to the pilgrim that the souls of Tolomea are, uniquely, sent to hell while their bodies are still on earth, where they are possessed by devils. Dante is here troping his master fiction: instead of "living" dead people, we now must contend with the idea of dead living people. As the outlines of the fiction become harder to hold onto, we succumb to it more readily, especially when the text reproduces our relation to it within itself, as occurs in the ensuing dialogue between the pilgrim and Alberigo: it seems that Branca Doria, a Genovese nobleman condemned to the ninth circle for the murder of his father-in-law, Michele Zanche (a Sardinian whom Dante has placed among the barrators), is in fact dead. The pilgrim is incredulous; Alberigo must be lying: "'Io credo,' diss'io lui, 'che tu m'in-ganni; / ché Branca Doria non morì unquanche, / e mangia e bee e dorme e veste panni'" ("'I believe,' I said to him, 'that you deceive me, for Branca Doria has not yet died, but eats and drinks and sleeps and puts on clothes'" [*Inf.* 33.139–41]). So the pilgrim is now in the reader's position, faced with an unbelievable truth, a "ver c'ha faccia di menzogna" (as earlier, in canto 28's version of this mirror game, the sinners played the reader's role). How does Alberigo—the creature in the fiction—persuade the pilgrim to believe him? By appealing to "reality," namely the fiction to which he belongs. His reply is one of the most remarkable intratextual moments within the *Commedia*, as the text buttresses the text, the fiction supports the credibility of the fiction: "'Nel fosso sù,' diss'el, 'de' Malebranche, / là dove bolle la tenace pece, / non era ancora giunto Michel Zanche, / che questi lasciò il diavolo in sua vece / nel corpo suo'" ("'In the ditch of the Malebranche above,' he said, 'there where boils the sticky pitch, Michel Zanche had not yet arrived when this one [Branca] left a devil in his place in his own body'" [*Inf.* 33.142–46]). With these references to the text of the *Inferno*—to the Malebranche and the boiling pitch of the *bolgia* of the barraters—the pilgrim is convinced; and the poet, who has mirrored and thereby mounted a sneak attack on the reader's reluctance to believe, concludes the canto by stating as simple fact what he learned from Alberigo: in this place he found—"trovai" (155)—a spirit whose soul was in Cocytus, while his body was on earth. Now that the fiction has been accepted as reality, reality—in a typically Dantesque inversion—can be revealed to be a fiction: "e in corpo *par vivo* ancor di sopra" ("and in body he still *appears alive* up above" [33.157]).

In between these concentrated rehearsals of the poem's poetics as a "ver c'ha faccia di menzogna" is the *Inferno*'s last extended narrative tour de force, Ugolino's refashioning of the "bestial segno" by which he is first characterized at the end of canto 32—his gnawing on Ruggieri's skull—into the more ornate and seductive *segno* of his oration in canto 33. Ugolino's consciousness of telling a story, the extreme narrative cunning by which he hopes to elicit the pilgrim's sympathy, have been amply documented in recent years.[46] For our present purposes, we should note that the self-consciousness of the episode encompasses an authorial self-scrutiny as well: Ugolino's narrative artistry after all includes the recounting of a dreamscape very like that of *Inferno* 1, in which allegorical wolves and hounds also course and signify. Moreover, the latent self-reflexive component of canto 33 is potentially more explosive than, for instance, the self-reflexive component of *Inferno* 5, which invests the poet's lyric past rather than his narrative present. If the prophetic dream is a narrative device that Ugolino can exploit, then surely it is a narrative device that Dante can exploit as well;[47] if Ugolino is too good a storyteller, then so too is the teller of the *Commedia*. Thus it is that the poet asserts his own narrative authority over Ugolino's with extraordinary force and aggressivity, issuing the ferocious invective against Pisa and drawing attention to himself, both as semiotic codifier of the "bel paese là dove 'l sì suona" ("beautiful land where *sì* sounds" [*Inf.* 33.80])[48] and as narrator with supreme artistic control over Ugolino's discourse: "Innocenti facea l'età novella, / novella Tebe, Uguiccione e 'l Brigata / e li altri due che 'l canto suso appella" ("Their youth, you new Thebes, made Uguiccione and Brigata innocent, *and the other two that the canto above names"* [*Inf.* 33.88–90]). This tercet ostentatiously reaffirms the narrator's authority over his text, the "canto" in which these names have been inscribed,[49] appropriating the word with which Ugolino had begun his speech, *rinovellare,* and interpreting it in terms of the poetics of the new. While Ugolino begins his speech with a Vergilian formula—"Tu vuo' ch'io rinovelli / disperato dolor" ("You want me to renew desperate sorrow" [*Inf.* 33.4–5])—that suggests he aims to renew himself through rhetoric, the poet ends the encounter with a double use of the adjective *novella* that tells us Ugolino will never be renewed: renewal is only for innocents (like Ugolino's children, whose *età novella* makes *innocenti*), those who will be "rinovellate di novella fronde" ("renewed with new foliage") at the end of *Purgatorio.* By contrast, Ugolino can only be new in the sense that Pisa is a *novella Tebe,* in a form of deadly repetition, like the *novelle spalle* conferred on the thieves by their hellish metamorphoses. The narrator's double appropriation of "new" in reply to Ugolino's bid for semiotic renewal is a way of truly ending him, shutting him down as absolutely as does the narrative, which passes on—toward the truly new—without a backward glance in the next verse's "Noi passammo oltre" (*Inf.* 33.91).

Ugolino's rhetoric aims to make us forget that for him family connections were always political connections, always ties to be exploited by his nocent greed as now in hell he tries to exploit his greed's innocent victims. And yet canto 33, taken as a whole, is not evasive; rather it is steeped in the people and events that shaped Ugolino's politics, a politics whose central node was Sardinia, a Pisan possession. Ugolino was the Sardinian vicar of Re Enzo, son of Frederic II;[50] Ugolino's son Guelfo married Elena, Enzo's daughter, and Ugolino's grandchildren inherited Enzo's Sardinian possessions. Ugolino's son-in-law, Giovanni Visconti, was also a power on the island as judge of Gallura, as was Giovanni's son, Ugolino's grandson, Nino Visconti, whom Dante hails in the valley of the princes by his Sardinian title: "giudice Nin" (*Purg.* 8.53). These connections begin to manifest themselves in *Inferno* 33 when Ugolino says that Ruggieri appeared to him, in his dream, as "maestro e donno" ("master and lord" [28]); *donno* is a Sardinianism that occurs only here and in *Inferno* 22, where it is used in the description of the Sardinian barraters. One is friar Gomita of Gallura ("frate Gomita, / quel di Gallura" [*Inf.* 22.81–82]), vicar of Nino Visconti, the lord or *donno* whose enemies he freed for money. The other is "donno Michel Zanche / di Logodoro" (*Inf.* 22.88–89), a Sardinian noble who originally sided with Genova rather than Pisa; he was killed by his Genovese son-in-law Branca Doria, either out of greed for his Sardinian holdings or because of his later leanings toward Pisa. Sardinia as a catalyst of greed figures in all these dramas, and indeed frate Gomita, betrayer of Nino Visconti, and Michel Zanche, betrayed by Branca Doria, talk of Sardinia: "e a dir di Sardigna / le lingue lor non si sentono stanche" ("in talking of Sardinia their tongues do not grow weary" [*Inf.*

22.89–90]). Sardinia unites all these sinners as the object of their greed and strife, and Ugolino was as rapacious a player (not for nothing does he see himself as a wolf in his dream) as the others. The Guelph Visconti and Ghibelline Gherardesca families, traditionally opposed, became allies to protect their Sardinian holdings, an alliance that led to the ill-fated shared magistracy of Ugolino and his grandson Nino. And, in the same way that the poet links the players by ties of Sardinian greed, so he links the two cities that both desired the island: canto 33 contains not only the fulmination against Pisa but also a concluding invective against Genoa, hell's last two civic apostrophes. These links are important for understanding the historical backdrop against which Ugolino betrayed and was betrayed; they also make canto 33 a repository of infernal themes and motifs. From the truthful lie reminiscent of Malacoda's with which the pilgrim deceives frate Alberigo, to "e cortesia fu lui esser villano" ("and it was a courtesy to be discourteous to him" [*Inf.* 33.150]), which echoes *Inferno* 20's similar manifesto of an inverted order, "Qui vive la pietà quand'è ben morta" ("Here pity lives when it is truly dead" [28]); from the pilgrim's questioning of Alberigo, "or se' tu ancor morto?" ("are you already dead?" [*Inf.* 33.121]), reminiscent of Nicholas III's earlier questioning of the pilgrim, to the explicit recalls of the pitch and the Malebranche in the pouch of barratry—canto 33 sums up the poetics of hell, as Ugolino sums up its perverted politics and failed humanity.[51]

*Inferno* 34 is a canto of transition, a canto whose narrative mode exists in the liminal space inhabited by the pilgrim: "Io non mori' e non rimasi vivo; / pensa oggimai per te, s'hai fior d'ingegno, / qual io divenni, d'uno e d'altro privo" ("I did not die and I did not remain alive; think now for yourself, if you have any wit, what I became, deprived of one and the other" [*Inf.* 34.25–27]). "Non mori' e non rimasi vivo": he is between life and death, salvation and damnation, light and darkness, good and evil.[52] He is in the space between the tenses, the past absolute and present that define Lucifer, whose essence is contained by the verse "S'el *fu* sì bel com'elli *è* ora brutto" ("If he *was* as beautiful as now he *is* ugly" [34]). He is in the space delineated by the transitional adverbs *oramai/oggimai*, used repeatedly in this canto, the space between "now" ("ora") on the one hand and "never" ("mai") on the other. He is a being dedicated to becoming, as indicated by the triple use of *divenni*: "Com'io divenni allor gelato e fioco" ("How I became then frozen and faint" [22]), "qual io divenni, d'uno e d'altro privo" (27), "s'io divenni allora travagliato" ("if I became confused then" [91]). He is engaged in the delicate task of transiting Lucifer, grasping Lucifer (both physically and metaphysically),[53] without remaining, like Lucifer, stuck in the eternal present of hell: "fitto è ancora sì come prim'era" ("he is still fixed as he was before" [120]). The pilgrim must transit the point of becoming, "quel punto ch'io avea passato" ("that point that I had passed" [93]); he must get beyond Lucifer, who generates real fear, but no passion. The text privileges the process of becoming, of transiting, not the creature who emblematizes the ground of transition, the core of what must be left behind. Even the application of the Geryon principle to Lucifer's physical awesomeness is accomplished quickly, almost routinely: "Oh quanto parve a me gran mara-viglia / quand'io vidi tre facce a la sua testa!" ("Oh how it seemed to me a great marvel when I saw three faces on his head!" [37–38]). Lucifer is repre-sented in such a way as to remind us that evil is the absence of good; from a narrative point of view, therefore, Lucifer is deliberately handled as a nonengaging, noninvolving, "nonpresent" anticlimax. So, the question is raised: if evil is absence, and some sinners are more present, does that mean that they are less evil?

We come back thus, at the end of the *Inferno*, to perhaps the canticle's chief problematic, which I believe can best be resolved by realizing that it is at heart a narrative problematic. In chapter 2 I discussed the (theological) problems raised by Dante's (narrative) need to institutionalize difference: are the souls of upper hell in any absolute sense better than those lower down, any less damned? In chapter 3 I raised the related issue of the "great" sinners, and suggested that souls like Francesca and Ulysses are indeed priv-ileged by Dante, not morally or eschatologically, but textually. Once again we must detheologize and ask: How could a poet effectively represent ab-sence without having established some presence to play against it? How could he fashion anticlimaxes, big or little, without fashioning climaxes as well? When the requirements of narrative conflict with the laws of justice, Dante must bow to narrative. By working relentlessly to situate us within his *speculum*, he seeks to reorient us: if we see things from inside, from within the *Commedia*'s possible world, then perhaps we will not notice that the laws that govern this ultimately textual universe are in fact less God's laws than his own.

*Chapter 5*

# PURGATORY AS PARADIGM: TRAVELING THE NEW AND NEVER-BEFORE-TRAVELED PATH OF THIS LIFE/POEM

> *Fr.* Nulla me deinceps accusatione turbaveris. Dic
> ingenue quicquid est, quod me transversum agat.
> *Aug.* Rerum temporalium appetitus.
>
> (Petrarch, *Secretum*)

THE NARRATIVE of the *Commedia* is a line intersected by other lines; it is a "vedere interciso da novo obietto," a seeing interrupted by new things, the *novi obietti* or *cose nove* that do not trouble angels. It is a voyage intersected by other voyages; each time the pilgrim meets a soul, his lifeline intersects another lifeline. In hell he encounters failed voyages, journeys that have ended in failure. Ulysses' special stature within the poem derives in no small measure from the fact that his lifeline concludes with a literal voyage that has literally failed, so that he, alone among the souls Dante encounters, unites the poem's formal and thematic values: he both represents a failed voyage (one among many), and he recounts a failed voyage (uniquely). While in *Inferno* and *Paradiso* the moving pilgrim encounters perfected voyages, voyages that have achieved either the stasis of failure or the peace of success, in *Purgatorio* all the intersecting lifelines are in motion, voyaging in time—just as on earth all parties in any encounter are moving forward along their respective lines of becoming. (In fact, because the *Purgatorio* swerves so fundamentally from the *Commedia*'s basic narrative structure, whereby a moving figure encounters stationary ones, the poet compensates by ritualizing the narrative components of the seven terraces, so that, if the pilgrim does not meet fixed souls, he does meet a fixed pattern of angels, encounters, and examples.)[1] Given its temporal dimension, the narrative of the second canticle is most akin, in its rhythm, to the narrative of life; its *cammino* is most similar to the "nuovo e mai non fatto cammino di questa vita" described in the *Convivio*, in a passage that provides the clearest exposition of life as voyage to be found in Dante's oeuvre:[2]

> . . . lo sommo desiderio di ciascuna cosa, e prima da la natura dato, è lo ritornare a lo suo principio. E però che Dio è principio de le nostre anime e fattore di quelle

simili a sé (sì come è scritto: "Facciamo l'uomo ad imagine e similitudine nostra"), essa anima massimamente desidera di tornare a quello. E sì come peregrino che va per una via per la quale mai non fue, che ogni casa che da lungi vede crede che sia l'albergo, e non trovando ciò essere, dirizza la credenza a l'altra, e così di casa in casa, tanto che a l'albergo viene; così l'anima nostra, incontanente che nel nuovo e mai non fatto cammino di questa vita entra, dirizza li occhi al termine del suo sommo bene, e però, qualunque cosa vede che paia in sé avere alcuno bene, crede che sia esso. E perché la sua conoscenza prima è imperfetta, per non essere esperta nè dottrinata, piccioli beni le paiono grandi, e però da quelli comincia prima a desiderare. Onde vedemo li parvuli desiderare massimamente un pomo; e poi, più procedendo, desiderare uno augellino; e poi, più oltre, desiderare bel vestimento; e poi lo cavallo; e poi una donna; e poi ricchezza non grande, e poi grande, e poi più. E questo incontra perché in nulla di queste cose truova quella che va cercando, e credela trovare più oltre.

The greatest desire of each thing, given first by nature, is to return to its beginning. And since God is the beginning of our souls and maker of those similar to himself (as is written: "Let us make man in our image and likeness"), the soul desires above all to return to him. And like the pilgrim who travels on a road on which he has never been, who thinks that every house he sees from a distance is the inn, and finding that it is not, redirects his belief to the next, and thus from house to house, until he comes to the inn; so our soul, as soon as it enters on the new and never before traveled path of this life, straightens its eyes to the terminus of its highest good, and then, whatever thing it sees that seems to have some good in it, the soul believes that it is that terminus. And because the soul's knowledge is at first imperfect, because it is neither expert nor learned, small goods seem to it to be big goods, and so from these it begins at first to desire. So we see children desire above all an apple; and then, proceeding further, a little bird; and then, further still, beautiful clothing; and then a horse; and then a lady; and then not great riches; and then great riches; and then more. And this happens because in none of these things does the soul find what it is looking for, and it believes that it will find it further on.

(*Conv.* 4.12.14–16)

This passage is virtually a blueprint for the *Commedia*. We begin with desire, the supreme desire to return to our origin; this desire provides the energy that moves the pilgrim along his road, a road on which he has never before traveled, one that is thus by definition new. In the same way that the pilgrim mistakes the houses that he sees along the road for the inn, the place of legitimate repose, so the soul on the new and never before traveled path of life mistakes the little goods that it encounters for the supreme good that it seeks. Our progress on the path of life is figured linguistically as successiveness: we desire something, "e poi, più procedendo," we desire something new, "e poi, più oltre," something new again, and so on as by virtue of a succession of *e pois* our desires grow ever greater, and we create what Dante will shortly describe as a pyramid of objects of desire. This rhythm of escalating desire figures the narrative rhythm of the poem, also a continuum in which forward progress is marked by encounters with successive new things. In particular, the *Convivio* passage figures the *Purgatorio*, where the desire to see and know new things is insistently underscored, where for the first time the pilgrim is among other pilgrims: "Voi credete / forse che siamo esperti d'esto loco; / ma noi siam peregrin come voi siete" ("You think perhaps that we are experts regarding this place, but we are pilgrims as you are" [*Purg.* 2.61–63]).[3] Like their counterparts in the *Convivio*, the voyagers in the second realm are repeatedly shown to be neither *esperti* nor *dottrinati* but rather strangers in a strange land, whose ignorance triggers their frequent *maraviglia*. Most importantly, the souls of purgatory are learning to devalue the *piccioli beni* by which they were tempted as they journeyed along the path of life, to exchange such goods for the supreme good to which they are now returning. The very idea of a return to the beginning ("lo ritornare a lo principio"), of a progression forward to the past,[4] finds its precise counterpart only in purgatory, where forward motion is a way of recuperating and redeeming the past, of returning to lost innocence and our collective point of origin, the garden of Eden. Only purgatory is the place where "tempo per tempo si ristora" (*Purg.* 23.84), where time is restored to us so that we can undo in time what we did in time.[5] Indeed, the experience of purgatory is the conversion of the old back into the new: the unmaking of memory, in which the once new has been stored as old.

No episode in *Inferno* or *Paradiso* captures the essence of the earthly pilgrimage like the Casella episode at the beginning of *Purgatorio*, whose structure faithfully replicates life's—and terza rima's—continual dialectic between forward motion and backward glance, voyage and repose, illicit curiosity and necessary desire. On the one hand the poet stages Cato's rebuke, thus acknowledging the idea of a premature repose, a lapse into misdirected desire. On the other the poet valorizes the object of desire that occasions the rebuke, the lyric whose sweetness "ancor dentro mi suona" ("still sounds within me" [*Purg.* 2.114]). The authority of the present tense and the adverb *ancora* prohibits us from crudely labeling the experience "wrong"; rather we must attend to both constitutive elements within the spiral of desire, fully present only in the second realm: both the desire that functions as goad (here Cato), and the desire that functions nostalgically (here Casella's song). One could restate the above by saying that the *Purgatorio* is the most Augustinian of Dante's three canticles. The *Inferno*, by contrast, draws on the spirit of the Old Testament, while the *Paradiso* is informed by saints of both newer and older vintage, such as Francis and Peter (though Benedict belongs to Augustine's middle period). Perhaps the much debated absence of Augustine from Dante's poem is related to the

Augustinian basis of the second realm: Augustinianism—like memory it-self—is a presence in purgatory more than in paradise, but there is in purga-tory, as we shall see, another vigorous spokesperson for the saint's thought, namely Beatrice. In other words, Dante uses Augustinian doctrine in the realm where separation from earthly objects of desire is still problematic, to provide the philosophical basis for such separation, much as Petrarch uses Augustinus in the *Secretum*; however, the Augustinus role is assigned to Beatrice, who in a sense therefore becomes a substitute Augustine.[6]

*Purgatorio* is the canticle in which the restless heart of the Christian pil-grim is most literally dramatized, embodied not only by Dante but by all the souls he meets. Its "plot" hinges on an Augustinian view of temporal goods as inherently dissatisfying because of their mortality, as necessarily dissatis-fying even when they are (in Augustine's words) "things perfectly legitimate in themselves, which cannot be relinquished without regret."[7] The tension between the legitimacy of the object of desire on the one hand and the need to relinquish it on the other is the tension that sustains the second canticle of the *Commedia*, the tension that Dante maximizes and exploits in order to create the bittersweet elegiac poetry of *Purgatorio*: "biondo era e bello e di gentile aspetto, / *ma* l'un de' cigli un colpo avea diviso" ("blond he was and beautiful and of gentle aspect, *but* a blow had divided one of his eye-brows" [*Purg.* 3.107–8]). The first verse renders Manfredi's desirability, which is the desirability of what Petrarch calls the "cosa bella mortal"; we want him as we want on earth, without thought of sublimation. Then, after evoking nostalgically the earthly object in its earthly beauty, the second verse, beginning with the adversative, tells us the problem: it is wounded, imperfect, fallen; or, to complete Petrarch's thought, "cosa bella mortal passa, et non dura" ("the beautiful mortal thing passes, and does not last" [*Canzoniere* 248.8]). The second verse brings us back to why there need be a purgatory, to the fact that even the most beautiful of earthly things is always compromised, wounded, mortal, that therefore we must learn to love different things, in a different way. The spiral of conversion that moves away from the noble temporal goods for which the soul feels a backward-turning love in the direction of their eternal counterparts is paradigmatically ren-dered in the concluding verses of *Purgatorio* 28, where the pilgrim "lapses" toward his classical poets and "converts" to Beatrice: "Io mi rivolsi 'n dietro allora tutto / a' miei poeti . . . poi a la bella donna torna' il viso" ("I turned all backward to my poets; then to the beautiful lady returned my face" [*Purg.* 28. 145–46, 148]).

The second canticle tells of the soul's voyage from desiring successive new things to becoming itself new: "Voi siete nuovi" says Matelda to the travel-ers in *Purgatorio* 28.76, and although she means "newly arrived," her words also adumbrate the souls' newly minted condition at purgatory's end. The theme of voyage is linked to the search for the new in a way that recalls the

*Convivio*'s pilgrim passage, where the traveler goes successively from one *bene*—one new thing—to the next. As in the paradigmatic Casella episode, the *Purgatorio* offers us both the necessary encounter with the new, with the "altra novità ch'apparve allora" ("other novelty that then appeared" [*Purg.* 26.27]) and the refusal to be detoured by the new, like the man who "vassi a la via sua, che che li appaia" ("goes on along his path, whatever appears to him" [*Purg.* 25.5]). In typical purgatorial language, Matelda constitutes a necessary detour, a "cosa che disvia / per maraviglia tutto altro pensare" ("thing that for wonder detours all other thought" [*Purg.* 28.38–39]), while the seven virtues who escort the pilgrim in the earthly paradise stop at the water as a guide stops "se trova novitate o sue vestigge" ("if he finds a new thing or its traces" [*Purg.* 33.108]). In fact, the importance of the *cosa nova* for the *Purgatorio* is such as to strongly support Petrocchi's restoration of "novità" in place of "vanità" in *Purgatorio* 31.60, where Beatrice castigates the pilgrim for having continued to pursue, after her death, "altra novità con sì breve uso" ("another novelty of such brief use"). Thus formulated, Beatrice's rebuke resonates with the voyage of life, the "vedere interciso da novo obietto," and with the reminder that she was the pilgrim's ultimate *cosa nova*.[8] *Novità* is a temporally charged way—a profoundly Augustinian way—of saying *vanità*, a synonym of *vanità* that says everything it says and more, by adding the temporal dimension of voyage and pilgrimage that is key to this temporal realm. The Augustinian basis of the second canticle is rooted in its temporality, its overwhelming concern to trace the will's transition—in time—from mortal to immortal objects of desire, from objects of "brief use" to objects that the soul can "enjoy" indefinitely. Beatrice's "con sì breve uso" is strikingly coincident with Augustine's injunction to use earthly things rather than enjoy them.[9] The dimension of time, transition, successiveness—so fundamental to Augustine's analysis of the human condition that even eating is analyzed from a temporal perspective (it spreads its snares of concupiscence in the transition, "in ipso transitu," from hunger to satiety)[10]—is the dimension in which the purgatorial soul undertakes what is an essentially Augustinian pilgrimage.

The Augustinian aspect of Dante's thought finds its gloss in the pilgrim passage of *Convivio* 4.12, which echoes *Confessions* 1.19: "non haec ipsa sunt quae a paedagogis et magistris, a nucibus et pilulis et passeribus, ad praefectos et reges, aurum, praedia, mancipia, haec ipsa omnino succedentibus maioribus aetatibus transeunt" ("For commanders and kings may take the place of tutors and schoolmasters, nuts and balls and pet birds may give way to money and estates and servants, but these same passions remain with us while one stage of life follows upon another"). Augustine's *passer* becomes Dante's *augellino*, Augustine's *aurum* becomes Dante's *ricchezza*; both authors are concerned with the transitoriness ("transeunt") of life and the successiveness of human desire, which remains constant in its inconstancy as it passes to the "succeeding older ages" of our lives—the "suc-cedentibus maoribus aetatibus." The pilgrim passage of *Convivio* 4.12 is translated into verse at the very heart of the *Purgatorio*, in canto 16's description of the newborn soul which, sent forth by a happy maker upon the path of life ("mossa da lieto fattore" [*Purg.* 16.89]), willingly turns toward all that brings delight ("volontier torna a ciò che la trastulla" [90]).[11] The voyage is perilous, and the simple little soul that knows nothing, "l'anima semplicetta che sa nulla" (16.88),[12] is distracted by the very desire that also serves as necessary catalyst and propeller for its forward motion: "Di picciol bene in pria sente sapore; / quivi s'inganna, e dietro ad esso corre, / se guida o fren non torce suo amore" ("First the soul tastes the savor of a small good; there it deceives itself and runs after, if guide or curb does not twist its love" [91–93]). The spiritual motion of the soul that runs after little goods— "piccioli beni" is the expression used in both the treatise and the poem—is explained in the *Convivio*, where we learn that this errancy occurs because, to the inexperienced soul, "piccioli beni le paiono grandi, e però da quelli comincia prima a desiderare." The crucial point at which the soul is deceived, the node where desire and spiritual motion meet free will and justice, provides the point of departure for the anatomy of desire that dominates the *Commedia*'s "mezzo del cammin," an analysis that responds to the following queries: to whom is the blame of the soul's self-deception to be charged, to the stars or to itself, and is there any guidance to help it on its way? (canto 16); in what different forms can the soul's self-deception manifest itself, i.e., what forms can misdirected desire assume? (canto 17); what is the process whereby such self-deception occurs, i.e., what is the process whereby the soul falls in love? (canto 18).

At the end of canto 17 we learn that love is the seed of all human activity, whether it be good or evil ("amor sementa in voi d'ogne virtute / e d'ogne operazion che merta pene" ["love is the seed in you of every virtue and of every act that merits suffering" (*Purg.* 17.104–5)]); this principle—which implies that love is the foundation for hell as well as purgatory—is restated at the outset of canto 18: "amore, a cui reduci / ogne buono operare e 'l suo contraro" ("love, to which you reduce all good action and its contrary" [*Purg.* 18.14–15]). In other words, desire is the motive force for all our actions. Again, the struggling traveler of *Convivio* 4.12 provides the model for the purgatorial meditation; in the *Convivio* too the seeker is driven by his desire from one "good" to the next, in search of the object of desire that will finally bring desire to an end: "Ciascun confusamente un bene apprende / nel qual si queti l'animo, e disira; / per che di giugner lui ciascun contende" ("Each of us confusedly apprehends a good in which the soul may rest, and this it desires; to reach this good each of us contends" [*Purg.* 17.127–29]). This view of life as a struggle along the pathway of desire, a view that profoundly informs the *Commedia*'s narrativity, is elaborated in canto 18, where we learn that the soul, seized by love, begins to desire, that desire is precisely the motion of the soul as it follows after the object it craves (which it seeks to apprehend, to possess), and that such motion will never cease—the soul will never rest—until the beloved object gives it joy: "così l'animo preso entra in disire, / ch'è moto spiritale, e mai non posa / fin che la cosa amata il fa gioire" (*Purg.* 18.31–33).

The second canticle's Augustinian thematic of spiritual motion finds its peculiarly Dantesque focus in canto 19's evocation of Ulysses.[13] It is here that the *dolce serena* of the pilgrim's dream, later exposed as a stinking, stuttering hag and thus the embodiment of the false and misleading desires expiated on purgatory's top three terraces, boasts that she was able to detour Ulysses from his path: "Io volsi Ulisse del suo cammin vago / al canto mio" ("I turned Ulysses, desirous of the journey, with my song" [*Purg.* 19.22–23]). This alignment of the Greek voyager with the *dolce serena* is of great significance within the poem's anatomy of desire. The terraces of avarice, gluttony, and lust purge affective inclinations toward goods that are false because, having seduced us with promises of full satisfaction (like the siren, who claims "sì tutto l'appago!" [19.24]), they are not in fact capable of delivering the ultimate satisfaction—*quies*, peace, freedom from craving—that we seek. Because of their mortality, these "beni" cannot make us truly happy, cannot offer us true repose, but only more time on the treadmill of desire, the treadmill of the new: "Altro ben è che non fa l'uom felice; / non è felicità, non è la buona / essenza" ("There is another good that does not make man happy; it is not true happiness, not the good essence" [*Purg.* 17.133–35]). The desiring purged on the top three terraces is characterized by excessive abandon vis-à-vis these seductive but misleading goods: "L'amor ch'ad esso troppo s'abbandona, / di sovr'a noi si piange per tre cerchi" ("The love that abandons itself too much to it is lamented above us in three circles" [*Purg.* 17.136–37]). The key word here is *troppo*, which echoes the original partition of love, capable of erring "per malo obietto / o per troppo o per poco di vigore" ("through an evil object or through too much or too little vigor" [*Purg.* 17.95–96]). The figure who stands within the *Commedia*'s metaphoric system for excess, abandonment of limits, transgression, trespass—in short, for *troppo di vigore*—is Ulysses.

I am suggesting that there is a programmatic reason for the insertion of Ulysses' name into the economy of *Purgatorio* at this point. Rather than focus on the siren/*femmina balba* and the identity of the lady who rudely unveils her, I believe that we can profitably consider this passage from the vantage of its provocative and unexpected naming of Ulysses, posing the question "Why Ulysses here?"[14] The siren's invocation of the Greek wayfarer serves first to remind us of what we already know, namely that he can be characterized in terms of his own false craving, the misplaced and misleading *ardore*—burning desire—that causes him to burn as a tongue of

flame in hell. More importantly, the presence of Ulysses serves to characterize the desire of the top three terraces as Ulyssean, to metaphorize avarice,
gluttony, and lust, so that we see these sins in the light of their root cause:
excessive desire, the pursuing of objects with *troppo di vigore*. As validation
of the Ulyssean thrust here conferred upon the final three terraces, we note
the presence of a tree upon the terrace of gluttony whose parent is none
other than the tree that Ulysses desired—metaphorically—to eat, the tree
from which Adam and Eve did indeed eat: "Trapassate oltre sanza farvi
presso: / legno è più sù che fu morso da Eva, / e questa pianta si levò da esso"
("Pass onward without drawing near; further up is a tree that was bitten by
Eve, and this plant was taken from that one" [*Purg.* 24.115–17]). This graft
from the tree of knowledge enjoins the souls in Ulyssean language ("Trapassate oltre") against Ulyssean trespass ("sanza farvi presso"), an injunction
that is built into the tree's very shape, which is inverted so that its branches
taper not toward the top but the bottom, "perché persona sù non vada" ("so
that none will go up it" [*Purg.* 22.135]). A generalized interdict of this sort
was uttered with respect to the pillars of Hercules, which were placed where
they are "acciò che l'uom più oltre non si metta" ("so that man will not go
beyond" [*Inf.* 26.109]). And what is the root cause of *trapassare oltre*? What
caused both Ulysses and Eve to ignore the interdicts they encountered?
According to the analysis of human motivation provided by the second canticle, they were spurred by twisted love, by misshapen desire—by variants of
the desire felt so keenly and underscored so emphatically on the terrace of
gluttony, as the souls gather around the graft from the tree "that was bitten
by Eve":

> Vidi gente sott'esso alzar le mani
>   e gridar non so che verso le fronde,
>   quasi bramosi fantolini e vani
> che pregano, e 'l pregato non risponde,
>   ma, per fare esser ben la voglia acuta,
>   tien alto lor disio e nol nasconde.

> I saw people under it raising their hands and crying out I know not what toward
> the leaves, like avid and desiring children who beg, and he whom they beg does
> not answer but—to make their longing more acute—holds high the object of their
> desire and does not hide it.

> (*Purg.* 24.106–11)

Dante handles gluttony in such a way as to deliteralize it; by invoking the
tree of knowledge and the restraints that Eve did not tolerate he forces us to
associate the sin purged on the sixth terrace with Eve's metaphorical gluttony—her eating of the tree of the knowledge of good and evil, her *trapassar
del segno*—and thus to see gluttony in a Ulyssean light anticipated by the

siren of canto 19. This expanded reading of the sins of concupiscence (for what I have said about gluttony can easily be applied to avarice and lust as well)[15] is confirmed in the *Purgatorio*'s final cantos, where Beatrice's view of the fallacy of earthly desire recalls both Augustine and the *dolce serena*: "e volse i passi suoi per via non vera, / imagini di ben seguendo false, / che nulla promession rendono intera" ("he turned his steps along a not true path, following false images of good that satisfy no promise in full" [*Purg.* 30.130–32]). The basic plot of the *Purgatorio*, like that of the *Vita Nuova*, is a courtly medieval inflection of the Augustinian paradigm whereby life—new life—is achieved by mastering the lesson of death. Because of the courtly twist, the pilgrim's original desire for Beatrice was not in itself wrong; indeed his desire for Beatrice led him to love "the good beyond which there is nothing to aspire" ("i mie' disiri, / che ti menavano ad amar lo bene / di là dal qual non è a che s'aspiri" [*Purg.* 31.22–24]).[16] What was wrong was his failure, after her death, to resist the siren song of the new, the *altre novità* that are false if for no other reason than that they are mortal, corruptible, confined to the present and doomed to die: "Le presenti cose / col falso lor piacer volser miei passi" ("Present things with their false pleasure turned my steps" [*Purg.* 31.34–35]).[17] Having encountered the lesson of mortality once, he should not have needed to be taught it again; like Augustine after the death of his friend, he should have learned the error of "loving a man that must die as though he were not to die"—"diligendo moriturum ac si non moriturum" (*Conf.* 4.8). Having learned, when Beatrice died, that even the most beautiful of mortal things, the most supreme of earthly pleasures, will necessarily fail us, Dante should have known better than to ever desire another "cosa mortale": "e se 'l sommo piacer sì *ti fallio* / per la mia morte, qual cosa mortale / dovea poi trarre te nel suo disio?" ("and if the supreme pleasure thus *failed you*, with my death, what mortal thing should then have drawn you into desire?" [*Purg.* 31.52–54]). A similar theologizing of courtly topoi along Augustinian lines is already evident in the *Vita Nuova*, whose protagonist is converted from desiring Beatrice's "mortal" greeting, which fails him, to desiring only "quello che non mi puote venire meno" (18.4), a phrase that will be punctually recast in the *Purgatorio*'s "sì ti fallio." "Beatitudine," as he calls it in the *libello*, is spiritual autonomy, the ability to relinquish even the best and most beautiful of earthly things—such as Beatrice's greeting, Casella's song, Manfredi's beautiful aspect. Not the cessation of desire, but the mastery of an infallible desire, is the goal; and indeed the pilgrim enters the earthly paradise full of a questing desire ("Vago già di cercar dentro e dintorno" ["Desirous already to search inside and about" (*Purg.* 28.1)]) that cannot go wrong.

So, the paradigm of the quest remains, but the quester can no longer err. Within this conceptual node, we can identify the purgatorial valence that will be assigned to the figure of Ulysses, the shadings particular to the only canticle in which everyone is questing, in which everyone must needs fly "con l'ale snelle e con le piume / del gran disio" ("with the slender wings and with the feathers of great desire" [*Purg.* 4.28–29]). We note that the verb *volgere*, used by Beatrice to indict the pilgrim ("e volse i passi suoi per via non vera"), and then by the pilgrim as he acknowledges the legitimacy of her rebuke ("Le presenti cose ... volser miei passi"), is the same verb used by the siren in her boast regarding Ulysses: "Io volsi Ulisse del suo cammin vago." In fact, the Ulyssean twist that Dante gives his Augustinian thematic is made explicit by Beatrice in her summation, where she says she intends to strengthen the pilgrim in any future encounters with sirens, any future exposure to their seductive songs: "e perché altra volta, / udendo le serene, sie più forte" ("and so that another time, hearing the sirens, you may be stronger" [*Purg.* 31.44–45]). Here we find the *Purgatorio*'s ultimate synthesis of the Ulyssean model (a man—in this case Dante—tempted by sirens) with Augustine's critique of false pleasure. Given that the sirens of verse 45 may be interpreted in the light of Cicero's *De finibus* as knowledge,[18] resistance to the sirens constitutes not only resistance to the false pleasures of the flesh but also resistance to the false lure of philosophical knowledge, a lure embodied in Dante's earlier itinerary by the *donna gentile*/Lady Philosophy of the *Convivio*,[19] the text that begins with the Ulyssean copula of desire and knowledge: "tutti li uomini naturalmente desiderano di sapere." As the pilgrim has learned restraint before the sweet siren in all her guises, so, in the earthly paradise, the griffin is praised for having resisted the sweet taste of the tree of knowledge: "Beato se', grifon, che non discindi / col becco d'esto legno dolce al gusto, / poscia che mal si torce il ventre quindi" ("Blessed are you, griffin, who do not tear with your beak from this tree sweet to the taste, for by it the belly is evilly twisted" [*Purg.* 32.43–45]). By resisting the temptation of knowledge, the griffin refuses to challenge God's interdict (the *interdetto* of *Purgatorio* 33.71, where the tree is glossed precisely in terms of the limits it represents, the obedience it exacts, and the consequent justice of the punishment meted to those who transgress). The temptation to which Adam/Ulysses succumb is the temptation that the griffin resists.

All the threads are tied in these cantos—the threads connecting gluttony, concupiscence, pride, curiosity, questing, loving, transgressing, Ulysses, the siren, Adam, and Eve[20]—as the Augustinian critique of misplaced desire proper to the *Purgatorio* converges with the theme of limits and transgression central to the poem as a whole, the theme embodied by Dante not only in the canonical figures of Adam and Lucifer but also in the more idiosyncratic and personal mythography of Ulysses. It is worth noting that the system of values that finds expression in the tied threads of *Purgatorio* was already, to a significant degree, present in the earlier works. We have seen that the purgatorial journey toward spiritual autonomy is adumbrated in the

*Vita Nuova*; so too, the *Convivio* explores the desire for knowledge in ways that portend the *Commedia*. Let us consider, for instance, the passage in *Convivio* 4.13 where Dante compares the desire for riches to the desire for knowledge. (It should be noted that riches, *le ricchezze*, are characterized in the *Convivio* in terms that strikingly anticipate the *dolce serena* of *Purgatorio* 19, as "false traditrici" and "false meretrici" who make promises of satisfaction they cannot fulfill, and who lead not to repose but to renewed desire.)[21] This being the *Convivio*, Dante's assessment of man's desire to know is comparatively sanguine and untroubled, and the successiveness of the desire for knowledge, with its many scaled opportunities for reaching "perfection," is sharply disjoined from the unilaterality of the desire for wealth, which leads only to increased desire:

> E così appare che, dal desiderio de la scienza, la scienza non è da dire imperfetta, sì come le ricchezze sono da dire per lo loro, come la questione ponea; ché nel desiderare de la scienza successivamente finiscono li desiderii e viensi a perfezione, e in quello de la ricchezza no.

> And so it appears that, on the basis of the desire for knowledge, knowledge itself is not to be called imperfect, as riches instead are to be called on the basis of the desire for riches, as the question posed; for in the desire for knowledge successively our desires conclude and come to perfection, and in desiring riches this does not happen.

> (*Conv.* 4.13.5)

Similarly, in an earlier passage on desire in *Convivio* 3.15, Dante invokes the miser to explain what the seeker after knowledge is not; the miser is doomed to failure, since, by pursuing the unattainable, he desires always to desire: "e in questo errore cade l'avaro maladetto, e non s'accorge che desidera sé sempre desiderare, andando dietro al numero impossibile a giugnere" ("and into this error falls the accursed miser, and he does not realize that he desires himself always to desire, going after a number impossible to reach" [*Conv.* 3.15.9]).[22] By contrast, the seeker after knowledge will satisfy his desire and fulfill his quest, in part because his quest is measured rather than gluttonously insatiable, and he realizes that there is a line he cannot cross: "E però l'umano desiderio è misurato in questa vita a quella scienza che qui avere si può, e quello punto non passa se non per errore, lo quale è di fuori di naturale intenzione" ("And so human desire is measured in this life by that knowledge which here can be had, and it does not pass that point except by error, which is outside of natural intention" [*Conv.* 3.15.9]).[23]

One could describe the distance between the *Convivio* and the *Commedia* in terms of the poet's growing concern about our Ulyssean lack of measure, our failure to respect the line that cannot be crossed, "quello punto [che l'umano desiderio] non passa se non per errore." Even in the treatise, Dante concludes his defense of the desire for knowledge by quoting St. Paul on the need for limits: "E però Paulo dice: 'Non più sapere che sapere si convegna, ma sapere a misura'" ("And so Paul says: 'Do not know more than is fitting, but know with measure'" [*Conv.* 4.13.9]). Moreover, the fact that Dante sees a basis of comparison between the desire for wealth and the desire for knowledge is significant, indicating the conceptual foundation for his mature ideology of an intellectual as well as a material cupidity and pointing forward to the *Commedia*'s composite image of Ulysses on the one hand and the wolf on the other. The *lupa* of *Inferno* 1 illuminates the negative side of the basic human condition whereby "disire è moto spiritale" and recalls Augustine's own reduction of all desire to spiritual motion, either in the form of "charity," desire that moves toward God, or "cupidity," desire that remains rooted in the flesh.[24] As cupidity, our dark desire, the *lupa* is quintessentially without peace, "la bestia sanza pace" (*Inf.* 1.58). Her restlessness and insatiability denote unceasing spiritual motion, unceasing desire: heavy "with all longings" ("di tutte brame" [49]), "her greedy craving is never filled, and after eating she is more hungry than before" ("mai non empie la bramosa voglia, / e dopo 'l pasto ha più fame che pria" [98–99]). Her limitless hunger is both caused by unsatisfied desire and creates the condition for ever less satisfaction, since, in Augustine's words, "When vices have emptied the soul and led it to a kind of extreme hunger, it leaps into crimes by means of which impediments to the vices may be removed or the vices themselves sustained" (*De doct. Christ.* 3.10.16). When the "antica lupa" is recalled as an emblem of cupidity on purgatory's terrace of avarice (again indicating the common ground that underlies all the sins of inordinate desire), her "hunger without end" is once more her distinguishing characteristic: "Maladetta sie tu, antica lupa, / che più che tutte l'altre bestie hai preda / per la tua fame sanza fine cupa!" ("Cursed be you, ancient wolf, who more than all the other beasts have prey, because of your deep hunger without end! [*Purg.* 20.10–12]). The "antica lupa," the "bestia sanza pace" of the poem's first canto, prepares us for *Purgatorio*'s rooting of all sin in desire and for the coupling of Ulysses, a wanderer who makes the mistake of enjoying the sights and sounds that he should merely use, with the "dolce serena": it is impossible to separate in categorical fashion avarice from greed, greed from lust, or any of the three from desire—including the desire for knowledge—that has become immoderately transgressive, that has gone astray.[25]

The *Convivio*'s assessment of the possibilities for human desiring is not so positive as to preclude the figure of the errant voyager. Thus, Dante offers the parable of the path that is shown and then lost ("e pongo essemplo del cammino mostrato [e poscia errato]"),[26] a story whereby one man makes his way across an arduous and snowy plain, leaving his tracks for those behind him, only to be followed by one who is incapable even of keeping to the path

laid out by his predecessor, and so loses himself: "e, per suo difetto, lo cammino, che altri sanza scorta ha saputo tenere, questo scorto erra, e tortisce
per li pruni e per le ruine, e a la parte dove dee non va" ("and, through his
own fault, the path that another without guidance knew how to follow, this
one with guidance loses, and wanders wrongly through the bushes and down
the steep slopes, and to the place where he should go does not go" [*Conv.*
4.7.7]). Still, despite the Ulyssean presence of the *cammino errato*, it should
be noticed that the parable puts great emphasis on the *cammino mostrato* as
well, devoting attention to the industry and skill of the guide who "per sua
industria, cioè per accorgimento e per bontade d'ingegno, solo da sé guidato, per lo diritto cammino si va là dove intende, lasciando le vestigie de li
suoi passi diretro da sé" ("by his own industry, by observation and the resources of intellect, guided only by himself, goes where he intended, leaving
the traces of his steps behind himself" [4.7.7]). Particularly striking is the
proto-Vergilian image of the tracks left for those who come behind, which
anticipates the description of the Roman poet as one "che porta il lume
dietro e sé non giova, / ma dopo sé fa le persone dotte" ("who carries the
light behind and helps not himself, but after himself makes people wise"
[*Purg.* 22.68–69]). While in the *Convivio* the guide is able to benefit from
his own *industria*, the *Commedia* will recombine the parable's elements so
that the guide fails, and instead the follower benefits from the guide's proffered help and reaches his goal. Indeed, in the poem the very idea of being
able to make one's way "per bontade d'ingegno, solo da sé guidato" will be
suspect.

Even more telling than the parable of the *cammino errato* is the predictive
value of our pilgrim passage from *Convivio* 4.12; here we already find the
association between misdirected desire and the voyager who will never reach
his goal. As we proceed from desire to desire, as our desires grow ever larger
and we quest more and more insatiably for the prize that eludes us, we may
deviate from the straight and truest path:[27]

Veramente così questo cammino si perde per errore come le strade de la terra. Che
sì come d'una cittade a un'altra di necessitade è una ottima e dirittissima via, e
un'altra che sempre se ne dilunga (cioè quella che va ne l'altra parte), e molte altre
quale meno allungandosi e quale meno appressandosi, così ne la vita umana sono
diversi cammini, de li quali uno è veracissimo e un altro è fallacissimo, e certi
meno fallaci e certi meno veraci. E sì come vedemo che quello che dirittissimo vae
a la cittade, e compie lo desiderio e dà posa dopo la fatica, e quello che va in
contrario mai nol compie e mai posa dare non può, così ne la nostra vita avviene:
lo buono camminatore giugne a termine e a posa; lo erroneo mai non l'aggiugne,
ma con molta fatica del suo animo sempre con li occhi gulosi si mira innanzi.

Truly thus this path is lost through error like the roads of the earth. For just as
from one city to the other there is by necessity one best and straightest road, and

another road that instead gets always further away (that is, which goes in another direction), and many others of which some get further and others come nearer, so in human life there are different paths, of which one is the truest and the other the most false, and some less false and some less true. And as we see that the path that goes most directly to the city fulfills desire and gives rest after weariness, while the one that goes in the contrary direction never brings fulfillment and can never bring rest, so it happens in our life: the traveler on the right path reaches his goal and his rest; the traveler on the wrong path never reaches it, but with great weariness of soul always with his greedy eyes looks ahead.

(*Conv.* 4.12.18–19)

In the figure of the traveler on the wrong path who never reaches his goal, never fulfills his quest and his desire, never finds peace but strains forward as with "great weariness of soul always with his greedy eyes he looks ahead," we have a full-fledged anticipation of the Ulysses figure within the *Commedia*: the *erroneo camminatore* whose greedy desire and ever forward-looking "occhi gulosi" lead him fatally to his death.[28] On the other hand, in the *buono camminatore* who reaches his goal and finds repose ("giugne a termine e a posa"), we find anticipated all the pilgrims of the *Commedia*, all the souls in the second realm. Given this realm's intimate tie to the concepts of pilgrimage and voyage, it is not surprising to find at its outset a particularly lucid synthesis of the *Convivio*'s two types of voyagers.

The presence of Ulysses as mariner saturates the first canto of *Purgatorio*, from the opening image of the poem as the "little ship of my intellect," to the closing cadenza about the deserted shore "that never saw any man navigate its waters who afterward had experience of return" ("che mai non vide navicar sue acque / omo, che di tornar sia poscia esperto" [*Purg.* 1.131–32]). No human navigator has ever seen these waters and returned to tell the tale; the pilgrim, on the other hand, looks "a l'altro polo" ("altro polo" is used only here in *Purgatorio* 1, twice, and in *Inferno* 26) and sees "quattro stelle / non viste mai fuor ch'a la prima gente" ("four stars never seen save by the first people" [23–24]). How can it be that, in the course of Ulysses' journey, "the night saw *all* the stars already of the other pole" ("*Tutte* le stelle già de l'altro polo / vedea la notte" [*Inf.* 26.127–28]), while now the other pole shows the pilgrim four stars that no one has seen since Adam and Eve? Whether the contradiction is meant to indicate the purely symbolic nature of these four purgatorial stars,[29] or whether the night somehow saw what Ulysses himself did not see, the dialectic between vision denied and vision vouchsafed is essential to this canto, whose themes of castigated pride and potentially broken laws ("Son le leggi d'abisso così rotte?" ["Are the laws of the abyss so broken?"] asks Cato in line 46) link it to its predecessor, *Inferno* 34, as surely as its style and tonality disjoin it. In the same way, the pilgrim—

of whose previous *follia* Vergil speaks in what the poem has coded as a Ulyssean lexicon—is purposely linked to the Greek sailor, only to be just as purposely disjoined: although his backward descent to the base of the mountain makes him appear a man who travels in vain until he returns to the road he has lost ("com'om che torna a la perduta strada, / che 'nfino ad essa li pare ire in vano" [119–20]), in fact this backward motion will serve to dissociate him from Ulyssean pride, bringing him to the reeds of rebirth rather than to the "perduta strada" of hell.[30]

Throughout these opening cantos of *Purgatorio* recur the images of travel: Dante and Vergil are "come gente che pensa a suo cammino, / che va col cuore e col corpo dimora" ("like people who think of their path, who go in heart and remain in body" [*Purg.* 2.11–12]); the souls dispersed by Cato move off toward the mountain's slope "com'om che va, né sa dove rïesca" ("like a man who goes, nor knows where he may come forth" [*Purg.* 2.132]). Throughout these cantos, also, runs the leitmotif of limits, of the non-Ulyssean humility that distinguishes our travelers from the *erroneo camminatore*. The newly arrived souls of purgatory are "rustic" ("selvaggia" [*Purg.* 2.52]) rather than "urbanely" self-confident;[31] not being "esperti d'esto loco," they look around "come colui che nove cose assaggia" ("like one who tastes new things" [*Purg.* 2.54]). In contrast to Ulysses, who sought to conquer the *nova terra*, to make it no longer new, these souls accept their status as "nova gente" (*Purg.* 2.58). In contrast to Ulysses, who in trying to reach purgatory was striving to be a new thing in the sense of something not envisioned by God, something not written into the divine script (the periphrasis for the shore, "che mai non vide navicar sue acque," anticipates the periphrasis for God, "Colui che mai non vide cosa nova"), these souls are new things in the sense that they will be made new, will be "remade like new plants, renewed with new leaf" at the canticle's end. Like the souls, the pilgrim too is God's "cosa nova": not an attempt to abrogate the laws and surprise God but a sign of God's providence, as Sapìa indicates when she exclaims that the pilgrim's journey is "sì cosa nuova . . . che gran segno è che Dio t'ami" ("such a new thing that it is a great sign that God loves you" [*Purg.* 13.145–46]).[32] This contrast is sustained in canto 3 through Vergil's discourse on human intellectual limits ("State contenti, umana gente, al *quia*" ["Content yourselves, human folk, with the fact that certain things are" (*Purg.* 3.37)]), through the description of the purgatorial souls as timid sheep, who are content to act without knowing the reason why ("e lo 'mperché non sanno" [84]), and finally through the temporal ban—the "divieto" of verse 144—that punishes the "presumption" ("presunzïon" [140]) of those who die excommunicate. In canto 4 we learn that to scale purgatory we must fly with the wings of great desire and then find contrasted the immoderate zeal of Phaeton's flight with the immoderate torpor of the negligent Belacqua;[33] at the same time, there is also the suggestion that Belacqua's negligence partakes of humility and might have something to teach the pilgrim, who—unlike Phaeton—will have to accept his limitations before climbing to the top of this mountain. Belacqua's friendly taunt, "Forse / che di sedere in pria avrai distretta!" ("Maybe before then you'll need to sit!" [*Purg.* 4.98–99]), will be picked up by Sordello's sterner reminder of limits—"sola questa riga / non varcheresti dopo 'l sol partito" ("not even this line would you cross after the sun's departure" [*Purg.* 7.53–54]), where the use of the verb *varcare* carries a Ulyssean reverberation.

In the *Purgatorio*, then, Dante takes great pains to establish the paradigm of the *erroneo camminatore* versus the *buono camminatore* and to associate the pilgrim with the latter. He sets up an implied model, a scale that measures various approaches to the divine and indicates the wide range of right movement, of acceptable—non-Ulyssean—flight. But, in a text whose fiction is that it is no fiction, and whose strategy is that there is no strategy, the matter is never so simple. Thus, in canto 3, the theme of human limits is allowed to embrace the ecclesiastical establishment, up to and including the pope: had the bishop of Cosenza, instructed to hunt Manfredi by Clement IV, been able to "read" the face of God that is his infinite mercy ("avesse in Dio ben letta questa faccia" [*Purg.* 3.126]), Manfredi's bones would not have been disinterred. The bishop, and with him his superior, was proved incapable of "reading," understanding and interpreting, the divine will.[34] In the same way, in canto 5, the mystery of divine predestination will baffle not only human agents, like the pope, but a devil, who will be infuriated by the inexplicable intervention of an angel on Bonconte's behalf: "Io dirò vero, e tu 'l ridì tra ' vivi: / l'angel di Dio mi prese, e quel d'inferno / gridava: 'O tu del ciel, perché mi privi?'" ("I will tell the truth, and you retell it among the living: the angel of God took me, and the one from hell cried, 'O you from heaven, why do you deprive me?'" [*Purg.* 5.103–5]). What Bonconte recounts cannot be logically explained or comprehended, since it belongs to the mystery of providence; it must be accepted on faith, as the truth: "Io dirò vero," says Bonconte. And, indeed, it must be the "truth," or else Dante would not be sanctioning what Bonconte said to him ("e tu 'l ridì tra ' vivi"), or else—in fact—Bonconte would not be where he is, in purgatory. In this fiction a soul, in this case Bonconte, tells the pilgrim that he is telling the truth; the poet repeats what the soul "said" to the pilgrim, along with the injunction to repeat it, and thereby presents it as the truth rather than as fiction. Ultimately, however, the fiction is a fiction, no matter how skillfully deployed, and the choice to save Manfredi, thereby branding the pope an incompetent reader of the divine text, like the choice to save Bonconte, is Dante's. Thus we come back to the word *presunzione* inscribed into the conclusion of canto 3: whose presumption is really at stake here, if not the poet's? The textual language employed in these episodes—not only the failure to read but also calling the Archiano's convergence with the Arno the place where the river loses its name, where its signifier is emptied of significance, "Là 've 'l vocabol suo diventa vano" (*Purg.* 5.97)—serves to highlight the metatextual implications: does Dante read God correctly, as he claims, or does he read like Clement, composing a text whose *vocaboli* are therefore *vani*?

I submit that the terms *presunzione* and *presumere* may be said to carry a Ulyssean charge in all Dante's works, that indeed they were invested by Dante with a special significance as early as the *Convivio* and the *De vulgari eloquentia*, before such a thematic could properly be dubbed "Ulyssean."[35] In other words, Dante has a history of using these words in contexts that indicate his ongoing concern with the problem of intellectual arrogance, the problem to which in the *Commedia* he gives dramatic and poetic shape with the figure of Ulysses. In the *De vulgari eloquentia* we find the first and programmatic use of the adjective as a qualifier for Eve, *presumptuosissima Eva*, who, in replying to the devil, became the first human to speak (1.4.2).[36] The sin of human presumption ("culpa presumptionis humane" [1.6.4]) leads to mankind's "third" fall; following the expulsion from the garden of Eden and the flood, in our foolish pride we presume yet a third time: "per superbam stultitiam presumendo" (1.7.3). The participle "presumendo" is immediately picked up by the next word, "Presumpsit," which powerfully begins the paragraph dedicated to the discussion of the linguistic diaspora occasioned by Nimrod's hubristic attempt to construct the tower of Babel: "Presumpsit ergo in corde suo incurabilis homo, sub persuasione gigantis Nembroth, arte sua non solum superare naturam, sed etiam ipsum naturantem, qui Deus est" ("So uncurable man, persuaded by the giant Nimrod, presumed in his heart to surpass with his art not only nature, but also nature's maker, who is God" [1.7.4]). The connection between pride and human endeavor—human "art" as it is called here and in a related passage in *Inferno* 11[37]—is a striking feature of this passage, and one that anticipates the *Commedia*; Nimrod's attempt to surpass not only nature but nature's maker will cause him to be remembered in each canticle of the poem, as part of an "artistic" constellation that also includes Ulysses and Phaeton.[38] Not surprisingly, then, in the *Commedia presumere* is invested with enormous self-consciousness; on both occasions in which Dante employs the verb (the noun occurs only in *Purgatorio* 3), he is referring to himself.[39] It appears in *Paradiso* 33, in the supreme moment of the pilgrim's nontransgressive transgression, where the verb's prideful connotations are redeemed through the grace of God: "Oh abbondante grazia ond'io presunsi / ficcar lo viso per la luce etterna" ("O abundant grace whereby I presumed to thrust my face through the eternal light" [82–83]). If the point here is the legitimate presumption that propels us toward our maker, the poem's other usage recoups its previous history in Dante's works; in answer to the pilgrim's query as to why Peter Damian alone was predestined to welcome him to the heaven of Saturn, the saint replies that the mystery of predestination is hidden in the abyss of God's will and that human beings should not presume to tackle such a question: "E al mondo mortal, quando tu riedi, / questo rapporta, sì che non presumma / a tanto segno più mover li piedi" ("And to the mortal world, when you return, bring back this message, so that it will not any longer presume to move its feet toward such a goal" [*Par.* 21.97–99]).

Here the poet advises himself, through the medium of Peter Damian, to advise the world not to seek presumptuously to know what cannot be known; like the passage in *Paradiso* 13 in which Dante, the great judger, condemns hasty judgments through the agency of St. Thomas, this passage betrays a protective awareness of the *Commedia*'s own Achilles' heel. As a self-proclaimed prophecy, the *Commedia* is a text whose basic program of revealing the state of souls after death participates in the very presumption it is supposed to warn the world against. Indeed, the *Commedia*'s only defense against such presumption is its aggressive assumption of the mantle of truth, its vigilant assertions that it is a true prophecy, vouchsafed by God in a vision. Dante is aware that he is only preserved from presumption by the divine investiture that he alone knows he received, and that only his ability to persuade us of this investiture's historicity (or of his sincerity in claiming its historicity) prevents us from considering him fraudulently self-deluded and self-promoting: as self-deluded and self-promoting as, for instance, the false prophets of *Inferno* 20, or the mendacious preachers of *Paradiso* 29.[40] This awareness dictates both the connection between artistry and pride that runs through his work and the (defensive) aggression he directs at any others—like the false prophets and the lying preachers—whose art it also is to present themselves as tellers of truth. This aggression toward rival claimants was first directed, in the course of Dante's career, against poets whose pretensions surpassed their abilities. Thus, when, in the *De vulgari eloquentia*, Dante condemns the Tuscan poets for their mad arrogance, he uses language that anticipates the *Commedia*'s lexicon of Ulyssean hubris;[41] the key word, *praesumptuositas*, used in adjectival form earlier in the treatise for Eve, now describes poets who try to go beyond their natural limits. They should desist from such presumption, and if nature or laziness has made them ducks, they should accept their lowly status (likewise Nimrod should have accepted the low position of human art in the mimetic hierarchy) and cease to imitate the star-seeking eagle: "et a tanta presumptuositate desistant, et si anseres natura vel desidia sunt, nolint astripetam aquilam imitari" (2.4.11). Poets like Guittone d'Arezzo, in other words, should not seek to imitate supreme poets, poets who seek the stars, poets like Dante; their (false) claims to tell truth should not interfere with his (true) claims.[42] The

question of presumption is thus intimately connected to the question of
access to truth, as Peter Damian tells us in the *Commedia* and as Dante had
already clarified in this passage from the *Convivio*:

> ché sono molti tanto presuntuosi, che si credono tutto sapere, e per questo le non
> certe cose affermano per certe; lo qual vizio Tullio massimamente abomina nel
> primo de li Offici e Tommaso nel suo Contra li Gentili, dicendo: "Sono molti
> tanto di suo ingegno presuntuosi, che credono col suo intelletto poter misurare
> tutte le cose, *estimando tutto vero quello che a loro pare, falso quello che a loro non
> pare.*"

> for there are many who are so presumptuous that they think they know everything,
> and on this basis they treat matters that are not certain as certain; which vice
> Cicero greatly abominates in the first book of the *De officiis* and Thomas in his
> *Contra gentiles* saying: "There are many so presumptuous in their intelligence
> that they think with their minds to be able to measure all things, *believing every-
> thing to be true which seems to them to be true, and false that which seems to them
> false.*"

(Conv. 4.15.12)

The *Convivio* foreshadows the dialectical bind in which the author of the
*Commedia* is caught, as he either ferociously condemns those who fail to
accept their limits[43] or wards off the possibility that he himself may not be
accepting his limits, that the authority of his authorship may cause him to
transgress against other authorities: "E prima mostrerò me non presummere
[contra l'autorità del Filosofo; poi mostrerò me non presummere] contra la
maiestade imperiale" ("And first I will demonstrate that I have not presumed [against the authority of the Philosopher; then I will show that I have
not presumed] against the imperial majesty" [*Conv.* 4.8.5]).[44] Looking again
at the episode in *Paradiso* 21 where Peter Damian denounces the pilgrim's
curiosity regarding predestination, we note that the pilgrim beats a retreat
from his daring original query to the humbler "Who are you?": "Sì mi
prescrisser le parole sue, / ch'io lasciai la quistione e mi ritrassi / a diman-
darla umilmente chi fue" ("So did his words impose a limit that I left the
question and drew back to asking humbly who he was" [*Par.* 21.103–5]).[45]
But the episode gives us a counter signal as well, in the form of the rhyme
words *abisso* and *scisso*, which send us back to one of the most daringly
transgressive passages in the poem and remind us that the pilgrim's retreat
cannot be simplistically equated with the poet's. Peter Damian tells the
pilgrim that the seraph whose eyes are most fixed on God would not be able
to answer his question, "for what you ask is so far advanced in the abyss of
the eternal decree that from every created vision it is cut off": "però che sì
s'innoltra ne lo *abisso* / de l'etterno statuto quel che chiedi, / che da ogne
creata vista è *scisso*" (*Par.* 21.94–96). This same rhyme occurs elsewhere

only in *Purgatorio* 6, where *abisso* also refers to the inscrutability of the divine will ("abisso / del tuo consiglio" as compared to "abisso / de l'etterno statuto"), where our awareness is also cut off—"scisso"—from understanding, and where the recollection of our eternal shortsightedness follows a query, addressed to God, of enormous presumption:

> E se licito m'è, o sommo Giove
>   che fosti in terra per noi crucifisso,
>   son li giusti occhi tuoi rivolti altrove?
> O è preparazion che ne l'*abisso*
>   del tuo consiglio fai per alcun bene
>   in tutto de l'accorger nostro *scisso*?

And if it be lawful for me, o supreme Jove who was crucified for us on earth, are your just eyes turned elsewhere? Or is it a preparation that in the *abyss* of your counsel you make for some good that is completely *cut off* from our perception?
(*Purg.* 6.118–23)

The new and never before traveled path of this poem entails bizarre reversals: on the one hand, we have a poet who invents a special penalty to castigate the presumption of anyone who challenges the authority of the church, a temporal ban ("divieto") of thirtyfold the amount of time passed by such a soul "in sua presunzïon"; on the other hand, this same poet presumes to ostentatiously include in the community of the saved, by his own—that is, "God's"—fiat, a soul who was notoriously cast out by one of God's chosen vicars. And, were questioning a pope not problematic enough, this poet presumes to question God himself, wondering all the while if it is licit so to do—"se licito m'è"—because he knows perfectly well that it is not.[46]

*Purgatorio* 6 is a canto in which the narrator steps out of bounds—both ideologically, in the lengthy invective that escalates into the questioning of divine justice, and narratologically, in that the invective is couched in the form of a digression: a literal swerving away from the narrative confines and off the narrative path. Ideological *transgressio* thus elicits narratological *digressio*.[47] Beginning in verse 76, the digression finds its pretext in the civic embrace of Vergil and Sordello and preempts the rest of canto 6; not until canto 7 does the interrupted encounter between the two Mantuan poets resume (the willed and programmatic nature of the interruption is further emphasized by its coincidence with the canto break).[48] There are signs of the coming disruption in the first part of the canto: the narrator has already slipped out of harness in lines 22–24, when he suggests to the still living Marie de Brabant that she begin to provide for her immortal soul;[49] the encounter with Sordello also elicits a brief apostrophe that momentarily arrests the narrative flow in midverse: "Venimmo a lei: o anima lombarda, / come ti stavi altera e disdegnosa" ("We came to him; O Lombard soul, how you were proud and disdainful" [*Purg.* 6.61–62]). Of particular importance is the attack on the integrity of Vergil's text that is staged between lines 28 and 48: the poet has the pilgrim wonder why it is that in the *Aeneid* prayer does not help Palinurus to cross the Acheron, while in purgatory prayer is a force for spiritual advancement; Vergil is forced to confront the fact that he was writing about souls whose prayers are disjoined from God, while the pilgrim is experiencing the requests of souls whose prayers have access to divine justice. In Vergil's murky explanation (the fact that he tells us that his text is clear on this point, "La mia scrittura è piana" [34], only highlights the obscurity of his gloss), the justice that will so exercise the poet later on in this canto is already present: "ché cima di giudicio non s'avvalla / perché foco d'amor compia in un punto / ciò che de' sodisfar chi qui s'astalla" ("for the summit of judgment is not lowered because the fire of love fulfills in one moment that which he who stays here must satisfy" [37–39]). Vergil has thus already posed, indirectly, the question of how justice can be bent by love without ceasing to be just (or how, by implication, it can fail to be bent by love without ceasing to be just).[50] He further anticipates the poet by inserting into his address a little authorial signpost: Vergil's "se ben si guarda con la mente sana" ("if with sound mind you consider well" [36]) will be echoed in the course of the digression by the poet's own "se bene intendi ciò che Dio ti nota" ("if you understand well what God tells you" [93]). These anticipations serve to underscore the disjunction between Vergil and Dante, *Aeneid* and *Commedia*. Prior to his great invective, an invective that is licit—if indeed it is, *se licito m'è*—precisely because he is one who interprets God's notations correctly, the poet stretches a textual cordon between his text and the *Aeneid*, confirming the latter in its errors and thus creating the space, the liminality, in which the *Commedia* can receive its mandate for prophetic transgression, for the literal trespass of the sign ("trapassar del segno") that is his "digression."

In the *Commedia* Dante uses the terms *digressione* and *digredire* only twice, on both occasions to usher in a full-fledged change in subject matter:[51] in *Purgatorio* 6 he uses the noun, congratulating Florence on "questa digression che non ti tocca" ("this digression that does not touch you" [128]); while in *Paradiso* 29 the poet concludes the invective against fraudulent preachers by announcing that it is time for us to turn our eyes back to the straight road (in this case, the straight road, the narrative path, is a discussion of the nature of angels), since we have digressed enough ("Ma perché siam digressi assai, ritorci / li occhi oramai verso la dritta strada" [127–28]). If we consider that the brunt of *Paradiso* 29's critique is that there exist unscrupulous preachers who tell falsehoods, inventions, and lies, we begin to discern the consonance between the poem's two self-proclaimed digressions: they are both metatextual moments, concerned with situating the text from which they pretend to depart with respect to other texts; in a word, far from being extraneous, they are integrally connected to Dante's campaign to be seen as a teller of truth. In his condemnation of false preachers, Dante's strategy is the fairly straightforward attack on other pretenders that we have already noted to be a staple of his career. The invective of *Purgatorio* 6, on the other hand, offers the more delicate dialectic between the author's awareness of his own potential for transgression and the express declaration of his status as a teller of truth, one whose words are corroborated by events, by history itself: "S'io dico 'l ver, l'effetto nol nasconde" ("If I tell the truth, the facts do not hide it" [*Purg.* 6.138]). The truly remarkable nature of the rupture in *Purgatorio* 6, moreover, is suggested by the steps that Dante takes to restore the fictive status quo that he has so emphatically sundered. In canto 7 Sordello will guide the pilgrim to the valley of the princes, showing him its denizens, in the same way that in canto 6 the poet offers to guide the emperor, exhorting him to "look" at what he has to show in the thrice repeated formula, "Vieni a veder" ("Come to see");[52] as the poet apostrophizes Albert I of Austria, accusing him of abandoning the garden of the empire, so Sordello notes that Albert's father, Rudolf I, could have healed the wounds that have been the death of Italy. Sordello might almost be said to "imitate" the poet, self-consciously drawing attention to his narrative role as Dante did in the digression: "Anche al nasuto vanno mie parole / non men ch'a l'altro" ("My words apply to the large-nosed one no less than to the other" [*Purg.* 7.124–25]). However, when Sordello echoes the poet in his use of "licito," it is not to suggest the possibility of transgression but rather the need to accept one's limits: "licito m'è andar suso e intorno; / per quanto ir posso, a guida mi t'accosto" ("it is permitted me to go up and around; as far as I am able, I will accompany you as guide" [*Purg.* 7.41–42]).

Sordello restores narrative normalcy and ideological humility, leading us back within the limits, both narratologically and theologically. Rather than attend to the unveiled voice of the poet, we once more learn our lessons at the hands of a figure within the fictive construct, one, moreover, who does not question the workings of providence: thus Sordello explains that if nobility is rarely passed on from father to son, it is because God wills it so (*Purg.* 7.121–23). Another figure within the fictive construct, Nino Visconti, refers to the mysteries of providence in a periphrasis that wonderfully literalizes the limits to our mental voyaging: God is "the one who so hides his first cause that there is no fording thereto" ("colui che sì nasconde / lo suo primo perché, che non lì è guado" [*Purg.* 8.68–69]). Nino is drawing attention to the singular grace that has brought the pilgrim to purgatory while alive, a grace that he effectively posits as the only answer to the poet's anguished query of canto 6; the text's reply to its author's "Vieni a veder" is Nino's echoing call to Currado to "come and see what God willed in his grace": "vieni a veder che Dio per grazia volse" (*Purg.* 8.66). And so we are folded back within the fiction; so *di-gressio*, trespass without the bounds, is channeled within, becoming the "trapassar dentro" of the author's address to the reader in canto 8: "Aguzza qui, lettor, ben li occhi al vero, / ché 'l velo è ora ben tanto sottile, / certo che 'l trapassar dentro è leggero" ("Reader, here sharpen well your eyes to the truth, for the veil is now so thin that certainly to pass within is easy" [19–21]). The digression has been righted by the restoration of the fiction (somewhat "thinner" than usual, perhaps, as a result of the preceding rupture): truth is under the veil, within the fiction, not only outside it, in the space of digression. And yet, finally, is not the fiction more transgressive than that which it corrects? What is more transgressive than Nino's call, when we consider that the object of God's grace whom Currado is summoned to see is none other than our author? The poet addresses us again, in canto 9, to alert us to the exalted nature of his theme and therefore of his art: "Lettor, tu vedi ben com'io innalzo / la mia matera, e però con più arte / non ti maravigliar s'io la rincalzo" ("Reader, you see well how I raise my matter, and therefore do not marvel if with more art I sustain it" [70–72]). The episode that follows is not known for its linguistic or poetic virtuosity, for its hold on the reader or its dramatic power; indeed, the description of the ritual encounter with the angel at purgatory's gate would hardly seem to qualify as an example of "più arte." To the extent, however, that art is measured by its access to truth, this passage may indeed be of the "highest," if, as Armour claims, it constitutes a supreme example of figural polysemy.[53] Apparently simple writing may not be so simple, may even be "exalted," if the literal veil covers not a fictitious truth, a metaphorical truth, but the actual—incarnate—truth. If the fiction tells truth then the retreat from the trespass of the digression is in fact not a retreat but an advance. The implications of the digression, with respect to *praesumptuositas*, are thus more intact than ever, as we—and the poet—approach the terrace of pride.

## Chapter 6

# RE-PRESENTING WHAT GOD PRESENTED: THE

# ARACHNEAN ART OF THE TERRACE OF PRIDE

ars adeo latet arte sua
(Ovid, *Metamorphoses*)

As it is, in the intricate evasions of as,
In things seen and unseen, created from nothingness,
The heavens, the hells, the worlds, the longed-for lands.
(*Wallace Stevens,*
"*An Ordinary Evening in New Haven*")

R EPRESENTATATION becomes an issue for the *Commedia* most
overtly on purgatory's terrace of pride, where the pilgrim encounters
a series of marble engravings that are rendered ecphrastically by the
poet, one form of representation thus representing another. This chapter
will explore the implications of that encounter, viewed as an authorial meditation on the principles of mimesis as they apply to Dante and to his art. As
traditionally constituted, the principles of mimesis are here immediately
violated; instead of art being inferior to nature, the art of the first terrace is
such that it puts nature to shame: "non pur Policleto, / ma la natura lì
avrebbe scorno" ("not only Polycletus, but nature would there be shamed"
[*Purg.* 10.32–33]). By proposing an art that surpasses nature, Dante proposes an art that is capable of going beyond verisimilitude, representation,
to become presentation, the *ver* itself—as though Nimrod (who figures
prominently among the examples of pride) had succeeded in his quest "to
surpass with his not only nature, but also nature's maker" (*DVE* 1.7.4).[1]
What kind of art equals reality and succeeds in making the dead look dead
and the living alive ("Morti li morti e i vivi parean vivi" [*Purg.* 12.67])? Not
until he has devoted much of canto 10 to a detailed representation of three
reliefs does the poet reveal their miraculous and literally supernatural
status, conferred by their divine artifex: "Colui che mai non vide cosa nova
/ produsse esto visibile parlare, / novello a noi perché qui non si trova" ("He
who never saw a new thing produced this visible speech, new to us because
here one does not find it" [*Purg.* 10.94–96]).[2] Concentrating on the fact that
the engravings are God's handiwork, Dante exegesis, focusing as usual on
what Dante says at the expense of what he does, has traditionally read the

terrace of pride as an exercise in humility and viewed the reliefs as a decorative way of underscoring Oderisi's remarks on the vanity of all human achievement.[3] But why does Dante choose to use the conceit of God as artist precisely in these cantos? Most crucially, why does he choose to posit a kind of supreme realism that is God's art, deliberately putting himself in the position of having to re-present God's realism with his own? If we argue, as does a recent article on these cantos, that "verisimilitude sets terrible traps into which even the most accomplished of readers can tumble,"[4] we maintain the illusion of a poet who is never compromised by his own actions. Rather, verisimilitude sets traps into which even the most cautious of poets can tumble—and Dante is not a cautious poet. By the same token, critics who "blame" characters like Oderisi for their imperfect signifying or who argue that Dante "corrects" the terrace of pride in that presumably more humble canticle, the *Paradiso*, have also succumbed to the hermeneutic imperatives structured by Dante into his poem.[5]

As examples of humility, the engravings of canto 10 are described in a leisurely crescendo that devotes twelve lines to the Annunciation, fifteen to David dancing before the Ark of the Covenant, and twenty-one to the story of Trajan and the widow. Like the singing that he hears as the gate of purgatory swings open, "ch'or sì or no s'intendon le parole" ("that now yes now no are the words understood" [*Purg.* 9.145]), the tableaux of the terrace of pride afflict the pilgrim with sensorial confusion:[6] whereas the account of the first engraving begins modestly enough, claiming only that the angel and the Virgin seem to speak, and thus that the pilgrim seems to hear, the second engraving not only confuses his ears, which seem to hear singing, but also his nose, which seems to smell incense burning. The struggle between the pilgrim's eyes, which know they are looking at an engraving, and his ears, which insist on the presence of sound, is rendered through a miniature debate between eyes and ears: "a' due mie' sensi / faceva dir l'un 'No,' l'altro 'Sì, canta'" ("made my two senses say, the one: 'No,' and the other: 'Yes, they sing'" [*Purg.* 10.59–60]). The confusion over the incense causes a similarly described discord between eyes and nose ("li occhi e 'l naso / e al sì e al no discordi fensi" ["my eyes and nose became discordant, with yes and no" (*Purg.* 10.62–63)]). The pilgrim's sense of sight, still capable of fighting the illusion of reality in front of the second engraving, yields to the magic of the reliefs in the third, where he believes that he sees the emperor's banners moving in the wind: "e l'aguglie ne l'oro / sovr'essi in vista al vento si movieno" ("and the eagles on the gold above them moved in one's sight in the wind" [*Purg.* 10.80–81]). Dante thus takes pains to depict a gradual overcoming of three of his five senses. Nonetheless, in the summarizing tercet that follows, he baptizes the engravings "esto visibile parlare" (*Purg.* 10.95), a phrase that insists on the representation of speech, rather than on the representation of incense or moving banners. The reason for this is that speech is a verbal medium, and—whereas the poet cannot even attempt to recreate God's incense for the reader—he can at least try to recreate God's speech.

According to Dante's conceit, God produced visible speech: "produsse esto visibile parlare." In other words, God produced the miracle of a visual medium that is endowed with the verbal medium of speech, such that the sculptures seem to speak; as compared to Augustine, who refers to signs like banners and military standards as "visible words," meaning simply that there are signs that are not verbal but visual, Dante means to appropriate for the visual sculptures the aural properties of language: they somehow speak, and as a result, they somehow live.[7] God, then, produced a kind of living art, and Dante's way of re-producing it is to resort to dialogue:

> La miserella intra tutti costoro
>   *pareva dir*: "Segnor, fammi vendetta
>   di mio figliuol ch'è morto, ond'io m'accoro";
> *ed elli a lei rispondere*: "Or aspetta
>   tanto ch'i' torni"; *e quella*: "Segnor mio,"
>   come persona in cui dolor s'affretta,
> "se tu non torni?"; *ed ei*: "Chi fia dov'io,
>   la ti farà"; *ed ella*: "L'altrui bene
>   a te che fia, se 'l tuo metti in oblio?";
> *ond'elli*: "Or ti conforta; ch'ei convene
>   ch'i' solva il mio dovere anzi ch'i' mova:
>   giustizia vuole e pietà mi ritene."

The poor woman among all these *seemed to be saying*: "My lord, avenge for me my son who is dead, whence I grieve"; *and he seemed to be answering*: "Now wait until I return"; *and she*: "My lord," like a person whom grief makes impatient, "if you do not return?"; *and he*: "The one who will take my place will do it for you"; *and she*: "Of what avail is someone else's good deed to you, if you forget your own?"; *and he*: "Now take comfort, for I must discharge my duty before I go—justice requires it and pity holds me here."

(*Purg.* 10.82–93)

This passage is Dante's attempt to make speech visible; his means is direct discourse held together by narrative connectors that become ever less obtrusive, eventually diminishing into the almost invisible "ed ei," "ed ella," "ond'elli."[8] The shift to dialogue is intended to inscribe the illusion of time into the text, to project it—like God's "visibile parlare"—into the fourth dimension. The text mimics speech, as the poet strives to recreate for the reader the confusion experienced by the pilgrim.[9] We recall that earlier the pilgrim's confusion was rendered by debates between his warring senses; this topos, whereby the eyes and ears are personified as speakers saying respectively yes and no, works to conflate the realm of the visual with the realm of the verbal, thus indicating the presence of a "visual speech." Significantly, whereas the earlier sensory debates were triggered by the engraving of David's dance, thus by "art," the visual debate of which Vergil speaks in line 117, the "tencione" engaged in by his eyes, is caused not by art but by "life" (or, more precisely, by life after death)—that is, by the perplexing shapes of the souls who inhabit this terrace.

The pilgrim's uncertainty as to what he sees—"non mi sembian persone, / e non so che, sì nel veder vaneggio" ("they do not seem to me persons, but I don't know what they are, my sight so wavers" [*Purg.* 10.113–14])—is redressed by Vergil, who, after noting that his eyes too "pria n'ebber tencione" ("first had debated" [117]), instructs his charge to look carefully and distinguish the human forms underneath the heavy stones they carry: "Ma guarda fiso là, e disviticchia / col viso quel che vien sotto a quei sassi" ("But look fixedly there, and disentangle with your eyes that which comes underneath those stones" [118–19]). Vergil's clearheadedness is, however, not reinforced by the poet, who ends canto 10 by once more blurring the distinctions between art and life; as earlier he accomplished this by way of an art that is described as real, now he turns to describing reality in terms of art. Thus, the contorted bodies of the approaching sinners are described as grotesque caryatids,[10] in a simile that forces us to think about what is real and what is not:

> Come per sostentar solaio o tetto,
>   per mensola talvolta una figura
>   si vede giugner le ginocchia al petto,
> la qual fa *del non ver vera rancura*
>   nascere 'n chi la vede; così fatti
>   vid'io color, quando puosi ben cura.

In the same way that, as corbel to support ceiling or roof, one sometimes sees a figure whose knees are joined to its chest, which sight—*although not real—creates real distress* in the one who sees it; just so did I see them fashioned, when I looked carefully.

(*Purg.* 10.130–35)

Although the caryatids are not real, the realism of their suffering bodies, their chests bent over to their knees, is such that it causes real pain in those who look at them: from their nonreal suffering—"del non ver"—comes the real distress—"vera rancura"—of the observer. This line, "la qual fa del non ver vera rancura," epitomizes the theme at the heart of this canto, the question the poet is posing throughout: what is reality, what is truth? The real people seem like sculptures, and the sculpted reliefs seem like real people: which is imitation and which is being imitated?

The canto's final sentence, following the simile of the caryatids, begins with "Vero è," a phrase that echoes "del non ver vera rancura" three lines above and subtly reinforces the narrator's claim to be a teller of truth, not merely a maker of art; the sentence continues by describing the appearance of the penitent prideful in greater detail:

Vero è che più e meno eran contratti
  secondo ch'avien più e meno a dosso;
  e qual più pazïenza avea ne li atti,
piangendo parea dicer: "Più non posso."

It is true that they were more or less contracted according as they had more or less on their backs; and he who had most patience in his acts, weeping, seemed to say: "I can no more."

(*Purg.* 10.136–39)

Canto 10 thus ends with a line of dialogue—"Più non posso"—ascribed by the narrator to the sufferers he observes but presented, interestingly, as direct discourse.[11] The phrase used to set up the direct discourse, "piangendo *parea dicer*," is much the same as that used earlier to set up the first words of the widow to the emperor: "La miserella intra tutti costor / *pareva dir*" (82–83). The presentation of the real sinners seems intended to recall the representation of the figured *vedovella*, as the use of direct discourse at the end of the canto recalls the divine dialogue of the third engraving. God's art is real, unlike other art; but then Dante's art, his text, is also an art that is charged with representing reality—as on this terrace it is charged with representing the reality of the reliefs. And so we find the programmatic use of a lexicon that blurs the boundary between the divine mimesis and the text that is charged with reproducing it: God's sculpted art is strangely textual, referred to as "un'altra *storia* ne la roccia imposta" ("another *story* imposed onto the rock" [52]), and "un'altra *istoria*, / che di dietro a Micòl mi biancheggiava" ("another *story*, that behind Michal was shining white" [71–72]). While the first two engravings are engraved, *intagliati* (the angel is "quivi intagliato in un atto soave" ["here engraved in a gentle act" (38)], the cart carrying the Ark of the Covenant "Era intagliato lì nel marmo stesso" ["was carved there in the same marble" (55)]), the third is "storïata," in the only use of *storiare* in the poem: "Quiv'era storïata l'alta gloria / del roman principato" ("here was *storied* the high glory of the Roman prince" [73–74]).[12] Thus, the *storia* of Trajan and the widow is "storïata," as though it were made of words rather than marble—as indeed it is.

The presentation of the examples of pride in canto 12 is also marked by an insistently representational lexicon. The sculpted vices are not on the *cornice*'s walls but trampled underfoot; as tombs bear signs identifying the remains within them ("portan *segnato* quel ch'elli eran pria" ["they bear the *signs* of what they were before" (*Purg.* 12.18)]), so these slabs are figured ("figurato") with designs more beautiful than those of earthly tombs because of the artistry—Dante uses "artificio," a hapax in the *Commedia*—of their divine maker:

> sì vid'io lì, ma di miglior sembianza
>   *secondo l'artificio, figurato*
>   quanto per via di fuor del monte avanza.

so I saw *figured* there as much as abuts from the mountain for a path, but of more beautiful appearance *because of the artistry*.

> (*Purg.* 12.22–24)

The figured ground is imitated by the figured text, which now launches into its own *artificio*, the acrostic whose *artificiosità*, frequently criticized, is in fact intended to imitate divine *artificio*:[13] of the thirteen tercets devoted to the thirteen examples of pride, four begin with "Vedea," four with "O," and four with "Mostrava," so that the first letters of the first twelve tercets spell VOM or UOM, graphically illustrating the role of pride in man's history.[14] The representational thrust of the reiterated "mostrava" hardly needs underscoring;[15] indeed, it should be noted that the words Dante chooses to build the *artificio* of *Purgatorio* 12 reflect the terrace's visual (*vedere*) and representational (*mostrare*) thematics, with the result that the acrostic is not an arbitrary appendage but is fully integrated into the text. The thirteenth tercet repeats the acrostic in condensed form, beginning each line with one of the three key words:

> Vedeva Troia in cenere e in caverne;
>   o Ilïón, come te basso e vile
>   *mostrava il segno* che lì si discerne!

I saw Troy in ashes and in caverns; O Ilium, how *the sign* that one discerns there *showed* you low and vile!

> (*Purg.* 12.61–63)

The "segno" representing Troy echoes the descriptions of Niobe, "*segnata* in su la strada" ("*marked* on the path" [38]), and Rehoboam, whose "segno" no longer threatens: "O Roboàm, già non par che minacci / quivi 'l tuo *segno*" ("O Rehoboam, now your *image* does not seem to threaten here" [46–47]).[16]

Rehoboam, son of Solomon, seems to have been assimilated to the sign that represents him: "'l tuo segno" establishes an identity between *res* and *signum* that reminds us that this is God's art, an art in which there is no gap between presentation and representation, is and as. It is noteworthy in this context that *segno* appears in the *Commedia* most often in the canto of providential history, *Paradiso* 6, where it refers to the imperial eagle: the "sacrosanto segno" (32), the "pubblico segno" (100), not a mere representational sign but the divine hieroglyph inscribed by God into the textuality of existence. Rhetorically, moreover, Dante's use of *segno* as a personified subject in *Paradiso* 6 has the effect of making the sign an actor, of achieving a conflation between the *signum* that represents and the *res* that does. The string of tercets in which *segno* governs the verb *fare* ("Tu sai ch'el fece" [*Par.* 6.37], "E sai ch'el fé" [40], "Sai quel ch'el fé" [43], "E quel che fé" [58], "Quel che fé" [61], "Di quel che fé" [73]) culminates in the lines where the *segno*, far from being a word, is the active force that constrains Justinian to find the words with which he now speaks: "Ma ciò che 'l segno che parlar mi face / fatto avea prima e poi era fatturo" ("But that which the sign that makes me speak had done before and after was to do" [82–83]). The poem's most concentrated use of *segno* and *segnare* belongs to the heaven of justice, the eagle's home; indeed, if viewed from the perspective of representational issues, this heaven seems fashioned as a kind of celestial extension of the terrace of pride. Not only does it contain the *Commedia's* only acrostic outside *Purgatorio* 12,[17] but also Dante's only use of the term *storia* outside *Purgatorio* 10: in *Paradiso* 19, *storia* refers to the actual events accomplished on earth by the eagle of justice, the events that men praise but fail to emulate ("commendan lei, ma non seguon la storia" ["they praise it [the memory of the eagle], but do not follow its example" (*Par.* 19.18)]). In fact, this heaven is full of pictorial, representational, textual, linguistic, and grammatical terminology: we note "consonante," "contesto," "dipingere," "dipinto," "emme," "essemplo," "favella," "figura," "image," "imagine," "imprenta," "incostro," "lettere," "nome," "penna," "ritrarre," "scrittura," "verbo," "versi," "vocabol," "vocale," "volume," and even *rappresentare*, in one of its two appearances in the poem.[18] Some relatively common words, like *scrivere*, appear in this heaven in unusual density; others, like "vocale," "consonante," and "contesto" (the past participle of *contessere*) constitute hapax legomena. The heaven of justice contains the poem's only verse to unite the verbs *leggere* and *scrivere* ("e quivi non è chi ragioni / di Cristo né chi legga né chi scriva" ["and none is there who speaks nor reads nor writes of Christ" (19.71–72)]); the very leitmotif of the *Paradiso*, the canticle's concern with the paradox of the one and the many, here finds a linguistico-grammatical focus in the conundrum of the eagle that sounds forth in the first-person singular while representing a collective that would normally use the first-person plural ("e sonar ne la voce e 'io' e 'mio,' / quand'era nel concetto e 'noi' e 'nostro'" ["sounding with its voice both 'I' and 'mine,' when it was in concept both 'we' and 'our'" (19.11–12)]).

The concern for representation that all this lexical activity denotes finds its fullest expression in the divine script whose letters are formed by the souls of this heaven:[19]

> Mostrarsi dunque in cinque volte sette
>   vocali e consonanti; e io notai
>   le parti sì, come mi parver dette.

"DILIGITE IUSTITIAM," primai
  fur verbo e nome di tutto 'l dipinto;
"QUI IUDICATIS TERRAM," fur sezzai.
Poscia ne l'emme del vocabol quinto
  rimasero ordinate . . .

They showed themselves then in five times seven vowels and consonants, and I
noted the parts as they were spelled for me. "DILIGITE IUSTITIAM" were the first
verb and noun of the whole design, "QUI IUDICATIS TERRAM" the last. Then, in the
M of the fifth word, they remained ordered . . .

(Par. 18.88–95)

Moving into the shape of an eagle, the souls become a pictogram of sorts: "la
testa e 'l collo d'un'aguglia vidi / rappresentare a quel distinto foco" ("the
head and the neck of an eagle I saw represented by that patterned fire" [Par.
18.107–8]). As God is an artist on the terrace of pride, so here he is a writer
and painter: "Quei che dipinge lì, non ha chi 'l guidi" ("He who paints there
has none who guides him" [Par. 18.109]). And, lest we miss the connection
to Purgatorio 10, it is underscored again in Paradiso 20, where we find
among the just souls of this heaven the same two figures who, with the
Virgin, served as purgatorial examples of humility: the introduction of
David as "il cantor de lo Spirito Santo, / che l'arca traslatò di villa in villa"
("the singer of the Holy Spirit, who transferred the ark from town to town"
[Par. 20.38–39]) cannot but recall the second engraving, in which David
performed his humble dance before the ark; likewise Trajan is "colui che . . .
la vedovella consolò del figlio" ("he who consoled the widow for her son"
[Par. 20.44–45]), in an overt reprise of the episode that forms the subject of
the third relief.[20]
    Dante's transposition of representational concerns from the terrace of
pride to the heaven of justice reflects a move from the sign in "art" to the
sign in "life." The storia told by the eagle does not seem to be but is God's
providential history; the segno of Paradiso 6 is not an artifact but the eagle—
history—itself. When God chooses to write, the signs he uses are human
souls. At the same time, however, that there is a bow toward the mimetic
hierarchy implicit in this transition, Dante's design works dialectically, for
the whole point regarding the divine art of Purgatorio 10 and 12 is that it is
equivalent to reality. The mimetic hierarchy is invoked only to be undercut:
this is art that is not so much lifelike ("verisimilar") as somehow akin to life
("ver") itself. This crucial fact about God's art is stated conclusively at the
end of the episode, where the submerged paradox is fully articulated: "Morti
li morti e i vivi parean vivi: / non vide mei di me chi vide il vero" ("The dead
seemed dead and the living alive: he who saw the truth saw no better than
I" [Purg. 12.67–68]). The onlooker who witnessed these events when they
first occurred, when they were "true"—"chi vide il vero"—did not see more

clearly than the pilgrim who observes them now, produced by God in such a way that what seems—"Morti li morti e i vivi *parean* vivi"—is also what is: "non vide mei di me chi vide *il vero*." In God's representation art and truth, seeming and being, have merged, have become one, so that there is ultimately no difference between being a sign in God's reality and a sign in his art: Rehoboam, the "segno" etched by God in the marble of *Purgatorio* 12, is as much a part of the providential design as the souls in the eagle, the "segno" fashioned by God in *Paradiso* 18. But the dialectical nature of Dante's design inscribes a more radical suggestion into our consciousness: the various techniques for blurring the boundary between art and life employed in the representation of the reliefs also serve to blur the distinction between God's representation and the representation that represents it. The speech patterns of the real sinners recall those of the *vedovella* for the same reason that the poet follows God's art with the simile of the caryatids, designed to sustain rather than lessen our confusion regarding the relative status of art and nature, imitator and imitated. Dante thus suggests an analogy between God's art and his own, the *storia* in which God's *storia* is *storiata*; his rhetorical strategies for rendering the "visibile parlare" of the engravings work to suggest the interchangeability of the two artists and to approximate on the page what God did in stone.[21] And what are Dante's textual goals if not the achievement of a supreme realism, an art in which "the dead seem dead and the living alive" (and—I cannot resist adding—in which the dead are alive and the living, occasionally, dead)?

Dante is not unaware of the dangers inherent in such goals, the dangers of claiming that his subject is "quella materia ond'io son fatto scriba" ("that matter of which I am made the scribe" [*Par.* 10.27]). His awareness causes him not to desist from what he is doing but to invoke the figure of Ulysses, who functions in the *Commedia* as a lightning rod placed in the poem to attract and defuse the poet's consciousness of his presumption in anointing himself *scriba Dei*. Among the examples of pride, therefore, we find Arachne, accompanied by the adjective "folle," which signals Ulysses and reminds us that she is his surrogate in the sphere of art:[22]

O folle Aragne, sì vedea io te
   già mezza ragna, trista in su li stracci
   de l'opera che mal per te si fé.

O mad Arachne, I saw you already half spider, wretched on the rags of the work that evilly by you was done.

(*Purg.* 12.43–45)

Although commentators have routinely indicated the *Metamorphoses* as the source of this exemplum, none to my knowledge has noted that Ovid's account of Arachne and Dante's terrace of pride share an authorial self-consciousness that is underscored by their common use of ecphrasis, or that the Ovidian story demonstrates the dangers of human representation in a way that is extremely suggestive in the context of *Purgatorio* 10–12.[23] Like Daedalus, Arachne is famous for her art ("non illa loco nec origine gentis / clara, sed arte fuit" ["she was famous not for place of birth or ancestry, but for her art" (*Metam*. 6.7–8)]), the art of weaving in which she will yield pride of place not even to Minerva.[24] Like Phaeton, whose steeds run wild ("ruunt" [2.167, 204]), Arachne, called "temeraria" ("reckless" [6.32]), rushes to her fate: "in sua fata ruit" (6.51). Ovid's language underscores the connection between textile pursuits and textuality: when Arachne challenges the goddess to a contest, the narrator describes how the contestants set up their webs ("intendunt . . . telas" [54]), how different colors are woven ("texitur" [62]) onto the loom, and finally how each embroiders into her fabric an ancient story ("vetus . . . argumentum" [69]). As God inscribes his warnings into stone, so Minerva (for whom Ovid interchanges verbs like "pingit" and "inscribit") attempts to warn her rival ("aemula" [83]) with embroidered examples ("exemplis" [83]). But, if the goddess's work is so effective that one of her figures appears to weep ("lacrimare videtur" [100]), Arachne's is such that not only does Europa seem to be looking back and calling to her companions on the shore, but an observer would think that the bull and the sea were real: "verum taurum, freta vera putares" (104).

Arachne, *aemula* indeed, matches verisimilitude with greater verisimilitude. Thematically, too, Arachne is the goddess's rival, answering Minerva's pictures of stately gods and humbled mortals with pictures of deceitful gods and violated mortals. Minerva's "text" is double: it shows the gods gathered for an artistic creation of sorts, the naming of Athens, and, in the corners, it depicts men and women changed from their original forms as punishment for their presumption; those who dared to emulate the gods ("nomina summorum sibi qui tribuere deorum" ["who attributed to themselves the names of the most high gods" (89)]) have become a frame to set off the gods' accomplishments. Arachne counters with an act of creation that is not only as accomplished as Minerva's—"Non illud Pallas, non illud carpere Livor / possit opus" ("Not Pallas, not Envy, could criticize that work" [129–30])—but that sets out to expose the gods' failings; her Olympians use their powers not to create a great city but to adopt other shapes in order to deceive and seduce. Both embroiderers weave miniature versions of the text that tells their tale, Ovid's *Metamorphoses*: Minerva shows the metamorphoses of men, Arachne the metamorphoses of gods, Ovid the metamorphoses of both.[25] In this passage, then, Ovid depicts a depicting strangely like his own; like Dante on the terrace of pride, he seems aware of the perils of his own project. In other words, Dante's representational awareness is informed by Ovid, as testified by the similarly Ovidian self-consciousness that inspires Dante's handling of another representational touchstone, the

Daedalus/Icarus story. Unlike later poets, Dante focuses not on the reckless sunward flight of the youth but rather, like Ovid, on the calculated risk of the creator.[26] For him the myth's protagonist is Daedalus, and its dramatic core is the drama of the artist's creation and consequent responsibility: while Icarus pitifully feels the unfeathering that dooms him ("Icaro misero le reni / sentì spennar per la scaldata cera"), his father is caught up in an agon of choice ("gridando il padre a lui 'Mala via tieni!'" [*Inf.* 17.109–11]). Thus, it is not Icarus who loses himself, but the father/artifex who loses his son, becoming "quello / che, volando per l'aere, il figlio perse" ("the one who, flying through the air, lost his son" [*Par.* 8.125–26]).

In the Latin poem, Minerva, enraged at the perfection of Arachne's mimesis, destroys her rival's representations ("rupit pictas" [131]); in *Purgatorio* 12, the Arachnean designs that proudly decorated Geryon's flanks have become "stracci / de l'opera che mal per te si fé," tattered remnants of the ill-conceived project on which she embarked. Arachne's will to transgress is crushed, like that of Ulysses. The terrace of pride is laced with Ulyssean language because of the poet's consciousness of being on the edge: is not his attempt to cross the boundary between nature and art, truth and imitation, animate and inanimate, a *varco folle*?[27] Thus, Dante's comparison of himself and Oderisi to yoked oxen—"Di pari, come buoi che vanno a giogo" ("Together, like oxen that go yoked" [*Purg.* 12.1])—is part of a strategy to counter the implicit charge that he is like presumptuous Uzzah. Uzzah's presumption is evoked in canto 10's second engraving of "the cart and the oxen, pulling the holy ark, *because of which men fear offices not given in charge*" ("lo carro e ' buoi, traendo l'arca santa, / *per che si teme officio non commesso*" [56–57]); Uzzah was struck down for daring to steady the Ark of the Covenant, and his fate serves as a warning to those who would take on a duty not expressly assigned to them, "officio non commesso." Dante, moreover, worries that he is considered a presumptuous Uzzah in the Epistle to the Italian cardinals, but, as he there explains, the analogy is not apt, because he directs his attention not to the ark itself but to the recalcitrant oxen who lead it astray.[28] Because Dante-poet's extraordinary handling of the terrace of pride cannot fail to make us wonder whether his is an *officio commesso*, he lets us know that he is not like Uzzah (or therefore like the other examples of pride whom Uzzah anticipates), nor like the recalcitrant oxen of the Epistle, but rather like a humble and well-behaved ox doing its assigned job, its *officio commesso*. Significantly, the same language was employed to communicate the all-important divine sanction accorded the pilgrim's journey, the poem's most clamorous example of otherwise presumptuous human activity: "Tal si partì da cantare alleluia / *che mi commise quest'officio novo*" ("Such a one departed from singing alleluia who *committed to me this new office*" [*Inf.* 12.88–89]), says Vergil to the centaurs, indicating that his "officio novo" of otherworld guide was assigned him by the highest authority.

For the same reason, Vergil addresses his charge in language that establishes him as a positive Ulysses, saying "Lascia lui e varca; / ché qui è buono con l'ali e coi remi, / quantunque può, ciascun pinger sua barca" ("Leave him and pass on; for here it is good that with wings and oars each push his boat as much as he can" [*Purg.* 12.4–6]). *Here*, in purgatory, it is good—"qui è buono"—to do what Ulysses should not have done: to push one's boat with wings and oars, to leap, to bound, to vault, to fly. A Ulyssean caveat is also woven into the Lord's Prayer that opens canto 11, where the extended gloss on humility takes on a pointedly Ulyssean tone:

> Vegna ver' noi la pace del tuo regno,
>   *ché noi ad essa non potem da noi,*
>   s'ella non vien, *con tutto nostro ingegno.*

> May the peace of your kingdom come toward us, *for we cannot reach it on our own,* if it does not come, *with all our intellect.*
>
> (Purg. 11.7–9)

By warning us that God's kingdom cannot be achieved "con tutto nostro ingegno," the souls recall the failed journeys of those who attempted to fly on what Beatrice will later call the short wings of reason ("la ragione ha corte l'ali" [*Par.* 2.57]). Other Ulyssean innuendos include the wavelike rock through which the travelers must pass, "una pietra fessa, / che si moveva e d'una e d'altra parte, / sì come l'onda che fugge e s'appressa" ("a cleft rock, that moved from one to the other side like the wave that flees and draws near" [*Purg.* 10.7–9]), Vergil's suggestion that "Qui si conviene usare un poco d'arte" ("Here we must use a little art" [*Purg.* 10.10]), which recalls Ulysses' *arte* in *Inferno* 26.61, and the appearances of *varco* or *varcare* in each of this terrace's three cantos, the only such geographical concentration of these terms in the poem.

Dante's evocation of Uzzah, a figure whom in the Epistle he associates with his own possible writerly presumption in daring to critique the Church, serves warning regarding the tensions at the core of this episode. At the center of *Purgatorio* 11, and thus at the center of the *cornice*, is Oderisi's famous speech on the "vana gloria de l'umane posse" ("vain glory of human powers" [91]), a speech that picks up the admonition inscribed into the Lord's Prayer and—combined with the chastening effect of God's miraculous art, an art that literally flanks canto 11—serves to bring us back to the idea of this terrace as an extended exercise in humility. And yet, also in Oderisi's speech, also at the terrace's center, are words that alert us to the fact that the apparent humility of this terrace cannot be taken at face value. I refer to the words Dante puts into the miniaturist's mouth regarding a third poet who will surpass his predecessors in "la gloria de la lingua" (*Purg.* 11.98); as Giotto surpassed Cimabue, so Guido Cavalcanti has surpassed Guido Guinizzelli, "e forse è nato / chi l'uno e l'altro caccerà del nido" ("and perhaps he is born who will chase the one and the other from the nest" [98–99]). This veiled but nonetheless powerful reference to his own poetic supremacy in prideful terms on the terrace of pride is far from casual; in fact, Dante will shortly tell us that when he returns to purgatory he expects to spend time on the terrace of pride, thus confirming the self-portrait generated by the assertion of his poetic pride in canto 11.[29] The poet deliberately writes Oderisi's prideful words and places them at the center of the terrace where they are most apposite but least expected, for the same reason that he makes the question of art and representation central to this terrace alone. For although we find figures of poets elsewhere, and the thematization of poetic concerns, nowhere else in the poem does the poet dramatize representation as he does on the terrace of pride. This is because there is no issue that cuts so close to the marrow of his own poetic pride: Dante celebrates himself as the poetic correlative of Giotto, an artist who was celebrated for aspiring to total verisimilitude,[30] because he knows—perhaps better than we—what is at stake in his imitation of the divine mimesis, as he knows that he has surpassed Guinizzelli and Cavalcanti, and as he knows that Oderisi's words on the vanity of earthly fame apply to no one as little as to himself. The answer to Oderisi's rhetorical question, "Che voce avrai tu più, se vecchia scindi / da te la carne, che se fossi morto / anzi che tu lasciassi il 'pappo' e 'l 'dindi,' / pria che passin mill'anni?" ("What more fame will you have if you put off your flesh when it is old than if you had died before leaving 'pappo' and 'dindi,' when a thousand years have passed?" [*Purg.* 11.103–6]), may be, for most of us, that it would make no difference at all whether we died as infants or as old men, but Dante knows—and intends us to know that he knows—that he is one to whom this rule does not apply. Oderisi's framing of the question in verbal terms—his reference to dying young as dying when one's speech is limited to baby talk, to "in-fancy" in its etymological sense of speechlessness, and his use of "voce" for "fama"—heightens our awareness of the passage's double-edged thrust: with respect to a divinely inspired poet, one invested with a divinely sanctioned poetic mission, it is important that he live beyond the ability to say "pappo" and "dindi," and it will be important in a thousand years.

The theme of fame running through these cantos takes the form of an emphasis on names that first surfaces in canto 11, where Omberto Aldobrandesco, after referring to the pilgrim as one "ch'ancor vive e non si noma" ("who still lives and does not name himself" [*Purg.* 11.55]), sets up the relation between names and pride: "Guiglielmo Aldobrandesco fu mio padre; / non so se 'l nome suo già mai fu vosco" ("Guiglielmo Aldobrandesco was my father; I do not know if his name was ever known to you" [59–60]). Later on, Oderisi's deflating discourse will provide a gloss to these verses by establishing the vanity of all names. First pointing to the mute Provenzan Salvani as one whose name once resounded through all Tuscany but now is barely remembered ("Toscana sonò tutta; / e ora a pena in Siena sen pispiglia" ["all Tuscany resounded, and now they barely whisper in Siena" (110–11)]), Oderisi makes fame a function of one's name: "La vostra nominanza è color d'erba, / che viene e va" ("Your renown is the color of grass, which comes and goes" [115–16]). Oderisi's point is that our "nominanza"—our fame, our glory, our "nameability"—is, like all human constructs, evanescent. This precept is frequently perceived as the central lesson of this terrace. But, in a prime example of how isolating a moral dictum from the prismatic polysemy of the text may prevent us from appreciating the implications of its unfolding action (and, in this sense, from noticing what the poet has actually done as compared to what he says), exclusive focus on Oderisi's words fails to take into account the challenge the text poses the miniaturist's lesson.[31] Thus, although Omberto condemns the excessive pride that was his undoing, he does not recoil from suggesting that his death is known to all the Sienese and to every person (but note Dante's choice of the term "fante": literally, every speaker) in Campagnatico: "ch'io ne mori', come i Sanesi sanno, / e sallo in Campagnatico ogne fante" ("I died of it, as the Sienese know, and as everyone in Campagnatico knows" [65–66]). The fact that his death—and thus his name—is on every tongue (hence the use of "fante") contrasts with Oderisi's statement, in the canto's next sequence, on the vanity of all names. By the same token, immediately following Oderisi's discourse, in fact right after he has explained that our "nominanza è color d'erba," the pilgrim responds by thanking the miniaturist for the lesson in humility ("Tuo vero dir m'incora / bona umiltà" ["Your true speech fills my heart with good humility" (118–19)]) and then asks, despite our *nominanza* being the color of grass: "ma chi è quei di cui tu parlavi ora?" ("but who is that one of whom you just spoke?" [120]). "Quelli è," Oderisi answers, "Provenzan Salvani" ("He is Provenzan Salvani" [121]), and once more the drama has exploded the moral lesson, for, in order for his presumption to be indicted, Provenzan's name must be registered.

My point is that, despite Oderisi's speedy substitution of his own name by Franco Bolognese's, and despite his insistence that earthly fame is but a breath of wind ("Non è il mondan romore altro ch'un fiato / di vento" [100–101]) that brings new names to the fore arbitrarily, merely because it changes its location ("e muta nome perché muta lato" [102]), the text, being historically grounded, requires names, cannot help but celebrate them. The same paradox may be observed in *Paradiso* 16, where the listing of Florentine families by name celebrates their historical specificity at the same time that it dramatically highlights their evanescence—these are names we no longer know. Since the *nomina*—the signs—used by this poet are grounded in things, are *consequentia rerum*, according to the dictum of the *Vita Nuova*, they are not mutable, not mere breaths of wind. In this text, names stand for historical existences, names are tied to essences, and essences are not evanescent but irreducible. Thus, Omberto, Provenzan, even Oderisi are *nomina* that must have their *nominanza*, for they are names in a text whose mode is akin to that of the reliefs, a text whose art is grounded in reality.[32] If one is such an artist, may not one be legitimately proud of one's *nominanza*? This is the question that haunts the absent name at the heart of this terrace, an absent name that is still in the poet's thoughts a few cantos later, when the pilgrim refuses to oblige Guido del Duca by stating his name and seems motivated less by humility than by the thought that he has not yet made a sufficient name for himself, i.e., that his fame has not yet achieved its full dimensions: "dirvi ch'i' sia, saria parlare indarno, / ché 'l nome mio ancor molto non suona" ("to tell you who I am would be to speak in vain, for my name does not yet much resound" [*Purg.* 14.20–21]). Although the use of the verb *suonare* echoes Oderisi's description of the renown once accorded Provenzan Salvani ("Toscana sonò tutta"), the pilgrim does not seem to have internalized the miniaturist's moral, at least not with respect to his identity as a poet. The verses's apparent humility and prideful core—"'l nome mio *ancor* molto non suona"—provides an emblem for the terrace of pride, where on the one hand the pilgrim learns humility while on the other the poet reproduces God's divine mimesis: visible speech, life itself.

Dante knows that the words Beatrice speaks to Vergil, when she greets him as one "di cui la fama ancor nel mondo dura, / e durerà quanto 'l mondo lontana" ("whose fame still lasts in the world, and will last as long as the world" [*Inf.* 2.59–60]), are true of himself. He knows that whatever fame can be had will be his. Indeed, he is extremely candid about his own fame, writing as early as the *De vulgari eloquentia* that the *vulgare illustre* confers on its practitioners greater fame than that of kings: "Nonne domestici sui reges, marchiones, comites et magnates quoslibet fama vincunt?" ("Do not its servants surpass in renown kings, marquises, counts, and magnates?" [1.17.5]). He does not consider this unimportant; rather, he deals with this self-knowledge by trying to put it into perspective, for instance by comparing textual life to eternal life in the Brunetto Latini episode. But for all that *Inferno* 15 sounds a clear warning against the accumlation of glory, reminding us that the form of immortality it confers is sterile at best, even here the issues are not as straightforward as they might appear to be. Here too the passage is Ovidian: Brunetto's claim to "live" in his text ("Sieti raccomandato il mio Tesoro, / nel qual io vivo ancora" ["Let me recommend to you my *Tesoro*, in which I live still" (*Inf.* 15.119–20)]) echoes the end of the *Metamorphoses*; Ovid will live—his poem's last word is "vivam"—as a result of the fame procured by what he calls, also in the poem's final verses, his *indelebile nomen*. That Dante associated the concept of *nominanza*—the fame one can achieve through one's name—with his classical authors is demonstrated by his use of the word: "nominanza" appears in the *Commedia* only in *Purgatorio* 11 and in *Inferno* 4, where it is also coupled with the verb *suonare* and refers to the classical figures of limbo. Dante suggests, scandalously enough, that the resounding of their honored "nominanza" has won them grace in heaven: "L'onrata nominanza / che di lor suona sù ne la tua vita, / grazïa acquista in ciel che sì li avanza" ("Their honored fame, which resounds in your life above, acquires grace in heaven that thus advances them" [*Inf.* 4.76–78]). The association is significant, for the same tensions that afflict Dante with regard to his classical authors afflict him with regard to his personal quest for *nominanza*. Dante's relationship to his own fame, like his relation to classical antiquity, is far more complex and tortured than is implied by the cliché that views him as relegating fame univocally to hell. His prehumanist *forma mentis* (I use this label with full consciousness of its inadequacy vis-à-vis a poet who was far too radical to be embraced or understood by the genuinely and merely prehumanist avant-garde of his own day)[33] is reflected in the ambivalent, indeed paradoxical, positions he forges both with respect to classical antiquity and with respect to the value of his own literary glory.

The dialectic between fame and evanescence that runs through the terrace of pride manifests itself in full paradoxical vigor in the heaven of Mars, where our love for earthly things that cannot last is cast in an epic mode. Having weaned both pilgrim and reader from the desire for earthly affectivity in the heaven of Venus, where eros rather than be celebrated even in redeemed form was deflected by politics, Dante stages the resurfacing of earthly affectivity—of "ardente affetto" (*Par.* 15.43)—when and where we no longer expect it, in the bellicose heaven of Mars, a historical triptych of thesis, antithesis, and synthesis: *Paradiso* 15 creates the mythical moment outside of time and history, *Paradiso* 16 returns us to the world of time and to the sorrow of history, while *Paradiso* 17 offers some measure of consolation, through the epic memorialization of history and those who achieved fame before they died.[34] This is the heaven where the first person historical reaches an apotheosis of personalized bliss, diving Glaucus-like into the profoundest depths "de la *mia* gloria e del *mio* paradiso" ("of *my* glory and of *my* paradise" [*Par.* 15.36]). And personalized bliss consists of the indelibly historical: a bloodline (Cacciaguida), a natal place (Florence), a language—the vernacular—that fathers and mothers delight to use ("l'idïoma / che prima i padri e le madri trastulla" [*Par.* 15.122–23]). Despite the pervading consciousness that "time goes around with its scissors" ("lo tempo va dintorno con le force" [*Par.* 16.9]), with the result that "your things all have their deaths"—"Le vostre cose tutte hanno lor morte" (*Par.* 16.79)—in this heaven *le nostre cose* are lovingly caressed. The narrator's proleptic warning against the love of that which does not last—"amor di cosa che non duri (15.11)—is balanced, even more proleptically, by the souls' desire for their dead bodies, expressed in the sequence that immediately precedes the pilgrim's ascent to Mars:

> Tanto mi parver sùbiti e accorti
>   e l'uno e l'altro coro a dicer "Amme!"
>   che ben mostrar disio d'i corpi morti:
> forse non pur per lor, ma per le mamme,
>   per li padri e per li altri che fuor cari
>   anzi che fosser sempiterne fiamme.

So sudden and eager both the one and the other chorus seemed to me in saying "Amen," that truly they showed desire for their dead bodies: maybe not only for themselves, but for their mothers, for their fathers, and for the others who were dear to them before they were eternal flames.

(*Par.* 14.61–66)

These souls are happily celebrating the future resurrection of their flesh, that most irreducible husk of selfhood, because only in the flesh will they fully experience their love for "those who were dear to them *before* they were eternal flames."[35] In other words, their desire for their dead bodies is an expression of their desire to love fully in heaven what they loved on earth: their "mamme," their "padri," and the "altri che fuor cari." The rhyme of *mamme* with *fiamme*, the flesh with the spirit, is one of Dante's most poignant envisionings of a paradise where earthly ties are not renounced but enhanced.

The tension of that rhyme between "mamme" and "fiamme" is explored and nuanced in the cantos that follow, where one of the "altri che fuor cari," one of the very "padri" imagined in canto 14, is brought forth. With him comes a full range of human affectivity and human caring, including affectivity of a rather dubious sort, such as that which motivates the pilgrim to glory in his ancestor's nobility. We remember the passage that opens *Paradiso* 16, where the poet marvels at the power of family lineage, "nobility of blood," which makes him take such pride in Cacciaguida (nor is the martyr immune from gratification at his descendent's own remarkable achievements) that he addresses him with the honorific *voi* despite being in heaven, where our desires cannot be skewed: "ché là dove appetito non si torce, /dico nel cielo, io me ne gloriai" ("for there where appetite is not twisted, I mean in heaven, I gloried in it" [*Par.* 16.5–6]). There is a paradox here, for the pilgrim is in paradise, where his appetite cannot err, and yet he indulges his pride in Cacciaguida in such a way as to cause Beatrice to indicate her awareness of his "transgression": she laughs, and the poet says that "she seemed the one who coughed at the first fault written of Guinevere" ("parve quella che tossio / al primo fallo scritto di Ginevra" [16.14–15]). The comparison seems compellingly clear: Guinevere's love led her to sin, to her "primo fallo." The lady of Malehaut's cough signified another's awareness of the transgression, as does Beatrice's laugh. But is the pilgrim's love a *fallo*? In order to inhabit the dialectical tension of these cantos, to experience the rhyme between "mamme" and "fiamme," we have to recognize that we are witnessing a paradox, for Beatrice does not cough but laughs. She does not censure—or censor—the pilgrim. Nor, in fact, does the poet, whose narrative moves from Beatrice's noncensoring laugh to the very words that the pilgrim spoke, words where the offending *voi* is repeatedly registered: "Voi siete il padre mio; / voi mi date a parlar tutta baldezza; / voi mi levate sì, ch'i' son più ch'io" ("You are my father, you give me all boldness to speak, you uplift me so that I am more than I" [16–18]). The interwoven *vois* and *mis* of these verses brandish the uncensored essence of these cantos: these are the cantos of the I's resurgence, the cantos of triumphant personal love, the cantos where the I is enhanced and enlarged ("so that I am more than I") by achieving a connectedness to its past—to its history, its dead self ("li vostri antichi" of 16.23), that part of its self that died but is still worth remembering.

These cantos are the *Commedia*'s epic core, complete with epic features like the "catalogue of ships"; the archaic and paradigmatically epic roll call from the *Iliad* takes new shape (via the *Aeneid*) in *Paradiso* 16's roster of forgotten but indelible Florentine names.[36] Here we find not the vanity of *nominanza* but the names that defy time and thwart oblivion; the fame of the "alti Fiorentini" may have been obscured by time ("nel tempo nascosa" [87]), but by naming them Cacciaguida seeks to restore their luster, and in some way, to restore them: "Io vidi li Ughi e vidi i Catellini, / Filippi, Greci, Ormanni e Alberichi" (88–89). By the same token, the later list of literally epic heroes (with its noteworthy assimilation of biblical heroes to those of medieval epic)—Joshua, Judas Maccabeus, Charlemagne, Roland, William of Orange and Renouard, Godfrey of Bouillon and Robert Guiscard—is prefaced by the statement that their renown is such that any muse would be rich with them: "fuor di gran voce, / sì ch'ogne musa ne sarebbe opima" (*Par.* 18.32–33). The poet stresses the act of naming—and thus memorializing—these heroes, each already recorded and remembered in his own epic, by his own muse: "quello ch'io nomerò" ("that one whom I will name" [18.35]) says Cacciaguida, echoed by the poet's "dal nomar Iosuè" ("at the naming of Joshua" [38]) and "al nome de l'alto Macabeo" ("at the name of the great Maccabeus" [40]). These names confer a kind of immortality because their bearers accomplished what Cacciaguida predicts of Cangrande, to wit, notable deeds: "notabili fier l'opere sue" (*Par.* 17.78). To the poet goes the epic task of recording—literally "noting"—these notable names and deeds, the task of remembering. If the passing of families is no surprise, given that cities themselves have their end ("poscia che le cittadi termine hanno" [*Par.* 16.78]), yet poets have the power, through the Muses, through their poetic gift, to grant longevity, not only to themselves but indeed to cities and kingdoms: "O diva Pegasëa che li 'ngegni / fai glorïosi e rendili longevi, / ed essi teco le cittadi e ' regni" ("O divine Pegasea, who make men of genius glorious and render them immortal, as they, through you, the cities and the kingdoms" [*Par.* 18.82–84]).

In these cantos of the *Paradiso*, Dante explores the ancient epic function of the poet who does not attenuate or flinch from the sorrows of the history he records but who yet invokes time's consolations—fame and memory—to counter time's scissors and their bitter corollary, the fact that "Le vostre cose tutte hanno lor morte." That all our things have their death is the fact that epics never forget (and with which they end: Hector's death, Turnus's death, Beowulf's death, Rodomonte's death), the fact that—in the gesture that makes them "epic"—they heroically and flimsily deny with words, the words that give life not only to the sung but to the singer. In epic fashion, Dante must tell the truth, because otherwise he fears to lose his future life among us, his readers, the ones who will call his time ancient: "temo di perder viver tra coloro / che questo tempo chiameranno antico" (*Par.* 17.119–20). And, true to the epic key of these cantos, Cacciaguida does not reprove the pilgrim for desiring life—"viver"—through his literary prowess; rather he incites him to tell the truth and provides him the literary formula most likely to guarantee his future life in words. The very coinage *infuturarsi*, used by Cacciaguida to refer to the pilgrim's future life in words, echoes the coinage *etternarsi* of the Brunetto episode;[37] but the *Paradiso* does not conform to the theological grid by confirming the vanity of literary immortality, the *Inferno*'s suggested impossibility of living in a text. Instead, these epic cantos recast Brunetto's message, empowering the poet to live in his words, among those "che questo tempo chiameranno antico." Nor does this poet grow indifferent to posterity's mandate; in the *Commedia*'s final canto, in a final epic surge, Dante still prays to be able to reach "la futura gente" with his poetry: "e fa la lingua mia tanto possente, / ch'una favilla sol de la tua gloria / possa lasciare a la futura gente" ("and make my tongue so powerful that one spark alone of your glory it may leave for future folk" [*Par.* 33.70–72]).

These issues, still vital in the *Paradiso*, are most exhaustively canvassed on purgatory's terrace of pride. Here the poet lets us know that his pride exists for good reason: if anyone's fame will endure, it will be his; if anyone's mimesis can rival God's, it is his. On the one hand these cantos tell of the enforced humility of the human artist, who—no longer tempted to "fly like

Daedalus" in the fashion of the falsifiers of *Inferno* 29—accepts his limits, constrained by a miraculous art, more real than nature herself, that he can never emulate. On the other hand these cantos speak of Dante's greatness and establish the poet as an Arachne, as *aemulus*; indeed, they constitute in themselves an Arachnean act of emulation. Thus, Dante's representation of God's art in *Purgatorio* 12 takes the form of a rivaling *artificio*: the acrostic spelling UOM, a form of visual poetry signifying man's sinful tendency toward pride, is also an example of the very pride it condemns, since it affords the poet—through the physical design of the letters on the page—a way of inscribing a visual art of his own into his representation of God's visual art and so of further conflating the two artists and their work. Similarly, the acrostic in the heaven of justice can be seen as the poet's imitation of the divine skywriting of that same heaven;[38] by carving the letters LUE into the text of *Paradiso* 19 Dante creates a visual reminder of and analogue to the letters DILIGITE IUSTITIAM QUI IUDICATIS TERRAM formed by the souls and written by God in the preceding canto. From this perspective, even the Lord's Prayer in *Purgatorio* 11 may be viewed dialectically. The prevailingly negative critical reaction to Dante's version of the Lord's Prayer is noted by Mario Marti, who ascribes it to a misunderstanding of the poet's intent: "S'è voluto mettere a confronto le terzine di Dante col dettato evangelico, come se il poeta avesse presunto di poter gareggiare e rivaleggiare con la spoglia essenzialità di Matteo" ("We have compared Dante's tercets to the evangelical script, as if the poet had presumed to contest and rival the stripped essentiality of Matthew").[39] In thus taking us to task for thinking that the poet might have presumed to rival the Gospel of Matthew, Marti unwittingly formulates the essence of this terrace's Arachnean poetics. For, why is the only prayer to be cited in full in the *Commedia* found on the terrace of pride? Although the glosses added to the words of the prayer are exhortations to humility, the presence of the prayer in canto 11 ensures that the terrace's central canto will contain an instance of the Arachnean art that distinguishes cantos 10 and 12: an instance of God's art (in this case, an instance of God's verbal rather than his visual art) elaborated, extended, commented on—in short, re-presented—by a man.

How then does Dante resolve the issues he seems to hold in unresolved resolution on the terrace of pride? What prevents us from concluding this chapter with the words Dante imagines in the mouths of the indignant Italian cardinals: "Who is this man who, not fearing the sudden punishment of Uzzah, raises himself toward the ark, wavering though it be?" ("et quis iste, qui Oze repentinum supplicium non formidans, ad arcam, quamvis labantem, se erigit?" [*Ep.* 11.9]).[40] His method is to extend the balanced tension of these cantos and, by embracing explicit paradox, to make it rigorous. The swath of metapoetic passages inscribed by Dante into his poem's core reaches its denouement on the terrace of wrath, at "live" center as it were, where not insignificantly the pilgrim experiences examples of meekness and anger in the form of ecstatic visions. These visions, which I believe Dante views as analogues to the *Commedia* itself, are dubbed "non falsi errori" (*Purg.* 15.117), in an elaboration of that original textual conundrum from the Geryon episode, "ver c'ha faccia di menzogna" (*Inf.* 16.124). With the paradox of nonfalse error Dante expresses the dilemma of art and provides the formula that synthesizes the various facets of the terrace of pride: all art is error, but some art—like his and God's—is nonfalse.

## Chapter 7

# NONFALSE ERRORS AND THE TRUE DREAMS OF THE EVANGELIST

> Mente ed umìle e più di mille sporte
> piene di spirti e 'l vostro andar sognando,
> me fan considerar che d'altra sorte
> non si pò trar ragion de vo' rimando.
> (*Onesto degli Onesti to Cino da Pistoia*)

ROM THE TIME OF Drythelm to the time of Charles the Fat, living voyagers traveled to the hereafter, leaving their bodies behind on earth to be returned to at journey's end. These journeys were considered to be 'real' by the men of the Middle Ages, even if they depicted them as 'dreams' (*somnia*)." So writes the historian Jacques Le Goff, in words that provide a context for Dante's experience.[1] Dante believed that his journey was, in some essential sense, real. But Dante differs from other medieval visionaries in at least one fundamental respect, namely, the immensity of his poetic gift: a gift that, paradoxically, induces subconscious suspensions of disbelief in his readers on the one hand and prevents them from taking him seriously as a visionary on the other. The claims of the "great prophet-visionaries of the twelfth and thirteenth centuries—Hildegard and Joachim, Mechthild and Marguerite," with whom Peter Dronke would like us to associate Dante,[2] are not as problematic to their readership as are Dante's—nor has their readership ever been as large. Dante's readers have, on the whole, always been able and willing to distinguish between a poet and a prophet, and they have categorized him as a poet. In fact, for all that Dante's early commentators felt the need to protect their poet from the charge of heresy by insisting on the allegory, it seems worth noting that Dante never succeeded in eliciting the attention from the Church that in our own day the novelist Salman Rushdie elicited from the Ayatollah Khomeini; for all that he put popes in hell, he never was condemned to death. (The Catholic willingness to accommodate commentators and glossators—the "decretalists" whom Dante so scorns[3]—is perhaps a factor here.) In other words, despite the confusion regarding the *theologus-poeta*, negative reactions like that of the Dominican Guido Vernani, and the placing of the *Monarchia* on the Index, Dante's audience—perhaps to his dismay (it seems to me at any rate distinctly possible that Dante, who considered himself not a decretalist but a new St. John, would have welcomed the dangers attendant on being taken more seriously as prophet and visionary)—considered him fundamentally a poet. Nor were they mistaken: Dante is a poet.[4] But—and this is crucial—he is a poet who used the means of poetry in the service of a vision that he believed to be true: a true dream, a nonfalse error.

While Dante scholars have been arguing among themselves as to whether the *Commedia* employs the allegory of poets or the allegory of theologians, elaborating a discourse that is not accessible even to other scholars of literature, historians of religion have gone ahead and calmly included Dante in their discussions of vision literature. In other words, while we continue to debate whether or not to consider the *Commedia* a vision, scholars in other disciplines have been working to understand the common ground that underlies all vision literature, including the *Commedia*. If we wish our more nuanced and complex sense of the *Commedia* to have any impact on such discussions, we must come to terms with the poem not only as a literary artifact but also as the record of a visionary experience. Cesare Segre's "*L'Itinerarium animae* nel Duecento e Dante" is a rare attempt by a literary scholar to deghettoize our reading of the *Commedia* by situating it among the lesser visionary works to which it is related. Perhaps because of our concern not to make the postivist error of seeing earlier visionary texts as sources of the *Commedia*, we tend to ignore them altogether, thus preserving Dante's text on its isolated high-culture peak. But, in fact, the question of literary dependence is problematic even with respect to the nongreat works that make up the bulk of the medieval visionary corpus, since, as Carol Zaleski points out, "it seems likely that at least some of these narratives reflect actual experience and as such cannot be reduced to a matter of mechanical literary dependence."[5]

As far as we can infer from Dante's elliptical comments, visionary sleep underlies the experience represented in the *Commedia*, whose author is "pien di sonno a quel punto / che la verace via abbandonai" ("full of sleep at that point when I abandoned the true path" [*Inf.* 1.11–12]), and whose vision draws to an end "perché 'l tempo fugge che t'assonna" ("because the time that puts you to sleep flees" [*Par.* 32.139]). These references to sleep at the beginning and end of the poem are important;[6] although the poet does not dwell on them, neither can they be conjured out of the text. I take their elusive presence as part of Dante's Pauline strategy, stemming from his need to veil in mystery the ultimate mode of an experience that he himself—like St. Paul—was unable to explain: "Scio hominem in Christo ante annos quatuordecim, sive in corpore *nescio*, sive extra corpus *nescio*, Deus scit, raptum huiusmodi usque ad tertium caelum" ("I know a man in Christ who fourteen years ago—whether in the body I *know not* or out of the body I *know not*, God knows—was caught up to the third heaven" [2 Cor. 12:2]).

In this way, we can bypass the choice we have presumed we have to make between Dante as a writer of realistic narrative (a "poet") and Dante as the recorder of a genuine mystical experience (a "visionary"). This is the choice that bedevils Michele Barbi as he attempts, in an influential passage, to gloss *Paradiso* 32.139, St. Bernard's "perché 'l tempo fugge che t'assonna":

> Non è qui il luogo di trattare la questione se Dante voglia far credere d'essere andato pei cieli col corpo o senza . . . io credo ch'egli voglia far intendere d'esserci stato corporalmente. Certo è che in tutta la *Commedia* dà a credere d'aver fatto un viaggio reale pei regni ultraterreni, non d'aver avuto una visione nel sonno.[7]

> This is not the place to treat the question of whether Dante wants us to believe that he journeyed through the heavens with his body or without . . . I believe that he wants us to understand him to have been there corporally. Certainly throughout the *Commedia* he gives us to understand that he took a real voyage through the otherworldly realms, not that he had a vision in sleep.

Barbi continues, hammering home the presumed incompatibility of vision with voyage:

> Dante non descrive una visione, ma un viaggio; e se s'incontra nel poema la parola *visione* riferita al complesso di ciò che descrive il poeta nell'opera sua (*Par.* 17.128), va intesa in senso oggettivo per "ciò che hai veduto."

> Dante does not describe a vision, but a voyage; and if one encounters in his poem the word *visione* referred to the entirety of what the poet describes in his work (as in *Par.* 17.128), it is to be understood objectively as "that which you saw." (295)

Despite the above, Barbi does in fact intuit the possibility that Dante could both insist he had been where he says he was and think he was the recipient of a true and prophetic vision. Although couched ambivalently, he comes close to proposing what I consider the correct solution—that of a visionary "waking sleep":

> O dobbiamo vederci un richiamo alla sua condizione di essere vivente, la quale non permette una troppo lunga vigilia . . . oppure s'intende che il poeta, rapito ormai nella contemplazione dei più profondi misteri, *quasi dormiens vigilaret* (son parole di S. Agostino a proposito del ratto di S. Paolo, e cfr. *Purg.* 29.144, ove l'autore dell'*Apocalisse* si vide "venir dormendo con la faccia arguta").

> Either we must see in the verse a recall of his condition as a human being, which does not permit too long a vigil . . . or we must understand that the poet, enraptured by now in contemplation of the most profound mysteries, was as though awake while sleeping, *quasi dormiens vigilaret*—these are words of St. Augustine's apropos the *raptus* of St. Paul, to be compared to *Purg.* 29.144, where the author of the Apocalypse is seen "to come forward sleeping with a piercing gaze." (294)

Here Barbi suggestively brings together, under the heading of waking sleep, Augustine's gloss of Paul's *raptus* in the twelfth book of the *De genesi ad litteram* and Dante's characterization of the old man representing the Apocalypse in the procession of the earthly paradise: Barbi represents Dante's condition as akin to that ascribed by Augustine to Paul and by Dante himself to the author of Revelation, whose "faccia arguta" pierces the veil to uncover the divine mysteries while he sleeps. Bernard's cryptic verse, "perché 'l tempo fugge che t'assonna," is thus to be understood with the help of Augustine on Paul: Dante is as though awake while sleeping, "quasi dormiens vigilaret," just like St. John, the author of the Apocalpyse. (It should be remembered that Dante entertained no doubts as to the identity of the apostle John, author of the fourth gospel, the "Vangelista" of *Inferno* 19, and John of Patmos, author of the Apocalypse.)[8] Even if Barbi's reading of Augustine is somewhat imprecise (Augustine's view of Paul's *raptus* is much less clear than Barbi suggests, nor have I been able to locate the words Barbi cites as Augustine's),[9] his reading of the *Commedia*—his linking of Dante's vision to Paul's and to John's—is, in my opinion, right on target. Barbi, however, goes on to attenuate the force of his insight, by denying that Bernard's words can refer to anything more than the vision of the last heaven; he denies, in the second passage cited above, that the word *visione* can refer to the sum of the pilgrim's experience, since Dante describes not a vision but a voyage. His ambivalence with respect to "perché 'l tempo fugge che t'assonna" has become canonical,[10] when, indeed, it has not been replaced by more absolute refusals to acknowledge the mystical quotient of Dante's experience.[11]

The excessive timidity with which we handle Dante's suggestions regarding what is clearly a mystical experience has its roots in the issues discussed in the first chapter: Dante's narrative realism and our desire to distinguish poets from prophets conspire to disallow this option. In other words, Dante's empiricism prevents us from acknowledging his mysticism. And yet Dante's empiricism is ultimately in the service of his mysticism; the problem is that the poetic strategies with which he constructs his empirical scaffolding are so effective that we are dissuaded from accepting their mystical foundation. We come full circle with Singleton's refusal to acknowledge the visionary nature of the *Commedia*, his paradoxical defense of the *Commedia*'s realism at the expense of its mysticism. Because he does not think in terms of a true vision, like the one revealed to St. John, Bernard's verse puts Singleton on the defensive; he is at pains to neutralize it so that it will not appear to contradict his tenet that the voyage described by Dante is real: "Since, within the poem, this journey to the afterlife has never been termed a *dream*, but has always been presented as *real*, it is not possible to understand this verse, with the verb *assonnare*, to contradict this fundamental postulate of the experience."[12] The irony of Singleton's position is that, in order to defend the historicity of the *Commedia*, he has recourse to reading it as metaphor: "*Assonnare* is thus not literal in its meaning but bears an allusion that makes it metaphorical. 'Sleep' is a falling away from the final experience, which must happen soon, for the mortal man's experience of the light of glory is most transitory." By the same token, the *sonno* of *Inferno* 1 must be taken metaphorically: "The 'sleep' is the sinful life in its forgetfulness of the good." Despite his insistence on the need to retrieve a medieval *forma mentis* in order to read the *Commedia*, Singleton fails to consider the most medieval possibility of all: a vision that is perceived—and conceived— as real.

While I am not suggesting that the sleep of the first canto must be taken exclusively in its literal sense, I am saying that its literal sense cannot continue to be summarily dismissed. I agree with Baldelli, who notes the critical contortions that have resulted from the refusal to accommodate the literal sense in *Paradiso* 32: "Sono passi che hanno tormentato i commentatori e specialmente quel *tempo* che *assonna*, è stato interpretato nei modi più incredibilmente contorti: ciò proprio perché se ne è rifiutata l'interpretazione letterale, recalcitrando a vedere nella *Commedia* una *visio in somniis*" ("They are passages that have tormented commentators, and especially that 'time' that 'puts to sleep,' which has been interpreted in the most incredibly contorted ways: this precisely because we have refused the literal interpretation, in our stubborn resistance to seeing in the *Commedia* a *visio in somniis*").[13] Such recalcitrance has, in one of the critical ironies that beset Dante studies, been a common feature among scholars who otherwise have little in common: Mazzoni, with his overt disapproval of all readers (including Guido da Pisa) who take the *Commedia* as more than a "poem," and Singleton, despite his insistence on the historical veridicity of the text, are in agreement that there is no visionary component to the pilgrim's "sonno."[14] This approach has continued to hold sway; recently, in support of an exclusively metaphorical reading of the pilgrim's sleep against the "misapprehension" occasioned by the word *sonno*, Anthony Cassell has insisted that "the metaphor of sleep as a symbol of habitual sin is a patristic commonplace."[15]

However, the possibility of experiencing a true vision while the body remains on earth in apparent sleep is an even more pervasive medieval commonplace, theorized by Augustine in book 12 of the *De genesi ad litteram* and adopted in an abundant popular literature. Thurkill is described as "lying senseless on his bed—as if oppressed with a heavy sleep—for two days and nights," while Tundale "lay dead for three days and three nights"; the monk of Evesham too appears almost dead, and returns to himself "as if waking out of a deep sleep."[16] Most importantly for our purposes, such a premise does not pave the way for an abstract and disembodied visionary experience; rather, these accounts are infused with an insistence on the physical reality of the experiences, an insistence that renders the status of the body highly ambiguous. Furseus, after returning, bears the physical marks of the fire that he had felt in his soul: "When he was restored to his body, and throughout his whole life, on his shoulder and jaw he bore the mark of the fire that he had felt in his soul, visible to all men" (55). Likewise Tundale suffers great physical torment,[17] while Thurkill's apparently lifeless body coughs at the same time as does his spirit in the otherworld. In his analysis of the generic elements that characterize visions and voyages, Segre claims that Dante chooses the vision as his model, then adds elements that pertain to the voyage, notably geographical precision and the presence of his journeying body.[18] In fact, what Dante does is to blur further the already blurred lines between vision and voyage, which are in any case much less clearly defined than Segre suggests. Segre's assertion that, in visions, "il viaggio viene compiuto dalla sola anima, mentre il corpo resta fermo" ("the journey is accomplished by the soul alone, while the body stays still" [13]) is insufficiently nuanced; as Zaleski declares, there is no "coherent rule for the interpretation of visions," precisely because of their ambiguity regarding the status of the body: "Many ambiguities remain, all related to a central question: was the visionary still attached to a body, and, if so, what bearing does this have on the validity of the vision?"[19] In maintaining an ambiguity that characterizes otherworld journeys of all periods,[20] Dante is deliberately following his avowed and greatest model, St. Paul, whose ambiguity regarding the corporeality of his *raptus* did not prevent the early Church fathers from viewing it as a real event.[21] Paul's uncertainty is carefully echoed by Dante at the beginning of *Paradiso* in Paul's own language: the apostle's "sive in corpore nescio, sive extra corpus nescio, Deus scit" becomes Dante's "S'i' era sol di me quel che creasti / novellamente, amor che 'l ciel governi, / tu 'l sai" ("If I was only that part of me that you created last [i.e., the soul], love that governs the heavens, you know it" [*Par.* 1.73–75]).[22] Dante thus intimates the presence of his body in heaven in a veiled and indirect manner that is undoubtedly suggested by the Pauline model.[23]

There need not be a conflict between "vision" and "voyage." To rid ourselves of any contradiction we need only fully accept the analogy that Dante proposes between himself and St. Paul. In choosing Paul as a model, Dante chooses a precursor who "went" as well as "saw"; further, he chooses a precursor who left his mode of going notoriously unexplained, so that an exegetical tradition grew up devoted to explaining what the apostle says he does not know and, increasingly, to debating whether or not Paul saw God in his essence. Dante adopts Augustine's controversial affirmative position on this question (adopted also by Thomas, presumably out of deference to Augustine).[24] Refining the nature of Dante's debt to Augustine, Francis X. Newman suggested that each canticle of the *Commedia* corresponds to one of Augustine's three categories of vision: in hell the pilgrim sees according to *visio corporalis*, in purgatory according to *visio spiritualis* or *imaginativa*, and in paradise according to *visio intellectualis*.[25] In light of Augustine's classification of John's vision as imaginative and Paul's as intellectual, Newman is able to draw a neat correlation to the endings of *Purgatorio* and *Paradiso*: "If the climax of *Paradiso* recalls the Pauline *raptus*, the masque which concludes *Purgatorio* recalls Apocalypse in its imaginative splendor" (69). However, his scheme contradicts the evidence of the poem, in which the pilgrim seems to be present in the flesh in all three realms; Dante does not tell us, as Newman's scheme would imply, that the pilgrim was corporeally in hell, imaginatively in purgatory, and intellectually in paradise but that he was corporeally in hell, purgatory, and (most problematically) paradise. Therefore, the three types of Augustinian vision can be applied, at best, as metaphors for the differences in tone between the three canticles. Likewise, the correspondences that exist between the Apocalypse and the end of *Purgatorio*, as well as between Paul's supreme vision and the end of *Paradiso*, may derive from Dante's acquaintance with the exegetes, and their hierarchical classification of Paul over John, without indicating that Dante applied their distinctions in a systematic fashion. In my opinion, it would be a mistake to perceive Dante as systematically following any one of his authorities in this matter.[26] Thus, although Paul's *raptus* is associated with the empyrean, and John's vision with the earthly paradise, Paul is cited as a model at the beginning of the poem, when the pilgrim names those whom he fears he is not. Paul is Dante's all-embracing model; moreover, Dante's sense of the interconnectedness of Paul and John is apparent in *Paradiso* 26.10–12, where the pilgrim, blinded as a result of having gazed at John (in an attempt to ascertain whether he was raised to heaven in the flesh), is compared to Paul, blinded by the vision on the road to Damascus. Regarding the manner of Dante's voyage through the otherworld, therefore, I suggest that we can do no better than to echo Augustine regarding Paul: "Apostolus certus se vidisse tertium coelum, incertus quomodo viderit" ("The apostle was certain that he saw the third heaven but uncertain as to how he saw it" [*De gen. ad lit.* 12.3]).[27]

The condition of a trancelike waking sleep is not only attested to throughout the visionary corpus but has been linked by artists of all times to the source of their inspiration. William Anderson, who takes Dante's visionary experience seriously, notes that:

> Many poets have described how they have found the ability to enter the realm of sleep and of dreams while retaining consciousness. Yeats described the state as a "waking trance," a paradoxical phrase that expresses the resolution of opposites, and Edwin Muir, who gives a long description of his experience of waking visions in his autobiography, believed that "poetic inspiration is a joining of the sleeping self with the conscious mind."[28]

Anderson also quotes Charles Lamb's dictum that "the true poet dreams being awake" (16). These testimonies are not inappropriate, for Dante indicates that he too views dreaming as a form of representation, related to other simulations of reality. Significant in this regard is Dante's decision to interlard *Purgatorio*, the canticle of dreams, with the examples of vices and corresponding virtues that are a narrative staple of each terrace. If dreams are a kind of internally staged representation that the poet externalizes, the exempla too are dramatic occurrences, shared didactic representations, that the poet must reproduce. In fact, all the exemplary vignettes of *Purgatorio*—not just the sculptural reliefs that Dante explicitly classifies as art—are forms of "art." The spoken exempla are imagined as a kind of living theater: theatrically patterned aural events obligingly performed by the souls in terza rima.[29] Particularly interesting are the exemplary lessons of the terrace of wrath, which, rather than being publicly staged like the other examples, take the form of ecstatic visions that the pilgrim experiences internally, like his dreams, thus providing an overt link between the oneiric and the exemplary representations. These visions are described by Dante in language similar to that which he uses for the sculptural reliefs on the terrace of pride: to render the "inner art" of the ecstatic visions as well as the "outer art" of the reliefs, the poet employs the verb *parere*, frequent direct discourse, and dialogue. These are the hallmarks of "visible speech," of extreme mimetic self-consciousness; and, indeed, as with the art of the terrace of pride, the visions of the terrace of wrath are implicitly representations of representations: distilled emblems for the art of the *Commedia* itself.[30] The use of *parere* is significant in this regard, since it has a long history of service in visionary contexts, beginning with the *Vita Nuova* and continuing with the dreams of the *Purgatorio*.[31] Rather than an indicator of diminished realism, it functions as a signpost of a heightened visionary reality, as in "Tanto gentile e tanto onesta pare," where the lady's miraculously sacramental presence sets a precedent for the *Commedia*; in this sonnet, as Contini explains, "*pare* non vale già 'sembra,' e neppure soltanto 'appare,' ma 'appare evidentemente, è o si manifesta nella sua evidenza'" ("*pare* does not mean 'she seems,' nor yet only 'she appears,' but rather 'she appears plainly, she is or she manifests herself in her manifestness'").[32]

*Parere* is a visionary term for Dante, a marker of counterfactual but true events, events like those recounted by St. John in the Apocalypse. It marks the pilgrim's encounter with the three beasts in the visionary penumbra of the first part of *Inferno* 1,[33] before the advent of a more historicized time with the arrival of Vergil in the canto's second half. *Parere* serves Ugolino as he recounts the dream borne to him by the "evil sleep that rent the veil of the future" ("'l mal sonno / che del futuro mi squarciò 'l velame" [*Inf.* 33.26–27]), his true and prophetic dream, the vision in which the wolf and its cubs are pursued and destroyed by eager hounds: "In picciol corso mi *parieno* stanchi / lo padre e ' figli, e con l'agute scane / mi *parea* lor veder fender li fianchi" ("After a brief run the father and sons *appeared* tired to me, and it *appeared* to me to see their flanks torn by sharp fangs" [*Inf.* 33.34–36]). Ugolino's narrative offers the only use of *sogno* in the *Inferno* ("e per suo sogno ciascun dubitava" ["because of his dream each one feared" (*Inf.* 33.45)]); the dreams of hell are hellish and fearsome, but they are not untrue.[34] Nor are infernal dreams lacking in representational self-consciousness, given that Ugolino's narrative, which includes the narrative of his dream, is among the canticle's most polished and adroitly self-referential performances. The *Inferno* may be said, then, to anticipate the concern with dreaming and representation that distinguishes the *Purgatorio*. Indeed, the theory of the true dreams of early morning, on which Dante will insist in purgatory, is first expressed in *Inferno* 26, in the poet's prophetic denunciation of his natal city: "Ma se presso al mattin del ver si sogna, / tu sentirai, di qua da picciol tempo, / di quel che Prato, non ch'altri, t'agogna" ("But if near morning one dreams the truth, you will experience, after a brief time, what Prato as well as others desire for you" [*Inf.* 26.7–9]). Whereas the true morning dreams of *Purgatorio* reflect the private sphere, representing the pilgrim himself or adumbrating what he will encounter on the next stage of his journey, in *Inferno* 26 the concept of dreaming leads directly to the public practice of civic and political prophecy; the poet, in the apocalyptic tones of a Hebrew prophet (in tones, in fact, that recall his political epistles, thoroughly imbued with the language of Old Testament prophecy), announces that—if his dreams are true—Florence will soon be subjected to the catastrophes invoked by the Tuscan cities under her dominion.[35] Here, the true morning dream expands to embrace the visionary ability of a prophet to forecast the events of an entire people (another sign, I would note, of how eclectically Dante uses the language of the visionary repertory). It seems not unrelated that in this same canto mention will be made of the prophet Elijah, viewed in the very moment of his proto-Pauline *raptus*, when his horses lift his chariot to the sky.[36]

The hallmarks of the visionary style are never more in evidence than in the rendering of the apparitions of the terrace of wrath, which appear and disappear like bubbles within water: "E come qui si tacque, / ciò che pareva prima, disparìo. / Indi m'apparve un'altra" ("And when she fell silent, that which first appeared, disappeared. Then there appeared to me another" [*Purg.* 15.92–94]). The pilgrim finds himself suddenly caught up— "tratto"—in what is explicitly called an *ecstatic* vision: "Ivi mi parve in una visïone / estatica di sùbito esser tratto" (*Purg.* 15.85–86). Not only is *tratto* reminiscent of the Pauline *ratto* to which the pilgrim is subjected in his first dream, but *estatica* occurs nowhere else in Dante's oeuvre.[37] The passage at the end of canto 15, following the first series of visions, reinforces their mystical character. The poet describes his soul as having to return to consciousness of the outer world; in so returning, he recognizes the nature of his visions as "not false errors": "Quando l'anima mia tornò di fori / a le cose che son fuor di lei vere, / io riconobbi i miei non falsi errori" ("When my soul returned outside to the things that are outside of it true, I recognized my not false errors" [*Purg.* 15.115–17]). The pilgrim is said to come back to reality "like a man unloosed from sleep" ("com'om che dal sonno si slega" [119]); his condition is underscored by Vergil, who accuses his charge of having walked half a league "like a man bent over by wine or sleep" ("a guisa di cui vino o sonno piega" [123]).[38] When the pilgrim attempts to explain, Vergil tells him he already knows the cause of his behavior; using the language of the visionary treatises, Vergil says that he did not ask what was wrong in the manner of someone "who looks only with an eye that does not see, when the body lies insensible" ("chi guarda pur con l'occhio che non vede, / quando disanimato il corpo giace" [134–35]). Vergil's phrasing, awkward as the description of one friend who knows the thoughts of another, works best as a transposed evocation of the pilgrim's visionary trance: the condition in which, as Augustine writes in the *De genesi ad litteram*, and as so many visionaries attest, the body lies apparently lifeless while the soul is rapt in contemplation. These suggestions regarding the extraordinary nature of the pilgrim's experience are developed in the opening sequence of canto 17, where the examples of wrath follow an apostrophe to the imagination in which the supernatural source of Dante's visions is explicitly confirmed:

> O imaginativa che ne rube
>   talvolta sì di fuor, ch'om non s'accorge
>   perché dintorno suonin mille tube,
> chi move te, se 'l senso non ti porge?
>   Moveti lume che nel ciel s'informa,
>   per sé o per voler che giù lo scorge.

> O imagination that sometimes steals us so away from the outside world that a man is unaware if around him sound a thousand trumpets, who moves you, if the senses give you nothing? A light moves you that takes form in heaven, either by itself or by the will [of God] that guides it down.

> (*Purg.* 17.13–18)

This passage picks up canto 15's emphasis on withdrawal from the outside world, the world "di fori" from which the soul departs to go deep within itself, later to return to the "cose che son fuor di lei vere"; in canto 17 the capacity of the imaginative faculty to remove us from the outer world so totally that we are effectively sealed off from its "things," its *cose*, is reiterated: "e qui fu la mia mente sì ristretta / dentro da sé, che di fuor non venìa / cosa che fosse allor da lei ricetta" ("and at this my mind was so gathered within itself that from without came no thing that was then received by it" [*Purg.* 17.22–24]).[39] What is now clarified is that the world "di fori" from which the pilgrim no longer receives any images is the world of sense perception, so that these images are instead afforded by a light from heaven, either generated by the stars or, as in the pilgrim's case, guided into the mind by God. Once again, an analogy with Pauline *raptus* would seem to be implied, since only a supernatural experience of the Pauline sort could adequately explain, from the perspective of an Aristotelian Thomist, the reception of images not proffered through the senses. Dante follows Aristotle and Aquinas in his belief that all knowledge comes through the senses, that images are based on empirical reality; as Beatrice says, "vostro ingegno . . . solo da sensato apprende / ciò che fa poscia d'intelletto degno" ("your intellect apprehends only through sense perception that which afterwards it makes fit for cognition" [*Par.* 4.40–42]).[40] Therefore, it seems likely that, in his deviation from this principle, Dante should also follow Aquinas, whose *quaestio* on Pauline ecstasy, "De raptu," contains an article devoted to "utrum Paulus in raptu fuerit alienatus a sensibus" ("whether St Paul in ecstasy was separated from his senses" [*ST* 2a2ae.175.4]). In affirming that the apostle was indeed separated from his senses, Thomas explains that human cognition derives from the apprehension of sense-objects and images:

> And the human intellect only turns to sense-objects through the medium of images. From these images he arrives at ideas of sense-objects, and while considering these ideas, judges of the realities and disposes of them. So in every operation in which our intellect abstracts from images, it needs also to abstract from the senses. (*ST* 2a2ae.175.4; Blackfriars 1969, 45:109)

But images cannot reveal the essence of God; therefore, a living man cannot see God without being separated from his senses:

> When the intellect of man is raised to the supreme vision of God's essence, it must be that the whole of a mind's intent is borne that way—to the extent that he grasps no other reality from images but is wholly borne to God. Hence it is impossible for a man, in this life, to see God in his essence without abstraction from the senses. (Ibid.)

Although the pilgrim's visions in *Purgatorio* are far from constituting an encounter with God in his essence, Dante's account of the workings of his image-making faculty, divorced from sense perception and guided from above, offers an explanation of how the ultimate vision too could be vouchsafed. Even the violence that Dante conjures through the verb *rapire* in the dream of the eagle and the verb *rubare* in canto 17 ("O imaginativa che ne *rube*") conforms to Thomas's assertion that rapture implies violence.[41]

The ecstatic visions are situated at the end of *Purgatorio* 15 and the beginning of *Purgatorio* 17, in such a way as to flank the poem's fiftieth canto; they suggest the kind of inspiration that created the *Commedia*, as though Dante inscribed, into the center of his narrative edifice, the kind of experience that brought it into being. Through these examples, Dante takes care to invoke at his poem's core, as he does at its extremes, the visionary sleep within which he saw and experienced all that weighty matter of which he was made the scribe. The visions of the center of purgatory lead through the rapt figure of the Apocalypse in the earthly paradise to the end of the poem,[42] where the poet compares himself to one who "sees while dreaming":

> Qual è colüi che sognando vede,
>   che dopo 'l sogno la passione impressa
>   rimane, e l'altro a la mente non riede,
> cotal son io, ché quasi tutta cessa
>   mia visïone, e ancor mi distilla
>   nel core il dolce che nacque da essa.

As is he who dreaming sees, and after the dream the impressed passion remains, and the rest does not return to the mind, such am I, for almost wholly my vision ceases, and still distills in my heart the sweetness that was born from it.

(*Par.* 33.58–63)

The pilgrim loses his vision as we lose our dreams, holding on to an essence, an emotion, an imprinted sentiment, for which we can find no adequate representation. Similarly, the visions of purgatory do not fade all at once but, like sleep that is broken by a sudden light, flicker before they entirely die out:

> Come si frange il sonno ove di butto
>   nova luce percuote il viso chiuso,
>   che fratto guizza prima che muoia tutto;
> così l'imaginar mio cadde giuso . . .

As sleep is broken when suddenly new light strikes on closed eyes, and, broken, it flickers before it entirely dies, so my visions fell away . . .

(*Purg.* 17.40–43)

Here too there is a Pauline analogy, since, according to Thomas, the visionary experience comports vanished knowledge whose impressions yet remain within the soul:

St Paul, after he had ceased seeing God in his essence, bore in mind what he had known in that vision, by means of some ideas which had remained in their usual state; so too when sense-realities vanish, some impressions remain in the soul. Subsequently turning back to such images he recalled the ideas. That is why he could not think of or express in words all the knowledge he had. (2a2ae 175.4; Blackfriars 1969, 45:109–11).

Visionary sleep and representation are connected again in the final cantos of the *Purgatorio*, where once more the representer takes it upon himself to re-present God's handiwork, thus creating another emblem for the project of writing the *Commedia*. As on the terrace of pride, where the poet recasts God's plastic art, and the terrace of wrath, where he renders the divinely inspired ecstatic visions, so the procession of the figures incarnating the books of the Bible in canto 29 constrains the poet to reproduce the Bible—God's divine word—through the medium of his human words. We could go further and note that Dante reproduces the Bible not as words but as things; the one text whose *verba* are in fact *res* are preserved by him as *res* in his *verba*. Not surprisingly, the description of the procession evokes cantos 10–12 (where, we remember, Dante finds occasion to rewrite the Lord's Prayer), with its painterly images (the seven candelabra paint the air with bands of color, as though they were paintbrushes) and its representational lexicon: besides such words as "dipignere," "pennelli," "colori," the use of "mostrava" for two of the biblical figures ("L'un si mostrava" [*Purg.* 29.136], "mostrava l'altro" [29.139]) recalls the acrostic of *Purgatorio* 12. Reminiscent of *Purgatorio* 17 is the emphasis on the senses, which are initially deceived by the supernatural panorama (the candelabra falsely give the impression of being trees); the verb *falsare* ("falsava nel parere" [29.44]) occurs elsewhere only in the *bolgia* of the falsifiers, also invested with a strong representational subtext, being marked by the presence of the master artifex Daedalus. The enormous self-consciousness that permeates Dante's representation of the procession in canto 29—from the invocation to the Muses and the use of such candidly self-presencing language as "quanto a mio avviso" ("as far as I can judge" [80]) and "com'io diviso" ("as I describe" [82]), to the caveat, self-administered by way of Phaeton's fiery end in the sun's errant chariot—has been glossed by Peter Hawkins, who writes:

> While throughout the canto we see the pilgrim rapt before the conjuration of God's Book, our own attention is repeatedly drawn away from the allegorical vision to the voice of the poet who brings it to us—the poet who, rather than disappearing from the text so that we too may follow Matelda's command to watch and listen, reaches out from the narrative to include us in the drama of his own representational act.[43]

Indeed, not only does Dante include us in the drama of his representational act but he tells us, in unmistakable and emphatic terms, that his representational act is to be considered on a par with those of the biblical prophets:

> Ognuno era pennuto di sei ali;
> le penne piene d'occhi; e li occhi d'Argo,
> se fosser vivi, sarebber cotali.
> A descriver lor forme più non spargo
> rime, lettor; ch'altra spesa mi strigne,
> tanto ch'a questa non posso esser largo;

> ma leggi Ezechïel, che li dipigne
>     come li vide da la fredda parte
>     venir con vento e con nube e con igne;
> e quali i troverai ne le sue carte,
>     tali eran quivi, salvo ch'a le penne
>     Giovanni è meco e da lui si diparte.

Each one was feathered with six wings, and the feathers were full of eyes; the eyes of Argus, if they were alive, would be like these. In describing their forms I will scatter no more rhymes, reader, for other spending constrains me so much so that I cannot be generous in this one. But read Ezekiel, who depicts them as he saw them come from the cold parts with wind and cloud and fire, and as you find them in his pages, so were they here, except that in the matter of the wings John is with me and departs from him.

(Purg. 29.94–105)

In this passage Dante instructs us regarding the appearance of the four animals representing the evangelists in the procession: each one has six wings, covered with eyes, as plentiful as the eyes of Argus, whose hundred watchful eyes were enlisted by Juno to guard her rival Io, as recounted by Ovid. Since the poet cannot spare the time to describe ("descriver") the gospel animals in greater detail, we are to read Ezekiel, who "paints them as he saw them"; in the matter of the number of their wings, however, we are to follow John, the seer who relived Ezekiel's vision and who agrees with Dante that they have six wings rather than four. The passage presents a visionary genealogy: Dante moves from Ovidian Argus, to an Old Testament prophet, to a prophet of the new dispensation, the author of the text that will appear at canto's end in visionary posture, as the *senex* who approaches "dormendo, con la faccia arguta" (144). Dante makes much of canto 29's visionary configuration, recalling Argus again in these cantos and again arranging for the classical monster to be followed by St. John. In canto 32, after witnessing the renewal of the tree by the griffin, the pilgrim falls asleep, and the poet refers to the sleep of Argus, when finally Mercury succeeded in dulling the monster's wakefulness by telling the story of Syrinx; when the pilgrim awakens, the poet compares his arousal to the awakening of the three apostles Peter, John, and James after their vision of the transfigured Christ:

> Quali a veder de' fioretti del melo
>     che del suo pome li angeli fa ghiotti
>     e perpetüe nozze fa nel cielo,
> Pietro e Giovanni e Iacopo condotti
>     e vinti, ritornaro a la parola
>     da la qual furon maggior sonni rotti,

e videro scemata loro scuola
    così di Moïsè come d'Elia,
    e al maestro suo cangiata stola;
tal torna' io . . .

As when Peter, John, and James, having been led to see the flowers of that apple tree whose fruit makes greedy the angels and holds perpetual weddings in heaven, and having been overcome, returned to the word by which greater sleeps were broken and saw their company lessened alike by Moses as by Elijah, and saw their master's garment changed, so I returned . . .

(*Purg.* 32.73–82)

As we learn from the gospels, Jesus took Peter, John, and James onto Mount Tabor, where he "was transfigured before them: and his face did shine as the sun, and his raiment was white as the light" (Matt. 17:2), and where there appeared also Moses and Elijah; after hearing God's voice from a cloud, they fell on their faces, remaining thus until Jesus touched them, saying, "Surgite, et nolite timere" ("Arise, and be not afraid" [Matt. 17:7]). As they came down from the mountain, Jesus charged them to tell no one what they had seen—their "vision"—until the son of man be risen from the dead: "Nemini dixeritis visionem, donec Filius hominis a mortuis resurgat" (Matt. 17:9).

Dante here compares himself, confronted with the visionary spectacle of the griffin renewing and transfiguring the tree of life, to the three apostles—"Pietro e Giovanni e Iacopo"—who see in vision the transfiguration of their Lord.[44] Like them he is awakened, by a light that rends his sleep like a veil ("un splendor mi squarciò 'l velo / del sonno" [*Purg.* 32.71–72]), and by a voice calling "Surgi: che fai?" (Arise, what are you doing?" [72]). But if sleep is a veil to be torn off, it also provides the disciples—and by analogy the pilgrim—with a foretaste of the fruit the angels eat, a foretaste of the beatific vision.[45] Indeed, the simile confirms the pilgrim's visionary abilities: it recalls the ecstatic visions of canto 15, where the pilgrim, as in the simile of canto 32, "returns" to himself ("tal torna' io");[46] it recalls canto 17, where the pilgrim's sleep is broken by the light of the angel as here it is rent by a "splendor," and as the apostles' sleep is broken by Christ's word, the "parola / da la qual furon maggior sonni rotti." The simile recalls Elijah, whose own *raptus* was already noted in *Inferno* 26; moreover, it allows Dante once again to compare himself to St. John. If the issue in these cantos is emphatically sight—Argus's sight, Ezekiel's sight, John's sight, Dante's sight—then the clarity of vision to which Dante aspires is that of John, whose vision he relives as John had relived Ezekiel's, and who foresaw the very vicissitudes of the Church that are revealed to the pilgrim in *Purgatorio* 32. As a telling periphrasis later in the poem reminds us, John is "quei che vide tutti i tempi gravi, / pria che morisse, de la bella sposa / che s'acquistò con la lancia e coi clavi" ("he who saw, before he died, all the grave times of the beautiful bride who was won with the spear and nails" [*Par.* 32.127–29]). John's is a triple appearance in the allegorical procession: he appears as one of the winged creatures figuring the gospels, as one of the minor Epistles (*Purg.* 29.142), and finally, "di retro da tutti" ("behind them all" [143]), as the sleepwalking *senex* figuring the Apocalypse. Dante introduces John's name, alone among the four evangelists, aligning him first with his precursor Ezekiel, and then with his fellow viewers of the transfiguration, thus alluding to his multiple roles.[47] Most importantly, John's Apocalypse is the major source for the *tableaux vivants* that the pilgrim witnesses in canto 32: a series of dramatic reenactments that relate historical truth in imagistic and phantasmagoric form.

*Purgatorio* 32's symbolic dramatizations of the afflictions of the Church constitute the *Purgatorio*'s final series of representations of representations, and once again they serve as a vehicle for clarifying the art of the *Commedia* itself. We tend to refer to the processional and apocalyptic sequences of these final cantos as an instance—perhaps the chief instance—of Dante's willingness to exploit the allegory of poets within a poem whose dominant mode is the allegory of theologians. There is no doubt much truth to this assertion; the procession's green, red, and three-eyed maidens are not of the same incarnate coin as Beatrice or Vergil. But the representational mode of the procession is also emblematic of the figural approach, at least to the degree that here too the poet has appropriated God's writing and made it conform to his: he takes the Bible and makes it into people. In the same way, the apocalyptic allegories of canto 32 are mixed with elements of Dante's figural allegory to forge a mode that is bizarrely and uniquely Dantesque. How can Beatrice both be "my lady" and also drive off the fox of heresy? How can the harlot who personifies the Church incite the giant to jealousy by looking at Dante? The poet breaks the frame of his symbolical dramas by inserting the first person singular of the figural mode, first calling Beatrice "la donna mia" in 32.122, then having the harlot turn her lascivious gaze "a me" in 32.155. Dante thus causes the two types of allegory to intersect and creates an emblem for the *Commedia*'s trademark intersecting of the universal with the singular, an intersecting that is never more on display than in these cantos, where the pilgrim's encounter with Beatrice and personal confession are literally enfolded by universal history. The marvelous fusions of these cantos—between the allegory of theologians and the allegory of poets, between the Johannine and the Ovidian—allow the poet to have his chariot sprout seven heads and ten horns, like the monsters of the Apocalypse, but still legitimately claim that "a similar monster was never seen before" ("simile mostro visto ancor non fue" [*Purg.* 32.147]).[48]

And yet Dante's debt to John is great, encompassing not only the saint's dragons and fornicators but also a self-referential attitude and a stress on the conjoined beginning and ending that is God. "Ego sum alpha et omega, principium et finis, dicit Dominus Deus" (1:8) is a refrain repeated through-out Revelation, up to the final "Ego sum alpha et omega, primus et novissimus, principium et finis" ("I am Alpha and Omega, the beginning and the end, the first and the last" [22:13]). God is first and last, "primus et novissimus"; "I make all things new"—"Ecce nova facio omnia" (21:5)—says the God who presides over this book of endings, of last things. In the *Commedia*, too, God makes things new: by causing the apocalyptic end of the purgatorial journey to coincide with Eden, the place of our beginnings, Dante causes mankind's first place to be transformed from the oldest place ("primus") to the newest of places—"novissimus" (not coincidentally does the poem's only use of "novissimo" belong to these cantos).[49] In this space the first and last, beginning and ending, Alpha and Omega intersect.[50] And, too, as in John, and as in many visionaries following John, this is a place of self-consciousness regarding the act of representation:[51] if the Lord instructs John to "write the things which thou hast seen, and the things which are, and the things which shall be hereafter" (1:19), so Beatrice enjoins the pilgrim, "Però, in pro del mondo che mal vive, / al carro tieni or li occhi, e quel che vedi, / ritornato di là, fa che tu scrive" ("Therefore, on behalf of the world that lives badly, fix your eyes on the chariot, and—when you have returned over there—make sure you write what you see" [*Purg.* 32.103–5]).[52] Again later, Beatrice instructs Dante to transcribe her words and the double defoliation of the tree that he has witnessed, "qual hai vista" (*Purg.* 33.56): "Tu nota; e sì come da me son porte, / così queste parole segna a' vivi" ("You note, and as they are uttered by me, so write these words for the living" [52–53]).[53] And if John ends his text by insisting that what he has written no one else should dare amend:

> For I testify unto every man that heareth the words of the prophecy of this book, if any man shall add unto these things, God shall add unto him the plagues that are written in this book: And if any man shall take away from the words of the book of this prophecy, God shall take away his part out of the book of life, and out of the holy city, and from the things which are written in this book. (Rev. 22:18–19),

so too Dante draws attention, uniquely, to the need to end at the end of *Purgatorio*, imposing upon himself the "curb" that his great precursor imposes on his readers.[54] The limits that Dante encounters at the end of *Purgatorio*, the "fren de l'arte" that he is constrained humbly to accept, might be intended to compensate for the uncurbed nature of canto 32, his "Apocalypse," which is the longest canto of the poem.

If John the Divine's representations are the fruits of his vision, the same may be said for Dante—or so Dante would have us understand. Eyes that see are, for Dante, frequently eyes that see in a state akin to sleep: besides Ugolino, we recall St. Dominic's godmother, who "saw in sleep the marvelous fruit that was to come from him and from his heirs" ("vide nel sonno il mirabile frutto / ch'uscir dovea di lui e de le rede" [*Par.* 12.65–66]). The

visionary cantos that conclude *Purgatorio* refer not only to the wakeful sleep
of the Apocalypse-*senex* but also to the sleep of Argus, in a passage that
underscores the connection between sleep and representation:

> S'io potessi ritrar come assonnaro
>   li occhi spietati udendo di Siringa,
>   li occhi a cui pur vegghiar costò sì caro;
> come pintor che con essempro pinga,
>   disegnerei com'io m'addormentai;
>   ma qual vuol sia che l'assonnar ben finga.

If I could depict how the pitiless eyes closed in sleep while listening about Syrinx—eyes whose wakefulness cost so dear—then as a painter who paints from his
model, I would draw how I fell asleep; but let someone else be the one who adequately represents the act of falling asleep.

> *(Purg.* 32.64–69)

Here the poet wishes that he could represent the experience of falling
asleep; if he could describe ("ritrar") the falling asleep of Argus's eyes,
then—like a painter imitating his model—he would draw ("disegnerei") his
own loss of consciousness.[55] But mimesis provides no way to feign in
words—*fingere*—the moment of falling into sleep; unlike Ezekiel, "che li
dipigne / come li vide," this *pintor* is unable to execute his painting. And so
he must pass to the next canvas, his awakening, recounted by way of the
simile of the awakened disciples. But before we in turn pass on, we must ask:
why does the poet draw attention to the representation of sleep? Does this
passage signal, as Hawkins has argued, the "narrowly aesthetic and ultimately self-serving preoccupations"—which for Hawkins are Ovidian—into
which Dante as poet is still capable of momentarily lapsing?[56] I think not, for
although these cantos indicate the superiority of Christian to classical visions, their pointed transition from Ovid to the Bible does not eliminate
Ovid from the *Commedia*; far from it, for the classical poet will come into
his own precisely as a source for Dante's attempts to render *trasumanar* in
*Paradiso*. The transition from Argus to St. John may remind us that Dante
sees better than Ovid, but it does not therefore signify that the poet's expressed desire to represent the Ovidian act of falling asleep is wrong. Ovid
is the poet of metamorphosis, and sleep is for Dante one of the great vehicles of metamorphosis: to represent the act that Dante denotes with the
verb *assonnare* would be to represent the very moment of change, the very
instant of transition into enlightenment, into the state that furnished Dante
the *materia* of his poem and St. Paul his experience of the third heaven.

Transition in the *Commedia* is regularly represented by sleep, a quintessentially liminal condition that participates in both life and death, standing on the thresholds of both worlds and fully committed to neither.[57]

Dante connects such liminality to transition of both a narrative and spiritual order: "Io non mori' e non rimasi vivo" ("I did not die, and I did not remain alive" [Inf. 34.25]) are the words with which he signals a moment of heightened transition, as the pilgrim faces Lucifer and the poet prepares to leave hell. The pilgrim's swoon on the shores of Acheron ("e caddi come l'uom cui sonno piglia" ["and I fell like the man whom sleep takes" (Inf. 3,136)]) and his first purgatorial dream take the metaphor of sleep as transition—sleep as vehicle for spiritual change—and render it literal: the pilgrim falls asleep in one place, and when he awakens he has reached another, he has progressed. While the second and third purgatorial dreams function less literally as vehicles of transition, they too prepare the pilgrim for forward movement; by anticipating the future, they make transition ideologically possible. But the verb assonnare is reserved by Dante for supreme transition, for the rapt reverence that overcomes him in the presence of Beatrice, the sound of whose name "mi richinava come l'uom ch'assonna" ("bowed me over like the man who falls asleep" [Par. 7.15]). This phrase yields the poem's only use of assonnare besides St. Bernard's "'l tempo fugge che t'assonna" and the two uses in the Argus passage of Purgatorio 32: "S'io potessi ritrar come assonnaro . . . ma qual vuol sia che l'assonnar ben finga." The somnolence that overcomes the pilgrim at Beatrice's name is related to the ecstatic torpor that overcomes him on the terrace of wrath, causing him to bend over, "a guisa di cui vino o sonno piega" (Purg. 15.123);[58] all these passages indicate a waking sleep, like that of the old man figuring the Apocalypse in the procession. As compared to Argus, who simply slept, and whose sleep led to his death, Dante refers to a less simple condition, a wakeful sleep that gives life, like the "letargo" that overcomes the pilgrim in the poem's last canto, as he perceives the form of the universe in a visionary instant:[59] this is a stupor, an "oppressio cerebri cum oblivione et continuo somno" ("oppression of the brain with oblivion and continual sleep"),[60] which enables vision rather than compromising it. The vision afforded the apostles in their sleep, the vision afforded the senex in his sleep, the "visïone / estatica" afforded the pilgrim on the terrace of wrath, the "letargo" afforded him at poem's end—all are analogues to the vision afforded Dante as author of this poem, analogues to the Commedia. If he could depict the assonnare of Argus's eyes, then, says Dante, he could depict "how I fell asleep," that is, how he entered the experience that would become his poem. What he wishes he could represent is the transition—the imperceptible movement in time, the flicker of an eyelid—into the visionary state that generated the nonfalse error of the Commedia, a state that was not visionary for Argus, who could only see while awake, but that is potentially visionary for all those—like the disciples, like Ezekiel, and like St. John—who can see while sleeping.

As the meeting place of endings and beginnings, the cantos of the earthly paradise form a particularly dense and striated node—a "pertrattato nodo"

(*Purg.* 29.133)—within the economy of the poem's narrative: their weight lends an ideological significance to a moment in the journey that otherwise would be less clearly posted. Despite appearances to the contrary (appearances dictated by Dante's adherence to the poetics of the new as a means for creating a life-mimetic text), the only absolute dividing line in Dante's multiply-divided world is the line between perdition and salvation, between hell on one side and purgatory and paradise on the other.[61] The narrative block of *Purgatorio* 28–33, six cantos of carefully layered historical masques and personal dramas encompassing the supreme drama of the exchange of one beloved guide for another, achieves a textual importance that offsets the much sharper ideological break between the first and second canticle and allows the second canticle to come to a culminating narrative pinnacle, to reach its own distinct conclusion. (The fact that one transition remains much sharper than the other, however, can be inferred from geography: we find ourselves in purgatory from the outset of *Purgatorio* 1, while the first part of *Paradiso* 1 is still situated in the earthly paradise.) Within the system of orchestrated tensions that structures the *Commedia*'s narrative, Dante works to counter the theological pull that unites purgatory to paradise, finding narrative means to link purgatory to hell: both realms share a conical shape (in fact, Dante's mythography of *Inferno* 34 institutes an intimate bond between the two, holding that purgatory was formed by the land that was excavated by Lucifer's fall) and require similar but inverted modes of travel (spirals down and to the left in hell, up and to the right in purgatory); both share the presence of Vergil as guide and father. These features work to override the forces that should compel us to link purgatory and paradise to the exclusion of hell; they belong to the *Commedia*'s system of narrative stresses, a system of checks and balances intended to create a structure of balanced tensions. Balanced tension is achieved by excluding each of the three realms from a system that embraces the other two, so that each realm is the "different" realm in one of three basic systems:

| HELL | PURGATORY | PARADISE | |
|------|-----------|----------|--|
| 1. X◄─────────────────────── SALVATION | | | Hell is different |
| 2. ETERNAL◄──────── X ──────────► ETERNAL | | | Purgatory is different |
| 3. SPIRALS/VERGIL─────────────────────────► X | | | Paradise is different |

The *Commedia* works like an arch, sustained by stresses that are not resolved but held in check by equal and opposing forces. Although the third of these three narrative systems is, conceptually, the most tenuous, from a narrative perspective it is extremely effective, to the point that I think most naive readers naturally link the first two realms. The linkage of hell and purgatory is greatly reinforced by the density and complexity of *Purgatorio* 28–33, by the way that these cantos tie up all the narrative strings generated thus far in the poem and provide an overwhelming sense of nexus and completion, most forcefully by staging the chiasmic scene of Vergil's departure and Beatrice's arrival.[62] The very singularity of the earthly paradise as a narrative block serves to bring the narrative journey to a kind of halt and to affect us forcefully as an ending.

If, however, Dante works to prevent purgatory from sliding into paradise, he also uses the second canticle to introduce a kind of discourse that will come into its own only in *Paradiso*. In the third canticle, the poet's increasing inability to narrate what he saw requires new solutions from the point of view of language and narrative; as we shall see, Dante forges a new "jumping" discourse for the moments in which the narrative line cannot be sustained, when the narrative *cammino* is fractured by ineffability. Such moments are anticipated in *Purgatorio*, where already there are occasions that reduce the poet to aphasia; one such is the falling into sleep that occurs before the transfigured tree, prompting the analogy with the three disciples. We recall that Dante wishes he could find the "essempro"—the model from life—that would allow him to depict his lethargy: "come pintor che con essempro pinga, / disegnerei com'io m'addormentai." Because he cannot, he is forced to pass on, to "jump," to leave a dropped stitch in the fabric of his narrative: "Però trascorro a quando mi svegliai" ("Therefore I pass on to when I awoke" [*Purg.* 32.70]). If narrative has power—Mercury's words put Argus to sleep, Christ's word awakened his disciples—it also has limits. This jump, this *trascorrere* of the narrative line because it has reached an event for which it can find no adequate signifier, anticipates a narrative condition that typifies the *Paradiso*, just as, with respect to content, the blindness that afflicts the pilgrim at the outset of *Purgatorio* 32 anticipates the failure and renewal of vision that will occur in the third realm. A canto that serves as a primer in the matter of the *Commedia*'s alternative styles is *Purgatorio* 9, the canto of the first dream: its two sections neatly juxtapose first the need to design a special discourse for a "fantastic" event, in the dream sequence, and then the return to sustained "normal" narrative in the sequence at the gate of purgatory. The difference between the two sections is set by the similes: whereas the first part (lines 1–42) contains numerous mythological comparisons, in which the pilgrim is linked to such as Ganymede and Achilles, the longer second part (lines 43–145) contains only the one simile of the Tarpeian rock, taken not from the "marvelous" storehouse of classical mythology but from sober Roman history. Whereas the dream sequence is marked by counterfactual language, by repeated uses of *parere* and *forse*, by reference to the "imagined fire" ("'ncendio imaginato" [*Purg.* 9.32]) into which the pilgrim is ravished by the eagle, the narrative of the pilgrim's arrival at the gate and the ritual imposed upon him by purgatory's angel guardian betrays no departure from "realism" (always granted that we accept the basic tenet of a journey to the beyond). Whereas the pilgrim's dream cannot be reconstructed as a straightforward narrative recounting of a straightforward event without losing its evocative connection to a mysterious and supernatural order, the order of *raptus* (when Vergil tries to reconstruct the earlier sequence in more "realistic" fashion, he succeeds in adding information but also in reducing it),[63] the latter section's narrative style is limpid to the point of simplicity, strikingly different from the convoluted astronomical periphrasis, also erotic and mythological, with which the canto opens.

Looking at the *Commedia* as a whole, we could say that the *Inferno* is composed mainly in the straightforward "realistic" manner, with the significant exception of the first part of canto 1; it is important to remember that Dante chooses to begin his narrative journey with a harbinger of alternatives to his dominant mode. The *Purgatorio* introduces longer "nonrealistic" passages, concentrated in the sections devoted to the dreams, the reliefs, the visions, and so forth; while in the *Paradiso* the ecstatic visionary mode comes into its own, and the proportion of text devoted to it increases. Before moving on to the *Paradiso*, and the attempt to anatomize Dante's narrative styles more systematically, I would like to consider the problematic nature of the term "realistic" in this context. In the world of nonfalse error, what seems less realistic need not be less true. The adjective *imaginato* tells an interesting story in this regard, for when Vergil uses it to suggest that the devils' pursuit is not real in *Inferno* 23, he is mistaken; and if the *imaginata caccia* of the *bolgia* of barratry is real, why not the *incendio imaginato* of the pilgrim's first dream? Maybe the eagle is the "erring" gloss of that for which Lucia is the "true" explanation, but if so the eagle is a nonfalse error. And the Virgin *imaginata* in the act of speech, the incense *imaginato* as its smoke enfolds the dancing Psalmist (both these uses belong to the exempla of *Purgatorio* 10), are equally "real."[64] These images are real, like the dream of the dreamer who wishes he were dreaming in the remarkable simile of *Inferno* 30: "Qual è colui che suo dannaggio sogna, / che sognando desidera sognare, / sì che quel ch'è, come non fosse, agogna" ("Like the one who dreams his hurt and, dreaming, wishes he were dreaming, so that what is, as though it were not, he craves" [136–38]). Here the dream is reality; the dreamer need dream no more. All the while that he craves reality, "what is" ("quel ch'è"), he is in possession of it, if he could but recognize the reality of his dream, the truth—nonfalsity— of his error. Like the dreamer, we must learn that there are other kinds of sight, other kinds of reality, first adumbrated at the very beginning of the poem; it is the *Purgatorio*'s task to insist on these other realities, on these other modes of seeing. Before acceding to the ultimate vision, the text instills respect for the mind that sees truth in "dreams": "dormendo, con la faccia arguta." Whether we call it a sleeping into sight or a dying into life, this is the condition in which, loosened from the flesh and unencumbered by the noisy distraction of conscious thought, our souls are rendered divinatory, prophetic, "divine":

> la mente nostra, peregrina
> più da la carne e men da' pensier presa,
> a le sue visïon quasi è divina

> our mind, pilgrim more from the flesh and less taken by thoughts, in its visions is
> almost prophetic. . . .

(Purg. 9.16–18)

The pilgrimage of Dante's mente peregrina is a pilgrimage in the footsteps of St. Paul, of St. John: the pilgrimage of a prophetic voyeur bent on recounting in pellucid verse the nonfalse errors of his divine imaginings.

*Chapter 8*

PROBLEMS IN PARADISE: THE MIMESIS OF TIME

AND THE PARADOX OF *PIÙ E MENO*

> But each for the joy of the working, and each, in his separate star,
> Shall draw the Thing as he sees It for the God of Things as They are!
> (*Rudyard Kipling, "When Earth's Last Picture Is Painted"*)

W E TURN NOW TO the *Paradiso* and to the problems of recounting the unrecountable. Due to our habit of conflating the
*Commedia*'s form with its content, the exegetical tradition has
produced a theologized reading of the third canticle that portrays it as cloy-
ingly serene (no doubt a factor in its undeserved reputation as boring). In
recent years, the old critical commonplace of a serene and problem-free
third canticle has been given a metapoetic twist; we hear now about the
difficulties of writing the *Inferno*, difficulties that presumably lessen as the
poem proceeds. As indicated earlier, such readings unacceptably theologize
the act of representation itself: Ugolino's "bestial segno," to take a commonly offered example, does not constitute a dire impasse for the *Commedia*, its potential end, nor does the encounter with Lucifer. The poetics of
the new, whereby the pilgrim is shown and the narrator relates encounters
with "le vite spiritali ad una ad una," provides adequate protection from any
such danger; the poet, the practicing poet whose praxis forged this text, is
not—practically speaking—imperiled. He may well be, in such episodes,
meditating on the perils of bestial signs and dead speech, but he is not in
personal danger of being stopped, derailed. Much more dangerous, from the
point of view of the writing writer, is the *Paradiso*.

Formally, the root problem of paradise is the problem of time, of the
temporality of narrative. If, in Paul Ricoeur's formulation, "the major tendency of modern theory of narrative . . . is to 'dechronologize' narrative,"
then Dante's third canticle is very modern.[1] Indeed, one could describe
Dante's project in *Paradiso* as the dechronologizing of narrative, as a struggle against the linearity of narrative that dramatizes the very temporality it
can never evade, since, as Ricoeur writes, "peregrination and narration are
grounded in time's approximation of eternity, which, far from abolishing
their difference, never stops contributing to it" (29). Most straightforwardly: "The world unfolded by every narrative work is always a temporal
world" (3). The questions we will pose in this and subsequent chapters are:

What happens when the world unfolded in narrative is supposed to be a world outside of time? What happens if the author of such a world is fully aware of the temporality of language and takes steps to counter it? What are the steps an author can take to counter what is finally not counterable?

Any attempt to answer these questions must be grounded in the key philosophical texts on which Dante drew in conceptualizing his representation of paradise, beginning with the Aristotelian definition of time as number and difference that appears in the *Convivio*:

> Lo tempo, secondo che dice Aristotile nel quarto de la Fisica, è "numero di movimento, secondo prima e poi"; e "numero di movimento celestiale," lo quale dispone le cose di qua giù diversamente a ricevere alcuna informazione.

> Time, according to Aristotle in the fourth book of the *Physics*, is "number of movement, according to before and after"; and "number of celestial movement," which disposes the things down here differently to receive information.

> (*Conv.* 4.2.6)

"For time is just this," writes Aristotle, "number of motion in respect of 'before' and 'after'" (*Physics* 4.11.219b1): "numerus motus secundum prius et posterius."[2] Time, therefore, comports otherness, difference, nonidentity, nonsimultaneity. (This is why, in the above passage from the *Convivio*, Dante can move directly from the definition of time to the notion of difference on earth, saying that "lo tempo . . . dispone le cose di qua giù *diversamente* a ricevere alcuna informazione.") Asking, "does [the 'now'] always remain one and the same or is it always other and other?" (*Physics* 4.10.218a9–10), Aristotle writes that "if the 'now' were not different but one and the same, there would not have been time" (4.11.218b27–28): "si non esset alterum nunc, sed idem et unum, non esset tempus."[3] For there to be time, there must be the other: the *alterum* as compared to the *unum*, the *prius* and *posterius* as compared to the *nunc*.

If time is difference, and if language is a function of time, then language is a differential medium, unable to express simultaneity. This conceptual wedding of language to time is found in the work of Augustine, who describes his return from ecstatic simultaneity in the vision at Ostia as a falling back into sound, language, and therefore time, in the form of beginnings and endings: "et remeavimus ad strepitum oris nostri, ubi verbum *et incipitur et finitur*" ("we returned to the sound of our own speech, in which each word *has a beginning and an ending*").[4] Book 11 of the *Confessions*, in particular, is a meditation on the temporality of narrative (Ricoeur not coincidentally begins his study with a chapter on this book). When God spoke from the clouds during Christ's transfiguration, saying, "Hic est filius meus dilectus," he caused his voice to sound in time ("temporaliter sonantia" [11.6]), to exist in a sequence with a beginning and an end. The syllables of the hymn "Deus, Creator omnium" also momentarily exist and then die away, like the syllables of "Hic est filius meus dilectus": sound does not stay still ("non stabat" [11.27]) but is transient, moving continuously toward its extinction. When caused by God to sound in time, therefore, his speech is like human speech. Otherwise, God's word is silent and eternal, and his will is read by the angels "without the aid of syllables inscribed in time"—"sine syllabis temporum" (13.15); unless God has specifically caused his voice to sound in time, as a sequence, it is immune to the scansion of time's syllables:

> For your Word is not speech in which each part comes to an end when it has been spoken, giving place to the next, so that finally the whole may be uttered. In your Word all is uttered at one and the same time, yet eternally. If it were not so, your Word would be subject to time and change, and therefore would be neither truly eternal nor truly immortal.
>
> (*Conf.* 11.7)

Our words exist in sequence—"ex ordine" (11.6); God's word exists all at once and forever—"simul ac sempiterne" (11.7). God is not difference but sameness, never *aliud* but always *ipsum*: "qui non es alias aliud et alias aliter, sed id ipsum et id ipsum et id ipsum" ("who art not another in another place, nor otherwise in another place: but the same and the very same, and the very self-same").[5] Time's syllables, on the other hand, are always *aliud*, never *ipsum*, always different and dying rather than simultaneous and eternal. In this meditation Augustine distills the essence of the problem of writing paradise: the "syllables of time," or, as we would say, the temporality of narrative.

The temporal status of language, never far from Dante's awareness in his theoretical writing, becomes critical for him in practical terms when he sets out to write the *Paradiso*. God is by definition eternal, and therefore, as underscored by Boethius's definition of eternity in the *Consolation of Philosophy*, simultaneous. Acknowledging Aristotle's doctrine of infinite time, Boethius yet claims that even if time has no beginning or ending, it cannot be called "eternal"—"aeternum"—because it does not comprehend and embrace all the space of its life at the same time—"simul." Eternity requires simultaneity: "Aeternitas igitur est interminabilis vitae *tota simul* et perfecta possessio" ("Eternity therefore is the perfect possession *altogether and at the same time* of an endless life" [*Phil. Cons.* 5.6.9–11]).[6] Over and over, Boethius stresses that what is not "simul" is not eternal: endless life is one thing, and God's ability to embrace the whole presence of an endless life together and at the same time is another. Endlessness should be called "perpetual"—"perpetuum"; while only the plenitude of presence in a never fading instant may be called "eternal"—"aeternum." Augustine too had contrasted the still presentness of eternity to the constant movement of time: "But in eternity nothing moves into the past: all is present. Time, on the other hand, is never all present at once" ("non autem praeterire quicquam in aeterno, sed totum esse praesens; nullum vero tempus totum esse praesens" [Conf. 11.11]). And for Aquinas, following both Boethius and Aristotle, eternity is a unified and simultaneous whole—"aeternitas est tota simul"—while time contains a before and after: "in tempore autem est prius et posterius" (ST 1a.10.4).[7] How then to put into the temporal continuum of language some inkling of the eternity and simultaneity of God? How to render a condition defined as beyond space and time in a medium that is intractably of space and time? Noting that "Augustine is vexed not only by the incommensurability of conventional language with an ineffable God but also by the paradox of even attempting to utter in temporal, vocal signs a notion such as that of eternity," Eugene Vance concludes that "Augustine denounces the whole attempt to speak in time about eternity in a language which is itself a perfect reflection of the temporal."[8]

An index of Dante's distance from Augustine is that he measures the problem of representing paradise in Augustinian terms but nonetheless goes forward with the project. And his project was enormous. Alone among the many whose descriptions of paradise testify, in Harry Levin's words, "with monotonous eloquence to the poverty of the human imagination,"[9] Dante attempts not just to represent paradise pictorially, as previous visionaries had done, but to inform his representation with metaphysical concerns about time and space. Noting that "medieval visions are more concerned with the realms of punishment than with heaven," Carol Zaleski distinguishes between visionary and contemplative discourse—the former concentrating on hell and purgatory and the latter on paradise—and indicates Dante's unique position as a conflater of the two:

> Few of these writers attempt a synthesis of the sort achieved by The Divine Comedy, however, with its fusion of visionary and contemplative discourse, and its equal treatment of hell, purgatory, and heaven. More often the territory is divided: vision literature, a didactic genre, concentrates on hell and purgatory, while contemplative writings specialize in what Jean Leclercq calls "devotion to heaven." This division of labor, though not absolute, reflects a widespread assumption that graphic images are appropriate for infernal or purgatorial subjects, but incommensurate with transcendent, heavenly experience.[10]

The "division of labor" outlined above is significant; the unique perspective that the visionary tradition offers us for assessing the Commedia is never more useful than with respect to the representation of paradise. A perusal of earlier visions reminds us that Dante is unusual even in giving equal time—textually speaking—to heaven.[11] Most importantly, we are reminded that there was no precedent for his agenda. If we imagine a contemporary poet attempting to graft into his poetry the concerns of modern theoretical physics, we may perhaps get a sense of what it meant for Dante to embrace in his paradise the discourse of medieval metaphysics.[12] Against the backdrop of what his visionary precursors did not do, we can better appreciate what Dante did, remembering that he need not have chosen to deal with that aspect of his subject that is least accessible to the narrator's art. He could have followed his predecessors in fashioning a more concrete paradise, whether pastoral or urban: either a supreme *locus amoenus*, the flowery fields and meadows of so many medieval visions or, following St. John in the Book of Revelation, a magnificent heavenly Jerusalem.[13] In other words, he could have adopted the restraint of previous composers of textual heavens, who make only few representational gestures toward the immaterial paradise favored by philosophers.[14]

Instead, relegating both the natural and the urban features of earlier heavens to his imagery, Dante sets out to do what no one before or since has done: to represent paradise as a state beyond the coordinates of space-time, beyond the continuum that defines our lives and thoughts. Rather than content himself with merely saying that heaven is eternal, he actively confronts the narrative implications of its timelessness, demonstrating the difference between asserting eternity and representing timelessness in his disparate treatments of hell and heaven. Thus, hell is defined as eternal, but in his representation of hell Dante never problematizes the concepts of space and time as he does in his representation of paradise; he never says (the very ludicrousness of the proposition is telling) that all the souls are really with Lucifer in Cocytus and only appear in various circles for the benefit of the pilgrim. Spatially, hell is treated as tangible and concrete, while temporally, the fact that it is eternal means only that it will last forever, that its torments are perpetual. Eternity in the context of hell signifies duration; as Aquinas notes, "The fire of hell is called eternal only because it is unending" (*ST* 1a.10.3; Blackfriars 1964, 2:143). In conceptualizing paradise, on the other hand, Dante moves from an interminable duration to an eternal present, to that which is outside of time altogether: the divine mind exists "in sua etternità di tempo fore" ("in his eternity outside of time" [*Par.* 29.16]). Dante seems to have applied to his two realms Boethius's distinction between perpetual endlessness and eternal timelessness: the air of hell is "without time"—"sanza tempo" (*Inf.* 3.29)—because it is starless and therefore endless, deprived of the measured time produced by the motion of the spheres, not because it is truly timeless and eternal, altogether outside of time, "in sua etternità di tempo fore."[15] Transcendence of space and time is the essence of Dante's paradise: God is "the point to which all times are present" ("il punto / a cui tutti li tempi son presenti" [*Par.* 17.17–18]), the being in whom all space and time converge, "where every where and every when is centered" ("'ve s'appunta ogne *ubi* e ogne *quando*" [*Par.* 29.12]). By the same token, the divine realm, the empyrean, is literally a utopia, a "no place," in that it contains all space but belongs to none: "in quella sola / è ogne parte là ove sempr'era, / perché non è in loco e non s'impola" ("in that alone is every part there where it always was, because it is not in space and it has no poles" [*Par.* 22.65–67]). In figuring his paradise, Dante immeasurably raises the representational stakes by setting out to render God's all-at-once-ness—his *totum simul*[16]—in language: in a system of differences parsed by the syllables of time.

Because all narrative exists in time, and a narrator can only represent one event at a time, Alessandro Manzoni, like all his storytelling brethren, was unable to represent the simultaneity of life. He complains that the separate lives of Lucia, don Rodrigo, and Renzo cannot be recounted simultaneously, as they occurred, but must—like his son's guinea pigs—be herded into the pen one by one:

> Avrebbe voluto fargli andar tutti insieme al covile; ma era fatica buttata: uno si sbandava a destra, e mentre il piccolo pastore correva per cacciarlo nel branco, un altro, due, tre ne uscivano a sinistra, da ogni parte. Dimodoché, dopo essersi un po' impazientito, s'adattava al loro genio, spingeva prima dentro quelli ch'eran più vicini all'uscio, poi andava a prender gli altri, a uno, a due, a tre, come gli riusciva. Un gioco simile ci convien fare co' nostri personaggi: ricoverata Lucia, siam corsi a don Rodrigo; e ora lo dobbiamo abbandonare, per andar dietro a Renzo, che avevam perduto di vista.

> He wanted to make them go all together into the pen, but it was wasted effort: one disbanded to the right, and while the little shepherd ran to chase it into the flock, another, two, three exited on the left, from all directions. So that, after losing his patience, he adapted to their ways, and pushed in first the ones who were nearest the entrance, then went to get the others, by one, by twos, by threes, as it happened. We must play a similar game with our characters: having taken care of Lucia, we ran to don Rodrigo; and now we must abandon him, to follow after Renzo, whom we had lost from sight.[17]

If the problem of time in narrative afflicts all narrators, we may find in the comparison of these two narratives an opportunity for noting how it afflicts Dante in the *Paradiso* more than most. Manzoni yearns to be able to represent the simultaneity of the events befalling his characters. He cannot because the medium in which he works—language—is subject to the laws of space and time that govern human existence: it is always *alterum*, never *unum*; always *prius* or *posterius*, never *nunc*. But Manzoni's limitation is less severe than Dante's, for his plot does not require him to make his characters somehow ontologically simultaneous, simultaneous in their essences; their separate existences as Lucia, don Rodrigo, and Renzo are not in themselves problematic, except in so far as he wishes that he could represent simultaneously the things that occurred within those separate existences at the same time. For Dante, on the other hand, in the *Paradiso*, the nonsimultaneity of language poses a special dilemma: it creates time and difference in a context where he wants to create eternity and unity. In other words, he wants to represent not merely the simultaneity of life but the simultaneity of heaven; not merely the simultaneity of many different events occurring at the same time but the simultaneity of a condition in which everything is the same at the same time. Not only does he want to represent separate existences simultaneously, but he wants to represent them as not separate.

We now turn to the philosophical paradox that serves as the thematic correlative of the *Paradiso*'s formal problematic. The formal problem of representing separate existences as yet not separate mirrors Dante's philosophical probing of the issue of the one and the many, already implicitly present in the canticle's first tercet: "La gloria di colui che tutto move / per l'universo penetra, e risplende / in una parte più e meno altrove" ("The glory of the one who moves all penetrates through the universe and shines in one part more and in another less" [*Par.* 1.1–3]). These three lines contain *in nuce* the core concerns of Dante's *Paradiso*, both philosophically and narratologically. The first two lines convey the unity of paradise, its all-in-one-ness: God's glory moves all—"tutto"—and penetrates the entire "universo," a word whose root meaning brings us face to face with the unity and oneness of God's creation. The oft-ignored third line is less sublime than its precedessors, which are supreme examples of Dante's ability to extract sublimity from syntactic simplicity.[18] The unprepossessing third verse is, however, critical, for it introduces difference into the realm of unity: here the world of the undifferentiated all gives way to a world that contains an "other" ("altrove"), a world that contains difference. With its strong central caesura highlighting the little word "più," the third verse also suggests the framework for accommodating difference within unity, the many within the one: it can be done by means of a hierarchy, by instituting *gradatio*, here hypostatized by the apparently humble but ever so important adverbs "più" and "meno," markers of difference throughout the *Commedia* that come into their own in the *Paradiso*. The question implicitly posed in the first tercet—how can the universe be one and yet receive God's light in differing degrees, "in one part more and in another less"—will be refracted throughout the canticle; it is the obsessive question of the *Paradiso*.[19] Thus, after recording Piccarda, the first of many apologists for the existence of difference, of "più e meno," in God's realm, the poet comments: "Chiaro mi fu allor come ogne dove / in cielo è paradiso, *etsi* la grazia / del sommo ben d'un modo non vi piove" ("Then it was clear to me how everywhere in heaven is paradise, although grace does not rain down in one way from the highest good" [*Par.* 3.88–90]). Everywhere is paradise and yet—the crude Latinism "etsi" serves as a textual pivot marking the two terms of the tercet's unresolved paradox—grace does not rain down equally.

The *Paradiso*'s source of tension is the Dantesque variant of the ancient dialectic between a self-sufficient God, independent of and hostile to multiplicity, and a creationist God, the loving maker of multiplicity.[20] If there were not the problem of the many, of the difference that the one must accommodate while still remaining one, there would be no *più e meno* to mar the unity of paradise. Patrick Boyde touches on this issue when he refers to Dante's "unease and suspicion in the presence of multiplicity," a posture that he relates to what he perceives as Dante's fundamental Neoplatonism.[21] I prefer to think in terms of paradox and tension deriving from Dante's double allegiance: his desire to synthesize Aristotelian sympathy for difference with the Neoplatonic One. Or, in the terms of Isaiah Berlin's essay *The Hedgehog and the Fox*, I am suggesting that Dante is less an archetypal hedgehog—less a monist—than is commonly assumed.[22] There is in his makeup an enormous dedication to the cause of difference and pluralism: to the individual, the specific, the many. Dante's view of the universe requires the many, in the same way that his incarnational poetics with its trademark investment in the irreducible historicity of the individual is dependent on multiplicity; both as philosopher and as poet, therefore, Dante is acutely conscious of the role of difference as the sine qua non of a Christian paradise as well as of this Christian poem. His commitment on this score causes him to document his repudiation of the Averroist doctrine that separates the possible intellect from the individual soul, in a passage where respect for the Arabic thinker is tempered by the need to condemn a belief that implicitly denies the individual's immortality qua individual:

> quest'è tal punto,
> che più savio di te fé già errante,
> sì che per sua dottrina fé disgiunto
>   da l'anima il possibile intelletto,
>   perché da lui non vide organo assunto.

This is such a point that it already caused to err one wiser than you, so that in his doctrine he disjoined the possible intellect from the soul because he saw no organ assumed by it.

(*Purg.* 25.62–66)

Multiplicity, then, is the safeguard of our singularity. The persistence of *più e meno* within the one testifies to the persistence of the individual soul as a uniquely differentiated being within the unity of the cosmos: difference must exist if we are to exist.

But if a Christian paradise requires the preservation of the individual's irreducible and essential self, it also gratifies our desire for nondifference, providing a solvent for the ego and a medium for the dissolution of the all too inescapable "I." How the many and the one can coexist, how difference can abide within the single and indivisible plenitude of the godhead—for God is supremely one and therefore "supremely existent and supremely undivided"[23]—is a paradox for which the ultimate emblem in Christian theology is the trinity. In the *Commedia*, this paradox will be vigorously and repeatedly articulated, for—as the *Paradiso*'s first three verses testify—Dante wants to render not only difference, the *più e meno* of the third verse, but also—and much more problematically—God's unity, the undifferentiated glory of the all-mover whose light is simultaneously all-embracing. The reading that follows is an attempt to chart Dante's course between the Scylla of unity and the Charybdis of difference: his plotting of a narrative strategy that attacks first the one, then the many, then the one again, then the many again, as he works to create a text that encompasses the illusion of the one and the many as coexistent and simultaneous. In practical terms, I shall approach the *Paradiso* by using words like "più," "meno," "differenza," and "differente" as markers of difference, as indices of the contradictions denoted by the persistence of the many within the one, contradictions inherent in the project of representing paradise. My use of these markers is dictated by Dante, who uses such language almost exclusively in the *Paradiso*: "differente," "differentemente," "differenza," "differire" (with the exception of one use in *Purgatorio* 25.53),[24] "diversamente," "distinzione," and "multiplicare" are all restricted to the third canticle, as though the poet were thus leaving traces of the struggle that marked its composition. For, as we know, and as Dante knew, the difference that cannot be avoided in figuring paradise is not only conceptual; it is also the difference incarnate in the medium of language, the multiplicity embodied in the narrative continuum that would express God's unified and simultaneous simplicity. We recall the syllables of the hymn that Augustine measures out one by one; we recall the characters in the novel that Manzoni can lead to their destinies only individually. The temporality of language is the ultimate basis for the persistence of difference in human representations of the divine. Number, difference, otherness, ticks and tocks, befores and afters, beginnings and endings, births and deaths: these are the components of the Aristotelian definition of time found in the *Convivio*, Dante's "numero di movimento, secondo prima e poi." Time and difference are exigencies with which Dante must deal in his representation of the reality outside time and difference: aware of this necessity, exploiting it as much as possible, he proceeds in the face of it to represent God's "etternità di tempo fore."

.   .   .   .   .

The one made the many: "distinctio et multitudo rerum est a Deo"—"the difference and multiplicity of things come from God" (*ST* 1a.47.1).[25] In the act that we call creation, God made difference, in Thomas's words, "so that his goodness might be communicated to creatures and re-enacted through them" (ibid.; Blackfriars 1967, 8:95). God's goodness required expression in multiplicity: "because one single creature was not enough, he produced many and diverse, so that what was wanting in one expression of the divine goodness might be supplied by another, for goodness, which in God is single and all together, in creatures is multiple and scattered" (ibid.). Taking a further step, Aquinas notes that from difference and multiplicity follows inequality, and that the inequality of things is also from God: "God's wisdom is the cause of inequality, as it is of distinction" (ST 1a.47.2; Blackfriars 1967, 8:99). To explain the presence of inequality, Thomas invokes Aristotle and the likeness of forms of things to numbers, "which vary by addition and subtraction":

> Now distinction of form always requires inequality, for, to quote the Metaphysics, forms of things are like numbers, which vary by addition or subtraction of units. So among the things of nature an ordered scale is observed; compounds are higher than elements, plants than minerals, animals than plants, and men than other animals, and under each of these headings we find one species more perfect than others.
>
> (ST 1a.47.2; Blackfriars 1967, 8:99)

In this passage, comparatives—più e meno for Dante, magis et minus for Aquinas—enter the world, manifestations of the inequality that results from difference, because "distinction of form always requires inequality": "Distinctio autem formalis semper requirit inaequalitatem." At the same time enter gradation, hierarchy, the "ordered scale" by which the various things of nature are arranged according to their greater or lesser perfection, some higher and some lower.[26] The Paradiso reflects the scholastic doctrine of creation, both with respect to the passage from the one to the many and in the insistence that the one remains one, for "although he is the One he can also make the many" (ST 1a.47.1; Blackfriars 1967, 8:95). This is a paradox on which Dante had already meditated; the Convivio offers a creationist passage in which the adversative conjunction "avvegna che" expresses the tension later embodied by "etsi" in Paradiso 3.89, the prepositional phrase "secondo più e meno" looks forward to Paradiso 1.3, and the adverb "diversamente" anticipates its running presence in the third canticle: "Ove è da sapere che la divina bontade in tutte le cose discende, e altrimenti essere non potrebbero; ma avvegna che questa bontade si muova da simplicissimo principio, diversamente si riceve, secondo più e meno, da le cose riceventi" ("Wherein it must be known that the divine goodness descends into all things, and that otherwise they could not be; but although this goodness moves from a supremely simple source, it is received differently, with respect to more and less, by the receiving things" [Conv. 3.7.2]).[27] In the Paradiso, the importance of the coexistence of unity and difference, equality and hierarchy, is signaled by the first two cantos, which treat the paradox first from the perspective of the one, and then from the perspective of the many.

The discourse on the order of the universe in canto 1 acknowledges difference but enfolds it into the all-embracing one, the all-engulfing "great sea of being." The discourse on the celestial influences in canto 2, on the other hand, makes a case for difference as a necessary feature of that same ordered universe. If canto 1 stresses unity, elaborating on the "gloria di colui che tutto move," canto 2 stresses difference, glossing "in una parte più e meno altrove." Together, they set the agenda for the rest of the *Paradiso*, both in terms of the canticle's overriding preoccupations and its narrative strategy of alternation, whereby the poet first stresses the one, then stresses the many, and so on from one to the other, in the hope that the diachronic package he offers us will convey some idea of the synchronic reality he experienced. The discourse of canto 1 reveals itself as a purveyor of unity in its emphasis on the quest for at-one-ness that motivates all God's creatures, and in its lexicon, with its unifying "tutte" (which echoes "La gloria di colui che *tutto* move"), "universo" (echoing "per *l'universo* penetra e risplende") and—a new addition to the lexicon of unity—"ordine":[28] "Le cose tutte quante / hanno ordine tra loro, e questo è forma / che l'universo a Dio fa simigliante" ("All things have order among themselves, and this is the form that makes the universe similar to God" [*Par.* 1.103–5]). The universal aspiration to identity with God, the prevailing quest for similitude with and absorption into the divine essence, is grandly and simply stated, then restated; the recapitulation maintains the emphasis on unity by repeating both "ordine" and "tutte" and then proceeds to acknowledge the difference out of which the unity is composed:

> Ne *l'ordine* ch'io dico sono accline
>     *tutte* nature, per *diverse* sorti,
>         *più* al principio loro e *men* vicine;
>     onde si muovono a *diversi* porti
>         per lo gran mar de l'essere, e *ciascuna*
>         con istinto a lei dato che la porti.

> In the *order* of which I speak *all* natures are inclined by *different* lots, *more* and *less* near to their beginning; wherefore they move to *different* ports across the great sea of being, and *each* with an instinct given to it that carries it.
>
> (*Par.* 1.109–14)

Multiplicity exists—lexically in the adjectives "diverse" and "diversi," the adverbs "più" and "men," the pronoun "ciascuna"—but it is more than balanced by the sequence's conceptual, verbal, and rhythmic apex: the "gran mar de l'essere," a metaphor that effectively absorbs the many into the oceanic one. The diverse ports to which we individually sail are all located on the great sea of being; none of us is so distinct as to be independent of this

PROBLEMS IN PARADISE   177

cosmic ocean. While the task of expressing unity is, for Dante as for the rest of us, much more difficult than the task of expressing difference (and so he premises his narrative with the disclaimer "vidi cose che ridire / né sa né può chi di là sù discende" ["I saw things that one who descends from up there neither has the knowledge or the ability to retell" (*Par.* 1.5–6)]), he has at his command singular resources of metaphoric language: only metaphor is able to placate the tension between the one and the many, with the result that images—from the great sea of being, to the heavenly clock that sounds "tin tin" with so sweet a note, to the culminating vision of the universe as a single volume bound by love—will carry the burden of expressing the non-differentiated One.

The image of the "gran mar de l'essere" is anticipated in canto 1 by the sea into which Glaucus plunges upon eating the metamorphic herb that makes him a god, the unifying medium that absorbs him and renders him similar to the other gods, their "con-sort" in the waters of being, alike them in his *sorte*, no longer different: "consorto in mar de li altri dèi" ("consort in the sea of the other gods" [*Par.* 1.69]). The image is reprised in the Ulyssean address to the reader that opens canto 2, where the *gran mare* has become our vicarious experience of paradise, the textual ocean—the *pelago*, the *alto sale*—from whose perilous watery expanses the poet warns those of us who sail in little boats, those who are not capable of following in his wake, taking care to stay "dinanzi a l'acqua che ritorna equale" ("ahead of the water that comes back equal" [*Par.* 2.15]). Here unity, indicated by the word "equale," another key addition to the *Paradiso*'s lexicon of nondifferentiation,[29] has taken on a threatening undertone: from the perspective of the human specks of difference that the deep can so easily cover over (as it covered over Ulysses, whose boat is whirled around "infin che 'l mar fu sovra noi richiuso" [*Inf.* 26.142]), the ability of these waters to cancel our differentiating presences, to come back *equal* after our light barks have passed over them, returning always—as though we had not existed—to a condition of unperturbed unity, is not without menace. The menace is to our sense of our selves as selves, as eternally existent and unabsorbed individual essences. Having alerted us to this threat, the poet will shortly address it, by way of the pilgrim's entrance into the sphere of the moon, a passage that is handled in such a way as to treat the paradox of consubstantiation: how can one body, one "corpo," copenetrate with another and yet remain unperturbedly itself? The moon is able to receive the pilgrim into itself while still remaining "unita,"[30] undifferentiated: "Per entro sé l'etterna margarita / ne ricevette, com'acqua recepe / raggio di luce permanendo unita" ("Into itself the eternal pearl received us, as water receives a ray of light while remaining united" [*Par.* 2.34–36]). How the pilgrim can cease to be "other" and become "one" with the moon while both he and it remain themselves is a question that the poet underscores, for—he says—it adumbrates a greater mystery, namely that of the coexistence of human nature with God's divine nature in one united being, the mystery that Dante will try to render at his poem's end:

S'io era *corpo*, e qui non si concepe
  com'*una* dimensione *altra* patio,
  ch'esser convien se *corpo* in *corpo* repe,
accender ne dovria più il disio
  di veder quella essenza in che si vede
  come nostra natura e Dio *s'unio*.

If I was *body*, and here we cannot conceive how *one* dimension can suffer *another*, which must occur if *body* enters *body*, this must kindle more our desire to see that essence in which is seen how our nature and God *united themselves*.

(*Par.* 2.37–42)

In this passage Dante renders the paradox: difference exists—"una," "altra," "corpo," "corpo"—but it is embraced and resolved into an all-encompassing unity; "unita" introduces the conundrum, while "s'unio" completes it. The verbal repetition, in this case of *corpo*, later on of *luce* ("da luce a luce" [145]), initiates a technique that the poet will use frequently in the third canticle, as a way of signifying the paradox of the thing that both is itself and is the other.[31]

*Paradiso* 2 digs deeply into the paradox of difference within unity; this canto, which contains the above two uses of *unire* and the poem's only use of *unitate*, provides at the same time the *Paradiso*'s first great manifesto for necessary difference. Taking its key from the mysterious consubstantiation of the pilgrim's body with that of the moon, the discussion begins by noting an apparent difference within the moon's body, namely its dark spots; because of these "segni bui," the moon is not equally luminous throughout. Following the Averroistic explanation that is endorsed by the *Convivio*, this element of diversity in heaven is explained as a material phenomenon by the pilgrim, who responds to Beatrice's instigation by suggesting that the spots are caused by a variation in the density of the moon's identical being:[32] "Ciò che n'appar qua sù diverso / credo che fanno i corpi rari e densi" ("That which appears to us as different up here is produced, I think, by bodies thin and thick" [59–60]). The variation in "rarity and density" of the moon's matter thus accounts for its differing degrees of luminosity. Beatrice repudiates this derivation of difference from a physical cause, assigning to it instead a metaphysical existence as a "formal principle" and arguing that all difference must have an ontological basis: rather than a single nature that is thicker or thinner, difference must be real and substantive, derived from different natures. Establishing an analogy between the moon, with its spots of difference, and the eighth sphere, with its many different stars, she explains (in language dense with the dialectic between the one and the many) that if Dante were correct in his reduction of the moon's difference to one physical cause, then the difference that characterizes the eighth sphere would in turn be destroyed:

La spera ottava vi dimostra *molti*
  lumi, li quali e nel quale e nel quanto
  notar si posson di *diversi* volti.
Se raro e denso ciò facesser tanto,
  *una sola* virtù sarebbe in *tutti*,
  *più e men* distribuita e altrettanto.
Virtù *diverse* esser convegnon frutti
  di princìpi formali, e quei, for ch'*uno*,
  seguiterieno a tua ragion distrutti.

The eighth sphere shows you *many* lights, which in their quality and in their quantity can be seen to be of *diverse* aspect. If thin and thick accounted for all this, *one* power only would be in *all* of them, distributed either *more or less* or the same. *Diverse* powers must be the fruits of formal principles, and those—but for *one*— would be destroyed according to your reasoning.

(*Par.* 2.64–72)

The difference represented by the moon's spots can no more be destroyed than the difference represented by the many diverse stars of the eighth sphere; if one has a metaphysical basis, then so does the other. And, as it turns out, far from being susceptible to destruction, the difference of the eighth sphere is essential to the workings of the universe. For, within the empyrean, "the heaven of divine peace" ("ciel de la divina pace" [112]), is the primum mobile, the heaven in which being is actualized, "un corpo ne la cui virtute / l'esser di tutto suo contento giace" ("a body within whose power lies the being of all that it contains" [113–14]); following the primum mobile comes the eighth sphere, which is responsible for differentiating the being that the primum mobile has caused to exist, for initiating the division of the one into the many, to be further carried out by each of the successive seven heavens:

Lo ciel seguente, c'ha *tante* vedute,
  quell'esser *parte* per *diverse* essenze,
  da lui *distratte* e da lui contenute.
Li altri giron per varie *differenze*
  le *distinzion* che dentro da sé hanno
  dispongono a lor fini e lor semenze.

The following heaven, which has so *many* stars, *divides* that being into *diverse* essences, *distinct* from it and contained by it. The other circles through various *differences* dispose the *distinctions* that they have within themselves to their aims and forms.

(*Par.* 2.115–20)

The making of difference is thus an essential part of the divine plan (given by theologians the label *opus distinctionis*);[33] through his heavens, God himself is responsible for creating the "diverse essenze," the "varie differenze." At the same time, now that Dante has delivered himself of this manifesto on behalf of difference, he can begin to reintroduce the paradoxical relation of necessary difference to necessary unity. Verse 117, "da lui distratte e da lui contenute," delineates a paradox: how can the "diverse essenze" created by the differentiating process of the eighth sphere be both distinct from it ("da lui distratte") and contained by it ("da lui contenute")?[34] In other words, how can the different stars of the eighth heaven be both part of that heaven and separate from it? What is still submerged in verse 117 comes into relief toward the end of the canto, where Dante attempts to graft the multiplicity whose coming into being he has just articulated onto the unity and order that dominates canto 1. In the same way that a single soul deploys "different members" ("differenti membra" [134]) conforming to "diverse faculties" ("diverse potenze" [135]), so a heaven generates multiplicity while still remaining one:[35] "così l'intelligenza sua bontate / *multiplicata* per le stelle spiega, / girando sé sovra sua *unitate*" ("so the heavenly intelligence unfolds its goodness, *multiplied* through the stars, itself circling upon its own *unity*" [136–38]). The heaven circles in self-contained and nondifferentiated unity: "sovra sua unitate." Unity exists. But difference too exists, as the lexicon of this canto has amply testified, and *Paradiso* 2 concludes by restating this fact, reminding us that differing degrees of light derive from different formal principles, different essences, and not merely from a single essence whose matter is more thinly or thickly distributed:

> Da essa vien ciò che *da luce a luce*
>   par *differente*, non da denso e raro;
>   essa è formal principio che produce,
> conforme a sua bontà, lo turbo e 'l chiaro.

> Thence comes that which seems *different from light to light*, not from thick and thin; this is the formal principle that produces, according to its excellence, the dark and the bright.

(*Par.* 2.145–48)

A new category of difference—"lo turbo e 'l chiaro"—has taken the place of the old category, "denso e raro"; and so the *Paradiso* goes.

In some of his works, notably the *De vulgari eloquentia* and the *Monarchia*, Dante displays a hostility toward difference and multiplicity. In the treatise on language, for instance, one of the vernacular's claims to superiority is its universality, the fact that the whole world, "totus orbis," uses it, despite its being divided into different pronunciations and vocabularies ("licet in diversas prolationes et vocabula sit.divisa" [1.1.4]). Speech itself is required because we, unlike angels, cannot enter into one another through a spiritual mirroring of each other's thoughts ("Nec per spiritualem speculationem, ut angelum, alterum alterum introire contingit" [1.3.1]), in other words because we are different from one another and cannot bridge the gap from one to the other: "alterum alterum." Although there is a passing reference to God as the maker of difference,[36] the treatise emphasizes not God's triumphant creation of difference but rather mankind's fall into difference: difference as castigation for our pride. This is the moral of the building of the tower of Babel, an activity to which we came united, assisting in the work with one same language ("una eademque loquela"), and from which we departed divided, diversified by many languages ("multis diversificati loquelis"), unable any longer to work on a common project ("ad idem commertium" [1.7.6]).[37] Linguistic differentiation leads to political fragmentation, a thread that runs through human history from the time of Nimrod to contemporary Italy; in treating the many dialects of the Italian peninsula, Dante extends the point first developed vis-à-vis the tower of Babel, namely that a common language is the prerequisite for a common political agenda. This theme is carried forward in the *Monarchia*, where the need to justify a single ruler leads to the explanation that what can be done by one—"per unum"—is better done by one than by many—"per plura": "Et quod potest fieri per unum, melius est per unum fieri quam per plura" (1.14.1). From this principle Dante derives another, namely that for something to be done by one is good, whereas for it to be done by many is evil: "quod fieri per unum est bonum, per plura simpliciter malum" (1.14.2). Proceeding to larger and larger conclusions, Dante goes on to align oneness—"unum"— with goodness and multiplicity—"multa"—with evil: "unum esse videtur esse radix eius quod est esse bonum, et multa esse eius quod est esse malum" ("to be one seems to be the root of what it is to be good, and to be many of what it is to be evil" [1.15.2]). The polarity established between the one and the many finally allows Dante to achieve a definition of sin as nothing but the disparagement of the one and a consequent progression toward the many: "peccare nichil est aliud quam progredi ab uno spreto ad multa" (1.15.3). Here, then, we do indeed find that "unease and suspicion in the presence of multiplicity" that Boyde views as a current of Dante's thought.[38] The posture of the *Paradiso*, on the other hand, as I have tried to show, reflects a willingness to accommodate difference as an essential aspect of the created universe. Emblematic of the *Paradiso* is the position Dante expresses in the late *Questio de aqua et terra*, where, writing of the stars of the eighth sphere, which differ in magnitude, luminosity, and in the figures of the constellations, he notes that such differences cannot be in vain: "differentie frustra esse non possunt" (71).

This is the attitude that will inform the *Paradiso*: the difference God made cannot be in vain, *differentiae frustra esse non possunt*. At the same time, this is an attitude with which Dante will struggle throughout the *Paradiso*, since it also accounts for the specter of disunity in the realm of unity, first dramatically played out in canto 3's encounter with Piccarda. The image of a pearl on a white forehead ("perla in bianca fronte" [*Par.* 3.14]) visually relays the idea of subtle shades of difference within an overarching unity (in this case the whiteness that encompasses both pearl and forehead), as, in the linguistic sphere, do the rhyme words "vòto" ("empty") and "voto" ("vow"): here the same sound encompasses two different meanings. Beatrice informs the pilgrim that the faint shapes he thinks are mirrored images are indeed true beings, *vere sustanze*, "qui rilegate per manco di voto" ("relegated here for unfulfilled vows" [30]). Her wording, the harsh verticality implied by her statement that these souls are "relegated" to the sphere in which we find them, is reinforced by Piccarda, whose discourse is a veritable model of ambivalence: if, on the one hand, she tells us that divine charity cancels difference, being "quella / che vuol simile a sé tutta sua corte" ("that which wants all its court similar to itself" [44–45]), on the other she fractures identity and similitude by claiming that "beata sono in la spera più tarda" ("I am blessed in the slowest sphere" [51]). Beatrice's vertical stress is heard once more in Piccarda's reference to her lot as one that "seems so lowly" ("par giù cotanto" [55]). These potentially invidious comparatives—we note Piccarda's deployment of the telltale "più"—impress the pilgrim, who articulates in the clearest possible terms the problem of finding some souls lower down than others; he assumes that they feel deprived, cut off from full membership in paradise and full participation in God's love.[39] Surely they desire to be higher up, where they can see more, participate more fully, and belong to the inner circle of God's "friends": "Ma dimmi: voi che siete qui felici, / disiderate voi più alto loco / per più vedere e per più farvi amici?" ("But tell me: you who are happy here, do you desire a higher place, in order to see more and to make yourselves more beloved?" [64–66]). The single *più* of Piccarda's first speech has been tripled by the pilgrim, who suggests, reasonably enough, that the souls must want a "*più* alto loco / per *più* vedere e per *più* farvi amici." He sees only the stigma of difference, and so Piccarda must explain further; rather than eliminate difference ontologically, she eliminates it psychologically. The souls, she says, do not experience difference, for their wills are quieted by God's love, which makes them desire only what they have; if they desired to be higher, their wills would be discordant with God's, which is impossible. In fact, the essence of paradise is conformity of the many to the one, with the result that the many are as pleased by their hierarchical disposition as is God (here the differential "di soglia in soglia" [82] is offset by the unifying *tutto* in "a tutto il regno piace" [83]); indeed their peace consists in conforming to his will, as the famous verse testifies: "E 'n la sua volontade è nostra pace." Piccarda's discourse renders conformity linguistically, most strikingly in the mirrored transitions from singular to plural happiness: "per ch'*una* fansi *nostre* voglie" ("so that *one our* wills are made" [81]); "E 'n la *sua* volontade è *nostra* pace" ("And in *his* will is *our* peace" [85]). She concludes by invoking the great metaphor of unity from *Paradiso* 1: God's will is the sea to which moves all the created universe—"quel mare al qual tutto si move / ciò ch'ella crïa o che natura face" ("that sea to which moves all that it creates or that nature makes" [86–87]).

The many are content to take their places in the "gran mar de l'essere," but they nonetheless exist, which is why Piccarda's energetic attempt to convey unity yields the following paradox: "Chiaro mi fu allor come ogne dove / in cielo è paradiso, *etsi* la grazia / del sommo ben d'un modo non vi piove" (*Par.* 3.88–90). Everywhere in heaven is paradise, i.e., all heavenly locations are equally good; nonetheless, at the same time, grace is not equally distributed. This is a notion we can accept only if we cease to think in terms of space; otherwise, we run into the problem of all celestial real estate being equally valued despite not receiving the same goods and services. Moreover, if grace is not distributed *d'un modo* (a phrase that doubles in the *Paradiso* for *igualmente*), then it must perforce be distributed *più e meno*. And so we return to the paradox of the *Paradiso*'s first tercet, which Dante does not so much attempt to resolve as hold up for scrutiny, perusing it first from one perspective and then from another. Given that the problem of the one and the many is not one that Dante can, in fact, "resolve," we nonetheless may note that our poet seems more to revel in it than to want to cover it over. Typical of his approach is his having Piccarda—that erstwhile champion of unity—immediately put the pilgrim's newfound understanding to the test by casually reintroducing difference into her speech, referring to St. Clare as a "donna più sù" ("lady higher up" [98]). Why this lack of interest in sustaining even a little longer the metaphorical unity purchased by the "gran mar de l'essere"? Besides the fact that he is representing a paradox, and thus deliberately privileging first one horn and then the other of his dilemma, Dante is also representing himself representing, needing difference in order to write. He dramatizes this need in the opening sequence of canto 4, which contains the description of the pilgrim's uncertainty faced with two questions he desires equally to ask:

Intra due cibi, distanti e moventi
   *d'un modo*, prima si morria di fame,
   che liber'omo l'un recasse ai denti;
sì si starebbe un agno intra due brame

di fieri lupi, *igualmente* temendo;
sì si starebbe un cane intra due dame:
per che, s'i' mi tacea, me non riprendo,
da li miei dubbi *d'un modo* sospinto,
poi ch'era necessario, né commendo.

Between two foods, *equally* distant and appetizing, a free man would die of hunger before he brought one to his teeth. So would a lamb stand between two cravings of fierce wolves, *equally* fearing; so would a dog stand between two does. Therefore, if I was silent, pushed *equally* by my doubts, I do not reprove myself, nor do I commend, since it was necessary.

(*Par.* 4.1–9)

Here the language of unity—"d'un modo," "igualmente"—has become the language of stasis; because the pilgrim finds the two questions he wishes to put to Beatrice equally enticing, he cannot ask either one. He is like a man between two equally distant and equally appetizing meals, like a lamb between two equally frightening wolves, like a dog between two equally appealing does. Each is an image of desire thwarted by sameness, prevented from issuing into action by parity, equality—by lack of difference. Suspended equally, the pilgrim is at a standstill; he cannot proceed, nor—figuratively—can the poem. Since the plot of the *Paradiso* is provided by the intellectual forward motion of the pilgrim, by the articulation of his various *dubbi* and the answers they elicit, his stasis figures the stasis that would overtake the text if difference, in the form of new doubts, new language, were not continually reintroduced.[40] And, indeed, Beatrice reactivates the plot precisely by establishing a hierarchy, announcing that "Queste son le question che nel tuo *velle* / pontano *igualmente*; e però pria / tratterò quella che *più* ha di felle" ("These are the questions that weigh *equally* in your will, and so first I will treat the one that has *more* poison" [*Par.* 4.25–27]). In order to move forward, to rupture the impasse experienced by the pilgrim, she converts *igualmente* to *più*, unity to difference: of the two questions that weigh "igualmente" on the pilgrim, she identifies one as in fact possessing "più di felle"—more poison—and proceeds to tackle it first. The difference that Beatrice invokes with the word *più* thus figuratively prevents the poem from grinding to a halt, stymied by premature unity. Difference is required for all temporal life, including the temporal life of this poem, and Dante indicates as much through Beatrice's behavior as well as through her lexical choices. With her combination of *velle* and *igualmente*, both together again only in the poem's final tercet (when the pilgrim's *disio* and *velle* are turning equally), he points us lexically to supreme unity and ultimate repose, to a state beyond *più e meno*, and thus also beyond poems: when the soul no longer reacts to difference by turning "to the sign of a *greater* desire" ("al segno di *maggior* disio" [*Par.* 3.126]), when instead it is equally turned, "come rota ch'*igualmente* è mossa" ("like a wheel that is *equally* moved" [*Par.* 33.144]), the journey will have come to an end.[41]

The presence of souls in the heaven of the moon has caused the pilgrim to wonder whether Plato's doctrine in the *Timaeus,* according to which souls come from and return to the natal stars that create their characters and dispositions, may be correct. This is the belief which Beatrice considers more dangerous to the pilgrim's mental health, and which she feels obliged to treat first. (The fact that she catalogues it second—"*Ancor* di dubitar ti dà cagione"—but discusses it first—"e però *pria* / tratterò"—is another way of underlining the temporal and hierarchical dimension to which the narrative is reconsigned after its figurative opening encounter with heavenly homology.) In order to disabuse the pilgrim of Plato's alarming identification of the soul with its star, Beatrice begins by categorically stating that all the souls in paradise are in the empyrean with God: they are not distributed, as he believes on the evidence of his meeting with Piccarda, from heaven to heaven, but are rather all at one in the first circle. Not the highest of the seraphim, not any of the saints, not even the Virgin, belongs to a different heaven from the souls the pilgrim has just met, nor do they possess a lengthier beatitude. Despite being united externally, however, the souls do differ internally, since each possesses a differing amount of bliss, according to each one's greater or lesser ability to experience the divine breath:

> D'i Serafin colui che *più* s'india,
>    Moïsè, Samuel, e quel Giovanni
>    che prender vuoli, io dico, non Maria,
> non hanno in altro cielo i loro scanni
>    che questi spirti che mo t'appariro,
>    né hanno a l'esser lor *più o meno* anni;
> ma *tutti* fanno bello il *primo* giro,
>    e *differentemente* han dolce vita
>    per sentir *più e men* l'etterno spiro.

Of the seraphim he who is *most* in God, Moses, Samuel, and whichever John you wish to take, I say, even Mary, do not have their seats in any other heaven from these spirits who have just now appeared to you, nor do they have for their being *more or less* years; but *all* make beautiful the *first* circle, and *differently* they have sweet life by feeling *more or less* the eternal breath.

(*Par.* 4.28–36)

Of the nine lines that make up this passage, the first seven are dedicated to canceling difference; even the subtle reminders of hierarchy that are verbally present (the seraph who is "most" in God, the numeral "first" in "primo giro") seem intended to pave the way for a more triumphant assertion of unity over hierarchy, culminating in "ma *tutti* fanno bello il primo giro." Like Piccarda, however, Beatrice here means to have it both ways, and after asserting unity for seven lines she resurrects hierarchy in the last two: "e *differentemente* han dolce vita / per sentir *più e men* l'etterno spiro." There is no difference in paradise, but then again, as wonderfully signified by the conquering adverb "differentemente," whose six syllables (five with ellision) spread over most of the pivotal verse in which it is situated, there is. What we have here is another restatement of the conceptual paradox first posed in the *Paradiso*'s first tercet, a more articulated rendering of canto 3's "Chiaro mi fu allor come ogne dove / in cielo è paradiso, *etsi* la grazia / del sommo ben d'un modo non vi piove."

In positing different degrees of beatitude, Dante is following his philosophical models. Thomas, for instance, poses the question "Can one be more blessed than another?" and replies in the affirmative, for happiness "admits of various degrees, and is not equal in every case" (*ST* 1a2ae.5.2).[42] The angelic doctor's elaboration is much like Beatrice's: "one can be more blessed than another, for the deeper his joy the more blessed he is. And in point of fact his joy can be deeper because he is more open and adapted to receive it" (ibid.; Blackfriars 1969, 16:121).[43] However, Dante's philosophical models do not have the problem of finding an adequate representation for the differing degrees of beatitude that render each of us unique and yet do not hinder us from fully participating in the unity and nondifferentiation of paradise. Dante now deals with the representational aspects of his problematic, projecting onto the souls a concern for representing themselves to the pilgrim which is in fact a displaced articulation of his own concerns as writer of this text:

> Qui *si mostraro*, non perché sortita
>   sia questa spera lor, ma *per far segno*
>   de la celestïal c'ha men salita.
> Così parlar conviensi al vostro ingegno,
>   però che solo da sensato apprende
>   ciò che fa poscia d'intelletto degno.
> Per questo la Scrittura condescende
>   a vostra facultate, e piedi e mano
>   attribuisce a Dio e altro intende;
> e Santa Chiesa con aspetto umano
>   Gabrïel e Michel vi *rappresenta*,
>   e l'altro che Tobia rifece sano.

Here *they showed themselves*, not because this sphere is allotted to them, but *to make a sign* of the celestial grade that has least height. It is necessary to speak in this way to your intellect, since only from sense perception does it apprehend that which later it makes worthy for understanding. For this reason Scripture conde-

scends to your faculty and attributes feet and hands to God while intending something else, and Holy Church with human aspect *represents* for you Gabriel and
Michael and the other who remade Tobit healthy.

(*Par.* 4.37–48)

The issue at hand is overtly representation, as we learn from "si mostraro,"
"per far segno," and "vi rappresenta"; specifically, it is the problem of how
to represent nonsensory, supernatural realities. This is a problem, Beatrice
explains, that the souls have sought to overcome for the sake of the pilgrim,
finding a way to represent in concrete sensory terms the nonsensory reality
of their spiritual condition. Because of the pilgrim's limitations, the souls
have chosen temporarily to dispose themselves in the various heavens that
correspond to their spiritual inclinations as a way of signifying the spiritual
reality that the pilgrim would otherwise be incapable of comprehending.
Moreover, as Beatrice adds in a corollary that sets up an implied analogy
between God's representation in the Bible and Dante's in the *Commedia*, in
the same way that the pilgrim would be unable to apprehend the souls'
differing grades of celestial beatitude were they not to adopt this crude form
of representing themselves, so, by extension, humans generally would be
unable to grasp the supernatural truths contained by the Bible, did that text
not condescend to lower those truths, making them sensory and thus palat-
able for human consumption. In sum, then, Plato was wrong: the souls in
paradise are not assigned to individual heavens, as they appear to be; they
only appear thus as a representational expedient, a fictive pedagogical con-
descension to the pilgrim's limited human faculties.

If this passage is candid in its highlighting of representation as an issue,
it is, however, far from candid in its ultimate goals, which are to displace
onto the souls—the author's fictional constructs—concerns that in fact belong to the author himself. It is as much a mistake for us to accept Beatrice's
words uncritically and at face value, overemphasizing the heavens' metaphorical status, as it was for an earlier critical tradition to neglect Beatrice's
caveat. For, although the hierarchy of the heavens may be presented as an
illusion, as a fictive expedient adopted for the sake of the pilgrim, in fact it
serves a practical poetic purpose that is far from fictional. From a narrative/
compositional point of view, in terms of what is actually on the page, the
divisions created by the various heavens are not fictional but accurate reflections of that most real of poetic realities: the difference of language itself. In
other words, the hierarchy of the heavens is not only helpful to the pilgrim,
as the poet tells us; it is also—as he emphatically does not tell us—a sine qua
non for the poet, who literally could not have written the third canticle
without it. The poet requires a way to stretch the third canticle through
time, to distend it. In the *Inferno* and *Purgatorio*, there is no obstacle to

creating a "distesa lingua," a narrative analogue to what Augustine calls the *distentio* of time;[44] the poet need only take us with him through the material realms he allegedly visited. But in the *Paradiso*, the representation of a non-material realm, such a format conflicts with basic conceptual presuppositions: this is the realm of unity, of souls all united in God, no longer differentiated by space and time. And yet, without the temporal/spatial/narrative continuum to which text and voyage subscribe in the first two canticles, the poet is, as De Sanctis noted without deriving the implications of his insight,[45] at a representational loss. If Dante is to compose with regard to his last imaginary world thirty-three cantos of narrative verse and not a mystical haiku, then that world must be supplied with some form of structural difference analogous to the circles and terraces that punctuate its two imaginary predecessors. The hierarchy of the heavens supplies the structural framework that is required if Dante is to write a *Paradiso* of the same textual dimensions as *Inferno* or *Purgatorio* (and we remember his anomalous standing among visionary authors for choosing to do so); it supplies the difference required to distend the last canticle through time.

The fact that Dante institutes the hierarchy because he needs it as a poet has proved critically elusive. Thus, Marguerite Mills Chiarenza warns us not to be persuaded by the fictitious hierarchy of the heavens into forgetting the unity of paradise and reminds us that the hierarchy is "an artificial structure which does not exist outside of the momentary need for it," since Dante's "vision was essentially 'in un punto solo,' which *punto* substituted and annulled a kind of paraphrase that led up to it."[46] Particularly valuable here is the correction of the common assumption that the diachrony of the narrative is also ideological (as assumed by those who divide *Paradiso* into 30 cantos of preamble followed by 3 cantos of "true" heaven); Chiarenza is seeing paradise whole, as Dante would have us see it. But she, in turn, is not remembering that although the diachrony of the narrative should not be projected onto the ideological structure, neither can it be caused to disappear: what Chiarenza omits from her analysis is the complicity between the poet and his paraphrase, the fact that Dante was obliged to invent something like the artifice of the heavens. While Chiarenza's explanation for the hierarchy's existence, her suggestion that the souls "stage this hierarchy because the pilgrim is not ready for a vision of totality" (81), is acceptable within the possible world of the *Commedia* (i.e., at the level of its *plot*), if we step outside of that world—if we detheologize our reading—then we realize that the hierarchy is a means of allowing the last canticle to exist. A similar point can be made regarding John Freccero's reading of this passage,[47] which on the one hand had the merit of drawing our attention to the metaphoric status of the heavenly hierarchy, but on the other has lulled us into implicitly accepting Dante's fiction, which we do whenever we refer to the "metaphor" of the heavens without remembering that the difference the heavens represent is real and unavoidable. When Freccero states as fact what is an illusion posing as fact, referring to the "extended metaphor of the *Paradiso*" (225), he is helping Dante to maintain an illusion of unity. By the same token, when he says that "the structure of the *cantica* depends, not upon a principle of *mimesis*, but rather upon metaphor" (222), he is essentially paraphrasing Beatrice.[48] Rather, we should say that the structure of the canticle depends upon mimesis claiming to be metaphor. Difference, mimetic structure, is present (how could it not be?), but it is pretending to be absent and thus camouflages itself as metaphor. In the *Paradiso* Dante feigns that the distinctions he creates are feigned because as a poet he requires these distinctions, but he also requires the illusion of their absence: i.e., the illusion of unity, which is created, in a medium that is necessarily diachronic, by first registering difference and then denying it. The solution is a fiction whereby the difference he needs as a poet is a metaphor supplied solely for the sake of the pilgrim. In other words, the divisions of the *Paradiso* are not fictional or metaphoric; rather, the claim that there are no divisions in the *Paradiso* is supremely fictional and supremely metaphoric. The *Paradiso*'s grandest illusion is the one whereby the poet hides the unavoidable difference that gives being to his text by simply having Beatrice (a creation of that same text) deny its existence.

The device whereby Dante entrusts the illusions of the *Paradiso* to a fictional character is one to which he has recourse more than once; thus, in canto 5, Beatrice is presented as the text's true cantor. After she speaks to the pilgrim at the beginning of the canto, we find the following verses: "Sì cominciò Beatrice questo canto; / e sì com'uom che suo parlar non spezza, / continüò così 'l processo santo" ("So Beatrice began this canto; and, as a man who does not break his speech, she thus continued the saintly process" [*Par.* 5.16–18]). This fascinating authorial intervention serves simultaneously to heighten and deflect the author's authority, his very presence: for indeed, who is the author, Dante or Beatrice?[49] Verses 1–15 of *Paradiso* 5 are made of direct discourse, Beatrice's words to her charge; verse 16 comments, "So did Beatrice begin this canto," thus eliding the role of Beatrice as speaker and the role of Dante as poet who later arranges her speech, choosing to place it at the beginning of the canto: somehow Beatrice has begun the canto, and Dante has conflated the representation with what it represents. In the same way, later in *Paradiso* 5 Dante both draws attention to the ongoing narrative process and simultaneously camouflages it, passing it off as Beatrice's "processo santo" rather than his own.[50] Beatrice's discourse on the prudence required of Christians in making vows is no sooner concluded than the author interjects, "Così Beatrice a me com'ïo scrivo" ("So Beatrice to me as I write" [85]), a verse that highlights the poet, the one who says "io scrivo" and yet devolves his narrative authority upon someone else, the person whose scribe he claims to be. He is a scribe, moreover, who has resigned not only the content of his text but even its disposition, its arrangement into beginnings, middles, and ends: if Beatrice "begins" canto 5, so Justinian "begins"—and "authors"—canto 6. Canto 5 begins with Beatrice's beginning, and it ends with the anticipatory preface to Justinian's beginning, placed at the end of canto 5 in order to preserve canto 6 from any marring of its authorial integrity, from the presence of any author other than its singer, the emperor who responds to the pilgrim "nel modo che 'l seguente canto canta" ("in the manner that the following canto chants" [*Par.* 5.139]). This verse, simultaneously the last line of canto 5 and the preface to canto 6, maintains the poet's ambidextrous narrative illusionism. On the one hand, it testifies, with the adjective "seguente," to an ongoing textual process that is presumably controlled by the poet (whose control was, moreover, underlined earlier by the veiled threat of narrative interruption: "Pensa, lettor, se quel che qui s'inizia / non procedesse" ["Think, reader, if that which here begins were not to proceed" (109–10)]). On the other hand, it gives the authorship of the "seguente canto" to Justinian, who will, fittingly, be its only *auctor*; no one else's words—not the poet's, not the pilgrim's, not Beatrice's—will be registered in canto 6. The passing of authorship from the writer/scribe to the speaker/singer is further expressed by the etymological figure "canto canta," in which the evocation of the common root *cantare* serves to move the "canto" from the written sphere, the sphere of the writer (Dante), to the oral sphere, the sphere of the cantor (Justinian).[51]

Justinian's canto contributes to the theme of the one and the many a tercet that valorizes diversity as a prerequisite for paradisiacal harmony and justifies the existence of different heavens by claiming them as necessary constituents in the blending of a harmonious heavenly polyphony, a unity made of many voices: "Diverse voci fanno dolci note; / così diversi scanni in nostra vita / rendon dolce armonia tra queste rote" ("Diverse voices make sweet notes; so diverse orders in our life render sweet harmony among these wheels" [*Par.* 6.124–26]). The following canto, instead, tells how mankind was cast by sin into a state of dissimilitude, of difference. In *Paradiso* 7, where Dante recounts the story of mankind's sin and redemption from the perspective of difference and unity, difference is not prized but viewed as the emblem of human estrangement from the divine. Christ redeemed humanity by reuniting it with its maker, from which it had distanced itself; his act of redemption was thus an act of uniting, of canceling difference: he "*united* to himself in his person" ("*unì* a sé in persona" [*Par.* 7.32]) our estranged nature, allowing it to become once more "questa natura al suo fattore *unita*" ("this nature *united* to its maker" [35]). As we learned from canto 1's first great tribute to divine unity, the order of the universe is the sign of its conformity, its similitude, to its creator: "Le cose tutte quante / hanno ordine tra loro, e questo è forma / che l'universo a Dio fa simigliante"

(*Par.* 1.103–5).[52] This point is reiterated in canto 7's discourse on creation, where Beatrice instructs us that the things that are made directly by God, without intermediaries, receive the gifts of immortality, liberty, and conformity, and that the greater the conformity of a creature the more pleasing it is to it maker, for God's ardor is most alive in those creatures that are most similar to him: "ne la più somigliante è più vivace" (75). On this backdrop of a God who prizes *somiglianza* and who "vuol simile a sé tutta sua corte" (*Par.* 3.45), Beatrice more effectively castigates the sin that made the "umana creatura" radically dissimilar, horribly different: "Solo il peccato è quel che la disfranca / e falla dissimìle al sommo bene" ("Only sin is what disfranchizes it and makes it dissimilar from the supreme good" [79–80]). Mankind's supreme madness, the act of Ulyssean "follia" to which Beatrice refers in line 93, was the arrogant intolerance of limits that caused us to abandon the original conformity and similitude by which we had been blessed[53] and to be expelled from a condition of plenitude into one of emptiness and privation—in short, into a state of desire. Sin empties—"colpa vòta"—and we can return to our former dignities only if we refill where sin has emptied ("se non rïempie, dove colpa vòta" [83]); sin separates and distances, and because of it human nature was cast out ("fu remota" [87]), exiled from likeness into unlikeness. Sin made the lack in mankind, the desire that is our birthright, the void that can only be filled by our arduous return to the similitude we forsook.

In a canto like *Paradiso* 7, which tells of man's fall into unlikeness, Dante's emphasis is on unity, and difference is viewed negatively. Even when discussing creation, therefore, the emphasis has shifted; it is not, in canto 7, on God's sublime act of differentiation, which he accomplishes with the assistance of the heavens, but rather on the benefits of being created directly by God, "without mediation" ("sanza mezzo" [*Par.* 7.142]), as compared to being subjected "to the influence of the new things" ("a la virtute de le cose nove" [72]).[54] Whereas, in *Paradiso* 2, a canto of necessary difference, the work of the heavens was viewed triumphantly, as a testament to the intricately coordinated operation of the great heavenly organism, in canto 7 we learn that those things which are created indirectly through the agency of the heavens are perishable, doomed to "come to corruption and to last but little" ("venire a corruzione, e durar poco" [126]). The heavens, as "new things" themselves, are destined to generate ever newer and newer things, things that are further and further distanced from the preserving likeness to the one true maker. This perspective is all the more notable by comparison to the following canto, where the pendulum has swung back, in typically Dantesque fashion, from an Augustinian view of difference as the *regio dissimilitudinis* to an Aristotelian appreciation of its benefits. Linguistically, difference is registered in the telltale phrase *più e meno*, used in the presentation of the souls of canto 8: the speed of their circling movement exemplifies their different grades of internalized beatitude, grades that (we now know) the external heavens only serve to figure forth; they move "in giro più e men correnti, / al modo, credo, di lor viste interne" ("in circle more or less swiftly according, I believe, to their internal sight" [*Par.* 8.20–21]). One of these circling souls, Charles Martel, will speak of the crucial role played by difference in the social sphere; his discourse is one of the *Paradiso*'s great testaments to beneficial multiplicity. Although the first part of his speech insists that the influences of the heavens are strictly controlled by divine providence, claiming that if they were not so controlled the effects of the heavens on the sublunary world "would be not works of art, but ruins" ("non sarebbero arti, ma ruine" [108]), his reasoning proceeds dialectically from the limitations of the heavens to their importance. Beginning with the Aristotelian premise that man is by nature a social animal, Charles moves to the corresponding need for difference: how could we function harmoniously and productively as citizens in a body politic if we did not live differently and undertake different duties, "se giù non si vive / *diversamente* per *diversi* offici?" ("if below men do not live *diversely* for *diverse* offices?" [118–19]).[55] The need for diversity is further underscored when Charles concludes: "Dunque esser *diverse* / convien di vostri effetti le radici" ("Therefore the roots of your effects need to be *diverse*" [122–23]). Indeed, he informs us that the heavens must intervene in the workings of nature precisely to create diversity, since nature left on its own would produce only similarity, in an endless undifferentiated generation of children identical to their parents: "Natura generata il suo cammino / simil farebbe sempre a' generanti" ("Generated nature would always make its path alike to that of the generators" [133–34]).

The index of the philosophical distance between cantos 7 and 8 is the word *simile*. While in canto 7 similitude is life, and sin has branded man as *dissimile* ("Solo il peccato è quel che la disfranca / e falla dissimìle al sommo bene" [79–80]), thrusting him into the *regio dissimilitudinis*, in canto 8, far from being prized, similitude must be countermanded: the things that are begotten would follow a path identical to their begetters—"Natura generata il suo cammino / *simil* farebbe sempre a' generanti"—did providence, in the form of the heavens, not intervene, creating beneficial difference.[56] In this context, *simile* signifies repetition, identity, stasis, and death, the opposite of life-quickening difference; in canto 7, by contrast, *simile* signifies conformity, identity, unity with—and therefore life in—the divine all-at-oneness.[57] The contrast between these cantos may be taken as symptomatic of the program Dante undertakes in the *Paradiso*, the program whereby he alternatingly privileges unity and privileges difference, in his quest to encompass both horns of his dilemma, both the Neoplatonic/Augustinian One and the Aristotelian/Thomistic Many. This is a program to which he adheres throughout the third canticle, having presented it in the first two cantos and developed it throughout the first nine. Before proceeding to the new narrative beginning that is signaled by the opening verses of *Paradiso* 10, we can conclude our overview of Dante's alternating strategy, his attempt to accommodate a synchronic paradox to the unfolding diachrony of his text, with Cunizza's formulation of the problem we have already repeatedly encountered:

> Cunizza fui chiamata, e qui refulgo
> perché mi vinse il lume d'esta stella;
> ma lietamente a me medesma indulgo
> la cagion di mia sorte, e non mi noia;
> che parria forse forte al vostro vulgo.

> I was called Cunizza, and I shine here because the light of this star conquered me. But happily I pardon in myself the reason of my lot, and it does not vex me—which might seem hard to comprehend to your vulgar minds.

> (*Par.* 9.32–36)

Anticipating the question that the pilgrim posed Piccarda, Cunizza volunteers the information that she is where she is because of her passionate and venereal nature. She is not grieved by her lowly position in the heaven of Venus; rather she finds in it a source of joy. In her present and perpetual indulgence of her former self-indulgence she finds the confirmation of her unique identity, the essence of what makes her Cunizza and no one else; she finds the "cagion di *mia* sorte." It is precisely this preservation of the historical that makes difference a commodity that cannot be relinquished—not even in paradise.

## Chapter 9

## THE HEAVEN OF THE SUN AS A MEDITATION
## ON NARRATIVE

> Potest etiam hoc, mendacio tollerando, per distinctionem
> dissolvi: mitior nanque est in adversarium solutio distinctiva;
> non enim omnino mentiens esse videtur, sicut
> interemptiva illum videri facit.
> *(Monarchia* 3.4.17)

> Since all progress of mind consists for the most part in
> differentiation, in the resolution of an obscure and complex
> object into its component parts, it is surely the stupidest of losses
> to confuse things which right reason has put asunder, to lose
> the sense of achieved distinctions . . .
> (Walter Pater, *Appreciations)*

T HE THEMATIC project of the heaven of the sun is a replay, in the
key of wisdom, of what Dante seeks to represent and promote
throughout the *Paradiso*: a paradise where difference is blended into
the one enough to achieve peace and harmony, but not enough to lose what
makes it itself, what makes it different. Such a paradoxical project requires
from the poet a perpetual balancing, as at one moment he emphasizes the
unity of paradise and at another he emphasizes the hierarchy that differen-
tiates—and disunifies—that unity. In the heaven of the sun the balancing
that underlies the *Paradiso* as a whole is focused on the two circles,[1] their
members, and the reciprocal praise that characterizes the presentations
of the two nonpresent saints, Francis and Dominic.[2] While the rhetorical structures and imagistic components of the two panegyrics have been
analyzed, critics have connected such formal aspects to thematic concerns:
if Dante dwells longer on St. Francis, and if the story of Francis's life has
appealed to more readers, it is because Dante is partial to the Franciscans and their cause; if the imagery of the two *vite* is related, it is because
Dante is underscoring the fundamental unity of the two saints' missions.[3]
Although these notions are not necessarily wrong, they fail to take into account Dante's awareness of the representational task he sets himself. Auerbach, in his reading of Francis's canto, makes much of the fact that the poet
does not stage an encounter between the pilgrim and one of the most vi-

brant figures of the age;[4] by employing another soul to recount the life of Francis, rather than having the saint speak for himself, Dante breaches his customary narrative mode in an explicit and elaborate fashion. Auerbach proposes that Dante wishes in this way to stress the mission over the man, a thematically oriented explanation that is refuted by the presence of St. Benedict in *Paradiso* 22, who tells how he founded the Benedictine order and condemns his degenerate followers, thus doing for himself what Thomas and Bonaventure are called upon to do for Francis and Dominic.[5]

If, as I believe, the heaven of the sun contains a meditation on the nature and constraints of narrative, cantos 11 and 12 have, within the heaven's economy, a (literally) central role. Having chosen two saints whose lives had already occasioned complex narrative traditions,[6] Dante responds to this previous textuality not with the usual fictive reality of an imagined encounter—his own textuality posing as reality—but with an explicitly narrative construct: his own textuality posing as someone else's textuality. By making Thomas and Bonaventure into narrators, Dante highlights narrative itself as an issue and also throws into silhouette his own narrative problems as artificer of this text. Thomas and Bonaventure are not only presenters; they are also representers. And, as is always Dante's poetic praxis, their representation is charged with the textual mission of reproducing thematic concerns at the level of language, of imitating formally what is most at stake thematically. Therefore, in line with this heaven's concern with making the many into one, Dante's task—the task he assigns Thomas and Bonaventure—is to make Francis and Dominic one rather than two, one rather than many. Dante tells us as much when he has Thomas say, "De l'un dirò, però che d'amendue / si dice l'un pregiando" ("I shall speak of one; although in praising one, one speaks of both" [*Par.* 11.40–41]), verses that I take not simply as courteous hyperbole but as a bold attempt to deny the Aristotelian precept that "to be diverse necessarily means to be unequal":[7] if to speak of one saint is to speak of both, then the two saints are one, are equal. In fact, this is an impossible claim, as Dante knows: he could speak of both saints when he speaks of one if he were content to tell only one story, or the same story twice, and so forgo individual identity, but such is not the case. And, of course, the claim that to speak of both saints is to speak of one is—from the standpoint of the two very different *vite* Dante composes—belied by his own text.

I am not suggesting that Dante claims, or in any way desires, the historical parity of Francis and Dominic; for Dante, both saints had uniquely necessary historical missions, and the elimination of the difference embodied by these missions would be harmful and counterproductive. Rather, I am suggesting that he is concerned with the linguistic and ultimately temporal obstacles to representational parity, which we could sum up as follows: he sets out to describe $x$ and $y$, and begins $x = a$; if he says $y = a$ he repeats himself, whereas if he says $y = b$ he creates difference. The paradoxical task of telling simultaneously of one and the other, in such a way as to preserve individual identity and yet to create no difference, is a microcosmic version of the task of writing the *Paradiso*: to represent as one, undifferentiatedly, figures who appear in time, in narrative sequence, separately. In the same way that Dante, in order to write a narrative, is constrained to create divisions—inequalities—in the *Paradiso* as a whole, so in the heaven of the sun he must either represent Francis and Dominic differently, and thus unequally (since, in Aquinas's words, "distinctio semper requirit inaequalitatem"), or write the same story twice. Likewise, in the same way that he pretends that the structural divisions that underlie the canticle as a whole do not exist, so he insists that there is no difference between the two saints, insists that to tell of one is to tell of both, that two can be made into one: "De l'un dirò, però che d'amendue / si dice l'un pregiando." In both cases, the poet's real narrative constraints compromise the fiction of celestial unity that he is dedicated to maintaining. Dante's problem—how best to represent equally the two saints—is the rhetorical extension of the paradox of heavenly space, whereby "ogne dove / in cielo è paradiso, *etsi* la grazia / del sommo ben d'un modo non vi piove" ("everywhere in heaven is paradise, although grace does not rain down in one way from the highest good" [*Par.* 3.88–90]). By crafting the parallel narratives of Francis and Dominic with such evident care, Dante draws attention to the problem of representational equality: how to represent them with the same spirit, how to endow them with the same grace and dignity, how to design them "d'un modo"? In other words, how to create the illusion of simultaneity within the constraints of a medium that is defined as sequentiality? How to evade the "syllables of time"?

The representational self-consciousness of the fourth heaven is at once apparent:

> Leva dunque, lettore, a l'alte rote
>   meco la vista, dritto a quella parte
>   dove l'un moto e l'altro si percuote;
> e lì comincia a vagheggiar ne l'arte
>   di quel maestro che dentro a sé l'ama,
>   tanto che mai da lei l'occhio non parte.
>
>   . . . . . . . . . . . .
>
> Or ti riman, lettor, sovra 'l tuo banco,
>   dietro pensando a ciò che si preliba,
>   s'esser vuoi lieto assai prima che stanco.
> Messo t'ho innanzi: omai per te ti ciba;
>   ché a sé torce tutta la mia cura
>   quella materia ond'io son fatto scriba.

Lift therefore, reader, your sight with me to the high wheels, straight to that part where one motion hits the other; *and there begin to look with desire upon the art of that master* who loves it within himself so much that his eye from it never parts. . . . Now remain, reader, upon your bench, thinking about that of which you have a foretaste, if you wish to be happy sooner than you tire. I have put before you; now eat for yourself—because *that matter of which I am made the scribe* twists all my attention to it.

(*Par.* 10.7–12, 22–27)

Having introduced himself as a scribe in a context where God is the artist and the universe is "l'arte / di quel maestro," the poet turns to his own *arte*, speaking of its inherent limitations:

Perch'io lo 'ngegno e l'arte e l'uso chiami,
    sì nol direi che mai s'imaginasse;
    ma creder puossi e di veder si brami.
E se le fantasie nostre son basse
    a tanta altezza, non è maraviglia;
    ché sopra 'l sol non fu occhio ch'andasse.

*Were I to call on genius, art, and practice, still I could not describe it so that it could be imagined;* but one can believe, and one can long to see. And if our fantasies fall short before such heights, it is no marvel since no eye can go beyond the sun.

(*Par.* 10.43–48)

In a later exhortation—"chi non s'impenna sì che là sù voli, / dal muto aspetti quindi le novelle" ("he who does not feather himself so that he flies up there, may await news from a mute" [10.74–75])—the poet implicitly likens himself to one who cannot speak, setting the stage for a heaven filled with speakers, and also for this heaven's paradoxes: if, as Thomas tells us, all the world craves news of the fifth and most beautiful soul in the first *corona* ("tutto 'l mondo / là giù ne gola di saper novella" [10.110–11]), who will be the newsbearer but our mute poet?[8]

The most long-winded of this heaven's speakers, St. Thomas, will also draw attention to his discourse as verbal artifact, in self-conscious passages like the following:

Se sì di tutti li altri esser vuo' certo,
    di retro al mio parlar ten vien col viso
    girando su per lo beato serto.

*If thus of all the others you wish to be certain, follow with your eyes behind my speech,* circling above along the holy wreath.

(*Par.* 10.100–102)

Or se tu l'occhio de la mente trani
*di luce in luce dietro a le mie lode,*
già de l'ottava con sete rimani.

If now you are bringing your mind's eye *from light to light behind my praises*, you
are already thirsting for the eighth.

(*Par.* 10.121–23)

His emphasis on language persists in his articulation of the pilgrim's need
for clear and "distended" discourse ("Tu dubbi, e hai voler che si ricerna / in
sì aperta e 'n sì distesa lingua / lo dicer mio" ["You doubt, and you wish my
speech to be distinguished in open and explicit language" (11.22–24)]) and
throughout his eulogy of Francis. We note the insistence on matching the
signifier to the signified that informs the etymological play on Assisi/Ascesi/
Orïente: "Però chi d'esso loco fa parole, / non dica Ascesi, ché direbbe
corto, / ma Orïente, se proprio dir vuole" ("Therefore let him who speaks of
this place not say 'Ascesi,' which would be to say too little, but 'Orient,' if he
wants to speak correctly" [11.52–54]). We note, further, the remarks, analogous to the poet's own such thoughts cited above, which deprecate his ability to adequately tell the story of "costui, la cui mirabil vita / meglio in gloria
del ciel si canterebbe" ("that one, whose miraculous life would better be
sung in the glory of heaven" [11.95–96]); the exhortation to the pilgrim that
mimics the poet's own exhortation to the reader ("Or, se le mie parole non
son fioche, / se la tua audïenza è stata attenta, / se ciò ch'è detto a la mente
revoche" ["Now, if my words are not faint, if your listening has been intent,
if what has been said you recall to mind" (11.133–35)]); and especially the
self-consciousness that prompts Thomas to provide the hermeneutic key to
his own discourse: "Ma perch'io non proceda troppo chiuso, / Francesco e
Povertà per questi amanti / prendi oramai nel mio parlar diffuso" ("But that
I may not proceed too covertly, you may now take Francis and Poverty to be
the lovers of my outspread speech" [11.73–75]). Bonaventure displays a
similar awareness of his role as speaker-narrator, and indeed of his role as
second narrator, whose discourse is motivated by previous discourse: "Ad
inveggiar cotanto paladino / mi mosse l'infiammata cortesia / di fra Tommaso e 'l discreto latino" ("The inflamed courtesy of brother Thomas and
his discerning speech moved me to praise so great a paladin" [12.142–44]).

Both eulogies are divisible into an introductory section, the *vita* proper
and a coda.[9] The two narratives are, moreover, essentially the verbal equivalents of the double rainbow invoked to describe the two circles of souls; they
are (despite Francis's *vita* being fifteen verses longer than Dominic's) "due
archi paralelli e concolori" ("two rainbows parallel and like in color"
[12.11]), "paralelli" in their structural similarities and "concolori" in their
shared imagery. Dante has been scrupulous in the allocation of connotative

elements: if the geographical periphrasis introducing Francis's birthplace points to the east, "Orïente," Dominic's periphrasis points west;[10] if there is etymological wordplay regarding Assisi in canto 11, canto 12 refers to the etymologies of the names of Dominic, his father, and his mother; if Francis's birthplace is a rising sun, an "orto" (11.55), Dominic is the cultivator of Christ's garden, Christ's "orto" (12.72, 104). This same principle of balance informs the metaphors that govern the *vite*: if Francis is portrayed chiefly as a lover and a husband, and if we think of his life in terms of the mystical marriage to Poverty, nonetheless Dominic's baptism is characterized as an espousal of faith and he is "l'amoroso drudo / de la fede cristiana" ("the amorous lover of the Christian faith" [12.55–56]); if Francis's life is modeled on Christ's, nonetheless the poem's first triple rhyme on "Cristo" belongs to the life of Dominic (12.71, 73, 75). In writing the life of Dominic, Dante seems to have been intent on picking up the rhetorical and metaphorical components of the life of Francis: if Francis is an "archimandrita" (11.99), a prince of shepherds in an ecclesiastical Greek locution, Dominic is not only "nostro patrïarca" (11.121), a term that displays the same linguistic provenance, but also a "pastor" (11.131), whose sheep are wandering from the fold. Although we think of Dominic as the more military, and of Francis as the more loving, in fact Francis is a *campione* as well as Dominic, and Dominic is a lover as well as Francis. Even the agricultural images of Dominic as the keeper of Christ's vineyard and as a torrent sent to root out heretical weeds are anticipated by Francis's return "al frutto de l'italica erba" ("to the harvest of the Italian fields" [11.105]) and reprised in the image of the Franciscans as tares that will be excluded from the harvest bin.

Dante, then, strove to fashion his two narratives as verbal analogues to the twin arcs of souls that "matched motion with motion and song with song": "e moto a moto e canto a canto colse" (12.6). Most intriguing from this perspective are the two introductions of fifteen verses each, devoted to emphasizing the identity of Francis and Dominic before embarking on their nonidentical stories. In the first case, Thomas begins by telling us that God chose two princes as guides for the church, whom he characterizes as respectively seraphic and cherubic, and concludes by insisting that it matters not a whit whose life is narrated first, since they worked to the same end:

> due principi ordinò in suo favore,
> che quinci e quindi le fosser per guida.
> L'un fu tutto serafico in ardore;
>     l'altro per sapïenza in terra fue
>     di cherubica luce uno splendore.
> De l'un dirò, però che d'amendue
>     si dice l'un pregiando, qual ch'om prende,
>     perch'ad un fine fur l'opere sue.

God ordained two princes on her behalf, who on this side and that should be her guides. One was all seraphic in his ardor; the other by his wisdom was a splendor of cherubic light. I shall speak of one; although in praising one, one speaks of both, whichever one takes, since their works were to one end.

(*Par.* 11.35–42)

The second introduction is organized chiastically with respect to the first.[11] Bonaventure concludes his preamble by calling the two saints two champions, explicitly referring us back to Thomas's initial "due principi": "e, *come è detto*, a sua sposa soccorse / con due campioni" ("and, *as was said*, he sustained his bride with two champions" [12.43–44]). He begins by stressing the need to complete what Thomas began, to complement his colleague's discourse with his own: "L'amor che mi fa bella / mi tragge a ragionar de l'altro duca / per cui del mio sì ben ci si favella" ("The love that makes me beautiful leads me to discourse of the other leader because of whom my own was so praised here" [12.31–33]). Like Thomas, Bonaventure stresses that where one champion is the other must be, since they work to one end:

Degno è che, dov'è l'un, l'altro s'induca:
   sì che, com'elli ad una militaro,
   così la gloria loro insieme luca.

Right it is that wherever is the one the other should be led in, so that, as they fought as one, so their glory should shine together.

(*Par.* 12.34–36)

What is striking about these passages is that these paeans to oneness are in fact hymns to difference. Language, in the form of inevitable little words like "l'un" and "l'altro," reveals and belabors difference, continually betraying the attempt to transform "one" in the sense of unique and hence different ("De *l'un* dirò") into "one" in the sense of identical, the same ("ad *un fine* fur l'opere sue"). The form points to difference while the content denies it, insisting that to speak of one is to speak of two, that one can be two. The disjunction between form and content becomes yet more apparent when we reconsider the tercet describing the trinity that opens this heaven—"Guardando nel suo Figlio con l'Amore / che *l'uno e l'altro* etternalmente spira, / lo primo e ineffabile Valore" ("Looking upon his son with the love that *the one and the other* eternally breathe forth, the first and ineffable power" [*Par.* 10.1–3])[12]—and compare it to Bonaventure's "Degno è che, dov'è *l'un, l'altro* s'induca." In referring to the persons of the trinity, the separateness inherent in "l'uno e l'altro" is minimized; the phrase is blanketed by its position between the participial construction of the first verse and the postponed subject of the third, the middle verse thereby serving as a pivot governing the harmonious disposition of the whole and mirroring the dialectical workings of the trinity itself. By contrast, in Bonaventure's "dov'è l'un, l'altro s'induca," the pronouns—militantly disjoined by a caesura rather than linked by a copula—are also militant disjoiners, telling us that the "due principi" are irretrievably "*due* principi," "*due* campioni," that despite their working "ad un fine," they will never be "un."

What is true ontologically is also true rhetorically: for all Dante's attempt to represent the two saints *d'un modo*, there is an inescapable measure of difference, if only because—since narrative exists in time—one must be presented first. Bonaventure's awareness of following Thomas reminds us that, in narrative as in time, what follows is inevitably conditioned by what precedes; most readers have shared Bonaventure's sense of belatedness, feeling (whether rightly or wrongly does not really matter) that the life of Dominic is conditioned by the life of Francis and not vice versa.[13] By leading us to believe that the life of Dominic is governed by a principle of compensation—that if Francis's adult life is highlighted, we will hear instead of Dominic's childhood—Dante leads us to think of narrative precedence: thus the remarkable disclaimer with which Thomas begins his story, when he goes out of his way to remind us that narrative order exists by telling us that it does not affect this particular narrative, since whichever saint is chosen ("qual ch'om prende") the other will also be praised, because to praise one is to praise both. In fact, as any narrator knows, it makes a great deal of difference (an illuminating idiom) what story we tell first: the order in which we relate events is the essence of plot making. Dante shows keen awareness of the strategic effects of narrative order in the *Convivio*, where he argues that one's most important point should be made last, since it will remain in the mind of the listener: "sempre quello che massimamente dire intende lo dicitore sì dee riservare di dietro; però che quello che ultimamente si dice, più rimane ne l'animo de lo uditore" ("always that which a speaker most intends to convey must be reserved for last, since what is said last most remains in the mind of the listener" [2.8.2]).[14] Following this precept, Dominic benefits from having his story told last, rather than suffering by comparison with Francis. Still, however we interpret the effects of the order in cantos 11 and 12, parity is impossible. Despite the disclaimers, parity is breached when one saint's story is recounted first. And when later in the poem Dante places Francis—but not Dominic—in the second tier of the rose, thus implicitly refuting Bonaventure's claim that where one is the other must be, he further ruptures the unity posed by this heaven.[15]

If, therefore, Dante takes pains to balance the representations of Francis and Dominic, as part of the balancing that informs this heaven, he also makes authorial decisions that undermine balance and draw attention to the impossibility of fully balancing or equalizing these two representations. Did he really want to represent Francis and Dominic *d'un modo*? Did he want to eliminate difference? He says he did (or rather, Thomas and Bonaventure say they do), but, in that case, why not—for starters—have Thomas call them both seraphim? Again we can see Dante striving to embrace both ends of his paradox. On the one hand, the traditional connotations of the seraphim and cherubim—love and knowledge—work to underscore the trinitarian accommodation of difference that is his theme, while on the other the names of the orders serve to create difference, and thus to undermine Thomas's next assertion: if we represent Francis as a seraph, and Dominic as a cherub, then one referent will not apply to both, and to speak of one is not to speak of both. Looking again at the famous tercet that presents the two saints for the first time, we see that it institutionalizes diversity/inequality by invoking a hierarchy that is buttressed by the telltale "l'un" and "l'altro":[16]

> L'un fu tutto *serafico* in ardore;
> *l'altro* per sapïenza in terra fue
> di *cherubica* luce uno splendore.

(Par. 11.37–39)

Here, as he embarks on the lengthy and complex balancing of the two biographies, Dante seems to call attention to the futility of his project in the very act of beginning it. How can we account for his apparently contradictory behavior? The answer lies in Dante's commitment to a paradoxical paradise, whose optical illusions are rendered with verbal sleights of hand that are intended to afford us an insight into how difference can coexist with unity, how it can be that "ogne dove / in cielo è paradiso, *etsi* la grazia / del sommo ben d'un modo non vi piove." The author's grace both confers and withdraws the illusion of raining equally on all parts of his textual paradise, with the result that, on the page as in heaven, our one certainty is that "d'un modo non vi piove."

.   .   .   .   .

Thus far I have traced the tensions, deriving from the need simultaneously to individuate and unify, that subtend the stories of Francis and Dominic, while suggesting that these tensions undergird the *Paradiso* as a whole. Having proposed that the heaven of the sun be read as an authorial meditation on narrative, I would like now to explore further the reflexive components of this meditation. It is not coincidental that this heaven should contain the deceptively simple verse that proclaims this poem's poetics; we remember the address to the reader in canto 10, which the poet concludes by telling us that his attention is constrained by "quella materia ond'io son fatto scriba." Dante's claim to be merely the scribe who writes down what the "verace autore" (*Par.* 26.40) composes, in other words his absolute claim to absolute truth, is the single most fascinating feature of his textuality. A poet is constrained by such a claim; it is a claim that requires constant tending, that must be tenaciously reinforced. Thomas's presentation of the first circle of wise men provides, almost incidentally, such reinforcement, since he adopts the same narrative strategies—modesty topoi, apostrophes to the listener/reader—adopted elsewhere by the poet. Further reinforcement is provided by the technique of making the end of a canto coincide with the end of a speaker's speech; thus, the last words of canto 11 are the last words of Thomas's condemnation of the Dominicans, a coincidence to which the first verse of the next canto promptly draws our attention: "Sì tosto come l'ultima parola / la benedetta fiamma per dir tolse" ("As soon as the blessed flame had spoken its last word" [12.1–2]). The end of canto 12 will coincide with the last words of Bonaventure, and the last word of canto 13 will once more be Thomas's. By minimizing framing material in this way Dante subtly reinforces our sense that these speakers really have taken the floor, that the text is really theirs, that there is no distinction between what they said and what he says they said. Boundaries between narrators are further blurred by the self-referential nature of the discourse; the "ultima parola" of canto 11 is Thomas's second verbatim citation of the cryptic verse he had first uttered in 10.96 ("u' ben s'impingua se non si vaneggia" ["where one can fatten well if one does not stray"]) and had subsequently restated in 11.25. In a speech act that could be taken as emblematic of the discourse-ridden nature of this heaven, he concludes his life of Francis with a layering of discourse within discourse: "e vedra' il corrègger che argomenta / 'U' ben s'impingua, se non si vaneggia'" ("and you will see the correction that is argued by 'where one can fatten well if one does not stray'" [11.138–39]). It is not surprising that the inattentive reader begins to lose track of the levels of speech, attributing to Thomas the narrative control that is in fact Dante's.

Indeed, Thomas is a champion of narrative, a champion of discourse—not only because he discourses so much, but because so much of what he says is a manifesto for difference, and hence for narrative. In canto 11, in the verses that lead up to the life of Francis, Thomas rehearses the two "doubts" or intellectual problems that were raised for the pilgrim by his earlier speech; they concern "ove dinanzi dissi: 'U' ben s'impingua,' / e là u' dissi: 'Non nacque il secondo'" ("where before I said: 'Where one fattens well,' and there where I said: 'A second was not born'" [25–26]). Technically, the life of Francis will be a gloss to the problem posed by "U' ben s'impingua," where it was stated that the members of the Dominican order can fatten if they do not stray, and Thomas's discourse on creation in canto 13 will be a gloss to his other self-citation, "Non nacque il secondo," which stated that no one ever arose whose wisdom was as profound as Solomon's. As he prepares to deal with the first dubbio, Thomas lays great stress on the need to make distinctions:[17] "e qui è uopo che ben si distingua" ("and here it is

needful that one distinguish well" [11.27]). Then, rigorously distinguishing—i.e., putting aside for the time being the question of Solomon—he
launches into providence's need for two princes to guide the church, and so
into the life of Francis and the corruption of the Dominicans, concluding
with a restatement of the problematic verse on the fat Dominicans, which
the pilgrim is now in a position to understand. Thomas returns to the need
for distinctions in canto 13, as he concludes his resolution of the second
*dubbio*. Having clarified that Solomon's wisdom was that of a king, in other
words having inserted into his argument a distinction that previously he had
not articulated, Thomas reproves the undiscriminating pilgrim, saying,
"Con questa distinzion prendi 'l mio detto" ("Take my words with this distinction" [13.109]), and advises him in future to move slowly in his thought
process, rather than being among the fools who come to conclusions without having distinguished, "sanza distinzione":

> E questo ti sia sempre piombo a' piedi,
>    per farti mover lento com' uom lasso
>    e al sì e al no che tu non vedi:
> ché quelli è tra li stolti bene a basso,
>    che *sanza distinzione* afferma e nega
>    ne l'un così come ne l'altro passo. . . .

> And let this always be lead to your feet, to make you move as slowly as a tired man,
> to either the "yes" or the "no" that you do not see; for he is well down among the
> fools who *without making distinctions* affirms and denies in one case just as in the
> other. . . .

> (*Par.* 13.112–17)

Thomas's rhetoric of differentiation—his use of *distinzione* and *distinguere*[18]—is part of the narrative self-consciousness that permeates this
heaven, demonstrated by phrases like "ove dinanzi dissi" ("where I said before" [11.25]), "e però miri a ciò ch'io dissi suso,/ quando narrai" ("and
therefore you wonder at what I said above, when I narrated" [13.46–47]),
"se ciò ch'io dissi e questo note" ("if you note that which I said and this"
[13.103]), "e se al 'surse' drizzi li occhi chiari" ("and if you direct your clear
eyes to 'there arose'" [13.106]). In the second and fourth examples, we find
that Thomas seems to have assimilated his spoken discourse to the written
discourse of the surrounding poem, using the preposition "suso" to refer to
what he said "above" ("ciò ch'io dissi suso") and telling the pilgrim to direct
his glance ("occhi chiari") at a previous utterance ("al 'surse'").[19] Thomas
himself is described in terms of his narrative function, as "la luce in che
mirabil vita / del poverel di Dio narrata fumi" ("the light in which the wondrous life of the poor man of God had been narrated to me" [13.32–33]). Of
the scant seven uses of *narrare* in the poem, two appear in this brief span of

*Paradiso* 13, referring to Thomas and his various discourses, all of which are paradigms for logical discursive narrativity, narrativity that proceeds from point one to point two without attempting to disguise or combat its necessary unfolding in time: thus, in the life of Francis, the narrative is propelled by logical formulas like "Pensa oramai" and "discerner puoi" ("Think now," "you can discern" [11.118, 123]). Far from disguising the relation of narrative to time, Thomas strips it bare in verses like "se ciò ch'io dissi e questo note" (13.103), where the pilgrim is advised to bear in mind "ciò ch'io dissi," i.e., what was said about Solomon in canto 10, and add it to what has just been said in canto 13; if one must store the past and add it to the present to make a complete narrative, narrative must exist in time. In the same way, Thomas projects the pilgrim's reaction were he to cease his explanation at a premature point:

> Or s'i' non procedesse avanti piùe,
> "Dunque, come costui fu sanza pare?"
> comincerebber le parole tue.

> Now if I were to proceed no further, "How, then, was that one without an equal?" your words would begin.

$$(Par. \ 13.88\text{–}90)$$

Here discourse is figured as an ongoing procession (*procedere* + "avanti piùe"),[20] in which logical connectors like "dunque" move the motion forward by providing a new question to answer, a new point of departure. In other words, discourse is presented as a system of *distinzioni*, a system of differences.

Thomas celebrates difference, and his mode of narration is explicitly based on difference; his presentation of the first circle of souls is a model for this kind of narrative, proceeding explicitly from "Questi che m'è a destra più vicino" ("This one who is nearest on my right" [10.97]) to "Quell'altro" ("that other" [10.103]), "L'altro ch'appresso" ("the other who next" [10.106]), "La quinta luce" ("the fifth light" [10.109]), and so forth. When he exhorts the pilgrim to follow behind his speech with his eyes ("di retro al mio parlar ten vien col viso" [10.101]), he figures his discourse as a line, a narrative path that stretches before the listener, articulated by logical hinges like the numerical tags assigned to certain souls along the way. We can go further and note that the repeated use of number in this heaven (the heaven of arithmetic according to the *Convivio*'s alignment of the heavens with the liberal arts)[21]—in phrases like "la quarta famiglia" ("the fourth family" [10.49]), "La quinta luce" (10.109), "non surse il secondo" ("there never rose a second" [10.114]), "l'ottava [luce]" ("the eighth light" [10.123]), "la prima rota" ("the first wheel" [13.12]), "quando narrai che non ebbe 'l secondo / lo ben che ne la quinta luce è chiuso" ("when I recounted that the good enclosed within the fifth light had no second" [13.47–48])—constitutes an invocation of time, given Dante's Aristotelian definition of time as number in the *Convivio*. The temporal/narrative path here invoked by Thomas is a miniversion of the temporal/narrative path followed by the reader of the *Commedia* as a whole, the discursive analogue to the journey in which the pilgrim is taken "per lo ciel, *di lume in lume*" ("through heaven *from light to light*" [*Par.* 17.115]) and is shown "le vite spiritali *ad una ad una*" ("lives of the spirits *one by one*" [33.24]). Thus, when Thomas as narrator figures his speech as a line, saying, "Or s'i' non procedesse avanti piùe," he is "imitating" Dante narrator, who had earlier exhorted us readers in precisely the same language:

> Pensa, lettor, se quel che qui s'inizia
> *non procedesse*, come tu avresti
> di più savere angosciosa carizia. . . .

> Think, reader, if that which here begins *were not to proceed*, how you would have an anguished desire to know more. . . .
>
> (*Par.* 5.109–11)

In other words, the basic narrative skeleton of the *Commedia* is linear, is based on a system of differences, is premised on the rules for narrative that are implicit in Thomas's celebration of order, of hierarchy, of *distinzione*.

But, as we saw when discussing the problems Dante faces in writing the lives of Francis and Dominic, there are occasions—and they arise increasingly in the *Paradiso*—when his basic narrative mode does not suit him, when the context dictates unity, not difference, and therefore he feels called upon to disguise or alter as much as possible the very nature of his textuality. The heaven of the sun presents in microcosm the problems that Dante faces as the narrator of the *Paradiso*, as he veers from the discursive mode favored by Thomas, the mode that subtends most of the poem, to a newer mode that will be called upon more and more frequently as he completes the final canticle. The shifts in register that mark this heaven are paradigmatic of the shifts that will dominate the *Paradiso*'s textuality: from the orderliness of Thomas's presentation of the souls, in canto 10, to the lyricism of that canto's ending passage, in which the linear roll call of souls is rounded into harmonious circularity by way of the simile of the clock:

> Indi, come orologio che ne chiami
>    ne l'ora che la sposa di Dio surge
>    a mattinar lo sposo perché l'ami,
> che *l'una parte e l'altra* tira e urge,
>    tin tin sonando con sì dolce nota,
>    che 'l ben disposto spirto d'amor turge;
> così vid'ïo la gloriosa rota

muoversi e render *voce a voce in tempra*
e in dolcezza ch'esser non pò nota
se non colà dove gioir s'insempra.

Then, like the clock that calls us at the hour in which the bride of God rises to sing matins to the bridegroom that he may love her, when *one part and the other* pulls and draws, sounding "tin tin" with notes so sweet that the well-disposed spirit swells with love; so did I see the glorious wheel move and render *voice to voice with such harmony* and sweetness that it cannot be known except for there where joy is everlasting.

*(Par.* 10.139–48)

Here, as in the verses describing the trinity cited before, the markers of difference—words like the ones Thomas uses in his visual tour of the wise men, words like the ones that dot the biographies of Francis and Dominic, to wit, words like "uno" and "altro"—are defused, their separateness harmonized by the unified workings of the celestial clock, a circularity in which the synchrony of voices is rendered by a verbal repetition ("voce a voce in tempra") that will be picked up in a later passage, where again the two circles move and sing as one: "e moto a moto e canto a canto colse" *(Par.* 12.6). The latter verse comes, not surprisingly, from a passage that is tonally very similar to the verses from the end of canto 10 cited above and that, like the clock simile, is also dedicated to generating a narrative mode radically different from the one championed by Thomas.

One could sketch the workings of this heaven in terms of shifts from a discursive logical mode based on embracing *distinzione,* that is, a mode that accepts the fundamental subjection of narrative to linear time, to a "lyrical" or "antinarrative" mode that rebels against the dominion of time.[22] Frequently the burden of this rebellion is carried by similes, like the simile of the clock, or the simile in which the wise men of canto 10 appear to the pilgrim like ladies who have temporarily ceased dancing as they wait for the music to begin once more ("donne mi parver, non da ballo sciolte, / ma che s'arrestin tacite, ascoltando / fin che le nove note hanno ricolte" ["they seemed to me ladies, not freed from the dance, but who stop silent, waiting until they have caught the new notes" (10.79–81)]); the incongruity of such an image is perhaps such as to destabilize all congruities, including those of narrative sequence. The openings of both cantos 12 and 13 are lyrical explosions dedicated to impressing upon us the unity of the two circles, a unity that has just been shattered by the preceding biographies, with their relentless privileging—and denial—of difference. When Dante tells us that difference does not exist, as in the introductory sections of the *vite,* he creates it; when he wholeheartedly wishes to create the illusion of lack of difference, he resorts not to statements about its presence or absence but to another kind of writing, one that does not (insofar as is humanly possible) make distinctions. In these passages, the text becomes an incandescent swirl of language, as the poet layers simile within simile, intending thus to disconnect the logical connectors of discourse à la St. Thomas:

> Come si volgon per tenera nube
>    due archi paralelli e concolori,
>    quando Iunone a sua ancella iube,
> nascendo di quel d'entro quel di fori,
>    a guisa del parlar di quella vaga
>    ch'amor consunse come sol vapori
>
> .  .  .  .  .  .  .  .  .  .  .  .  .
>
> così di quelle sempiterne rose
>    volgiensi circa noi le due ghirlande,
>    e sì l'estrema all'intima rispuose.

As two rainbows parallel and like in color curve through a thin cloud when Juno commands her handmaid, the outer rainbow born from the one within, like the voice of that wandering nymph whom love consumed as the soul does vapors . . . so the two garlands of those eternal roses curved around us, and so the outer garland answered to the inner one.

(Par. 12.10–15, 19–21)

As one rainbow is born from within another, "nascendo di quel d'entro quel di fori," so similes give birth to similes, in a play of language whose ultimate recourse to metaphor (indeed to the *Paradiso*'s first use of the rose: "quelle sempiterne rose") attempts to disguise its origins in discursive thought, in *distinzioni*.

If this heaven is about the centeredness of differing human perspectives around an all-embracing divine point, it is also about the attempt of a human poet to represent such centeredness. How to replace the eccentricity of language with the concentricity of heaven? Concentricity—the idea that different beings, represented as different points on the circumferences of different circles, can have the same center, can be united around one central truth—is the hallmark of this heaven, whose goal is the demonstration that all points on the circumference are equidistant from the center, so that "nel vero [si fanno] come centro in tondo." Typically, the "centro in tondo" imagery is here applied to language and belief; the pilgrim's thoughts are being harmonized with Thomas's discourse: "Or apri li occhi a quel ch'io ti rispondo, / e vedräi il tuo credere e 'l mio dire / nel vero farsi come centro in tondo" ("Now open your eyes to what I answer you, and you will see your belief and my discourse become in the truth as the center in a circle" [13.49–51]). Moreover, the image anticipates the magnificently recapitulatory verse that opens the heaven's last canto: canto 14 begins with "Dal centro al cerchio, e sì dal cerchio al centro" ("From the center to the circumference and so from the circumference to the center"), used to describe the movement of water in a round vase. The poet here recalls that the currents of speech created by Thomas, who stands on the circle's circumference, and by Beatrice, who stands at its center, seemed to him like water moving from the circumference of a vase to its center and back again; in other words, the image of concentricity is employed to describe waves of discourse, "per la similitudine che nacque / del suo parlare e di quel di Beatrice" ("because of the similitude that was born of his speech and that of Beatrice" [14.7–8]). Thus, the image of concentricity, the most basic image of this heaven, is devoted to visualizing currents of language as they move about the pilgrim. What this passage, with its unique use of "similitudine" (a hapax that adds another intensely self-conscious word to this heaven's roster), tells us is that language must be viewed as part of this heaven's subject; the heaven of the sun is about the possibility of concentricity not only among different schools of thought, as represented by the wise men, but also among different forms of expression, as represented by the different registers—the "narrative" and the "antinarrative"—employed by the poet.

The poet's two registers could be seen as his approximations of two kinds of divine discourse, one based on difference and one freed from temporality, like Beatrice, who is significantly defined in canto 10 as "quella che sì scorge / di bene in meglio, sì subitamente / che l'atto suo per tempo non si sporge" ("the one who guides me so from good to better, so immediately that her act does not extend into time" [37–39]). Beatrice's movements toward the good are so immediate that they do not extend into time; Beatrice's poet, on the other hand, can only attempt the illusion of a language that does not extend into time, and the story of the last canticle will increasingly be the story of such an attempt. But God also writes with difference, in a mode that the poet can more faithfully approximate; thus Thomas quotes divine discourse, recounting Solomon's reaction "quando fu detto 'Chiedi'" ("when 'Ask' was said to him" [13.93]).[23] Thomas's matter-of-fact citation of God's speech reminds us that the act of creation—"lo discorrer di Dio sovra quest'acque" ("the moving of God upon these waters" [Par. 29.21])—is a form of discursiveness ("discorrer"), of differentiation. In fact, the word distinzione, which we have seen used twice in Paradiso 13 by Thomas, occurs only in two other places in the poem, both in the Paradiso, both in the context of God's creation, his sublime act of differentiation,[24] and in canto 13 itself the doctrine of creation focuses on the difference wrought by nature (compared to an artist with a trembling hand) upon God's unity, his "segno / idëale" ("ideal sign" [68–69]). Thomas's celebration of difference thus seems rooted in an analogy between creative acts; God creates the universe by creating difference ("giù d'atto in atto" ["down from act to act" (13.62)]), and man likewise is able—by distinguishing and differentiating—to create and sustain logical thought. What Thomas, not for nothing an Aristotelian, celebrates is the positive side of time: the ability to separate, to distinguish, to relish each thing for itself, mirroring God's "d'atto in atto" with our "ad una ad una." Indeed, the heaven of the sun as a whole could be viewed as a celebration and justification of difference (the sun itself is defined as the measurer, the parser of difference, the sphere that "col suo lume il tempo ne misura" ["with its light measures time for us" (10.30)]), including the form of difference that is narrative. In the opening address to the reader the poet tells us that the proper workings of the heavens depend upon a necessary divergence of their motions from the straight path: "se la strada lor non fosse torta, / molta virtù nel ciel sarebbe in vano" ("if their path were not twisted, much potency in heaven would be in vain" [10.16–17]). In other words, sometimes the path should be twisted; sometimes difference, rather than unity, is called for. (As to how we are to know when "la strada" should be "torta," the answer must involve Thomas's injunction: "e qui è uopo che ben si distingua.") Dante thus begins this heaven with a strikingly peremptory apostrophe whose lesson is precisely the moral basis of difference, difference as a positive and necessary factor in the functioning of the universe.

Rhetorically, Dante tries to have it both ways, as his use of that representative phrase, *l'uno e l'altro*, indicates. On the one hand, the expression denotes balance, harmony: Freccero, citing three examples of this construction—"che l'uno e l'altro etternalmente spira" (10.2), "dove l'un moto e l'altro si percuote" ("where the one motion strikes the other" [10.9]), "e l'un ne l'altro aver li raggi suoi" ("and one to have its rays within the other" [13.16])—refers to the "parallel syntax" used by Dante to render the celestial motions of this heaven, and indeed all these examples come from contexts where Dante is creating unity.[25] In canto 10 all uses of *l'uno e l'altro* point toward unity: besides the trinity and the heavenly cross cited above, we find the celestial clock, "che l'una parte e l'altra tira e urge" (142), and "Grazïan, che l'uno e l'altro foro / aiutò sì che piace in paradiso" ("Gratian, who aided one and the other forum such that it pleases in paradise" [104–5]). These examples present necessary difference, a difference that somehow simultaneously exists and is resolved into a higher unity, thus—like Gratian—pleasing paradise. The same language that helps to convey this mysterious coexistence, and that operates as parallel syntax in the examples from canto 10, functions, however, as adversative syntax in the biographies of the two saints, polarizing rather than unifying. In cantos 11 and 12 Dante divides the expression, using it to create unadulterated rather than resolved difference in referring to Francis and Dominic: "L'un fu tutto serafico in ardore; / l'altro per sapïenza in terra fue" (11.37–38); "Degno è che, dov'è l'un, l'altro s'induca" (12.34); "Se tal fu l'una rota de la biga . . . ben ti dovrebbe assai esser palese / l'eccellenza de l'altra" ("If such was the one wheel of the chariot, the excellence of the other should be clear" [12.106,

109–10]). The last usage of canto 12 is a reference to the errors of the two competing factions of the Franciscan order ("ch'uno la fugge e altro la coarta" [126]), and thus a political variant of the difference stressed by these cantos.

Canto 13 seems to achieve a balance between the unity of canto 10 and the difference of cantos 11 and 12: its first two usages ("e l'un ne l'altro aver li raggi suoi" [16], "che l'uno andasse al primo e l'altro al poi" ["so that one should go first and the other after" (18)]) belong to the lyrical "antinarrative" opening and are akin to the examples from canto 10, while the succeeding usages belong to Thomas's celebration of logical discrimination as a positive force. As he sets out to clarify the second *dubbio,* Thomas reemphasizes the order with which he has proceeded from one problem to another ("Quando l'una paglia è trita . . . a batter l'altra dolce amor m'invita" ["When one straw is threshed sweet love invites me to beat the other" (13.34, 36)]); he criticizes those who treat all issues in the same way ("che sanza distinzione afferma e nega / ne l'un così come ne l'altro passo" [116–17]) and warns that the differences we think we see may not correspond to what is ("Non creda donna Berta e ser Martino, / per vedere un furare, altro offerere, / vederli dentro al consiglio divino" ["Let not dame Bertha and sir Martin, if they see one steal and another offer, believe to see them within the divine counsel" (139–41)]). In a sense, Thomas achieves a redeemed difference, looking forward to the one usage of *l'uno e l'altro* in the last part of this heaven: in canto 14, the phrase reaffirms the unity of canto 10, returning to the unified behavior of the two circles ("e l'uno e l'altro coro a dicer 'Amme!'" ["both the one and the other chorus in saying 'Amen'" (62)]). Thomas's achievement is brought about by his affirmation of the apostrophe's lesson on the value of difference and especially by his linking of God with difference in his discourse on creation. In confirming that Adam and Christ were infused by God with as much knowledge as has been given to human nature, Thomas refers to God as "quel valor che l'uno e l'altro fece":

> Tu credi che nel petto onde la costa
>   si trasse per formar la bella guancia
>   il cui palato a tutto 'l mondo costa,
> e in quel che, forato da la lancia,
>   e prima e poscia tanto sodisfece,
>   che d'ogne colpa vince la bilancia,
> quantunque a la natura umana lece
>   aver di lume, tutto fosse infuso
>   *da quel valor che l'uno e l'altro fece....*

You believe that into the breast from which the rib was drawn to form the beautiful cheek whose palate costs dear to all the world, and into that which, pierced by the lance, both before and after so much satisfied that of every sin it clears the scale, was infused—*by that power which made both the one and the other*—whatever light is permitted to human kind. . . .

(*Par.* 13.37–45)

God is thus the maker of difference in its highest form, the maker of difference that can redeem difference, as Christ, "[che] prima e poscia tanto sodisfece," is able to redeem all of time, all the linear narrativity of *prima e poscia.* A being in time who can redeem time: this is the dialectic adumbrated by a verse like "che l'uno andasse al primo e l'altro al poi," in which unified celestial movement is expressed in the language of diversity,[26] or by the simile of the clock, where eternity is manufactured ("s'insempra" ends both simile and canto) via the material representation of time itself. In the same way, Dante himself is a dialectical being. On the one hand, his entrance into the heaven of the sun is marked by atemporality, since he is not aware of his arrival "se non com'uom s'accorge, / anzi 'l primo pensier" ("except as a man is aware before the first thought" [10.35–36]); his awareness exists outside of temporal or narrative succession, "before the first thought." On the other, if he is to continue his experience of this heaven, the pilgrim must move from unity to difference, and so the rapt ecstasy of his thanks to God is fragmented by the splendor of Beatrice's smile, which divides his attention, diversifying his unified mind and causing it to move from one thing to many, "più cose": "mia mente unita in più cose divise" (10.63).[27] He is naturally a creature of *distinzioni*, able thus to approximate one form of divine discourse. However, although in one creation passage God is the maker of "le distinzion" (*Par.* 2.119), in another, the one in which he "discourses" over the waters, we learn that he himself was "sanza distinzïone in essordire" ("without distinction in beginning" [*Par.* 29.30]), that "né prima né poscia procedette / lo discorrer di Dio sovra quest'acque" ("neither before nor after preceded the moving of God upon these waters" [29.20–21]). Whereas man, who exists within the bounds of "prima e poscia," is exhorted by Thomas to create difference, God, who existed before "prima e poscia," may both create difference and be without it in his essence; unlike the "artista / ch'a l'abito de l'arte ha man che trema" ("artist who in the practice of his art has a hand that trembles" [13.77–78]), God does dispose of a "segno / idëale," even if he does not choose to employ it. In this heaven we view the problems of a poet who faces not only the challenge of difference but also of its absence, who would like to represent not only in Thomas's manner but also in the manner suggested by Beatrice's movement, "[che] per tempo non si sporge." When Dante says that he is freed from the vanities of earth, "da tutte queste cose sciolto" (11.10), he knows that he is (alas!) not freed from the temporal/spatial exigencies of narrative.

And thus we come back to the heaven's central representational node, to the stories of Francis and Dominic and the paradoxes that adhere to them.

Earlier I discussed the rhetorical balancing through which Dante seeks to create a sense of equality in these representations and drew attention to the introductory sections of the *vite* as repositories of difference. There is also, as commentators have noted, an overall sense of difference conferred by the asymmetrical treatment Francis and Dominic receive in the *Commedia* as a whole. The figure of Dominic is contained within this heaven, where he is named twice (10.95, 12.70), while the figure of Francis, named only once in this heaven (11.74), appears and is named elsewhere in the poem: in hell, where he is said to have unsuccessfully litigated with a devil for the soul of Guido da Montefeltro (*Inf.* 27.112); in the heaven of Saturn, where Benedict cites Francis along with himself and St. Peter as one of the great founders of an ecclesiastical movement (*Par.* 22.90); and in the empyrean, where he appears in the rose, linked again to Benedict: "Francesco, Benedetto e Augustino" (*Par.* 32.35). In the same way that Francis is a greater presence throughout the poem than Dominic, he is a more pervasive presence in the heaven of the sun, where his love for Lady Poverty will be recalled in references to his early followers as the "primi scalzi poverelli" ("the first barefoot poor ones" [12.131]) and to Francis himself as the "poverel di Dio" ("poor man of God" [13.33]).[28] These uses of the term *poverello*—which serve as fervent reminders of what Dante considered most noteworthy about St. Francis's life, namely his embrace of a Christlike poverty—support those who have maintained that the asymmetry of the biographies in favor of Francis is related to Dante's political sympathies for the Franciscan spirituals, the wing of the order that provoked papal displeasure through its militant insistence on ecclesiastical renewal through poverty. These critics note that Bonaventure's reproof of the leader of the conventuals is stronger than his reproof of the leader of the spirituals, and that the very presence of two of Francis's *poverelli* among the souls of the second circle constitutes a further oblique indictment of the conventuals.[29] One could add that the presence of Joachim of Flora among the souls of the second circle, and Dante's explicit confirmation of Joachim's status as a prophet ("il calavrese abate Giovacchino / di spirito profetico dotato" ["the Calabrian abbot Joachim, endowed with prophetic spirit" (12.140–41)]), are also signs of his leaning toward the spirituals, since Joachim's prophecies were interpreted and used by the spirituals in such a way as to buttress their cause.

The issue of prophecy is an important one in this heaven and is another indication of its highly reflexive content. Dante's sources for the lives of Francis and Dominic made much of prophecies that foretold the coming and working together of the two saints; in a passage used by the Franciscan biographers, Joachim wrote "erunt duo viri, unus hinc, alius inde" ("There will be two men, one over here, the other over there").[30] Prophecy is a central motif of the heaven: not only do we find Joachim, "di spirito profetico dotato," but also the Hebrew prophet Nathan, explicitly called "Natàn profeta" (12.136), Dominic's mother, who is made a prophet by virtue of the saint in her womb ("che, ne la madre, lei fece profeta" ["who, in his mother, made her a prophet" (12.60)]), and Dominic's godmother, who foresaw the nature of her godson's future accomplishments in a prophetic dream. Dante's stress on prophecy in this heaven is related to the heaven's concern with narrative, his own narrative, for to write a text defined as true—and here we come back to the verse inscribed at the heaven's threshold, in which the poet speaks of "quella materia ond'io son fatto scriba"—is to write a prophetic text. And, since one of Dante's principal textual strategies is to support his most perilous behavior by means of polemics against anyone who might dare to act similarly—but does not, in his view, benefit from divine authority to do so—it is not surprising to find in this heaven a great indictment, put in the mouth of Thomas, against those who have the temerity to judge prematurely: "Non sien le genti, ancor, troppo sicure / a giudicar" ("Let not folk be too sure in judging" [13.130–31]).[31] It goes without saying that those who judge prematurely and incorrectly are false prophets, while those who judge prematurely and correctly—like Joachim, Nathan, Dominic's mother and godmother, and Dante himself—are true prophets.[32] From this perspective, the philosopher Siger's "invidïosi veri" ("invidious truths" [10.138]) take on a new relevance with respect to a poet whose own mission, to be conferred in the next heaven by Cacciaguida, will be to tell unpopular truths;[33] the *Commedia* itself is an *invidioso vero*, and its poet is one whose special brand of assertive anxiety is revealed by such phrases as "se 'l vero è vero" ("if the truth be true" [10.113]). Since the first "vero" of this phrase is the Bible, and the Bible is written by God, the *verace autore*, it follows that the truth is true; since the *Commedia* is written by the scribe of the *verace autore*, it further follows—in Dante's own version of Siger's syllogisms—that in his case too " 'l vero è vero."

As we have seen, Dante tells us quite a lot in this heaven about the problems of writing this poem; we shall conclude by noting that he also presents a vision of the hermeneutic choices available to its author, a vision that corresponds to the alternatives he called in the *Convivio* allegory of poets and allegory of theologians. The life of Francis is implicitly labeled an example of the allegory of poets, that is to say personification allegory, by Thomas, who provides instructions as to how his story should be read:[34]

> Ma perch'io non proceda troppo chiuso,
> Francesco e Povertà per questi amanti
> prendi oramai nel mio parlar diffuso.

> (*Par.* 11.73–75)

Here we find all the hallmarks of personification allegory: its obscurity ("troppo chiuso"), its *quid pro quo* substitution of one set of figures for another ("Francesco e Povertà *per* questi amanti"), and its promise of real meaning to be revealed only later, when the literal sense is discarded and the allegorical key is revealed ("prendi *oramai*"). By contrast to this presentation of the allegory of poets, the method used by writers who do not claim to be God's scribe, canto 12 provides an exposition of the other way of writing, God's way of writing, the way in which biblical exegetes said the Bible was written, in which signs are the things themselves:

> Oh padre suo *veramente* Felice!
>   oh madre sua *veramente* Giovanna,
>   se, interpretata, val come si dice!

> Oh father of him *truly* Felice! Oh mother of him *truly* Giovanna, if, interpreted, this means what it says!

> (*Par.* 12.79–81)

Here Bonaventure, talking about Dominic's parents Felice and Giovanna, tells us that Felice is truly happy and that Giovanna is truly the grace of God because their names, when interpreted (*interpretare* is another intensely textual hapax), i.e., construed according to their etymological and therefore true significance, mean what they say.[35] In other words, their names are not arbitrary signs imposed from without—in the way that the allegorical significance is imposed onto the literal meaning in personification allegory—but are their essences, are the truth. Likewise we learn that Dominic is named *Domenico* (the possessive of *Dominus*, and thus "belonging to the Lord") so that his name may correspond to his reality:

> e perché fosse qual era in costrutto,
>   quinci si mosse spirito a nomarlo
>   del possessivo di cui era tutto.

> and so that he might be in his name what he indeed was, a spirit moved from here to name him with the possessive of him whose he wholly was.

> (*Par.* 12.67–69)

To use the *Vita Nuova*'s formula, "nomina sunt consequentia rerum": names or signs are consequences of things, so that the name is the thing in truth, as Beatrice is truly—"veramente"—a bringer of beatitude. These names that are the truth, that—like Ascesi converted to Orïente—are a speech that signifies properly and fully rather than abbreviatedly ("non dica Ascesi, chè direbbe corto, / ma Orïente, se proprio dir vuole"), constitute a gloss on Dante's own way of writing, on his prophetic text. It is not unrelated that of the *Commedia*'s four uses of *profeta/profetico*, three appear in *Paradiso* 12, or that the legends of Francis and Dominic insist on prophetic dreams—true dreams—as harbingers of the saints' coming: Innocent III dreamt of supporters for the crumbling Lateran, and Dominic dreamt of a companion to aid in his struggle.[36] Dante is a poet who believed that he learned the truth directly from God, receiving it in a prophetic dream of the kind experienced in canto 12 by Dominic's godmother, who sees the future—the truth—in her sleep: "vide nel sonno il mirabile frutto / ch'uscir dovea di lui e della rede" ("saw in sleep the wondrous fruit that was to come from him and from his heirs" [65–66]). Although ordinary folk—"donna Berta" and "ser Martino"—err when they attempt to deduce God's judgment on the basis of what they see ("Non creda donna Berta e ser Martino, / per vedere un furare, altro offerere, / vederli dentro al consiglio divino" [13.139–41]), our poet has been appointed God's scribe and as such is capable of seeing at least as far into the divine counsel as is necessary to write his poem.

The biographies of Francis and Dominic present the methods available to their author declaratively, as well as through their own formal choices. Naive readers, those reading the cantos for the first time who have not yet learned to see the poet's balancing of structure and rhetoric, experience the two stories as very different, and they usually prefer the story of Francis. In fact, although the two *vite* are superficially similar, "due archi paralelli e concolori" in the ways we discussed before, they are—with respect not to structure or imagery but narrative mode—profoundly different. Simply put, Dante tells the life of Francis as a story, adopting an explicitly narrative vein to which readers easily respond; we all love a story. The saint is born, he becomes a youth and falls in love, confronts his father for the sake of his love—it matters not to the seductive narrative line that the lady is called Poverty—attracts disciples, obtains papal approval for his order, preaches in the East, returns to Italy, receives the stigmata, and dies. This is narrative at its most graspable and most pleasurable. By contrast, the infant Dominic in his mother's womb is the subject of arcane visions and etymological discussions that retard what narrative line there is, and there is very little: although we learn that the saint became a great doctor and fought the heretics, his life is told not by way of a story line proceeding from birth to death but by way of a multitude of similes and metaphors that creates for the reader not the comfortable linearity of canto 11 but rather a pastiche of elusive impressions.[37] These characteristics of the two biographies recall the two kinds of writing displayed by this heaven as a whole, which we labeled "narrative" and "antinarrative"; indeed, the two *vite* seem to conform to this fundamental anatomy of poetic styles. In which case, we can end by adding one last element, and creating one more chiasmus, to be weighed in the poetic scales that balance Francis and Dominic: narratologically, canto 11 demonstrates the mode that is the *Commedia*'s backbone, while canto 12 demonstrates the essential but more peripheral mode that will allow the *Paradiso* to be written; hermeneutically, the reverse is true, since canto 11 proclaims an allegorical method that is essential but peripheral, while canto 12 proclaims the literally prophetic mode that is the foundation of the *Commedia*'s unique form of representation, that makes it what it is.

Rhetorical Breakdown of the Eulogies in *Par.* 11 and 12

| | Francis/Franciscans | Dominic/Dominicans |
|---|---|---|
| INTRO 1 (15 lines) | Two princes to guide the bride of Christ<br><br>Seraphic | Two princes to guide the bride of Christ<br>Cherubic |
| VITA 1 (75 lines) | Geographical periphrasis: east<br>A sun was born<br>Etymological play Ascesi/Oriente<br>"Orto" = birth<br>Marriage to Lady Poverty<br>Association with Christ (Poverty on the cross, stigmata), who is named three times<br>"Archimandrita" = prince of shepherds | |
| CODA 1 (22 lines) | Worthy to maintain Peter's bark | Worthy to maintain Peter's bark<br>"Nostro patriarca"<br>Dominicans are sheep<br>"Pastor"<br>The plant of the order is splintered |
| INTRO 2 (15 lines) | They fought together in Christ's army<br>Two champions to succor the bride of Christ | They fought together in Christ's army<br>Two champions to succor the bride of Christ |
| VITA 2 (60 lines) | | Geographical periphrasis: west<br>Lover of the Christian faith<br>Holy athlete<br>Espousals between him and faith<br>Etymological play on Domenico, Felice, Giovanna<br>The farmer chosen by Christ for his "orto" ( = garden)<br>First triple rhyme on "Cristo"<br>Christ's messenger and familiar<br>The keeper of the vineyard<br>A torrent to root out heretical weeds |
| CODA 2 (21 lines) | The other wheel of the chariot that defends the Church<br>Franciscans are the neglected wheel track (of the chariot)<br>Franciscans are a cask covered with mold<br>Bad Franciscans are tares that will be excluded from the harvest bin<br>The order is a volume and its members are pages | One wheel of the chariot that defends the Church |

*Chapter 10*

# THE SACRED POEM IS FORCED TO JUMP:
# CLOSURE AND THE POETICS OF ENJAMBMENT

> An *end-stopped* line is one—as you'll have guessed—
> Whose syntax comes, just at its end, to rest.
> But when the walking sentence needs to keep
> On going, the *enjambment* makes a leap
> Across a line-end (here, a rhyming close).
> (John Hollander, *Rhyme's Reason*)

> my readers . . . will see in the tell-tale compression
> of the pages before them, that we are all hastening
> together to perfect felicity.
> (Jane Austen, *Northanger Abbey*)

IN ANSWER TO Cacciaguida's exhortation to sound forth his will and his desire, the pilgrim responds by explaining the diegetic problems—problems of disequality and difference—that beset all mortals:

> L'affetto e 'l senno,
>   come la prima *equalità* v'apparse,
>   *d'un peso* per ciascun di voi si fenno,
> però che 'l sol che v'allumò e arse,
>   col caldo e con la luce è sì *iguali*,
>   che tutte *simiglianze* sono scarce.
> Ma voglia e argomento ne' mortali,
>   per la cagion ch'a voi è manifesta,
>   *diversamente* son pennuti in ali;
> ond'io, che son mortal, mi sento in questa
>   *disagguaglianza*, e però non ringrazio
>   se non col core a la paterna festa.

Affect and intelligence, as soon as the first *equality* appeared to you, became *of one weight* for each of you, because the sun that illumined you and burned you with its heat and with its light is so *equal* that all other *likenesses* are scarce. But desire and expression in mortals, for the reason that is manifest to you, are *diversely* feathered in their wings; so that I, who am mortal, feel myself in this *disequality*, and therefore I give thanks only with my heart for the paternal welcome.
(*Par.* 15.73–84)

The pilgrim cannot adequately give thanks to Cacciaguida because, not yet being a blessed soul in paradise, his affective and intellective faculties ("L'affetto e 'l senno") have not yet been made equal ("iguali"), of one weight ("d'un peso"), by the first equality ("la prima equalità"), God. The condition of blessedness is precisely a condition of perfect balance, perfect equality: a balance expressed here by the paired nouns and verbs referring to our two faculties ("v'allumò" / "arse", "caldo" / "luce") and by the chiasmus that links "v'allumò" with "luce" and "arse" with "caldo"; an equality whose lexicon points forward to the poem's penultimate verse, which features the adverb "igualmente." What is absent, of course, from the poem's finale is the corollary that in *Paradiso* 15 follows the adversative turn ("Ma voglia e argomento ne' mortali") from eternity to mortality and from equality to difference: when dealing with *mortali*, allowance must be made for imbalance, for difference, for the fact that our wings are diversely ("diversamente") feathered. The pilgrim cannot express his thanks because he is mortal and, being mortal, a creature of difference; never (in a typically Dantesque move) have the disadvantages of mortality been more stunningly expressed than in the simplicity of "ond'io, che son mortal" followed by the enjambment that isolates and highlights the word that forms a hemistich, the magnificently protracted "disagguaglianza."

Dante tells us, in the above passage, about mortal *disagguaglianza*, and— most signficantly for our purposes—he relates this condition of difference that we mortals routinely inhabit to our speech, our diegesis, our narrative: because of the *disagguaglianza* that is factored into any mortal's natural state, the pilgrim is at a loss for words to treat the super-natural surroundings and events in which he, most unnaturally, finds himself. What obtains for the pilgrim within the possible world of paradise is, as is frequently the case on Dante's circular scales, precisely the opposite of what obtains for the poet within the reality of praxis and the written poem: while the pilgrim is blocked by his disequality, the poet is empowered by the very *disagguaglianza* that he must, in the third canticle, nonetheless forswear. As the poem heads toward the *uguaglianza* of its ending, as it is deprived of the fuel of *disagguaglianza*, it stutters; early instances of such stuttering are the first sets of "Cristo" rhymes, located in the life of Dominic in *Paradiso* 12 and in the passage, toward the end of *Paradiso* 14, relating the miraculous appearance of Christ within the cross of Mars. These triple rhymes of *Cristo/ Cristo/Cristo* signify not only the incommensurability of Christ to anything other than himself but also the inevitable death of terza rima;[1] as difference in the form of three different rhymes gives way to identity, homology, and stasis, the poem begins to die. Not for nothing was the biography of Dominic identifiable as an "antinarrative" narrative, while the passage containing the *Cristo* rhymes in canto 14 contains one of the poet's most explicit disavowals of his narrative ability; because he cannot find an adequate referent, an "essempro degno" for what he saw, he will leave it untold in the hope that the reader will take up his own cross and achieve his own vision:

Qui vince la memoria mia lo 'ngegno;
  ché quella croce lampeggiava Cristo,
  sì ch'io non so trovare essempro degno;
ma chi prende sua croce e segue Cristo,
  ancor mi scuserà di quel ch'io lasso,
  vedendo in quell'albor balenar Cristo.

Here my memory overcomes my genius; for that cross so flashed forth Christ that I do not know how to find a worthy referent. But he who takes his cross and follows Christ will yet forgive me for what I leave out when he sees Christ flash in that dawn.

(*Par.* 14.103–8)

The lapse in content that occurs at this juncture finds its formal correlative in the triple rhyme that threatens to stop the narrative, puncturing the seamless web of terza rima. The *Cristo* rhymes speak to us, therefore, of the future of the *Commedia*: of the point when there will no more (new) rhymes, no more difference, no more *essempri* (*degni* or otherwise), no more poem. The *Cristo* rhymes are precisely an instance of linguistic and diegetic *uguaglianza*; as the poem moves toward the equality of its ending, toward that talismanic *igualmente*, it testifies to the fact that, in life as in language, unity is death and difference is life. But if, in Stanley Fish's terms, the *Paradiso* is a self-consuming artifact, it is one whose author plots its demise to the letter.[2] Dante achieves the ending of his poem by structuring ever more *uguaglianza* into the *disagguaglianza* of his narrative line, causing the narrative ever more frequently to skip over some element of the journey that is not translatable into language, such as the love in Beatrice's eyes at the beginning of canto 18:

              e qual io allor vidi
  ne li occhi santi amor, *qui l'abbandono*:
non perch'io pur del mio parlar diffidi,
  ma per la mente che non può redire
  sovra sé tanto, s'altri non la guidi.

and what love I then saw in the saintly eyes *I here abandon it*; not only because I distrust my speech, but because my memory cannot return so far over itself, unless another guide it.

(*Par.* 18.8–12)

In the last chapter I discussed the interlayering, within the heaven of the sun, of two distinct narrative modes, one "narrative," and the other "lyrical" or "antinarrative." I now propose that we can chart Dante's handling of his poem's long struggle with closure in terms of the strategic alternation of these two modes, the modes of *disagguaglianza* and *uguaglianza*: the former ("narrative") is discursive, logical, linear, "chronologized," and (if we form a category based on the *Paradiso*'s stress on man's two faculties) intellective; the latter ("lyrical") is the opposite, i.e., nondiscursive, nonlinear or circular, "dechronologized," and affective.[3] The former is based on an Aristotelian sense of time as duration and continuum, "numero di movimento, secondo prima e poi," while the latter is based on an Augustinian sense of time as an indivisible instant: "In fact the only time that can be called present is an instant, if we can conceive of such, that cannot be divided even into the most minute fractions, and a point of time as small as this passes so rapidly from the future to the past that its duration is without length."[4] The lyrical or antinarrative mode, of which canto 23 is a prime example, is resistant to subdivision and hence to logical exposition, and is characterized by apostrophes, exclamations, heavily metaphoric language, and intensely affective similes. It represents nothing less than Dante's attempt to forge an oxymoron, an adynaton, a paradox: namely linguistic/diegetic *uguaglianza*, "equalized" language. As the *Commedia* reaches its terminus, the dosage of *uguaglianza* in the text's narrative admixture is increased, with the upper reaches of *Paradiso* offering the poem's highest proportion of antinarrative textuality.

Although theoretically the beginning of the end of the poem could be located at any point along the diegetic line, including the first verse, we will begin our study of the end's beginning rather further along, in the heaven of Saturn. After the lengthy series of initial cantos offering little in the way of the drama that entertains the reader in the *Inferno*, the *Paradiso* undertakes with the new beginning of canto 10 a dramatic upswing that reaches its apogee in the Cacciaguida cantos. The affective personal involvement of the Cacciaguida cantos gives way in turn to the impersonal and intellective tension that governs the heaven of justice; the move to the impersonal is signaled by Beatrice, when she tells the pilgrim to turn away and listen, since "non pur ne' miei occhi è paradiso" ("not only in my eyes is paradise" [*Par.* 18.21]). Instead of the dramatically personal concerns that were treated in the heaven of Mars, in the heaven of Jupiter Dante examines the austere and impersonal issues of justice and predestination, a topic that does however contain an implicit affective focus in its necessary connection to the figure of Vergil. In dramatic terms, the heaven of Jupiter is the first step in a narrative downswing that follows the heaven of Mars and that is fulfilled in the heaven of Saturn, where there is no longer even the implied affectivity inherent in the tension surrounding the problem of the virtuous pagans to provide some dramatic interest. And yet in this narrative nadir, in this quiet contemplative heaven of the contemplatives where the chief protagonists are Saints Peter Damian and Benedict, in this plainsong, nonpyrotechnical heaven whose modest dimensions make it the canticle's briefest (stretching only from the beginning of canto 21 to circa two thirds of the way through canto 22), one can discern the first narrative signposts pointing indisputably to the journey's end. Against a thematic backdrop that alludes retrospectively to the two previous heavens—the pilgrim's query as to why Peter Damian alone was chosen to welcome him recalls the issue of predestination that dominates the heaven of Jupiter, while the saint's somewhat chilly reply ("né più amor mi fece esser più presta" ["nor did more love make me more solicitous" (*Par.* 21.67)]) contrasts with the affectionate warmth of Cacciaguida's welcome—the heaven of Saturn establishes clearcut prospective signals, narrative "firsts." For the first time the ascent to a new heaven is not accompanied by Beatrice's smile, which she withholds for the same reason that this sphere is the first to be experienced without "la dolce sinfonia di paradiso" ("sweet symphony of paradise" [59]); they have reached a stage where the pilgrim's mortal senses are until further tempering incapable of tolerating either the divine smile or the divine song, "onde qui non si canta / per quel che Bëatrice non ha riso" ("wherefore here we do not sing for the same reason that Beatrice did not smile" [62–63]). Moreover, the ladder that the pilgrim sees is the first of the heavenly hieroglyphs to give the impression of reaching all the way to the empyrean, all the way to journey's end: "vid'io uno scaleo eretto in suso / tanto, che nol seguiva la mia luce" ("I saw a ladder rising up so far that my sight did not follow it" [29–30]).

Saturn, the last of the planetary heavens, is thus designed, in this interlocking terza rima universe where each beginning is an ending and each ending a beginning, as a first step toward the end. Saint Benedict is concerned lest the pilgrim be delayed in reaching his lofty goal ("alto fine" [22.35]), and the emphasis on reaching the goal and fulfilling desire continues in the ensuing dialogue: the pilgrim wants to see Benedict in "discovered form" ("con imagine scoverta" [60]), a privilege that will be granted him in the empyrean. Benedict tells the pilgrim that his wish will be fulfilled ("s'adempierà" [62]) where all wishes are fulfilled ("s'adempion" [63]); pointing the way forward to the "ultima spera" ("last sphere" [62]), he offers one of the canticle's most straightforwardly paradoxical definitions of the empyrean, the place that contains all places but is itself uncontained: "in quella sola / è ogne parte là ove sempr'era, / perché non è in loco e non s'impola" ("in that alone is every part there where it always was, for it is not in space and it has no poles" [65–67]). Canto 22's spate of "ending words" continues: after the pilgrim has been raised to the sphere of the fixed stars, Beatrice informs him that he has come so near to the final blessedness ("ultima salute" [124]) that he must prepare his eyes for the journey's final leg by looking down at the distance he has traversed (a paradigmatic application of the mythic law whereby one must go down before going up).[5] And so, following the *Commedia's* last address to the reader (*Par.* 22.106–11), we encounter the *Commedia's* first look back, carefully situated at a simultaneous end/beginning: the end of a canto and the beginning of the nonplanetary heavens. The controlled Orphism of this experience is a potent indicator of how far we have come from *Purgatorio* 9, where the angel who guards the portal warned the travelers not to look back, because "di fuor torna chi 'n dietro si guata" ("he who looks back returns outside" [132]). If now Beatrice issues the contrary order, instructing the pilgrim to do what the angel warned against, it is because he has achieved such perspective that looking back is no longer perilous; by the same token, if the old perils exist no longer, the journey must be almost over. Looking back is no longer a nostalgic lapse, mandated by excessive desire; it is, instead, an action whose paradoxes exemplify the paradoxes of the *Paradiso* as a written form. Theoretically, the pilgrim looks back in order to acknowledge the perspective he has developed, to demonstrate his total freedom from any desire for the object of his attention. And yet the text certainly harbors a latent desire in this passage, the same desire that it harbors in all the diatribes and invectives whose content condemns the earth but whose existence displays their love for something that cannot be merely scorned and put aside. The poignant tenderness of the prayer to Dante's natal stars that precedes the looking back, in which the poet gives postvisionary present-tense thanks to the constellation Gemini for his genius and evokes the Tuscan air into which he was born, reintroduces the personal affective strand of the *Paradiso* and contrasts mightily with the learned indifference that is about to be directed toward the "aiuola che ci fa tanto feroci" ("threshing floor that makes us so fierce" [151]). The supremely dialectical combined gesture of thankful prayer and Orphic turn, both acknowledging and refuting the umbilical cord that ties the poet to his past, deposits us at its newest new beginning, its first "nondead" ending, its first beginning of the end in absolute terms, canto 23.

*Paradiso* 23 anticipates *Paradiso* 33; it is a rehearsal for the beatific vision that in some ways delivers more and frustrates less than the finale, granting us the vision of Christ as man, as lucent being ("lucente sustanza" [*Par.* 23.32]). With canto 33, it is the *Paradiso's* most extended attempt to deploy the mode of *uguaglianza* in a sustained fashion, for a space of significant narrative duration, and it displays, perhaps more explicitly than its celebrated successor, all the hallmarks of the *Paradiso's* antinarrative mode. Canto 23 is devoted to subverting linearity and narrativity, which it does both within itself, by fragmenting and absconding what could be called its plot, and also within the macronarrative of the canticle as a whole, where it performs a key role: Dante aims to take the pressure off his poem's ultimate ending by staging staggered anticipated "pre-endings," multiple endings that work to camouflage the absolute finality of the end in the same way that the multiple infernal incipits were intended to blur the artifice of textual incipience. By working to defuse some of the narrative pressure that is accumulated as the reader approaches *Paradiso* 33, Dante greatly increases his chances of carrying off one of the representational wagers of all time.

The antinarrativity of canto 23 also makes the point that although we humans like stories with beginnings, middles, and ends, stories composed of *disagguaglianza*, such is not God's way; to the extent that the narrativity of canto 23 is attempting to participate in what it describes, an *excessus menti* and a foretaste of the beatific vision, it is obliged to eschew the orderly time-bound narrative structures that would, for instance, represent the Annunciation before the Advent rather than vice versa. Indeed, the hysteron proteron that marks the address to the reader in canto 22, where the poet conflates time by reversing it, telling us that he saw and entered Gemini more speedily than we would draw out and put our finger into a fire ("tu non avresti in tanto tratto e messo / nel foco il dito" [22.109–10]), is carried over at a narrative level to canto 23, whose "plot" is governed by a kind of hysteron proteron writ large. Not surprisingly, canto 23 is a text that challenges its readers; resistant to subdivision and hence to exposition, it is difficult to teach because of its lack of linearity and, for the same reason, difficult to read.[6] Having by this point built up a certain reservoir of confidence in their ability to tackle the *Paradiso* and lulled into a sense of mastery by the easy narrativity of canto 22, first-time readers experience canto 23 as a severe setback: suddenly there is no narrative thread to hold on to, no clearly marked plot segments that allow us to divide the text into its differential components. If "divide and conquer" is the hegemonic law of reading as well as geopolitics, then a text like *Paradiso* 23 is constructed precisely with a view to resisting our attempts to make sense of it, to conquer it. It is forged in such a way as to frustrate division, parsing, and syllabification; it jumps about from one impression, one image, to the next: two tercets for this, three for that, never a sustained narrative line that the reader can grasp. Rather, we are plunged into that textual ocean of which the poet warned us at the outset of *Paradiso* 2; if at that point our boats were deemed "picciolette barche," very likely incapable of following "dietro al mio legno che cantando varca" (*Par.* 2.3), now the poet himself seems potentially underequipped for his Ulyssean task:

> Ma chi pensasse il ponderoso tema
> e l'omero mortal che se ne carca,
> nol biasmerebbe se sott'esso trema:
> non è pareggio da picciola barca
> quel che fendendo va l'ardita prora,
> né da nocchier ch'a sé medesmo parca.

But he who thinks of the ponderous theme and the mortal shoulder that is burdened with it will not blame it for trembling beneath the load; it is not a crossing

for a little boat, this which my bold prow now cleaves, nor for a helmsman who
would spare himself.

(*Par.* 23.64–69)

The antinarrative textual components of *Paradiso* 23—apostrophes, exclamations, metaphoric language, and affective similes—are used by the
poet to fracture his text;[7] moments of plot are interrupted by an apostrophe,
exclamation, or lyrical simile, deployed as a means of preventing a narrative
line from forming. Canto 23 opens with a simile of attendant desire, the
simile of the mother bird, in which Dante demonstrates an ability, arguably
never achieved in Italian again, to control a register of *dolcezza* uncloyed by
even the least trace of sentimentality.[8] Love and desire govern all who wait
at this dawn, and the language sets a tone of untrammeled affectivity:
"amate fronde" ("beloved leaves" [1]), "dolci nati" ("sweet offspring" [2]),
"aspetti disïati" ("desired aspects" [4]), "ardente affetto" ("ardent love"
[8]), "vaga" ("desirous" [13]), "disïando" ("desiring" [14]). Onto this backdrop of loving expectancy burst "the hosts of Christ's triumph" ("le schiere /
del trïunfo di Cristo" [19–20]); the pilgrim witnesses an Advent of Christ in
what could be characterized, with the reader's indulgence, as a brief interlude (three tercets, verses 16–24) of "plot," happening, or event. The last
verse of this interlude has already left plot in abeyance, confessing that the
author must pass over the joy in Beatrice's eyes without finding the language
to describe it ("che passarmen convien sanza costrutto" [24]), when we are
apparently further derailed by the canto's second great lyrical simile, the
mysterious and beautiful comparison of the moon shining among the other
stars to a blazing sun:[9] the movement from "Quale ne' plenilunïi sereni /
Trivïa ride tra le ninfe etterne" ("As in clear skies at full moon Trivia laughs
among the eternal nymphs" [25–26]) to "un sol che tutte quante l'accen-
dea" ("a sun that lit them all" [29]) actually marks the abrupt transition
back into plot, as through the living light of the sun-Christ shines the very
substance of his resurrected flesh. The pilgrim's intolerance of such a sight
is followed by a seeming non sequitur, the exclamatory apostrophe of verse
34, "Oh Bëatrice, dolce guida e cara!"; the sweet guide's brief explanation of
the force that has overwhelmed him (35–39) is in turn interrupted by a third
simile, comparing the lightning burst within a cloud to the dilation of the
pilgrim's mind as, nourished by such incomparable spiritual feasts, it expands to the point of leaving itself, in a moment of literal ec-stasis: "la
mente mia così, tra quelle dape / fatta più grande, di sé stessa uscìo" ("my
mind thus, having become greater amid those feasts, departed from itself"
[43–44]). Ecstasy in turn gives way to the unrecoverability of such an experience by his memory: "e che si fesse rimembrar non sape" ("and what it
became it does not remember" [45]).[10] Typical of Dante's fracturing textual
tactics in *Paradiso* 23 is the transition directly from verse 45's confession of

the inadequacy of memory, a recurrent theme of *Paradiso* 33 as well, to Beatrice's direct discourse in verse 46 ("Apri li occhi e riguarda qual son io" ["Open your eyes and look at what I am"]); only after her spoken tercet does the narrative recount the pilgrim's return to his senses, like that of one who awakens "di visïone oblita e che s'ingegna / indarno di ridurlasi a la mente" ("from a forgotten vision and who strives in vain to recall it to memory" [50–51]), in a passage that too will find its systematic echo in the poem's finale.

With respect to plot, Beatrice has now offered to renew the smile that was suspended at the outset of canto 22, saying that the pilgrim has been rendered capable of withstanding it (46–48). With respect to narrative, Beatrice's offer occasions the lengthy (fifteen-verse) metapoetic passage that takes center stage in many readers' recollections of canto 23 and by which it is essentially sundered in half: after embarking on the negative invocation in which he claims that not even the sounding forth in unison of all those tongues that were ever fattened by the Muses' milk could help him to sing a thousandth part of the truth of Beatrice's smile (55–60), so that, in figuring paradise, the sacred poem is forced to jump (61–62), Dante brings his ship to shore with the tercets cited earlier on his weighty theme and daring prow (64–69). Not only does this passage break the narrative thread, tenuous as it is, that runs through the canto, but it announces that such breaks are programmatic, are indeed required, and that the only way to persist in weaving textuality at this stage of the journey is at the price of occasional holes in the fabric:

> e così, figurando il paradiso,
> > convien saltar lo sacrato poema,
> > come chi trova suo cammin riciso.

> and so, figuring paradise, the sacred poem is forced to jump, like one who finds his path cut off.

> > > > > > (*Par.* 23.61–63)

While much attention has been accorded these lines for their redefinition of the *comedìa* as a "sacrato poema," critics have tended to pass over the statement that here the sacred poem must "jump, like one who finds his path cut off." And yet these verses make explicit Dante's active pursuit of a new kind of discourse; they express the concerted attempt to abandon straightforward narrativity for a more fractured, less discursive, less linear, ultimately more "equalized" or "unified" textuality. The path that is cut off is precisely the narrative path, the path that has faithfully recorded "le vite spiritali ad una ad una" (*Par.* 33.24). We have reached the point where the poet, a wayfarer on a textual *cammino* of his own, finds his path cut off, so that there is no way forward unless he jumps over the empty space to where the path resumes on the other side.[11] The sacred poem is forced to *jump*: the *saltar* that results is the best description we can give—because it is Dante's own—of the antinarrative discourse that characterizes the high *Paradiso*. Moreover, *saltare* bears a true comedic pedigree, both as a humble variant of the proud Ulyssean *varcare* (Dante could have written "convien varcar lo sacrato poema" but did not, which is why, in my translation, the sacred poem jumps rather than leaps), and as a term that recalls the biblical *sermo humilis* of the psalm most linked to the *Commedia*'s poetics. The image of the jumping poem is no more preposterous than that of the skipping mountains in "In exitu Israel de Aegypto"; this psalm was quoted as recently as the preceding canto, where we find the "Iordan vòlto retrorso" ("Jordan turned back" [*Par.* 22.94]) and the sea in flight ("e 'l mar fuggir" [95]), images that in their original context immediately precede the jumping mountains:

> Mare vidit, et fugit;
> Iordanis conversus est retrorsum.
> Montes exsultaverunt ut arietes,
> Et colles sicut agni ovium.

> The sea saw it and fled: Jordan was driven back. The mountains skipped like rams, and the little hills like lambs
>
> (Psalm 113.3–4)[12]

In a divinely defined poetics, the inappropriate becomes paradoxically *conveniens*: the sacred poem must jump, just as the mountains bizarrely skip, and as David—the divinely inspired cantor of those mountains—shames his haughty wife by humbly dancing and leaping before the sacred ark.[13] With respect, moreover, to a possible classical source for Dante's *saltare*, I would suggest the appositeness of the Aristotelian axiom, "Natura non facit saltus."[14] If nature does not jump, creating instead a great chain of graded and interlocked being (much like terza rima), it may have occurred to Dante that art, no matter how mimetic, might eventually be constrained to break nature's laws, the better to abide by its own.

*Paradiso* 23 continues in the jumping mode, resuming with three tercets of plot (70–78): the speech in which Beatrice suggests that the pilgrim direct his gaze toward the garden of Christ's souls, first among whom is the rose in which the word was made flesh, prompts a return to "the battle of the weak brows" ("la battaglia de' debili cigli" [78]); not only will this last phrase be picked up in the image of the pilgrim's drinking eyelashes of *Paradiso* 30, but the garden metaphor, and the Marian rose in particular, both of mystical derivation, anticipate the empyrean. Once more a simile intervenes: as he has in the past seen a field of flowers lit by a ray of light that comes through a rent cloud (the "fratta nube" of line 80 provides a verbal

228 CHAPTER 10

icon for the canto's fracturing of discourse), so now the pilgrim gazes on the heavenly hosts without seeing the source of the light that illumines them (79–84). If the second term of this simile constitutes a flash of plot, a momentary interlude of information, it is as suddenly converted to sentiment by the apostrophe that—in a move typical of canto 33 as well—follows and interrupts; the poet briefly stops the "action" to address the benign power that raised itself, ascending, and that, by withdrawing, made it possible for him to gaze on the splendors that remained (85–87). Then, the narrator tells us, the pilgrim concentrates on the brightest light, and the passage that follows is the canto's most uninterrupted narrative, distinguished however by its sweetly melodic and intensely affective language: a torch formed as a circle in the likeness of a crown wheels around the queen of heaven in this replay of the Annunciation, singing with a sweetness that would make the sweetest of earthly songs sound in comparison like a bolt of thunder (88–108). The angel's song is nothing less than Dante's rendering of the "voce modesta,/ forse qual fu da l'angelo a Maria" ("modest voice, perhaps as it was from the angel to Mary" [*Par.* 14.35–36]). A supreme example of Dantesque apparent simplicity, we notice that every verse, but for the one between the two tercets, is enjambed:

> Io sono amore angelico, che giro
> 	l'alta letizia che spira del ventre
> 	che fu albergo del nostro disiro;
> e girerommi, donna del ciel, mentre
> 	che seguirai tuo figlio, e farai dia
> 	più la spera supprema perché lì entre.

> I am angelic love, and I circle the high happiness that breathes from the womb that was hostel of our desire; and I will circle you, lady of heaven, while you follow your son and make more brilliant the highest sphere because you enter there.
> 												(*Par.* 23.103–8)

The angel circles—"giro," "girerommi"—and the angel's language circles; the enjambing of the verses makes the angelic song a literal "circulata melodia": "Così la circulata melodia / si sigillava" ("So the circulated melody sealed itself" [109–10]).

Enjambment is a rupture that unifies: the rupture of the syntax engenders the unifying of the verse, the *circulata melodia*. The *circulata melodia* that describes both the angel's circling movement and his song is an apt if untranslatable label for the entire canto, itself a "circulated melody." For the result of fracturing the discourse, of jumping about rhetorically—from plot to invocation to apostrophe to a simile to some more plot followed by another simile and another apostrophe—is, paradoxically enough (in an effect similar to that produced, on a local scale, by enjambment),[15] to create

a peculiarly unified or equalized linguistic texture: a texture from which
*disagguaglianza* has been to some degree banished, a *circulata melodia*. The
jumping discourse that governs canto 23 could be seen as a kind of macro-
enjambment: enjambment operating not between individual verses but between segments of a canto. The jumping discourse is obtained by way of a
poetics of enjambment, by way of a rupture that unifies. Canto 23 is in fact
a strangely cohesive text, one that could be plucked entire out of the narrative fabric of the *Commedia*.[16] Its unity is conferred by its lack of easy divisibility, its defiance of linear narrativity, in a word, by the fact that it jumps.
Sealed by its last great affective simile, in which the souls are said to reach
after the departing Virgin in the manner of an infant who, after taking milk,
extends its arms toward its mother (121–26), canto 23 constitutes the measure by which we can henceforth gauge Dante's alternations between the
modes of *uguaglianza* and *disagguaglianza* as he enters the poem's final
stretch. Not surprisingly, in that we still have ten cantos to go, the poet will
apply the brakes in the cantos that follow, which on the whole are marked
by a return to difference.

If *Paradiso* 23 is the canto of *affetto*, *Paradiso* 24 is just as surely written
under the sign of *intelletto*, devoted to handling the great irrational leap
that is faith in eminently rational fashion. It is the first and perhaps the most
characterized by *disagguaglianza* of the three examination cantos; although
I would not consider any of the three to be dominated by the jumping mode
of *uguaglianza*, the admixture of lyrical language increases as we reach the
examination on *caritas* of canto 26.[17] In canto 24, on the other hand, with
the exception of some elements in the opening passage that refer back to
canto 23—most significantly, the poet's reuse of the verb *saltare* to denote
his representational failure ("Però salta la penna e non lo scrivo" ["Therefore my pen jumps and I do not write it" (25)]) in a programmatic confirmation of what might have otherwise seemed like a bizarre and idiosyncratic
usage[18]—we find a discourse that is logical, linear, and scholastic to the
point of being legalistic. Not for nothing is *Paradiso* 24 the only canto in the
poem to contain both the verb "silogizzar" (77) and the noun "silogismo"
(94), neither used disparagingly.[19] If the textual emblem for canto 23 and
the mode of *uguaglianza* is the phrase "circulata melodia," the textual emblem for canto 24 and the mode of *disagguaglianza* is the adverb "diffe-
rente-/mente" (16–17), situated in a passage dedicated to explaining the
differing velocities displayed by the individual souls as they whirl about, a
passage that spells difference in its lexicon of "first" and "last," "fast" and
"slow," "more" and "less":

> E come cerchi in tempra d'orïuoli
>   si giran sì, che 'l *primo* a chi pon mente
>   quïeto pare, e l'*ultimo* che voli;

così quelle carole, *differente-*
*mente* danzando, de la sua ricchezza
mi facino stimar, *veloci* e *lenti*.
Di quella ch'io notai di *più* carezza
vid'ïo uscire un foco sì felice,
che nullo vi lasciò di *più* chiarezza. . . .

And as the wheels within the fittings of clocks revolve, so that to one who observes the *first* seems quiet and the *last* to fly, so did those circles, *differently* dancing, *fast* and *slow*, give me the measure of their riches. From the circle that I noted as *most* precious I saw come out a fire so happy that none did it leave behind of *more* clarity. . . .

(Par. 24.13–21)

The second and final presence of the adverb "differentemente" in the *Commedia* also constitutes the poem's only instance of a single word divided by enjambment between two verses. Various commentators suggest that Dante thereby shows his awareness of the formation of Italian adverbs from an adjective and the noun *mente*; I would add that he thus inscribes into the text a reminder that different minds—individual and irreducible *differenti menti*—are required for the sweet symphony of paradise.[20] But even more noteworthy, in my opinion, is the point touched upon by Tommaseo, namely that Dante, by dividing the adverb, actually portrays difference;[21] in other words, once more form is content in the *Commedia*, as Dante employs the most literal of graphic differentiations to make the meaning of the word *differentemente* incarnate in his poem. Whereas in canto 23 enjambment engenders *circulata melodia*, the emphasis falling on the unity created by the rupture that unifies, in canto 24 enjambment incarnates difference, the emphasis falling rather on the rupture.

Another indicator of the mode of *disagguaglianza* is the famous simile of the bachelor student who prepares himself for questioning (*Par.* 24.46–51): as compared to the similes of canto 23, which engage the reader affectively in such a way as to impress a feeling, attempting to convey almost subliminally at least *il millesimo del vero* experienced by the pilgrim, the simile of the *baccialier* is quintessentially nonlyric; it belongs to the narrative mode and in fact constitutes in itself a little narrative, a brief but recognizable story with a logical structure not at all akin, for instance, to canto 23's mystical confrontation in simile of a female pagan moon with the sun-Christ.[22] Logical structure is everywhere apparent in canto 24, which proceeds clearly and rigorously from point to point; Dante wants to exemplify a syllogistic form of reasoning that manages to be precise and yet untainted by sophistry, and has St. Peter congratulate the pilgrim on his mastery of precisely such a discourse (79–81). Even the contradictions fundamental to this poem and its poetic authority are confronted analytically, through the syllogistic method. Thus, the problematic of true textuality that runs through these cantos, having been broached by canto 23's redefinition of the *Commedia* as a "sacrato poema" and picked up by the reference in canto 24 to St. Paul as the "veracious pen" ("verace stilo" [61]), leads to a probing of the basis of the Bible's own textual authority: why, comes the startling question, does the pilgrim hold the Old and New Testaments to be "divina favella" ("divine discourse" [99]); because of the "works that followed," i.e., the miracles that confirmed the biblical accounts, is the reply. But St. Peter continues an analysis that leaves very little to be taken on faith, pointing out the circularity of the pilgrim's argument: the Bible's divine authorship is proved by the successive miracles, and yet the only authority for the existence of those miracles is the same text whose authority they in turn guarantee. Although Dante sets up the circular argument in order to reach outside it, to counter the syllogistic stalemate by bringing in God, whose presence in history in the form of Christianity is declared to be so great a miracle that none other is needed (106–11), he has implicitly demonstrated his awareness of the inherent logical frailty of all guarantees of divine inspiration. One wonders in what way Dante would answer such a question with regard to his own claims to a *divina favella*; would the actual conversion of his readers be the only sufficient proof of his divine inspiration? Ever more vigorous assertions of the reality of divine inspiration constitute the poet's only reply: toward the end of canto 24, he tells us of "la verità che quinci piove / per Moïsè, per profeti e per salmi, / per l'Evangelio e per voi che scriveste / poi che l'ardente Spirto vi fé almi" ("the truth that rains down from here through Moses, the prophets and the psalms, through the Gospel and through you who wrote after the burning spirit made you holy" [135–38]); in canto 25 he calls his poem a "poema sacro" (1) and coins the term "tëodia" (73) for one of the psalms; in canto 26 he refers to the "autorità che quinci scende" ("authority that descends from here" [26]) and calls God the "verace autore" (40).[23]

St. John's inquisition on love in the first part of canto 26 presents an interesting attempt to balance the affective and the intellective modes: on the one hand, the pilgrim is told to compensate for his physical blindness by reasoning (i.e., by using the eyes of his mind) and to distinguish more accurately by straining his thoughts through a finer sieve; on the other, the erotic register frequently recalls *Inferno* 5, *Purgatorio* 24, or even, in the case of the teeth with which love bites, the *petrosa* "Così nel mio parlar."[24] A mixed bag compared to the other examination cantos, canto 26 concludes with the interview with Adam. The first man is the last of the *vite spiritali* the pilgrim meets,[25] constituting a kind of human Alpha and Omega and recalling Dante's earlier designation of God as the Alpha and Omega of all his writing: "Lo ben che fa contenta questa corte, / Alfa e O è di quanta scrittura / mi legge Amore o lievemente o forte" ("The good that makes happy this court is the Alpha and Omega of whatever writing Love reads to me, either soft or loud" [*Par.* 26.16–18]). And, indeed, we are rapidly approaching the no-place that is both Alpha and Omega: the primum mobile, both the last material heaven and the heaven from which the nature of the whole universe begins ("La natura del mondo . . . quinci comincia" [*Par.* 27.106, 108]), is yet a no-place, since "questo cielo non ha altro dove / che la mente divina" ("this heaven has no other where but the divine mind" [109–10]).[26] How, textually, does Dante set off this last place that is the first place that is no place? With canto 27's last look back at earth, an occurrence that we could label the end of the beginning of the end, just as the first look back in canto 22 was the beginning of the beginning of the end. The self-consciousness of the *Paradiso*'s last backward glance is such that it looks back not only at the earth but also at its textual predecessor: the narrator situates himself with respect to the time that has passed since he looked down before ("Da l'ora ch'ïo avea guardato prima" [79]), and reprises the word "aiuola" used for the earth previously. The point of this reflexiveness is to mark the second look back as the end point of a narrative arc (cantos 22 to 27) that was started by the first look back (an arc that I have called the beginning of the end) and, therefore, as a new beginning:[27] geographically speaking, the two downward glances frame the heaven of the fixed stars, a heaven consecrated to difference and dialectic, which gives way to the equality of the primum mobile, whose parts are so uniform ("sì uniforme son" [101]) that there is no way of knowing which section was chosen for the pilgrim's entry.[28]

　　The entrance into the primum mobile is marked by absolute vitality, supremity, and uniformity: "Le parti sue vivissime ed eccelse / sì uniforme son, ch'i' non so dire / qual Bëatrice per loco mi scelse" ("Its parts, supremely alive and exalted, are so uniform that I cannot say which part Beatrice chose as place for me" [*Par.* 27.100–102]). But the discourse of unity—the discourse that tries to give a name to God—is sustained for only twenty-one verses (100–120), verses in which the poet relies on paradox (the all-places that is no-place), chiasmus ("amor"/"virtù"/"luce"/"amor" [111–12]), negation ("Non è suo moto per altro distinto" ["Its motion is not determined by another's" (115)]), and metaphor: time hides its roots in the vase of the primum mobile, while its leaves are the visible and measurable motion of the lower heavens (118–19). Then the poem jumps, as though the effort of sustaining such a discourse were too great, and we pass from the roots and leaves of time to an exclamatory apostrophe to human greed: "Oh cupidigia, che i mortali affonde / sì sotto te, che nessuno ha podere / di trarre li occhi fuor de le tue onde!" ("O cupidity, who so drowns mortals under you that none has power to pull his eyes out from your waves!" [121–23]). There is, in fact, a striking contrast between the uniformity of the primum mobile and the narrative texture of the canto designated to introduce us to this newest of realms: canto 27 is a kind of political/polemical variant of a jumping canto, whose narrative insignia is the jumping prefix *tras-* (*trascolorare* [19, 21], *trasmutare* [34, 38], *trapassare* [75]). True to the transgressive and transformational poetics suggested by the five-times re-current *tras-*, this canto of Ulysses' final enjambed "varco / folle" (82–83) is capable of dizzying leaps, veering within a brief compass from the inebri-ated bliss of its opening hosannah to the papacy's stinking sewer, and again, in a transition that leaves us gasping, from the high physics that locates the roots of time in the primum mobile to the *cupidigia* that submerges mortals beneath its metaphoric waves.[29]

The very universe is revealed to be both Alpha and Omega in the primum mobile; the cosmos itself is turned inside out as Dante struggles to render the idea of an unmeasurable motion that contains the roots of all mensura-tion. In order to render the paradox of the no-place that is all-places, the nonmeasured that is all-measurer ("Non è suo moto per altro distinto, / ma li altri son mensurati da questo" ["Its motion is not determined by an-other's, but the others are measured by this" (*Par.* 27.115–16)]), Dante inverts the universe; the vision he presents in canto 28, where the pilgrim views God as the infinitely bright and infinitely tiny point at the center, and the various angelic intelligences as revolving circles growing ever larger and slower as they grow more distant from the point, creates a visual paradox with respect to the notion of the universe we have held thus far. By forcing us to complement the circumference model of the universe with a centrist one, Dante is trying to make us come to grips with the paradox of a deity that is "enclosed by that which he encloses" ("inchiuso da quel ch'elli 'nchiude" [*Par.* 30.12]), both center and circumference, both the deep (Au-gustinian) within and the great (Aristotelian) without, both "lyric" and "epic." At the same time, since Dante decides to have Beatrice account rationally for the visual paradox he has launched, rather than simply deploy-ing it without attempting an explanation, *Paradiso* 28 proceeds to become a great intellective canto, akin to *Paradiso* 2 in its reliance on the language of difference. Linguistic *disagguaglianza* is registered in the usual way, with *più* and *meno*:

> Così l'ottavo e 'l nono; e ciascheduno
> *più* tardo si movea, secondo ch'era
> in numero distante *più* da l'uno;
> e quello avea la fiamma *più* sincera
> cui *men* distava la favilla pura,
> credo, però che *più* di lei s'invera.

Thus the eighth and the ninth [circles]; and each moved *more* slowly, according as it was in number *more* distant from the one; and that one had the *most* clear flame that was from the pure spark *least* distant, because, I believe, it intruths itself *more* in it.

(*Par.* 28.34–39)

Verse 36 in particular, in which "numero" (the many) and "l'uno" (the one) confront each other across the abyss mediated by "distante più," could be taken as an emblem of the problematic that Dante cannot seem to leave alone, and against which he now once more pits himself. As previously the pilgrim was puzzled by the oneness that is claimed for the various heavens, when in fact they appear different, and grace does not rain down on them *d'un modo*, now he clamors to understand the fundamental oneness of the material and the spiritual universes, which also appear different and which—he says—do not go together or coincide: "non vanno *d'un modo*" (56). If his desire is to have an end ("se 'l mio disir dee aver fine" [52]), to find fulfillment, he must hear further "come l'essemplo / e l'essemplare non vanno d'un modo" ("why the model and the copy do not go in one way" [55–56]).

Dante has chosen to set up two models of the universe—one material, "sensibile" (the "mondo sensibile" of verse 49 is the world accessible to the senses), the other spiritual, beyond sense perception—and then to pose the question: how can the two models coexist? How can they *andare d'un modo*? How can they be one? He further chooses to have Beatrice provide a rational answer to the problem. Before looking at her answer, I would like to stress the obvious: Dante has found a way to render dramatically the pilgrim's transgression of time and space, to literalize the coexistence of the physical and the metaphysical. After all, the pilgrim is somehow *in* the primum mobile of the physical universe, at the same time that he sees the primum mobile of the metaphysical universe circling around the fiery point. So, whether or not the two universes can be made to coexist in rational discourse (they cannot), the poet has made them coexist in his fictive reality; at the level of the *Commedia*'s plot, the phenomenon that Beatrice tries to explain has already occurred.

Beatrice's explanation hinges on the verb *corrispondere* and the noun *consequenza*, both hapaxes in the *Commedia*. These terms are the key to her dilemma; she can set up correspondences—proportionally harmonious relations—between the two universes, but she cannot coalesce them, cannot in words collapse the physical and the metaphysical into one. (What Dante told us at the beginning of *Paradiso* was true: "Trasumanar significar *per verba* / non si poria.") She thus explains that the larger the material heaven the more blessedness it must contain, so that the largest material heaven perforce corresponds to the most blessed of the spiritual heavens, the one that loves most, knows most, is closest to God, and hence the smallest; if the pilgrim will readjust his perspective, looking not at the appearance of things ("la parvenza / de le sustanze") but at their inherent worth ("a la virtù"), he will see a proportional correspondence between the most worthy of the material heavens (the largest and the fastest) and the most worthy of the spiritual heavens (the smallest and the fastest):

Li cerchi corporai sono ampi e arti
    secondo il più e 'l men de la virtute
    che si distende per tutte lor parti.
Maggior bontà vuol far maggior salute;
    maggior salute maggior corpo cape,
    s'elli ha le parti igualmente compiute.
Dunque costui che tutto quanto rape
    l'altro universo seco, *corrisponde*
    al cerchio che più ama e che più sape:
per che, se tu a la virtù circonde
    la tua misura, non a la parvenza
    de le sustanze che t'appaion tonde,
tu vederai mirabil *consequenza*
    di maggio a più e di minore a meno,
    in ciascun cielo, a süa intelligenza.

The corporeal circles are wide and narrow according to the more and less power that extends through all their parts. Greater goodness makes for greater blessedness; a greater body contains greater blessedness, if its parts are equally perfect. Therefore this heaven, which carries off with it the rest of the universe, *corresponds* to the circle that loves most and knows most; so that, if you bring your measure to bear on the power and not on the appearance of the substances that appear to you as circles, you will see a marvelous *correspondence* of greater to more and smaller to less in each heaven with respect to its intelligence.

(*Par.* 28.64–78)

The apparent rigor of this passage, its "scientific" flavor, is enhanced by Beatrice's persistent use of difference-imprinted language (as in "secondo il più e 'l men de la virtute"), which gives an impression of quantification and precision. Logical forms are observed; the argument follows "a rigorous syllogism."[30] And, as a result, the pilgrim is satisfied, his mind—after Beatrice provides him her "clear response" (86)—is compared to a sky cleared of clouds by a northwest wind. But is Beatrice's really a "risponder chiaro"? Has Beatrice really blown away the clouds or has she created them? What she assuredly has not done is show why "l'essemplo / e l'essemplare non vanno d'un modo." Dante here attempts, as on other occasions, to "pull the clouds" over our eyes through Beatrice's verbal ingenuity, which consists in instructing us to substitute *virtù* for *la parvenza*. But our human understanding relies on appearance, on what we can learn through our senses; as a result, Beatrice's linguistic substitution provides an elegant but merely linguistic solution to the problem, a verbal sleight of hand: "tu vederai mirabil consequenza / di maggio a più e di minore a meno, / in ciascun cielo, a süa intelligenza." The correspondence of "maggio" to "più" and of "minore" to "meno" may be *mirabile*, but it does not succeed in collapsing the two universes into one on the page. Words necessarily make do for substance in Beatrice's reply, which cannot find the verbal *essemplo* to wed to what the pilgrim sees—the *essemplare*.[31] Just as "lo turbo e 'l chiaro" takes the place of "denso e raro" at the end of *Paradiso* 2 without getting rid of the root problem of difference, which has merely been shifted from a phrase denoting material causality to one denoting a spiritual principle, so in *Paradiso* 28 Dante attempts to elide the gulf between the physical and metaphysical worlds with a bridge of language, a tightrope of difference.

Such gallant verbal assaults on the unknowable belong to quintessentially intellective cantos. Canto 28, with its alliterative play on *vero* and *vedere*,[32] privileges the truth that is seen by the intellect over the loving motion of the will, and thus difference over unity; the angels move toward similitude, circling "per somigliarsi al punto quanto ponno" ("to be as like to the point as they can" [101]), but the amount of likeness they achieve is determined by their individual ability to see: "e posson quanto a veder son sublimi" ("and they can to the degree that they are exalted in sight" [102]). Dante explicitly upsets the balance between love and intellect by proclaiming the priority of the latter: the state of blessedness is founded on the act that sees, we learn, and not on the act that loves, which follows after (109–11).[33] As the canto that treats the angelic orders, *Paradiso* 28 has ample opportunity to engage the lexicon of *disagguaglianza*, particularly in the form of numbers; the angels are arranged in numerically assigned orders, by grade, in a hierarchy: "In essa gerarcia son l'altre dee: / prima Dominazioni, e poi Virtudi; / l'ordine terzo di Podestadi èe" ("In this hierarchy are the other divinities: first Dominations, and then Virtues; the third order is of the Powers" [121–23]). Given the importance of the concept of hierarchy in discussions of Dante's paradise, it is worth noting that the word *gerarcia* appears in the entire *Commedia* only this once, in a passage that justifies difference precisely by appealing to the orderly and harmonious hierarchy in which it is disposed; the arrangement is one of mutual combined attraction and exigency, in which each link in the chain both directs its gaze worshipfully above and exerts a force on what lies below: "Questi ordini di sù tutti s'ammirano, / e di giù vincon sì, che verso Dio / tutti tirati sono e tutti tirano" ("These orders all gaze upward and compel downward, so that they are all pulled toward God and they all pull" [127–29]). "Tutti tirati sono e tutti tirano": there is no weak link in this chain, since an equal pressure is exerted throughout. As with a similar tercet in *Paradiso* 2 that it closely echoes— "Questi organi del mondo così vanno, / come tu vedi omai, di grado in grado, / che di sù prendono e di sotto fanno" ("These organs of the universe so proceed, as you now see, from grade to grade, for they take from above and influence below" [121–23])—one could take canto 28's description of interlocking units that are poised equally in either direction—upward and downward, or, we could say, forward and backward—as an apt representation not only of the great chain of being but also of the great chain of language that unifies the vast universe of this poem: of *terzine* too it may be said that "di sù prendono e di sotto fanno." The metapoetic cast we might ascribe to this passage presages the canto that follows, where the discussion of angels in a numbered hierarchy gives way to a discussion of the original making of all number and hierarchy, angelic and otherwise, and where God's creation, his "discursive" act, "lo discorrer di Dio sovra quest'acque" ("the moving of God upon the waters" [*Par.* 29.21]), raises a mirror to the discursive act that creates the poem, one discursive *fabbro* mirroring the other. There is perhaps no greater metapoetic moment in the *Commedia* than *Paradiso* 29, a canto that has therefore been unavoidably present from the outset of this study; it is not coincidental that my opening definition of human life and Dantesque narrativity as a "vedere interciso da novo obietto" comes from this text.

With the sublime cadenza that marks his greatest metaphysical verse (we think, for instance, of *Paradiso* 13's "Ciò che non more e ciò che può morire" [52]), Dante represents the act of creation as an opening: "s'aperse in nuovi amor l'etterno amore" ("the eternal love opened itself in new loves" [*Par.* 29.18]). In the balance between "nuovi amor" and "l'etterno amore" hangs all the universe, and in the contrast between the eternal love and the new loves that it generates is all the splendor and pathos of created existence, the whole problematic of the *novo*; although "nuovi amor" is here a positively charged reference to the angels, we remember *Paradiso* 7, where we learned that free being is not subject to "la virtute de le cose nove" ("the power of the new things" [72]). How, and more importantly why, the eternal should give rise to the corruptible, the one should make way for the many, is the question posed in the dialectic between *l'etterno amore* and *nuovi amor* and framed by the two aspects of God's creation that Dante chooses to emphasize within the paradox of a timeless discursiveness. For God's creation is timeless, immune from the difference that characterizes all human actions, movements, and discourses: God creates "in sua etternità di tempo fore" ("in his eternity outside of time" [*Par.* 29.16]), his gesture preceded by neither a "before" nor an "after" ("né prima né poscia procedette" [20]); the triple creation of form, matter, and their union knows no interval between its inception and fulfillment ("che dal venire / a l'esser tutto non è intervallo" [26–27]), but takes its being all together and at once, "sanza distinzïone in essordire" ("without distinction of beginning" [30]). While I cannot vouch for the extent of Dante's etymological imagination or guarantee an intentional metapoetical subtext to his use of the verb *discorrere* for God's movement over the deep, the discursive thrust Dante confers on the creation needs no inventing:[34] God "discourses" so that his reflected light can discourse back to him, can (employing direct discourse) "say 'I exist'" ("dir 'Subsisto'" [15]). God's creation outside of time evokes the potency of a prelapsarian narrative: the image of what writing could be if it too could be outside of time, if it were without befores and afters, without intervening intervals, without distinctions, successiveness, or difference, without beginnings, middles, or ends. Within the metaphoric universe of this poem, God's moving over these waters, "quest'acque," cannot fail to recall Ulysses' watery journey, or, therefore, the poet's, and there are yet other acts of discursive creation here inscribed; that proto-Ulysses, Adam, gave linguistic existence to the creatures when he named them in the garden of Eden, and Dionysius, as we just learned at the end of canto 28, named and thereby "distinguished" the various angelic orders: "li nomò e distinse com'io" ("he named and distinguished them as I" [Par. 28.132]). Only God's "distinguishing," however, succeeds in being "sanza distinzïone"; only he can create an ordered universe of beginnings, middles, and ends—placing pure act at the "summit" ("cima" [Par. 29.32]) of his creation, pure potentiality at the bottom ("la parte ima" ["the lowest part" (34)]) and a mixture of the two "in the middle" ("nel mezzo" [35])—without participating in the intervals, hierarchies, gradations, and distinctions that he creates.

Writing and word crafting are implicated throughout Paradiso 29, from Jerome's mistaken scribblings on the moment of angelic creation ("Ieronimo vi scrisse" [Par. 29.37]), to "the truth" on this topic that is "written in many places by the writers of the holy spirit" ("ma questo vero è scritto in molti lati / da li scrittor de lo Spirito Santo" [40–41]), and ultimately to the false preachers whom Beatrice so fervently indicts in the canto's second half, those who arrogantly replace the divine writ ("la divina Scrittura" [90]) with their own "invenzioni": "Per apparer ciascun s'ingegna e face / sue invenzioni; e quelle son trascorse / da' predicanti e 'l Vangelio si tace" ("To make an appearance each one strives and makes his inventions; and those are elaborated by the preachers while the Gospel is silent" [94–96]). In the mendacious inventio of the false preachers, who dare to elaborate their own invenzioni while ignoring the word of God, as they take turns shouting their "favole" (104) from the pulpits of Florence, in such inventio—a false and vulgar discursiveness whose emblem is the direct discourse that Christ did not utter ("Non disse Cristo al suo primo convento: / 'Andate, e predicate al mondo ciance'" ["Christ did not say to his first company: 'Go, and preach idle stories to the world'" (109–10)])—Dante finds a perverted and distorted reflection of the inventiveness that created the universe and, more polemically, of the inventiveness that created his poem. He, of course, is not like the lying preachers, his inventions are not akin to theirs; and the discussion of angelic memory that is the pretext for the distancing diatribe becomes in many ways a summa of his poetics, of his inventio. Angels do not have memory, because they do not need it, because they see all things at once in the face of God; as a result their sight is not intercepted by new objects, and they have no need to remember by means of divided thought: "però non hanno vedere interciso / da novo obietto, e però non bisogna / rememorar per concetto diviso" (79–81). The philosophers who ascribe the faculty of memory to angels (comprising some who believe they are telling the truth, and others who do not) are dreaming without being asleep: "sì che là giù, non dormendo, si sogna, / credendo e non credendo dicer vero" ("so that down there, not sleeping, men dream, believing and not believing that they speak truth" [82–83]). Dante makes such a point of denying memory to angels (arguing much more forcefully on this topic than Aquinas, for instance),[35] because he wants to appropriate memory exclusively as the basis of human life and human creativity: language is a function of memory, which in turn is a function of time, and both are the exclusive province of human beings and human poets—angels need never remember, and they need never write poems. Dante, moreover, signals the connection of this passage to the wellspring of his own poetics with the words *dormire, sognare, credere, dire vero*, used to characterize those who hold to the mistaken doctrine of angelic memory: while those teachers are false dreamers, whose "dreams" are consciously forged while they are awake and then spread among the people either in good faith or in bad, Dante is one whose dreams come to him not "non dormendo," but—like St. John—"dormendo, con la faccia arguta." The point is that the *Commedia* is not Dante's invented dream, his *invenzione*, crafted by him while awake, but an inspired dream, given to him in a waking sleep, by the same God who gave true script to "li scrittor de lo Spirito Santo."

Beatrice proceeds to accuse philosophers of abandoning the one true path, the single path of truth, for the multiplicity of appearance: "Voi non andate giù per un sentiero / filosofando" ("You do not go down one path in philosophizing" [*Par.* 29.85–86]). The philosophical *sentiero* so often abandoned is another figure for the line of becoming that haunts Dante's imagination, applied to life ("il cammin di nostra vita"), to narrative ("il cammin riciso"), and now to thought; the same figure appears again, reinvested with a narrative significance, toward the end of canto 29, when Beatrice exhorts the pilgrim to turn back to the "straight road" ("la dritta strada" [128]) after their "digression" on the mendacious preachers: "we have digressed enough," she tells him, "siam digressi assai" (127). Our minds go back to angelic intellection: because angels "non hanno vedere interciso / da novo obietto," they are incapable of digressing; once more the point has been made that a narrative journey, a journey predicated on memory, time, and difference, on "rememorar per concetto diviso," is a profoundly human undertaking. Human creators digress, they remember, and they are constrained by time; indeed, Beatrice wants to return to the "dritta strada" so that the way may be shortened along with the time ("sì che la via col tempo si raccorci" [129]), in other words, so that their discussion may be commensurate with the time at their disposal. Situated as it is toward the canto's end, this verse suggests that the temporal limits Beatrice speaks of are textual limits as well; the conflation of the journey's experiential "time" with the text's actual dimensions, which *lo fren de l'arte* is bound to respect, alerts us to the poet's metapoetic awareness in precisely the same way that Jane Austen alerts us when she writes that her readers see "in the tell-tale compression of the pages before them, that we are all hastening together to perfect felicity."[36] And, given the telltale compression of his pages as well, Dante is of course alluding not only to the end of canto 29, in experiential terms the end of the primum mobile, but also to the end of the poem, in experiential terms the end of the journey; thus, Beatrice's "sì che la via col tempo si raccorci" in the closing section of canto 29 is echoed by Bernard's "Ma perché 'l tempo fugge che t'assonna" in the closing section of canto 32. The end of canto 29 marks not just another canto ending but a larger closure within the narrative arc we have been tracing: we could say that cantos 22–27 (from one backward glance to the other, corresponding to the heaven of the fixed stars) constitute the beginning of the beginning of the end, cantos 28–29 (the primum mobile) the middle of the beginning of the end, and cantos 30–33 (the empyrean) the end of the beginning of the end.[37] The anxiety that informs these cantos, beginning with "sì che la via col tempo si raccorci," is the anxiety of the impending end, the anxiety of having to end without delivering the satisfaction that only God could deliver. The limits Dante ultimately faces (invoked by the Ulyssean motifs woven into the poem's final cantos) are limits that not even he can overcome.

As prelude to the new beginning of canto 30, and as conclusion to cantos 28–29, Beatrice leads the pilgrim back to "la dritta strada," picking up the issue of angelic nature where she left off; "Questa natura" in 29.130 hearkens back to verse 71's "angelica natura." The path to which she reconducts him after their detour is none other than the master path of *Paradiso*, as once more the problem of the one and the many absorbs Dante's explanatory energies. The numerical multiplicity of the angelic nature is beyond human expression ("Questa natura sì oltre s'ingrada / in numero, che mai non fu loquela / né concetto mortal che tanto vada" ["This nature forms so many *grades* in *number* that never was there speech or mortal concept that could go so far" (130–32)]); a reading of the prophet Daniel indicates that no definitive count may be reached, since "'n sue *migliaia* / determinato *numero* si cela" ("in his *thousands* a definite *number* is hidden" [134–35]). (It is worth noting that *numero*, talisman of time and difference, appears only in the *Paradiso*, six times in all, and is concentrated in cantos 28 and 29, occurring twice in each canto, while the verb *numerare*, a hapax, appears in canto 29.) Each of these innumerable splendors receives the divine light in its own way ("per tanti modi" [137]), so that, since each angel's ability to love is premised on its access to the light of truth ("a l'atto che concepe /

segue l'affetto" ["affection follows upon the act that conceives" (139–40)]), each loves "diversamente" (141). The pilgrim is now better able to see the breadth of the eternal goodness, which can shatter itself ("si spezza") into so many countless fragments, all the while remaining one as before: "poscia che tanti / speculi fatti s'ha in che si spezza, / uno manendo in sé come davanti" ("since it has made itself into so many mirrors in which it is shattered, one remaining in itself as before" [143–45]). Here Beatrice, at the end of the last of the *Paradiso*'s great creation cantos, echoes an earlier such; St. Thomas's discourse on creation in canto 13 describes the divine light mirroring itself into the nine angelic beings while still remaining eternally one: "quasi specchiato, in nove sussistenze, / etternalmente rimanendosi una" (*Par.* 13.59–60). With its echoing restatement of the *Paradiso*'s fundamental paradox canto 29 ends, and with a final metapoetic reminder: for, also paradoxically, the more the *Commedia*'s narrative line is shattered, the more—pace Beatrice, who in canto 5 "com'uom che suo parlar NON spezza, / continüò così 'l processo santo" (16–18)—the *processo santo si spezza*, the more it too achieves the unity of *uguaglianza*, "uno manendo in sé come davanti."[38]

Canto 30 is in many ways like canto 23, another rehearsal for the absolute finale.[39] Geographically and thematically, *Paradiso* 30 proclaims its anticipatory function with respect to the poem's ultimate ending more explicitly than does its forerunner; after all, this is the canto in which the travelers enter the empyrean, and in which the pilgrim's visions are proleptically termed "prefaces," still shadowy and veiled, of the truth that is to come: "son di lor vero umbriferi prefazi" ("they are of their truth shadow-bearing prefaces" [*Par.* 30.78]). Canto 30 will slip out of the mode of *uguaglianza* before its ending, in order to permit Beatrice her final indictment of human cupidity in general and of the papacy in particular. Nonetheless, much of *Paradiso* 30 testifies to the "jumping" mode as we characterized it with respect to canto 23, wherein the "plot" is subjected to various tactical pressures that fragment it; and, in fact, as in canto 23, there is a lengthy metapoetic protest in which the poet announces the cutting off of the narrative line that he has been following up to now, using a Latinism, *preciso*, that rhymes with and is etymologically related to the earlier *riciso*.[40] From the first day that he saw her face until this moment, his song has prevailed, his pursuit of it has never been cut off: "non m'è il seguire al mio cantar preciso" (30). But now, for the first time—and we notice how, as befits his construction of a self-consuming artifact, Dante is constrained to demote his earlier failure in canto 23, which now turns out not to have existed, in order to claim priority for this, his newest, failure—his path is truly cut off; as earlier it behooved him to jump ("convien saltar lo sacrato poema"), now it behooves him to desist in his poetic pursuit, in *il seguire al mio cantar*, his songful segueing: "ma or convien che mio seguir desista / più dietro a sua bellezza, poetando, /

come a l'ultimo suo ciascuno artista" ("but now I must desist from following further behind her beauty in making poetry, as at his ultimate must each artist" [31–33]). Although longer than its predecessor (seven tercets as compared to five), and situated toward the canto's beginning rather than at the middle, the metapoetic interlude of canto 30 again takes its point of departure from Beatrice's excessive beauty, as calmly resistant to the coming telos as the poet instead is urgently hurtling toward it. It is this sense of the ending that tinges these verses with an anxiety that was not present earlier, and that expresses itself in the double *seguire*'s insistence on the line, the long narrative path that extends back to the furthest recesses of the poet's past, all the way back to the *Vita Nuova* and its "stilo de la sua loda," echoed here in the "loda" of verse 17. In order to convey its compelling concern with textuality's telethetic linearity, encoded into the repeated *infino a*, the passage is best cited in full:

> Se quanto *infino a qui* di lei si dice
>   fosse conchiuso tutto in una loda,
>   poca sarebbe a fornir questa vice.
> La bellezza ch'io vidi si trasmoda
>   non pur di là da noi, ma certo io credo
>   che solo il suo fattor tutta la goda.
> Da *questo passo* vinto mi concedo
>   più che già mai da punto di suo tema
>   soprato fosse comico o tragedo:
> ché, come sole in viso che più trema,
>   così *lo rimembrar* del dolce riso
>   la mente mia da me medesmo scema.
> *Dal primo giorno* ch'i' vidi il suo viso
>   in questa vita, *infino a* questa vista,
>   non m'è *il seguire* al mio cantar preciso;
> ma or convien che *mio seguir* desista
>   *più dietro* a sua bellezza, poetando,
>   come a *l'ultimo suo* ciascuno artista.
> Cotal qual io la lascio a maggior bando
>   che quel de la mia tuba, che *deduce*
>   l'ardüa sua matera *terminando* . . .

If what has been said of her *as far as here* were all included in one praise, it would be little to accomplish this task. The beauty that I saw transmodes itself not only beyond us, but certainly I believe that only her maker enjoys it all. By *this pass* I concede myself vanquished more than ever before either a comic or tragic poet was overcome by a point in his theme; for, like the sun to the sight that most trembles, so the *remembrance* of the sweet smile weakens my mind from myself. *From the first day* that I saw her face in this life *as far as* this sight, the *following* of my singing has not been cut off; but now I must desist from *following further behind* her beauty in making poetry, as at *his ultimate* must each artist. Such as I leave her to a greater heralding than that of my trumpet, which *draws to a close* its arduous material . . .

(*Par.* 30.16–36)

Prior to this passage, Dante had related the fading of the vision first vouchsafed him in canto 28, the vision of the triumph ("trïunfo" in 30.10 recalls its previous use, the "trïunfo di Cristo" of canto 23) that plays eternally around the point that seems "enclosed by that which it encloses." God is "inchiuso da quel ch'elli 'nchiude" (*Par.* 30.12), and the echo of "inchiuso" by "conchiuso" a few verses later, in the metapoetic passage cited above, suggests the similarly paradoxical nature of the poet's task: if he could gather up everything he has ever said about Beatrice, bundling up all the past temporality and dispersed multiplicity of the long line of words he has left behind him, and make this multiplicity into one—one supreme lyric, one ultimate word of praise, "conchiuso tutto in *una loda*"—then he would, in the poetic sphere, be doing the equivalent of what God does when he binds the many quires of the universe "in un volume" ("in one volume" [*Par.* 33.86]). If he could say it all "in una loda" he need not have written the many quires of this poem; if he could express himself not discursively but simultaneously he would be like the angels. But he is not an angel, he is instead possessed of memory, "lo rimembrar del dolce riso": the *rimembrar* that at least allows him to re-collect what he cannot collect all at once, and then to transcribe what has been re-collected; the *rimembrar* that exists to compensate for the fact that his mental sight is—unlike that of angels— "interciso," but whose existence also guarantees that his song will ultimately be cut off ("riciso" or "preciso"), since his transcription will stumble when his memory fails. And so the sacred poem is forced to jump, and *Paradiso* 30 does just that, jumping not from simile to simile in the mode of canto 23 but from vision to vision, from one *umbrifero prefazio* to the next. The pilgrim is swathed by a living light that gives him a power beyond his own, kindling in him the ability to see the empyrean in a sequence of phantasmagoric images: he sees light in the form of a river whose banks are clothed in gemlike flowers, whose effulgence emits living sparks coursing between its shores and its depths, a river that later—after the pilgrim rushes to its banks like an infant desiring milk and drinks of it with his lashes, in two imagistic replays of canto 23—appears to him transformed into a circle, whereupon he sees the two courts of heaven made manifest, the sparks as angels and the flowers as saints. An apostrophe interrupts, an exclamatory tercet in which the poet prays to the divine light itself for the power of language to express what he saw: "O isplendor di Dio, per cu' io vidi / l'alto trïunfo del regno verace, / dammi virtù a dir com'ïo il vidi!" ("O splendor of God whereby I saw the high triumph of the true realm, give me the power to say how I saw it!" [*Par.* 30.97–99]). The narrator resumes: the light is distended in a circular shape ("in circular figura" [103]), around which rise the many tiers— more than a thousand ("più di mille soglie" [113])—that seat the blessed; the whole is compared to a hillside mirrored in water at its base ("E come clivo in acqua di suo imo / si specchia" [109–10]). In the next tercet the image of a hill, expressed through simile, "jumps," becoming the vision of a rose, which is introduced without even the warning or preparation of a preceding *come*: suddenly the "clivo" of verse 109 has become, in verse 117, "questa rosa."[41] The rose is repeated ("Nel giallo de la rosa sempiterna" ["In the yellow of the eternal rose" (124)]), before yielding in turn to the final vision, that of a city ("Vedi nostra città quant'ella gira" ["See our city how much it encircles" (130)]); "nostra città" signals the transition (by way of the empty throne that awaits Henry VII) into the political invective that closes the canto.[42]

From a river banked with springtime flora to a verdant amphitheater to a redolent rose to a celestial Jerusalem: Dante's representational phantasmagoria slides from one image to another in a classic example of the *Paradiso*'s jumping discourse. And yet, as cued by the final image's connection to the political theme that provides Beatrice her last speech, canto 30 displays, beginning with the thousand tiers of the heavenly hillside, a mixed mode, in which the language of difference coexists with the language of mystical unity. The same tercet that provides one of the canto's most spectacular imagistic jumps, from the *clivo* to the unheralded rose, a tercet that is both metaphoric and exclamatory in true jumping fashion, is also infused with linguistic *disagguaglianza*: "E se l'*infimo* grado in sé raccoglie / sì grande lume, quanta è la larghezza / di questa rosa ne l'*estreme* foglie!" ("And if the *lowest* rank contains in itself so great a light, how vast is the amplitude of this rose in its *farthest* leaves!" [115–17]). The rose is in fact the perfect example of the mixed discourse of canto 30: it is a lyric image that can be used (as will be apparent in cantos 31 and 32) in a nonlyric way, pressed into the service of hierarchy and difference.[43] But whereas the following cantos will exploit the rose's latent hierarchical value, its possession of what the tercet cited above calls "l'infimo grado" and "l'estreme foglie," in canto 30 the emphasis is still squarely on its affective connotations; in the verses "Nel giallo de la rosa sempiterna, / che si digrada e dilata e redole / odor di lode al sol che sempre verna" ("In the yellow of the eternal rose that extends in grades and dilates and exudes odor of praise to the sun that makes spring always" [124–26]), only the verb "digrada" points forward to the hierarchical language of the next two cantos, and it is more than compensated by the lyrical force of the tercet as a whole. If canto 30 is, in its entirety, less a *circulata melodia* than canto 23, it yet contains such hallmarks of *uguaglianza* as the triple rhyme on *vidi*,[44] deployed at the peak of visionary intensity in which the flowers and the sparks resolve themselves into heaven's two courts. It also contains the unique passage in which the last word of each verse is repeated as the first word of the next verse, in a kind of miniaturized application of the Provençal *capfinidas* technique:

> Noi siamo usciti fore
> del maggior corpo al ciel ch'è pura *luce*:
> *luce* intellettüal, piena d'*amore*;
> *amor* di vero ben, pien di *letizia*;
> *letizia* che trascende ogni dolzore.

We have come out from the greatest body to the heaven of pure *light*: intellectual *light*, full of *love*; *love* of true good, full of *happiness*; *happiness* that transcends every sweetness.

(Par. 30.38–42)

Attenuating the hierarchy of intellect over love that was imposed in canto 28, these verses are a graphic and aural incarnation of head-tailed circularity, a textual Alpha and Omega that gathers the ongoing spiral of terza rima into a net of verbal unity.

With regard to the formal disposition of the *Paradiso*'s final six cantos, we have hitherto noted a 2 + 4 arrangement: two cantos constituting, geographically, the primum mobile, and diegetically, the middle of the beginning of the end (cantos 28–29); and four cantos constituting, geographically, the empyrean, and diegetically, the end of the beginning of the end (cantos 30–33). From the point of view of alternations in narrative mode, however, one could view the same sextet as forming a 3 + 3 arrangement: two cantos of *disagguaglianza* (28–29), followed by one canto of *uguaglianza* (30); and again, two cantos of *disagguaglianza* (31–32), followed by one canto of *uguaglianza* (33). In both sets of three, the logical/discursive/ intellective cantos set the stage for the explosions of unity that follow, a unity that can best be achieved—in the nonunified medium of language— negatively: by not doing what has just been done, by rejecting the discourse that was privileged in the cantos of difference. In other words, cantos 28–29 allow canto 30 to be forged as the antithesis of themselves, and likewise, cantos 31–32 prepare for the poem's finale. The pattern in the two sets is basically the same, with the proviso that while cantos 28–29 move from more difference in canto 28 to less in canto 29, cantos 31–32 move from less difference in canto 31 to more in canto 32, the better to offset canto 33. The *variatio* employed in the buildup cantos thus causes the pattern to be markedly more pronounced in the second trio, in which a canto of maximum difference immediately precedes a canto of maximum unity. With respect to the latter trio's first canto, the intellective stamp of canto 31 is evident from its opening verse, from the strong metrical beat that falls on the verse's centerpiece, the intellectualizing "dunque" that mediates between "In forma" on the one hand and "di candida rosa" on the other. A word that has over the centuries been earmarked for use by teachers and scholars, *dunque* here hastens the passage from canto 30's lyrical rose redolent of praise to the more prosaic rose of cantos 31 and 32:[45] a categorized and hierarchical rose whose form is to be explained, unfolded, shorn of all mystery. "In forma dunque di candida rosa" ("So, in the form of a white rose" [*Par*. 31.1]) announces the narrator, at the same time announcing the explanatory and didactic functions of these cantos, whose duty is to explore the shape and content of paradise, encompassing its form—the "forma general di paradiso" as it will later be called (*Par*. 31.52)—in the language of formal exposition. As compared to canto 33's metaphoric vision of the universe bound by love in one volume, a vision wherein the poet thinks he saw, because he still feels, the universal form of things ("La forma universal di questo nodo" ["The universal form of this knot" (*Par*. 33.91)]), in cantos 31 and 32 the poet's task is not to feel the form of things so much as to explain, describe, and, as much as possible, divulge it. In these cantos, and especially in canto 32, his is to reason why; not to try to communicate a private and transrational emotion but to sustain a rational, discursive, and public inquest into the *forma general di paradiso*.

With regard to the discursive mode of canto 31, one could point to its three important similes of completed quest, all similes that recount, in the form of little stories, rather than similes that im-press. Like the simile of the bachelor student in canto 24, they describe the pilgrim, not what he sees. They are similes that figure trajectory and pilgrimage (the motif of pilgrimage itself, rarely rendered explicit in the *Commedia*, appears twice in canto 31); they figure the line from there to here, from *da* to *a*, prepositionally inscribed into the famous verses that constitute the second term of the simile of the barbarians arrived in Rome: "ïo, che *al* divino *da* l'umano, / *a* l'etterno *dal* tempo era venuto, / e *di* Fiorenza *in* popol giusto e sano, / di che stupor dovea esser compiuto!" ("I, who *to* the divine *from* the human, *to* the eternal *from* time had come, and *from* Florence *to* a people just and sane, with what amazement must I have been full!" [37–40]). Similarly, the simile of the Croatian pilgrim come to view the Veronica heightens the sense of a long and arduous journey that has been successfully brought to completion by recounting in direct discourse the voyager's thoughts as he faces the icon; his "Segnor mio Iesù Cristo, Dio verace, / or fu sì fatta la sembianza vostra?" ("My lord Jesus Christ, true God, was then your image made thus?" [107–8]) gives dramatic shape not only to his own mininarrative but to the enveloping narrative of the *Commedia*'s pilgrim, who is nearing the point at which he too may hope to see Christ's face. For throughout this canto of pilgrims, linear journeys, and much-desired arrivals one senses also, not coincidentally, the presence of the narrative line, the narrative journey, whose own arrival, so long deferred, approaches as well; not for nothing does the simile of the pilgrim who looks around the temple of his vow make mention of his already hoping—barely arrived as he is—to *tell again* how the temple was: "e spera già *ridir* com'ello stea" (45). The narrative continues, as the naked difference of the verse relating the substitution of Beatrice by Bernard proclaims ("*Uno* intendëa, e *altro* mi rispuose" ["*One* I intended, and *another* answered me" (58)]), and if it draws to its terminus ("A terminar lo tuo disiro" ["To terminate your desire" (65)] is the mission given by one guide to the other), it has not yet terminated, but is rather engaged in a preterminal celebration of itself: the pilgrim's last words to Beatrice insist on the long journey behind them, on the "tante cose quant'i' ho vedute" ("many things which I have seen" [82]), the many paths and many modes—"per tutte quelle vie, per tutt'i modi" (86)—that she has been empowered to employ for his salvation. The consummation of all paths is at hand, as Bernard tells the pilgrim: "Acciò che tu assommi / perfettamente . . . il tuo cammino" ("So that you can perfectly bring to conclusion your journey" [94–95]). But before the poet can perfectly bring his path—the diegetic *cammino*—to completion, he has two great tasks before him: the task of rendering ultimate unity, in canto 33, and before that, in canto 32, the task of trying one more time to understand and rationalize the place of difference in a singly-bound universe.

Canto 31 concludes with Bernard's injunction to the pilgrim to seek out heaven's queen, and with the "affetto" (141) felt by Bernard for his beloved, which makes the pilgrim's eyes even more "ardenti" (the canto's last word) as they gaze upward; canto 32 echoes (but grammatically varies) the preceding *affetto* in its opening description of Bernard, "Affetto al suo piacer" ("Lovingly intent on his delight"). Just as a strain of Marian affectivity runs through both cantos 31 and 32, delivering them from unrelieved *disagguaglianza*, so canto 31 inaugurates canto 32's final disquisition on the *Paradiso*'s consuming topic. Accordingly, canto 31 begins by demystifying the glinting sparks of canto 30, comparing the labor of the angels to that of bees as they descend into the flower "di banco in banco" ("from rank to rank" [*Par.* 31.16]), pollinating peace and love. "Di banco in banco" is the cue: the issue of the one and the many, which will receive its last great airing in canto 32, is now explicitly brought forward, in verses that are precise recapitulations of the *Paradiso*'s first tercet; as there "La gloria di colui che tutto move / per l'universo penetra, e risplende / in una parte più e meno altrove," so here "la luce divina è penetrante / per l'universo secondo ch'è degno" ("the divine light penetrates through the universe according to its worthiness" [*Par.* 31.22–23]).[46] The words "secondo ch'è degno" encapsulate a problematic that will be recalled in Beatrice's departure for her specific and inalienable seat, the "trono che suoi merti le sortiro" ("throne that her merits have allotted to her" [*Par.* 31.69]), where "merti" encompasses the ideas of free will and individual merit, while "sortiro" alludes to grace, providence, predestination. The same verb reappears in canto 32, where Francis, Benedict, and Augustine are allotted, under John the Baptist, to divide the rose vertically ("cerner sortiro" [34]) on one side, as on the other such division ("cotanta cerna" [30]) falls to the Hebrew women seated under Mary.[47] The passage leading up to the *dubbio* signaled by the verb *sortire* is riddled with difference, with individuality; not only is the rose arranged in a vertical hierarchy ("puoi tu veder così *di soglia in soglia / giù digradar,* com'io ch'a *proprio nome /* vo per la rosa giù *di foglia in foglia*" ["you may thus see *from rank to rank* in *gradation* downward, as I with *each name* go down through the rose *from petal to petal*" (*Par.* 32.13–15)]), but it is divided horizontally as well. Its bottom half contains the souls of innocent children who died before they had power of choice; in this section of the rose, therefore, seating is in no way related to one's individual merit: "per nullo proprio merito si siede" ("one is seated for no merit of one's own" [42]). And yet, despite the lack of merit, they are still hierarchically arranged, some lower and some higher, some *più* and some *meno.* This is the fact that engages the pilgrim in a final bout with his most unresolved *dubbio,* a *dubbio* whose hold on his imagination is indicated by Bernard's repetition: "Or dubbi tu e dubitando sili" ("Now you are doubtful and, doubting, you are silent" [49]). The final *dubbio* of the *Paradiso* is essentially its first, and exhibits the same preoccupation with unequally proportioned grace that has marked the pilgrim throughout his ascent. But the issue has never been more starkly raised than here, because never before was individual merit so totally excluded from the equation, leaving only the inexplicable variable, the incomprehensible component: God's grace.

The pilgrim's last intellectual dilemma regards the presence of difference in the realm of unity and equality, and it reflects what can only be called Dante's obsession with justice, an obsession that causes him to worry not only about the damnation of the meritorious but even about greater and lesser degrees of beatitude among the saved.[48] What motivates him to carry this concern to the very threshold of the beatific vision? What could be so important about the distribution of these saved infants? The answer, in one word, is justice: the fixation on justice that motivates Beatrice's indecorous final words on Boniface, so distressing to many readers. At stake for Dante is nothing less than the existence of the nonarbitrary. Where is the justice in distributing hierarchically—differentiatedly—souls for whom there is no criterion of merit? Can the divine will be unjust? Can paradise, whose perfect order depends on its reflection of an infallible justice, be not ordered but merely arbitrary? These are the terrifying thoughts that Bernard undertakes to answer, and that he does not so much reason away as deny. For although Bernard, much like Beatrice faced with the incommensurable universes in canto 28, confidently proclaims that he will loosen the hard knot of the pilgrim's doubt, in fact his reply consists of assertions, not explana-tions.[49] He asserts that within the divine realm no arbitrariness can exist, nothing can be a matter of chance ("Dentro a l'ampiezza di questo reame / casüal punto non puote aver sito" ["Within the width of this realm no point of chance can have a place" (*Par.* 32.52–53)]); having thus stated as fact what he cannot prove, he derives as a corollary of his unproven assertion the justness of the children's collocation. Given that there is no arbitrariness in God's realm, the children cannot have been arranged arbitrarily, "sine causa"; a cause for their being more and less excellent among themselves must exist: "e però questa festinata gente / a vera vita non è *sine causa* / intra sé qui *più e meno eccellente*" ("and therefore this company that hastened to true life is not without cause among itself *more and less excellent*" [58–60]). Now he has baldly said it: they are, through no fault of their own, *più e meno eccellenti*. Once more, and for the last time, *più e meno* is the *Commedia*'s herald of difference, of Dante's ceaseless worrying at an issue that will not go away (for, if the *Paradiso* were to go on as long again, this problem would never be resolved). Once more, *più e meno* ushers in the language of *di-sagguaglianza*, displayed in a passage that offers the poem's last use of *diver-samente*, its last use of *differente*, and its last use of *differire*:

> Lo rege per cui questo regno pausa
>   in tanto amore e in tanto diletto,
>   che nulla volontà è di più ausa,
> le menti tutte nel suo lieto aspetto
>   creando, a suo piacer di grazia dota
>   *diversamente*: e qui basti l'effetto.
> . . . . . . . . . . . .
> Dunque, sanza mercé di lor costume,
>   locati son per gradi *differenti*,
>   sol *differendo* nel primiero acume.

The king, through whom this kingdom reposes in such love and such delight that no will dares for more, creating all the minds in his happy aspect, at his pleasure bestows grace *diversely*; and here let the fact suffice. . . . Therefore, without merit of their conduct, they are located in *different* grades, *differing* only in their first acuteness of vision.

(*Par.* 32.61–66, 73–75)

The existence of difference is thus reaffirmed in the *Paradiso*'s penulti-mate canto, and its harsh presence is the more symptomatic in that it is idiosyncratic. For Dante moves beyond theological speculation with regard to baptized infants precisely in the direction of difference; while, for Bonav-enture and Aquinas, equality of grace for infants is the norm, to which there may be exceptions, for Dante "diversity in degrees of grace is the norm—is, indeed, a structural principle in the Empyrean—and to this extent his doctrine clearly differs from that of either of these two predecessors."[50] We could add that Dante goes to great lengths to highlight the apparently arbitrary nature of God's behavior, first by giving the scriptural example of God's differentiation between Esau and Jacob, from which is derived the corollary that we are graced "according to the color of our hair": "secondo il color d'i capelli" (70). There follow some of the *Commedia*'s most brutally dogmatic verses, outlining the historical conditions that govern the salvation of infants: from Adam to Abraham the faith of the parents is required, from Abraham to Jesus circumcision is a prerequisite, and after Christ, in "the time of grace" ("'l tempo de la grazia" [82]), salvation depends on baptism (76–84). In this passage Dante draws attention to the nub of his concern; by laying stress on the apparent arbitrariness of God's law, as of God's choice of Jacob over Esau, Dante confronts his worst nightmare and affirms his belief in a grace that, by eternal law ("etterna legge" [55]), is allotted as justly—"giustamente" (56)—as the ring fits the finger. God bestows his grace as he pleases, "a suo piacer"; on the basis of God's assignment, which we must assume to be just, and irrespective of any personal merit, we differ among ourselves. Before attempting to gather all difference into the *totum simul* of the wheel that equally is turned, Dante takes this final opportunity to put its existence forcefully and unequivocally into the record.

The *disagguaglianza* of canto 32 is a factor in its linguistic texture as well; this canto of conceptual difference is marked by narrative divisibility and approachability, its arduous intellectual problems offset by its relative diegetic simplicity. Although the "divina cantilena" ("divine song" [97]) performed by Gabriel for the Virgin puts us in mind of the "circulata melodia" of canto 23, canto 32 is not a lyrical canto (and in fact the angel's performance is not recorded, as it was in canto 23), but one whose linearity and limpidity serve to prepare for the circularity and density of what lies ahead. Bernard's injunction to gaze on the face that most looks like that of Christ— "Riguarda omai ne la faccia che a Cristo / più si somiglia" ("Look now upon the face that most resembles Christ" [85–86])—since only its brightness can prepare one to see Christ (the command coincides with the poem's last set of *Cristo* rhymes), recalls the naive anthropomorphism of the Croatian pilgrim before the Veronica and heightens our own inevitable desire for an encounter that will never occur, for the kind of resolution to this poem that Dante knows to be out of the question but nonetheless dangles in front of us. The issue of physical resemblance, physical likeness, raised by the verb *somigliare* in verse 86, points forward to the end of the journey as an at-oneness, as the achievement of a likeness that the likeness of the repeated *Cristo* rhymes underscores. Difference is, of course, still present in the fact that there is a face that resembles Christ's more than any other, or an angel who unites as much as may be—"quant'esser puote" (110)—of vigor and joy; it is especially present in the suggestion that the pilgrim penetrate God's brilliance as much as is possible—"quant'è possibil" (144)—that is, as much as may be achieved by his specific and eternally differentiated historical self. But, in order for him to achieve anything at all, they must first pray; otherwise, if he relies on his own powers—his own wings—he risks falling back rather than moving beyond: "ne forse tu t'arretri / movendo l'ali tue, credendo oltrarti" ("lest, perhaps, you go backward, moving your wings, and thinking to go forward" [145–46]). The Ulyssean cast of this passage, its wings, its embedded oltre, brings to the forefront of the reader's consciousness the ongoing problematic of transgression, already anticipated in the previous canto's recollection of Phaeton (the sun is "il temo / che mal guidò Fetonte" ["the pole that Phaeton badly guided" (31.124–25)]). Canto 33 will display an insistent Ulyssean lexicon that begins in the prayer to the Virgin, where Bernard remarks that whoever wants grace and does not turn to her is one whose "disïanza vuol volar sanz'ali" ("desire seeks to fly without wings" [Par. 33.15]), and where the orator's replication of "prieghi" and "priego" recalls Inferno 26 (nor is the hapax "orator," in 33.41, insignificant, given Ulysses' own status as the composer of the "orazion picciola").[51] This lexicon perseveres throughout the final canto in the pilgrim's "ardor del desiderio" ("ardor of desire" [48]), his "oltraggio" ("going beyond" [57]), his daring ("ardito" [79]) and presumption ("presunsi" [82]), culminating in the wings—"le proprie penne" (139)—that are unequal to the final flight.

We could say, for the sake of argument, that Paradiso 33 begins at the end of the preceding canto, in canto 32's last verse, the only last verse to conclude, in Petrocchi's edition of the Commedia, with a colon rather than a period, exclamation point, or question mark.[52] Paradiso 32 is in fact the only canto in the poem to terminate without benefit of a conceptual full stop, to reach closure with a verb of beginning (cominciare) and a demonstrative adjective ("questa") pointed toward the future: "E cominciò questa santa orazione" ("And he began this sainted oration"). This verse, whose "cominciò" so aggressively inscribes incipience into finality, further bespeaks circularity by virtually repeating the same canto's third verse, "e cominciò queste parole sante" ("and he began these sainted words" [Par. 32.3]); the echo at the canto's end of a verse that we associate with its beginning is another way of reinforcing the reader's sense of arriving at a beginning, rather than an end. "E cominciò questa santa orazione" marks the newest new beginning within the unfolding diegesis; by keeping this marker of the new outside of canto 33, Dante signals his will to refuse the new, to exile difference. While not suggesting that this is possible, or that Dante thinks it so, I do suggest that Dante means to strive, and to strive heroically, and that he therefore finds a new way to use the techniques elaborated in the course of Paradiso: he "enjambs" the end of canto 32, causing the poem to jump. As befits the paradox of enjambment, a rupture that unifies, the location of "E cominciò questa santa orazione" thus achieves two goals: first, it keeps out of an antinarrative canto a blatant signpost of narrativity; second, the open-ended ending, by building a bridge to canto 33, by resisting the division into two cantos, the difference between 32 and 33, constitutes a preview and emblem of the unified discourse that Dante works to forge in canto 33. Again, Dante's is a symbolic gesture, which will, of course, not actually be able to exile diegetic *disagguaglianza* from canto 33; like a condensed version of the *Paradiso* as a whole, or indeed of the *Commedia*, canto 33 will have its narrative ups and downs, its moments of *più*, poetically speaking, and its moments of *meno*. In any medium, like language, that proceeds by difference, such must be the case, as Bernard essentially reminds us when he invokes the long *cammino* that the pilgrim has traveled, characterizing him as an adventurer whose path has been parsed out by encounters with the new, encounters experienced in temporal succession, one by one: "*da l'infima* lacuna / de l'universo *infin qui* ha vedute / le vite spiritali *ad una ad una*" ("*from the lowest* pit of the universe *up to here* he has seen the spiritual lives *one by one*" [*Par.* 33.22–24]). And yet, the enjambed ending of canto 32 is indicative of Dante's search for the impossible: for a unified discourse that fuses the many into the one, a *circulata melodia* made by denying beginnings and endings, by evading the narrative distinctions that have sustained the poem till now, *ad una ad una*, and without which the *Paradiso* itself could not have been written. Canto 33 is Dante's supreme attempt to engage the fractured, circular, equalized mode of *ugua-glianza*; in it the jumping style of canto 23 is put to use in the sapient construction of an antinarrative that is not, however, antimimetic. Rather, the mimesis of canto 33 seeks to approximate the circling, surging, orgasmic approach of the soul to the fulfillment of its heart's desire.[53]

If we divide canto 33, searching for the *disagguaglianza* that it resists, we begin by distinguishing the oratorical prelude of the canto's first third, its first forty-five verses (consisting of Bernard's prayer in the present tense, 1–39, and the coda that introduces the narrative past tense, 40–45), from the ensuing "story" of the pilgrim's final ascent.[54] This story can, I believe, be viewed as three circular waves of discourse (like the rippling motion of water in a round vase that is compared to waves of spoken speech at the beginning of canto 14)—three *circulate melodie*, three "jumps"—by which the poet zeroes in on his poem's climax; he approaches and backs off, approaches and backs off again, and finally arrives. Each of these circular movements is made up of three textual building blocks used by the poet to keep the text jumping, to prevent a narrative line from forming: brief moments of "plot," where the pilgrim does something or something happens to him, alternate with impassioned statements about the poet and with apostrophes to the divinity.[55] The first of the circular movements, which I would posit from lines 46 to 75, articulates most clearly the three textual components: it begins with a sequence of pure plot, in which Dante narrates what happened in the past tense, first stating unequivocally that "l'ardor del desiderio in me finii" ("I brought to completion the ardor of my desire" [48]) and then describing how he looked upward, training his gaze more and more ("più e più" now takes the place of "più e meno") along the divine ray (46–54). Even in this relatively straightforward and "narrative" recounting, we note the slippage that is typical of this canto, as Dante inaugurates the technique of coupling the adversative "ma" with the time-blurring adverb "già" that will be reprised to such effect in the poem's conclusion: Bernard signals to the pilgrim to look up, "ma io era / già per me stesso tal qual ei volea" ("but I was already of my own such as he wanted me" [50–51]). We now move into the present tense, as the poet takes the stage, telling us that thenceforward his vision was greater than his speech can express, since his memory yields before such a going beyond, before "tanto oltraggio" (57). In three remarkable and quintessentially affective similes, the poet then figures both his gain and his loss: he is as one who sees in dream, but who after his vision retains only the imprinted sentiment, the "passione impressa" (59); in the same way that his vision ceases, leaving behind a distilled sweetness in his heart, so does snow melt under the sun, so in light leaves cast to the wind were the Sibyl's oracles lost: "Così la neve al sol si disigilla; / così al vento ne le foglie levi / si perdea la sentenza di Sibilla" (64–66). At this point, in an abrupt "jump" away from the lyrical peak formed by these similes, which impress upon us emotionally (working to transfer to us the "passione impressa" experienced by the pilgrim) what cannot be understood rationally, we move into a prayer/apostrophe, also in the present tense, in which the poet begs that his tongue may be granted the power to tell but a little of what he saw; beginning with the vocative "O somma luce" ("O highest light" [67]), this segment takes us to the end of the first circular movement, verse 75.

Whereas the first movement circles paradigmatically from "event" to the poet's inability to recount that event, to his appeal for help in verbalizing what he has thus far not proved able to express, the second movement, which encompasses lines 76 to 105, is less articulated. Again, it begins with a moment of plot, which contains what is probably the canto's most straightforward statement of arrival, situated in a passage whose rhyme words offer a veritable archeology of the *Commedia*'s thematics; afraid to look away lest he be lost ("smarrito" [77]), the pilgrim is daring ("ardito" [79]) enough to sustain the light and so reaches his journey's end: "i' giunsi / l'aspetto mio col valore infinito" ("I joined my sight with the infinite goodness" [80–81]). Immediately, as though that conjoining of the individual one ("io," "mio") with the infinite One were not sustainable at a narrative level, the text jumps into an exclamatory tercet as the poet apostrophizes

the grace that permitted his *oltraggio*: "Oh abbondante grazia ond'io presunsi / ficcar lo viso per la luce etterna, / tanto che la veduta vi consunsi!"
("O abounding grace whereby I presumed to drive my gaze along the eternal
light, so far that my sight was there consumed!" [82–84]). The apostrophe
in turn jumps into an attempt to say what was seen within that light, and we
are thrust into the poem's ultimate metaphor of unity: within its depths he
saw "legato con amore in un volume, / ciò che per l'universo si squaderna: /
sustanze e accidenti e lor costume / quasi conflati insieme" ("bound with
love in one volume that which through the universe is unquired: substances,
accidents, and their relations, as though conflated together" [86–89]). This
ineffable perception of the "forma universal," felt rather than comprehended (his recollection is affective, not intellective; he believes he saw the
"forma universal" because he *feels* joy as he speaks of it, "dicendo questo, mi
sento ch'i' godo" [93]), this "punto solo" is the source for him of greater
wonder and oblivion than are for us the twenty-five centuries that have
passed since Neptune first viewed the Argo: "Un punto solo m'è maggior
letargo / che venticinque secoli a la 'mpresa / che fé Nettuno ammirar
l'ombra d'Argo" ("A single moment is to me greater oblivion than are
twenty-five centuries to the enterprise that made Neptune wonder at the
shadow of the Argo" [94–96]). We, in other words, who have been forgetting the object of Neptune's wonder, the sight of the Argo's shadow, for
twenty-five hundred years, have in all that time lost less of Neptune's vision
than Dante has already lost of his. The instability of the analogy is structural, since the "punto solo" is analogous both, as object of the vision, to the
Argo and, as duration of the vision, to the twenty-five centuries;[56] making
the tercet even more impossible to hold onto is the fact that its main action
is forgetting: active, continual, endlessly accreted forgetting. Infinitely fascinating and suggestive, infinitely impenetrable and dense, conceptually and
syntactically illogical, but somehow offering a glimpse into the dialectic between simultaneity and eternity, point and duration, conflation and extension, the Neptune analogy is a fitting emblem for the poetics of *Paradiso* 33,
its ability to conflate all time into "un punto solo" unmatched even by the
canto's final verses.

A tercet of plot in which the pilgrim continues to gaze on the divine light
("Così la mente mia, tutta sospesa, / mirava fissa, immobile e attenta, / e
sempre di mirar faceasi accesa" ["So my mind, all suspended, gazed fixed
immobile and intent, and was in gazing ever more enkindled" (97–99)]), is
followed by a passage that is essentially the poem's last contribution to
Dante's long meditation on conversion, desire, and the will: the effect of
gazing on that light is to make impossible any dis-conversion, any consent-
ing to turn from it toward another sight ("che volgersi da lei per altro aspetto / è impossibil che mai si consenta" [101–2]).[57] At this point begins the
last, and longest, of canto 33's three *circulate melodie*. The transitional ad-

verb "Omai" starts off the final movement by telling us that we are reaching finality; the poem cannot continue much longer, because the poet's speech is becoming ever more insufficient, as "short" with relation to his task as that of a suckling infant: "Omai sarà più corta mia favella, / pur a quel ch'io ricordo, che d'un fante / che bagni ancor la lingua a la mammella" ("Now will my speech be more short, even with respect to what I remember, than that of an infant who still bathes his tongue at the breast" [106–8]). With this recall of the previous two cantos of antinarrative "infantile" speechlessness, cantos 23 and 30, Dante jumps into plot, warding off—as he prepares to render figuratively the final mysteries and paradoxes of the trinity and the incarnation—the specter of difference. Thus, his posture is defensive: not because the light into which he gazed was changing—for it was one and only one, "simple" (109) rather than various, so untouched by time or difference as to be "always what it was before" ("è sempre qual s'era davante" [111])—but because of changes within himself, the light was transformed. Within the luminous substance there appeared three circles of three colors and one dimension, two reflecting each other like rainbows and the third mediating equally in between: "e l'un da l'altro come iri da iri / parea reflesso, e 'l terzo parea foco / che quinci e quindi igualmente si spiri" ("the one by the other as rainbow by rainbow seemed reflected, and the third seemed fire that from this side and from that equally is breathed" [118–20]). The language of difference that we remember from the heaven of the sun—"l'un da l'altro," "quinci e quindi"—is registered, only to be canceled by the language of *uguaglianza*, by "iri da iri," and by the "igualmente" that anticipates the end of the poem.[58] But the effort to sustain the narrative line is too great, and the poet breaks in, first to exclaim again about the "shortness" of his speech (121–23) and then to address the eternal light that alone knows itself, is known by itself, and, knowing, loves itself (124–26): the apostrophe's trinitarian language moves the poet back into plot, into confronting the ultimate mystery of the incarnation, of the second circle that is painted within itself, in its same color, with our human image, "nostra effige" (131). Like a geometer who concentrates all his energies on squaring the circle but cannot find the principle he needs (an intellective rather than affective simile, but devoted to the intellect's failure), such is the pilgrim before that final paradox, "that new vision": "quella vista nova" (136).

The "vista nova" of verse 136 marks the poem's last beginning of the end, its last *cosa nova*, its newest encounter with the new. The verse that contains it is the tenth from the end, a fact that is certainly not coincidental, as it is not coincidental that, upon removing canto 33's prelude of forty-five verses, there remain precisely one hundred lines of text. These one hundred lines, if renumbered with verse 46 as verse 1, confirm the three circular movements suggested above by giving them numerological significance: line 75, the end of the first movement, is now line 30; line 105 is now line 60; and—a happy ending for any *dantista*—the poem's last line is now, by virtue of divine renumbering in God's invisible ink, line 100.[59] Moreover, canto 33's final *circulata melodia* of forty verses can be further subdivided at the "vista nova" ten lines from the end, so that the *Commedia*'s final one hundred verses recapitulate the threes and ones of its basic structure in the scheme thirty plus thirty plus thirty plus ten. Thematically, too, this last new beginning is a recapitulation of so many others: as in canto 28 the pilgrim wished to understand "come l'essemplo / e l'essemplare non vanno d'un modo," now he wants to know "come si convenne / l'imago al cerchio e come vi s'indova" ("how the image conforms to the circle and how it inwheres itself" [137–38]), but there is no longer a Beatrice to answer these unanswerable questions. The sacred poem is forced to jump; and it does, sprung by disjunctive conjunctions that reverse the text's direction from verse to verse, managing both to communicate an "event" and to conflate all narrativity into a textual approximation of the *igualmente* to which we hasten: "*ma* non eran da ciò le proprie penne: / *se non che* la mia mente fu percossa / da un fulgore in che sua voglia venne" ("*but* my own wings were not for such, *if not that* my mind was struck by a flash in which its desire came" [139–41]). Another jump occurs as the poet speaks of his poetic failure one last time ("A l'alta fantasia qui mancò possa" ["Power here failed the high fantasy" (142)]), and still another as he records a final event with a final time-defying adversative ("*ma già* volgeva il mio disio e 'l *velle*" ["*but already* my desire and will were moved" (143)]), and then the *Commedia* finally ends, leaving us, "sì come rota ch'*igualmente* è mossa" ("like a wheel that *equally* is moved" [144]), alone with "l'amor che move il sole e l'altre stelle" ("the love that moves the sun and the other stars" [145]). For, it is at least possibile to experience the end of this poem as a being stranded in an eternal present, on a very high peak that was attained by dint of following behind the voice, the all-making voice, that suddenly is no more. The "I" that has led us for so long does not return; it leaves us there, in that vast emptiness, without it. And not all this canto's fearful symmetry can compensate for that loss, for the fact that this poem too must die.

## TRANSITION: HOW CANTOS BEGIN AND END

C ANTO BEGINNINGS are divided by Ettore Paratore into those where the connection to the preceding canto is firm ("inizi di salda connessione," of which he posits sixteen in the *Inferno*, ten in the *Purgatorio*, and eight in the *Paradiso*), and those where the connection is looser ("di connessione più lassa").[1] Concentrating on the *Inferno*, he subdivides beginnings that maintain a firm connection into two types: (1) those in which the beginning marks the addition of something new; (2) those in which the previous ending is completed or reiterated without the introduction of a new event. Although I did not model my analysis on Paratore's, having preferred to categorize canto endings rather than canto beginnings (closure seemed somewhat more palpable and quantifiable than incipience), his emphasis on the introduction of the new coincides with my approach, and his overall findings, with respect to the slackening of the *Commedia*'s transitions as the poem proceeds, are fully endorsed by my own.

The difference between canticles is highlighted by such an exercise. Once again, the *Inferno* is the "crowded" canticle, the one for which the basic division I apply to canto endings—between transition and lack of transition—is most useful but also most in need of complication and subdivision. With respect to the *Purgatorio* and *Paradiso*, my findings are offered more for the sake of comparison than because I find them entirely satisfactory. Here the distinction between transition and nontransition is less workable, since the transitions of these canticles are frequently so diffuse that it is difficult to pinpoint them with any precision; as a result, my decisions to classify an ending as transitional or not may seem increasingly subjective and arbitrary.

This inquiry ultimately serves to address the concept of the canto, which it probes by investigating the canto's boundaries. What is a canto? How does it function? Why does Dante choose to invent the division into cantos, rather than divide his poem into long books of the sort Vergil uses in the *Aeneid*? Conceptually, I believe that the choice of the canto is connected to Dante's obsession with the new; the division into cantos renders the spiraling rhythm of new dawns and new dusks, the incessant new beginnings and endings that punctuate the line of becoming. Formally, I believe that the roots of the canto are to be sought in Dante's vernacular apprenticeship. A long canzone is roughly the length of a canto (Dante's longest canzone is "Doglia mi reca," which at 158 lines is longer than most cantos).[2]

In the *Inferno* we note how frequently canto endings coincide with changes of locale, with literal forward movement, and we note that such correspondence occurs less frequently as the poem proceeds (which is one of the reasons that it becomes progressively more difficult to assess whether a canto ending is transitional or not). As the canto's boundaries coincide less and less with clear-cut fictive and/or geographical boundaries, the question of precisely what a canto serves to delimit becomes, if anything, more intriguing. Indeed, the lack of coincidence between literal transition and textual transition causes us to wonder about the nature of transition itself. What features must be present for a transition to occur? What principles are at work in the *Paradiso*, where canto endings never coincide with literal movement, and where canto beginnings are so spectacularly rhetorical?[3] I have not undertaken to answer such questions (to which I was alerted by the surprising complexities of this little undertaking) but merely to put in front of the reader some data that might provide a useful starting point for further investigation.

A canto ending may, moreover, mark the ending of a narrative segment without registering a sense of an ending; in other words, we may know with hindsight that a canto ending corresponds to the end of a geographical region, but not realize this as we read the canto ending itself. (Such unregistered transitions become frequent in the *Paradiso*, but there is a case in the *Inferno* as well.) In these instances I have classified the canto ending as nontransitional, since it is the explicit registering of transition in the closing verses, the active pressing into service of the formal delimiter, that I have taken as my guideline. Thus, as I indicate in the following tables, there are cantos that, according to Wilkins, "end with the ending of the account of a particular region,"[4] but whose endings I nonetheless consider nontransitional, because there is no way to tell as we read the canto ending that a transition is about to occur.

## Inferno Endings

### Transition

#### PURE FORWARD MOTION

*Inf.* 1. "Allor si mosse, e io li tenni dietro": the model of a pure forward motion ending.

*Inf.* 2. "intrai per lo cammino alto e silvestro": although "intrai" indicates entry into the new, this still seems categorizable as a "Pure Forward Motion" ending in that it does not really register the presence of the new.

*Inf.* 10. Transition begins in verse 133, "Appresso mosse a man sinistra il piede," concluding in the canto's final verse "che 'nfin là sù facea spiacer suo lezzo" (136); although, as Wilkins notes, the travelers do not leave the sixth circle, they certainly move forward.

*Inf.* 11. The transition is marked by Vergil (rather than by the narrator) in four verses, beginning "Ma seguimi oramai che 'l gir mi piace" (112) and concluding "e 'l balzo via là oltra si dismonta" (115).

*Inf.* 14. The transition is again marked by Vergil in four verses: "Omai è tempo da scostarsi / dal bosco; fa che di retro a me vegne: / li margini fan via, che non son arsi, / e sopra loro ogne vapor si spegne" (139-42).

*Inf.* 20. "Sì mi parlava, e andavamo introcque."

*Inf.* 21. Forward motion with the devils as escort, beginning "Per l'argine sinistro volta dienno" (136), and concluding "ed elli avea del cul fatto trombetta" (139).

*Inf.* 22. "E noi lasciammo lor così 'mpacciati."

*Inf.* 23. "ond'io da li 'ncarcati mi parti' / dietro a le poste de le care piante."

ENTRY INTO THE NEW/TRANSITION ACCOMPLISHED

*Inf.* 4. "E vegno in parte ove non è che luca": the model for this category.

*Inf.* 6. The quasi-formulaic nature of these endings is well demonstrated by canto 6's four-verse finale, which is echoed in canto 7: "Noi aggirammo a tondo quella strada, / parlando più assai ch'i' non ridico; / venimmo al punto dove si digrada: / quivi trovammo Pluto, il gran nemico."

*Inf.* 7. Compare this ending to that of canto 6: "Così giramm0 de la lorda pozza / grand'arco, tra la ripa secca e 'l mézzo, / con li occhi vòlti a chi del fango ingozza. / Venimmo al piè d'una torre al da sezzo."

*Inf.* 9. "passammo tra i martìri e li alti spaldi": the last verse (133) concretizes the transition registered earlier ("e noi movemmo i piedi inver' la terra" [104]).

[*Inf.* 17. Entry into the new is accomplished in verse 133, "così ne puose al fondo Gerïone," but transition is delayed by Geryon's departure; see listings under "Transition Initiated" below.]

*Inf.* 19. "Indi un altro vallon mi fu scoperto."

*Inf.* 27. Transition begins in verse 133, "Noi passamm' oltre," concluding "a quei che scommettendo acquistan carco" (136).

[*Inf.* 31. Like *Inf.* 17: Entry into the new is accomplished, "Ma lievemente al fondo che divora / Lucifero con Giuda, ci sposò" (142–43), but delayed by the giant's departure; see "Transition Initiated" below.]

*Inf.* 34. "E quindi uscimmo a riveder le stelle."

TRANSITION INITIATED BUT DELAYED

1. Closure is signified (twice by the pilgrim's fall), but transition is delayed until the next canto.

*Inf.* 3. "e caddi come l'uom cui sonno piglia."
*Inf.* 5. "E caddi come corpo morto cade."
*Inf.* 18. "E quinci sian le nostre viste sazie": Vergil's concluding emphasis on satiety suggests the transition to come.

2. Withdrawal of a companion; transition is postponed until after the departure.

*Inf.* 12. "Poi si rivolse e ripassossi 'l guazzo": Nesso's retreat.
*Inf.* 15. Brunetto's departure begins "Poi si rivolse" in verse 121 (like Nesso's at the end of canto 12), and concludes "e parve di costoro / quelli che vince, non colui che perde" (123–24).
*Inf.* 17. "si dileguò come da corda cocca": Geryon departs after depositing the travelers in the eighth circle.
*Inf.* 31. "e come albero in nave si levò": Antaeus's departure is evoked in a simile, as is Geryon's.

## No Transition

*Inf.* 8. "tal che per lui ne fia la terra aperta": the canto ends *in medias res*, with Vergil's words announcing the arrival of the *messo*, who does not appear until midway through canto 9.
*Inf.* 13. "Io fei gibetto a me de le mie case": the canto ends with the words of the Florentine suicide. Although transition occurs in the fourth verse of the next canto (same pattern as canto 6), there is no hint of it at the end of canto 13 (unless in a sense of closure conveyed by what is said; see canto 26 below).
*Inf.* 16. "che 'n sù si stende e da piè si rattrappa": the canto ends *in medias res*, with the arrival of Geryon, described in the following canto.
*Inf.* 24. "E detto l'ho perché doler ti debbia!": the canto ends with Vanni Fucci's prophecy; his story continues into the next canto.
*Inf.* 25. "l'altr'era quel che tu, Gaville, piagni": the canto ends with the narrator's identification of one of the thieves, without a clear transition.
*Inf.* 26. "infin che 'l mar fu sovra noi richiuso": the canto ends within Ulysses' narrative, without a clear transition, but with perhaps a sense of closure conveyed by the verse's content.
*Inf.* 28. "Così s'osserva in me lo contrapasso": the canto ends with the words of Bertran de Born.
*Inf.* 29. "com'io fui di natura buona scimia": the canto ends with the words of Capocchio.
*Inf.* 30. "ché voler ciò udire è bassa voglia": the canto ends with Vergil's rebuke.
*Inf.* 32. "se quella con ch'io parlo non si secca": the canto ends *in medias*

*res*, with the pilgrim's query to Ugolino, whose story resumes in the following canto.

*Inf.* 33. "e in corpo par vivo ancor di sopra": the canto ends with the narrator's comment on what he has seen. Although, as Wilkins notes, this is a canto whose ending coincides with the ending of a geographical region, Dante offers no narrative signpost to this effect, thus anticipating a procedure that he will frequently adopt in the *Paradiso*.

## In Sum

Twenty-three endings register transition of some kind or another; these transitions become more complex and less straightforward as the canticle progresses. Of the eleven canto endings that do not register clear transition, a concentration is found in the last third of the canticle.

The question of nontransitional endings would be further complicated if one were to take into account the sense conveyed by spoken discourse; thus, the final verse of canto 26, spoken by Ulysses, conveys a sense of closure that is, for instance, less palpable in the final verse of canto 29, spoken by Capocchio. The same could be observed, perhaps, of the final verses of cantos 24 and 28, spoken by Vanni Fucci and Bertran de Born respectively, as compared to the final verse of canto 32, spoken by the pilgrim and dedicated to bridging the gap between cantos 32 and 33. I raise this matter in order to alert the reader to my inconsistency; although I have essentially ignored such vague categories as a "sense of closure" for the *Inferno*, where clearer markers are in evidence, I have been less strict a constructionist for *Purgatorio* and *Paradiso* (see, for instance, my comments to *Purg.* 27). It should be kept in mind, therefore, that if one were to use as strict a guideline for the later canticles as for the first, there would be far fewer transitional endings in *Purgatorio* and *Paradiso* than is suggested by my findings below.

## PURGATORIO ENDINGS

### Transition

*Purg.* 2. "né la nostra partita fu men tosta": a rare purgatorial example of straightforward transition.

*Purg.* 4. Vergil's words mark transition, beginning "Vienne omai" (137) and concluding "cuopre la notte già col piè Morrocco" (139).

*Purg.* 8. "se corso di giudicio non s'arresta": Corrado's words begin with a dismissal ("Or va" [133]), giving a sense of closure and imminent transition to the canto's conclusion.

*Purg.* 9. "ch'or sì or no s'intendon le parole": the narrator's words conclude the extended description of the opening of purgatory's gate. Although in themselves they hardly seem transitional, the context signals transition, most insistently with the angel's "Intrate" (131).

*Purg.* 12. Transition is begun in verse 115 ("Già montavam su per li scaglion santi"), and unfolds, with typical purgatorial retardation, for twenty-one verses, through the pilgrim's discovery of the missing P from his forehead, to the explicit, "a che guardando, il mio duca sorrise" (136).

*Purg.* 14. Another delayed transition; Guido del Duca's dismissal in verse 124 ("Ma va via, Tosco, omai") is followed by the examples of envy and by Vergil's concluding commentary: "onde vi batte chi tutto discerne" (151).

*Purg.* 15. "Questo ne tolse li occhi e l'aere puro": *Inferno*-like entry into the new.

*Purg.* 16. "Così tornò, e più non volle udirmi": transition is marked by the departure of a companion, again like *Inferno*.

*Purg.* 18. "e 'l pensamento in sogno trasmutai": forward motion *Purgatorio*-style, where dreams coincide with transitions.

*Purg.* 19. Hadrian's dismissal ("Vattene omai") in verse 139; the canto ends with his reference to Alagia, in verse 145: "e questa sola di là m'è rimasa."

*Purg.* 20. Transition is initiated in verse 142, "Poi ripigliammo nostro cammin santo," and is maintained until the explicit: "così m'andava timido e pensoso" (151).

*Purg.* 24. The canto ends with the recitation of a beatitude, "esuriendo sempre quanto è giusto!," which (given the earlier "S'a voi piace / montare in sù" [139–40]) functions as a marker of transition.

*Purg.* 26. "Poi s'ascose nel foco che li affina": Arnaut withdraws.

*Purg.* 27. "per ch'io te sovra te corono e mitrio": Vergil's concluding discourse conveys a sense of an ending, even if we do not know that they are his last words.

*Purg.* 28. "poi a la bella donna torna' il viso": spiraling forward motion.

*Purg.* 33. "puro e disposto a salire a le stelle."

## No Transition

*Purg.* 1. "subitamente là onde l'avelse": the narrator comments on the renewed reed, without indicating a clear transition.

*Purg.* 3. "ché qui per quei di là molto s'avanza": Manfredi on prayer.

*Purg.* 5. "disposando m'avea con la sua gemma": Pia's words.

*Purg.* 6. "ma con dar volta suo dolore scherma": the narrator on Florence.

*Purg.* 7. "fa pianger Monferrato e Canavese": Sordello's words.

*Purg.* 10. "piangendo parea dicer: 'Più non posso'": the imagined words of a soul.

*Purg.* 11. "Quest'opera li tolse quei confini": Oderisi's words.

*Purg.* 13. "ma più vi perderanno li ammiragli": Sapìa's words.

*Purg.* 17. "tacciolo, acciò che tu per te ne cerchi": Vergil's words.

*Purg.* 21. "trattando l'ombre come cosa salda": Statius's words. Although this ending coincides with the end of a region, there is no narrative signpost to this effect.

*Purg.* 22. "quanto per lo Vangelio v'è aperto": the recitation of the examples of temperance initiates the terrace of gluttony; Dante offsets the static pattern of each terrace by placing a segment that marks the beginning of a terrace at the end of a canto (see canto 25).

*Purg.* 23. "lo vostro regno, che da sé lo sgombra": the pilgrim to Forese.

*Purg.* 25. "che la piaga da sezzo si ricuscia": the narrator's comment regards the just-recited examples of chastity; see canto 22.

*Purg.* 29. "fermandosi ivi con le prime insegne": the canto ends *in medias res*; stopping the procession suspends the drama, indicating something is about to happen.

*Purg.* 30. "di pentimento che lagrime spanda": the canto ends *in medias res*, with Beatrice's rebuke.

*Purg.* 31. "quando ne l'aere aperto ti solvesti?": the canto ends *in medias res*, with Beatrice's unveiling.

*Purg.* 32. "a la puttana e a la nova belva": the departure of the giant and the whore signals the end of the *tableaux vivants*; on the other hand, this transition seems overpowered by the overarching lack of transition created by the ongoing drama involving the pilgrim and Beatrice.

## In Sum

As compared to *Inferno*, where there are twenty-three transitional endings and eleven nontransitional endings, in *Purgatorio* the proportions are fairly equal; there are sixteen transitional endings and seventeen nontransitional endings. One could make a different case for some of these endings, however; see, for instance, my comments to canto 32.

## PARADISO ENDINGS

### Transition

*Par.* 1. "Quinci rivolse inver' lo cielo il viso": the model of a *Paradiso* "transitional" canto ending, even serving as a model for the first verses to indicate literal movement ("Beatrice in suso, e io in lei guardava . . . giunto mi vidi ove mirabil cosa / mi torse il viso a sé" [2.22, 25–26]).

*Par.* 3. A typically "loose" but still present transition, signaled by the registration of a new doubt: Piccarda disappears, the pilgrim reconverts his gaze to Beatrice ("e a Beatrice tutta si converse" [127]), whose brilliance makes him slower in his questioning, as declared in the explicit, "e ciò mi fece a dimandar più tardo" (130).

*Par.* 4. "e quasi mi perdei con li occhi chini": the pilgrim's response to Beatrice's renewed brilliance before responding to his latest *dubbio*.

*Par.* 5. "nel modo che 'l seguente canto canta": the postponement of Justinian's discourse to the "seguente canto" creates a wholly artificial, metapoetically imposed transition.

*Par.* 14. "perché si fa, montando, più sincero": the narrator's reference to Beatrice's growing beauty gives a hint of transition in the idea of "montare."

*Par.* 21. "né io lo 'ntesi, sì mi vinse il tuono": the thunder confers a heightened sense of closure; it should be noted, however, that (in a typical *Paradiso* nontransitional transition) no change of venue is forthcoming.

*Par.* 22. "poscia rivolsi li occhi a li occhi belli": a variant of *Par.* 1.

*Par.* 23. "colui che tien le chiavi di tal gloria": the introduction of St. Peter indicates a change of narrative direction.

*Par.* 24. "sì nel dir li piacqui!": transition is implied by the pilgrim's successful completion of his exam.

*Par.* 25. "per non poter veder, benché io fossi / presso di lei, e nel mondo felice!": the pilgrim is deprived of the sight of Beatrice, a change in his condition that signals a change in narrative direction as well.

*Par.* 31. "li suoi con tanto affetto volse a lei, / che ' miei di rimirar fé più ardenti": the culmination of Bernard's command that the pilgrim gaze upon the Virgin.

## No Transition

*Par.* 2. "conforme a sua bontà, lo turbo e 'l chiaro": Beatrice's words.

*Par.* 6. "assai lo loda, e più lo loderebbe": Justinian's words.

*Par.* 7. "che li primi parenti intrambo fensi": Beatrice's words; despite marking the end of a region, there is no narrative signpost to this effect.

*Par.* 8. "onde la traccia vostra è fuor di strada": Charles Martel's words.

*Par.* 9. "tosto libere fien de l'avoltero": Folquet's words; see canto 7.

*Par.* 10. "se non colà dove gioir s'insempra": the narrator.

*Par.* 11. "'U' ben s'impingua, se non si vaneggia'": Thomas's words.

*Par.* 12. "e mosse meco questa compagnia": Bonaventure's words.

*Par.* 13. "ché quel può surgere, e quel può cadere": Thomas's words.

*Par.* 15. "e venni dal martiro a questa pace": Cacciaguida's words.

*Par.* 16. "né per divisïon fatto vermiglio": Cacciaguida's words.

*Par.* 17. "né per altro argomento che non paia": Cacciaguida's words.

*Par.* 18. "ch'io non conosco il pescator né Polo": the narrator's invective.

*Par.* 19. "che dal fianco de l'altre non si scosta": the eagle's invective.

*Par.* 20. "con le parole mover le fiammette": the narrator; see canto 7.

*Par.* 26. "come 'l sol muta quadra, l'ora sesta": Adam's words.

*Par.* 27. "e vero frutto verrà dopo 'l fiore": Beatrice's prophecy.
*Par.* 28. "con altro assai del ver di questi giri": Beatrice's words.
*Par.* 29. "uno manendo in sé come davanti": Beatrice's words; see canto 7.
*Par.* 30. "e farà quel d'Alagna intrar più giuso": Beatrice's words.
*Par.* 32. "E cominciò questa santa orazione": the narrator.
*Par.* 33. "l'amor che move il sole e l'altre stelle": the narrator.

## In Sum

The *Paradiso*'s canto endings are substantially "looser" than the *Purgatorio*'s; eleven are transitional (some more convincing than others), leaving twenty-two nontransitional endings. The proportions are thus the inverse of the *Inferno*'s, where twenty-three canto endings are transitional, and eleven are nontransitional.

# NOTES

1. "Dante profeta," in *Dante e la cultura medievale*, 2d ed. rev. (1941; rpt., Bari: Laterza, 1949), 336–416.

2. "Non artificio letterario, ma vera visione profetica ritenne Dante quella concessa a lui da Dio" (376).

3. Benedetto Croce, *La poesia di Dante*, 2d ed. rev. (Bari: Laterza, 1921): "con tale ipotesi s'introdurrebbe nel genio di Dante una troppo grande mistura di demenza" (61).

4. "Dante fu vero profeta, non perchè i suoi disegni di riforma politica ed ecclesiastica si siano attuati (riconosciamo, anzi, che, dato il corso naturale degli avvenimenti, erano inattuabili, quali si sono rivelati), ma perchè, come tutti i grandi profeti, seppe levare lo sguardo oltre gli avvenimenti che si svolgevano sotto i suoi occhi, e additare un ideale eterno di giustizia" (415). Before reaching this concluding generality, Nardi takes Dante's pretensions even more seriously, rebutting the charge that the Florentine's prophecies were unverified by history by pointing out that the same can be said of Old Testatment prophecies: "Si può rispondere che altrettanto accadde per la restaurazione del trono di David, annunziata come imminente dagli antichi profeti" (409).

5. To study Dante's handling of his precursors is necessarily to study his truth claims, since he consistently formulates the difference between his poetry and that of his predecessors in terms of truth versus falsehood: he secures the credibility of his text by constructing situations designed to reveal the incredibility of his precursors' texts. My own interest in the relation between the *Commedia*'s intertextuality and its truth claims, as framed in *Dante's Poets: Textuality and Truth in the "Comedy"* (Princeton, N.J.: Princeton University Press, 1984), led me to this study of what could be termed the relation between the *Commedia*'s metatextuality and its truth claims. Because, in fact, this is a sequel of sorts, the reader will encounter frequent references to *Dante's Poets* in the following pages, for which I beg indulgence; when building upon previous arguments, it seemed more opportune to refer than to repeat.

6. Nardi's emphasis on prophecy can also be seen to have roots in figural exegesis, which is, after all, a form of retroactive prophecy. See Erich Auerbach, "Figura," 1944, rpt. in *Scenes from the Drama of European Literature* (Gloucester, Mass.: Peter Smith, 1973), especially section 2, "*Figura* in the Phenomenal Prophecy of the Church Fathers."

7. "Dante *Theologus-Poeta*," 1976; rpt. in *Studies in Dante* (Ravenna: Longo, 1980), 39–89; quotation, 64–65.

8. "Il punto sull'Epistola a Cangrande," in *Lectura Dantis Scaligera* (Florence: Le Monnier, 1960).

9. In the opening paragraph of his *De reprobatione monarchiae*, Vernani speaks of vessels used by the devil, "mendax et perniciosi pater mendacii," that tempt with a

beautiful exterior while containing poison within. Among such vessels is the author of the *Commedia*: "Inter alia vero talia sua vasa quidam fuit multa fantastice poetizans et sophista verbosus, verbis exterioribus in eloquentia multis gratus, qui suis poetici fantasmatibus et figmentis, iuxta verbum philosophie Boetium consolantis, scenicas meretriculas adducendo, non solum egros animos, sed etiam studiosos dulcibus sirenarum cantibus conducit fraudulenter ad interitum salutifere veritatis" (*Il più antico oppositore politico di Dante: Guido Vernani da Rimini. Testo critico del "De reprobatione monarchiae,"* ed. Nevio Matteini [Padova: CEDAM, 1958], 93). Adopting to his own ends the inside/outside model used by Dante's commentators to point to the allegorical truth beneath poetry's fictitious veil, Vernani likens the poetry of the *Commedia* to the Boethian sirens who lead away from truth with their "dulcibus cantibus."

10. Charles S. Singleton, *"Commedia": Elements of Stucture* (Cambridge: Harvard University Press, 1954), 90.

11. "Indeed, with some Dante scholars, so strong has the persuasion been that such a view of the allegory of the *Divine Comedy* is the correct one [i.e., that the allegory of poets is the correct one] that it has brought them to question the authorship of the famous letter to Can Grande. This, in all consistency, was bound to occur" (86). See, for instance, Hollander's rebuttal of John Scott on this issue, "Dante *Theologus-Poeta*," 55, n. 36.

12. Neither scholar seems aware of the other; Singleton's 1954 monograph contains no reference to Nardi, and Nardi's 1960 essay makes no mention of Singleton.

13. Regarding the response to "Dante profeta," Giorgio Padoan sustains that "si deve pur ammettere che la 'communis opinio' ha finito col lasciare piuttosto in ombra quest'aspetto del poema, limitandosi, semmai, a ripetere formule generali e generiche in cui si riconosce una qual certa affinità tra la *Comedìa* e la letteratura di 'visioni,' senza peraltro affrontare, con la chiarezza e la risolutezza necessaria, le delicate implicanze che ne risultano" (31). This concern was voiced in 1965, in "La 'mirabile visione' di Dante e l'Epistola a Cangrande," rpt. in *Il pio Enea, l'empio Ulisse* (Ravenna: Longo, 1977), 30–63.

14. An example of the former tendency is Anthony K. Cassell, whose *Dante's Fearful Art of Justice* (Toronto: University of Toronto Press, 1984), and *"Inferno" I*, Lectura Dantis Americana (Philadelphia: University of Pennsylvania Press, 1989), show little appreciation for the ways in which poetry can undermine theological certitude. Most remarkable is Cassell's claim that the pilgrim's tribute to Vergil in the poem's first canto "rings hollow and even self-serving" (*"Inferno" I*, 89); such comments take the Robertsonian principle that a theological perspective may reveal an embedded irony within the text to such an extreme that they begin to sound like a parody of their own method. On the other side, see Aldo Scaglione's rebuttal of Cassell's reading of Pier della Vigna, "Dante's Poetic Orthodoxy: The Case of Pier della Vigna," *Lectura Dantis: A Forum for Dante Research and Interpretation* 1 (1987): 49–59, where a stylistic approach is excessively divorced from Dante's ideology.

15. Nicolò Mineo asserts the centrality of such concerns in *Profetismo e apocalittica in Dante* (Catania: Università di Catania, 1968), as does Gian Roberto Sarolli in *Prolegomena alla "Divina Commedia"* (Florence: Olschki, 1971).

16. For Padoan's description of the debate between Mazzoni and Nardi, with full bibliography, see "La 'mirabile visione,'" 40–41.

17. Padoan cites Francesco da Buti: "'fu' io': cioè fu' io Dante, e questo si de' intendere ch'elli ci fu *intellettualmente*, ma *non corporalmente*, ma *finge* secondo la lettera ch'elli vi fusse corporalmente" ("La 'mirabile visione,'" 42).

18. *Dante and Medieval Latin Traditions* (Cambridge: Cambridge University Press, 1986).

19. While Padoan justifies the Epistle's inclusion of "fictivus" as a "modus tractandi" of the *Commedia* ("La 'mirabile visione,'" 51), Dronke takes it as indicating that the composer of the Epistle believes the poem to be a fiction, and thus as a sign that the Epistle is not Dante's (*Dante and Medieval Latin Traditions*, 127). More frequently, the presence of "fictivus" has been used to bolster the anti-Singletonians (cf. Hollander, "Dante *Theologus-Poeta*," 64 n. 53).

20. "*Comedìa*: Notes on Dante, the Epistle to Cangrande, and Medieval Comedy," *Lectura Dantis: A Forum for Dante Research and Interpretation* 8 (1991): 26–55; quotation, 42. Other attempts to disprove Dante's paternity focus on the *cursus*; see Dronke, Excursus I, "The *Epistle* to Cangrande and Latin Prose Rhythm," in *Dante and Medieval Latin Traditions*, and Henry Ansgar Kelly, *Tragedy and Comedy from Dante to Pseudo-Dante* (Berkeley: University of California Press, 1989), appendix 2, "The Analysis of Prose Cadences," and appendix 3, "Cadence Analysis of the *Epistle to Cangrande*." With respect to the "politics" surrounding the Epistle's authenticity, see my "For the Record: The Epistle to Cangrande and Various 'American Dantisti,'" *Lectura Dantis: A Forum for Dante Research and Interpretation* 6 (1990): 140–43.

21. What Singleton left veiled is elaborated by Hollander, who grafts onto Singleton's perhaps deliberate reticence an ironic poet who "creates a fiction which he pretends to consider not to be literally fictitious, while at the same time contriving to share the knowledge with us that it is precisely fictional" ("Dante *Theologus-Poeta*," 86). Hollander's incongruous sense of Dante as ironic, parodic, and humorous in these matters is the logical consequence of his refusal to believe that Dante believes; thus, with respect to the Geryon episode's insistence on veracity, he comments: "One senses behind Dante's passage an authorial wink, lest we take it for a nod: 'I know you won't believe this (why should you?—I don't either), but the convention of my poem compels me to claim historicity even for such as Geryon'" (76).

22. *On Christian Doctrine*, trans. D. W. Robertson, Jr. (Indianapolis: Bobbs-Merrill, 1958), 142.

23. "Scripts for the Pageant: Dante and the Bible," *Stanford Literature Review* 5 (1988): 75–92; quotation, 85.

24. The citations from *Tundale's Vision*, written in 1149, are from *Visions of Heaven and Hell before Dante*, ed. and trans. Eileen Gardiner (New York: Italica Press, 1989), 160, 171, 175, 177, 195. In *Otherworld Journeys: Accounts of Near-Death Experiences in Medieval and Modern Times* (New York: Oxford University Press, 1987), Carol Zaleski remarks that "a close look at the narrators' remarks in the longer vision stories reveals an intricate set of literary conventions, woven together to form a defense of both the style and the content of the narrative" (81).

25. The dangers of metaphoric language are, in my opinion, overstated by Giu-

seppe Mazzotta, who claims that the *Commedia* "also tells the story of the persistent ambiguity of metaphoric language in which everything is perpetually fragmented and irreducible to any unification" (*Dante, Poet of the Desert* [Princeton, N.J.: Princeton University Press, 1979], 269). The denial of all significance is as reductive in its way as the undiluted confidence in significance that it counters; neither position does justice to the complexity of Dante's achievement.

26. *Confessions*, trans. R. S. Pine-Coffin (London: Penguin, 1961). The Latin text is from the Loeb edition, 2 vols. (Cambridge: Harvard University Press; London: Heinemann, 1976). It is worth noting that Augustine stops himself after "if I had been Moses" to insert the parenthetical "for we are all of the same clay and man is nothing unless you remember him" (the insert is repositioned in the above translation but may be seen in its correct position in the Latin epigraph at the beginning of this chapter). I draw attention to this defensive move on Augustine's part, intended to defuse the possible hubris of his self-association with Moses, because it is a feature of "true rhetoric" that will figure prominently in the *Commedia*.

27. *Dante and Difference: Writing in the "Commedia"* (Cambridge: Cambridge University Press, 1988), 100.

28. "Authenticating Realism and the Realism of Chaucer," *Thought* 39 (1964): 335–58; quotation, 343.

29. "Dante's Addresses to the Reader," *Romance Philology* 7 (1954): 268–78.

30. "It would seem strange to me that Professor Auerbach, the author of such excellent works as "Dante the Poet of This World" and "Mimesis" did not think (or not primarily think) of the possibility that Dante's addresses are meant to be in the service of—precisely!—*Mimesis*, of the description of the other world carried out with the vividness, or realism, with which things of this world may be described, and I can attribute Auerbach's failure to draw the consequences of Mimesis for our particular problem only to that understandable tendency of the scholar to tire of those very categories he has most superbly developed in other works of his. 'The authority and the urgency of a prophet'—this interpretation smacks more of the arrogantly hieratic solemnity of Stefan George or of certain would-be religious poses applied to Dante by certain American critics than of the urbane thisworldliness and the subtle flair for artistry and its techniques that have ever characterized Erich Auerbach's writings" ("The Addresses to the Reader in the *Commedia*," *Italica* 32 [1955]: 143–65; quotation, 158).

31. *The Idea of the Book in the Middle Ages* (Ithaca, N.Y.: Cornell University Press, 1985), 143. A similar view is put forward by Giuliana Carugati, who sees the addresses to the reader as deliberate unmaskings of the poem's realism, indictments of the *menzogna* through which the poet must pass on his way to redemptive silence; see *Dalla menzogna al silenzio: La scrittura mistica della "Commedia" di Dante* (Bologna: Il Mulino, 1991), chapter 3.

32. For instance, the self-consciousness of *Inf.* 13, in which Dante secures the credibility of his own text by insisting on the incredibility of Vergil's text (see *Dante's Poets*, 212), is read by Gellrich as an instance of hermeneutic failure on the part of the pilgrim (*The Idea of the Book*, 148). His reading demonstrates the effectiveness of the very self-protecting authorial strategies whose presence in the *Commedia* he denies, strategies that encourage us to develop perspective on the pilgrim rather than on the poet.

33. In a comment that anticipates a good deal of Gellrich's book, Bloomfield writes that "all authenticating devices not only authenticate but also call attention to the need for authentication and hence to the inauthenticity of the work of art" ("Authenticating Realism," 340). As for Dante's application of what I shall call the Geryon principle, treated in chapter 3, its psychology is well understood by Spitzer ("To give the reader 'something to do' about a matter difficult to imagine is a psychological inducement to make him accept this subject matter" ["The Addresses to the Reader," 152]), and its rhetoric by Michael Riffaterre: "narrative verisimilitude tends to flaunt rather than mask its fictitious nature" (*Fictional Truth* [Baltimore: Johns Hopkins University Press, 1990], 21).

34. Unfortunately, it is also difficult to persuade one's colleagues otherwise; in my own case, I would disagree with John G. Demaray's assessment of me as one who takes a "modern idealist posture that the 'only external referent' upon which Dante based the truth of the *Commedia* is a transcendent God" (*Dante and the Book of the Cosmos* [Philadelphia: The American Philosophical Society, 1987], 42n). That is what Dante tells us, not what I believe.

35. See chapter 3, note 4 for the reference.

36. See Mowbray Allan, "Does Dante Hope for Virgil's Salvation?," *MLN* 104 (1989): 193–205; and, for a more detailed discussion of the narrative choices that determine Dante's handling of Vergil, see my response, "Q: Does Dante Hope for Vergil's Salvation? A: Why Do We Care? For the Very Reason We Should Not Ask the Question," *MLN* 105 (1990): 138–44, 147–49.

37. Henry Louis Gates, Jr., Introduction to *PMLA* 105 (1990): 11–22; quotation, 15.

38. See *Il genere e i suoi confini* (Turin: Stampatori, 1980), where Conte refers to "la filologia della struttura narrativa" (112). The fact that Conte is writing of the *Aeneid*, a text that has always been subject to literary analysis, should make it clear that I am not suggesting that the *Commedia* has been deprived in this regard or that its reception has been strictly analogous to that of the Bible (for which see Robert Alter, *The Art of Biblical Narrative* [New York: Basic Books, 1981]).

39. While Harold Bloom deplores those readers who "have learned to read Dante precisely as they would read theology," he does not seem to understand to what extent Dante himself is responsible for this state of affairs; see *Ruin the Sacred Truths: Poetry and Belief from the Bible to the Present* (Cambridge: Harvard University Press, 1989), 46.

40. See Robert Durling's comment on the word "forma" in Dante's poem "Amor, tu vedi ben che questa donna": "The term *forma* used of the poem in the *commiato*, then, does not refer to the stanza form as something *external* to the deeper meanings of the poem. . . . For Dante, the term *forma* carries its full metaphysical valency" (Robert M. Durling and Ronald L. Martinez, *Time and the Crystal: Studies in Dante's Rime Petrose* [Berkeley: University of California Press, 1990], 396).

41. Earlier treatments of the narrative dimension of the *Commedia* are more engaged in stylistic analysis than in the ideological implications of large-scale narrative strategies. See, for instance, Edoardo Sanguineti, *Interpretazione di Malebolge* (Florence: Olschki, 1961), and Tibor Wlassics, *Dante narratore: Saggi sullo stile della "Commedia"* (Florence: Olschki, 1975). Also interesting are Philippe Sollers, "Dante et la traversée de l'écriture," in *L'écriture et l'expérience des limites* (Paris: Seuil,

1968), 14–47, and Jacqueline Risset, *Dante scrittore* (1982; trans. Milan: Mondadori, 1984).

42. *Dante's "Inferno": Difficulty and Dead Poetry* (Cambridge: Cambridge University Press, 1987), 435.

43. *Dante's "Paradiso" and the Limitations of Modern Criticism: A Study of Style and Poetic Theory* (Cambridge: Cambridge University Press, 1978), 36, 162.

44. See his critique of Eliot and others who show a "thorough mistrust of any element that might purely be ornamental" (*Dante's "Paradiso"*, 173).

45. Erich Auerbach, *Mimesis* (1946; rpt., Princeton, N.J.: Princeton University Press, 1974), 184: "Of the characters which appear in it, some belong to the recent past or even to the contemporary present and (despite *Par.* 17.136–38), not all of them are famous or carefully chosen."

46. *Dante's Poets*, 282.

47. "Infernal Irony: The Gates of Hell," 1984, rpt. in *Dante: The Poetics of Conversion*, ed. Rachel Jacoff (Cambridge: Harvard University Press, 1986), 98.

48. The analogy between the *De genesi ad litteram*'s three types of vision and the *Commedia*'s three canticles will be further discussed in chapter 7.

49. Kirkpatrick's book on the *Inferno* is a prime example of this fallacy at work, as is Tambling's discussion of the "Ugolino impasse," discussed below in chapter 4, note 49.

50. The work on narrative of such as Hayden White (see, for instance, *The Content of the Form: Narrative Discourse and Historical Representation* [Baltimore: Johns Hopkins University Press, 1987]) has not made inroads among *dantisti* of either a traditionalist or deconstructionist bent. For the former, see Steven Botterill, who follows Freccero's mistaken assumptions: "Narrative requires representation—of characters, places, events, encounters—and to some extent it requires drama, or at least the sense of things happening. This sense is strongest by far in *Inferno*, just as Dante's representational anxieties are most acute there, so that the progress of the poem as a whole is what Freccero calls 'a gradual attenuation of the bond between poetry and representation'" ("*Dante Studies* and the Study of Dante," *Annali d'italianistica*, 8 (1990): 88–102; quotation, 98). For the latter, see Carugati, who creates a false distinction when she writes that "la terza cantica è segnata dalla prevalenza del discorso filosofico-teologico sulla narratività pura" (*Dalla menzogna al silenzio*, 85).

51. "The Irreducible Dove," *Comparative Literature* 9 (1957): 129–35; quotation, 129.

## CHAPTER 2
### INFERNAL INCIPITS

1. The idea of a narrative journey is profoundly Dantesque. The metaphor narrative = path informs Dante's oeuvre, manifesting itself in the *Vita Nuova*'s use of such expressions as "E uscendo alquanto del proposito presente" (10.3) and "Ora, tornando al proposito" (12.1). Similar expressions emphasizing the literal meaning of "digression" may be found throughout the *Convivio*, where textual detours are followed by textual returns that are frequently highlighted by serving as chapter openings: "e qui lasciando, torno al proposito" (1.12.12); "Tornando al proposito"

(2.9.1); "Partendomi da questa disgressione . . . ritorno al proposito" (3.10.1); "è da ritornare al diritto calle" (4.7.1); "Ritornando al proposito" (4.24.1). All these uses of *tornare* are preceded by a use of *digressione*. More overt exploitation of the metaphor includes narrative voyaging both by land and by sea. The *Convivio*'s author must navigate "lo pelago del loro [the canzoni's] trattato" (1.9.7): "lo tempo chiama e domanda la mia nave uscir di porto; per che, dirizzato l'artimone de la ragione a l'òra del mio desiderio, entro in pelago con isperanza di dolce cammino e di salutevole porto" (2.1.1). His narrative quest at times involves *camminare*: "per che via sia da camminare a cercare la prenominata diffinizione" (4.16.4); "è da vedere come da camminare è a trovare la diffinizione de l'umana nobilitade" (4.16.9); "E per lo cammino diritto è da vedere, questa diffinizione che cercando si vae" (4.16.10).

2. *The Sense of an Ending* (1966; rpt., London: Oxford University Press, 1968), 7. The classical injunction invoked by Kermode is Horatian (*Ars poetica* 148), while, as biblical precedent for the *Commedia*'s beginning, commentators cite Isaiah: "In dimidio dierum meorum vadam ad portas inferi" (38:10). Noting that "mi ha sempre colpito il fatto che l'esordio della *Commedia* invece di dire *In principio*, come sarebbe lecito aspettarsi, dica *Nel mezzo*," Guglielmo Gorni suggests that the *Commedia* begins in the middle out of deference to the "grandi testi ispirati" that begin at the beginning: Genesis ("In principio creavit Deus coelum et terram"), the Gospel of John ("In principio erat Verbum"), and the *Vita Nuova*, which begins "Incipit vita nova"; see "La teoria del 'cominciamento,'" in *Il nodo della lingua e il verbo d'amore* (Florence: Olschki, 1981), 175–76.

3. Aristotle is actually referring to the moment, which he considers indistinguishable from time: "Now since time cannot exist and is unthinkable apart from the moment, and the moment is a kind of middle-point, uniting as it does in itself both a beginning and an end, a beginning of future time and an end of past time, it follows that there must always be time: for the extremity of the last period of time that we take must be found in some moment, since time contains no point of contact for us except in the moment. Therefore, since the moment is both a beginning and an end, there must always be time on both sides of it" (*Physics* 8.1.251b18–26; in the translation of R. P. Hardie and R. K. Gaye, in *The Basic Works of Aristotle*, ed. Richard McKeon [New York: Random House, 1941]).

4. Dante's concept of the new brings to mind the linguistic formulation that structures all discourse into binaries variously called given/new, old/new, known/new; see Ellen F. Prince, "On the Given/New Distinction," *Proceedings of the Chicago Linguistic Society* 15 (1979): 267–78.

5. The equivalence *vita = cammino*, whose primitive origins are discussed by G. B. Bronzini ("'Nel mezzo del cammin . . .'", *Giornale storico della letteratura italiana* 155 [1978]: 161–77), permeates Dante's work, from the *Vita Nuova*'s "via d'Amor" and "cammino de li sospiri" to the *Monarchia*'s longed-for port ("Et cum ad hunc portum vel nulli vel pauci, et hii cum difficultate nimia, pervenire possint, nisi sedatis fluctibus blande cupiditatis genus humanum liberum in pacis tranquillitate quiescat" [3.15.11]); again, the voyage of life may be by land or by sea. The *Convivio* contains a number of full-fledged parables based on the metaphor of life as a path; besides the lengthy pilgrim passage (4.12.15–19) from which I cite above, there is the "essemplo del cammino mostrato" (4.7.5–7) and the extended comparison of death to journey's end (4.28.2–8). Shorter examples from the *Convivio* include: "l'uomo

che . . . disviato si rinvia" (3.8.19); "cammino di questa brevissima vita" (3.15.18);
"proposi di gridare a la gente che per mal cammino andavano, acciò che per diritto
calle si dirizzassero . . . io intendo riducer la gente in diritta via" (4.1.9); "la nave de
l'umana compagnia dirittamente per dolce cammino a debito porto correa" (4.5.8);
"pochi per male camminare compiano la giornata" (4.13.7); "noi potemo avere in
questa vita due felicitadi, secondo due diversi cammini, buono e ottimo, che a ciò ne
menano" (4.17.9); "così questi umani appetiti per diversi calli dal principio se ne
vanno, e uno solo calle è quello che noi mena a la nostra pace" (4.22.6); "dico che
questa prima etade è porta e via per la quale s'entra ne la nostra buona vita" (4.24.9);
"così l'adolescente, che entra ne la selva erronea di questa vita, non saprebbe tenere
lo buono cammino, se da li suoi maggiori non li fosse mostrato" (4.24.12).

6. Augustine describes memory as a great storehouse in *Confessions* 10.8, noting
in 10.11 that memories that have been stored too long have to be thought out again
as though they were new, "nova."

7. A passage from the *Convivio*, in which the "continuo sguardare" of the angelic
intelligences is compared to the "riguardare discontinuato" of man, provides an opportune gloss: Philosophy "è donna primamente di Dio e secondariamente de l'altre
intelligenze separate, per continuo sguardare; e appresso de l'umana intelligenza per
riguardare discontinuato" (3.13.7).

8. The editor and translator is Kenelm Foster, Blackfriars 1968, 9:150–57.

9. I use "difference" as Dante uses it ("In astratto significa il 'differire' tra due o
più elementi" [Fernando Salsano, *ED*, s.v. "differenza"]), and much as St. Thomas
uses *distinctio*: "any type of non-identity between objects and things. Often called
diversity or difference" (T. Gilby, Glossary, Blackfriars 1967, 8:164). In other words,
as will be apparent from the discussion of time and difference in chapter 8, my usage
is essentially Aristotelian.

10. Lucia Battaglia Ricci writes of "il momento in cui l'*iter* fisico e cognitivo del
poeta è spezzato più o meno violentemente dall'insorgere di un 'altro'" (*Dante e la
tradizione letteraria medievale* [Pisa: Giardini, 1983], 122). Marino Barchiesi's reading of *Inf.* 20 contains three pages entitled "La poetica della 'novitate'" where, in an
effort to contextualize the canto's incipit ("Di nova pena mi conven far versi"), he
catalogues the same verses noted here and cites *Convivio* 2.6.6: "potentissima persuasione [è], a rendere l'uditore attento, promettere di dire nuove e grandissime
cose" ("Catarsi classica e 'medicina' dantesca," *Letture classensi* 4 [1973]: 11–124,
esp. 16–18). More telling is another *Convivio* passage that establishes the connection
between the new and the path of life: "de le nuove cose lo fine non è certo; acciò che
la esperienza non è mai avuta onde le cose usate e servate sono e nel processo e nel
fine commisurate. Però si mosse la Ragione a comandare che l'uomo avesse diligente
riguardo ad entrare nel nuovo cammino" (1.10.2–3).

11. The verse cited above marks the end of the encounter with Guido da Montefeltro. Other examples are "E poi ch'a riguardar oltre mi diedi" (*Inf.* 3.70), which
signals the pilgrim's abrupt departure from the souls in hell's vestibule, who are still
being described in the preceding verse, and "Noi passammo oltre" (*Inf.* 33.91), which
marks the end of the Ugolino episode.

12. For other relevant citations, see Vincenzo Mengaldo, ed., *De vulgari eloquentia*, 33; he is glossing the passage at the end of the treatise's first chapter in which
Dante affirms the superiority of the natural to the artificial (and hence of the vernac-

ular to Latin). The first and third of the three reasons given for the vernacular's superiority (the human race used it first, the whole world uses it, it is natural) are in fact related, since both are connected to its priority. The hierarchy that informs the treatise—first God, then nature, then art—is articulated in *Inf.* 11.99–105.

13. Gianfranco Contini traces Dante's "ricorrente topos del nuovo": "il proponimento 'di dicer di lei quello che mai non fue detto d'alcuna,' alla fine della *Vita Nuova*; 'la novità che per tua forma luce, / che non fu mai pensata in alcun tempo,' nella sestina doppia; 'novum aliquid atque intentatum artis,' di essa appunto nel *De Vulgari*, che a sua volta si apre vantando il proprio inedito contenuto ('Cum neminem ante nos de vulgaris eloquentiae doctrina quicquam inveniamus tractasse'); 'maxime latens' e 'ab omnibus intentata' la materia della *Monarchia*" ("Un'interpretazione di Dante," 1965, rpt. in *Un'idea di Dante* [Turin: Einaudi, 1976], 103–4).

14. This is the case, for instance, with respect to *Inf.* 7's "nove travaglie e pene," which Natalino Sapegno glosses as "impensabili, inaudite" (*La Divina Commedia*, 3 vols. [Florence: La Nuova Italia, 1968], 1:79). Domenico De Robertis's gloss of "cosa nova" in "Donne ch'avete" is better: "mai vista, straordinaria" (125). The adjective's temporal resonance is never more present than in Dante's single use of the superlative: following Latin usage, the "novissimo bando" (*Purg.* 30.13) is the Last Judgment. For biblical, patristic, and Provençal uses of *nuovo*, see Alberto Del Monte, "'Dolce stil novo,'" *Filologia romanza* 3 (1956): 254–64.

15. On the "dyadic beginning and ending" of Dante's cantos, see John Freccero, "The Significance of *Terza Rima*," 1983, rpt. in *Dante: The Poetics of Conversion*, ed. Rachel Jacoff (Cambridge: Harvard University Press, 1986), 261. Still useful is J. S. P. Tatlock, "Dante's *Terza Rima*," *PMLA* 51 (1936): 895–903.

16. The analogy between terza rima and the spiral is noted by Freccero, who defines the spiral as the "geometric representation of forward motion which is at the same time recapitulatory" ("The Significance of *Terza Rima*," 263; see also "Dante's Pilgrim in a Gyre," 1961, and "Infernal Inversion and Christian Conversion: *Inferno* XXXIV," 1965, rpt. in *Dante: The Poetics of Conversion*). Planetary motion is spiral motion for Dante by virtue of the epicycle, which is essentially a regression that then resumes its forward path; the wedding of cosmic spirals with poetic spirals in the poem "Al poco giorno" is underscored by Robert M. Durling and Ronald L. Martinez, *Time and the Crystal: Studies in Dante's Rime Petrose* (Berkeley: University of California Press, 1990), 122–23. On spirals in general, see Pierre Gallais, who writes exuberantly that "the spiral is the fundamental characteristic—on our planet—of the Living" ("Hexagonal and Spiral Structure in Medieval Narrative," *Yale French Studies* 51 [1974]: 116).

17. Benvenuto glosses the encounter with Statius: "'Noi,' ambo, 'ci volgemmo subito,' ad rem novam, quia nondum viderant in toto circulo isto animam liberam, solutam et laetam nisi istam" (*Comentum super Dantis Aldigherii "Comoediam,"* ed. J. P. Lacaita, 5 vols. [Florence: Barbèra, 1887], 4:4).

18. The *ri-* verbs of *Inf.* 1 (concentrated in the canto's first half: "ritrovai" [2], "rinova" [6], "ridir" [10], "rimirar" [26], "ripresi" [29], "ritornar" [36], "ripigneva" [60], "ritorni" [76], "rimessa" [110]) constitute the pulsing life-mimetic reminders that, for Dante, spiral motion—and therefore, I would add, life itself—is "a series of conversions" ("The Significance of *Terza Rima*," 265). At the end of *Purgatorio*,

however, the reiterated *ri*-prefix signifies achieved conversion, rebirth, the end of
spiral motion, and initiation into (virtuous) circularity.

19. In his third Epistle, to Cino, Dante answers in the affirmative the question
"utrum de passione in passionem possit anima transformari" (2). For a geneology of
desire from the classics to Dante, see Franco Ferrucci, "La dialettica del desiderio,"
*Il poema del desiderio: Poetica e passione in Dante* (Milan: Leonardo, 1990), 221–64.

20. "For time is just this—number of motion in respect of 'before and after'"
(*Physics* 4.11.219b1–2); "time is the number of motion or itself a kind of motion"
(8.1.251b12–13); "For time is by its nature the cause rather of decay, since it is the
number of change, and change removes what is" (4.12.221b1–2); "But of time some
parts have been, while others have to be, and no part of it *is*" (4.10.218a5–6). The
first of the above definitions is cited in the *Convivio*: "Lo tempo, secondo che dice
Aristotile nel quarto de la Fisica, è 'numero di movimento, secondo prima e poi'"
(4.2.6).

21. To the theological reading of this verse exemplified by John Freccero, "The
Firm Foot on a Journey Without a Guide," 1959, rpt. in *Dante: The Poetics of Conversion*, we may add Ferrucci's reminder that a *piede* is also a metrical unit, in his
metapoetical reading of *Inf.* 1, "Il colle, il sole, il pelago, la selva," *Il poema del desiderio*, 47–90.

22. I do not agree with Anthony Cassell's view, put forth in *"Inferno" I*, Lectura
Dantis Americana (Philadelphia: University of Pennsylvania Press, 1989), that the
attempt to climb the mountain is in itself wrong; nor, therefore, do I see the canto's
first sixty verses as one homogeneous failure but rather as a series of failures and
(aborted) successes, starts and stops, ups and downs. The net result is certainly
failure, but I would stress a more textured approach to the "basso loco" reached by
the pilgrim in verse 61.

23. Antonino Pagliaro writes that canto 2 "strutturalmente costituisce una paren-
tesi, poiché il terzo [canto] si può riattaccare al primo senza che si avverta alcuna
lacuna," and that "il canto secondo costituisce un anello dialettico fra il proemio,
dove si ha la proposizione del tema, e l'inizio della trattazione" (*Ulisse: Ricerche
semantiche sulla "Divina Commedia,"* 2 vols. [Messina: G. D'Anna, 1967], 1:91, 113).
Similarly, Rachel Jacoff and William Stephany note that "the closing line of Canto
2 is so close to that of Canto 1 that the plot of *Inferno* seems to proceed directly from
the end of the first canto to the opening of the third" (*"Inferno" II*, Lectura Dantis
Americana [Philadelphia: University of Pennsylvania Press, 1989], 3).

24. Pagliaro calls *Inf.* 1 "Il proemio" and *Inf.* 2 "Il prologo"; see the two chapters
so named in *Ulisse*, vol. 1. Francesco Mazzoni, *Saggio di un nuovo commento alla
"Divina Commedia": "Inferno," Canti I-III* (Florence: Sansoni, 1967), comments on
p. 151 that "sul piano strutturale" canto 2 is "il prologo alla prima cantica (come il
precedente lo era a tutta l'opera)."

25. Benvenuto calls *Inf.* 1 proemial, a canto "in quo prohemizatur ad totum
opus," and *Inf.* 2 "similiter prohemiali": "Postquam in praecedenti primo capitulo
prohemiali autor noster fecit propositionem ... in isto secundo capitulo similiter
prohemiali more poetico facit suam invocationem" (Lacaita, *Comentum* 1:21, 73).
Jacoff and Stephany refer to the "'detached' quality" of the two introductory cantos
(*Inferno II*, 1). It is worth noting that the first two cantos of *Purgatorio* and *Paradiso*
seem to form proemial packages as well.

26. *Cominciare* appears in canto 2 six times; in no other canto do combined uses of *cominciare* and *incominciare* exceed four appearances. For the importance of *cominciare* and *cominciamento*, see Gorni, "La teoria del 'cominciamento,'" and Jacqueline Risset, *Dante scrittore* (1982; trans. Milan: Mondadori, 1984), 22–23. For *cominciare* in the *Vita Nuova* and the analogies between this canto and VN 18–19, see my "'Cominciandomi dal principio infino a la fine': Forging Anti-Narrative in Dante's *Vita Nuova*," in *"Gloriosa donna de la mente": A Commentary on the Vita Nuova*, ed. Vincent Moleta (Florence: Olschki, 1993).

27. No noun or verb form of *disio* or its variants occurs in *Inf.* 1; the first usage is Beatrice's "vegno del loco ove tornar disio" (2.71).

28. Jacoff and Stephany discuss the link between words and deeds in canto 2, noting that "characters move physically only *after* they have been moved spiritually, and it is words that move them," and point to Beatrice's verse cited above as the "paradigm for the relationship of words to motion within the canto as a whole" (*"Inferno" II*, 5).

29. *Entrare* denotes thematic transition—a new beginning—as early as the *Vita Nuova*: "E questo dico, acciò che altri non si maravigli perché io l'abbia allegato di sopra, quasi come *entrata* de la *nuova* materia che appresso vene" (30.2).

30. A first-time reader of the *Commedia* can measure his "performance" by comparing himself to the pilgrim; on this basis, swooning at Francesca is understandable, whereas weeping for Ugolino is not. Our uneducated perspective develops in synchrony with Dante's: thus, like the pilgrim, we pay little heed when we first learn, in canto 1, that Vergil will eventually leave us with Beatrice ("con lei ti lascerò nel mio partire" [123]); like the pilgrim again, we will be heartbroken when Vergil's departure actually occurs.

31. Vergil's question to Beatrice ("Ma dimmi la cagion che non ti guardi / de lo scender qua giuso in questo centro / de l'ampio loco ove tornar tu ardi" [82–84]) is not required by the "plot" of *Inf.* 2, i.e., the concern to justify the pilgrim's voyage, and seems to exist in order to provide the poet an opportunity to establish certain ground rules about hell before proceeding any further: "Temer si dee di sole quelle cose / c'hanno potenza di fare altrui male; / de l'altre no, ché non son paurose" (88–90). This is an example of *Inf.* 2 functioning as prologue to the canticle, rather than as prologue to the poem.

32. *Quivi* and *qui* are not the same word. Giovanni Nencioni points to the "frequente equivoco di ritenerlo [*quivi*] un sinonimo antico di *qui*, mentre il suo significato è 'lì,' come del resto indica la sua etimologia" (*Il testo moltiplicato*, ed. Mario Lavagetto [Parma: Pratiche Editrice, 1982], 93).

33. Dante's decision to create a special category of souls on the threshold of hell, to "distinguere e tener appartati di qua dall'Acheronte, nell'Antinferno, i pusillanimi, di contro a tutti gli altri dannati," has long caused critical turmoil: "I problemi suscitati dalla collocazione degli Ignavi nell'Antinferno son ben percepiti dal Buti, il quale si preoccupa da un lato di distinguerli dai Limbicoli (che vedremo nel canto 4) e dagli Accidiosi" (Mazzoni, *"Inferno," Canti I-III*, 364, 358).

34. On the Acheron as marking the division between "reality" and "vision," see Dino S. Cervigni, "L'Acheronte dantesco: morte del Pellegrino e della poesia," *Quaderni d'italianistica* 10 (1989): 71–89. Again, I would suggest a less absolute boundary.

35. With reference to both groups of neutrals, human and angelic, found in canto 3, Silvio Pasquazi writes: "I teologi non conoscevano tale categoria di dannati, così come la tradizione biblica ed evangelica non conosce la schiera degli angeli imbelli, ignorata anche dalla teologia e dall'angelologia tomistica" (*ED*, s.v. "Antinferno," 1:301).

36. For the growth of the theology of purgatory, still very fluid in Dante's time, see Jacques Le Goff, *The Birth of Purgatory*, trans. Arthur Goldhammer (1981; Chicago: University of Chicago Press, 1984). With regard to the popular vision tradition, Alison Morgan notes: "The doctrine of Purgatory as a place emerged definitively only as the last visions of the afterlife were being composed. Far from adopting the conventional solution as is commonly believed, Dante created his own solution to the problem—there does not seem to have been a convention. All visions up to and including the twelfth-century texts present Hell and Purgatory jumbled together as one realm of the other world; in 1206 Thurkill distinguishes for the first time between them, but suggests no systematic approach to the classification of sin in Purgatory" (*Dante and the Medieval Other World* [Cambridge: Cambridge University Press, 1990], 132).

37. For the proposal regarding the negligent, see Silvio Pasquazi in the *ED*, s.v. "Antipurgatorio." For Sordello's classification, see Marco Boni, *ED*, s.v. "Sordello."

38. See *The Door of Purgatory: A Study of Multiple Symbolism in Dante's Purgatorio* (Oxford: Clarendon, 1983), 100.

39. Canto 8's function as a thematic recapitulator is emblematized by the nostalgic bittersweetness of its third verse—"lo dì c'han detto ai dolci amici addio"—with its quintessentially antepurgatorial pun on *addio*, while its programmatic recalls of *Purgatorio* 1 and 2 serve to complete a narrative cycle: the sweet notes of the hymn recall the singing in canto 2, while the angels hearken back to that canto's celestial boatman; the references to the four stars and to Eve recall canto 1, as do the repeated evocations of "this morning"—"stamane."

40. "Sono i primi dannati che il poeta incontra, ed egli ha tenuto a istituire fin dall'inizio, mediante un esempio trasparente, il concetto del 'contrapasso'" (Mazzoni, "*Inferno*," *Canti I–III*, 389).

41. Intense speculation regarding the identity of this soul has marked the exegetical tradition from the beginning: although the first commentators concurred in believing him to be Celestine V, the pope's canonization created a controversy that, typically, centered on the desire to "evitare a Dante la taccia di eresia" (Mazzoni, "*Inferno*," *Canti I–III*, 401). In my opinion, Dante would have been perfectly capable of condemning even a beatified Celestine, and I agree with Giorgio Padoan that the political climate and Dante's leanings toward the Franciscan spirituals make Celestine the most convincing candidate (see "'Colui che fece per viltade il gran rifiuto,'" 1962, rpt. in *Il pio Enea, l'empio Ulisse* [Ravenna: Longo, 1977], 64–102). At the same time, Mazzoni is correct to insist that the character of verse 60 is "volutamente lasciato nell'ombra" (390), although he fails to grasp the full textual implications of the poet's enforcement of anonymity.

42. Another example of the text's participation in the reality it is seeking to represent is the famous crux of *Inf.* 10.63. The misunderstanding between the pilgrim and Cavalcante de' Cavalcanti, based on the linguistic obscurity of the verb *ebbe*, is replicated between narrator and reader: the textual obscurity of "forse cui Guido

vostro ebbe a disdegno" generates an analogous "misunderstanding" on the part of the reader, who is condemned to eternal uncertainty as to its meaning—as Cavalcante is condemned to eternal (at least in the text) premature certainty regarding his son's death. In both the "real" and the textual contrapassos, failure of communication and concomitant misinterpretation are the issues at stake. Still another example is the text's willful blurring of the identity of the three thieves in *Inf.* 25; by using *l'uno* and *l'altro* instead of their names, the poet makes it difficult for the reader to keep track of their identities, thus conferring on them textually the same loss of self that is their infernal contrapasso.

43. The "I" of hell's portal presents itself as confidently and unquestioningly, and as mendaciously, as the "I" on the computer screen of a bank's automatic teller that announces, "Sorry, I am temporarily out of service." An exception to our critical credulity regarding these verses, discussed in chapter 1, is Freccero's "Infernal Irony: The Gates of Hell" (1984, rpt. in *Dante: The Poetics of Conversion*).

44. Although we cannot simply take Vergil's explanation at face value, it is clear that the nature of sin for these souls is different from the rest of hell; see G. Busnelli, "La colpa del 'non fare' degl'infedeli negativi," *Studi danteschi* 23 (1938): 79–97.

45. Canto 4's last verses also constitute an implicit commentary on the text to which they belong; for the narrative as for the pilgrim, forward motion requires that we be led "per altra via," by way of alterity, the new. This is a canto in which the poet conflates the pilgrim's journey and his own journey, the "via lunga" and the "lungo tema," by registering the inexorable forward motion of both: Vergil says to the pilgrim, "Andiam, ché la via lunga ne sospigne" (22), and the narrator says to us, "Io non posso ritrar di tutti a pieno, / però che sì mi caccia il lungo tema, / che molte volte al fatto il dir vien meno" (145–47). It seems appropriate that this gloss on the workings of his own *lungo tema*, on its adherence to the poetics of the new, should belong to the canto where Dante is accepted by Homer, Vergil, Ovid, Lucan—those writers of *lunghi temi* par excellence—as their poetic equal.

46. The word *limbo* is derived from the ablative of Latin *limbus*, meaning border, hem, edge, fringe. Mazzoni comments "etimologicamente, 'orlo' (della veste). Quindi, margine esterno dell'Inferno" ("Saggio di un nuovo commento alla *Commedia*: il canto IV dell'*Inferno*," *Studi danteschi* 42 [1965]: 29–206; quotation: 89).

47. It is thus not surprising that there have been critics who have considered limbo part of "antehell," including Pasquazi, who counters the explicit determination of its status as *primo cerchio* by noting the features that make it different (see *ED*, s.v. "Antinferno").

48. Giorgio Padoan attests eloquently to Dante's conscious and deliberate flouting of theological thought on limbo, and to the concerned reactions of the fourteenth-century commentators, in "Il Limbo dantesco," 1969, rpt. in *Il pio Enea, l'empio Ulisse*, 103–24. Dante's concept of limbo is contrasted to that of various theologians by Mazzoni, "Il canto IV," 70–80.

49. Dante's paradoxical handling of Vergil, the more loved as he is the more explicitly superseded, is treated by me in *Dante's Poets: Textuality and Truth in the "Comedy"* (Princeton, N.J.: Princeton University Press, 1984), chapter 3.

50. I do not agree with Mazzoni's contention that the ending of canto 4 should be read as a return to the limbo that exists outside the noble castle, and that "non sarà da considerarsi prolettico rispetto alla atmosfera del canto seguente" ("Il canto IV,"

203). The proleptic nature of canto 4's final verses is confirmed by canto 5's first word: "*Così* discesi del cerchio primaio . . ."

51. For Florence as the infernal city, see Joan Ferrante, *The Political Vision of the "Divine Comedy"* (Princeton, N.J.: Princeton University Press, 1984), esp. chapter 1.

52. Umberto Bosco traces the growth of character development in the early cantos of *Inferno*, sustaining that canto 5 provides "il nostro primo incontro di lettori con un'individualità ben rilevata" and that, therefore, "Francesca segna una svolta nell'effettuale poesia dantesca, dovuta a un impatto col contemporaneo" ("La svolta narrativa nei primi canti dell'*Inferno*" in *Dal Medioevo al Petrarca: Miscellanea di studi in onore di Vittore Branca* [Florence: Olschki, 1983], 251–54; quotation, 253). Although he places the point of rupture in canto 5, Bosco offers as confirmation of his thesis canto 6: "Ormai un nuovo 'stile' di poesia è trovato: il canto 6 ha come scena Firenze. . . . Il reale occupa ormai lo spazio inventivo: Ciacco, il poeta può averlo conosciuto di persona" (253).

53. Ettore Paratore offers a brief but cogent analysis of transitional techniques in the opening pages of his "Analisi 'retorica' del canto di Pier della Vigna," *Studi danteschi* 42 (1965): 281–85. E. H. Wilkins analyzes and tabulates discrepancies between cantos and regions in "Cantos, Regions, and Transitions in the *Divine Comedy*" (*The Invention of the Sonnet and Other Studies in Italian Literature* [Rome: Edizioni di Storia e Letteratura, 1959], 103–10). For a breakdown of the *Commedia*'s explicits, see the Appendix.

54. The symmetry that precedes canto 7 and the change that it inaugurates are noted by Wilkins: "Each one of the four cantos that follow the Prologue of the *Divine Comedy* begins with the beginning of an account of a region not previously visited, and ends precisely with the ending of an account of a regional visit" ("Cantos, Regions, and Transitions," 103). Wilkins comments on the monotony that would have resulted if the symmetry had been maintained and applauds the fact that "variation begins in Canto 7"; however, he sees the variation "not as the result of a deliberate artistic decision, but as the unforeseen outcome of a decision made for didactic reasons" (104).

55. The adverb *ormai* will be frequently used to mark transitions; in verse 97 it is coupled with *or*, creating an untranslateable urgency.

56. I would suggest that the adjective "diversa," for which Sapegno finds no suitable gloss ("qui sarà da intendere 'aspra, malagevole'") serves to signal the presence of difference, the entrance into the new.

57. The monsters of hell belong to the poetic synchrony of these early cantos. Up to now each new circle (and thus each new canto) has been guarded by a new monster: Minos in the second circle (canto 5), Cerberus in the third circle (canto 6), Plutus in the fourth circle (canto 7). By waiting until canto 8 to introduce the guardian of the fifth circle, Phlegyas, Dante maintains some of the symmetry between episode and canto that he violates by leaving the fourth circle before the end of canto 7.

58. Judson Boyce Allen dedicates chapter 3 of *The Ethical Poetic of the Later Middle Ages: A Decorum of Convenient Distinction* (Toronto: University of Toronto Press, 1982) to the *distinctio* or outline as practiced by medieval writers and critics; he notes that "canto 11 of the *Inferno* is a distinctio on the kinds of sin" (154). Dante's sympathy with what Augustine calls the "scientia definiendi, dividendi,

atque partiendi" (*De doctrina Christiana* 2.35.53) is evidenced by the presence of the *divisioni* in the *Vita Nuova* and surfaces throughout his work: in the *Convivio*, for instance, he characterizes the writer's task as a "mestiere di procedere dividendo" (2.12.10), while Vergil punctuates one of his discourses in the *Commedia* with "se dividendo bene stimo" (*Purg.* 17.112).

59. Alessandro D'Ancona, in *I precursori di Dante* (Florence: Sansoni, 1874), notes the genre's previous lack of plastic realism: "la descrizione difetta di quella virtù plastica, così propria di Dante che a noi par quasi di conoscere graficamente e architettonicamente i luoghi da lui rappresentati" (30). In "L'*Itinerarium animae* nel Duecento e Dante," *Letture classensi* 13 (1984): 9–32, Cesare Segre sums up the differences between Dante and his visionary precursors as "Virgilio, la filosofia, la realtà" (25).

60. The vision of hell presented by Dante's Italian precursor Bonvesin de la Riva (ca. 1240–ca. 1313), in his *De scriptura nigra*, suffers if anything from too much order. Ruggero Stefanini compares Bonvesin's hell to Giacomino da Verona's *De Babilonia civitate infernale* (13th century): "The *Babilonia* is a pullulating chaos, bereft of any articulation or sense of perspective. . . . By contrast, Bonvesin distances and orders this same material, turning it into an inventory of twelve punishments which he presents one after the other, each headed by its ordinal number" (Bonvesin de la Riva, *Volgari scelti*, trans. Patrick S. Diehl and Ruggero Stefanini [New York: Peter Lang, 1987], 129). A hypothesis as to why Dante chose precisely canto number eleven for his taxonomy of sin is offered by Victoria Kirkham, "Eleven Is for Evil: Measured Trespass in Dante's *Commedia*," *Allegorica* 10 (1989): 27–50.

61. These categories of sinners seem to anticipate Dante's concepts of antehell, limbo, and antepurgatory. Alison Morgan comments that "the *Vision of Tundale* shows the most complex approach to the classification of sin among the twelfth-century texts" (110) and notes the following grounds for comparing it to *Inferno*: "the explicit separation of one class of sinner from another; the gradual increase in gravity of sin and corresponding torment as we travel deeper into the pit of Hell; the distinction between sins deserving of punishment in upper Hell and those deserving of punishment in lower Hell, with the offering of a principle according to which the two types are differentiated; the assignment of monsters or guardians to the various classes of sinner, and finally the change in mood as the area of purgation of minor sins is reached" (*Dante and the Medieval Other World*, 112). Citations are from *Visions of Heaven and Hell before Dante*, ed. and trans. Eileen Gardiner (New York: Italica Press, 1989), 162, 180, 181.

CHAPTER 3
ULYSSES, GERYON, AND THE AERONAUTICS OF NARRATIVE TRANSITION

1. On flight imagery and the metaphysics of ascent in the *Commedia*, see Hugh Shankland, "Dante 'Aliger,'" *Modern Language Review* 70 (1975): 764–85; Shankland argues persuasively that Dante is aware of the relation between his last name and Vergil's coinage *aliger*, "wing bearing." His later essay focuses on flight imagery and Ulysses; see "Dante *Aliger* and Ulysses," *Italian Studies* 32 (1977): 21–40.

2. The early dichotomy is noted by Natalino Sapegno, "Ulisse," *Letture classensi* 7 (1979): 93–98. In what follows I make no attempt to give an exhaustive résumé

of the Ulysses *querelle* but rather to highlight those critical writings that have proved most useful to me. Ample references may be found in Anthony K. Cassell, "*Ulisseana*: A Bibliography of Dante's Ulysses to 1981," *Italian Culture* 3 (1981): 23–45.

3. Mario Fubini, "Il peccato d'Ulisse" and "Il canto XXVI dell'*Inferno*," in *Il peccato d'Ulisse e altri scritti danteschi* (Milan: Ricciardi, 1966), 1–76. Much of this material is repeated in Fubini's "Ulisse" in the *ED*. His supporters include Sapegno, in the previously cited essay, Antonino Pagliaro ("Ulisse," in *Ulisse: Ricerche semantiche sulla "Divina Commedia*," 2 vols. [Messina: G. D'Anna, 1967], 1: 371–432), Fiorenzo Forti ("'Curiositas' o 'fol hardement'?," in *Magnanimitade: Studi su un tema dantesco* [Bologna: Pàtron, 1977], 161–206), and Lino Pertile, "Dante e l'ingegno di Ulisse," *Stanford Italian Review* 1 (1979): 35–65.

4. John A. Scott, "L'Ulisse dantesco," in *Dante magnanimo* (Florence: Olschki, 1977), 117–93, provides a review of the critical issues raised in the debate over Ulysses; his stated goal is to right the balance that had tipped too far toward Ulysses' heroic aspect. On the problems with knowing what sin to ascribe to this *bolgia*, see John Ahern, "Dante's Slyness: The Unnamed Sin of the Eighth Bolgia," *Romanic Review* 73 (1982): 275–91. The poet's avoidance of a label has provided fertile soil for the collocation fallacy discussed in chapter 1; Pertile, for instance, claims that the nature of Ulysses' discourse is not a cause for damnation, "ché se fosse un falsario di parole, dovremmo trovarlo più giù nell'Inferno insieme al suo commilitone Sinone" ("Dante e l'ingegno d'Ulisse," 42). For another example of the fallacy at work, see note 34 below.

5. Scholars who have emphasized the *orazion* itself as the manifestation of Ulysses' sinfulness include Giorgio Padoan, "Ulisse 'fandi fictor' e le vie della sapienza," 1960, rpt. in *Il pio Enea, l'empio Ulisse* (Ravenna: Longo, 1967), 170–99, and Anna Dolfi, "Il canto di Ulisse: occasione per un discorso di esegesi dantesca," *Forum Italicum* 7–8 (1973–1974): 22–45.

6. "La tragedia di Ulisse," 1937, rpt. in *Dante e la cultura medievale*, 2d ed. rev. (Bari: Laterza, 1949), 153–65. Nardi's position is endorsed by Amilcare A. Iannucci, who comments that "it is difficult not to see in Ulysses' 'mad flight' a conscious act of rebellion against a divine law, and, more specifically, a re-enactment of the Fall" ("Ulysses' *folle volo*: The Burden of History," *Medioevo romanzo* 3 [1976]: 410–45; quotation, 426).

7. "Con l'ammirazione per l'eroe che scaglia la sua vita nell'ignoto contrasta appunto, nella coscienza di Dante, la riprovazione del folle ardimento, per parte del teologo" ("La tragedia di Ulisse," 165).

8. "Ulisse e la tragedia intellettuale di Dante," in *La struttura morale dell'universo dantesco* (Rome: Ausonia, 1935), 26–40.

9. For Freccero, Ulysses' voyage is an allegory of Dante's own previous intellectual adventurism, especially as represented by the philosophical detour of the *Convivio*; see "Dante's Prologue Scene," 1966, and "Dante's Ulysses," 1975, rpt. in *Dante: The Poetics of Conversion*, ed. Rachel Jacoff (Cambridge: Harvard University Press, 1986). The same line of argument is pursued by David Thompson in "Dante's Ulysses and the Allegorical Journey," 1967, rpt. in *Dante's Epic Journeys* (Baltimore: Johns Hopkins University Press, 1974). Maria Corti sees Ulysses as a symbol of the radical Aristotelians, an *in malo* version of what Siger represents *in bono*; see *Dante a un nuovo crocevia* (Florence: Libreria Commissionaria Sansoni, 1981), 85–97.

10. Fubini writes of "un certo gusto dannunziano a cui inconsapevolmente ha ceduto il severo studioso" (*ED*, s.v. "Ulisse," 5:806).

11. For Cassell, "Ulysses, far from being the exceptional paragon imagined by romantic-minded critics, was chosen by the Poet as the exemplary ambitious, dissembling pretender to noble counsel, one whose aims and posturing advice were as deceptive as the rest of the 'lordura' held in this ditch of Malebolge"; see *Dante's Fearful Art of Justice* (Toronto: University of Toronto Press, 1984), 95.

12. Fubini's thesis shows obvious strains as he argues that "certo Ulisse va incontro a un limite, a un limite che aveva ignorato e che gli s'impone con quella catastrofe, ma non è, ripeto, una punizione" and that "soprattutto non vi è parola di 'divieto'" (*ED*, s.v. "Ulisse," 5:807, 808).

13. Vergil is also a sinner who is named in each canticle, but as a major protagonist of the poem, rather than as a figure encountered only once. Nimrod appears in *Inf.* 31, is listed among the examples of pride in *Purg.* 12, and is invoked by Adam in *Par.* 26. He attests to the indissoluble link between pride and creativity: our creativity leads to the invention and use of language, and our pride is responsible for its disruption. Another figure mentioned in each canticle is Phaeton, not a sinner in the *Commedia* but a further emblem of the problematic that both Ulysses and Nimrod represent.

14. On Dante's use of *folle/follia*, associated with excess and intellectual pride, see Umberto Bosco, "La 'follia' di Dante," 1958, rpt. in *Dante vicino*, 2d ed. (Caltanisetta: Sciascia, 1972), 55–75. For textual recalls of Ulyssean motifs, see Franco Fido, "Writing Like God—or Better? Symmetries in Dante's 26th and 27th Cantos," *Italica* 63 (1986): 250–64.

15. Croce's strictures against the stretches of "non poesia" in the *Commedia* echo those of Edgar Allan Poe vis-à-vis *Paradise Lost* in "The Philosophy of Composition": "What we term a long poem is, in fact, merely a succession of brief ones—that is to say, of brief poetical effects. It is needless to demonstrate that a poem is such, only inasmuch as it intensely excites, by elevating, the soul; and all intense excitements are, through a psychal necessity, brief. For this reason, at least one half of the *Paradise Lost* is essentially prose—a succession of poetical excitements interspersed, *inevitably*, with corresponding depressions (*Literary Criticism of Edgar Allan Poe*, ed. Robert L. Hough [Lincoln: University of Nebraska Press, 1965], 22–23).

16. Likewise, vis-à-vis Nardi's alignment of Ulysses with Lucifer, also considered anachronistic, D'Arco Silvio Avalle points out that the *Libro de Alexandre*'s Alexander the Great is explicitly compared to Lucifer; see "L'ultimo viaggio di Ulisse," in *Modelli semiologici nella "Commedia" di Dante* (Milan: Bompiani, 1975), 60.

17. "'Né dolcezza di figlio,'" 1965, rpt. in *Dante vicino*, 173–96.

18. I refer the reader to Scott, who demonstrates four fundamental oppositions: Ulysses vs. Aeneas, Ulysses vs. Cato, Ulysses vs. Solomon, and Ulysses vs. Dante. Another way to state the terms of the critical debate would be to divide critics into those who see Ulysses as a precursor of the pilgrim and those who see him as his antithesis; see Adriano Bozzoli, "Ulisse e Dante," *Convivium* 34 (1966): 345–53. Jurij M. Lotman writes "Ulisse è l'originale doppio di Dante" (96); see "Il viaggio di Ulisse nella *Divina Commedia* di Dante," *Testo e contesto* (Bari: Laterza, 1980), 81–102.

19. Although not elaborated systematically, Giuseppe Mazzotta suggests a similar position: "He will reappear again, even in *Paradiso*, as a constant reminder to the poet of the possible treachery of his own language and the madness of his own

journey" (*Dante, Poet of the Desert* [Princeton, N.J.: Princeton University Press, 1979], 105). More explicitly, Giuliana Carugati views Ulysses "come figura emblematica di un tema che, debordando dai confini del canto 26 dell'*Inferno*, assume valore di struttura portante, di metafora centrale della scrittura dantesca" (*Dalla menzogna al silenzio: La scrittura mistica della "Commedia" di Dante* [Bologna: Il Mulino, 1991], 89).

20. It is worth noting that an anonymous story ascribing the authorship of the *Commedia* to the holy spirit ("che quello libro di Monarchia si dovesse e potesse bene intitolare a Dante, ma la Comedia più tosto allo Spirito Sancto che a Dante") offers *Purg.* 24 as its clinching argument: "Non vedi tu che dice qui chiaro che, quando l'amore dello Spirito Sancto lo spira dentro al suo intellecto, che nota la spirazione, e poi la significa secondo che esso Spirito gli dicta e dimostra? volendo dimostrare che le cose sottili e profonde, che trattò e toccò in questo libro, non si potevano conoscere sanza singulare grazia e dono di Spirito Sancto" (*Dante, secondo la tradizione e i novellatori,* ed. Giovanni Papanti [Leghorn: Vigo, 1873], 85–88).

21. The advantage is compounded by the fact that, as Augustine points out, there is no way to check as to the truth of the scribe's transcription: "But how should I know whether what he [Moses] said was true? . . . Since, then, I cannot question Moses, whose words were true because you, the Truth, filled him with yourself, I beseech you, my God, to forgive my sins and grant me the grace to understand those words, as you granted him, your servant, the grace to speak them" (*Conf.* 11.3; trans. R. S. Pine-Coffin [London: Penguin, 1961]).

22. *Impresa* is a Ulyssean term in the *Commedia*, appearing twice regarding the pilgrim's undertaking in *Inf.* 2, once regarding the poet's undertaking in *Inf.* 32, and in a way calculated to conflate pilgrim and poet in *Par.* 33.

23. For Hawkins, see "Virtuosity and Virtue: Poetic Self-Reflection in the *Commedia*," *Dante Studies* 98 (1980): 1–18; citing Dante's "chastening conversation with Oderisi" (12), his humble "willingness to fly 'di retro al dittator'" (13), and the "redeemed poesis" (14) of *Paradiso*, Hawkins concludes that "the story of Ulysses is rewritten by the 'tempered' life of the pilgrim and the 'tempered' pen of the poet" (15). For Taylor, see "From *superbo Ilïón* to *umile Italia*: The Acrostic of *Paradiso* 19," *Stanford Italian Review* 7 (1987): 47–65; since the acrostic of *Purg.* 12 "edges dangerously close to Lucifer's presumption," it "requires revision" (55), which Dante provides in the acrostic of *Par.* 19 (for the manner in which the second acrostic is alleged to correct the first, see chapter 6, note 17).

24. See *Dalla menzogna al silenzio*, 79; the two poles of Carugati's reading, "mensonge" versus "Silence," are derived from Michel De Certeau's study of the mystical enterprise as a linguistic enterprise, *La fable mystique* (Paris: Gallimard, 1982).

25. "The Fate of Writing: The Punishment of Thieves in the *Inferno*," *Dante Studies* 102 (1984): 51–60; quotation, 55.

26. "The Imageless Vision and Dante's *Paradiso*," *Dante Studies* 90 (1972): 77–91; quotation, 81.

27. *Dante and Difference: Writing in the "Commedia"* (Cambridge: Cambridge University Press, 1988), 125.

28. Of this apostrophe, Anna M. Chiavacci Leonardi writes that "tutto il testo è costruito sulle parole stesse pronunciate da Ulisse nell'Inferno" (*La guerra de la pietate* [Naples: Liguori, 1979], 171). For Lucia Battaglia Ricci, the Ulyssean passages cited here indicate that "non è l'eroe Dante a essere l'antagonista di Ulisse, ma il

Dante narratore" (*Dante e la tradizione letteraria medievale* [Pisa: Giardini, 1983], 173). Our positions differ however, since Battaglia Ricci couples Ulysses/Dante–narrator in order to set up the same reversal usually operated with respect to Ulysses/Dante–pilgrim: the Ulyssean imagery used by the poet in the *Paradiso* indicates how confident and secure a guide he is to his readers, how unlike Ulysses to his crew, and how sure of a positive outcome to his voyage. The Ulyssean elements of the address of *Par.* 2 are treated also by Gino Rizzo, "Dante's Ulysses," *Arts: The Journal of the Sydney University Arts Association* 12 (1984): 7–21, and Carugati, *Dalla menzogna al silenzio*, 99–103.

29. It is difficult, in the context of so explicit a statement of poetic originality, not to see a double meaning in the locution "nove Muse."

30. Robert Hollander gathers together all these passages under the rubric of "Dante's Voyage," chapter 5 of *Allegory in Dante's "Commedia"* (Princeton, N.J.: Princeton University Press, 1969). For him, however, the Neptune analogy contains the following figural identities: "The Pilgrim is Jason, on the way to getting the Fleece; the Poet is Neptune, watching him do so" (230–31). And yet Jason is identified with the poet in *Par.* 2, since it is the poet who will create in us the wonder elicited by Jason from his crew, and there is no doubt that Neptune's wonder serves as a figure for the wonder of the pilgrim in the face of "La forma universal di questo nodo" (*Par.* 33.91). By the same token, Glaucus serves as a model for the pilgrim, not the poet, in *Par.* 1: "tal dentro mi fei, / qual si fé Glauco nel gustar de l'erba / che 'l fé consorto in mar de li altri dèi" [67–69]). Apropos Glaucus, we might note that his "gustar de l'erba" is a variant of Adam's "gustar del legno," indicating once again how fine is the line between transgression and transformation.

31. On the "words that tie Ulysses' experience to Dante's in the first canto of the poem," see Hollander, *Allegory in Dante's "Commedia*," 120.

32. Whether registered negatively, as a fear, or positively, as an aspiration, a comparison indicates a likeness, with the result that *Inf.* 2.32 constitutes a classic example of the content signifying in one way while the form signifies in another.

33. One reader who states this view very clearly is Jorge Luis Borges, in the essay on the *Commedia* contained in *Seven Nights*, trans. Eliot Weinberger (New York: New Directions, 1984): "To what do we owe the tragic weight of this episode? I think there is an explanation, the only valid one, and that is that Dante felt, in some way, that he was Ulysses. I don't know if he felt it in a conscious way—it doesn't matter. In some tercet of the *Commedia* he says that no one is permitted to know the judgments of Providence. We cannot anticipate them; no one can know who will be saved and who condemned. But Dante has dared, through poetry, to do precisely that. He shows us the condemned and the chosen. He must have known that doing so courted danger. He could not ignore that he was anticipating the indecipherable providence of God. For this reason the character of Ulysses has such force, because Ulysses is a mirror of Dante, because Dante felt that perhaps he too deserved this punishment. Writing the poem, whether for good or ill, he was infringing on the mysterious laws of the night, of God, of Divinity" (24).

34. For a reading of the canto in this key, see my "True and False See-ers in *Inferno* XX," *Lectura Dantis: A Forum for Dante Research and Interpretation* 4 (1989): 42–54. Apropos the connection between Ulysses and the diviners, Alessandro Chiappelli demonstrates the collocation fallacy in his denial of any such link: "E se invece fosse colpa quel suo voler *veder troppo*, come di lui disse il Petrarca, ei forse

starebbe invece fra i miseri che fan petto delle spalle" ("L'Odissea dantesca," in Pagine di critica letteraria [Florence: Le Monnier, 1911], 314).

35. In seeking to achieve God's perspective, from which there is nothing new to see because everything has been foreseen, the diviners are the opposite of Neptune, who sees not no new things but plenty of them: "Tra l'isola di Cipri e di Maiolica / non vide mai sì gran fallo Nettuno, / non da pirate, non da gente argolica" (Inf. 28.82–84). Note the phrasing "non vide mai," which anticipates "mai non vide" in Purg. 10.94.

36. In light of Rocco Montano's suggestion that Ulysses' quest for knowledge degenerates into vana curiositas ("I modi della narrazione di Dante," Convivium 26 [1958]: 546–67), it is worth noting that St. Thomas, in his critique of curiosity as a vice that derives from the "inordinateness of the appetite and effort to find out," includes those who seek "to foretell the future by recourse to demons" (ST 2a2ae.167.1; trans. and ed. Thomas Gilby, Blackfriars 1972, 44:203). Cato is contrasted to Ulysses by Scott in part for his refusal to ask an oracle for a message and thus go beyond the limits set for human knowledge. On Ulysses and the sin of curiosity, see also Albert E. Wingell, "The Forested Mountaintop in Augustine and Dante," Dante Studies 99 (1981): 9–48.

37. See Michael Riffaterre, Fictional Truth (Baltimore: Johns Hopkins University Press, 1990), 21 and 30, where the author also notes that "signs of fictionality in a text are not veiled or blunted or compensated for by corrective verisimilitude that suspends disbelief; rather, it is these very signs that point to a truth invulnerable to the deficiencies of mimesis or to the reader's resistance to it" (33). Riffaterre's list of "signs pointing to the fictionality of fiction" include many used by Dante: "authors' intrusions; narrators' intrusions; multiple narrators; humorous narrative that acts as a representation of the author or of a narrator or that suggests an outsider's viewpoint without fully intruding; metalanguage glossing narrative language; generic markers in the titles and subtitles, in prefaces, and in postfaces; emblematic names for characters and places; incompatibilities between narrative voice and viewpoint and characters' voices and viewpoints; incompatibilities between viewpoint and verisimilitude, especially omniscient narrative; signs modifying the narrative's pace and altering the sequence of events (backtracking and anticipation, significant gaps, prolepsis, and analepsis); mimetic excesses, such as unlikely recordings of unimportant speech or thought (unimportant but suggestive of actual happenings, of a live presence, creating atmosphere or characterizing persons); and, finally, diegetic overkill, such as the representation of ostensibly insignificant details, the very insignificance of which is significant in a story as a feature of realism" (29–30).

38. For a full-fledged exposition of the analysis regarding Dante's use of comedìa, tragedìa, and tëodìa that informs this paragraph, see the last chapter of Teodolinda Barolini, Dante's Poets: Textuality and Truth in the "Comedy" (Princeton, N.J.: Princeton University Press, 1984).

39. The paradigm that emerges from the Eclogues is of particular significance because these works belong to the last years of Dante's life, 1320–1321, and, in the case of the second eclogue, perhaps to his last months (see Cecchini's introduction to his edition, 648–49). One could see these texts as proposing a final succinct statement of Dantesque poetics, in which we move from the first eclogues's defense of comica verba (2.52) to the second's suggestion that the province of such verba is mira vera.

40. It is significant that both these passages constitute addresses to the reader, moments of exposed narrativity, as discussed in chapter 1.

41. "Dante *Theologus-Poeta*," 1976, rpt. in *Studies in Dante* (Ravenna: Longo, 1980), 76.

42. "Gerione non rappresenta soltanto la frode come categoria morale, ma anche come categoria estetica: egli è anche *la personificazione della menzogna poetica*" ("Comedìa," 1971; rpt. in *Il poema del desiderio* [Milan: Leonardo, 1990], 99). Ferrucci reads Geryon as Dante's indication to us that his poem is merely metaphorical, made of lies; he is seconded by Carugati, *Dalla menzogna al silenzio*, 68–70. In *Dante's Poets*, 214 and passim, I disagree with Ferrucci's position, taking Geryon rather as Dante's paradoxical confirmation that the *comedìa*, even when it appears to be lying, always tells truth. A similar position is that of Zygmunt G. Barański, who claims that Dante makes explicit his poem's sharing in the allegory of theologians "by associating his 'comedy' with Geryon, who, as a divinely created *mirabile*—and hence like the Bible and the universe in general—was an *allegoria in factis* and not simply *in verbis*" ("The 'Marvellous' and the 'Comic': Toward a Reading of *Inferno* XVI," *Lectura Dantis: A Forum for Dante Research and Interpretation* 7 [1990]: 72–95; quotation, 87).

43. The last interpretation is that of Antonio Lanza, who provides a resume of critical reactions in "L'allegoria della corda nel canto XVI dell'*Inferno*," *Rassegna della letteratura italiana* 84 (1980): 97–100.

44. *Semantica di Gerione: Il motivo del viaggio nella "Commedia" di Dante* (Rome: Bulzoni, 1984). Franco Masciandaro also stresses the relation between the Geryon episode and the first canto in "Appunti sulla corda di Gerione e la cintura-serpente della dialettica," *Revue des études italiennes* 25 (1979): 259–72; for him the cord represents the excessively confident intellectualism associated with the *Convivio*.

45. The traditional interpretation is supported by Mario Marti: "Ebbene, dirò subito che fra la compatta interpretazione degli antichi, che videro nella corda aggroppata e ravvolta il simbolo della frode, e le numerosissime spiegazioni dei moderni esegeti, che vi colsero o la buona fede, o la continenza, o la castità (e in questo caso s'identificherebbe col cordiglio francescano), o l'umiltà, o la contrizione, o la mortificazione della carne, o la legge e l'osservanza della legge, o la temperanza, o la dirittura della coscienza morale, o altro ancora, io sto con gli antichi" ("Tematica e dimensione verticale del XVI dell'*Inferno*," 1968; rpt. in *Studi su Dante* [Galatina: Congedo, 1984], 74).

46. On the Geryon similes, see Richard H. Lansing, *From Image to Idea: A Study of the Simile in Dante's "Commedia"* (Ravenna: Longo, 1977), 124–27. Uberto Limentani notes that *Inf.* 17 contains more similes (15) than any other canto in the poem and suggests that the "constant and exceptionally frequent use of comparisons serves to make Geryon and the circumstances of his extraordinary appearance more credible" (*Dante's "Comedy"* [Cambridge: Cambridge University Press, 1985], 49). Marino Barchiesi comments that canto 17 "è il più ricco di comparazioni, brevi e lunghe, adunate intorno alla presenza simulatrice di Gerione" ("Arte del prologo e arte della transizione," *Studi danteschi* 44 [1967]: 147).

47. The description of the suicides' souls as bound "in questi nocchi" (*Inf.* 13.89) is anticipated by the branches of their wood, "non rami schietti, ma nodosi e 'nvolti" (13.5).

48. This emphasis is certainly related to "la lonza a la pelle *dipinta*" (*Inf.* 16.108), "che di pel *macolato* era coverta" (*Inf.* 1.33).

49. Speaking of the book of his life in *Par.* 17, according to the conflation between life and text that is a hallmark of his poetics from the time of the Vita Nuova, Dante writes of Cacciaguida that "si mostrò spedita / l'anima santa di metter la trama / in quella tela ch'io le porsi ordita" (100–102).

50. Mercuri sees Phaeton and Icarus as allusions to Ulysses (*Semantica di Gerione*, 85); he connects these two figures to Arachne, writing "Dante è esempio di umiltà antitetico agli 'exempla' di superbia incarnati da Icaro, Fetonte, Aracne e Gerione" (153). On the pilgrim as a "corrected" Phaeton, see Kevin Brownlee, "Phaeton's Fall and Dante's Ascent," *Dante Studies* 102 (1984): 135–44.

51. The third use of *navicella* occurs in the tableaux of the earthly paradise, where it refers to the chariot that represents the church: "O navicella mia, com' mal se' carca!" (*Purg.* 32.129). In these three usages Dante seems to give us instances of three fundamental voyages: the voyage of the individual life in the first, the voyage of the text in the second, and the voyage of providential history in the third.

52. A similar pun occurs in a similarly metapoetic canto, to be discussed shortly, *Inf.* 8: when the pilgrim refers to Vergil as "O caro duca mio, che più di sette / volte m'hai sicurtà renduta e tratto / d'alto periglio che 'ncontra mi stette" (97–99), we are reminded that Vergil has escorted his charge through seven previous cantos.

53. Dante equates himself to Paul in *Par.* 1 and to the disciples in *Purg.* 32; he also draws an analogy between his own visionary experience and that of St. John, to be discussed in chapter 7. Guido da Pisa writes as follows: "Unde ait nos admonens quod illi vero, quod habet faciem mendacii, debemus claudere labia quousque possumus, idest tantum tacere debemus quousque necessitas postulabit. Et ideo beatus Paulus Apostolus, licet raptus fuerit usque ad tertium celum, tamen quia illud verum faciem falsi poterat in auribus audientium generare, ideo illud annis xiiii occultavit. Et Christus mandavit illis tribus apostolis qui suam transfigurationem viderant, quod nemini dicerent visionem quousque ipse fuisset a mortuis suscitatus. Nam si ante suam resurrectionem illam visionem dixissent, audientes nullatenus credidissent. Sed probata et manifestata resurrectione, illud tale verum iam non habuerit faciem falsi, sed veri" (*Expositiones et glose super "Comediam" Dantis*, ed. Vincenzo Cioffari [Albany: State University of New York Press, 1974], 306).

54. On Geryon and the falcon imagery of the *Purgatorio*, see Mercuri, *Semantica di Gerione*, 163–64.

55. Although critics like Mercuri and Masciandaro have made much of the relation between *Inf.* 16 and *Inf.* 1, less attention has been paid to the importance of *Inf.* 8 in this progression of new beginnings. Amilcare A. Iannucci discusses Christ's descent into hell as typological model for both *Inf.* 2 and 9: "Queste intrusioni divine risolvono il pauroso dilemma del pellegrino e fanno sì che il viaggio prima possa iniziare e poi possa continuare" ("Dottrina e allegoria in *Inferno* VIII, 67–IX, 105," *Dante e le forme dell'allegoresi*, ed. Michelangelo Picone [Ravenna: Longo, 1987], 122).

56. Both words occur for the first time in canto 3 vis-à-vis Charon, and for the second time in canto 8 vis-à-vis Phlegyas. The third use of *nocchiero* refers to the angel in *Purg.* 2.

57. This represents the first appearance of *barca*, whose last appearance is in the

Ulyssean passage of *Par.* 23; Phlegyas's "barca" is also called "legno," like the ship in the address of *Par.* 2.

58. In demonstrating that "Dante's aeronautical imagination proves every bit as lively and exact as Leonardo's," Glauco Cambon compares Geryon's movement to that of the *angelo nocchiero* (*Dante's Craft* [Minneapolis: University of Minnesota Press, 1969], 86). Mercuri notes that "Gerione può essere considerato l'antitesi dell'angelo nocchiero" (*Semantica di Gerione*, 22). Shankland makes the comparison to Ulysses, pointing out that "the wing navigation of this 'celestial nocchiero' can be read as a serene enactment of the extravagant rhetorical phrase which the foolhardy human captain had used to describe the eager start of his adventure" ("Dante *Aliger* and Ulysses," 30).

59. The *correre* of the purgatorial ship-text ("Per correr miglior acque alza le vele / omai la navicella del mio ingegno") echoes the *correre* of Phlegyas's boat in *Inf.* 8.

60. Mark Musa stresses the suspense generated by the last line of canto 7 and the interruption created by the flashback in canto 8; whereas the flashback is normally interpreted as extending through verse 12 of canto 8, i.e., until the arrival of Phlegyas, Musa argues (unconvincingly, in my opinion) for its extension through 8.81 (see "At the Gates of Dis," in *Advent at the Gates* [Bloomington: Indiana University Press, 1974], 65–84). Aldo Vallone outlines the history of the biographical explanation of the flashback in "A proposito di *Inf.* VIII, 'Io dico, seguitando,'" *Dal Medioevo al Petrarca: Miscellanea di studi in onore di Vittore Branca* (Florence: Olschki, 1983), 285–87.

61. The use of *già* is important; it signifies forward motion, the antithesis of hell. The *già* at the end of canto 8 looks forward to the emphatic adverb that greets the angel's arrival in canto 9: "E già venìa su per le torbide onde / un fracasso d'un suon" (9.64–65). The poet uses *già* to manipulate narrative time, most tellingly in the final verses of the poem, where its use in "ma già volgeva il mio disio e 'l *velle*" helps create the illusion of all time conflated into an eternal present. Edoardo Sanguineti refers to Dante's *già* as a "'iam' narrativo," and notes its frequent use in canto openings (*Interpretazione di Malebolge* [Florence: Olschki, 1961], 72n and 257).

62. G. A. Borgese writes of the Filippo Argenti episode that "structurally, Dante proves able for the first time to handle three persons at once: Argenti, Virgil, and himself" ("The Wrath of Dante," *Speculum* 13 [1938]: 184). Pride—with its Ulyssean connotations—is present not only through the devils, but also through the figure of Argenti, whose anger stems from his pride; see Forti, "Il magnate non magnanimo: la *praesumptio*," in *Magnanimitade*, 137–60.

63. "Sol si ritorni per la folle strada" also echoes "io sol uno" in *Inf.* 2.3; the pilgrim's fear leads him to renounce his journey in canto 2 and again in canto 8: "ritroviam l'orme nostre insieme ratto" (8.102).

64. I do not agree with Kirkpatrick, *Dante's "Inferno": Difficulty and Dead Poetry* (Cambridge: Cambridge University Press, 1987), that the poet is ashamed of the "dead poetry" of hell; rather, being able to emulate God's *scritta morta* is a source of pride. Being aware of the dangers of such pride does not mean that it is not genuine, as we shall see in chapter 6.

65. The semiotic nature of these signals is stressed by the questions the pilgrim addresses to his guide: "Questo che dice? e che risponde / quell'altro foco? e chi son quei che 'l fenno?" (*Inf.* 8.8–9).

66.  Giorgio Bàrberi Squarotti describes the angel as a source of impetuous movement able to break "l'incanto infernale e demoniaco, che ha congelato così a lungo il movimento"; see "L'interruzione del viaggio," *L'artificio dell'eternità* (Verona: Fiorini, 1972), 225.

67.  Vergil's word seems to have lost ground since canto 2, where it was not "parola tronca" but "parola ornata." Although Vergil's cautionary verses ("Volgiti 'n dietro e tien lo viso chiuso; / ché se 'l Gorgón si mostra e tu 'l vedessi, / nulla sarebbe di tornar mai suso" [9.55–57]) demonstrate his susceptibility to the pagan Furies, it is possible that his advice—although given for the wrong reasons—is not wrong per se. There are occasions in hell when backward motion is necessary, when the wrong turn becomes the right turn. The principle is best dramatized by the use of hell's denizens— Geryon, Antaeus, and Lucifer—as vehicles in the pilgrim's progress; in fact, the entire journey through hell is itself an example of backward motion becoming forward motion, the wrong way becoming the right way. In hell, a perverse place, the apparently "perverse order" of backward motion, of "andare indietro e non innanzi" ("Ciascuna cosa che da perverso ordine procede è laboriosa, e per consequente è amara e non dolce, sì come dormire lo die e vegghiare la notte, e andare indietro e non innanzi" [*Conv.* 1.7.4]), may be the most appropriate. It is interesting that both of the *Inferno*'s significant deviations from the pilgrim's usual infernal progress to the left, instances of right rather than left turns, should occur in transitional cantos, cantos 9 and 17: perhaps these "wrong" turns to the right are connected to the need to go backward in order to spiral forward.

68.  Barchiesi considers the art of transition in Western literature and the narrative technique of *ordo artificiosus* in "Arte del prologo e arte della transizione," 156–77. Battaglia Ricci characterizes the *Commedia*'s narrative structure as a contamination of medieval parataxis (*ordo naturalis*) with epic hypotaxis (*ordo artificiosus*) in *Dante e la tradizione letteraria medievale* (156–57). E. H. Wilkins notes the interruptions of cantos 8 and 17 in "Cantos, Regions, and Transitions in the *Divine Comedy*" (*The Invention of the Sonnet and Other Studies in Italian Literature* [Rome: Edizioni di Storia e Letteratura, 1959], 105).

69.  Paolo Cherchi notes that *Inf.* 17 "follows a mortise technique"; see "Geryon's Canto," *Lectura Dantis: A Forum for Dante Research and Interpretation* 2 (1988): 31–44; quotation, 34.

70.  Again, the adjective *solo* in canto 17 echoes canto 8 ("Sol si ritorni") and canto 2 ("io sol uno"); the pilgrim is excluded from Vergil's colloquy with Geryon as he was by his guide's negotiations with the devils.

71.  Marti asks why the symbol of fraud should be treated before the pilgrim has finished exploring the circle of violence, pointing out that the encounter with the usurers and the arrival of Geryon are narrative units that could be substituted for each other without affecting the lengths of their respective cantos. He concludes that Dante wishes to preserve the Florentines of canto 16 from the degredation that makes the usurers quasi participants in the "bassa vita delle incipienti Malebolge" ("Tematica e dimensione verticale del XVI dell'*Inferno*," 77).

72.  Canto 16's transitional concerns resonate in the particularly forward-looking justification of his journey offered by the pilgrim in verses 61–63 ("Lascio lo fele e vo per dolci pomi / promessi a me per lo verace duca; / ma 'nfino al centro pria convien ch'i' tomi") and in the sodomites' equally farsighted *captatio benevolentiae*, with its

anticipation of *Inferno*'s last verse and reference to a future when the pilgrim will look back on this present as the past: "Però, se campi d'esti luoghi bui / e torni a riveder le belle stelle, / quando ti gioverà dicere 'I' fui,' / fa che di noi a la gente favelle" (82–85).

73. The pilgrim's backward motion from the usurers to Geryon is emphasized: "torna'mi in dietro da l'anime lasse" (17.78). Geryon responds to Vergil's instructions to move out and down in a spiral configuration ("moviti omai: / le rote larghe, e lo scender sia poco" [97–98]) by backing up from his berth: "Come la navicella esce di loco / in dietro in dietro" (100–101).

## CHAPTER 4
## NARRATIVE AND STYLE IN LOWER HELL

1. Robin Kirkpatrick comments with respect to the opening of canto 18 that it has "far more the appearance of a true beginning than the oblique and hesitant opening of *Inferno* I" (*Dante's "Inferno": Difficulty and Dead Poetry* [Cambridge: Cambridge University Press, 1987], 237).

2. On the *descriptio loci* of *Inf.* 18 and its Vergilian antecedents, see Edoardo Sanguineti, chapter 1 of *Interpretazione di Malebolge* (Florence: Olschki, 1961), and Marino Barchiesi's *lectura* of canto 18, "Arte del prologo e arte della transizione," *Studi danteschi* 44 (1967): 115–207. Sanguineti's book is notable for its ideological motivation as well as its practical criticism; the author intends his "lettura narrativa dei canti di Malebolge" (xx) as a methodological challenge to Crocean emphasis on the *Commedia*'s "lyrics." Although Sanguineti's thirteen chapters on each of Malebolge's thirteen cantos more often provide detailed individual canto readings than one overarching *lettura narrativa*, his attempt generates insights into the poem's narrative dimension.

3. Jurij M. Lotman notes that for Dante the worst of sins is "un uso falso dei segni" ("Il viaggio di Ulisse nella Divina Commedia di Dante," *Testo e contesto* [Bari: Laterza, 1980], 92). On the *Inferno* as a whole, see also Fredi Chiappelli, "Il colore della menzogna nell'*Inferno* dantesco," *Letture classensi* 18 (1989): 115–28.

4. "In quanto alla forma, la parola fa sì che il nostro verso proemiale proponga, con esemplare sinteticità, quello che costituirà l'aspetto più singolare dell'intero canto, vale a dire l'accostamento di linguaggio elevato e linguaggio violentemente realistico" ("Arte del prologo," 126).

5. Dante's Malebolgian poetics seem to savor Augustine's recommendations in *De doctrina Christiana* 4.22.51: "But no one should think that it is contrary to theory to mix these three manners; rather, speech should be varied with all types of style in so far as this may be done appropriately. For when one style is maintained too long, it loses the listener. When transitions are made from one to another, even though the speech is long, it proceeds more effectively" (trans. D. W. Robertson, Jr. [Indianapolis: Bobbs-Merrill, 1958], 158). The fourth book of *De doctrina Christiana* is particularly concerned with the role of rhetoric in true discourse.

6. See *Interpretazione di Malebolge*, 14, and "Arte del prologo," 190–92. The coupling of classical with contemporary figures is a feature of exemplary literature; see Carlo Delcorno, "Dante e l'Exemplum' medievale," *Lettere italiane* 35 (1983): 3–28.

7. On the linguistic shift between cantos 26 and 27, see Teodolinda Barolini, *Dante's Poets: Textuality and Truth in the "Comedy"* (Princeton, N.J.: Princeton University Press, 1984), 228–33; for the significance of classical/contemporary couples, which may also be read as fictional/real, see the reading of Sinon and Master Adam, 233–38.

8. I would like to remind the reader that I am not referring to what is funny, not even in the sophisticated dress of "play." In my opinion, Dante's use of the terms *comedìa* and *tragedìa* must be understood in the context of truth and falsehood.

9. For the connection between Vergil and Jason, see Giuseppe Mazzotta, *Dante, Poet of the Desert* (Princeton, N.J.: Princeton University Press, 1979), 158.

10. Vergil's "parola ornata" finds expression most often in his use of the *captatio benevolentiae*; Cato responds to Vergil's *captatio* with the rebuke "non c'è mestier lusinghe" (*Purg.* 1.92). The four occurrences of *lusinga/lusingar* seem to outline a gradual calling into question of ornate speech. *Lusinga* first appears in relation to fraud, in *Inf.* 11's resume of Malebolge ("ipocresia, lusinghe e chi affattura" [58]); it recurs in the pouch of the flatterers, juxtaposed to Jason's *parole ornate*, in Alessio's self-indictment ("Qua giù m'hanno sommerso le lusinghe" [18.125]). The final two uses both point to the limits of *captatio benevolentiae*: the infernal perspective is expressed by Bocca's "mal sai lusingar per questa lama!" (32.96), and the purgatorial by Cato's "non c'è mestier lusinghe."

11. The use of *rime aspre* belongs mainly to the *bolgia* of the flatterers; starting from line 101, we find rhyme words like "s'incrocicchia," "nicchia," "scuffa," "picchia," "muffa," "zuffa," and "zucca." These are noted by Barchiesi, "Arte del prologo," 198. H. Wayne Storey points to the harsh rhymes at the beginning of canto 18, including -*oscio*, "used only once by Dante" (31); see "Mapping Out the New Poetic Terrain: Malebolge and *Inferno* XVIII," *Lectura Dantis: A Forum for Dante Research and Interpretation* 4 (1989): 30–41.

12. Although Dante works to undercut the consistently high style associated with classical epic, his point is not that high style is always wrong, but that a mixed style alone can capture all reality. The high style of canto 19 is, in any case, biblically rather than classically inspired; its rhetorical hallmarks will reappear in later political invectives, such as that of *Purg.* 6. Regarding "the violent oscillations in style marking, for example, *Inferno* 19, 20, and 21, which imitate the Bible, the classics, and the *comico-realistici*," Zygmunt G. Barański comments: "The *Comedy* embodies a truly middle style: a midpoint at which every kind of expression and literary genre, and every subject can come together within a single structure" ("'Significar *per verba*': Notes on Dante and Plurilingualism," *The Italianist* 6 [1986]: 5–18; quotation, 12).

13. Kirkpatrick characterizes the shift differently: "It is one of the most surprising features of the transition from Canto 18 to Canto 19 that Dante should [have] exchanged the ugly triviality of the one for the scriptural simplicity of the other: 'low' language now becomes *sermo humilis*" (*Dante's "Inferno"*, 255). The language of canto 19 seems to me less biblical *sermo humilis* than biblical grandiloquence.

14. "Hanc veritatem etiam Gentiles ante tubam evangelicam cognoscebant" (*Mon.* 2.9.7).

15. Sanguineti's crusade against romantic psychologizing readings of the *Commedia* leads him to ridicule D'Ovidio's suggestion that the autobiographical insert is connected to the sacreligious aspect of canto 19 as a whole. Despite D'Ovidio's heated phrasing, far too involved by today's cool critical standards, he hits on the key

point when he writes that this is a canto where the poet takes on "un peccato essenzialmente sacrilego, e non ci sarebbe mancato altro che egli medesimo non fosse del tutto libero dalla taccia di un sacrilegio!" (see *Interpretazione di Malebolge*, 41n). It is worth remembering that Sanguineti is unusual among Italian Dantists of the early 1960s, since he not only sustains an anti-Croce polemic but also routinely critiques earlier Italians like D'Ovidio in favor of such as Spitzer and Singleton.

16. The only other words in the *Commedia* specifically labeled true are Beatrice's; see *Dante's Poets*, 280n, for an elaboration of this point.

17. See *Dante's Poets*, 215–22, and my *lectura*, "True and False See-ers in *Inferno* XX," *Lectura Dantis: A Forum for Dante Research and Interpretation* 4 (1989): 42–54, where Dante's revision of the *Aeneid* is seen as investing not only the epic's content but its style, which is parodied in the excursus on Mantova.

18. Ciampolo, as he is called by commentators, seems to be reacting to Dante's and Vergil's accents; the speech habits of guide and pilgrim constitute another semiotic theme that will be developed in Malebolge.

19. Malacoda's lie in canto 21 is balanced by a further semiotic abuse in canto 22, where Ciampolo promises to summon his comrades by whistling, the sign that indicates the coast is clear (103–5). These abuses of sign systems by humans and devils are offset, ironically, by the behavior of animals: dolphins help sailors by signaling impending storms ("fanno segno / a' marinar" [*Inf.* 22.19–20]).

20. Sanguineti refers to the "amplificazione catalogica dei segnali" in the exordium of canto 22 (*Interpretazione di Malebolge*, 121). Augustine refers to the trumpet in his discussion of signs in the opening chapters of book 2 of *De doctrina Christiana*.

21. The response from one tower to another is described with the phrase "render cenno" (*Inf.* 8.5).

22. The same association is pointedly achieved at the beginning of *Inferno* 14, where we are faced with divine art—"di giustizia orribil arte"—and with the human whose job it is to narrate it: "A ben manifestar le cose nove, / dico che" (6–8). The independent reality conferred by the first verses of canto 21 will further manifest itself; as Sanguineti points out, this episode is exceptional for the "libero giuoco vitale, quell'autonomia drammatica" (*Interpretazione di Malebolge*, 141) that will allow Dante and Vergil to be forgotten while Ciampolo and the devils take center stage.

23. He comments apropos the opening of canto 22 that the author "vult se excusare de turpi recitatione quam fecit supra in Capitolo precedenti in fine, per id quod scribit Socrates, dicens: 'Que facere turpe est, ea nec dicere honestum puto'" (Guido Biagi, ed., "*La Divina Commedia*" *nella figurazione artistica e nel secolare commento*, 3 vols. [Turin: Unione Tipografico-Editrice Torinese, 1924–1929], 1:531). More perceptively, Jacopo della Lana writes of the end of canto 21: "Circa la quale locuzione si pò excusare l'Autore a chi l'acusasse de parladura porca e villana sì in questo logo commo eziamdeo in lo XVIII° Capitolo de Tayde, che la materia del logo lo constrenge, zoè l'Inf., in lo quale è omme dexordinazione" (Biagi, *La Divina Commedia* 1:529).

24. For Domenico De Robertis, the exordium is marked by "epicità" ("In viaggio coi demòni," *Studi danteschi* 53 [1981]: 1–29). On the episode's stylistic registers, see Leo Spitzer, "The Farcical Elements in *Inferno*, Cantos XXI-XXIII," *MLN* 59 (1944): 83–88; Vittorio Russo, "*If* XXII o del 'grottesco sublime,'" *Il romanzo teo-*

*logico* (Naples: Liguori, 1984), 95–123; and, most recently, Michelangelo Picone, who reads cantos 21–22 against the backdrop of "comic" Romance cultural modalities, as embodied by the *jongleurs* and by texts such as the *Roman de la Rose* and the *Fiore* ("Giulleria e poesia nella *Commedia*: una lettura intertestuale di *Inferno* XXI–XXII," *Letture classensi* 18 [1989]: 11–30). For the "carnevalizzazione del canto 21," see Piero Camporesi, "Il carnevale all'inferno," in *Il paese della fame* (Bologna: Il Mulino, 1978), 23–51; I disagree, however, with Camporesi's suggestion that the ludic mode enters the *Inferno* against Dante's will. Rather, it enters as part of the narrative variety hymned by Tommaseo: "Sembra quasi che, dopo sfoggiata nel XX° Canto erudizione profana, e nel XIX° dottrina sacra e poetico sdegno, in questi due voglia riposare la propria mente e de' lettori con imagini che ben s'addicono al titolo del Poema. All'aridità del II° Canto abbiamo così veduta succedere la bellezza del III°; e alle enumerazioni del IV° la grande poesia del seguente; e alla disputa sulla Fortuna il furor dell'Argenti, e a questo la venuta dell'Angelo e le scene del Farinata e del Cavalcanti; e dopo la scolastica precisione del Canto XI° e le enumerazioni del XII°, il Canto dei suicidi; e dopo la descrizione de' fiumi d'Inf., la scena con Brunetto e coi tre Fiorentini; e innanzi alla tromba che suona pe' simoniaci, la faceta rappresentazione di Venedico, d'Alessio, di Taide. Varietà mirabile se pensata; se inavvertita, più mirabile ancora" (Biagi, *La Divina Commedia* 1: 529).

25. Boccaccio may have had this episode in mind when he composed *Decameron* 4.2, the story of frate Alberto and madonna Lisetta: the friar's leap to safety into the Grand Canal and away from Lisetta's irate brothers seems modeled on Ciampolo's leap into the pitch. To support this reading, I would point out that 4.2 is Boccaccio's Venetian story, and that the *bolgia* of the barraters begins with the simile of the Venetian arsenal; most importantly, 4.2 is an anomolous story for the *Decameron*, in that friar Alberto's wit does not ultimately serve to save him. Like Ciampolo, Alberto is playing in a no-win game, a *nuovo ludo*. Note that, with respect to a sinner, *nuovo* has assumed an inverted hellish significance; it refers to the incapacity to move forward, to ever be "new." Similar usages are the "color novo" and "novelle spalle" attained by the thieves during their dead-ended metamorphoses (*Inf.* 25.119, 139). By contrast, when referring to the pilgrim, the adjective conserves its positive valence, implying his capacity for rebirth and forward movement; see *Inf.* 23.71–72.

26. Kirkpatrick refers to "the 'humble' speech of the fable" (*Dante's "Inferno,"* 279). A further intertextual complication is the echo of Cavalcanti's "e vanno soli, senza compagnia, / e son pien' di paura" ("Io non pensava che lo cor giammai," 51–52).

27. "Far from being wrong, the pilgrim's wish to listen is right, for his is the comedic desire to confront evil and to bear witness to all of reality, including Hell" (*Dante's Poets*, 238).

28. Guido uses *istra*, a variant of *issa*: "O tu a cu' io drizzo / la voce e che parlavi mo lombardo, / dicendo 'Istra ten va, più non t'adizzo'" (*Inf.* 27.19–21). Bonagiunta uses *issa* to signal his conversion to understanding: "'O frate, issa vegg'io,' diss'elli, 'il nodo / che 'l Notaro e Guittone e me ritenne / di qua dal dolce stil novo ch'i' odo!'" (*Purg.* 24.55–57).

29. See Robert Hollander, "Virgil and Dante as Mind-Readers (*Inferno* XXI and XXIII)," *Medioevo romanzo* 9 (1984): 85–100.

30. Dante's understanding of *mo* and *issa* could be described in the terms Zygmunt G. Barański uses for the "I" of *Par.* 26, i.e., as "an *avant la lettre* instance of neo-Saussurean 'arbitrariness of the signifier'" ("Dante's Biblical Linguistics," *Lectura Dantis: A Forum for Dante Research and Interpretation* 5 [1989]: 105–43; quotation, 126).

31. See Mark Musa's notes to this canto, *Dante's "Inferno"* (Bloomington: Indiana University Press, 1971), 202.

32. Joan Ferrante notes that "normally, we think of art imitating nature (cf. *Inf.* 11.97–105), but here nature seems to imitate art, using its tools just long enough to deceive its audience" ("Good Thieves and Bad Thieves: A Reading of *Inferno* XXIV," *Dante Studies* 104 [1986]: 83–98; quotation, 87). The semiotic meditation of lower hell will offer another example of nature as an imperfect artist in *Inf.* 31, where she is congratulated for having left off the art of making giants: "Natura certo, quando lasciò l'arte / di sì fatti animali, assai fé bene / per tòrre tali essecutori a Marte" (49–51). All these passages depend on the mimetic hierarchy articulated in *Inf.* 11.

33. Guido Almansi glosses this episode's "stupenda turpitudine," noting, with respect to the following passage, that "l'adesione, ovviamente, non è geometrica o matematica, bensì squisitamente sessuale" ("I serpenti infernali," in *L'estetica dell'osceno* [Turin: Einaudi, 1974], 37–88; quotations, 41, 66).

34. In "Dante's Anti-Virgilian *Villanello* (*Inf.* XXIV, 1–21)," *Dante Studies* 102 (1984): 81–109, Margherita Frankel reads the simile as written in "two distinct styles, one highly literary and rhetorically ornate, the other humble like an Evangelical parable" (92). From this perspective, one could see the simile as initiating the hybrid style of cantos 24–25.

35. She writes of the "imprevedibile alleanza tra registri stilistici tradizionalmente antitetici" and of a "discorso letterario di provenienza ora petrosa ora stilnovistica, ora giocoso-realistica ora biblica, ora virgiliana ora dottrinaria" (*Dante e la tradizione letteraria medievale* [Pisa: Giardini, 1983], 28–29). Sanguineti too discusses Malebolge's last two cantos in these terms, noting canto 29's "modulazioni di narrato al tutto imprevedibili" (*Interpretazione di Malebolge*, 322) and characterizing canto 30 as a supreme example of Dantesque "politonalità" (337).

36. Hugh Shankland points out that Dante's "dei remi facemmo ali" is "actually a reversal of the Virgilian tag *remigium alarum*, that is 'delle ali remi,' originally applied to the sure flights of Mercury and Daedalus in *Aeneid* 1.301 and 6.10" ("Dante *Aliger* and Ulysses," *Italian Studies* 32 [1977]: 21–40; quotation, 30). The image recurs in Ovid's account of Icarus's fall: the boy's wings melt, and he beats his naked arms to no avail, "remigioque carens" ("lacking oarage" [*Metam.* 8.228]). Thus, the image that Dante adopts as his chief emblem for Ulysses is associated in Vergil and Ovid with both Icarus and Daedalus, setting up the *Commedia*'s twofold analogy: as a frightened flyer, the pilgrim is compared to Icarus; as an artist who completes his flight, Dante is analogous to Daedalus, who arrived at Cumae.

37. The above verses are, in order of citation, *Metamorphoses* 8.188–89, 195, 215, 220, 234. The text is from the Loeb edition by F. J. Miller, 2 vols. (1916; rpt., Cambridge: Harvard University Press; London: William Heinemann, 1971 [vol. 1] and 1968 [vol. 2]).

38. See E. R. Curtius, "The Ape as Metaphor," *European Literature and the Latin Middle Ages* (1948; Princeton, N.J.: Princeton University Press, 1973), 538–40, and,

for a reading similar to mine, see Steven Botterill, "*Inferno* XXIX: Capocchio and the Limits of Realism," *Italiana 1988: Selected Papers from the Proceedings of the Fifth Annual Conference of the American Association of Teachers of Italian*, ed. Albert N. Mancini et al. (River Forest, Ill.: Rosary College, 1990), 23–33. Curtius's account does not include the passage in the *Convivio* in which Dante denies that parrots speak as men or that apes act as men; their representation is not real, because not guided by reason: "Onde è da sapere che solamente l'uomo intra li animali parla, e ha reggimenti e atti che si dicono razionali, però che solo elli ha in sé ragione. E se alcuno volesse dire contra, dicendo che alcuno uccello parli, sì come pare di certi, massimamente de la gazza e del pappagallo, e che alcuna bestia fa atti o vero reggimenti, sì come pare de la scimia e d'alcuno altro, rispondo che non è vero che parlino né che abbiano reggimenti, però che non hanno ragione, da la quale queste cose convegnono procedere; né è in loro lo principio di queste operazioni, né conoscono che sia ciò, né intendono per quello alcuna cosa significare, ma solo quello che veggiono e odono ripresentare" (3.7.8–9). Unlike apes, the falsifiers possess reason and are therefore responsible for their imitations. In the context of poetic imitation, we recall the anonymous sonnet "In verità questo libel di Dante / è una bella simia de' poeti," connected by Guglielmo Gorni to *Inf.* 29 in "Cino 'vil ladro': parola data e parola rubata," *Il nodo della lingua e il verbo d'amore* (Florence: Olschki, 1981), 138.

39. I follow Robert Hollander's suggestion that the adverb *qui* in "punisce i falsador che qui registra" refers to the text of the *Commedia*; see "Dante's 'Book of the Dead': A Note on *Inferno* XXIX 57," *Studi danteschi* 54 (1982): 31–51, where Hollander also notes that the alchemists are "perversely reminiscent of the poet's role of fabricator" (34).

40. Ephialtes' desire to be "esperto" recalls Ulysses' ardor to become "del mondo esperto" and his subsequent call for "l'esperïenza, / di retro al sol, del mondo sanza gente" (*Inf.* 26.98, 116–17). The Ulyssean stamp imprinted on the sin of pride in *Inf.* 31 will be confirmed in *Purg.* 12, where the examples of pride rehearse the same transgressive configuration: Lucifer, the giants, including Nimrod, and—as stand-in for Ulysses—Arachne.

41. The canto's first three words can thus be taken, out of context, to announce its theme.

42. The idea of traversing is present in the *De vulgari eloquentia*, where Dante discusses the dual nature of language in terms of mankind's need to traverse the distance between the rational and the sensual, using the verb *pertransire*: "Quare, si tantum rationale esset, pertransire non posset; si tantum sensuale, nec a ratione accipere nec in rationem deponere potuisset" (1.3.2). One could look at the *Commedia* as a project that on the one hand seeks to eliminate the need for passage between the sensual sound (signifier) and its rational meaning (signified), by making them indivisible, and on the other is aware of the impossibility of a task whose consummation would make us like angels. In this sense, the *Commedia* is, like the tower of Babel, an "ovra inconsummabile" (*Par.* 26.125).

43. The use of *convenire* in 32.2 echoes the infernal decorum of the previous canto, which dictated that Nimrod speak gibberish since he is one "cui non si convenia più dolci salmi" (31.69); the poet, too, is one for whom "sweeter psalms" are not currently appropriate. By the same token, the poet's "rime aspre e chiocce" echo

Plutus's "voce chioccia" (*Inf.* 7.2; these are the only instances of *chioccia* in the poem).

44. Dante had long striven for what Gianfranco Contini calls "la conversione del contenuto nella forma": in the verses "Così nel mio *parlar* voglio esser aspro / com'è ne li *atti* questa bella petra," we see an earlier version of *Inf.* 32's *dir* and *fatto.* (For Contini's comment, see his edition of Dante's *Rime* [1946; rpt., Turin: Einaudi, 1970], 165.) In the same canzone the poet tells us that the weight that submerges him "è tal che non potrebbe adequar rima" (21). Dante most likely had his earlier experiment with hard speech in mind as he composed *Inf.* 32: the canzone's last stanza begins, "S'io avessi le belle trecce prese," a verse that will be echoed in "S'io avessi le rime aspre e chiocce." Moreover, in canto 32 the optative hair pulling of the canzone becomes "reality" when the pilgrim pulls the hair of Bocca degli Abati. For other echoes of the *petrose* in Cocytus, see Robert M. Durling and Ronald L. Martinez, *Time and the Crystal: Studies in Dante's Rime Petrose* (Berkeley: University of California Press, 1990), 217–23.

45. See Giovanni Papanti, ed., *Dante, secondo la tradizione e i novellatori* (Leghorn: Vigo, 1873), 151–53.

46. See Giorgio Bàrberi Squarotti, "L'orazione del conte Ugolino," *Lettere italiane* 23 (1971): 3–28; Piero Boitani, "Ugolino e la narrativa," *Studi danteschi* 53 (1981): 31–52.

47. In "Ugolino e la narrativa," Boitani categorizes both Dante's exordium of canto 32 and Ugolino's dream as narrative authenticating devices, referring explicitly to Bloomfield's "Authenticating Realism and the Realism of Chaucer"; see chapter 1 for discussion of Bloomfield's essay.

48. Dante is here reminding us of the treatise in which he classifies the various languages spoken in the *bel paese*, and where he first refers to Italian as the *lingua di sì.* For further connections between the *De vulgari eloquentia* and this portion of the poem, in which we are made to witness man's "betrayal of his very essence as speaker, according to the definition in the treatise" (137), see Donna L. Yowell, "Ugolino's 'bestial segno': The *De Vulgari Eloquentia* in *Inferno* XXXII-XXXIII," *Dante Studies* 104 (1986): 121–43.

49. The writerly context that has absorbed the originally oral "canto" is denoted by the adverb "suso"; the poet refers to the children whose names are registered "above," in the written text. I do not agree with Jeremy Tambling, for whom Ugolino "is going beyond representation, going into the stark withdrawal about which there is nothing to say," and who sees in the episode the signs of an "Ugolino impasse" whereby "a writer who continued in the *Inferno* mode would soon have to cease writing altogether" (*Dante and Difference: Writing in the "Commedia"* [Cambridge: Cambridge University Press, 1988], 81–82). This interpretation depends on suspending awareness of the composing poet, who demonstrates no difficulty in moving beyond Ugolino, who suffers no impasse, no drying up of his tongue as he responds to Ugolino's narrative with the scathing indictment of Pisa. It is not enough to say, "The address to Pisa is a separate thing" (82). Why conclude that a text that is about absence of signification itself participates in the absence of signification it represents?

50. See Simonetta Saffiotti Bernardi's entry, "Ugolino," in the *ED*; apropos Ugo-

lino's vicarship, she comments that "probabilmente il conte usava questo titolo di vicario, oramai privo di contenuto, per legittimare le sue pretese sarde" (5:795).

51. Canto 33 also encompasses stylistic extremes, since, as Piero Boitani points out, Alberigo's tone is as "low" as Ugolino's is "high" (see *"Inferno* XXXIII," *Cambridge Readings in Dante's "Comedy,"* ed. Kenelm Foster and Patrick Boyde [Cambridge: Cambridge University Press, 1981], 70–89, esp. 86).

52. The condition of the neutrals, of whom Dante writes at the outset of the journey—as now he is at the end—that "mai non fur vivi" (*Inf.* 3.64), is perhaps akin to this one, making them souls who never transited transition.

53. With the words "per cotali scale . . . conviensi dipartir da tanto male" (*Inf.* 34.82, 84), Vergil echoes "Omai si scende per sì fatte scale," canto 17's first formulation of participatory transition. Kathleen Verduin reads the episode as the pilgrim's participation in the "essentially deathful condition of the devil" ("Dante and the Sin of Satan: Augustinian Patterns in *Inferno* XXXIV. 22–27," *Quaderni d'italianistica* 4 [1983]: 208–17; quotation, 211).

CHAPTER 5
PURGATORY AS PARADIGM

1. For the basic narrative structure of each terrace and the variations applied to it, see Enrico De' Negri, "Tema e iconografia del *Purgatorio,*" *Romanic Review* 49 (1958): 81–104.

2. Michelangelo Picone writes a brief history of the pilgrimage metaphor in *Vita Nuova e tradizione romanza* (Padua: Liviana, 1979); see chapter 5, "*Peregrinus amoris*: la metafora finale," where he concludes his resume with this passage from the *Convivio,* in which the metaphor is presented "al massimo delle sue potenzialità espressive" (152). The importance of this passage for the *Commedia* is noted by Bruno Basile, "Il viaggio come archetipo: note sul tema della 'peregrinatio' in Dante," *Letture classensi* 15 (1986): 9–26.

3. The typology of Exodus, of pilgrimage, is further signaled by the psalm, "In exitu Israel de Aegypto" in *Purg.* 2. As Peter Armour explains, this typology applies in a unique way to purgatory: "the *Inferno* and the *Paradiso* do not actually refer to the Exodus, for the souls there are not going anywhere"; "the path of purification is a single, continuous road to be started in this life and completed in the next" ("The Theme of Exodus in the First Two Cantos of the *Purgatorio,*" *Dante Soundings,* ed. David Nolan [Dublin: Irish Academic Press, 1981], 59–99; quotations, 77, 79). Pilgrimage motifs in the *Vita Nuova* and the *Commedia* are treated by Julia Bolton Holloway, *The Pilgrim and the Book* (New York: Peter Lang, 1987), chapter 3, and John G. Demaray, *Dante and the Book of the Cosmos* (Philadelphia: The American Philosophical Society, 1987).

4. Giovanni Cecchetti uses the happy expression "nostalgia del futuro" to describe the condition of the souls in purgatory in "Il *peregrin* e i *navicanti* di *Purgatorio,* VIII, 1–6: saggio di lettura dantesca," *A Dante Symposium in Commemoration of the 700th Anniversary of the Poet's Birth,* ed. W. De Sua and G. Rizzo (Chapel Hill: University of North Carolina Press, 1965), 159–74; quotation, 168. I disagree with Cecchetti's insistence that nostalgia for the past is completely absent from the verses at the beginning of *Purg.* 8, and from the *Purgatorio* in general; the poetic tension of

the second canticle, carefully manipulated by the poet, is generated from the inter-play between the souls' double nostalgia. They do, as Cecchetti says, want to return home, but they are not yet completely sure where home is.

5. The importance of the verse "dove tempo per tempo si ristora" is discussed by Ricardo J. Quinones, *The Renaissance Discovery of Time* (Cambridge: Harvard University Press, 1972), 72, and by me in *Dante's Poets: Textuality and Truth in the "Comedy"* (Princeton, N.J.: Princeton University Press, 1984), 46–47. See also Luigi Blasucci, "La dimensione del tempo nel *Purgatorio*," *Studi su Dante e Ariosto* (Milan: Ricciardi, 1969), 37–64, and Franco Masciandaro, *La problematica del tempo nella "Commedia"* (Ravenna: Longo, 1976), chapter 5.

6. A balanced discussion of Augustine's role in the works of both Dante and Petrarch is provided by Carlo Calcaterra, *Nella selva del Petrarca* (Bologna: Cappelli, 1942). Recently, Augustine's absence from the *Commedia* has been taken up by Peter S. Hawkins, "Divide and Conquer: Augustine in the *Divine Comedy*," *PMLA* 106 (1991): 471–82. Hawkins focuses on the intertextual presence of Augustine in Vergil's discourse of *Purg.* 15. Interestingly, he too concentrates on a purgatorial presence, which he also sees as mediated through a substitute figure, who in his more political reading is Vergil.

7. The passage from the *Enchiridion* is cited by Jacques Le Goff, *The Birth of Purgatory*, trans. Arthur Goldhammer (1981; Chicago: University of Chicago Press, 1984), 71. Le Goff does not relate Augustine's analysis to Dante's purgatory; in fact, his chapter on Dante, the weakest in the book, makes very little use of the material that his own previous chapters provide.

8. See above, chapter 2, for Beatrice as a *cosa nova*. In his edition, Petrocchi supports "*novità* nel senso di 'giovanile esperienza,' 'immatura passione,' o magari 'altra passione per donna giovine'" (*La Commedia secondo l'antica vulgata* 3:538). While these meanings are certainly legitimate, I think this passage provides a key example of the benefits of taking Dante's use of *novo* more literally, as in "nuovo e mai non fatto." *Purgatorio* 10's periphrasis for God as "Colui che mai non vide cosa nova" is also profoundly Augustinian, considering Augustine's struggle to "dismiss any idea of 'newness' in the will of God" (Paul Ricoeur, *Time and Narrative*, trans. Kathleen McLaughlin and David Pellauer [1983; Chicago: University of Chicago Press, 1984], 26).

9. "Some things are to be enjoyed, others to be used, and there are others which are to be enjoyed and used. Those things which are to be enjoyed make us blessed. Those things which are to be used help and, as it were, sustain us as we move toward blessedness" (*On Christian Doctrine* 1.3.3; trans. D. W. Robertson, Jr. [Indianapolis: Bobbs-Merrill, 1958], 9).

10. *Confessions* 10.31: "But the snare of concupiscence awaits me in the very process of passing from the discomfort of hunger to the contentment which comes when it is satisifed" (trans. R. S. Pine-Coffin [London: Penguin, 1961]). The Latin is from the Loeb edition, 2 vols. (Cambridge: Harvard University Press; London: Heinemann, 1977).

11. Voyage imagery to describe the unfolding of the human soul is also found in *Purg.* 25; a human fetus is still in transit when a plant has already arrived: "questa è in via e quella è già a riva" (54).

12. Points of contact between authors frequently spell out their divergences as

well, and it should be noted that Dante's beautiful image of the newborn soul as a little girl, "che piangendo e ridendo pargoleggia" (*Purg.* 16.87), expresses a relative innocence that is certainly not Augustinian. Indeed, the very passage in *Confessions* 1.19 cited above begins with a disclaimer of the innocence of childhood.

13. Giorgio Padoan brings together Augustine and Dante's Ulysses in "Ulisse 'fandi fictor' e le vie della sapienza," 1960, rpt. in *Il pio Enea, l'empio Ulisse* (Ravenna: Longo, 1977), 170–204; drawing attention to the medieval tradition whereby wandering at sea signifies the soul's inclination toward false goods, Padoan cites, among other texts, a passage from Augustine's *De beata vita* (181–84). John Freccero points to resemblances between Augustine's allegory of voyage and *Inf.* 26 in "The Prologue Scene," 1966, rpt. in *Dante: The Poetics of Conversion*, ed. Rachel Jacoff (Cambridge: Harvard University Press, 1986), esp. 20–23.

14. Robert Hollander's reading, which leads to the conclusion that "Ulysses was precisely such a sailor; Dante is so no longer," is representative of a prevalent approach toward this episode, whereby the siren and Ulysses are situated within the poem's moral allegory but the question of their local significance, of why Ulysses is invoked *here*, is never really posed. See "*Purgatorio* XIX: Dante's Siren/Harpy," in *Dante, Petrarch, Boccaccio: Studies in the Italian Trecento in Honor of Charles S. Singleton*, ed. Aldo S. Bernardo and Anthony L. Pellegrini (Binghamton, N.Y.: Medieval and Renaissance Texts and Studies, 1983), 77–88; quotation, 86.

15. Petrarch engages in a metaphorically expanded reading of the sins of concupiscence in his Augustinian *Secretum*, where he treats ambition and the desire for glory as forms of avarice.

16. Augustine does not conceive of erotic objects of desire as vehicles toward God, a fact that Petrarch (more attuned to the historical Augustine than Dante) dramatizes in the *Secretum*: the Augustinus figure consistently refutes Franciscus's courtly rationalizations of his love for Laura as a path toward virtue.

17. Dante's use of *falso* as qualifier for *piacer* recalls Augustine's invocation of God as "dulcedo non fallax, dulcedo felix et secura" in *Confessions* 2.1.

18. "It is knowledge that the Sirens offer, and it was no marvel if a lover of wisdom held this dearer than his home" (*De fin.* 5.18; trans. H. Rackham [Cambridge: Harvard University Press; London: William Heinemann, 1971]). The *De finibus* is brought to bear on Dante's sirens by Joseph Anthony Mazzeo, "The 'Sirens' of *Purgatorio* XXXI, 45," *Medieval Cultural Tradition in Dante's Comedy* (1960; rpt., New York: Greenwood Press, 1968), who shows that the two terms of Beatrice's rebuke (the sirens of 31.45 and the *pargoletta* of 31.59) stand "for the temptations of the mind as well as the temptations of the flesh" (209). For the literary and autobiographical implications of the *pargoletta* qua temptation of the flesh, see Sara Sturm-Maddox, "The *Rime Petrose* and the Purgatorial Palinode," *Studies in Philology* 84 (1987): 119–33.

19. The connection between the siren of *Purg.* 19 and Lady Philosophy is elaborated by Colin Hardie, "*Purgatorio* XIX: The Dream of the Siren," *Letture del "Purgatorio"*, ed. Vittorio Vettori (Milan: Marzorati, 1965), 217–49.

20. Among the threads that are tied is the one linking Dante's two key sins: *superbia* (the crucial sin in the private sphere) and *cupidigia* (the crucial sin in the public sphere) are both forms of *il trapassar del segno*. Hardie stipulates, I believe correctly, that the siren "should turn out to be complex and comprehensive": "She should

personify the whole range of seven [sins], just as the sin of Adam can be shown to include elements of the whole gamut from superbia to luxuria" ("*Purgatorio* XIX," 236–37).

21. See *Convivio* 4.12, and note the adjective *nuovo*, always part of Dante's discourse of desire: "Promettono le false traditrici sempre, in certo numero adunate, rendere lo raunatore pieno d'ogni appagamento; e con questa promissione conducono l'umana volontade in vizio d'avarizia. . . . Promettono le false traditrici, se bene si guarda, di torre ogni sete e ogni mancanza, e apportare ogni saziamento e bastanza; e questo fanno nel principio a ciascuno uomo, questa promissione in certa quantità di loro accrescimento affermando: e poi che quivi sono adunate, in loco di saziamento e di refrigerio danno e recano sete di casso febricante intollerabile; e in loco di bastanza recano *nuovo termine*, cioè maggiore quantitade a desiderio e, con questa, paura grande e sollicitudine sopra l'acquisto. Sì che veramente non quietano, ma più danno cura, la qual prima sanza loro non si avea" (4–5). Referring generically to "quanto la verace Scrittura divina chiama contra queste false meretrici" (8), Dante underlines the social ills caused by a desire that can never be satisfied, that is always new: "E che altro cotidiana pericola e uccide le cittadi, le contrade, le singulari persone, tanto quanto lo *nuovo raunamento* d'avere appo alcuno? Lo quale raunamento *nuovi desiderii* discuopre, a lo fine de li quali sanza ingiuria d'alcuno venire non si può" (9).

22. The *Convivio*'s *avaro maladetto* also figures in the fourth strophe of the canzone "Doglia mi reca," where Dante writes of a miser who follows a "dolorosa strada," and to whom the pursuit of gain will bring no peace (note the Ulyssean cast to the lexicon, e.g., "folle volere"):

Corre l'avaro, ma più fugge pace:
oh mente cieca, che non pò vedere
lo suo folle volere
che 'l numero, ch'ognora a passar bada,
che 'nfinito vaneggia.

The miser is cursed for having desired what can only be desired in vain, for having hungered without finding satisfaction, for having accomplished nothing:

dimmi, che hai tu fatto,
cieco avaro disfatto?
Rispondimi, se puoi, altro che "Nulla."
Maladetta tua culla,
che lusingò cotanti sonni invano;
maladetto lo tuo perduto pane,
che non si perde al cane:
ché da sera e da mane
hai raunato e stretto ad ambo mano
ciò che sì tosto si rifà lontano.

For the importance of this canzone in forecasting the moral basis of the *Commedia*, see my "Dante and the Lyric Past," *Cambridge Companion to Dante*, ed. Rachel Jacoff (Cambridge: Cambridge University Press, 1993).

23. On *Convivio* 3.15's assessment of the desire for knowledge, in comparison to that of St. Thomas, see Bruno Nardi, *Dal "Convivio" alla "Commedia": Sei saggi danteschi* (Rome: Istituto Storico per il Medio Evo, 1960), 66–75. In *La felicità mentale* (Turin: Einaudi, 1983), Maria Corti makes too much of the alleged theological orthodoxy of the treatise's fourth book in comparison to its predecessors, basing herself in part on the issue of the desire for knowledge. The distance between *Convivio* and *Commedia* on this topic remains much more striking than the distance between *Convivio* 3 and *Convivio* 4.

24. "I call 'charity' the motion of the soul toward the enjoyment of God for His own sake, and the enjoyment of one's self and of one's neighbor for the sake of God; but 'cupidity' is a motion of the soul toward the enjoyment of one's self, one's neighbor, or any corporal thing for the sake of something other than God" (*On Christian Doctrine* 3.10.16).

25. Anthony K. Cassell makes the point that the "*lupa* suggests something including, yet more encompassing than, the fully realized sin of *avaritia* or *cupiditas* in its extreme manifestations: the wolf represents the temptation of the sins of incontinence or concupiscence in the broadest sense" ("*Inferno*" *I*, Lectura Dantis Americana [Philadelphia: University of Pennsylvania Press, 1989], 68).

26. For this passage I have followed the edition of G. Busnelli and G. Vandelli (2d ed., rev. A. E. Quaglio, 2 vols. [Florence: Le Monnier, 1964]), in order to use their bracketed emendation. In his edition Cesare Vasoli comments that "Busnelli e Vandelli aggiungono [*e poscia errato*], richiamandosi al testo della canzone ('cui è scorto il cammino e poscia l'erra'). Ma l'aggiunta non sembra indispensabile" (598).

27. Despite the fact that men take different paths ("ché l'uno tiene uno cammino e l'altro un altro"), there is only one true path: "Sì come dice l'Apostolo: 'Molti corrono al palio, ma uno è quelli che 'l prende,' così questi umani appetiti per diversi calli dal principio se ne vanno, e uno solo calle è quello che noi mena a la nostra pace" (*Conv.* 4.22.6).

28. The theme of "occhi gulosi" is recalled in the pilgrim's own *occhi vaghi* of *Purg.* 10 ("ch'a mirare eran contenti / per veder novitadi ond'e' son vaghi" [103–4]), which echo an earlier passage where his *mente* is similarly *vaga*, desirous of new sights: "la mente mia, che prima era ristretta, / lo 'ntento rallargò, sì come vaga" (*Purg.* 3.12–14).

29. This is Charles Singleton's position in *Journey to Beatrice* (1958; rpt., Baltimore: Johns Hopkins University Press, 1977), 141–203; he mentions Ulysses as one who may have seen the stars (147) but does not elaborate.

30. Backward motion is forced upon the false prophets of *Inf.* 20; likewise the proud Christians addressed by the poet in the apostrophe of *Purg.* 10 have faith in their "retrosi passi" (123). Like flight on the wings of desire, therefore, backward motion can be coded positively or negatively. This double coding is typical of *Purgatorio* (where the poet frequently assigns a positive valence to what had seemed like an exclusively negative code): in the verses cited above, for instance, the "perduta strada" is in fact positive, the road that the traveler has lost and hopes to find, and partakes only contrastively of the negative "perduto" of *Inf.* 26.84.

31. The similes of *Purg.* 26.67–69 and *Par.* 31.31–36 are based on the same contrast between "humble" countryside and "expert" *urbs*.

32. The pilgrim's status as a legitimate non-Ulyssean *cosa nova* is underscored in

the next canto by Guido del Duca, for whom the grace accorded to Dante is a "cosa che non fu più mai" (14.15).

33. Dante uses a periphrasis for the sun's path to introduce Phaeton into the discourse, referring to "la strada / che mal non seppe carreggiar Fetòn" (*Purg.* 4.71–72).

34. The simoniac pope Nicholas III uses similar textual language when he expresses his wonder at the presumed early arrival of Boniface in hell: "Di parecchi anni mi mentì lo scritto" (*Inf.* 19.54).

35. The entries "presumere," "presuntuoso," "presunzione" in the *ED* by Francesco Vagni speak, corrrectly, of "una temerarietà di ordine intellettuale" but fail to elaborate in terms of Dante's longstanding concern with this problematic. In a *quaestio* entitled "De praesumptione," *ST* 2a2ae.21 (Blackfriars 1966, ed. and trans. W. J. Hill), Aquinas comments that presumption "occurs by turning towards God in ways that are inordinate, much as despair takes place by turning away from God" (33:103), and that the sinner suffers from a lack of moderation, "hoping to obtain pardon without repentance or glory without merits" (105). Noting the fine line between genuine hope and presumption ("'Presumption' is sometimes used to describe what really is hope, because genuine hope in God when looked at from the vantage point of the human situation almost seems like presumption" [107–9]), Aquinas concludes by making the connection between presumption and pride: "presumption appears to spring directly from pride; implying, in effect, that one thinks so much of himself that he imagines God will not punish him nor exclude him from eternal life in spite of his continuing in sin" (113). Augustine offers a Ulyssean description of presumption in the *Confessions*, commenting on "the difference between presumption and confession, between those who see the goal that they must reach, but cannot see the road by which they are to reach it, and those who see the road to that blessed country which is meant to be no mere vision but our home" (7.20).

36. In "Dante's Biblical Linguistics," *Lectura Dantis: A Forum for Dante Research and Interpretation* 5 (1989): 105–43, Zygmunt G. Barański notes that Dante rewrites Genesis in proposing that Eve was the first to speak and suggests that "the reference to Eve as the first speaker is a smokescreen . . . a pseudo-problem introduced to give a veneer of logical legitimation and the appearance of a valid philosophical *quaestio* to the ensuing discussion" (118). I would suggest, rather, that Eve is introduced as the epitome of *praesumptuositas*, Dante's overriding concern at this point in the treatise; indeed, for whom else could he so legitimately employ the redolent superlative, *presumptuosissima Eva*? I would add, moreover, that the issue of female speech is an obsessive one with Dante, who will end up reversing the silence of the lyric lady and the mis-speech of Eve with that most loquacious of literary ladies, the *Beatrix loquax* of Paradiso. Once more Dante's path is anomalous: the traditions he inherits boast female abstractions like Boethius's Filosofia who speak authoritatively, in a voice that is coded as non-gender-specific, i.e., masculine, and female nonabstractions who either do not speak or speak within the province of the gender-specific. In Beatrice Dante creates a historicized object of desire—not a personification—who yet speaks, indeed, in the *Paradiso*, speaks "like a man," unconstrained by the content or modality normatively assigned to female speech. In this ability to at least imaginatively reconcile the woman as a sexual and simultaneously intellectual presence, Dante was not followed by the humanists, who, in the accounts of recent

feminist scholarship, were not particularly generous to their female counterparts, according them a voice only at the price of their sexuality.

37. The *De vulgari eloquentia* stresses Nimrod's failure to respect the mimetic hierarchy, whereby human "art" follows nature, which in turn follows God (*Inf.* 11.99–105). Rather than be content with the position of human art at the bottom of the hierarchy, Nimrod seeks to make it surpass not only nature, but also God, thus lifting it to the top of the ladder.

38. See chapter 3, note 13 for this grouping. Joan M. Ferrante, in "A Poetics of Chaos and Harmony," *Cambridge Companion to Dante*, points out that *arte* is the most used noun "core rhyme" in the *Commedia* (core rhymes are "rhyme groups in which one of the rhyme words is contained within the other two as if it were their core"); suggestively enough, the last appearance of *arte* in the poem shortly follows the last reference to Phaeton in *Par.* 31.125. Also suggestive, from the point of view of Dante's "Ulyssean" art, is the fact that, according to Ferrante's data, the second most present noun core rhyme word is *ali*.

39. The adjective appears once, with reference to Provenzan Salvani, who was "presuntüoso / a recar Siena tutta a le sue mani" (*Purg.* 11.122–23), in a context redolent of poetic pride.

40. With respect to the false prophets, and Dante's perception of the fundamental similarity between their calling and his own, leading to the defensiveness that therefore dictates his handling of them, see my "True and False See-ers in *Inferno* XX," *Lectura Dantis: A Forum for Dante Research and Interpretation* 4 (1989): 42–54.

41. "Post hec veniamus ad Tuscos, qui propter amentiam suam infroniti titulum sibi vulgaris illustris arrogare videntur. Et in hoc non solum plebeia dementat intentio" (1.13.1).

42. Guittone d'Arezzo, because of the religious pretensions of his postconversion poetry became, for Dante, the example par excellence of the poet who goes beyond his limits, who "fishes for the truth and has not the art" (*Par.* 13.123); for Dante's views of Guittone, see *Dante's Poets*, 85–123.

43. "E oh stoltissime e vilissime bestiuole che a giusa d'uomo voi pascete, che presummete contra nostra fede parlare e volete sapere, filando e zappando, ciò che Iddio, che tanta provedenza hae ordinata! Maladetti siate voi, e la vostra presunzione, e chi a voi crede!" (*Conv.* 4.5.9). In the *Questio de aqua et terra* as well, Dante writes that certain questions "proceed either from much foolishness or from much presumption, because they are above our intellect" ("vel a multa stultitia vel a multa presumptione procedunt, propterea quod sunt supra intellectum nostrum" [75]), and that we must desist from trying to understand the things that are above us, and search only as far as we are able: "Desinant ergo, desinant homines querere que supra eos sunt, et querant usque quo possunt" (77). Also in the *Questio* Dante defines the habitable earth as extending from Cadiz, on the western boundaries marked by Hercules, to the Ganges ("a Gadibus, que supra terminos occidentales ab Hercule positos ponitur, usque ad hostia fluminis Ganges" [54]), thus evoking Ulysses both through the Herculean interdict of *Inf.* 26 and the mad flight beyond Cadiz of *Par.* 27. In the *Epistole*, the Florentines are cast as mad and presumptuous transgressors (Dante uses the very word "transgredientes" for those "who transgress divine and human laws" [*Ep.* 6.5]), puffing themselves up in their arrogant rebellion ("presumendo tumescunt" [*Ep.* 6.4 and passim]); by contrast, the poet is

endowed with a prophetic mind that does not err ("si presaga mens mea non fallitur" [*Ep.* 6.17]).

44. Other examples of this authorial concern are the passage in which Dante argues that it would be presumptuous to discuss ("presuntuoso sarebbe a ragionare") the limit that God put on our imaginations (*Conv.* 3.4.10), as it is also presumptuous to attempt to speak of Cato ("O sacratissimo petto di Catone, chi presummerà di te parlare?" [*Conv.* 4.5.16]). On questions of authority in the *Convivio*, see Albert Russell Ascoli, "The Vowels of Authority (Dante's *Convivio* IV.vi.3–4)," in *Discourses of Authority in Medieval and Renaissance Literature*, ed. Kevin Brownlee and Walter Stephens (Hanover, N.H.: University Press of New England, 1989), 23–46.

45. Sapegno's comment on "prescrisser" ("imposero un freno alla mia voglia di sapere") clarifies the passage's Ulyssean component, as does the consonance between "a tanto segno più mover li piedi" (*Par.* 21.99) and "il trapassar del segno." Daniello's gloss situates the *segno* toward which we are not to move within the context of the *trapassar del segno*: "*Prescrivere* propriamente significa assegnar termine ad alcuna cosa, il quale da essa non si possa trapassare" (quoted by Sapegno, *La Divina Commedia*, 3 vols. [Florence: La Nuova Italia, 1968], 3:267).

46. Dante frequently registers a high level of defensive anxiety in the vicinity of his critiques of the Church. Thus, in the Epistle to the Italian cardinals we find him defending himself from the charge of being infected with the presumption of Uzzah ("Oze presumptio" [*Ep.* 11.12]). For further discussion of Uzzah, see chapter 6.

47. Giuseppe Mazzotta notes the importance of the digression, reading it however as an index not of transgression but of alienation, as a sign that "a rupture exists between history and the text" (*Dante, Poet of the Desert* [Princeton, N.J.: Princeton University Press, 1979], 136).

48. Mark Musa notes that "the interruption that is part of the narrative (when Sordello prevents Virgil from finishing his sentence) is followed by an interruption of the narrative itself" and that Dante "has interpolated between the first and second stages of Sordello's embrace the longest auctorial intervention in the whole of the *Divine Comedy*, interrupting narrative time with auctorial time" (*Advent at the Gates: Dante's "Comedy"* [Bloomington: Indiana University Press, 1974], 97–98).

49. Marie is warned lest she find herself, after her death, in a worse flock than the one to which her treachery consigned Pierre de la Brosse; the brief "digression" is occasioned by the sight of Pierre among the group of souls who died violent deaths: "Pier da la Broccia dico; e qui proveggia, / mentr'è di qua, la donna di Brabante, / sì che però non sia di peggior greggia" (*Purg.* 6.22–24).

50. Both questions will be reprised in the heaven of justice, a heaven whose subtext is, to a great degree, the justice of Vergil's own damnation. See *Par.* 20.94–99, where the eagle will articulate the paradox of the dialectic between God's love and God's justice, already touched upon by Vergil in *Purg.* 6.

51. Sergio Corsi, "Per uno studio del 'modus digressivus,'" *Studi di italianistica: In onore di Giovanni Cecchetti*, ed. P. Cherchi and M. Picone (Ravenna: Longo, 1988), 75–89, argues that Dante conceived of the *modus digressivus* according to the wider canons of classical and medieval rhetoric (as encompassing formal shifts, like similes or descriptions of place and time), rather than in the more limited modern sense of major shifts in content. By contrast to the *Commedia*, the term *digressione* appears with some frequency in the *Convivio* (see the *ED* entry by Fernando Sal-

sano). For Dante's self-conscious use of metaphors of departing and returning with respect to the voyage of discourse, see chapter 2, note 1.

52. The anaphoric "Vieni a veder" (in lines 106, 112, 115; repeated four times if we count "Vien, crudel, vieni, e vedi la pressura" in 109) derives from the Apocalypse, where it is also repeated four times: "Veni, et vide" is the command that each of the four beasts issues to St. John (Apoc. 6:1, 3, 5, 7). Dante's presentation of himself as a prophetic truth-teller thus gains an implicit alignment of his text with the Book of Revelation; in fact, since Dante is the speaker, the analogy is between him and the four beasts on the one hand and between the negligent emperor and John as visionary witness on the other. More often, as we shall see in chapter 7, Dante is content to align himself with the author of the Apocalypse, whose four beasts figure prominently in the procession of the earthly paradise.

53. See Peter Armour, *The Door of Purgatory: A Study of Multiple Symbolism in Dante's "Purgatorio"* (Oxford: Clarendon, 1983), who points out that, because the episode of *Purg.* 9 "involves symbols and not personalities, [it] is one of the purest examples of polysemy in the *Comedy* and as such is one of the simplest episodes technically, if not conceptually" (144). One could propose an additional metapoetic polysemy with respect to the three steps leading up to purgatory's gate: each step could be taken to represent one of the *Commedia*'s canticles, associating *Inferno* with the self-knowledge of the mirroring step, *Purgatorio* with the penitential suffering of the cracked and burned step, and *Paradiso* with Christ's redemptive blood and flaming passion as reflected in the third step. This reading, whereby the poet has inscribed a reference to his poem into the canto's figural symbolism, would further support Armour's case for the importance of this passage vis-à-vis the *Commedia* as a whole.

CHAPTER 6
RE-PRESENTING WHAT GOD PRESENTED

1. The passage from the *De vulgari eloquentia*, quoted in full in the previous chapter, strikingly anticipates the apparent overturning of the mimetic hierarchy in *Purg.* 10. Nimrod is always connected, for Dante, with the pride inherent in human creativity, human "work": thus, the "gran lavoro" that figures with him on the terrace of pride (*Purg.* 12.34), the "ovra inconsummabile" linked to him by Adam (*Par.* 26.125).

2. The verb *trovare*, with its technical thrust as the Romance equivalent of *invenire*, informs a passage in the *Convivio* where Dante explicitly opposes men— "trovatori"—to God, "fattore": "però che di queste operazioni non fattori propriamente, ma li trovatori semo. Altri l'ordinò e fece maggior fattore" (4.9.6). The same opposition is found in *Purg.* 10, where men, *trovatori* by nature, are not able to "find" such art ("novello a noi perché qui non si trova"), and God is not a finder but a maker, a "fabbro" (99).

3. The theological approach is exemplified by Maria Simonelli, "Il canto X del *Purgatorio*," *Studi danteschi* 33 (1955–1956): 121–45. Recent critical attention has been fueled by our collective interest in metapoetic matters; the following selective bibliography testifies to the ongoing critical fascination elicited by these self-conscious cantos in our self-conscious times: Ferruccio Ulivi, "Dante e l'interpreta-

zione figurativa," *Convivium* 34 (1966): 269–92; Dante Isella, "Gli 'exempla' del canto X del *Purgatorio*," *Studi danteschi* 45 (1968): 147–56; H. Gmelin, "Il canto X del *Purgatorio*," in *Letture scelte sulla "Divina Commedia"*, ed. G. Getto (Florence: Sansoni, 1970), 619–28; Francesco Tateo, "Teologia e 'arte' nel canto X del *Purgatorio*," in *Questioni di poetica dantesca* (Bari: Adriatica, 1972), 139–71; Gloria K. Fiero, "Dante's Ledge of Pride: Literary Pictorialism and the Visual Arts," *Journal of European Studies* 5 (1975): 1–17; Giuseppe Mazzotta, *Dante, Poet of the Desert* (Princeton, N.J.: Princeton University Press, 1979), 237–52; Robert L. Montgomery, *The Reader's Eye: Studies in Didactic Literary Theory from Dante to Tasso* (Berkeley: University of California Press, 1979), 70–77; James Thomas Chiampi, "From Unlikeness to Writing: Dante's 'Visible Speech' in Canto Ten *Purgatorio*," *Mediaevalia* 8 (1982): 97–112; Page DuBois, *History, Rhetorical Description and the Epic* (Cambridge: D. S. Brewer, 1982), 58–68; P. Giannantonio, "I superbi (*Purgatorio*, X)," in *Endiadi* (Florence: Sansoni, 1983), 169–97; Nancy J. Vickers, "Seeing is Believing: Gregory, Trajan and Dante's Art," *Dante Studies* 101 (1983): 67–85; Teodolinda Barolini, *Dante's Poets: Textuality and Truth in the "Comedy"* (Princeton, N.J.: Princeton University Press, 1984), 274–78; Tobia R. Toscano, "Il canto X del *Purgatorio*," *Critica letteraria* 12 (1984): 419–39; Marilyn Migiel, "Between Art and Theology: Dante's Representation of Humility," *Stanford Italian Review* 5 (1985): 141–59; Carolynn Van Dyke, *The Fiction of Truth* (Ithaca, N.Y.: Cornell University Press, 1985), 229–46; Shirley Adams, "*Ut pictura poesis*: The Aesthetics of Motion in Pictorial Narrative and the *Divine Comedy*," *Stanford Italian Review* 7 (1987): 77–94; Karla Taylor, "From *superbo Ilïón* to *umile Italia*: The Acrostic of *Paradiso* 19," *Stanford Italian Review* 7 (1987): 47–65. Also interesting is the discussion of *Purg.* 10 in the context of Franciscan spirituality by Ronald Herzman, "Dante and Francis," *Franciscan Studies* 42 (1982): 96–114.

4. This is the opening sentence of Migiel, "Between Art and Theology."

5. For an example of the former tendency, see Van Dyke, *The Fiction of Truth*, whose reading is discussed in note 31 below; the idea that Dante corrects the terrace of pride in *Paradiso* is presented by Taylor, "From *superbo Ilïón*," whose argument is premised on the newfound authorial humility that Dante allegedly acquires in the third canticle.

6. For an analysis of the various sounds heard by the pilgrim as the gate opens, see Denise Heilbronn, "*Concentus Musicus*: The Creaking Hinges of Dante's Gate of Purgatory," *Rivista di studi italiani* 2 (1984): 1–15.

7. *De doctrina Christiana* 2.3.4: "et sunt haec omnia quasi quaedam verba visibilia" (*Patrologia Latina* 34: 37). DuBois notes that Dante's phrase *visibile parlare* "echoes Vergil's *non ennarrabile textum* of *Aeneid* VIII" (*History, Rhetorical Description and the Epic*, 62). The echo is suggestive, but more for the Dantesque reversal than for similarities in outlook: Vergil writes of the ineffable fabric of Aeneas's shield, a plastic reality that cannot be translated into language, while Dante refers to discourse that has achieved a plastic reality; Vergil addresses his inability to narrate, to describe what he sees, while Dante comments that such art is not seen on earth, not that he cannot describe it.

8. Isella notes the "nessi elementari" of the dialogue, suggesting that they help to create the scene's "illusorietà sensoriale" ("Gli 'exempla' del canto X," 156), while Vickers comments that the scene of Trajan and the widow "erases its own narrative

to leave us listening to a dialogue depicted by God, His 'visible speech'" ("Seeing is Believing," 69). In "Per un'analisi della struttura significante del dialogo nella *Divina Commedia*," *Letture classensi* 17 (1988): 9–21, Nicolò Mineo refers to the "poetica dell'animazione, oltre che dell'illusione" (11–12) epitomized by the above passage.

9. The reader is at this stage already struggling to keep a grip on reality; as Chiampi points out, in "From Unlikeness to Writing," the language of the canto's opening sequence confuses the reader both spatially, by making the mountain appear to move, and temporally, by indicating the time in a less than straightforward periphrasis. For the reading that holds that the mountain itself moves, see Giannantonio, "I superbi," 172–73.

10. Although the term "caryatids" is generally reserved for the draped female figures of classical architecture, discussions of *Purg.* 10 frequently appropriate the usage; see Valerio Mariani, *ED*, s.v.

11. With respect to these words spoken by the sinners, Toscano points out that "ancora un discorso immaginato chiude il canto del 'visibile parlare'" ("Il canto X," 439). Giovanni Fallani has drawn attention to the caryatids of Civita Castellana, one of which bears the inscription "Non possum quia crepo" (*Dante e la cultura figurativa medievale*, 2d ed. [Bergamo: Minerva Italica, 1976], 193–97).

12. *Storia* and *storiato* were employed in the Middle Ages for graphic representations with an extended or "narrative" dimension, and the term certainly conserves a textual orientation for Dante, who uses it as "narrazione" in the *Convivio* with respect to his own poetry and that of others; see Domenico Consoli, *ED*, s.v. Montgomery comments: "*Storie* is the correct word, for what Dante here describes are indeed 'speaking pictures,' capsule narratives" (*The Reader's Eye*, 70). The past participles "intagliato" in verses 38 and 55 and "storïata" in verse 73, which initiate each of the three scenes, are part of a series of past participles that bear the representational burden in *Purg.* 10 and 12: "intagliato" (10.38), "imaginata" (10.41), "imposta" (10.52), "intagliato" (10.55), "imaginato" (10.62), "effigïata" (10.67), "storïata" (10.73), "atteggiata" (10.78), "segnato" (12.18), "figurato" (12.23), "segnata" (12.38).

13. In "Gli esempi di superbia punita e il 'bello stile' di Dante," *Poesia e storia nella "Divina Commedia"* (Naples: Perrella, 1920), 233–52, E. G. Parodi defends the artifice of *Purg.* 12 on the basis of medieval delight in ornamentation. Although Parodi refers more than once to the *artificio* that informs the examples of pride, his references to Dante's artifice harbor no sense of its self-consciousness, as witnessed by the fact that Dante was the first to use the word *artificio* in the context of these exempla. Similarly, Carlo Delcorno calls the examples of pride "tra le più artificiose prove di bravura che Dante abbia tentato," defending the passage as an example of "gusto medievale" ("Dante e l'Exemplum' medievale," *Lettere italiane* 35 [1983]: 3–28; quotation, 15).

14. The acrostic of *Purg.* 12 was first noted by A. Medin in 1898 (see Lia Baldelli in the *ED*, s.v. "acrostico"; Delcorno cites Moore's contribution as well ["Dante e l'Exemplum' medievale," 17]). A more recent claim for an acrostic DIQ in *Purg.* 10.67–75, intended to stand for DIO in contrast to UOM in *Purg.* 12, is wholly unconvincing (Philip R. Berk, "Some Sibylline Verses in *Purgatorio* X and XII," *Dante Studies* 90 [1972]: 59–76). Equally farfetched is Richard Kay's claim to have discovered an acrostic system that works as a key to the sources of the entire

poem ("Dante's Acrostic Allegations: *Inferno* XI–XII," *Alighieri* 21 [1980]: 26–37). In fact, the arbitrariness with which these modern exegetes posit acrostics strikes one as the latest manifestation of the ancient art of perusing Dante's text less for its poetic than its cryptographic value. Whereas the alleged acrostics of Berk and Kay are based on the single appearance of the first letter of a tercet, in *Purg.* 12 we find words rather than letters and multiple rather than single appearances: four repetitions of the word "Vedea," four repetitions of the vocative particle "O," and four repetitions of "Mostrava." To posit an acrostic on the basis of single letters is to reduce the poet to a maker of crossword puzzles; for this reason, and because I see no substantial gain as far as the reading that would result, I also find unconvincing J. P. Th. Deroy's suggestion that the initials of the tercets that run from *Par.* 33.19–33 spell IOSEP, although the proposed word is per se more persuasive than DIQ ("Un acrostico nella preghiera di San Bernardo," in *Miscellanea dantesca* [Utrecht: Het Spectrum, 1965], 103–13).

15. Dante's sense of *mostrare* as linked to representation is illustrated by his statement, from the *Convivio*, that "le parole sono fatte per mostrare quello che non si sa" (1.2.7).

16. If we were to apply the three categories of pride that we find in canto 11— pride of family (Omberto Aldobrandesco), pride in art and self (Oderisi), and pride of power (Provenzan Salvani)—to the examples of canto 12, the "artistic" or vainglorious group would consist of the central tetratych: Niobe, Saul, Arachne, and Rehoboam. Arachne is such a compelling example of artistic hubris that her presence makes the scheme seem to work; although the others are not artists, Niobe's pride in her children is pride in artistry of sorts, and Saul's self-involvement is suggested by his death "in su la *propria* spada" (40). Also interesting in this regard is the textual lexicon ("segnata," "segno") that distinguishes this group.

17. The invective against the Christian princes in *Par.* 19 contains three tercets that begin with "Lì si vedrà," followed by three that begin with "Vedrassi," and three that begin with the conjunction "E" (115–41). This acrostic, which spells LUE, "plague," because the Christian princes are the plague of Christendom, was noted by F. Flamini in 1903 (see the *ED*, s.v. "acrostico") and, although generally accepted, has been accorded less favor than the acrostic of *Purg.* 12. Thus, Giovanni Reggio objects that this scheme is less symmetrical than that of the terrace of pride, since the invective continues beyond the acrostic, and rigid correspondence between tercet and exemplum is not maintained; he prefers to see the passage as demonstrating "l'artificio dell'anafora" (*La Divina Commedia*, ed. and comm. Umberto Bosco and Giovanni Reggio, 3 vols. [Florence: Le Monnier, 1979], 3:327–28). In my opinion the second acrostic, based like the first on the repetition of words rather than isolated letters, can stand; in this case too there is visual terminology ("Lì si vedrà" and "Vedrassi") that relates the acrostic to the pictorial and representational concerns of the heaven in which it is situated. While the findings of this chapter provide circumstantial evidence for the validity of both acrostics by linking the cantos that contain them (in a much repeated quote, Savi-Lopez gives as his reason for not accepting either acrostic the fact that they appear in such disparate contexts; see the *ED*), I do not endorse Karla Taylor's line of reasoning: beginning with a conclusion masked as a premise ("It seems proper to assume . . . that in a poem with two acrostics, they are related to one another" ["From *superbo Ilïón*," 49]), Taylor proceeds to add *I* and *M*

(the letters invoked by Dante to mark the good and evil deeds of Charles of Anjou in verses 128–29) to LUE, achieving LUEIM, an anagram for UMILE. A procedure with no textual basis is then supported by appealing to suspect hermeneutic principles: "The acrostic of *Purgatorio* 12 requires revision" (55); moreover, it requires an unintelligible revision, so that its unintelligibility can indicate Dante's conversion from prideful artist to the humility of an imperfect writer.

18. The other appearance of *rappresentare* occurs in *Par.* 4, in a passage discussed in chapter 8.

19. The representational concerns of this heaven have been noted by John Leavey, "Derrida and Dante: Differance and the Eagle in the Sphere of Jupiter," *MLN* 91 (1976): 60–68, and, more substantially, by John Ahern, who comments that "the Heaven of Jupiter is the most important single episode in an elaborate, self-referential strategy which unfolds in the *Comedy*'s last eighteen cantos" ("Dante's Last Word: The *Comedy* as a *liber coelestis*," *Dante Studies* 102 [1984]: 1–14; quotation, 9). DuBois considers the M formed by the souls in the heaven of the just "the paradisiacal equivalent of the *ekphraseis*" of the terrace of pride (*History, Rhetorical Description and the Epic*, 69).

20. For the suggestion that Trajan is the common denominator of the *Commedia*'s three instances of divine writing, identified as the inscription on the gate of Hell, the visible speech of the terrace of pride, and the script of the eagle in the sphere of Jupiter, see Robert Hollander, *Allegory in Dante's "Commedia"* (Princeton, N.J.: Princeton University Press, 1969), 297–300.

21. A related strategy may be found in the invective of *Paradiso* 19 where Dante insists that the corrupt princes whom he is condemning in his book will also be condemned in God's book, "quel volume aperto / nel qual si scrivon tutti suoi dispregi" (113–14), thus suggesting the interchangeability of the two books. Dante further reinforces the complicity of the two authors and their books by describing the sins of the European princes in bookish metaphors: a pen will move to record Albert's destruction of Bohemia (115–17); the good deeds of Charles II of Anjou will be marked with the letter *I*, signifying one, while his evil deeds will be marked with the letter *M*, signifying one thousand ("segnata con un i la sua bontate, / quando 'l contrario segnerà un emme [128–29]); the indictment against Frederic II will be registered in the book of justice with shortened, cut-off letters, in order to indicate his insignificance by writing much in a small space ("la sua scrittura fian lettere mozze, / che noteranno molto in parvo loco" [134–35]).

22. The alignment of Arachne with Phaeton, Icarus, and Ulysses was discussed in chapter 3. The examples of pride, headed by Lucifer, include another "Ulyssean" figure, namely Nimrod.

23. The self-conscious components of Arachne's tale have been much discussed by students of Ovid; see especially Eleanor Winsor Leach, "Ekphrasis and the Theme of Artistic Failure in Ovid's *Metamorphoses*," *Ramus* 3 (1974): 102–42, who comments that ecphrases "offer the artist an opportunity to speak in *propria persona* and to make us aware of the self-consciousness of his art through his attention to the fictional artistry of some other creator" (104). For further discussion of the Ovidian timbre of Dante's self-consciousness regarding the dangers of representation, see my "Arachne, Argus, and St. John: Transgressive Art in Dante and Ovid," *Mediaevalia* 13 (1989): 207–26.

24. Arachne's story is told in *Metamorphoses* 6.1–145; as Leach points out, it is one of a series of contests between human artists and gods that occur in books 5 and 6. The Latin text is from the Loeb Classical Library edition, trans. F. J. Miller, 2 vols. (1916; rpt., Cambridge: Harvard University Press; London: William Heinemann, 1971 [vol. 1] and 1968 [vol. 2]). Translations are mine.

25. In response to W. S. Anderson's suggestion that Ovid's own art is like Arachne's asymmetrical and "baroque" tapestry, as compared to Minerva's balanced and "classicistic" work, Leach comments that "it is not Arachne's tapestry alone, but the two scenes in combination that form a mirror of the *Metamorphoses*" ("Ekphrasis and the Theme of Artistic Failure," 117). For Anderson, see his review of Brooks Otis's *Ovid As an Epic Poet*, *American Journal of Philology* 89 (1968): 93–104. Ovid's identification with Arachne is sustained also by Leonard Barkan, *The Gods Made Flesh* (New Haven, Conn.: Yale University Press, 1986), 1–4.

26. For developments in the tradition, see John H. Turner, *The Myth of Icarus in Spanish Renaissance Poetry* (London: Tamesis, 1976), who notes that Dante is "the first to link the myths of Icarus and Phaeton, treated quite differently by classical poets" (24).

27. Dante's interest in crossing the boundaries between the animate and the inanimate goes back to *Vita Nuova* 25, where he discusses the propriety of having treated Love as an animate being, "come se fosse corpo" (2), and adduces as justification the behavior of classical poets, who "hanno parlato a le cose inanimate, sì come se avessero senso e ragione" (8). He gives an example from the *Aeneid*, in which "parla la cosa che non è animata a le cose animate" (9), an example from Lucan, in which "parla la cosa animata a la cosa inanimata" (9), an example from Horace, in which "parla l'uomo a la scienzia medesima sì come ad altra persona" (9), and an example from Ovid (which, interestingly, corresponds to his own case, the handling of Amor), in which "parla Amore, sì come se fosse persona umana" (9).

28. "Nec Oze presumptio quam obiectandam quis crederet, quasi temere prorumpentem me inficit sui tabe reatus; quia ille ad arcam, ego ad boves calcitrantes et per abvia distrahentes attendo" (*Ep.* 11.12).

29. See *Purg.* 13.136–38. One could make a case for canto 13 as a "backup" canto that works to reinforce the themes of the terrace of pride (whose paradigmatic function is underlined by the neat breakdown, exclusive to it, of narrative components by canto: examples of the virtue corresponding to the vice in canto 10, encounters with souls in canto 11, examples of the vice in canto 12). Thus, in addition to the confession of the pilgrim's own leaning toward pride, we find: the use of *segno* in 13.7 and 146; the reference to the pilgrim as a "cosa nuova" (13.145), echoing "Colui che mai non vide cosa nova"; the emphasis on the idea *nomina sunt consequentia rerum* in 13.109–10; and the presence of Sapìa who, with her "ardita faccia" (13.121), is a worthy aunt for the "presuntüoso" (11.122), Provenzan Salvani.

30. Boccaccio writes that Giotto succeeds in rendering objects such that they appear to be the thing itself, with the result that spectators are confused, believing the painting to be real: "[Giotto] ebbe uno ingegno di tanta eccellenzia, che niuna cosa dà la natura, madre di tutte le cose e operatrice col continuo girar de' cieli, che egli con lo stile e con la penna o col pennello non dipignesse sí simile a quella, che non simile, anzi piú tosto dessa paresse, in tanto che molte volte nelle cose da lui fatte si truova che il visivo senso degli uomini vi prese errore, quello credendo esser

312 NOTES TO CHAPTER 6

vero che era dipinto" (*Decameron* 6.5.5). Boccaccio seems to be following in the tradition established by Ovid in his description of Arachne's art in the *Metamorphoses*, as well as that established by Dante in *Purg.* 10–12.

31. Although Van Dyke notices that Oderisi "elegizes earthly fame even as he denounces it" (*The Fiction of Truth*, 236), she blames the miniaturist as an imperfect signifier of virtue, rather than positing the problem within the poet. Therefore, despite her sensitivity to the ambivalences in the passage, she ends up essentially admonishing us to stay within the framework prescribed by Dante: "Such manifestly poetic passages, resonant with Dante's own lyric voice and his own artistic concerns, always invoke a personal and aesthetic frame of reference that seems to override the allegorical one. But of course it does not. We cannot forget where this discussion of poetry occurs and what judgement has been rendered on the absolute devotion to art" (237).

32. The point that the text is grounded in reality is neatly underscored at the end of canto 11, where Oderisi tells the pilgrim that life itself will gloss his obscure words: "Più non dirò, e scuro so che parlo; / ma poco tempo andrà, che ' tuoi vicini / faranno sì che tu potrai chiosarlo" (139–41).

33. Far from embracing Dante, the avant-garde in the form of Giovanni del Virgilio respectfully reproved him for the use of the vernacular (and, in fact, the laurel crown was awarded not to Dante but to Albertino Mussato for his Latin tragedy *Ecerinis*). One could think of Dante as always already "postmodern," never merely avant-garde, remembering Contini's formulation: "L'impressione genuina del postero, incontrandosi in Dante, non è d'imbattersi in un tenace e ben conservato sopravvissuto, ma di raggiungere qualcuno arrivato prima di lui" ("Un'interpretazione di Dante," 1965; rpt. in *Un'idea di Dante* [Turin: Einaudi, 1970], 111).

34. For the value of history in these cantos, see Jeffrey T. Schnapp, *The Transfiguration of History at the Center of Dante's "Paradise"* (Princeton, N.J.: Princeton University Press, 1986). Schnapp sees in these cantos the blazon of Dante's "poetics of martyrdom," noting that "the martyr is the precise Christian equivalent to the Classical epic hero" (216). I have stressed, rather than Dante's repudiation of the classical epic mode, the surprising degree to which he retains it.

35. This feature of heaven, viewed as a place of reunion with our dear ones, is still immensely popular. A recent *Newsweek* Poll showed that 77 percent of Americans believe in a heaven, while Andrew Greeley reports that "Americans look forward to a heaven where they reunite with earthly relations" (*Newsweek*, March 27, 1989, p. 53). Nor is this feature lacking in theological currency: Augustine "cannot believe that the draught [of God's fountain] intoxicates [Nebridius] so that he forgets me" (*Conf.* 9.3; trans. R. S. Pine-Coffin [London: Penguin, 1961]). And, in his Letter to Italica, the bishop of Hippo consoles the widow: "We have not lost our dear ones who have departed from this life, but have merely sent them ahead of us, so we also shall depart and shall come to that life where they will be more than ever dear as they will be better known to us, and where we shall love them without fear of parting" (*PL* 33:318; trans. in Colleen McDannell and Bernhard Lang, *Heaven: A History* [New Haven, Conn.: Yale University Press, 1988], 60). Dante's "disio d'i corpi morti" is ripe for reevaluation in the light of recent historical work on the body in the Middle Ages (e.g., Caroline Walker Bynum, "Material Continuity, Personal Survival and the

Resurrection of the Body: A Scholastic Discussion in Its Medieval and Modern Contexts," *Fragmentation and Redemption: Essays on Gender and the Human Body in Medieval Religion* [New York: Zone Books, 1991], 239–97); see Rachel Jacoff's forthcoming study on the discourse of the body in the *Commedia*.

36. Raymond Adolph Prier discusses the catalogue style in Homer, linking it to ecphrasis, in *Thauma Idesthai: The Phenomenology of Sight and Appearance in Archaic Greek* (Tallahassee: Florida State University Press, 1989). Epic predilection for processions is treated in "Epic and Empire," *Comparative Literature* 41 (1989): 1–32, by David Quint; to my mind, however, Quint's analysis of the imperialist component of epic excessively downplays the genre's haunted consciousness of death.

37. For correspondences between *Inf.* 15 and the Cacciaguida cantos, see Schnapp, *The Transfiguration of History*, 199 and 236n.

38. Ahern notes that "God's message formed by the stars on the sky corresponds to the acrostic on the reader's page" ("Dante's Last Word," 9).

39. See "L'effimero e l'eterno: la meditazione elegiaca di *Purgatorio* XI," in *Studi su Dante* (Galatina: Congedo, 1984), 102.

40. Dante answers this question by saying that he is one of the least of the sheep of Christ's flock. The continuity between the Epistle and the *Commedia* thus includes the poet's self-identification first with one humble animal and then with another.

CHAPTER 7
NONFALSE ERRORS AND THE TRUE DREAMS OF THE EVANGELIST

1. *The Birth of Purgatory*, trans. Arthur Goldhammer (1981; Chicago: University of Chicago Press, 1984), 177. In fact, such visions predate Drythelm and postdate Charles the Fat; see Howard Rollin Patch, *The Other World* (1950; rpt., New York: Octagon Books, 1980), Carol Zaleski, *Otherworld Journeys: Accounts of Near-Death Experience in Medieval and Modern Times* (New York: Oxford University Press, 1987), Alison Morgan, *Dante and the Medieval Other World* (Cambridge: Cambridge University Press, 1990).

2. *Dante and Medieval Latin Traditions* (Cambridge: Cambridge University Press, 1986), 127.

3. See *Par.* 9.133–35: "Per questo l'Evangelio e i dottor magni / son derelitti, e solo ai Decretali / si studia, sì che pare a' lor vivagni." In the *Monarchia*, where Dante treats the Decretals less harshly, he nonetheless explicitly subordinates them to Scripture and to those inspired writers, like Augustine, who were aided by the Holy Spirit: "Sunt etiam Scripture doctorum, Augustini et aliorum, quos a Spiritu Sancto adiutos qui dubitat, fructos eorum vel omnino non vidit vel, si vidit, minime degustavit. Post Ecclesiam vero sunt traditiones quas 'decretales' dicunt: que quidem etsi auctoritate apostolica sunt venerande, fundamentali tamen Scripture postponendas esse dubitandum non est, cum Cristus sacerdotes obiurgaverit de contrario" (3.3.13–14).

4. As Cesare Segre puts it: "Dante non ci inganna e non si inganna: l'imponenza architettonica della sua 'visione' è frutto di lunghe, lucide veglie" ("L'Itinerarium animae nel Duecento e Dante," *Letture classensi* 13 [1984]: 9–32; quotation, 21).

5. *Otherworld Journeys*, 34. For a summary of the debate as to whether the visions' borrowings were conscious or unconscious, see Morgan, *Dante and the Medieval Other World*, 12.

6. Ignazio Baldelli connects Bernard's "perché 'l tempo fugge che t'assonna" to the beginning of the poem, by way of the saint's preceding reference to "Lucia, che mosse la tua donna / quando chinavi, a rovinar, le ciglia" (*Par.* 32.137–38): "Probabilmente le due terzine alludono all'inizio del 'sonno' di Dante (Lucia che manda Beatrice a Dante 'quando chinavi, a rovinar, le ciglia') e alla fine appunto dello stesso 'sonno' ('perché il tempo fugge che t'assonna'), cioè all'inizio e alla fine del sogno-visione" ("Visione, immaginazione e fantasia nella *Vita Nuova*," in *I sogni nel Medioevo*, ed. Tullio Gregory [Rome: Edizioni dell'Ateneo, 1985], 1–10; quotation, 9).

7. *Problemi di critica dantesca, Prima serie* (Florence: Sansoni, 1934), 294.

8. According to the *New Catholic Encyclopedia* (New York: McGraw-Hill, 1967), "Most modern scholars posit different authors for the Fourth Gospel and the Apocalypse" (1:654). Gian Roberto Sarolli, in the *ED*, does not acknowledge any uncertainty: "Fu ed è comunemente ritenuto autore del quarto *Vangelo*, delle tre *Epistole* che vanno sotto il suo nome, e dell'*Apocalisse*" (s.v. "Giovanni").

9. Barbi gives no reference for "quasi dormiens vigilaret," saying only that they are words of Augustine's with regard to Paul's *raptus*. One assumes that the citation comes from Book 12 of Augustine's *De genesi ad litteram*, which is dedicated to 2 Corinthians 12:2–4. The closest match that I find to Barbi's citation is in 12.5.14, where the clause "et non quasi dormiens evigilaret" belongs to a context full of references to ecstatic sleep but does not in itself mean what Barbi seems to take it to mean. Augustine has posed the question, "How is Paul certain about the vision seen but uncertain about the manner in which he saw it?" and suggests that Paul "could not tell whether he was in the body (as a man's soul is in his body but withdrawn from the bodily senses while he is awake or asleep or in ecstasy, though his body is said to be alive) or whether he actually went out of the body, so that his body would lie in death until, the vision over, his soul would be reunited with his dead members. In the latter case he would not awaken as if from sleep ["et non quasi dormiens evigilaret"] nor return to his senses as one coming from an ecstasy, but from death he would truly come to life again." (The Latin text is in *Patrologia Latina* 34:458; the translation is that of John Hammond Taylor, *The Literal Meaning of Genesis*, in *Ancient Christian Writers* [New York: Newman Press, 1982] 42:184–85.) Emilio Pasquini in the *ED*, s.v. "assonnare," picks up "quasi dormiens vigilaret" from Barbi but gives no reference; he does the same in "Le metafore della visione nella *Commedia*," referring to the "riscontri stabiliti dal Barbi col 'quasi dormiens vigilaret' di sant'Agostino" (*Letture classensi* 16 [1987]: 129–51; quotation, 147–48).

10. See Pasquini in the *ED*, s.v. "assonnare," and Sapegno, who quotes Barbi and—refreshingly—opts for the second, more mystical, interpretation of the verse, with the following caveat: "L'ultima interpretazione è senz'altro da preferire; ma è anche vero che sulla condizione mistica, in cui si svolge l'ultima fase del suo itinerario a Dio, Dante sorvola, qui come altrove, sì che l'accenno riesce alquanto oscuro e persino ambiguo" (*La Divina Commedia*, comm. Natalino Sapegno [Florence: La Nuova Italia, 1968], 3:409).

11. Giovanni Reggio draws back altogether from Barbi's suggestion regarding a mystical experience: "Forse è meglio, togliendo all'espressione ogni connotazione

mistica, dato che Dante non ha mai, specie in questi ultimi canti, sottolineato una sua condizione di tal genere, considerarla in puri termini linguistici" (*La Divina Commedia*, comm. Umberto Bosco and Giovanni Reggio [Florence: Le Monnier, 1979], 3:534).

12. Citations are from the commentary volumes of *The Divine Comedy*, trans. and comm. Charles S. Singleton, 6 vols. (Princeton, N.J.: Princeton University Press, 1970–1975).

13. "Visione, immaginazione e fantasia nella *Vita Nuova*," 9. Tibor Wlassics supports the minority opinion, writing that *sonno* "comprende *anche*, in primo luogo come sempre nella *Commedia*, il senso letterale" ("L'onirismo dell'*incipit*: appunti su *Inferno* I, 1–63," *Letture classensi* 18 [1989]: 31–39; quotation, 34). In more general terms, Allen Mandelbaum calls for a reconsideration of "what is, after all, a worthy macro-hypothesis: the *Commedia* itself as a massive dream vision—a venerable hypothesis fallen into disuse, a hypothesis that, in a century that begins with the publication of the *Traumdeutung*, may merit complex rehabilitation" ("'Ruminando e mirando': la capra di Dante," in *I linguaggi del sogno*, ed. V. Branca, C. Ossola, S. Resnik [Florence: Sansoni, 1984], 407–16; quotation, 407). While denying that the entire *Commedia* is a vision, Antonino Pagliaro notes the importance of conserving the literal meaning of the initial *sonno* ("Il proemio," in *Ulisse: Ricerche semantiche sulla "Divina Commedia"*, 2 vols. [Messina: G. D'Anna, 1967], 1:6).

14. In his *Saggio di un nuovo commento alla "Divina Commedia": "Inferno," Canti I–III* (Florence: Sansoni, 1967), Francesco Mazzoni notes that, with regard to the ancient commentators, "soltanto Guido da Pisa intese poi la terzina come unicamente letterale, in armonia con la sua interpretazione generale del poema come 'visio per somnium': 'Hic manifeste apparet *quod suas visiones in somno finxerit vidisse*, et sic confirmat dictum superius positum'" (56).

15. Neither Cassell, in his monograph on the poem's first canto, (*"Inferno" I*, Lectura Dantis Americana [Philadelphia: University of Pennsylvania Press, 1989], 3–4), nor Dino S. Cervigni, in his study of sleep and dreams in the *Commedia*, entertain any deviation from the Singletonian line. Cervigni states that "the Pilgrim's journey commences with a sleep which is to be interpreted metaphorically," and again that "this initial sleep needs to be interpreted metaphorically, within a biblical and patristic context" (*Dante's Poetry of Dreams* [Florence: Olschki, 1986], 10, 165).

16. *Thurkill's Vision* is dated 1206; *Tundale's Vision* 1149; and *The Monk of Evesham's Vision* (called Eynsham by Morgan), 1196. Quotations are from *Visions of Heaven and Hell before Dante*, ed. and trans. Eileen Gardiner (New York: Italica Press, 1989), 235, 150, 199.

17. The author of *Tundale's Vision* writes: "For he suffered the most incredible and intolerable kinds of tortures, the order of which is without name," going on to refer to him as "this man, who saw and suffered," i.e., who underwent both vision ("saw") and voyage ("suffered"); see *Visions of Heaven and Hell before Dante*, 150.

18. "Scelto il modello della visione, Dante si avvicina per qualche elemento al viaggio. . . . È sconosciuto alle visioni, e comune nei viaggi, l'impegno (variabile secondo i testi) nel fornire le coordinate geografiche e cronologiche. . . . Questa confluenza di visione e viaggio ha come centro la persona fisica di Dante, che infatti narra un viaggio che sarebbe stato compiuto corporeamente, come quelli dei viaggiatori, e a differenza dai visionari" (20–21). Alessandro D'Ancona classifies the *Comme-*

*dia* as belonging to "la forma della Visione" in *I precursori di Dante* (Florence: Sansoni, 1874), 100.

19. *Otherworld Journeys*, 90. Owen in *St. Patrick's Purgatory*, for instance, is congratulated for making his journey to the otherworld "soul and body, while you are still alive" (*Visions of Heaven and Hell before Dante*, 138). These are the very ambiguities probed by Augustine in the twelfth book of the *De genesi ad litteram*, a text Zaleski does not discuss. Moreover, as Nicolò Mineo points out, nothing prevents a visionary from having a vision of himself in the flesh: "sia in un sogno che in una visione può accadere che il soggetto veda se stesso compiere azioni e niente esclude che possa vedersi compiente azioni in corpo" (*Profetismo e apocalittica in Dante* [Catania: Università di Catania, 1968], 196). Mineo, however, does not adopt this position for himself, arguing rather that the *Commedia's* first canto is free of any element "che possa far pensare ad una visione in sogno o in estasi" (196); likewise, although he classifies Bernard's "t'assonna" as "un termine che può dirsi tecnico delle esperienze mistiche" (288), he denies that it refers to the voyage as a whole (289 n. 420).

20. See James D. Tabor, *Things Unutterable: Paul's Ascent to Paradise in Its Greco-Roman, Judaic, and Early Christian Contexts* (Lanham, Md.: University Press of America, 1986). Tabor surveys the heavenly journey in antiquity (a different set of otherworld journeys from that surveyed by Zaleski) and arrives at a significantly similar conclusion regarding the ambiguous status of the body: "In so many of the texts which report some kind of ascent, it is simply unclear whether the journey was thought to be in or out of the body" (121).

21. Tabor notes that "The early church fathers invariably treated the account as an objective, straightforward report of a highly privileged revelation given to Paul" (*Things Unutterable*, 1).

22. As Sarolli notes, Dante here translates Paul's "Deus scit" with his "tu 'l sai" ("La visione dantesca come visione paolina," in *Prolegomena alla "Divina Commedia"* [Florence: Olschki, 1971], 114). For other parallelisms between Dante's and Paul's descriptions of their visions, see Giuseppe Di Scipio, "Dante and St. Paul: The Blinding Light and Water," *Dante Studies* 98 (1980): 151–57; more generally, see Giorgio Petrocchi, "San Paolo in Dante," in *Dante e la Bibbia*, ed. Giovanni Barblan (Florence: Olschki, 1988), 235–48.

23. As Sapegno comments: "E non vuol esser dubbio, anzi attestazione solenne; come se dicesse: 'Dio lo sa che salivo veramente con tutto me stesso, e non con l'anima soltanto'" (3:10).

24. Joseph Anthony Mazzeo notes that "St. Augustine's account of the visions of Paul and Moses runs against the mainstream of theological and mystical speculation" ("Dante and the Pauline Modes of Vision," in *Structure and Thought in the "Paradiso"* [1958; rpt., New York: Greenwood, 1968], 197 n. 15); he reviews the theological controversy regarding Paul's vision, as well as the passages in which Dante aligns himself with the apostle. Roland Potter, ed. and trans. of the volume of the *ST* that contains "De raptu," reacts to Thomas's conclusion that "it is better to say that he [Paul] did see God in his essence" as follows: "The guarded conclusion is based on the authority of Augustine and on St Paul's own words as read by St Thomas. Scripture however does not compel us to believe that St Paul saw the divine essence. 'Third heaven,' 'paradise,' 'things that cannot be told' can all be understood of some profound mystical experience which yet falls far short of that vision of

heaven. . . . Modern theologians generally do not admit that Moses and St Paul saw the divine essence" (Blackfriars 1969, 45:104–5). In *ST* 1a.12.11, Thomas asks whether any man in this life can see God's essence; his reply, though basically negative, anticipates the exception of St. Paul, to be treated more fully later: "God can work miracles with minds as well as bodies, in either case raising them beyond the normal order of things to a supernatural level. Thus he may raise up certain minds to see his essence in this life but not by making use of their bodily senses. Augustine says that this is what happened to Moses, the teacher of the Jews and to St Paul, the teacher of the gentiles. We will deal with this more fully when we come to speak of ecstasy" (trans. Herbert McCabe, Blackfriars 1964, 3:39).

25. "St. Augustine's Three Visions and the Structure of the *Commedia*," *MLN* 82 (1967): 56–78. Newman, whose contribution has been central to the work of John Freccero and Marguerite Chiarenza, seems unaware of Murray Wright Bundy, who in 1927 made the same point: "No one has, however, pointed out the striking similarity of Dante's conception of vision and that of Augustine's *De genesi ad litteram*, and especially the correspondence of the three canticles of the poem to the three kinds of vision described in the tractate—'corporeal,' 'spiritual,' and 'intellectual'" ("Dante's Theory of Vision," *The Theory of Imagination in Classical and Mediaeval Thought* [Urbana: University of Illinois Press, 1927], 233).

26. More typical of Dante's procedure is what we find in the Epistle to Cangrande, where a medley of very different visionary texts are yoked together: Paul's *raptus*, the Gospel of Matthew on the disciples' vision of the transfigured Christ, Ezekiel, Richard of St. Victor's *De gratia contemplandi*, St. Bernard's *De consideratione*, St. Augustine's *De quantitate animae* (*Ep.* 13.79–80). According to Mazzeo, these authorities, all cited in the Epistle to buttress 2 Cor. 12:2–4, were not in agreement on the question of Paul's vision: while Augustine in the *De quantitate* "describes what could easily be read as a direct intuition of the divine essence and alludes to a number of people who have had, and are still having, such an experience . . . St. Bernard [was] absolutely certain that no man in this life, neither a man of wisdom, nor a saint, nor a prophet, can have that direct vision of God, which is the prerogative of the blessed, and still be in this mortal flesh" ("Dante and the Pauline Modes of Vision," 90). On the other hand, Steven Botterill has provided a contextual analysis of the Epistle's three biblical and three nonbiblical references in support of his contention that "all six references are linked by their concern with mystical experience, or rather their demonstration that such experience is even possible in this life"; see "'Quae non licet homini loqui': The Ineffability of Mystical Experience in *Paradiso* I and the *Epistle to Can Grande*," *Modern Language Review* 83 (1988): 332–41; quotation, 335. It is noteworthy in this regard that Dante represents Bernard as having tasted the beatific vision while alive: he is "colui che 'n questo mondo, / contemplando, gustò di quella pace" (*Par.* 31.110–11).

27. Thomas cuts through the complicated morass of Augustine's speculations by focusing on the question of Paul's uncertainty and cites from the chapter whose heading I have quoted above: "And Augustine writes, 'If the Apostle remained in doubt, who among us can have any certainty?' Those who propound an opinion on this subject speak more from conjecture than from certitude" (*ST*, Blackfriars 1969, 45:117). In *De genesi ad litteram* 12.3.8, Augustine writes "unde illo dubitante, quis nostrum certus esse audeat?" (*PL* 34:456; the heading is in column 455).

28. *Dante the Maker* (1980; New York: Crossroad, 1982), 15. The poet Andrea Zanzotto's view of poetic creation is very similar to Muir's: "Che è avvenuto dunque nel momento in cui si effettuava la 'produzione' di un testo poetico? Si è realizzata una specie di diplopico dormiveglia, per cui da una parte un soggetto procedeva progettando, dall'altra invece procedeva generando 'come in sogno,' mettendosi a disposizione di quell'allucinatorio 'dettato interiore' da sempre noto ai poeti" ("Una poesia, una visione onirica?," in *I linguaggi del sogno*, 501–9; quotation, 504). It is perhaps worth noting that Australian aborigines refer to their art works as "dreamings."

29. The theatricality of the exempla of *Purgatorio* reminds me of *Thurkill's Vision*, where the sinners are required to perform their sins for the devils in an infernal amphitheater—a *nuovo ludo* indeed! Franco Ferrucci notes that the dreams of purgatory are "una teatralizzazione interna di momenti visionari" ("Dal poema narrativo alla sacra rappresentazione," *Il poema del desiderio* [Milan: Leonardo, 1990], 202).

30. As Jacqueline Risset notes: "Ogni esempio deve essere decifrato al volo, nel passo stesso, nella continuità della scalata; in questo senso è—come ogni spettacolo della *Commedia—emblema*, ma è anche molto di più: è, in qualche modo, emblema dell'emblema" (*Dante scrittore* [1982; trans. Milan: Mondadori, 1984], 115–16).

31. Benvenuto Terracini connects *parere* to the mysticism of the *Vita Nuova*; see "La prosa poetica della *Vita Nuova*," *Analisi stilistica* (Milan: Feltrinelli, 1966), 209–49, esp. 219. Cervigni, *Dante's Poetry of Dreams*, discusses Dante's use of *parere* in the *Vita Nuova* and in the dreams of *Purgatorio*.

32. Gianfranco Contini, "Un sonetto di Dante," 1947; rpt. in *Un'idea di Dante* (Turin: Einaudi, 1976), 23–24.

33. Wlassics points to the repeated presence of *parere* in *Inf.* 1 as well as to its use by Ugolino ("L'onirismo dell'*incipit*," 34–35). His intriguing comparison of this episode to the film convention whereby "il regista metteva le scene 'viste in sogno' in una specie di cornice di nebbia" (34) incites me to a further comparison. Dante attains the status of "truth" for his (often fantastic) fiction by treating it with mimetic verisimilitude, a verisimilitude that is intentionally heightened by contrast to the "dreamlike" handling of the (less fantastic) events that befall the pilgrim in canto 1. In the same way, the television film made by the BBC of Paul Scott's *The Jewel in the Crown* moves from real black-and-white footage of India during World War II to the fictive narrative, filmed in color, i.e., treated with full mimetic verisimilitude according to the conventions of this genre; the opening newsreels serve to "garner reality" for the fictive events, which seem more "real" to the viewer than do the actual events recorded in black-and-white.

34. According to Thomas, even demons can at times prophesy truths: "Demonic prophets do not always speak from a demonic revelation, but sometimes by divine inspiration, as is clearly stated of Balaam, to whom it is said the Lord spoke, although he was a prophet of demons" (*ST*, Blackfriars 1969, 45:47).

35. The very syntax of the prophetic denunciation of *Inf.* 26, "If my dreams are true, then you will . . .," recalls the denunciation of Florence in the Epistle to the Florentines: "Et si presaga mens mea non fallitur, sic signis veridicis sicut inexpugnabilibus argumentis instructa prenuntians, urbem diutino merore confectam in manus alienorum tradi finaliter, plurima vestri parte seu nece seu captivitate deperdita, perpessuri exilium pauci cum fletu cernetis" (*Ep.* 6.17). For a resume of

thematic and stylistic characteristics typical of Hebrew prophecy, see Mineo, *Profetismo*, 73–75; for the impact of the prophets' pictorial images on Dante's visual imagination, see Anderson, *Dante the Maker*, 299.

36. The Bible's "there appeared a chariot of fire, and horses of fire . . . and Elijah went up by a whirlwind into heaven" (2 Kings 2:11) is recalled in Dante's reference to " 'l carro d'Elia al dipartire, / quando i cavalli al cielo erti levorsi" (*Inf.* 26.35–36).

37. *Rapire* appears five times in the *Commedia*, twice in the context of the dream of the eagle, whose Pauline connotations are reinforced by the poem's only use of the participial form *ratto*, analogous to Latin *raptus* (*Purg.* 9.24). Cervigni comments that "the similarities of the terms employed in describing the two experiences [Paul's and Dante's] can hardly be overlooked. Paul was kidnapped ('raptum' and 'raptus'); Dante's assumption is also likened to a mythological abduction ('Ganimede . . . ratto al sommo consistoro') and the seer dreamed that the eagle *kidnapped* him ('e me rapisse')" (*Dante's Poetry of Dreams*, 106). The noun *estasi* is never used by Dante, the adjectival form only in *Purg.* 15.86.

38. St. Thomas notes the possibility of confusing divine possession with madness or drunkenness: people might make the mistake of looking upon "speakers with tongues as mad—just as the Jews thought that the Apostles speaking with tongues were drunk" (*ST* 2a2ae.176.2; Blackfriars 1969, 45:125). Jacopone da Todi, a true mystic, uses drunkenness to describe Christ's rapture of love:

> Como ebrio per lo mondo spesso andavi,
> menàvate l'Amor com' om venduto;
> en tutte cose Amor sempre mustravi,
> de te quasi neiente perceputo,
> ché, stando ne lo templo, sì gridavi:
> "A bbever vegna chi à sustinuto,
> sete d'amor à 'uto,    che lli sirà donato
> Amor esmesurato,    qual pasce cun dolzore."
>
> ("Amor de caritate," 203–10)

39. The pilgrim's experience of an inner ecstasy, the fruit of a mind that is gathered within itself, "ristretta / dentro da sé," recalls Augustine's discovery of God within himself in *Confessions* 7.10: "Under your guidance I entered into the depths of my soul, and this I was able to do because your aid befriended me. I entered, and with the eye of my soul, such as it was, I saw the Light that never changes casting its rays over the same eye of my soul, over my mind" (trans. R. S. Pine-Coffin [London: Penguin, 1961], 146). On the importance of this passage, see Ewert H. Cousins, " 'Intravi in intima mea': Augustine and Neoplatonism," *Archivio di filosofia* 51 (1983): 281–92.

40. The use of language like "sensato" in the above citation echoes that most Aristotelian of medieval lyric texts, namely Cavalcanti's "Donna me prega." *Par.* 4 elaborates Vergil's discourse of *Purg.* 18, where he explains that our faculty of apprehension derives images from true beings, objective existences: "Vostra apprensiva da esser verace / tragge intenzione" (*Purg.* 18.22–23). In the *Convivio* Dante notes that the human intellect is limited by its dependence on *fantasia* and on sense perception: "dico che nostro intelletto, per difetto de la virtù da la quale trae quello ch'el vede, che è virtù organica, cioè la fantasia, non puote a certe cose salire (però che la

fantasia non puote aiutare, ché non ha lo di che), sì come sono le sustanze partite da materia" (3.4.9). Robert L. Montgomery discusses Dante's use of the terminology of Aristotelian faculty psychology in *The Reader's Eye: Studies in Didactic Literary Theory from Dante to Tasso* (Berkeley: University of California Press, 1979); counter to Murray Wright Bundy's stress on the Platonism of Dante's theory of the imagination, Montgomery emphasizes instead the "persistent materiality of the *Commedia*" (84).

41. "Rapture adds something to ecstasy. For ecstasy implies simply 'standing outside oneself' as when a person is placed outside his usual disposition. But rapture ('being caught up') adds a note of violence to this" (*ST* 2a2ae 175.2; Blackfriars 1969, 45:101).

42. Textually as well, there are anticipations of the end of the poem in these passages: in *Purg.* 15.127 we find the only occurrence of "larve" prior to *Par.* 30.91; verses 25 and 54 from *Purg.* 17, "Poi piovve dentro a l'alta fantasia" and "così la mia virtù quivi mancava," recombine to form *Par.* 33's "A l'alta fantasia qui mancò possa" (142).

43. "Scripts for the Pageant: Dante and the Bible," *Stanford Literature Review* 5 (1988): 75–92; quotation, 81.

44. The disciples' vision is featured in the Epistle to Cangrande, where it is offered as the first exemplary gloss to Pauline *raptus*, as an example of the condition in which the intellect, after transcending human reason, does not remember what happened outside of it: "Ecce, postquam humanam rationem intellectus ascensione transierat, quid extra se ageretur non recordabatur" (*Ep.* 13.79). Matthew's account is specifically mentioned: "Et hoc est insinuatum nobis in Matheo, ubi tres discipuli ceciderunt in faciem suam, nichil postea recitantes, quasi obliti" (*Ep.* 13.80). There is also a reference to the transfiguration in *Monarchia* 3.9.11.

45. The slight negative connotation to sleep in the image of the veil will be retrieved and elaborated by Beatrice in *Purg.* 33, where twice she characterizes sleep and dreams as sources of human confusion: the pilgrim is to stop speaking "com'om che sogna" (33); his wit is sleeping ("Dorme lo 'ngegno tuo" [64]) if it fails to understand the significance of the inverted tree. I would explain these apparently contradictory usages in terms of the basic paradigm "ver c'ha faccia di menzogna": the nonfalse error that is the *Commedia* is not without its Geryonesque component of *menzogna*, alluded to in *Purg.* 32's *fingere* ("ma qual vuol sia che l'assonnar ben finga"). Beatrice's harsh remarks may be rooted in her awareness of the necessary *fingere* in all discourse, all "dreaming."

46. Compare "Quando l'anima mia tornò di fori" from *Purg.* 15.115 to the simile's double use of *tornare*: the apostles "return" ("ritornaro a la parola"), as does the pilgrim ("tal torna' io"). Cervigni, who reads Dante's sleep in *Purg.* 32 as analogous to Adam's, notes Augustine's gloss of Adam's sleep as not *sopor* but *ecstasis*, and concludes: "Like Adam, Dante also, the new Adam, is infused with a sleep which is tantamount to an ecstasis" (*Dante's Poetry of Dreams*, 179).

47. The connection between apocalyptic vision and the transfiguration was made as early as *St. Peter's Apocalypse*, a mid-second-century "account of Peter's vision of the apocalypse at the time of the Transfiguration of Christ before the Apostles. In addition to seeing Jesus and Moses and Elias in their heavenly glory, Peter and the disciples see a vision of the otherworld" (Gardiner, ed., *Visions of Heaven and Hell*

*before Dante*, 237). In *De genesi ad litteram* 12.2.5, Augustine offers Peter, John, Ezekiel and Isaiah as visionary counterparts to Paul: "Hence, if Paul saw Paradise as Peter saw the dish sent from heaven; as John, what he described in the Apocalypse; as Ezekiel, the plain with the bones of the dead and their resurrection; as Isaiah, God seated and before Him the seraphim and the altar from which the live coal was taken to cleanse the lips of the prophet; it is obvious that he could have been unable to determine whether he saw Paradise in the body or out of the body" (trans. John Hammond Taylor, 17–18). In *City of God* 22.29, Augustine brings together as visionaries Paul, John, and Elisha.

48. On Dante and the Apocalypse, see Peter Dronke, *Dante and Medieval Latin Traditions*, chapter 3; Eugenio Corsini, "A proposito dei rapporti di Dante con l'*Apocalisse*," *Letture classensi* 8 (1979): 77–84; Sergio Cristaldi, "Dalle beatitudini all'*Apocalisse*: il Nuovo Testamento nella *Commedia*," *Letture classensi* 17 (1988): 23–67); Peter Armour, *Dante's Griffin and the History of the World* (Oxford: Clarendon, 1989), chapter 7.

49. Dante textually underscores his view of the earthly paradise as both Alpha and Omega: canto 30, which contains *novissimo* ("novissimo bando" [13]) also registers three uses of *antico*, a frequency matched only by *Par.* 16's evocation of ancient Florence. Moreover, these "last" cantos constitute a newest "new beginning," marked in canto 28 by the *selva antica*'s echoing of the *selva oscura*. In a spiraling text, each ending is a beginning, and each beginning an ending; never is this clearer than with respect to the major new beginning marked by *Purg.* 28 and already initiated in *Purg.* 27 (where the backward glances woven into the textual fabric are at least as strong; see Zygmunt G. Barański, "Structural Retrospection in Dante's Comedy: The Case of *Purgatorio* XXVII," *Italian Studies* 41 [1986]: 1–23).

50. Carlo Ossola notes Dante's daring attempt to "raggiungere nello spazio dell'origine il tempo della fine (l'Apocalisse nel Paradiso terrestre)"; see "'Coi piè ristetti e con li occhi passai': Sospensione e compimento del tempo nel *Purgatorio*," in *L'arte dell'interpretare: Studi critici offerti a Giovanni Getto* (Cuneo: L'Arciere, 1984), 45–66; quotation, 50.

51. The writerly self-consciousness of later visionaries frequently takes the form of invoking John, precisely as in *Purg.* 29. Giacomino da Verona mentions the beauties spoken of by "san Çuano . . . entro l'Apocalipso" (*De Ierusalem celesti*, 32). The *Pearl* poet repeatedly refers us to John: "In Apocalypse it may all be read / As he set it forth, the apostle John"; "As John the apostle saw it of old / I saw the city beyond the stream . . . As he beheld it in sacred dream / In Apocalypse, the apostle John"; "As John had named them in writ divine / Each stone in order by name I knew" (17.1, 2, 3, trans. Marie Borroff [New York: Norton, 1977]).

52. Mineo discusses the presence of the Apocalypse in the last cantos of *Purgatorio*, drawing attention to the pilgrim's prophetic investiture by Beatrice, the "obbligo di *denuntiatio*" (*Profetismo*, 254). The requirement to recount what has been seen is common to medieval visions as well: in St. Paul's *Apocalypse*, the angel says, "I will show you what you must describe and tell openly" (*Visions of Heaven and Hell before Dante*, 28). Wetti is reluctant to reveal what he has learned and is scolded by his angel guide, "What God wishes and commands you to do, through me, do not dare put off" (75); he tells his fellow monks that "I was commanded with so much obligation to declare this in public that I am afraid I will be condemned without

322 NOTES TO CHAPTER 7

pardon if I am struck silent and cannot reveal what I saw and heard" (78). Thurkill requires a second vision to remind him to reveal his first: "In his great simplicity, however, he hesitated to relate his vision, until on the following night St. Julian appeared to him and gave him orders to reveal everything that he had seen, because he said he had been taken from his body for the purpose of making public all he had heard" (235). The author further notes that "he related his vision plainly and openly in English," reminding us of the importance in this regard of Dante's choice of Italian.

53. Ossola notes that Beatrice's authorization, with its emphasis on exact transcription ("e sì come . . . così"), "sembra non porre diaframma tra la natura del dettato e le possibilità dello scriba" ("'Coi piè ristetti,'" 66 n. 42). Perhaps her strict instructions betray her awareness of the power of narrative to transform "reality" in the telling; she uses the word "narrazion"—a hapax—to refer to her own discourse, putting the poet in the position of narrating her narration. Canto 33's lexicon is saturated with metapoetic terminology: besides the poem's only use of narrazione and one of seven uses of narrare, it is one of few cantos in which segnare is used twice, and the only canto in Inferno or Purgatorio in which scrivere occurs more than once (thrice).

54. Although Dante does not, like the prophet, threaten interpolaters with divine retribution, he does invent a rhyme scheme that, as J. S. P. Tatlock points out, guards his text against interpolation by copyists (see "Dante's Terza Rima," PMLA 51 [1936]: 895–903).

55. Shirley Adams discusses this passage in the context of medieval painting and its treatment of moments of transition; see "Ut pictura poesis: The Aesthetics of Motion in Pictorial Narrative and the Divine Comedy," Stanford Italian Review 7 (1987): 77–94.

56. "Transfiguring the Text: Ovid, Scripture and the Dynamics of Allusion," Stanford Italian Review 5 (1985): 115–39; quotation, 127. For Hawkins, Dante's interest in representing his own falling asleep is "a pointless (one might even saw sterile) preoccupation" (126). For a fuller discussion of Dante's use of Ovid in this passage, see my "Arachne, Argus, and St. John: Transgressive Art in Ovid and Dante," Mediaevalia 13 (1989): 207–26.

57. Guido da Pisa interprets the "mezzo del cammin" as signifying sleep, so that the poem's first verse means "While asleep I found myself . . ."; his authority is Aristotle: "Medium namque vite humane, secundum Aristotilem, somnus est" (Expositiones et glose super "Comediam" Dantis, ed. Vincenzo Cioffari [Albany: State University of New York Press, 1974], 10). Pagliaro comments: "In effetti, Aristotele nel De generatione animalium afferma che il sonno è territorio intermedio fra il vivere e il non vivere, e altrove accenna che il sonno nell'uomo prende la metà della vita" ("Il proemio," 4).

58. Sapegno makes the connection between "mi richinava come l'uom ch'assonna" and the terrace of wrath, as well as with the dream state the pilgrim enters at the end of Purg. 18, and St. Bernard's use of assonnare: "La similitudine dell'uomo assonnato, che a taluno è parsa inopportuna, può esser meglio intesa, se la riaccostiamo a due luoghi del Purg., 15.118–23 e 18.87 e 144–45, nel primo dei quali la sonnolenza rappresenta l'uomo rapito fuori dei sensi e nel secondo prelude a una visione profetica; in Par. 32.139, lo stesso vocabolo assonna esprime probabilmente una condizione di astrazione e di estasi" (La Divina Commedia 3:85). Giovanni Reg-

gio's negative reaction to this reading in the Bosco-Reggio commentary, which notes "ma qui si parla di *reverenza* (v. 13) non di rapimento estatico" (*La Divina Commedia* 3:104), is typical of the antimystical current in Dante studies.

59. Interestingly, "letargo" rhymes with "Argo," the only other "Argo" in the poem (which in this case is not the monster but Jason's ship, also supplied by Ovid), suggesting that the later *letargo* is intended to recall the swoon of *Purg.* 32.

60. Benvenuto comments: "*m'è maggior letargo*, idest maior infirmitas memorie; est enim 'letargum,' ut tradunt Hippocras, Galienus, Avicenna et alii physici, oppressio cerebri cum oblivione et continuo somno, quasi dicat: 'plus me sopit et smemorat'" (Guido Biagi, ed., "*La Divina Commedia*" *nella figurazione artistica e nel secolare commento*, 3 vols. [Turin: Unione Tipografico-Editrice Torinese, 1924–1929], 3:742).

61. Le Goff, *The Birth of Purgatory*, notes that Latin Christendom "had difficulty deciding whether Purgatory should be made more like Hell or more like Heaven" (205), and that Bonaventure "places Purgatory nearer to Paradise than to Hell, at least to the extent that the guides to both of these realms, as Dante would call them, are good angels" (252). There is no doubt that for Dante purgatory is—theologically—closer to paradise; those in hell are on the other side of the great divide cited by Cato regarding his wife, "che di là dal mal fiume dimora" (*Purg.* 1.88). Indeed, much of *Purg.* 1 is devoted to establishing the unbridgeable gulf that separates the two realms. I cannot therefore concur with Le Goff's assessment that Dante "clearly saw [Purgatory] as a Hell of limited duration" (341), except within the limited context of the punishments suffered eternally in one case and temporally in the other.

62. For the staged dimensions of this event, see my "Q: Does Dante Hope for Vergil's Salvation? A: Why Do We Care? For the Very Reason We Should Not Ask the Question," *MLN* 105 (1990): 138–44. For symmetries and specularities in cantos 28–33, viewed as a "macrosequence," see Bruno Porcelli, "Progressione e simmetria nella sequenza di *Purg.* XXVIII–XXXIII," *Studi e problemi di critica testuale* 35 (1987): 141–55.

63. Ruggero Stefanini points out the synchrony between the first dream and that which it interprets, as compared to the diachrony that prevails in the second and third dreams, which preannounce what has not yet occurred. Even in the first dream, he notes, the conceptual synchrony is countermanded by narrative reality: "Anche nel 9 canto, comunque, la sincronia dei due interventi (quello reale di Lucia e quello figurato dell'aquila, che ne è il riflesso e il chiarimento onirico) viene necessariamente a rompersi per le imprescindibili esigenze della progressione diegetica, cosicché, a livello testuale, l'aquila finisce per precedere Lucia proprio come, più mimeticamente nei confronti del *narratum*, la strega-sirena precede la descrizione delle ultime tre cornici e Lia viene prima di Matelda" ("I tre sogni del *Purgatorio*: struttura e allegoria," in *Studies in the Italian Renaissance: Essays in Memory of Arnolfo B. Ferruolo*, ed. G. P. Biasin, A. N. Mancini, N. J. Perella [Naples: Società Editrice Napoletana, 1985], 43–66; quotation, 46). I would suggest that the necessary diachrony of narrative is exploited by Dante in canto 9 in order to offer, with two accounts of the same event, an implicit commentary on two discrete modes of narration.

64. The truths told by the "erronea fantasia" are manifest as early as *Vita Nuova* 23, where Dante insists on "lo errare che fece la mia fantasia" as he is visited by a vision of Beatrice's death: the "errors" he imagines will shortly be proved true. The

chapter provides another link to the visionary tradition in its treatment of the body/ soul nexus. As Thurkill's lifeless body coughed on earth at the same time as his spirit in the afterlife, so Dante wept not only in the *imaginazione* but in reality: "e non solamente piangea ne la imaginazione, ma piangea con li occhi, bagnandoli di vere lagrime" (23.6).

## CHAPTER 8
## PROBLEMS IN PARADISE

1. *Time and Narrative* (1983; trans. Chicago: University of Chicago Press, 1984), 30. Jacqueline Risset notes the modernity of *Paradiso* in *Dante scrittore* (1982; trans. Milan: Mondadori, 1984), 141–42.

2. The translation of the *Physics* by R. P. Hardie and R. K. Gaye is from *The Basic Works of Aristotle*, ed. Richard McKeon (New York: Random House, 1941). See also: "It is clear, then, that time is 'number of movement in respect of the before and after,' and is continuous since it is an attribute of what is continuous" (4.11.220a24–26). The Latin for the first passage is "hoc enim est tempus, numerus motus secundum prius et posterius" (cited by Enrico Berti, *ED*, s.v. "Fisica"); for the second, "Quod quidem igitur tempus numerus motus secundum prius et posterius sit, et continuum (continui namque), manifestum est" (cited by Cesare Vasoli, in his edition of the *Convivio*, 535).

3. The Latin text is cited by Cesare Vasoli, *ED*, s.v. "tempo."

4. *Confessions* 9.10 in the translation by R. S. Pine-Coffin (London: Penguin, 1961). The Latin is from the Loeb Classical Library edition, 2 vols. (Cambridge: Harvard University Press; London: Heinemann, 1979).

5. *Confessions* 12.7 in the 1631 translation of William Watts, from the Loeb edition.

6. The Latin text of the the *Consolation of Philosophy* is cited in the Loeb Classical Library edition, ed. H. F. Stewart and E. K. Rand (Cambridge: Harvard University Press; London: Heinemann, 1936). The following discussion is based on book 5, prose 6.

7. Blackfriars 1964, 2:144; ed. and trans. Timothy McDermott. *Quaestio* 10 treats the eternity of God, "De aeternitate Dei." In it Thomas defends and confirms Boethius's definition of eternity from *Consolation of Philosophy* 5.6. His Aristotelian allegiance, on the other hand, is demonstrated by his discussion of time; in the course of his argument, he notes that we can only come to know eternity by way of time, which "nihil aliud est quam *numerus motus secundum prius et posterius*" (136).

8. "Saint Augustine: Language as Temporality," in *Mervelous Signals: Poetics and Sign Theory in the Middle Ages* (Lincoln: University of Nebraska Press, 1986), 34–50; quotation, 42–43. For a more positive assessment of Augustine's views with respect to the limits and powers of language, stressing the saint's belief in a "redeemed rhetoric," see Marcia Colish, *The Mirror of Language: A Study in the Medieval Theory of Knowledge* (1968; rev. ed., Lincoln: University of Nebraska Press, 1983), chapter 1.

9. *The Myth of the Golden Age in the Renaissance* (Bloomington: Indiana University Press, 1969), appendix A, "Paradises, Heavenly and Earthly," 169.

10. *Otherworld Journeys: Accounts of Near-Death Experience in Medieval and*

NOTES TO CHAPTER 8   325

*Modern Times* (New York: Oxford University Press, 1987), 93; the quote in the preceding paragraph is from page 58.

11. At 752 lines, Bonvesin de la Riva's treatment of the twelve glories of paradise in the *De scriptura aurea* is almost as long as his treatment of the twelve punishments of hell in the *De scriptura nigra*, which runs to 908 lines. However, Bonvesin describes heaven in great part by contrasting its joys to the earthly and infernal torments from which the blessed are exempt, concluding his paradise in typical fashion: "Dear God, what a dolt, madman, and fool he is who loses such treasure by begging off! How valiant and wise he is, what a paragon he is who acquires such a great possession by well-doing!" (*Volgari scelti*, trans. Patrick S. Diehl and Ruggero Stefanini [New York: Peter Lang, 1987], 202).

12. It seems worth noting that two of the thinkers whose physics and metaphysics Dante most absorbs, Aristotle and Augustine, are still not entirely eclipsed by today's physics (which has come to include metaphysics); both are cited by Stephen W. Hawking in *A Brief History of Time* (New York: Bantam, 1988). Hawking concludes his book by openly addressing the metaphysical concerns that have devolved onto physicists, given that "the people whose business it is to ask *why*, the philosophers, have not been able to keep up with the advance of scientific theories" (174). Hawking's last words—how can one *not* think of Dante?—are "for then we will know the mind of God." Also intriguing from this perspective is Mark A. Peterson's suggestion that Dante anticipates an Einsteinian cosmology; see "Dante and the 3-Sphere," *American Journal of Physics* 47, n. 12 (Dec. 1979): 1031–35.

13. In *Heaven: A History* (New Haven, Conn.: Yale University Press, 1988), 70–80, Colleen McDannell and Bernhard Lang offer a resume of medieval heavens, emphasizing the shift from the "paradise garden," derived from Genesis, to the "heavenly city," derived from the Book of Revelation. The texts in *Visions of Heaven and Hell before Dante*, ed. and trans. Eileen Gardiner (New York: Italica Press, 1989), demonstrate a mixture of natural and urban elements. *Tundale's Vision* (1149) combines the features of the *locus amoenus* with more "urban" delights: walls of silver, gold, and precious gems, bejeweled thrones enveloped in silk, many-colored silk pavilions. The monk of Evesham (1196) proceeds from a plain with fragrant flowers to a wall of crystal and steps leading to a throne of glory. In *Thurkill's Vision* (1206) paradise is a church containing a beautiful garden. Giacomino da Verona (13th c.) bases his vision of paradise as a heavenly Jerusalem in *De Ierusalem celesti* on the Apocalypse, as does the author of the Middle English *Pearl* (late 14th c.), while Bonvesin de la Riva's celestial city owes much to Giacomino.

14. At the end of *Tundale's Vision*, we find the following attempt to despatialize and detemporalize paradise, i.e., to create a sense of the *totum simul*: "Therefore from the place in which they now stood, they saw not only all the glory that they saw before but even the pain of the punished whom we spoke of above. Finally—which greatly amazes us—they were able to see the orb of the earth as if under one beam of the sun. For not anyone could weaken the sight, once it is given by the creator, to see all of creation. In a wonderful way, while they were standing in the same place in which they had been standing before, not turning themselves around, they still saw everything both in front of and behind them" (*Visions of Heaven and Hell*, 192).

15. Noting that "the fire of hell is called eternal only because it is unending," Thomas continues: "But the pains of hell include change, for we read in *Job* that *they*

*shall pass from waters of snow to excessive heat.* In hell then there is not true eternity, but rather time; hence the psalm saying *their time shall last for ever"* (1a.10.3; Blackfriars 1964, 2:143).

16. Benvenuto glosses *Par.* 33's image of the universe bound in one volume, a great image of all-at-once-ness, thus: *"in un volume,* quasi dicat: 'totum simul'" (Guido Biagi, ed., *"La Divina Commedia" nella figurazione artistica e nel secolare commento,* 3 vols. [Turin: Unione Tipografico-Editrice Torinese, 1924–1929], 3:742). On the image's self-referentiality with respect to the volume in which it is situated, see John Ahern, "Binding the Book: Hermeneutics and Manuscript Production in *Paradiso* 33," *PMLA* 97 (1982): 800–809. The same image is cited by Zaleski to make her point that the *Paradiso* contains, unusually, both motifs associated with journey narratives (e.g., the glance back at earth) and motifs associated with mystical literature (e.g., the vision of all creation fused into one); see *Otherworld Journeys,* 90–91.

17. *I promessi sposi,* chapter 11, page 189, in the edition of Lanfranco Caretti (Milan: Mursia, 1979).

18. Paul R. Olson, "Theme and Structure in the Exordium of the *Paradiso," Italica* 39 (1962): 89–104, analyzes the first tercet's "great decrescendo of sonority" from the opening verse to the "lowly—one can even say prosaic—adverbial expressions of line 3" (97–98).

19. McDannell and Lang point out that "a preoccupation with heavenly rank and hierarchy, while acknowledging the relative equality of the blessed, is a common theme in medieval texts" (*Heaven: A History,* 77). In "The Paradox of Equality and Hierarchy of Reward in *Pearl," Renascence* 33 (1981): 172–79, Anne Howland Schotter notes that "the central theological paradox of the Middle English *Pearl* is the simultaneous equality of reward and inequality of rank in heaven, whereby the blessed souls enjoy the same amount of beatitude, and yet have different statuses" (172). The *Pearl* poet's concern with this paradox is reflected in his recurrent use of the adverbs "more" and "less," reminiscent of Dante's "più" and "meno": "Then the less, the more remuneration, / And ever alike, the less, the more" (10.5); "'Of more and less,' she answered straight, / 'In the Kingdom of God, no risk obtains'" (11.1; trans. Marie Borroff [New York: Norton, 1977]).

20. This tension is described by Arthur O. Lovejoy: "But the God in whom man was thus to find his own fulfilment was, as has been pointed out, not one God but two. He was the Idea of the Good, but he was also the Idea of Goodness; and though the second attribute was nominally deduced dialectically from the first, no two notions could be more antithetic. The one was an apotheosis of unity, self-sufficiency, and quietude, the other of diversity, self-transcendence, and fecundity. . . . There was no way in which the flight from the Many to the One, the quest of a perfection defined wholly in terms of contrast with the created world, could be effectually harmonized with the imitation of a Goodness that delights in diversity and manifests itself in the emanation of the Many out of the One" (*The Great Chain of Being* [1936; rpt., New York: Harper and Row, 1960], 82–84).

21. Noting that "unease and suspicion in the presence of multiplicity" are "characteristic of Neoplatonism through the ages," Boyde elaborates: "Consciously [Dante] remained deeply committed to the biblical view that Creation was 'very

good'; but subconsciously he seems to have entertained misgivings about the goodness of a universe which could not be perfect because it was neither 'simple' nor
'one'" (*Dante Philomythes and Philosopher: Man in the Cosmos* [Cambridge:
Cambridge University Press, 1981], 219).

22. In *The Hedgehog and the Fox: An Essay on Tolstoy's View of History* (New
York: Simon and Schuster, 1953), Berlin distinguishes between the "hedgehog," who
searches for an underlying principle of unity, and the "fox," who focuses instead on
difference: "Dante belongs to the first category, Shakespeare to the second; Plato,
Lucretius, Pascal, Hegel, Dostoevsky, Nietzsche, Ibsen, Proust are, in varying degrees, hedgehogs; Herodotus, Aristotle, Montaigne, Erasmus, Molière, Goethe,
Pushkin, Balzac, Joyce are foxes" (2). Most have agreed with Berlin's assessment of
Dante, but I note with interest the following remark of Leo Spitzer's: "Tolstoy is
explained by Mr. Berlin as a born 'fox' who unsuccessfully attempted to make himself over into a 'hedgehog.' In my opinion Dante was born a fox type of writer and
became a *successful* hedgehog" ("The Addresses to the Reader in the *Commedia*,"
*Italica* 32 [1955] 165n. 9).

23. The quotation is from *ST* 1a.11.4; Blackfriars 1964, 2:167. *Quaestio* 11 treats
the "oneness of God," "De unitate Dei"; article 4 discusses whether God is supremely one. The reply is premised, not coincidentally, on a *sed contra* that invokes
the unity of the trinity: "On the other hand Bernard says that *among all the things we
say are one the unity of the divine Trinity takes pride of place*" (167).

24. The one use of *differente* outside of *Paradiso* (which Fernando Salsano in the
*ED* claims as a present participle of the verb rather than an adjective; see s.v. "differire") belongs to the *Commedia*'s discourse on the generation of the soul and refers
to the process whereby human life is differentiated from vegetative life: "Anima fatta
la virtute attiva / qual d'una pianta, in tanto differente / che questa è in via e quella
è già a riva" (*Purg.* 25.52–54). This passage treats in microcosmic terms the process
of creation that will be treated in universal terms in *Par.* 1 and 2. In the *Convivio* too,
Dante discusses the microcosm in the language of the macrocosm, with reference to
the causes of differences between human beings, the "differenza de le nostre anime"
(4.21.2). Following a biological discussion that anticipates *Purg.* 25, he writes: "E
però che la complessione del seme puote essere migliore e men buona, e la disposizione del seminante puote essere migliore e men buona, e la disposizione del Cielo
a questo effetto puote essere buona, migliore e ottima (la quale si varia per le constel-
lazioni, che continuamente si transmutano), incontra che de l'umano seme e di
queste vertudi più pura [e men pura] anima si produce" (4.21.7).

25. *Quaestio* 47 treats "De distinctione rerum in communi," translated by T.
Gilby as "the plurality in general of things" (Blackfriars 1967, 8:91). The following
translations from this *quaestio* are Gilby's, although not the citation in the previous
sentence.

26. The concept of gradation, of *magis et minus*, is sufficiently important from
Aquinas's perspective that it constitutes his fourth way of proving God's existence:
"The fourth way is based on the gradation observed in things. Some things are found
to be more good, more true, more noble [aliquid magis et minus bonum et verum et
nobile], and so on, and others less. But such comparative terms describe varying
degrees of approximation to a superlative. . . . Something therefore is the truest and

best and most noble of things, and hence the most fully in being; for Aristotle says that the truest things are the things most fully in being" (1a.2.3; Blackfriars 1964, 2:15–17).

27. These ideas appear in other passages of the *Convivio* as well: "Ciascuna forma sustanziale procede da la sua prima cagione, la quale è Iddio, sì come nel libro Di Cagioni è scritto, e non ricevono diversitade per quella, che è simplicissima, ma per le secondarie cagioni e per la materia in che discende" (3.2.4); "Ché avvegna che Dio, esso medesimo mirando, veggia insiememente tutto, in quanto la distinzione de le cose è in lui per [lo] modo che lo effetto è ne la cagione, vede quelle distinte" (3.12.11).

28. *Ordine* appears once in the *Inferno* (in the sense of sacred orders), twice in *Purgatorio*, and thirteen times in the *Paradiso*. *Universo*, which appears five times in *Inferno* and eight times in *Paradiso*, demonstrates an affinity for *tutto*: "che 'l mal de l'universo tutto insacca" (*Inf.* 7.18), "discriver fondo a tutto l'universo" (*Inf.* 32.8), "in tutto l'universo" (*Par.* 19.44).

29. The importance of the adverb *igualmente* for the *Paradiso*'s rhetoric of unity is anticipated in the single usage of *Inferno*, which belongs to the discourse on Fortune in canto 7, a discourse that deals precisely with the themes of distribution and allocation that will dominate the third canticle. The speech opens with a description of God as the universal and equal distributor of his light: "Colui lo cui saver tutto trascende, / fece li cieli e diè lor chi conduce / sì, ch'ogne parte ad ogne parte splende, / distribuendo *igualmente* la luce" (*Inf.* 7.73–76). Sapegno notes that these lines anticipate the first two verses of *Paradiso*; he does not mention that the *Paradiso*'s third verse will crucially modify their import, changing *igualmente* to *più e meno* (*La Divina Commedia* [Florence: La Nuova Italia, 1968], 1:83). One wonders whether the *Inferno*'s unproblematized presentation of God's distributory process is to be charged to Vergil, the speaker in canto 7, or to the poet's as yet insufficiently developed appreciation of the paradox he treats in *Paradiso*.

30. *Unire* too is a word that comes into its own in the third canticle: it occurs once in *Inferno*, once in *Purgatorio*, and six times in *Paradiso*.

31. Joan M. Ferrante addresses this point in "Words and Images in the *Paradiso*: Reflections of the Divine," in *Dante, Petrarch, Boccaccio: Studies in the Italian Trecento in Honor of Charles S. Singleton*, ed. Aldo S. Bernardo and Anthony L. Pellegrini (Binghamton: Medieval and Renaissance Texts and Studies, 1983), 115–32, where she notes that the "repeated word gives the sense of difference as well as of similarity," and that the verbal repetition of *corpo* reflects the essence of a paradise in which beings are "at once identical and distinct" (121).

32. In the *Convivio* Dante writes that the shadow in the moon "non è altro che raritade del suo corpo, a la quale non possono terminare li raggi del sole e ripercuotersi così come ne l'altre parti" (2.13.9). See Bruno Nardi, "La dottrina delle macchie lunari nel secondo canto del *Paradiso*," *Saggi di filosofia dantesca*, 2d ed. (Florence: La Nuova Italia, 1967), 3–39, who concludes that "la soluzione del problema delle macchie lunari, formulata da Dante in questo canto del *Paradiso*, implica e impegna tutto un sistema cosmologico di derivazione del molteplice dall'uno e di causalità divina nel mondo" (38). Nardi's stress on the Neoplatonic component of Beatrice's discourse is pushed to extremes in Robert M. Durling and Ronald L. Martinez, *Time*

*and the Crystal: Studies in Dante's Rime Petrose* (Berkeley: University of California Press, 1990), 227–32.

33. See Boyde, *Dante Philomythes* 265, for the suggestion that Dante had a more "advanced" view of the *opus distinctionis* than Aquinas.

34. In the *Questio de aqua et terra*, given as a lecture on January 20, 1320, Dante explains that while the eighth sphere has unity with respect to its substance, it nonetheless has multiplicity with respect to its powers: "licet celum stellatum habeat unitatem in substantia, habet tamen multiplicitatem in virtute" (70). It was necessary that the starry sphere possess the difference in its parts that we see, in order that it might influence different powers through different organs: "oportuit habere diversitatem illam in partibus quam videmus, ut per organa diversa virtutes diversas influeret" (70).

35. The analogy between microcosm and macrocosm reminds the reader of *Purg.* 25 on the generation of the human soul; indeed, *Par.* 2's "girando sé sovra sua unitate" recalls *Purg.* 25's description of the self-knowing soul "che vive e sente e sé in sé rigira" (75). The discourse on the generation of the soul also shares with the later discussion of the moon's spots a refutation of Averroes, who in both instances posits single substances where Dante sees diversity.

36. Dante wonders rhetorically whether God, who differentiated far greater things, could not have caused a few words to sound, to be differentiated, in his encounter with Adam: "Ipso distinguente qui maiora distinxit?" (*DVE* 1.4.6).

37. The passage that follows continues to make the point that language diversification is the punishment for sin. As each group of builders becomes a linguistic unit, with its "one" individual language, Dante deploys the terminology that used to signify unity in such a way as to underscore the unity that is no more: "Solis etenim in *uno* convenientibus actu *eadem loquela* remansit: puta cunctis architectoribus *una*, cunctis saxa volventibus *una*, cunctis ea parantibus *una*; et sic de *singulis* operantibus accidit" (1.7.7). By the same token, the *gramatica* was invented as a means for circumventing the debilitating effects of difference. Its inventors wanted to offset the possibility that linguistic mutability and differentiation would prevent us from coming into contact with the thoughts either of the ancients or of those who are geographically distant, those whom difference of place has rendered different: "illorum quos a nobis locorum diversitas facit esse diversos" (1.9.11). Language, rather than rendering us more different, should be the means for reaching those whom *diversitas facit esse diversos*. Despite the Augustinian pessimism that imbues the *De vulgari eloquentia*'s early chapters on man's pride, in this tribute to the inventors of the *gramatica* we can see the stirrings of a typically Dantesque activism that will blossom in his attempts to mold the Italian language of his day.

38. In writing of Dante's participation in the "almost mystical reverence for the One which seems such a constant feature of Neoplatonist sensibility and thought" (*Dante Philomythes*, 219), Boyde draws particular attention to the first book of the *Monarchia*.

39. The pilgrim thinks in human terms and assumes that where there are degrees, caused by multiplicity, there is likely to be envy. The fact that love does not suffer diminishment by sharing is explained doctrinally in *Purgatorio*, precisely as a corrective to the sin of envy, and expressed dramatically in *Paradiso*, where the souls wel-

330 NOTES TO CHAPTER 8

come the pilgrim's arrival by exclaiming, "Ecco chi crescerà li nostri amori" (5.105).
(Compare the *Pearl*: "The more the merrier in blessedness! / Our love is increased
as our numbers swell, / And honor more and never the less" [15.1].) *Purgatorio's*
doctrinal passage anticipates *Paradiso* in its vigorous use of the adverb *più*, emblematic of the underlying paradox of undiminished but much apportioned love:

ché, per quanti si dice *più* lì 'nostro,'
tanto possiede *più* di ben ciascuno,
e *più* di caritate arde in quel chiostro.

. . . . . . . . . . . . . . .

E quanta gente *più* là sù s'intende,
*più* v'è da bene amare, e *più* vi s'ama

(*Purg.* 15.55–57, 73–74)

Dante explicitly raises the issue of envy among the saints in paradise in the *Convivio*,
explaining that there is no envy because each soul reaches the limit of his personal
beatitude: "E questa è la ragione per che li Santi non hanno tra loro invidia, però che
ciascuno aggiugne lo fine del suo desiderio" (3.15.10). Modern imaginings of heaven,
according to Zaleski, have removed the problem: "For many people in our own day,
however, the plurality of heavens seems at last to have lost its rationale; the very
notion of ranking souls offends democratic instincts" (*Otherworld Journeys*, 60).

40. The paradigm is set forth in *Par.* 1, where the pilgrim is overwhelmed by desire
to understand the newness that he is experiencing: "La novità del suono e 'l grande
lume" (82); his desire is assuaged by Beatrice, who opens her mouth "a quïetarmi
l'animo commosso" (86). But his quietude is short-lived; as soon as he is divested of
the "primo dubbio" (94), he is enveloped in a new one: "dentro ad un nuovo più fu'
inretito" (96). The quest that leads the pilgrim toward *quietude*, spiritual satiety,
necessarily leads the poet to literal *quiet*, i.e., to silence.

41. At the disappearance of Piccarda's silhouette, the pilgrim "converts" his
glance to Beatrice, who marks the sign of a greater desire: "La vista mia, che tanto lei
seguio / quanto possibil fu, poi che la perse, / volsesi al segno di maggior disio, / e a
Beatrice tutta si converse" (*Par.* 3.124–27). The Latinism *velle* appears only in *Par.* 4
and at the end of the poem. On the Thomistic precedents for the opening of *Par.* 4,
see Warren Ginsberg, "Place and Dialectic in *Pearl* and Dante's *Paradiso*," *English
Literary History* 55 (1988): 731–53; Ginsberg sees in the pilgrim's stasis at the beginning of the canto "a human counterpart of the perfect peace the blessed enjoy"
(747).

42. The *quaestio* treats "De adeptione beatitudinis," the article "utrum unus
homo possit esse beatior altero" (ed. and trans. Thomas Gilby, Blackfriars 1969,
16:120). The arguments denying that one man can be happier than another, against
which Thomas takes his stand, are instructive with respect to the pilgrim's assumptions regarding equality and the potential for envy:

(1) According to Aristotle, happiness is *the reward of virtue*, and for the works of
virtue the recompense is equal. Recall the parable of the labourers in the vineyard *who received every man a penny*, which, comments Gregory, *signifies an equal
return in eternal life*. Consequently, one man will not be happier than another.
(2) Besides, beatitude is the highest good. And what can be higher than the high-

est? Therefore the beatitude of one cannot be higher than that of another. (3) Further, since it is complete and sufficient good, happiness brings man's desires to rest. This it would not do if some available good were still wanting: if nothing were wanting then, of course, there could be no greater good. Either, then, a man is not happy, or if he is, then no other could be happier than he is. (Blackfriars 1969, 16:121)

Interestingly, the *Pearl* poet too makes use of the parable of the vineyard to deal with this problem. See also *ST* 1a.12.6, where Aquinas answers affirmatively the question, "Is God's essence seen more perfectly by one than by another?" Again, the issue pivots on equality: "If therefore all saw the essence of God equally, all would be equal in eternal life; but this is contrary to what St Paul says, *Star differs from star in brightness*" (ed. and trans. Herbert McCabe, Blackfriars 1964, 3:21). Regarding degrees of bliss, see also 1a.62.9.

43. Gilby comments that "the underlying philosophy here is of the greater and less, *magis et minus*, in analogical values" (Blackfriars 1969, 16:121).

44. Dante's St. Thomas refers to "distesa lingua" in *Par.* 11.23, while Augustine uses the term *distentio* in relation to time in *Confessions* 11.23.

45. Francesco De Sanctis sees better than most the paradox on which the *Paradiso* is founded: "Il concetto del paradiso è il progressivo svanire della forma, e la forma è il sostanziale della poesia"; "Nel paradiso cristiano . . . il concetto sta spogliato di forma, anzi in opposizione con la forma, fuori della poesia; e non di meno Dante dee darvi una forma se vuole innalzarlo a poesia" (*Lezioni sulla "Divina Commedia,"* ed. Michele Manfredi [Bari: Laterza, 1955], 285–86). He was particularly acute in noting that "per condurre innanzi il suo poema Dante è ridotto ad una semplice scala quantitativa" and "non rimane ad esprimere questa gradazione *se non un più ed un meno*, più luce, meno luce" (287; italics mine).

46. "The Imageless Vision and Dante's *Paradiso*," *Dante Studies* 90 (1972): 77–91; quotations, 80–81. Or, as Susan Noakes puts it: "To write infinity, he writes the vision over and over" ("Dante's *Vista Nova: Paradiso* XXXIII.136," *Quaderni d'italianistica* 5 [1984]: 151–70; quotation, 168).

47. See "*Paradiso* X: The Dance of the Stars," 1968, rpt. in *Dante: The Poetics of Conversion,* ed. Rachel Jacoff (Cambridge: Harvard University Press, 1986), 221–44.

48. The same can be said of Jeremy Tambling, who, writing twenty years after Freccero, simply gives a Derridean gloss to his paraphrase of Beatrice: "The *Paradiso*'s whole structure, whole set of significations, is provisional, temporary, deferring meaning, because the 'actual' vision is not reducible to words" (*Dante and Difference: Writing in the "Commedia"* [Cambridge: Cambridge University Press, 1988], 154).

49. The brief inserted simile of line 17, "e sì com'uom che suo parlar non spezza," insists on identifying Beatrice as a "man." The switching of genders reinforces the conflation between Beatrice and Dante.

50. Sapegno recognizes the narrativity implicit in "processo" in his gloss: "svolgimento, filo, del discorso" (*La Divina Commedia* 3:58).

51. It is a measure of Dante's writerliness, in early fourteenth-century Italy, that he plays with the notion of orality. For the writerly culture of thirteenth-century Italy and the case of Monte Andrea da Firenze, see H. Wayne Storey, "Transferring

Visual Ambiguity from Manuscript to Modern Edition," *Romance Philology* 43 (1989): 154–80.

52. Albert E. Wingell notes the Augustinian flavor of these verses in "The Forested Mountaintop in Augustine and Dante," *Dante Studies* 99 (1981): 9–48, esp. 11. In "La nozione di 'deificatio' nel *Paradiso*," *Letture classensi* 9–10 (1982): 39–72, Rosetta Migliorini Fissi situates Dante's concept of *somiglianza* within the writings of St. Bernard.

53. Adam's sin is described in terms redolent of Ulysses/Phaeton/Icarus as the inability to tolerate any curb to his will: "Per non soffrire a la virtù che vole / freno" (*Par.* 7.25–26). The canto's later use of the term *follia* to describe mankind's Adamic sin further confirms the Nardian reading of Ulysses discussed in chapter 3.

54. This verse resonates with the God "che mai non vide cosa nova" (*Purg.* 10.94) and the poet who is charged with "ben manifestar le cose nove" (*Inf.* 14.7).

55. The same language is used in the *Convivio*, where the ship of state requires a helmsman, who "considerando le *diverse condizioni del mondo, ne li diversi e necessarii offici* ordinare abbia del tutto universale e inrepugnabile officio di comandare" (4.4.6; italics mine).

56. A passage in the *Convivio* views life as a progression from similarity to dissimilarity, in which we are propelled by our natural desires toward differentiation, thus becoming different from one another and ultimately choosing different paths: "E sì come ne le biade che, quando nascono, dal principio hanno quasi una similitudine ne l'erba essendo, e poi sì vengono per processo dissimigliando; così questo naturale appetito, che de la divina grazia surge, dal principio quasi si mostra non dissimile a quello che pur da natura nudamente viene, ma con esso, sì come l'erbate quasi di diversi biadi, si simiglia. E non pur ne li uomini, ma ne li uomini e ne le bestie ha similitudine; e questo appare, ché ogni animale, sì come elli è nato, razionale come bruto, sé medesimo ama, e teme e fugge quelle cose che a lui sono contrarie, e quelle odia. Procedendo poi, sì come detto è comincia una dissimilitudine tra loro, nel procedere di questo appetito, ché l'uno tiene uno cammino e l'altro un altro" (4.22.5–6).

57. Dante writes as follows on *assimilatio* in the *Convivio*: "Ove è da sapere che discender la virtude d'una cosa in altra non è altro che ridurre quella in sua similitudine, sì come ne li agenti naturali vedemo manifestamente; che, discendendo la loro virtù ne le pazienti cose, recano quelle a loro similitudine, tanto quanto possibili sono a venire ad essa. Onde vedemo lo sole che, discendendo lo raggio suo qua giù, reduce le cose a sua similitudine di lume, quanto esse per loro disposizione possono da la [sua] virtude lume ricevere. Così dico che Dio questo amore a sua similitudine reduce, quanto esso è possibile a lui assimigliarsi" (3.14.2–3).

CHAPTER 9
THE HEAVEN OF THE SUN AS A MEDITATION ON NARRATIVE

1. Commentators have noted that the first circle is composed primarily of rationalists, while the second is dominated by mystics; see Fiorenzo Forti, "Le Atene celestiali: i magnanimi del sapere," in *Magnanimitade* (Bologna: Pàtron, 1977), 49–81, esp. 68.

2. Scholars have followed the lead of the sixteenth-century commentator Ber-

nardino Daniello in noting that Dante's system of reciprocal praise is grounded in early custom; Franciscans and Dominicans commemorated the feast days of their founders with sermons preached by a member of the other fraternity. G. Mestica quotes Daniello as follows: "Nel principio di tali religioni nel giorno della festa di san Francesco avevano in costume i francescani di far predicare uno di quelli di san Domenico, il quale la vita del santo laudava, perchè *Laus in ore proprio sordescit*; all'incontro i domenicani nel dì solenne del santo facevan predicar uno di quelli di san Francesco" ("San Francesco, Dante e Giotto," *Nuova Antologia* 27 [1881]: 3–39, 403–43; quotation, 406). In "Le mistiche nozze di frate Francesco con madonna Povertà," *Giornale dantesco* 6 (1898): 49–82, Umberto Cosmo emphasizes that Francis and Dominic were linked by written and oral tradition prior to Dante ("Storia e leggenda già li avevano indissolubilmente uniti insieme" [59]); making the same point, Mestica cites Bonaventure's references to the two saints as "duo magna luminaria . . . duae tubae . . . duo Cherubim . . . duae stellae lucidae" ("San Francesco, Dante e Giotto," 407). Umberto Bosco notes that the pairing of Thomas and Bonaventure was also traditional by Dante's time; see "San Francesco (XI del *Paradiso*)," 1964, rpt. in *Dante vicino*, 2d ed. (Caltanisetta: Sciascia, 1972), 316–41, esp. 319 n. 3.

3. Some useful *lecturae* of canto 11, in the order of their composition, are: Alfonso Bertoldi, "Il canto XI del *Paradiso*," *Lectura Dantis* (Florence: Sansoni, 1903); Umberto Cosmo, "I due ultimi grandi campioni della chiesa e il valore della loro missione: l'eroe della povertà," in *L'ultima ascesa*, 1936, 2d ed., rev. Bruno Maier (Florence: La Nuova Italia, 1965), 121–40; Erich Auerbach, "St. Francis of Assisi in Dante's *Commedia*," 1944, rpt. in *Scenes from the Drama of European Literature* (Gloucester, Mass.: Peter Smith, 1973), 79–98; Alberto Chiari, "Ispirazione francescana nel canto dantesco di S. Francesco," *Lettere italiane* 2 (1950): 65–77; Bruno Nardi, "Il canto di S. Francesco," *L'Alighieri* 5 (1964): 9–20. Helpful readings of canto 12 include: Alfonso Bertoldi, "Il canto XII del *Paradiso*," *Lectura Dantis* (Florence: Sansoni, 1912); Filippo Crispolti, "Il canto XII del *Paradiso*," *Lectura Dantis* (Florence: Sansoni, 1923); Umberto Cosmo, "Il campione della scienza divina e la condanna delle deviazioni francescane," in *L'ultima ascesa*, 141–55; Leone Cicchito, "Il canto di Dante a San Domenico," *Miscellanea francescana* 48 (1948): 306–28; Antonio Di Pietro, "Canto XII," *Lectura Dantis Scaligera: "Paradiso"* (Florence: Le Monnier, 1971), 421–41. See also the articles on Francis and Dominic in the *ED*, by Stanislao da Campagnola and Gian Roberto Sarolli, respectively.

4. Noting that "from the entrance of Francis into the *Comedy*, we should expect one of the highlights of concrete life painting in which the *Comedy* is so rich" ("St. Francis," 80), Auerbach feels called upon to justify what he considers a poetically less effective procedure: "The personal reality of the saint had to be subordinated to his office, it had to shine forth from the office. It was for this reason that Dante did not describe a meeting in which the saint could reveal or express himself in an intimate way; instead he wrote a *Vita*, a saint's life" (93). My point is not to criticize what Dante has done but to draw attention to it as a deliberate narrative choice.

5. Saint Benedict's discourse in canto 22 is an abbreviated version of the similar discourses found in cantos 11 and 12: he tells the story of his life in lines 37–45 (note the one-verse geographical periphrasis with which he launches his autobiography, reminiscent of the lengthy periphrases with which Thomas and Bonaventure begin their biographies); he presents the other contemplative souls in lines 46–51 (in the

same way that Thomas and Bonaventure present their circles of souls); he condemns his degenerate order in lines 73–96 (in language that reminds us of Bonaventure's condemnation of the Franciscans in the coda of canto 12).

6. On Dante's sources for his biographies of Francis and Dominic, see Mestica, "San Francesco, Dante e Giotto" and Cosmo, "Le mistiche nozze," and the *lecturae* by Bertoldi, Crispolti, and Bosco; also Umberto Cosmo, "Noterelle francescane," *Giornale dantesco* 7 (1899): 63–70, and Michele Barbi, "Sulle fonti della vita di S. Francesco," and "Per la questione francescana," in *Problemi di critica dantesca, Prima serie* (Florence: Sansoni, 1934), 323–57. As compared to earlier commentators, who stress Dante's dependence on his sources, Bosco emphasizes the poet's willingness to alter them. On the importance of the oral tradition, and its merging with the written tradition of the early biographers, see Raoul Manselli, "Tradizione orale e redazione scritta a proposito di Francesco d'Assisi," in *Dal Medioevo al Petrarca: Miscellanea di studi in onore di Vittore Branca* (Florence: Olschki, 1983), 17–27.

7. Patrick Boyde paraphrases St. Thomas paraphrasing Aristotle: "'To be diverse necessarily means to be unequal, because the *differentiae* are either added or subtracted: *formae rerum sunt sicut numeri*" (*Dante Philomythes and Philosopher: Man in the Cosmos* [Cambridge: Cambridge University Press, 1981], 131). In St. Thomas's words: "Distinctio autem formalis semper requirit inaequalitatem, quia, ut dicitur in VIII *Metaph*. 'formae rerum sunt sicut numeri, in quibus species variantur per additionem vel subtractionem unitatis'" (*ST* 1a.47.2). For the context of this citation within the *Summa*, see chapter 8.

8. These plays on speech and muteness are further thrown into relief by the fact that the pilgrim is mute for the duration of this heaven, indeed from 9.81, his last words in the sphere of Venus, to 14.96, his first words upon entering Mars.

9. See the chart at the end of this chapter for a breakdown of the structures and rhetorical components of the eulogies. Kenelm Foster offers a contrastive analysis of the biographies in terms of three moments in the saints' lives: realization of vocation, formal approval, and epilogue; see "Gli elogi danteschi di S. Francesco e di S. Domenico," *Dante e il francescanesimo* (Cava dei Tirreni: Avagliano, 1987), 231–49.

10. Bertoldi, "Il canto XII," points out that Santa Croce, the Franciscan church, is situated in the eastern part of Florence, while Santa Maria Novella, the home of the Dominicans, is in the western part of the city (47 n. 27). Silvio Pasquazi deals at length with the cosmic significance of the two geographical periphrases heralding the saints' birthplaces; see "San Francesco in Dante," *Studi in onore di Alberto Chiari*, 2 vols. (Brescia: Paideia, 1973), 2:939–70.

11. The introduction of canto 11 begins with three tercets on the workings of providence (28–36), followed by two tercets more specifically concentrated on the two saints (37–42); the introduction of canto 12 reverses this order, providing first two tercets on the two saints (31–36), and then moving into three tercets on the workings of providence (37–45). The inverted order in which the second biography and presentation of souls occurs with respect to the first biography and presentation of souls also forms the figure ABBA, as does the disposition of "serafico"/"ardore"/ "sapïenza"/"cherubica" in 11.37–39. Enzo Noè Girardi points out that chiasmus is the figure by which the heaven of the sun as a whole is organized ("La struttura del Paradiso e i canti del Sole," *Studi in onore di Alberto Chiari* 1:629–52, esp. 638);

chiasmus is, indeed, a figure that allows Dante a rhetorical approximation of unified circularity within the linear medium of language. Particularly interesting from this point of view are the uses of chiasmus in *Par.* 14.28–30 and 40–51, in one case to express the paradox of the trinity and in the other to describe the parallel movements of the intellect and the will in the achievement of beatitude.

12. References to the trinity are particularly dense in this heaven, occurring also in 10.50–51, 13.25–27, 13.53–57, 14.28–30, 14.40–42, 14.49–51.

13. It is interesting to note to what extent the critical debate on these cantos has unwittingly mirrored the metatextual currents here being discussed, either by privileging Francis over Dominic, that is, by claiming that Dante privileges Francis over Dominic, or by feeling obliged to defend canto 12 from the charge that it is inferior to canto 11. Thus, Mestica tells us that although Dante pairs Francis with Dominic, he leans toward the former, an opinion Bertoldi reiterates, as does Cosmo; while, on the other hand, Cicchito and Pasquazi come to Dominic's aid. To add to the confusion, and to mirror even more faithfully the tensions with which Dante is dealing, variants of these positions can be held by the same author: Crispolti tells us that Francis's canto is "più poetico" ("Il canto XII," 21) and then responds to those critics who, moved by alleged anti-Dominicanism, "hanno affermato che Dante, anche pareggiando in apparenza i due santi, lascia intendere quanto San Domenico gli sembrasse inferiore a San Francesco" (27); the truth is, he tells us, that Innocent III dreamed of both saints holding up the Lateran, that Dante considered them both essential, and that "il maggior valore del canto di San Francesco fu un affare d'arte, non di giudizi agiografici" (28). In the same vein, Jacqueline Risset comments on "l'estrema, asimmetrica ammirazione [per San Francesco] che il testo, quasi suo malgrado, porta alla luce" (*Dante scrittore* [1982; trans. Milan: Mondadori, 1984], 148). Of course, the text could simply be reflecting reality: Foster (himself a Dominican) tells us that Dominic, with respect to Francis, was a "santo senza confronto meno popolare" ("Gli elogi danteschi," 231).

14. The *Convivio*'s editor points to *Purg.* 30: "continüò come colui che dice / e 'l più caldo parlar dietro reserva" (71–72).

15. Dante's explicit reference to Francis's exalted location forces the pro-Dominic critical faction into some unconvincing postulates in order to keep the balance from tilting. While Crispolti theorizes that Dante means to honor the Franciscan order (which was totally new, while the Dominican order "era una estensione ed applicazione della Regola agostiniana" ["Il canto XII," 28]), Pasquazi suggests that Dante omits mentioning Dominic's position in the rose because "non voleva metterlo più in alto o più in basso rispetto a San Francesco" ("San Francesco," 946), thus implicitly admitting that it would not be possible to attain parity were both saints named; again, "distinctio semper requirit inaequalitatem." Speculation has also resulted from the fact that we do not see Francis and Dominic in the heaven of the sun but merely hear of them, and do not know with certainty to which heaven either belongs; see Luca Bufano, "Note sulla posizione e il significato di San Francesco nel *Paradiso*," *Italica* 63 (1986): 265–77.

16. The hierarchical value of these verses is exploited by Daniello: "L'uno, che fu san Francesco, fu tutto serafico, cioè tutto acceso di ardente carità, come sono i Serafini, primo coro degli Angeli; l'altro san Domenico, fu, mentre visse qua giù in terra, per sapienza uno splendore di cherubica luce. *E pone san Francesco più ap-*

*presso a Dio, rassomigliandolo ai Serafini*" (quoted by Mestica, "San Francesco, Dante e Giotto," 408; italics mine). Pasquazi counters that Dante uses the attributes "seraphic" and "cherubic" to refer respectively to the Father and the Son of the trinity, and that therefore they do not militate against equality: "Posto, dunque, che il rapporto serafi-cherubi è analogo alla relazione Padre-Figlio, e posto che il Figlio è coeguale e coeterno con il Padre, ne deriva una pariteticità fra serafi e cherubi e, dunque, un'ulteriore pariteticità fra i due Fondatori e fra i due Ordini" ("San Francesco," 946). But this is to beg the question, since the paradox of the trinity is the ultimate embodiment of the problem (one vs. many) with which Dante is here grappling.

17. Critics have pointed to the appropriate behavior of Dante's Thomas: Foster notes that in the *Convivio* "the figure of St Thomas was associated in a special way with *discrimination*, conceived as a quality both intellectual and moral though rooted specifically in the human reason whose task it is to 'discern the relations between things'" ("St Thomas and Dante," *The Two Dantes* [Berkeley: University of California Press, 1977], 63), while Ettore Bonora suggests that the saint's powers of discrimination cause Dante to fashion for him a "discreto latino" ("Di fra Tommaso il discreto latino," *Giornale storico della letteratura italiana* 164 [1987]: 161–80).

18. As this heaven's "markers of difference," *distinzione* and *distinguere* are appropriately philosophical and scholastic in tone; see Erwin Panofsky, *Gothic Architecture and Scholasticism* (New York: Meridian, 1957), on *distinctio* as an essential component of the medieval *forma mentis*. Dante's sense of the relation between *differenza* and *distinzione* may be inferred from the following passage: "Li altri giron per varie differenze / le distinzion che dentro da sé hanno / dispongono a lor fini e lor semenze" (*Par.* 2.118–20).

19. Here too Thomas the narrator is imitating Dante the narrator, who earlier in this heaven had adopted the same technique of referring to what he had said "above": the sun is in conjunction "con quella parte che sù si rammenta" (*Par.* 10.31). In Dante's assimilation of the oral to the written we have a further index of his writerliness; rather than leave traces of an oral poetics in a written text, he does the opposite, submitting even what should properly, according to the fiction, be treated as oral to the hegemony of the written.

20. As noted in chapter 2, note 1, the metaphor narrative=path informs Dante's oeuvre. Examples from the *Convivio* sometimes include *procedere* and *processo*: "è da ritornare al diritto calle de lo inteso processo" (4.7.1); "In questa parte adunque si procede per via probabile" (4.18.2). *Processo* in the sense of narrative *cammino* occurs in the *Commedia* as well, in Beatrice's "processo santo" (*Par.* 5.18).

21. "E lo cielo del Sole si può comparare a l'Arismetrica per due proprietadi: l'una si è che del suo lume tutte l'altre stelle s'informano; l'altra si è che l'occhio nol può mirare. E queste due proprietadi sono ne l'Arismetrica: ché del suo lume tutte s'illuminano le scienze, però che li loro subietti sono tutti sotto alcuno numero considerati, o ne le considerazioni di quelli sempre con numero si procede" (*Conv.* 2.13.15–16). Dante goes on to relate number to the beginnings of things, "li principii de le cose naturali, li quali sono tre, cioè materia, privazione e forma" (17), and to note that, according to Pythagoras, number, in the form of odd or even, is at the basis of everything: "per che Pittagora, secondo che dice Aristotile nel primo de la Fisica, poneva li principii de le cose naturali lo pari e lo dispari, considerando tutte le cose

esser numero" (18). This passage is highly suggestive as to why there is a great creation discourse in this heaven; as Dante here tells us, this heaven is related to number, and number is at the root of creation.

22. I am aware, of course, that the entire *Commedia* is a narrative, so that there is no passage that is not narrative in the basic sense of the term, and also that my opposing of the terms "narrative" and "lyrical" raises questions regarding generic boundaries (narratives may display lyric qualities and vice versa). My use of these terms will be further clarified in the next chapter.

23. Dante is here referring to the biblical account in which God appears to Solomon in a dream and instructs him to ask for whatever he wants, eliciting the following reply: "Dabis ergo servo tuo cor docile, ut populum tuum iudicare possit, et *discernere inter bonum et malum*" (3 Kings 3:9; italics mine). *Par.* 13's emphasis on *distinguere* and *distinzione* is surely related to Solomon's request for the ability to "discernere inter bonum et malum."

24. The other uses of *distinzione* belong to 2.119 and 29.30. In using *distinzione* in the context of creation, Dante is following established practice; cf. Aquinas's "De distinctione rerum in communi" (*ST* 1a.47).

25. See "*Paradiso* X: The Dance of the Stars," 1968, rpt. in *Dante: The Poetics of Conversion*, ed. Rachel Jacoff (Cambridge: Harvard University Press, 1986), 242. Peter Dronke comments similarly on 10.2 and 9 in "The First Circle in the Solar Heaven," *Dante and Medieval Latin Traditions* (Cambridge: Cambridge University Press, 1986), 84.

26. In light of Petrocchi's suggestion that *primo* may here be the equivalent of *prima* ("resta pur sempre ammissibile *primo* neutro e perciò sinonimo dell'avverbio *prima*" ["*La Commedia*" *secondo l'antica vulgata* 4:207]), we can relate the verse "che l'uno andasse al primo e l'altro al poi" to the *Convivio*'s definition of time as "numero di movimento, secondo prima e poi."

27. Foster notes that "Dante's forgetting Beatrice in verses 59–60 is a step on what the theologians called the *via negativa*, the way of renunciation; his then being brought back by her smile from unity to multiplicity is a reminder that he is not yet at the end of that way" ("The Celebration of Order: *Paradiso* X," in *The Two Dantes*, 127). Indeed, if he were not brought back from unity to multiplicity, the poem would end: forward motion—for both the pilgrim and the poet—requires multiplicity, i.e., difference.

28. References to poverty in this heaven provide an index of the pervasiveness of Francis's presence: besides calling his followers the "primi scalzi poverelli" in 12.131, Dante refers to them as "la gente poverella" in 11.94. This heaven also contains a reference to "poveri giusti" (12.89) in the context of the life of Dominic (another attempt at balance?) and the poem's only use of "poverella" as a noun (the poor widow of Luke 21:2 in 10.107).

29. See Di Pietro, "Canto XII," and Manselli, "francescanesimo," in the *ED*. Discussions of Dante's political leanings inevitably run into the prophecy of *Par.* 12.118–20, in which the tares ("il loglio") are excluded from the harvest bin. The question is: who is the *loglio*? Cosmo concludes that the extremist spirituals are being condemned ("Noterelle francescane," *Giornale dantesco* 8 [1900]: 166–82, esp. 177–82), while Manselli, arguing forcefully for Dante's spiritualist tendencies, claims that Dante maintains balance by condemning the extremists of both wings, spirituals and

conventuals. Attilio Mellone demonstrates that Dante's position on poverty is that of the spiritualist Ubertino da Casale: "con la presentazione globale della povertà francescana [Dante] si situa senza equivoco nella corrente spirituale" ("Il S. Francesco di Dante e il S. Francesco della storia," *Dante e il francescanesimo*, 13–73; quotation, 43). For a more moderate position, see Charles T. Davis, "Poverty and Eschatology in the *Commedia*," *Dante's Italy* (Philadelphia: University of Pennsylvania Press, 1984), esp. 48–53.

30. Many commentators view *Par.* 11.36, "che quinci e quindi le fosser per guida," as an echo of "erunt duo viri, unus hinc, alius inde."

31. Textual echoes in this section of *Par.* 13 suggest that Guittone d'Arezzo is one of those "who fish for the truth and have not the art" (123); see Teodolinda Barolini, *Dante's Poets: Textuality and Truth in the "Comedy"* (Princeton, N.J.: Princeton University Press, 1984) 283 n. 104. A primary example of a poetic precursor who drew Dante's ire by making claims that prefigured his own, it should be remembered that Guittone wrote lauds for both Francis and Dominic, thus prefiguring Dante's poetic interest in the two saints. A group whose condemnation is certainly related to the prophetic claims Dante makes for himself is that of the false prophets, whose backward motion is perhaps echoed in that of the errant Franciscan order, which "è tanto volta, / che quel dinanzi a quel di retro gitta" (*Par.* 12.116–17). It is worth noting that the term *mirabile*, which has prophetic overtones in the *Commedia*, appears three times in the heaven of the sun referring to Francis and Dominic ("mirabil vita" [11.95], "mirabile frutto" [12.65], "mirabil vita" [13.32]), and in adverbial form brackets the episode of the false prophets in hell (*Inf.* 20.11; 21.6).

32. As noted in chapter 1, any metatextual study has to come to terms with the poet as truth-teller, and thus with "Dante profeta" in the larger sense; it happens that these cantos are particularly rich in references to prophets in the more specific sense as well. In "Spirito profetico duecentesco e Dante," *Letture classensi* 13 (1984): 49–68, Guglielmo Gorni asks: "se la profezia, nella *Commedia*, non ha statuto di frammento entro l'opera, bensì è una struttura latente e persistente, che emerge e quasi si coagula in singoli episodi, in quali punti precisi del poema Dante fa emergere la coscienza metatestuale di questo fatto decisivo nella costruzione della sua 'visione'?" (50). The heaven of the sun answers Gorni's query tellingly by combining an eruption of "coscienza metatestuale" with an interest in prophecy. That the prophet Nathan serves in the *Commedia* as a "*typus prophetae* e *per consequens* quale *typus Dantis*" is asserted by Gian Roberto Sarolli (*ED*, "Natàn"; see also "Dante Scriba Dei," in *Prolegomena alla "Divina Commedia"* [Florence: Olschki, 1971]). The association of Francis with Elijah and Dominic with Enoch, posited by Dante's contemporaries and discussed by Pasquazi, "San Francesco," further links this heaven to prophecy and eschatology; contrary to Pasquazi, I think this analogy only serves to heighten the figure of Francis, since Elijah is obviously more important to Dante than Enoch, whom he never mentions.

33. Against scholars who have sought to attenuate the precision of Dante's language, Dronke emphasizes that, according to Dante, "what Siger 'syllogized' were ideas ill-received but true" ("The First Circle," 144).

34. There is a suggestive discrepancy between Dante's glossed Francis and the saint's own insistence on an unglossed existence; according to Robert Brentano, Francis wanted his rule observed "*ad litteram, ad litteram ad litteram, sine glossa, sine*

*glossa, sine glossa"* ("Francis of Assisi's Gloss of Matthew 6:34," *Dal Medioevo al Petrarca*, 37–46; quotation, 38).

35. On the importance of this canto's divine onomastics, see Cicchito's *lectura* and Sarolli, who comments that it is not "un mero 'gioco di parole'—come finora è parso alla dantologia—ma una ben ferma e chiara istanza soteriologica ed esemplare" (*ED*, s.v. "Domenico").

36. The *Commedia* contains three instances of *profeta*, of which two occur in *Par.* 12 (the third is in *Par.* 24.136: "per Moïsè, per profeti e per salmi"), and one instance of *profetico*, which is applied to Joachim in the same canto. Canto 12 also contains another prophetic term, *presago*, used only here ("e fanno qui la gente esser presaga" [16]). We should not forget the prophecy of the *loglio* in *Par.* 12.118–20, or that God spoke to Solomon in a dream: "Apparuit autem Dominus Salomoni per somnium nocte" (3 Kings 3:5). On Innocent's dreams, see Howard Needler, *Saint Francis and Saint Dominic in the "Divine Comedy,"* Schriften und Vorträge des Petrarca-Instituts Köln, 23 (Cologne: Krefeld, 1969), 18. Dominic's dream, as recounted by Passavanti, is described by A. Sorrentino, "L'unità concettuale dei canti XI e XII del *Paradiso* e una leggenda riferita dal Passavanti," *Giornale dantesco* 30 (1927): 45–51. Alain Boureau places such dreams in the context of hagiography in *"La Légende dorée": Le système narratif de Jacques de Voragine* (Paris: Cerf, 1984), 167.

37. It is noteworthy that, unlike Dominic, Francis dies: his narrative proceeds from beginning to end in the most literal sense, reaching the total closure achieved by epics that end with the hero's death. Carlo Delcorno draws a sharp distinction between canto 11, "[che] è costruito per nuclei narrativi" (308), and canto 12: "Al contrario il canto 12 è poverissimo di elementi propriamente narrativi, e sovrabbonda di similitudini e di metafore" (309); see "Cadenze e figure della predicazione nel viaggio dantesco," *Lettere italiane* 37 (1985): 299–320. Cicchito too notices in the representation of Dominic "una varietà d'immagini disparate che ne spezza e confonde la figurazione" ("Il canto di Dante a San Domenico," 320).

CHAPTER 10
THE SACRED POEM IS FORCED TO JUMP

1. John Freccero notes that "the forward movement of *terza rima* is interrupted in the *Paradiso*, where the name of Christ, *Cristo*, appears in rhyme only with itself" ("The Significance of *Terza Rima*," *Dante: The Poetics of Conversion*, ed. Rachel Jacoff [Cambridge: Harvard University Press, 1986], 267). For the importance of these rhymes within the whole, see Thomas Elwood Hart, "The *Cristo*-Rhymes and Polyvalence as a Principle of Structure in Dante's *Commedia*," *Dante Studies* 105 (1987): 1–42.

2. Stanley Fish, *Self-Consuming Artifacts: The Experience of Seventeenth-Century Literature* (Berkeley: University of California Press, 1974), ch. 1. The relevance of Fish's discussion to the *Paradiso* was pointed out by Peter Hawkins: "Using the example of the *Phaedrus*, Fish describes the experience of reading such a work as a mimetic re-enactment of the Platonic ladder, with each successive 'rung' rejected even as it is negotiated, until finally the whole structure is thrown over, leaving the reader with him- or herself—and with whatever enlightenment has grown within" ("Dante's *Paradiso* and the Dialectic of Ineffability," *Ineffability: Naming the Un-*

*namable from Dante to Beckett*, ed. Anne Howland Schotter [New York: AMS Press, 1984], 5–21; quotation, 9). An emblem of the *Paradiso*'s functioning as a self-consuming artifact is its treatment of the moonspots, discussed at such length in canto 2 but no longer visible when the pilgrim looks down at the end of canto 22: "Vidi la figlia di Latona incensa / sanza quell'ombra che mi fu cagione / per che già la credetti rara e densa" (139–41).

3. The word "lyrical," effusively bandied about, and in a vague counterpoint with something else, is a hallmark of criticism on the third canticle (see, for instance, the resume provided by Gioacchino Paparelli, "Il *Paradiso*," *Cultura e scuola* 4 [1965]: 391–405), which I have tried to revive in more precise fashion, without engaging in too many lyrical effusions of my own. By "lyrical" I intend to denote certain textual characteristics that, as Aldo Scaglione points out with reference to enjambment, become paramount in the *Paradiso*: "It may seem paradoxical that the *Paradiso*—the Cantica which to Romantic ears sounded inferior to the *Inferno* because it lacked its dramatic emotionalism—would display more numerous cases of functional, expressive *enjambement*, because there LYRICAL emotion more frequently runs ahead of the forms" ("Periodic Syntax and Flexible Meter in the *Divina Commedia*," *Romance Philology* 21 [1967]: 1–22; quotation, 17). I also mean to denote an authorial intention to dechronologize narrative, a project whose roots I trace as far back as the *Vita Nuova*; see my "'Cominciandomi dal principio infino a la fine': Forging Anti-Narrative in Dante's *Vita Nuova*," in "*Gloriosa donna de la mente*": *A Commentary on the Vita Nuova*, ed. Vincent Moleta (Florence: Olschki, 1993). I do not share the desire to stigmatize one type of discourse and laud another that frequently motivates the word "lyrical" in *Paradiso* criticism; this tendency is still present, for instance, in Anna M. Chiavacci Leonardi, *Lettura del "Paradiso" dantesco* (Florence: Sansoni, 1963), who suggests that "l'alta fatica dei discorsi teologici è forse il prezzo che Dante paga per i suoi momenti lirici più puri" (115).

4. *Confessions* 11.15, trans. R. S. Pine-Coffin (London: Penguin, 1961).

5. Carol Zaleski notes that "the critical glance back at the earth is a common episode in otherworld journey narratives" (*Otherworld Journeys* [New York: Oxford University Press, 1987], 90); in *Things Unutterable: Paul's Ascent to Paradise in Its Greco-Roman, Judaic, and Early Christian Contexts* (Lanham, Md.: University Press of America, 1986), James Tabor cites an archaic backward glance that is strangely reminiscent of the *Commedia*, from "bread basket" to "aiuola": "My friend, cast a glance at how the land appears! The land has turned into a furrow . . ., and the wide sea is just like a bread basket" (70).

6. Although Lino Pertile begins his *lectura*, "Stile e immagini in *Paradiso* XXIII," *The Italianist* 4 (1984): 7–34, by calling canto 23 "uno dei canti più semplici di tutta la *Commedia*" (7), he in fact demonstrates that the canto's apparent "simplicity" (deriving from its lack of characters and events, its "vuoto narrativo" [14]) "finisce insomma per essere più complessa e misteriosa della complessità stessa" (7). Pertile's essay is a detailed rhetorico-linguistic demonstration of canto 23's complex circularity, in which he exhorts us to observe "come nel testo ogni tentativo di narrare si risolva, per la natura stessa della materia, in enunciati consecutivi, comparativi ipotetici, o interrogativi indiretti" (13).

7. Pertile notes the presence of six major similes and three exclamations, as well as commenting on the canto's "linguaggio fortemente caratterizzato in senso affet-

tivo" ("Stile e immmagini," 17), "vera poesia lirica" (22), "penetrazione affettiva e sentimentale, più che logica e razionale" (22), and "linguaggio altamente metaforico" (23).

8. The same perfectly tuned sweetness is found in the opening tercet of *Purg.* 8, whose final verse ("lo dì c'han detto ai dolci amici addio") is even rhythmically reminiscent of the equivalent verse in *Par.* 23 ("la notte che le cose ci nasconde").

9. For the rhetorical means by which this simile achieves its effects, see Aldo Scaglione, "Imagery and Thematic Patterns in *Paradiso* XXIII," in *From Time to Eternity: Essays on Dante's "Divine Comedy"*, ed. Thomas G. Bergin (New Haven, Conn.: Yale University Press, 1967), 137–72.

10. Manuela Colombo derives verses 40–51 from Richard of St. Victor; see "L'ineffabilità della 'visio mystica': il XXIII canto del *Paradiso* e il *Benjamin Major* di Riccardo da San Vittore," *Strumenti critici*, n.s. 1 (1986): 225–39, rpt. as chapter 4 of her monograph, *Dai mistici a Dante: Il linguaggio dell'ineffabilità* (Florence: La Nuova Italia, 1987), which mainly treats the history and usage of the Latin *ineffabilis* and the Italian *ineffabile*. Umberto Bosco cites Gregory the Great on the soul's dilation in "Il trionfo di Cristo (XXIII del *Paradiso*)," 1964, rpt. in *Dante vicino*, 2d ed. (Caltanisetta: Sciascia, 1972), 342–68.

11. Rather than supplying metaphoric obstacles obstructing the poet's metaphoric path, it seems preferable to maintain his image; cutting off suggests not the presence of an obstacle but the absence of path, as in the already registered absence of *essempli degni*. As Philippe Sollers puts it: "le 'poème sacré' doit 'sauter,' accepter son manque" ("Dante et la traversée de l'écriture," *L'écriture et l'expérience des limites* [Paris: Seuil, 1968], 43).

12. "In exitu" is Psalm 113 in the Vulgate, and Psalm 114 in the King James translation, both cited above. The verb *exsultare*, rendered "to skip" in the King James version, means "to spring vigorously," "to leap," or "to jump up"; interestingly, the modern Latin version of the Psalms approved by Pius XII in 1945 substitutes *saltare*: "Montes saltarunt ut arietes, / Colles ut agnelli." The apostles are figured as mountains in *Par.* 25.38–39, in language that the commentators derive from the Psalms.

13. With reference to *Purg.* 10.65, "trescando," Natalino Sapegno comments "danzando," pointing out that "*tresca* era un ballo saltato, di origine e di uso popolare"; he also cites Daniello's interpretation of "trescando alzato" as "in atto di saltare" (*La Divina Commedia* [Florence: La Nuova Italia, 1968], 2:110).

14. Patrick Boyde discusses "a very important axiom in the Aristotelian theory, which was usually stated in the form: *Natura non facit saltum*" (*Dante Philomythes and Philosopher: Man in the Cosmos* [Cambridge: Cambridge University Press, 1981], 129). And see Marino Barchiesi's elegant comment, in "Arte del prologo e arte della transizione," *Studi danteschi* 44 (1967): "Come è stato detto giustamente, a differenza della natura (o, almeno, della natura tradizionale), l'arte *facit saltus*" (141).

15. The increased use of enjambment in the *Paradiso* is noted by Valerio Lucchesi, "The Dantean Stamp," *The World of Dante*, ed. Cecil Grayson (Oxford: Clarendon Press, 1980), 166–97, who claims that "there is ample evidence and justification for calling the *Paradiso* the *cantica* of the open rhythms" (180). Joan Ferrante offers the only actual data I have come across: "While the instances of strict enjamb-

342 NOTES TO CHAPTER 10

ment in Purgatory number in the tens and twenties per canto, and are usually fewer than fifteen per canto in Hell, they rise to the thirties, forties and fifties in Paradise" ("A Poetics of Chaos and Harmony," *Cambridge Companion to Dante*, ed. Rachel Jacoff [Cambridge: Cambridge University Press], 1993).

16. From this perspective, one could invert Croce's dictum that posited the greatest number of "lyrics" in the *Inferno*; such passages are in fact more frequent in the *Paradiso*.

17. Let me remind the reader that Dante's text is far too rich and complex for these categories ever to obtain absolutely; thus, I would agree with Bosco that "gli esami sono intrisi di lirismo e culminano in esso" ("Teologia e non teologia negli ultimi canti del *Paradiso*," *Letterature comparate: Problemi e metodo. Studi in onore di E. Paratore* [Bologna: Pàtron, 1981], 3:1219–36; quotation, 1220), while at the same time affirming their basic identity as intellective rather than affective cantos.

18. The opening of canto 24 also includes the "affezione immensa" (7) that the pilgrim feels for the souls and Beatrice's maintaining of the mystical garden imagery in her request that they "water" him with their wisdom.

19. Both other uses belong to the heaven of the sun, and are less unambiguously positive; see *Par.* 11.2 ("quanto son difettivi silogismi") and 10.138 ("silogizzò invidïosi veri").

20. A possible confirmation of the play on *differenti menti* could be found in the later remark that God created "le menti tutte" (*Par.* 32.64). Giovanni Reggio notes "la spezzatura dell'avverbio nei suoi due elementi, dove è evidente la coscienza della sua formazione da un aggettivo e dalla parola *mente*" (*La Divina Commedia*, ed. and comm. Umberto Bosco and Giovanni Reggio, 3 vols. [Florence: Le Monnier, 1979], 3:398); see also Scaglione, who notes in "the extremely rare *enjambement* by etymological tmesis" an "echo of *trobar clus* techniques" ("Periodic Syntax," 19).

21. "Qui la spezzatura ritrae anco la differenza" (Guido Biagi, ed., *"La Divina Commedia" nella figurazione artistica e nel secolare commento*, 3 vols. [Turin: Unione Tipografico-Editrice Torinese, 1924–1929], 3:532).

22. Scaglione notes, with respect to the Trivia image, that "the vehicle and tenor lack even a logical relationship" (162), adding that in canto 23 we witness an "example of broad, lyrical, 'intuitive' texture rather than close logical context, and particularly of an image that is more a consequence of the 'spirit' or state of mind of the canto than of the logic of the immediate comparison" ("Imagery and Thematic Patterns in *Paradiso* XXIII," 171).

23. For the self-authorizing language of these cantos, see Kevin Brownlee, "Why the Angels Speak Italian: Dante as Vernacular *Poeta* in *Paradiso* 25," *Poetics Today* 5 (1984): 597–610, as well as Teodolinda Barolini, *Dante's Poets: Textuality and Truth in the "Comedy"* (Princeton, N.J.: Princeton University Press, 1984), esp. 268ff.

24. The reading and writing of "questa corte" (*Par.* 26.16) recalls *Inf.* 5, while the image of Love reading to the pilgrim recalls *Purg.* 24; John's question asking "con quanti denti questo amor ti morde" (51) echoes "co li denti d'Amor già mi manduca" ("Così nel mio parlar," 32).

25. Dante does not "meet" Bernard in the same way: as a guide, the saint is moved by Beatrice to come to Dante ("mosse Beatrice me del loco mio" [*Par.* 31.66]), as Vergil was moved by Beatrice and Beatrice was moved by love.

26. See Bruno Nardi, "La dottrina dell'Empireo nella sua genesi storica e nel pen-

siero dantesco," *Saggi di filosofia dantesca*, 2d ed. (Florence: La Nuova Italia, 1967), 167–214, who comments apropos these verses: "A guardar bene, l'Empireo, nel pensiero di Dante, serve a saldare la rottura del dualismo teologico, fra il mondo spirituale e l'universo sensibile, in una perfetta e continua unità" (209). Nardi's conclusions, however, err in the direction of making Dante's heaven too Neoplatonic.

27. The narrative dimension of the backward glance is underscored lexically by the juxtaposed beginnings, middles, and ends of the verse that describes the distance traveled by the pilgrim as "the arc that the first climactic zone makes from its middle to its end": "l'arco / che fa *dal mezzo al fine il primo* clima" (*Par.* 27.80–81).

28. By contrast, he knows precisely at what point he entered the heaven of the fixed stars. The adjective *uniforme* is also used to characterize the primum mobile in the *Questio de aqua et terra*: "Et cum primum mobile, scilicet spera nona, sit *uniforme* per totum et per consequens *uniformiter* per totum virtuatum" (68). Dante continues on from this passage to discuss the *diversitas* of the eighth heaven.

29. For John A. Scott, canto 27's "drammaticità si fonda non solo su un alternarsi tra 'violenza' e 'serenità' verbale, ma su tutta una serie di opposizioni assai spiccate" ("Immagini tematiche di *Paradiso* XXVII," *Dante magnanimo* [Florence: Olschki, 1977], 195–237; quotation, 234).

30. See the Bosco-Reggio commentary, *La Divina Commedia* 3:465; Reggio labels verse 67 the major premise of the syllogism and verse 68 the minor premise.

31. Daniel M. Murtaugh notes that "Beatrice's solution of the problem—a proportion between dimension in the 'essemplo' and velocity in the 'essemplare'—really has the effect of reducing both images to the same convertible status as signs, with their final reality not in themselves, but in what they refer to" ("'Figurando il paradiso': The Signs That Render Dante's Heaven," *PMLA* 90 [1975]: 277–84; quotation, 281). I would add that Dante sets himself up to fail; the pilgrim's use of the metapoetic terminology *essemplo* and *essemplare* indicates the poet's deliberate dramatization of his dilemma. In other words, Beatrice is supposed to "trick" us, but we are also supposed to notice her doing it. On the other hand, it should be noted that a physicist has suggested that Dante's language in this passage does not fail, but is an accurate representation of a 3-sphere; see Mark A. Peterson, "Dante and the 3-Sphere," *American Journal of Physics* 47, n. 12 (Dec. 1979): 1031–35. Particularly suggestive in Peterson's reading, to my narrative sensibility, is his claim that in canto 28 Dante resolves an "unsatisfactory feature of the Aristotelian cosmology" with regard to what would happen when he, "as narrator of the *Paradiso*, got to the 'edge' or 'top' of the universe" (1031). According to Peterson, Dante resolves the problem of describing the edge of the universe by conceptualizing a 3-sphere, which "has no boundary; every point is interior" (1032): "In Canto 27 Dante looks down into the first semi-universe and sees the earth ('this little threshing floor') far below him. At the beginning of Canto 28 he *turns around* and *looks up* into the second semi-universe" (1034). Peterson's thesis is attractive, and can, I believe, coexist with my reading, for if physicists one day succeed in finding the "unified theory" that will accommodate both the general theory of relativity and quantum mechanics (the very large and the very small, the *essemplo* and the *essemplare*!), they will not, I fear, be able to express their discovery in a language that we pilgrims will understand.

32. For *vero* as the leitmotif of canto 28, see Gianfranco Contini, "Un esempio di poesia dantesca (il canto XXVIII del *Paradiso*)," in *Un'idea di Dante* (Turin: Einaudi,

1970), 191–213. On the other hand, Dante's richness and resistance to being pigeon-holed is well served by Riccardo Scrivano's recent insistence on the canto's mystical currents, particularly the Bonaventurian exemplarism implicit in the use of *essemplo* and *essemplare*, "termini assolutamente bonaventuriani, che mettono in luce che qui si tratta di conoscenza mistica e non intellettuale, filosofica" (*"Paradiso* 28," *Quaderni d'italianistica* 10 [1989]: 269–85; quotation, 277). By the same token, Anna Maria Chiavacci Leonardi points to canto 28's beautiful verses on the angelic orders that flower "in questa primavera sempiterna" (116) as the stylistic forerunners of the "rosa sempiterna" that constitutes the lyrical zenith of canto 30 ("Il canto XXX del *Paradiso*," *Paragone* 308 [1975]: 3–34).

33. A major thematic thread of the *Paradiso* is the poet's treatment of the two approaches toward beatitude: the desire to know God he translates into vision, and the desire to love God he translates into circular motion. Not only does he take great care to strike a balance between seeing/knowing and wanting/loving, treating them in chiasmically circular fashion in passages such as *Par.* 14.40–51, but he gives us mixed signals regarding their priority: his handling of St. Francis, for instance, provides an instance in which Dante signals the priority of loving over knowing. Although canto 28 establishes the priority of knowing over loving, I would argue that Dante works to blur this hierarchy and reintroduce circular balance before the end of the poem. Support for this view is offered by Lino Pertile's demonstration that the semantic sphere of desire in *Paradiso* extends equally to the affective and the intellective; see "'La punta del disio': storia di una metafora dantesca," *Lectura Dantis: A Forum for Dante Research and Interpretation* 7 (1990): 3–28.

34. Dante could hardly have failed to take note of the semantic shift that provided his culture the word *cursus*, used metaphorically and "discursively" for the various Latin prose rhythms. In this very canto Dante will use figuratively and discursively the past participle of the verb *trascorrere* ("trascorse" in verse 95, meaning "elaborated" and referring to the "invenzioni" of the fraudulent preachers), derived like *discorrere* from Latin *currere*, in a move that suggests he could likewise play on the relation between *discorrere* and its past participle, *discorso*.

35. In "Il canto XXIX del *Paradiso*," *Convivium*, n.s. 24 (1956): 294–302, Bruno Nardi sustains that Dante's position on angelic memory counters that of St. Thomas: "L'osservazione muove da un principio schiettamente aristotelico-averroistico, e colpisce non solo Duns Scoto, come pretendeva il Bodrero, ma lo stesso San Tommaso" (301). Stephen Bemrose comments, more moderately, that "although St Thomas is just as emphatic as Dante that angelic contemplation is uninterrupted, he does not bring this in to the argument about whether or not they have memory" (*Dante's Angelic Intelligences: Their Importance in the Cosmos and in Pre-Christian Religion* [Rome: Edizioni di Storia e Letteratura, 1983], 75). Although Aquinas insists, like Dante, on uninterrupted angelic contemplation (*ST* 1a.58.1), he is less fervid in denying any form of memory: "Again, 'memory' may be ascribed to them [angels], if the term is used in the Augustinian sense as a faculty of 'mind,' but not if used for a part of the sentient soul" (1a.54.5; Blackfriars 1968, 9:89–91, ed. and trans. Kenelm Foster).

36. *Northanger Abbey*, the penultimate page (London: J. M. Dent, 1906).

37. I am aware of having already used two of these labels, when I referred to the first look back as "the beginning of the beginning of the end" and the last look back

as "the end of the beginning of the end." The seeming inconsistency is the result of a rhetorical problem that afflicts the one who would describe the self-consuming artifact as well as the one who would create it, stemming from the very nature of the beast, whose continued progress depends on and requires constant demotions of all that precedes. Thus, the backward glances should from our current vantage be degraded into "beginning of the beginning of the beginning of the end" and "end of the beginning of the beginning of the end"; more appalling still is the thought that such labeling could theoretically be applied all the way back to the poem's first beginning . . . of the end.

38. In nominal form, *spezzare* has had some currency in Dante criticism; see Luigi Malagoli on the "spezzature" of Dante's style in *Linguaggio e poesia nella "Divina Commedia"* (Genoa: Briano, 1949) and Robin Kirkpatrick's discussion of Malagoli in *Dante's "Paradiso" and the Limitations of Modern Criticism* (Cambridge: Cambridge University Press, 1978), 130–37.

39. Most readings of canto 30 refer to it as marking, in Prudence Shaw's words, "the beginning of the end of the *Comedy*" ("*Paradiso* XXX," *Cambridge Readings in Dante's "Comedy"*, ed. Kenelm Foster and Patrick Boyde [Cambridge: Cambridge University Press, 1981], 191–213; quotation, 191). Fewer comment on the relation of canto 23 to canto 30, other than to note the presence in both of a great ineffability passage.

40. It is worth noting that *interciso*, from the passage in which the angels do not have "vedere interciso / da novo obietto" (*Par.* 29.79–80) also rhymes with and is formed from the same stem as *preciso* and *riciso*; again, Dante is conflating the narrative path, now interrupted, with the path of life, interrupted for humans but not for angels. See Chiavacci Leonardi, "Il canto XXX del *Paradiso*," 10–11, for a comparison of the metapoetic passages of cantos 23 and 30; also on both, more generally, see Francesco Tateo, *Questioni di poetica dantesca* (Bari: Adriatica, 1972), chapter 7.

41. As Chiavacci Leonardi puts it: "mentre l'attenzione logica, il primo piano sintattico, è rivolta all'ampiezza ('e se l'infimo grado in sé raccoglie—sì grande lume, quanta è la larghezza'), subentra come casualmente, come si parlasse di cosa già nota, la grande immagine: 'di questa rosa ne l'estreme foglie!'" ("Il canto XXX del *Paradiso*," 20).

42. For the city image and its political program, see John Scott: "After the word 'città' the political thread that runs through the whole of Dante's poem becomes most apparent" ("*Paradiso* XXX," *Dante Commentaries*, ed. David Nolan [Dublin: Irish Academic Press, 1977], 159–80; quotation, 172).

43. Peter Dronke notes that "since Antiquity, in both profane and sacred contexts, the rose had at times epitomized the paradox of unity and multiplicity" ("Symbolism and Structure in *Paradiso* 30," *Romance Philology* 43 [1989]: 29–48; quotation, 41).

44. Although it is customary to point out that this is the *Commedia*'s only triple rhyme on any word other than *Cristo*, in fact, as Prudence Shaw notes ("*Paradiso* XXX," 207), there is a triple rhyme on "per ammenda" in *Purg.* 20.65–69.

45. I mean no censure to this *dunque*, and in fact would agree with Scaglione, who, noting Dante's ability (unusual in medieval verse) to use adverbs and conjunctions that "retain their full ratiocinative value" comments: "One has only to think of the

sublimely natural *dunque* [of *Par.* 31.1], tying the start of a Canto with the preceding discourse in a smooth flow, which lifts even the most prosaic elements of speech, the matter-of-fact connecting links of *sermo humilis*, to the level of poetry" ("Periodic Syntax," 8 n. 19).

46. Canto 31's fifth verse, "la gloria di colui che la 'nnamora," completes its evocation of the *Paradiso*'s opening tercet.

47. For the *ordo* of the souls within the rose, see Giuseppe Di Scipio, *The Symbolic Rose in Dante's "Paradiso"* (Ravenna: Longo, 1984).

48. Dante seems to be studying the formula of merit and grace as the twin components of beatitude from every possible perspective, and to have found in the virtuous pagans and the infants an opportunity to ponder the two extreme cases: while a saved pagan poses an instance of an exceptionally meritorious soul initially lacking in grace, a saved infant presents the opposite configuration, lacking merit and possessing only grace. These two extreme cases meet in limbo, home for both the virtuous pagans who are not graced, and the infants who do not meet the conditions for salvation outlined in *Par.* 32.

49. The same point is made by Steven Botterill, "Doctrine, Doubt and Certainty: *Paradiso* XXXII.40–84," *Italian Studies* 42 (1987): 20–36, who notes that "this doctrinal passage consists, not of argument, but of a series of assertions" (28).

50. Botterill, "Doctrine, Doubt and Certainty," 33.

51. As part of the Ulyssean program of the last canto, Dante draws an implicit comparison between Ulysses and Bernard and their two very different *orazioni*. But there is also a comparison to be made between the pilgrim and Bernard, as two cultivators of *preghiera*; interestingly, while the noun "prieghi" occurs more often in *Par.* 33 than in any other canto, and the verb "priego" is also registered there twice, "preghiera" is used only in *Inf.* 26, with respect to the pilgrim's prayer to speak to Ulysses, and in *Purg.* 11, with respect to the Lord's Prayer chanted by the souls. Steven Botterill notes the historical Bernard's eloquence, commenting, with respect to Dante's fictive saint, that the efficacy of his speech, "combined with his narrative position at the poem's climax, makes Bernard the supreme rebuke to all those characters in the *Commedia* who stand condemned for using language improperly or inadequately" ("Life after Beatrice: Bernard of Clairvaux in *Paradiso* XXXI," *Texas Studies in Literature and Language* 32 [1990]: 120–36; quotation, 132).

52. Unfortunately, Petrocchi offers no comment on the ending of *Par.* 32; on punctuation in general he offers only the brief paragraph "L'interpunzione" ("*La Commedia" secondo l'antica vulgata* 1:472). Nor does the *ED* contain information on the subject. In Petrocchi's edition, the following other deviations from the period occur: *Inf.* 24, exclamation; *Purg.* 24, exclamation; *Purg.* 31, question; *Par.* 24, exclamation; *Par.* 25, exclamation. In a facsimile of a 1337 manuscript, *Il Codice Trivulziano 1080 della "Divina Commedia"* (Milan: Hoepli, 1921), none of the final verses that bear distinctive punctuation in modern editions are marked differently from the others; and, although the last word of *Par.* 32 is not followed by as clear a *punctus* as we find throughout, the same may be said of the end of *Par.* 18.

53. In my opinion, no text more deliberately exemplifies what Robert Scholes calls "the orgastic pattern of fiction" than *Par.* 33 (see *Fabulation and Metafiction* [Urbana: University of Illinois Press, 1979], 26–28). This is not surprising, but a

reminder that even the most sublime of mystical unions must borrow its referentiality from its humble physical analogue. In E. H. Wilkins's more austere presentation, canto 33 constitutes "the supreme instance of Dante's use of his technique of gradual approach" ("Gradual Approach in the *Divine Comedy*," *The Invention of the Sonnet and Other Studies in Italian Literature* [Rome: Edizioni di Storia e Letteratura, 1959], 101).

54. Many of the *lecturae* of *Par.* 33 pay more attention to the prayer than to what follows; this is the case, for instance, with Mario Fubini, "L'ultimo canto del *Paradiso*," in *Il peccato d'Ulisse e altri scritti danteschi* [Milan: Ricciardi, 1966], 101–36, and Enzo Esposito, "Il canto dell'ultima visione (*Par.* XXXIII)," *Letture classensi* 7 (1979): 13–26. Criticism on this canto wavers between those who attempt to describe what Dante has done (e.g., Piero Boitani, "The Sibyl's Leaves: A Study of *Paradiso* XXXIII," *Dante Studies* 96 [1978]: 83–126), and those who stress the inadequacy of language at such a juncture (for an extreme case, see Giuliana Carugati, "Dante 'Mistico'?", *Quaderni d'italianistica* 10 [1989]: 237–50, who critiques the poet's lack of originality).

55. Kenelm Foster notes that after the prayer "the vision itself is then stated in a succession of alternated exclamations and precise descriptions," which "fall into three graded divisions, each corresponding to a stage in the voyager's approach to the completest possible sight of the nature of God" ("Dante's Vision of God," *The Two Dantes* [Berkeley: University of California Press, 1977], 83). Wilkins comments that "the attempted statements of increasing achievement are separated by recognitions of inadequacy and by exclamations of gratitude and rapture" ("Gradual Approach," 101).

56. "Un punto solo," for Eugene M. Longen, "may properly be understood to mean not only the moment of vision and the moment after the vision, but the substance of the vision as well"; he comments also on the passage's "infraction of the rules of both logic and grammar" ("The Grammar of Apotheosis: *Paradiso* XXXIII, 94–99," *Dante Studies* 93 [1975]: 209–14). On the "punto solo" as eternity, the Augustinian instant, see Francesco Tateo, "Il 'punto' della visione e una reminiscenza da Boezio," in *Questioni di poetica dantesca*, 203–16.

57. Dante goes on to explain that within the light the good, which is the will's object ("ch'è del volere obietto" [103]), is fully gathered, and that outside of it is defective all that within it is perfect ("e fuor di quella / è defettivo ciò ch'è lì perfetto" [104–5]). The use of "defettivo" in the context of desire recalls the *Convivio*'s definition of desire as "manifesto difetto" ("ché nullo desidera quello che ha, ma quello che non ha, che è manifesto difetto" [3.15.3]), as well as the *Vita Nuova*'s quest for "quello che non mi puote venire meno" (18.4).

58. The importance of the heaven of the sun is underscored by these echoes of it at the poem's end; we have moved from *Par.* 12's "due archi paralleli e concolori" (11) to the greater mystery of three circles "di tre colori e d'una contenenza" (33.117).

59. I had originally, without consideration of factors like length or symmetry, placed the end of the second movement at line 108, beginning the third movement with the reentry into plot of verse 109. The discovery of the invisible ink thus served both to confirm and correct my reading.

APPENDIX
TRANSITION: HOW CANTOS BEGIN AND END

1. See the opening pages of "Analisi 'retorica' del canto di Pier della Vigna," *Studi danteschi* 42 (1965): 281–336. Unfortunately, although Paratore writes of "quella nuova tecnica di connessione più lassa, a onda più lenta e più larga, che contraddistingue la maggioranza dei canti del *Paradiso*" (282), he does not give us his data for *Purgatorio* and *Paradiso*, so that we do not know, for instance, which are the *Purgatorio*'s ten "inizi di salda connessione." Guglielmo Gorni discusses the sources of the *Commedia*'s incipits in "La teoria del 'cominciamento,'" *Il nodo della lingua e il verbo d'amore* (Florence: Olschki, 1981), 143–86, as well as offering an "Indice alfabetico dei capoversi dei canti della *Commedia*."

2. In *Dante's Poets: Textuality and Truth in the "Comedy"* (Princeton, N.J.: Princeton University Press, 1984), 107–8, I touch on canzone length in Dante, Arnaut, and Guittone, noting that the *Commedia* is "the equivalent of many canzoni stitched together." Gorni makes a similar point: "Non mi pare che . . . si sia mai guardato ai canti della *Commedia* come a un insieme di cento canzoni, fornite di altrettanti incipit" (164).

3. For the reader's information, literal forward (or upward) movement in the *Paradiso* occurs at the following points: transition to the moon in *Par.* 2.25; transition to Mercury in *Par.* 5.93; transition to Venus in *Par.* 8.13; transition to the sun in *Par.* 10.34; transition to Mars in *Par.* 14.83; transition to Jupiter in *Par.* 18.61; transition to Saturn in *Par.* 21.13; transition to the fixed stars in *Par.* 22.111; transition to the primum mobile in *Par.* 27.99; transition to the empyrean in *Par.* 30.38. These passages are in themselves worthy of study, for the ways in which their rhetoric both accomplishes and masks the necessary transition.

4. See "Cantos, Regions and Transitions in the *Divine Comedy*," *The Invention of the Sonnet and Other Studies in Italian Literature* (Rome: Edizioni di Storia e Letteratura, 1959), 103–10.

# INDEX

acrostic, 127–29, 141, 308n.14, 309n.17
Adam, 49, 52, 58, 106, 108, 112, 211,
  231, 238, 283n.13, 320n.46, 329n.36,
  332n.53
Adams, S., 307n.3, 322n.55
address to the reader, 14, 223, 224, 287n.40
Aeneas, 11, 57
Aesop's *Fables*, 82–84, 86, 87
Ahern, J., 282n.4, 310n.19, 313n.38, 326n.16
Alanus, 10
Alberigo (frate), 94–95
Albert the Great, 3
Allan, M., 271n.36
allegory, 4–11, 20; of poets, 4, 5, 7, 158,
  214–15; of theologians, 4, 5, 7, 10, 16,
  158, 214
Allen, J. B., 280n.58
Almansi, G., 295n.33
Alter, R., 271n.38
Anderson, W. S., 149, 311n.25, 319n.35
angels, 18, 22, 23, 236–37, 238–40, 243
antehell, 33, 36, 39, 41
antepurgatory, 33, 34, 39. *See also* valley of
  princes
Arachne, 64, 130–31, 132, 141, 296n.40
Argus, 156, 157, 160, 161, 163
Aristotle, 25, 39, 49, 153, 169, 173, 175, 191,
  192, 195, 221, 227, 233, 274n.9, 322n.57,
  343n.31; *Physics*, 21, 276n.20. *See also*
  time
Armour, P., 34, 121, 298n.3, 306n.53,
  321n.48
Arnaut, Daniel, 348n.2
Ascoli, A. R., 305n.44
Auerbach, E., 5, 10, 14, 18, 194–95, 333n.3
Augustine, Saint, 9, 13, 101–10, 124, 148,
  167, 174, 188, 191, 221, 233, 248, 274n.6,
  312n.35, 313n.3, 347n.56; *City of God*,
  321n.47; *Confessions*, 3, 12, 103, 107,
  167–69, 284n.21, 299n.10, 300nn. 12 and
  17, 303n.35, 312n.35, 319n.39, 331n.44;
  *De doctrina Christiana*, 11, 12, 110, 131,
  281n.58, 291n.5, 293n.20, 299n.9,
  302n.24, 307n.7; *De genesi ad litteram*, 19,
  146, 147, 149, 152, 316n.19, 317n.25,
  321n.47; *De quantitate animae*, 317n.26;
  *Enchiridion*, 102. *See also* time
Austen, J., 218, 240

authenticating device, narrative, 15, 19, 32,
  59, 94, 286n.37
Avalle, D. S., 283n.16
Averroes, 173, 178, 329n.35

Baldelli, I., 147, 314n.6
Baldelli, L., 308n.14
Barański, Z., 10, 287n.42, 292n.12, 295n.30,
  303n.36, 321n.49
Bàrberi Squarotti, G., 290n.66, 297n.46
Barbi, M., 145–46, 314n.9, 334n.6
Barchiesi, M., 76, 274n.10, 287n.46, 290n.68,
  291n.2, 292n.11, 341n.14
Barkan, L., 311n.25
Barolini, T., 18, 267n.5, 269n.20, 270n.32,
  271nn. 34 and 36, 277n.26, 279n.49,
  285n.34, 286n.38, 292n.7, 293nn. 16 and
  17, 294n.27, 299n.5, 301n.22, 304nn. 40
  and 42, 307n.3, 310n.23, 322n.56,
  323n.62, 338n.31, 340n.3, 342n.23
Basile, B., 298n.2
Battaglia Ricci, L., 11, 91, 274n.10, 284n.28,
  290n.68
Beatrice (selections), 24, 30, 102–3, 107,
  138–39, 158, 163, 188–90, 222, 226, 242–
  43, 247, 277n.30, 299n.8, 303n.36,
  320n.45, 322n.53, 342n.25
beginnings/endings, 22, 26–47, 67, 71–72,
  74–75, 88, 101, 161–62, 220, 221–24, 232,
  240, 251–56, 345n.37. *See also* Appendix
Belacqua, 33, 113–14
Bemrose, S., 344n.35
Benedict, Saint, 101, 195, 221–22, 248
Benvenuto da Imola, 25, 49, 276n.25,
  323n.60, 326n.16
Berk, P. R., 308n.14
Berlin, I., 173
Bernard, Saint, 9, 145–46, 161, 240, 247,
  314n.6, 316n.19, 317n.26, 342n.25
Berni, Francesco, 3
Bertoldi, A., 333n.3, 334nn. 6 and 10,
  335n.13
Bertran de Born, 60, 90
Bible, 11, 16, 155, 214, 231; Apocalypse, 11,
  78, 79, 146, 149, 154, 158, 159, 161,
  306n.52; 2 Corinthians, 8, 144, 148; Deu-
  teronomy, 14; Genesis, 12, 273n.2; Isaiah,
  273n.2; John, 273n.2; 2 Kings, 319n.36; 3

350 INDEX

Kings, 337n.23, 339n.36; Luke, 337n.28;
Matthew, 141, 157, 317n.26; Psalms, 227
Blasucci, L., 299n.5
Bloom, H., 271n.39
Bloomfield, M., 14, 271n.33, 297n.47
Boccaccio, G., 7, 52, 82, 311n.30
Bocca degli Abati, 93–94
Boethius, 168–69, 170
Boitani, P., 297nn. 46 and 47, 298n.51,
347n.54
Bonaventure, Saint, 195, 198, 200–201, 203,
213, 215, 249, 323n.61, 333n.2, 344n.32
Boni, M., 278n.36
Boniface VIII, 79, 94, 248, 303n.34
Bonora, E., 336n.17
Bonvesin de la Riva, 281n.60, 325nn. 11
and 13
Borges, J. L., 285n.33
Borgese, G. A., 289n.62
Bosco, U., 52, 280n.52, 283n.14, 333n.2,
334n.6, 341n.10, 342n.17
Botterill, S., 272n.50, 296n.38, 317n.26,
346nn. 49, 50, and 51
Boureau, A., 339n.36
Boyde, P., 173, 181, 329n.33, 334n.7,
341n.14
Bozzoli, A., 283n.18
Branca Doria, 94, 96
Brentano, R., 338n.34
Bronzini, G. B., 273n.5
Browne, Sir Thomas, 48, 74
Brownlee, K., 288n.50, 342n.23
Brunetto Latini, 16, 71, 136, 140
Bufano, L., 335n.15
Bundy, M. W., 317n.25, 320n.39
Busnelli, G., 279n.44
Buti, Francesco da, 49, 63, 269n.17
Bynum, C. W., 312n.35

Cacciaguida, 18–19, 60, 137, 138–40, 218–
19, 221, 222
Calcaterra, C., 299n.6
Cambon, G., 289n.58
Camporesi, P., 294n.24
Cangrande della Scala, 139
Carugati, G., 53, 54, 270n.31, 272n.50,
284n.19, 285n.28, 287n.42, 347n.54
caryatids, 125–26, 130
Casella, 101, 103, 107
Cassell, A., 50, 51, 147, 268n.14, 276n.22,
282n.2, 283n.11, 302n.25
Cato, 77, 101, 112, 113, 305n.44, 323n.61

Cavalcanti, Cavalcante de', 278n.42
Cavalcanti, Guido, 133, 134, 294n.26,
319n.40
Cecchetti, G., 298n.4
Cecchini, E., 286n.39
Celestine V, 278n.41
Cervigni, D. S., 277n.34, 315n.15, 318n.31,
319n.37, 320n.46
Charles Martel, 192
Charon, 68
Cherchi, P., 290n.69
Chiampi, J. T., 307n.3, 308n.9
Chiappelli, A., 285n.34
Chiappelli, F., 291n.3
Chiarenza, M. M., 54, 188, 317n.25
Chiari, A., 333n.3
Chiavacci Leonardi, A. M., 284n.28, 340n.3,
344n.32, 345nn. 40 and 41
Ciacco, 43
Cicchito, L., 333n.3, 335n.13, 339nn. 35 and
37
Cicero, 108
Cino da Pistoia, 48
circulata melodia, 228–29, 230, 244, 250,
252, 254, 256
classical/contemporary couples, 76–77, 83,
88–89
Clement V, 114, 115
Colish, M., 324n.8
collocation fallacy, 15, 19, 33, 282n.4,
286n.34
Colombo, M., 341n.10
comedìa, 8, 59, 61, 67, 76, 77, 78, 81, 83, 226
Consoli, D., 308n.12
Conte, G. B., 17
Contini, G., 150, 275n.13, 297n.44, 312n.33,
343n.32
contrapasso, 35, 46, 47
Corsi, S., 305n.51
Corsini, E., 321n.48
Corti, M., 50, 302n.23
Cosmo, U., 333nn. 2 and 3, 334n.6, 335n.13,
337n.29
Cousins, E. H., 319n.39
Crispolti, F., 333n.3, 334n.6, 335nn. 13 and
15
Cristaldi, S., 321n.48
Croce, B., 4, 7, 10, 11, 51, 267n.3, 283n.15,
291n.2, 293n.15, 342n.16
Cunizza, 193
Currado Malaspina, 120–21
Curtius, E. R., 295n.38